6-28 d. Expected production costs, $527,500

6-29 b. Budgeted net income, $100,000

6-30 Difference in net income, $2,000

6-31 Variable cost variances, 82,000 U

6-32 c. Efficiency variance, $7,000 U

6-33 a. Price variance, $500 U

6-34 a. 2. Efficiency variance, $1,600 U

6-35 a. 3. Efficiency variance, $375 U

6-36 a. Total usage variance $400 U

6-37 b. Florimene, efficiency variance, $200 F

7-15 Total variance, $2,800 U

7-16 a. Efficiency variance, $2,250 U

7-17 a. Spending variance, $325 U

7-18 Spending variance, $150 U

7-19 b. Volume variance, $4,000 U

7-20 a. Budget variance, $2,500 U

7-21 b. Volume variance, $7,500 F

7-22 Total variance, $6,000 F

7-23 Volume variance, $3,000 U

7-24 b. Volume variance, $14,000 U

7-25 b. 121,000 hours

7-26 Material price variance, $250 U

7-27 Labor rate variance, $1,600 U

7-28 Volume variance, $500 F

7-29 b. Volume variance, $13,500 U

7-30 a. Spending variance, $1,000 U

7-31 c. Budget variance, $200 F

7-32 Budget variance, $2,000 U

7-33 c. 3,300 hours

7-34 Volume variance, $600 F

7-35 Budget variance, $300 U

7-36 Case A, a. 4,600 hr., c. $6,900; Case B, i. 10,000 hr., j. 9,800 hr.; Case C, q. 1,000 r., r. 1,100 hr.

7-37 c. Rate variance, $820 U; f. Budget variance, $225 U

7-38 b. 25,000 lb,; e. $4.20 per hr.

7-39 b. $20,000 U; f. $280,000 U

7-40 a. 9) Volume variance, $7,500 F; b. Net income, $756,400

8-20 Co. A, Branch 1, Segment margin, $10,000

8-23 c., Bingle, 25%; Company, 6.15%

8-24 b., Company, .625; c., Company, 1.56%

8-25 Segment 3, a. 23%; b. 1.3, c. 30%

8-26 c. 10%

8-27 Banana Division, b. $8,200

8-28 a. 12.5%

8-29 $100,000 disadvantage

8-31 b. 3. Hoe, 41.7%; Company, 7.7%; c. Hoe, $95,000

8-32 c. 3. Pine, 16%; Company, 5,5%; d. Pine, $2,500

8-33 ROI with new product, 17.8%

8-34 a. 1. Year 3, 53.3%; 3. Year 3, 16.7%

8-35 c. 1. 7.6%; 3. 16%; f. 1. 7.6%; 3. 22.9%

8-36 a. 3. 10%; b. Plan A, 3. 13.6%; Plan D, 3. 26.1%; c. 16,500 units

8-37 a. Appliance, 13.8%; b. Special Parts, (16.7%); f. 1. 25%; 2. $62,500 advantage

8-38 a. 3. $8,300,000

9-15 b. 30,000 units

9-16 b. 15,333 units

9-17 c. 8,000 dresses

9-18 b. $5.59 per unit

9-19 a. $3.67 per box

9-20 50%

9-21 b. $2,500,000

9-22 c. $400,000

9-23 $222,222

9-24 $450,000

9-25 b. $80,000

9-26 a. 26%

9-27 c. 16 2/3%

9-28 $750,000

9-29 c. 50 sets; d. 2. 2,667 sets

9-30 a. 2. $1.70 per book; c. 2. 27,333 copies

9-31 c. 152,423 units

9-32 a. 15,000 units; c. 19,125 units; e. $28.33 per unit

9-33 b. 12,000 pipes; d. $325,000 f. $52,500

9-34 b. $4.50 per box; c. $1,920,000

9-35 a. 7,000 albums; c. 16,800 albums

9-36 b. 29 dogs; c. 2. 47 dogs; e. $1.97 per dog per night

9-37 b. 29,167 batteries; d. $71 per battery; f. 7,500 batteries

9-38 a. 28,000 pizzas; c. $.87 or 17.4%; d. 3,530 coupons

9-39 b. $2,000,000; d. $60,000

9-40 a. 2. $1,333,333; b. Plan C, $2,200,000

9-41 a. 33%; c. 2. BW, $360,606 needed increase; d. $10,000

9-42 b. 2. 38,542 units; d. $112,400; e. 2. $215,385; f. 10,000 units

10-16 $1,500 in favor of new

10-17 $40,000 in favor of new

10-19 $2,000

10-20 b. $7,000 better to process further

10-21 Product W, $64,000

10-23 $11,000 in favor of make

10-24 $2.50 per unit

10-25 $100,000 increase

10-26 Twink, contribution margin per hr., $.67

10-27 b. E-Z Sit, $6,000 more profitable

10-28 $3,000 in favor of remachining

Managerial Accounting:
An Introduction

Managerial Accounting: An Introduction

Pierre L. Titard, *Ph. D., CPA*
University of South Alabama

The Dryden Press
Chicago New York Philadelphia San Francisco
Montreal Toronto London Sydney
Tokyo Mexico City Rio de Janeiro Madrid

Acquisitions Editor: James Walsh
Developmental Editors: Elizabeth Widdicombe/Susan Layton
Project Editor: Brian Link Weber
Design Director: Alan Wendt
Managing Editor: Jane Perkins
Production Manager: Mary Jarvis

Text and cover design by Bernard Arendt
Copy editing by Beverly Peavler, Naples Editing Service

Address orders to:

383 Madison Avenue
New York, New York   10017

Address editorial correspondence to:

One Salt Creek Lane
Hinsdale, Illinois   60521

Library of Congress Catalog Card Number: 81-67243
ISBN: 0-03-061556-9
Printed in the United States of America
345-016-98765432

CBS College Publishing
The Dryden Press
Holt, Rinehart and Winston
Saunders College Publishing

To
Barbara, Michael, Marcie, Laura, and Brian

Contents

Contents

Preface

Managerial Accounting: An Introduction is a text designed for a first course of one-semester or one-quarter length in managerial (management) accounting. It is especially suited for the second course of a financial/managerial sequence, or a third course following a two-semester, or two-quarter sequence of accounting principles courses, in which managerial topics were not included.

The text focuses on the use of accounting data internally by managers in making decisions for their firms, to include both manufacturing and nonmanufacturing businesses. Accounting is emphasized as a communication discipline that provides managers the financial data they need to make decisions. In all cases, the "why" is stressed, along with the "how to."

Organization

A major strength of this text is its organization. As written, the sequence of chapters is well-organized for student understanding and comprehension. It provides a logical flow of concepts from one chapter to the next, which helps make it a very teachable text. However, the organization is flexible enough that chapters can be sequenced as desired by the instructor to best meet course objectives. Examples of this flexibility are included below; and the Instructor's Manual provides course outlines that show several possible sequences.

Part One, Managerial Accounting Concepts provides the basic concepts students should have in order to best comprehend the subsequent chapters that emphasize planning, controlling, and decision making. Because cost behavior concepts provide a basic foundation needed in later chapters, they are included early in the text as Chapter 2. Note that this topic is not presented merely as a part of cost-volume-profit analysis (as is often done), but rather is the subject of a separate chapter. This is done because cost behavior applies to a number of important areas of managerial accounting; and separate coverage at this early stage makes the application of the concepts easier later in the course.

Chapter 3, Accounting for Manufacturing Costs allows students to receive the minimum of manufacturing accounting concepts needed as essential background before proceeding to managerial accounting applications. This avoids the need to cover the details of job order and process costing, which are the topics of Chapter 13.

Chapter 4, Contribution Approach to Decision Making, provides students with one of the basic managerial tools—the contribution approach income statement. Upon completion of this chapter, along with the first three chapters, students are prepared for applications of managerial accounting provided in Parts Two and Three.

Part Two, Managerial Accounting for Planning and Controlling, includes four chapters that present *budgeting, flexible budgets and standard costs, overhead analysis,* and *responsibility accounting and performance measurement.* Because the details of fixed overhead analysis, as shown in Chapter 7, are separated from the presentation of standards costs, Chapter 6, the instructor has the flexibility to defer or omit discussion of fixed overhead analysis, if desired. The appendix to Chapter 7 allows the instructor to present the journal entries for a standard cost system if this is a course objective.

Part Three, Managerial Accounting Techniques for Decision Making, shows how the manager uses accounting data in decision-making situations. This part includes chapters on *cost-volume-profit analysis, relevant cost, capital budgeting,* and *quantitative techniques.*

Chapters 1 through 12 provide the basis for a strictly managerial accounting course. **Part Four, Cost Accounting Concepts,** includes *Chapter 13, Cost Accounting Systems* and *Chapter 14, Cost Allocation.* These chapters are ideal for instructors who desire a stronger cost emphasis. They could be presented following Chapter 3 or Chapter 4.

Part Five, Special Topics, contains chapters that, strictly speaking, are considered more financial than managerial, specifically, *Chapter 15, Statement of Changes in Financial Position, Chapter 16, Financial Statement Analysis,* and *Chapter 17, Inflation Accounting.* Managers, of course, must be knowledgeable in these areas. However, a primary reason for their inclusion in this text is to provide flexibility in structuring the second course of a two-course financial/managerial sequence. Often instructors prefer to cover the topics found in Chapters 15 and 16 in the second course, rather than the first. The text allows that flexibility. If desired, these two chapters can easily be covered as the first two chapters in the course. Chapter 17 is important because *Statement of Financial Accounting Standards No. 33* requires supplementary inflation-adjusted data for many firms. Consequently, students will later be exposed to such data and should be familiar with it.

Finally, the text contains appendices to six chapters. These allow the instructor to expand coverage or to go into more depth in specific topics, as desired.

Features

The text is designed to help students learn. A major feature is that it is written in an extremely clear manner, with numerous exhibits that are thoroughly explained. Other specific features of this text include the following:

1. Outstanding selection of author-prepared assignment material This includes an abundance of CPA and CMA exam problems.

2. Learning objectives preceding each chapter These let students know expected outcomes from studying the chapter. In addition, the Instructor's Manual relates each learning objective to specific questions, exercises, and problems.

3. Use of bold face type for key terms and concepts Such emphasis highlights important items for students and makes reference and review easier.

4. Review problem with solution following each chapter This provides students with an opportunity to solve a problem and check the solution against the text solution. It also reinforces concepts presented in the chapter.

5. Short titles for exercises and problems These help organize the assignment material and assist the instructor in making assignments.

6. End of text glossary This provides a ready reference of key terms and definitions. Since it is at the end of the text (rather than the end of each chapter), students can easily look up a term without paging through the text. In addition, the glossary has a unique feature in that both the chapter *and* page number reference where the term is first used in the text is included for each term.

7. Two color The second color highlights key concepts and illustrations and helps improve overall text readability.

Supplements

Instructor's Manual The emphasis is on "Instructor" because it's more than just an "answer book." In addition to the author-prepared solutions to questions, exercises, and problems, the instructor's manual relates each learning objective to specific questions, exercises, and problems, making the learning objectives truly functional. Furthermore, the manual provides time and level of difficulty ratings for exercises and problems, check figures, chapter outlines, suggested assignments, and helpful comments to the instructor. It is also perforated for ease in making transparencies.

 Study Guide Co-authored by Dr. C. Edward Cavert, Northern Virginia Community College, a specialist in the design of instructional material to help students learn, the study guide truly "guides" students through the material. It is a unique type of study guide, seldom found accompanying accounting texts.

 Test Bank Prepared by Dr. Keith A. Russell, University of South Alabama, the test bank provides a large number and variety of true-false and multiple-choice questions, as well as problems for each chapter. This allows the instructor to choose those test items desired in constructing an exam. In addition, the test bank includes several examinations, based on those chapters that could logically be tested together.

Acknowledgments

I appreciate the work done by C. Edward Cavert on the study guide and by Keith A. Russell on the test bank, as well as the helpful comments and suggestions they provided regarding the text. Their supplements provide excellent complements to the text.

The text material has been thoroughly class tested. In this respect, I thank the students at the University of South Alabama who participated in the class testing. I also thank my colleagues at South Alabama, Adel M. Novin, Franklyn H. Sweet, and A. Jeannette Sylvestre, for their help and cooperation in class testing. The suggestions and comments they provided were especially beneficial.

I am indebted to Eamon J. Duignan, Robert B. King, and Jose F. Medina, students at the University of South Alabama, for their efforts in working the exercises and problems included in the text. Checking their results with mine has helped to minimize any errors in the preparation of the solutions. In addition, Professor Esther D. Flashner, Hunter College of the City University of New York, has thoroughly checked the solutions to exercises and problems in the Instructor's Manual. For this, I am most grateful.

John A. Caspari, Bradley University, and Kung H. Chen, University of Nebraska—Lincoln, provided an intensive review of the manuscript in its early stages. Their help is most appreciated. In addition, I am thankful for the many helpful comments provided by the following reviewers: Ted R. Compton, Ohio University; J. A. DeFatta, Northeast Louisiana University; John Durham, Northern Arizona University; B. J. Greenwald, Missouri Western State College; Larzette G. Hale, Utah State University; Raj Kiani, California State University, Northridge; William C. Kilpatrick, Colorado State University; Donald Krause, Oakland University; Robert MacDonald, University of Wisconsin, Eau Claire.

I am grateful for the skilled typing assistance, as well as the patience and understanding, provided by Mary Ellen Beasley, Pat Robinson, and Mary Jo Schmid.

The staff at The Dryden Press did an outstanding job in the preparation of this book. For this, I thank Flora Foss, Mary Jarvis, Susan Layton, Beverly Peavler, Jane Perkins, James Walsh, Brian Weber, and Alan Wendt. In addition, I am especially grateful to Liz Widdicombe of Dryden for her untiring efforts on my behalf as developmental editor of the text.

I thank the American Institute of Certified Public Accountants and the Institute of Management Accounting of the National Association of Accountants for their permission to use problem material from past CPA and CMA examinations. Such problems are indicated as "AICPA adapted" and "CMA adapted." I also thank the Financial Accounting Standards Board for permission to reprint schedules from *Statement of Financial Accounting Standards No. 33,* "Financial Reporting and Changing Prices."

Two special notes of appreciation are in order—one to Richard W. Metcalf, who first provided me with the inspiration and determination to write this book—and the other to John C. Neifert, without whose confidence, encouragement, and insistence this book would have never been written.

Finally, I thank my wife, Barbara, for her patience, understanding, and encouragement throughout this project.

Pierre L. Titard

Part One

Managerial Accounting Concepts

Chapter 1   Introduction to Managerial Accounting

Learning
Objectives

The purpose of this chapter is to provide you with an overview of managerial accounting. The chapter describes the role of managerial accounting and contrasts that role with the role of financial accounting. Studying this chapter will enable you to:

1. Define *managerial accounting.*

2. Describe differences and similarities between managerial accounting and financial accounting.

3. Describe the need for managerial accounting in both profit-oriented and not-for-profit organizations.

4. Define *responsibility accounting* and describe its relationship to managerial accounting.

5. Recognize levels of management and distinguish between line and staff responsibilities.

6. Describe the functions of management.

7. Identify types of decisions made with the help of managerial accounting.

8. Describe the role of the controller in managerial accounting.

9. Describe the significance of the Certificate in Management Accounting program.

Chapter Topics

The major topics included in this chapter are:

> The Role of Accounting in Decision Making
> Comparison of Financial and Managerial Accounting
> Objectives of an Organization
> Organization and Management of a Business Firm
> The Need for Managerial Accounting
> The Certified Management Accountant

The first question you might ask as you begin a course in managerial accounting is "What is managerial accounting?" This chapter answers that question by explaining the nature of managerial accounting and how it relates to financial accounting. The chapter also discusses the users of managerial accounting information and the reasons that managerial accounting is necessary for both profit-oriented and not-for-profit organizations.

To understand the nature of managerial accounting, it is a good idea first to review the role of accounting in general—particularly financial accounting, since that is a subject with which you are probably already familiar.

The Role of Accounting in Decision Making

Accounting can be defined simply as a discipline that communicates financial information for decision making. This definition has wide application, but the emphasis is always on "communicates." Accounting communicates information externally through formal financial statements so that decisions can be made about the firm; it also communicates information internally so that management can make decisions for the firm. Thus, accounting is usually classified as either **financial accounting (external)** or **managerial accounting (internal).**

Financial Accounting

Financial accounting requires a precise system for accumulating and reporting financial information. There are a number of acceptable ways to accumulate and report such information. Nevertheless, a comprehensive formal accounting system is based on the accrual basis of accounting, uses the double entry system of bookkeeping, and requires a standardized system of reporting. The reporting system includes four external financial statements—income statement, balance sheet, statement of changes in owner's (or stockholders') equity, and statement of changes in financial position—which may vary somewhat from one firm to another but which have the same relative format. A financial accounting course teaches details for accumulating information and reporting it through these four formal financial statements.

Many firms must prepare these statements in conformity with generally accepted accounting principles. Firms registered with the Securities and Exchange Commission (SEC), as well as many other firms, must have their financial statements audited by certified public accountants. CPAs report on the fairness of financial statement presentation in conformity with generally accepted accounting principles.

Although owners and managers of a business firm are interested in and may use the information reported on formal financial statements, the primary purpose of such statements is to communicate to individuals and interested parties outside the firm the current financial position and results of operations of the firm. From this information, outside parties make decisions such as whether to extend credit to the firm, whether to invest in it by buying stock, or whether to disinvest in it by selling stock. They may also compare firms to decide which appears to be a better credit risk or investment opportunity.

External financial statements play a major role in our system's economic growth. The communication of information on financial statements enables individuals to make decisions about firms which, in turn, affect economic growth. Without external financial statements, these decisions would be very difficult, if not impossible, to make.

Managerial Accounting

Managerial accounting (often called *management accounting*) communicates financial information internally so that management can make intelligent decisions for the firm. The information generated for managerial accounting, then, is used primarily for internal purposes; it may or may not be contained in external financial statements.

Since internal information needs differ among firms, there are no standard reports for internal financial information. However, many types of internal decisions are common to many firms; therefore, it is possible to discuss managerial accounting concepts that are applicable to almost any firm and to illustrate certain types of internal reports, even though their specific format may vary among firms. Types of decisions that might be based on managerial accounting information are discussed later in this chapter.

Comparison of Financial and Managerial Accounting

Financial accounting and managerial accounting serve different but complementary purposes. Unfortunately, they are sometimes written about in terms of "financial versus managerial." That is inaccurate, because there is no conflict between the two. Accounting communicates information for decision making. The decision-making needs of most firms are both external and internal; and the accounting system should be developed to provide information for both communication needs. Therefore, both financial and managerial accounting are required. Both may draw their data from the same sources. With this in mind, let us examine some of the differences and similarities between the two types of accounting, realizing that peculiarities of each are based on the information needs of the users of each.

Differences

Generally Accepted Accounting Principles External financial statements of publicly reported companies are prepared in conformity with generally accepted accounting principles. Generally accepted accounting principles, commonly referred to as GAAP, provide standards against which outside users of financial statements can evaluate a firm or measure differences among firms. Although there are criticisms and differences of opinion about certain specific elements and applications of GAAP, they provide enough standardization in external reporting so that, in general, outsiders can make decisions about a firm based on its financial statements.

There is no standardization in reporting for internal decision making. Managers can use a variety of managerial accounting techniques to help them make decisions. The information and format for reporting vary depending on the type of decision, type of firm, and desires of management.

The use of generally accepted accounting principles is not a requirement for managerial accounting. Management can develop and report internal information in any way desired.

When firms are audited by independent auditors, the CPAs are concerned with the presentation of external financial statements. Many CPA firms do provide management advisory, or consulting, services to help management to develop internal financial information. However, the primary role of the CPA is to audit financial statements to determine their fairness of presentation in conformity with generally accepted accounting principles. Thus, managerial accounting does not normally fall under the scrutiny of the CPA.

Terminology Financial accounting terminology is relatively standardized. Some principles, concepts, and financial statements may be known by more than one term, such as "balance sheet" and "statement of financial position." Nevertheless, there is a fair degree of standardization; and, in many cases, preferred terminology exists.

Since managerial accounting does not have a formal rule-making body, its terminology is less standardized. As a result, you will sometimes find managerial accounting terms used differently in different situations.

Mandatory Requirement There is no mandatory requirement for a firm to use managerial accounting concepts, as there is for many firms to prepare financial statements in conformity with GAAP. External reporting is an end in itself. Managerial accounting is a part of the broader process of management. As a result, financial accounting is mandatory and managerial accounting is not. Even firms with no external reporting requirements that force them to conform to GAAP must maintain financial accounting records in a manner acceptable to the Internal Revenue Service.

Although there are no requirements for managerial accounting, from a practical standpoint, the economic survival of a firm may depend more on managerial accounting than on financial accounting.

Type of Information External financial statements are based on historical cost and reflect what has happened in the past. Many users of these statements look at the information with an idea of predicting future economic performance of the firm. The Financial Accounting Standards Board (FASB) now requires certain companies to provide some data adjusted for inflation.[1] However, generally accepted accounting principles still require that statements be presented at historical cost.

Managerial accounting, on the other hand, often requires projections of the future and predictions on various elements of the enterprise, such as sales and related expenses. In addition, certain aspects of managerial accounting are frequently concerned with replacement costs rather than historical costs. Data for managerial accounting is frequently based on estimates rather than on historical transactions.

From this you can see that financial information used in managerial accounting may be less objective than that used in financial accounting.

[1]This requirement is discussed fully in Chapter 17.

That in no way reduces the importance of managerial accounting. Firms need to make decisions about the future; and projections for the future are naturally less precise than historical facts.

Subject of Reports Financial accounting, for the most part, reports on the business as a whole (although the FASB, as well as the SEC, require certain information to be reported externally based on product lines).[2] Managerial accounting may involve the business as a whole, but it also involves details of predictions and performance of specific operating units of a firm, as well as performance of individuals. This is discussed more fully later in this chapter.

Similarities

Basic Accounting System Although many differences exist between financial accounting and managerial accounting, a properly designed accounting system accumulates information that can be used for both. We normally think of the accounting system's gathering information for financial reporting purposes, since it is required to do so. However, often the information gathered for financial statements is also used as part of the managerial process. Where necessary, the accounting system can be flexible enough to provide supplementary information that can be used for managerial purposes.

To illustrate, managerial accounting often involves projections of sales. A first step in projecting sales might be to analyze past sales. Information on past sales is reported in a ledger account and on previous financial statements and is readily available for managerial purposes. Managerial accounting, however, is concerned not only with total sales for the firm but also with the breakdown of sales by such elements as geographical areas; product lines; individual products; and individual stores, managers, and salespersons. This causes no conflict between financial accounting and managerial accounting. Since the total sales figure for a firm is an accumulation of sales from each of the reporting elements, the accounting sytem can meet managerial accounting needs by accumulating information on each of the reporting elements, such as each state, store, or individual. The use of computers makes the collection and summarization of this type of information a relatively simple and economical process.

Overall Objective As stated earlier, financial and managerial accounting are also similar in that both have the overall objective of communicating information. The types of decisions based on the information provided by each may differ, but both represent sources of information for users.

Objectives of an Organization

Any organization for which financial information is needed is called an **entity.** This term covers both profit-oriented and not-for-profit organizations. To this point, discussion has related to accounting for business enti-

---

[2]"Financial Reporting for Segments of a Business Enterprise," *Statement of Financial Accounting Standards No. 14* (Stamford, Connecticut: Financial Accounting Standards Board, December 1976).

ties. However, accounting is used in not-for-profit organizations as well. These two types of entities have different external reporting objectives, but their internal accounting needs are quite similar.

Profit-Oriented Organizations

Profit-oriented organizations are referred to as business firms; they operate businesses in which they sell products or provide services in order to generate revenue. In so doing, they incur expenses. The difference between revenue and expenses is either net income or net loss.

It is often said that the objective of a business firm is to maximize profits. There are arguments against this generalization. For example, if maximization of profits disregards environmental considerations, then profit maximization may have to take a back seat. Environmental considerations often require incurring certain expenses or foregoing certain actions that might be profitable but that would damage the environment. Today business firms have many objectives, including concern for the environment, for their employees, and for the communities in which they operate. Nevertheless, if the economic system is to survive, businesses must earn an adequate return on their investment. Thus, while one can question whether profit maximization is the firm's only objective, business firms do attempt to make decisions that will provide maximum profits given the constraints inherent in today's society.

For external purposes, the measurement of profits is based on an accounting system that reports information in conformity with generally accepted accounting principles. In addition, all firms, including those that do not have public reporting requirements, must conform to reporting requirements of the Internal Revenue Service, which in some areas parallel GAAP. Managerial accounting is concerned with using accounting information that results in decisions that maximize profits by increasing revenue, decreasing expenses, or doing both.

Not-for-Profit Organizations

Not-for-profit organizations are typified by such entities as schools; hospitals; libraries; charitable organizations; and local, state, and federal governments. The primary objective of these entities is to provide services to the community.

External financial reporting requirements for such organizations often differ from those for profit-oriented organizations. Some entities, such as local and state governments, maintain accounting systems designed to reflect the type of information appropriate for these entities. However, our concern is not with external reporting.

Since the role of managerial accounting is to help business firms increase profits, you might wonder what place it has in not-for-profit organizations. Since such organizations usually obtain their resources from taxes, contributions, or charges (such as hospital bills) to the general public, society has an interest in their operation. Specifically, these entities are expected to operate as efficiently as possible, making the best use of their resources. The burden on society for additional taxes, contributions, or unnecessary charges is increased if they do not do so. From this you can see that managerial accounting is used in not-for-profit organizations to help managers reduce expenses and use resources efficiently in order to provide society with the best services at the least cost.

The concentration of economic transactions in U.S. society is in profit-oriented organizations. Therefore, most of the discussion, examples, and problems in this text center on business firms. Nevertheless, because managerial accounting is equally appropriate for not-for-profit organizations, these types of entities are also discussed and illustrated where appropriate.

Organization and Management of a Business Firm

The three basic forms of business organizations are single proprietorship, partnership, and corporation. Managerial accounting is important in all three types of organizations, whether small or large. In order for certain management and managerial accounting concepts to be more easily illustrated, an organization chart for a hypothetical supermarket chain, Dixie Fair Food Stores, Inc., is shown in Exhibit 1.1. An illustration of a large firm is used in order to show the management relationships inherent in that type of firm. However, small firms also make decisions based on managerial accounting concepts.

Since managerial accounting is part of the management process, it is useful to discuss management concepts and functions before looking at specific applications of managerial accounting.

Segments of an Organization

As stated earlier, the external financial statements of a business report the financial position and results of operation for the business as a whole. Internally, management must have information regarding all of the individual aspects of the business.

Dixie Fair Food Stores is divided into five major functional areas: store operations, finance, transportation, personnel, and purchasing. Store operations is further divided according to states, areas within states, individual stores within areas, and departments within stores. Each part of the organization is a **segment**—an area of activity about which accounting information is desired. For Dixie Fair Food Stores, each of the five major functional areas is a segment. In addition, each state, each area within a state, each store, and each store department is a segment.

The actual names given to segments vary among firms—they may be called departments, branches, divisions, or the like. Department stores are normally divided into departments, such as furniture department, housewares department, and appliance department. However, Sears, Roebuck designates its departments as divisions. For General Motors, though, divisions represent major segments, such as Chevrolet Division, Cadillac Division, and Buick Division. Thus, titles do not give any indication of a segment's size.

Exhibit 1.1 Dixie Fair Food Stores, Inc.

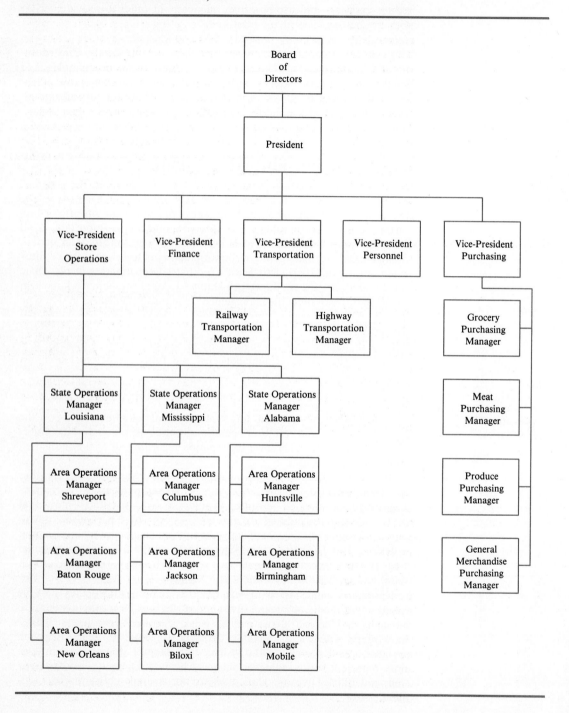

For our purposes, the important thing to understand is that management must have information from internal reports on various segments in order to make decisions about them. Segment reporting is a part of what is called **responsibility accounting**—a system of accounting under which managers are given decision-making authority and responsibility for activities occurring within specific areas of a company. **Authority** is the power or right to make decisions; **responsibility** is the requirement to be answerable or accountable for the results of decisions. A manager should never be given responsibility without authority, and authority always entails responsibility. Thus, a manager who has authority to make decisions about a particular segment also has responsibility for the ultimate results of that segment. For example, Dixie Fair's Shreveport area manager is given authority to make certain decisions that allow his area stores to meet profit goals. If his area fails to meet profit goals, he is responsible. He must determine the problem and make the necessary corrections. If he fails, top management might step in.

The concept of responsibility accounting is an important part of managerial accounting. This concept is discussed more fully in Chapter 8.

Management Concepts

The term *management* has already been used in this chapter; it is important to understand what it means. **Management** is defined as a collective group of individuals who direct the operations of an entity. In any business firm, a manager is an individual who has the authority to make decisions regarding specific aspects of operations. As previously mentioned, with authority comes responsibility. Thus, managers are considered responsible for decisions within their areas of authority, whether the results are favorable or unfavorable. It is important that clear lines of authority be established. One of the primary functions of managerial accounting is to provide information, based on lines of authority, to assist in evaluation of managerial performance.

Management Levels A single proprietorship may have only one manager, the owner, who is responsible for all decisions regarding the firm's operations. As firms grow, more people are needed to make decisions, and several levels of managerial responsibility are created. Although the terminology is not absolute, management of large organizations can normally be classified as: **(1) top management, (2) middle management,** and **(3) lower management.**

In the Dixie Fair Food Stores chain (Exhibit 1.1), the president and five vice-presidents are top management. The state operations managers, the transportation managers, and various purchasing managers are middle management. Depending on the firm's philosophy, the area operations managers may be considered middle management or lower management; the distinction between middle and lower management is not always clear-cut. The exhibit does not show the individual stores. However, individual store managers are lower management. Each store has a produce department, a meat department, a grocery department, and a general merchandise department (housewares and other nonfood items). Depending on store size, each of these departments may have a manager. If so, they are also considered lower management.

The board of directors is not generally considered management. The board sets overall policy and direction for the firm. Top management is charged with the implementation of policy decisions provided by the board and is responsible for seeing that the direction of the firm is consistent with the board's expectations. Middle and lower management are concerned primarily with the day-to-day decisions necessary for the firm to operate.

Exhibit 1.1 does not illustrate all areas of management for Dixie Fair Food Stores; for example, lower-management personnel under the transportation managers and under the purchasing managers have responsibilities for their particular areas.

Line and Staff   Another important management concept is the distinction between line and staff. Managers with line authority have direct responsibility for satisfying the goals of the company, while staff personnel serve primarily in advisory and service roles.

In Exhibit 1.1, store operations is clearly a line function, because the primary goal of the company is to operate retail food stores. The vice-president of store operations has line authority over the state operations managers. In turn, state operations managers have line authority over the area operations managers in their respective states; and the area operations managers have line authority over store managers within their areas. Naturally, each store manager has line authority over each person working in the store.

On the other hand, the vice-president of finance and the vice-president of personnel are staff. Neither has line authority over areas headed by the three other vice-presidents. They may recommend policies or procedures to the president regarding their respective areas; the president may then direct that corresponding actions be taken. However, the staff managers themselves have no authority to require action by any other element of the business. Within each staff area, however, managers have line authority. For example, the vice-president of finance and the vice-president of personnel have line authority over individuals in their respective areas.

In this illustration, the exact nature of the transportation and purchasing functions is not clear, as it relates to line and staff. Since these functions exist primarily to serve store operations, they can legitimately be called staff functions. Nevertheless, because of their importance for this firm, top management might consider them line functions. In any event, they have no line authority over store operations; but within each area, managers have line authority over their subordinates.

From this discussion, it is clear that the distinction between line and staff is based primarily on the area of responsibility. The president has line authority over the entire firm and is therefore responsible for the entire operation. Normally, unless the company as a whole is in serious trouble, the president is not held responsible for problems in a single area. However, the president is responsible for seeing that problems get solved. In some cases, this may mean replacing the manager responsible for the troubled area.

**Functions of
Management**

Management theory is not an exact science. However, many management theorists agree that all management activity can be fit in a framework of three primary functions:[3]
1. Planning.
2. Organizing.
3. Controlling.
Each function is discussed separately below. However, it should be understood that, in practice, isolation of the functions is sometimes difficult. In any business, all functions are normally occurring at the same time; and the interrelationships among them sometimes make one indistinguishable from the others.

Although not normally named among formal functions of management, *decision making* is involved in all three functions. Indeed, it is the reason managers exist. This section discusses it separately in order to highlight its importance.

Planning A business cannot survive if management allows things to just happen. Management must set organizational goals. **Planning** is determining in advance what steps are needed to satisfy these goals. It includes short-run planning, such as deciding how late to stay open during the holidays or deciding on the number of employees to work on a particular day, and long-range planning, such as planning for new stores, equipment, or products. Long-range planning is often called **strategic planning,** because it considers a firm's strategy for achieving its organizational goals. Planning is a part of decision making because a plan, in effect, represents a decision as to how to achieve a particular objective.

Organizing **Organizing** includes two functions: (1) establishing an organizational structure and (2) communicating plans to people responsible for its implementation. The first function includes determining which employees will perform which jobs; this is often depicted on an organization chart.

An organization will not run unless somebody tells somebody else what to do. Therefore, the second function of organizing includes the issuing of instructions to specific employees to carry out certain actions. This is sometimes referred to as **directing.** For example, a store manager assigns employee hours, designates which employees are to work in which area, and provides specific instructions as to how store procedures, such as ringing up sales on the cash register, are to be carried out.

Organizing also includes coordinating elements to insure that organizational goals are carried out. Note the close relationship between planning and organizing. You can see that organizing includes an element of planning and decision making. Like planning, organizing is an everyday function.

Controlling **Controlling** is a function that insures adherence to management plans. It is important in both small and large organizations at all levels of management.

[3]Richard M. Hodgetts, *Management Theory, Process, and Practice,* 3rd ed. (Hinsdale, Ill.: The Dryden Press, 1982), pp. 53–58.

Controlling becomes particularly significant where middle and top managers are unable to personally observe all the everyday operations of each business segment. Thus, they rely extensively on internal reports. Reports of actual results are compared with planned results. When significant deviations occur, management takes steps to determine the reason for such deviations and provides corrective action, if appropriate. The information provided management in these reports is often called **feedback.** For example, assume that the planned sales for a particular month for the Jackson area of the Dixie Fair Food Stores is $3 million but that the state operations manager for Mississippi receives a sales report showing actual monthly sales of $2.5 million. The manager must take steps to determine why the expected result was not achieved and, depending on the reasons, must make decisions regarding the Jackson area. Unless management compares results with expectations in this manner, the planning process is not as effective as it could be.

Decision Making All functions of management include decision making. Managerial accounting is designed to provide management with information for accomplishing the functions of planning, organizing, and controlling; however, it also focuses on specific types of decisions. The types of decisions in which it is particularly helpful are discussed in the next section.

The Need for Managerial Accounting

Some of the information management needs to perform the functions described in the preceding section is of a nonaccounting type, such as the quality of the firm's product versus that of a competitor, the advantage of one particular location for a new store over that of another, and the effect on employees' morale of a proposed management decision. However, much of the required information is accounting information. In many cases, accounting information is combined with nonaccounting information in order for a manager to have the best possible data with which to make a decision. As previously mentioned, external financial statements do not generally provide all the information necessary for internal use. Therefore, managerial accounting is needed to provide information structured for use in internal decision making.

Types of Decisions

Since the type of decision depends on the firm, there is no catalog of internal decisions made by using accounting information. Nevertheless, it is possible to discuss various types of decisions that use it. (These types are presented more fully in subsequent chapters.)

One of the most important decisions a firm must make regards the price at which to sell its product. Many factors affect pricing. Management needs to know the cost data associated with the product being sold and must also consider whether it is pricing on a long-run basis or for a short-run, nonrecurring situation. External financial statements are no help in determining this, but managerial accounting techniques are quite helpful.

A firm must often decide whether to make a particular item for its own use or to buy it. This is called (naturally enough) a make-or-buy decision, and information for it is provided by internal accounting.

Whether to expand is another common type of decision. For example, suppose the board of directors of Dixie Fair Food Stores is interested in expanding operations from the three states in which it now has stores. How does it go about making this type of decision? As you might expect, it is not easy. But managerial accounting provides management with data upon which to base its decision.

Looking at Dixie Fair Food Stores again, assume that one of the stores in the Mobile area appears to be losing money. Should the store be closed? Information can be made available to management to help it decide.

Every business has some type of equipment, even if it is nothing more than a cash register or a typewriter. Large manufacturing firms have millions of dollars invested in equipment. Decisions must be made regarding the timing of equipment replacement, as well as the type of new equipment to be bought. The use of managerial accounting provides information for this decision-making task.

One of a manager's most important jobs is the evaluation of subordinate managers. Unfortunately, incorrect decisions on managerial performance are often made simply because management does not understand how to use accounting information properly. Such poor evaluation methods lead to poor morale, and subsequently to poor performance for the company as a whole. The proper use of internal accounting information assists in the evaluation of managerial performance. Thus, it is vitally important that management make proper use of accounting data for this purpose.

It is important to realize that internal accounting information does not make decisions for management but merely provides a basis for them. The types of decisions discussed here and in later chapters are not all-inclusive; these examples, however, should provide you with an understanding of the concepts necessary for making various types of decisions using internal accounting information.

Role of the Controller in Managerial Accounting

In a large firm, the individual in charge of the accounting function is referred to as the **controller** (or *comptroller*). You are no doubt aware of the role of the controller in the accumulation of financial information and in the preparation of financial statements for external reporting. The controller plays an equally important role in gathering, compiling, reporting, and interpreting internal accounting information. As stated earlier, much of the information used for external purposes is used internally as well; in addition, the accounting system can be tailored to accommodate and gather information needed exclusively for internal purposes.

The controller is responsible for developing accounting information to help management control business operations. Normally, a number of accountants work under the controller. In addition to preparing external financial statements, tax returns, and SEC reports, they perform tasks needed specifically for internal reporting, such as preparing budgets.

The controller performs a staff function. Although the relationship is not shown in Exhibit 1.1, the controller for Dixie Fair Food Stores is subordinate to the vice-president of finance. The controller has line authority over the accountants and other employees in the controller's office.

The role of the controller was enhanced in the 1970s.[4] Inflation had reduced business profits. Management, needing help in making decisions to improve its financial situation, turned to the controller, because decisions related to profit objectives rely extensively on accounting information.

With a knowledge of managerial accounting concepts, the controller can provide data that helps management understand the significance of internal accounting reports. Neither the controller nor the internal accounting reports can make the decision for management. But without such information, management's decisions will not be as good as they otherwise would be.

The Certified Management Accountant

You are probably familiar with the Certified Public Accountant (CPA) designation and its meaning and significance. The CPA certificate primarily recognizes the holder's having met specific requirements relative to examination, education, and experience in the field of public accounting. The requirements include an all-encompassing knowledge of accounting, with particular emphasis on financial accounting and auditing.

A parallel program has been developed to recognize professional competence in the field of managerial accounting. This program was created in 1972 by the National Association of Accountants (NAA), an organization interested in promoting managerial accounting. The NAA created the Institute of Management Accounting (IMA), which is responsible for establishing and maintaining the program leading to a **Certificate in Management Accounting (CMA).** The CMA designation for the managerial accountant carries the same prestige as the CPA designation for the public accountant, although it has no force of law.

The CMA examination covers five areas: (1) managerial economics and business finance; (2) organization and behavior, including ethical considerations; (3) public reporting standards, auditing, and taxes; (4) periodic reporting for internal and external purposes; and (5) decision analysis, including modeling and information systems. The coverage of the CMA examination parallels, to some extent, that of the CPA examination. However, the CMA examination places more emphasis on managerial accounting and on other nonaccounting disciplines. The exam is designed to insure that people who receive the CMA designation have a broad background and understanding of all aspects of accounting and business. In addition to passing the examination, an individual must also meet certain experience requirements before being awarded a CMA certificate.

Summary   Managerial accounting is concerned with the development of internal accounting information to help managers make decisions. Managerial accounting uses all appropriate data in whatever way necessary to assist in

[4]"The Controller: Inflation Gives Him More Clout with Management," *Business Week,* August 15, 1977, pp. 84–95.

this decision-making process. In contrast, financial accounting has as its basis the preparation of financial statements in conformity with generally accepted accounting principles. These statements are issued to external parties so that they can make decisions about the firm.

Managerial accounting information is used for both profit-oriented and not-for-profit entities. Profit-oriented businesses are concerned primarily with maximizing profits, given the constraints of society. Not-for-profit organizations are concerned with the efficient use of resources. Thus, both types of entities can use managerial accounting in achieving their objectives.

Managerial accounting revolves around management concepts and the functions of management. Managers are concerned with planning, organizing, and controlling, all of which include decision making. Managerial accounting helps managers to perform all these functions.

The types of decisions that can be made with managerial accounting information are varied, depending on the size and type of firm. Internal accounting information does not make decisions; rather, it provides management with a basis upon which it can make intelligent decisions. Controllers play an important role in managerial accounting because they have the expertise to accumulate the appropriate information, prepare internal reports, and help management to interpret the reports.

Accountants who meet the rigid requirements of the Institute of Management Accounting are now formally recognized by the award of the Certificate in Management Accounting. This designation has helped to provide an even greater status to the already important field of managerial accounting.

Questions

1-1 Define *managerial accounting.*

1-2 If there are no official "rules" for managerial accounting, as there are for financial accounting, how can managerial accounting be systematically studied?

1-3 Describe differences between managerial accounting and financial accounting.

1-4 In what ways are financial accounting and managerial accounting similar?

1-5 Why is managerial accounting important for profit-oriented organizations?

1-6 Since not-for-profit organizations, by definition, are not concerned with making profits, why should they use managerial accounting concepts?

1-7 Define *responsibility accounting.*

1-8 What is the difference between authority and responsibility?

1-9 How is responsibility accounting related to managerial accounting?

1-10 List the three levels of management.

1-11 What is the difference between line and staff?

1-12 How does the management function of planning differ from that of organizing?

1-13 Where does decision making fit into the functions of management?

1-14 Indicate which function of management is primarily involved in the following decisions:

    a. Deciding on sales quotas.
    b. Deciding to open a new store.
    c. Deciding to drop a product line.
    d. Deciding individual employees' days off.
    e. Promoting a manager.
    f. Pricing a product.

1-15 Since managerial accounting is concerned with management decision-making, and since controllers perform a staff function, why is their role important in managerial accounting?

1-16 What is the Certificate in Management Accounting program?

1-17 What is the relationship between the CPA certificate and the CMA certificate?

Chapter 2   Cost Behavior

Learning Objectives

The purpose of this chapter is to provide you with a knowledge of how costs behave and why cost behavior is important to managers and to the managerial accountant. The chapter describes the various classifications of cost behavior and illustrates their application. Studying this chapter will enable you to:

1. Distinguish between *cost* and *expense*.

2. Describe the importance of a knowledge of cost behavior in applying the management functions of planning and controlling.

3. Define and illustrate graphically the major types of cost behavior patterns.

4. Distinguish among the types of cost behavior patterns.

5. Distinguish between committed fixed costs and discretionary fixed costs.

6. Use a scatter chart.

7. Apply the high-low points method.

8. Apply the method of least squares. (Appendix)

Chapter Topics

The major topics included in this chapter are:

    The Meaning of Cost Behavior
    Variable Cost
    Fixed Cost
    Step-Variable Cost
    Mixed Cost
    Appendix: Applying the Method of Least Squares

In financial accounting, expenses incurred in the course of operations are usually classified according to functions. The major expense items on an income statement are costs of goods sold, selling expenses, and administrative expenses (often called general and administrative expenses). Selling expenses and administrative expenses are classified together as operating expenses. For internal analysis and decision making, a knowledge of how these expenses react to changes in various types of activity, such as sales, is crucial. The reaction of cost to changes in activity is called **cost behavior.** Activity is often called **volume.**

Knowledge of cost behavior is an important part of practically all types of internal decision making. It should be considered in accounting for manufacturing costs (Chapter 3); it is required for budgeting (Chapters 5 through 7); and responsibility accounting and the evaluation of managerial performance depends on the concepts of cost behavior (Chapter 8). Finally, data for specific decisions frequently include a requirement for a knowledge of cost behavior patterns (Chapters 9 through 12). Thus, the importance of understanding cost behavior concepts cannot be overemphasized.

The Meaning of Cost Behavior

Cost Versus Expense

Cost is the amount of resources given up in order to receive some good or service. Expenses, matched with revenue on the income statement, are **expired costs.** Costs that have been incurred but not yet used up are assets, or **unexpired costs.** As the assets are used up, the costs expire. At that time the expired costs are shown as expenses on the income statement. There is, then, a technical difference between *cost* and *expense*. All expenses are costs, but not all costs are expenses. For example, if a firm buys a three-year insurance policy and pays $600 in advance, the $600 is a cost. But it is not yet an expense; it is an asset called "prepaid insurance." At the end of the first year, $200 of the asset has been used up. The cost of insurance protection for the year was $200. This $200 cost is classified as insurance expense. The remaining $400 cost is still an asset, which will become an expense over the next two years. In this chapter, the term *cost*, when used in the discussion of cost behavior, refers to an expired cost (an expense).

Costs on the Income Statement

As previously mentioned, the major functional classifications of costs on the income statement are cost of goods sold, selling expenses and administrative expenses. Selling expenses and administrative expenses are further classified into natural classifications. **Natural classification** is a means of identifying expenses according to the title that best describes their nature, such as salaries, rent, depreciation, and utilities. Internally, these classifications are important because management needs to control costs as they are incurred. For example, knowing the total administrative expense is too high is not enough. Management must know the dollar amount of each natural classification. In addition, management must also know how these amounts change with changes in business activity. Thus, management must have a knowledge of cost behavior.

Cost Behavior

If you stop your car to wait for a long train to go by, you may turn off the motor. Why? Because you know letting it run will waste energy and money. There is a relationship between the motor running and the consumption of gasoline. There is, therefore, a relationship between the motor running and the cost of using gasoline. This is a practical example of cost behavior.

Business firms and not-for-profit organizations incur a variety of costs. Being able to plan and control these costs helps them to operate efficiently.

Management can use knowledge of how costs behave to plan and control them.

The two basic cost behavior patterns are variable and fixed. Other cost behavior patterns—such as step-variable cost and mixed cost—are combinations of these two basic ones. The next sections discuss these patterns.

Variable Cost

Cost vary in direct proportion to the volume

A variable cost is one that changes in total in direct proportion to changes in a specific activity. Cost of goods sold for a merchandising firm—a firm that purchases merchandise for resale—is an example of a variable cost. As sales increase, cost of goods sold increases proportionately. In this case, sales is the activity against which variable cost varies.

To illustrate, assume that a paper carrier sells newspapers for $.20 each. He pays the publisher $.15 for each paper sold. For the paper carrier, the cost of newspapers sold is a variable cost. If no papers are sold, there is no cost of goods sold. If 100 papers are sold for $20, total cost of goods sold is $15. This variable cost behavior is illustrated in Exhibit 2.1. The activity, number of newspapers sold, is plotted on the horizontal axis. Total cost of newspapers sold is plotted on the vertical axis.

The unbroken diagonal line is the variable cost line. The dotted line

Exhibit 2.1 Variable Cost

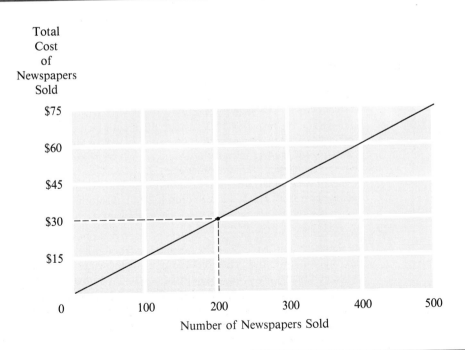

would not usually be shown, but it has been added to show how to read the graph. For example, if the paper carrier sells 200 papers, a dotted line is extended vertically to the variable cost line. From that point on the variable cost line, a horizontal dotted line is extended to the vertical axis, showing the total cost of newspapers sold to be $30.

The graph shows that as the *total* number of newspapers sold increases, *total* cost increases in direct proportion. Note the emphasis on *total*. Unit cost—that is, the cost per newspaper—does not change; but total cost does. This does not mean that unit cost can never change. Rather, it means that a variable cost is one in which total cost changes as activity changes even though the cost per unit remains the same regardless of activity.

When a cost behaves as shown in Exhibit 2.1, it is said to be *strictly* variable. This means that it varies in direct proportion to the activity. Whenever the term *variable cost* is used, it is assumed to mean strictly variable.

The importance of understanding the concept of variable cost is illustrated in later chapters. However, it should be evident already that when managers are trying to estimate future costs, knowing that certain costs vary in relation to some activity is essential. For if they can estimate the activity, such as total sales, they can estimate the cost, such as cost of goods sold.

Fixed Cost

A **fixed cost** is one that does not change in total in relation to changes in a specific activity within a relevant range of time or activity. The key phrase here is **relevant range,** a period of time or range of activity within which a fixed cost does not change. Fixed costs do not remain fixed forever. However, within some relevant range, some costs do not change.

A company vice-president's salary is considered a fixed cost. Say his or her salary for next year is going to be $4,000 per month; this amount will not change regardless of changes in sales or any other activity. Such fixed cost behavior is illustrated in Exhibit 2.2.

In this case, the relevant range is units sold. This graph does not mean that salary expense could not change during the year. If it were decided to increase (or decrease) the vice-president's salary, salary expense would change. But the change would not be caused by changes in sales; it would be based on management's decision.

Because fixed costs can change at the discretion of management, they can be further classified as either committed or discretionary.

Committed Fixed Costs

An organization that starts a business plans to be in business for a long time, perhaps forever. As long as the firm intends to stay in business, certain costs are unavoidable; the firm will have to incur these costs just to stay in business. Such costs are called **committed costs**—costs that must be incurred in order for a firm to accomplish its long-range organizational goals—and they cannot be easily modified from one year to the next.

For example, depreciation expense is normally considered a committed cost. While it is true that management might purchase new assets and dispose of old assets, very few businesses can operate without some commit-

Exhibit 2.2 Fixed Cost

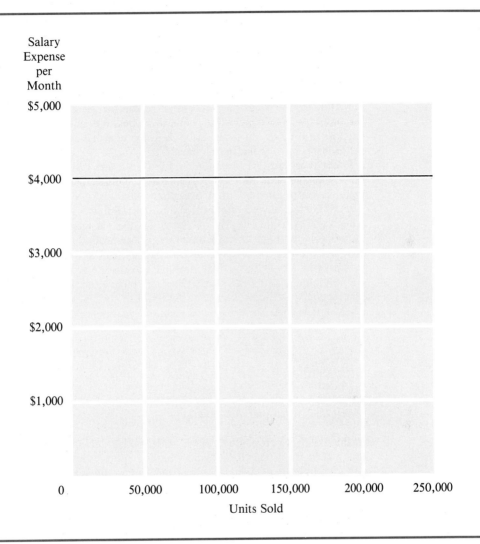

ment to property, plant, and equipment. Thus, although the amounts might change, there will always be depreciation expense. Changes in the amount of depreciation expense are normally the result of long-range planning by management.

Another example of committed costs is top management salaries. The salary of a corporation's president continues regardless of other economic factors that might result in layoffs of members of the work force. This cost is committed because the company will always have a president. It is fixed because the amount will be the same regardless of the activity level.

**Discretionary
Fixed Costs**

*discretionary by the
whims of mgt.
eg. R & D
Advertising
Training Programs*

Discretionary fixed costs are those fixed costs that management has the option of modifying from one year to the next without changing the firm's ability to accomplish its long-range goals. Discretionary costs are also called *programmed costs*.

Advertising is a good example of this type of cost. Large businesses typically contract with an advertising agency to spend a certain amount on advertising for a period of time. For example, a firm may contract to spend $150,000 on advertising for 19X1. The $150,000 is a fixed cost for 19X1. For 19X2, the firm may decide to continue the contract for $150,000, to increase the amount, or to decrease the amount. Thus, the amount of advertising expense to be incurred from one year to the next is based on management action each year; it is discretionary.

Other examples of discretionary fixed costs are research and development, management training programs, and maintenance programs. Do not be misled into thinking that discretionary costs are optional or "frill" costs. The difference between committed and discretionary is based on management's ability to take action to change such costs. Discretionary costs are more easily adjusted upward (or perhaps downward). However, their importance to the survival or profitability of the firm may be equal to that of committed costs. For example, although advertising is a discretionary cost, eliminating it may reduce sales. Thus, complete elimination of advertising may change the firm's ability to accomplish its long-range goals. Fixed maintenance costs can be reduced from one year to the next. But, as any car owner knows, neglecting maintenance results in more costs in the long run because it leads to the need for expensive overhauls or early replacement of equipment.

Reduction in research and development costs for drug companies and computer companies may be to their long-run disadvantage. These companies must keep abreast of technological developments to survive; thus, research and development is essential.

At this point, we are not concerned with making decisions as to the appropriate amount of costs for a firm. What is important to understand now is that the amount of fixed cost incurred can be affected by management action. Because these costs are influenced by management, the line between discretionary costs and committed costs is sometimes a fine one. Determining which classification a cost should be placed in is sometimes a matter of judgment.

Step-Variable Cost

A step-variable cost is one that changes as a particular activity changes, but not in direct proportion to changes in the activity. In this respect, it is not strictly variable. Sometimes it may be considered fixed, because it may not change within a relevant range of activity. It differs from a fixed cost, however, in that it is more easily changed than the previously described fixed costs; and these changes are caused by some change in volume rather than by management decision. This type of cost is most commonly represented by certain types of selling and administrative expenses that do not change in direct proportion to changes in sales.

To illustrate, assume that each of the Dixie Fair Food Stores described in Chapter 1 hires checkout clerks on the basis of sales volume. An increase in sales requires more clerks; but the number of clerks needed is not in direct proportion to dollar sales. Each checkout clerk is paid $600 per month. Past experience has shown that each clerk is capable of handling up to $50,000 of sales per month. This cost behavior is illustrated in Exhibit 2.3.

Looking at the graph, you can see that the cost for clerks is not strictly variable. As sales rise, so does the salary expense; but it rises in a step-like

Exhibit 2.3 Step-Variable Cost

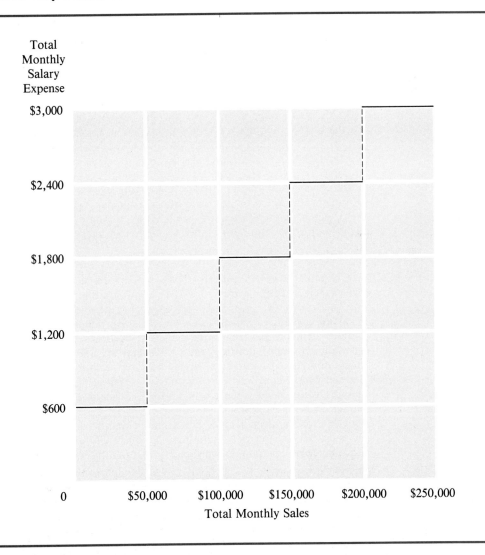

fashion. For up to $50,000 of sales, the firm incurs a cost of $600 per month as salary expense. If sales are between $50,001 and $100,000, the cost rises to $1,200. A store with an expected volume of $250,000 in sales requires five checkout clerks for a cost of $3,000 per month.

As a practical matter, step-variable cost behavior is not quite this simple. In the store that has sales of $250,000 per month, all five clerks are not working all the time. For example, you will normally find all checkout counters in a supermarket being used on a Saturday morning, while only a few of them are being used on a Monday morning. Deciding how many clerks to have working at any one time is not always easy, although there are techniques for doing it. The store manager must balance the increased cost of additional clerks against customers' irritation at having to stand in line.

We also assume individuals are paid on the basis of a forty-hour week. Since stores are open more than forty hours per week, the example indicates that a total of 200 clerk-hours per week are needed in order to handle the monthly volume of $250,000. The manager must allocate these hours on the basis of expected volume. On Monday mornings there may be only two clerks; but on Saturdays there may be five.

Realistically, if two clerks are needed for a monthly volume of $100,000, the store does not need to hire another clerk if sales are expected to be $100,001. At some point, however, two individuals will not be able to handle the sales and additional help will be needed. Determining this point is not an exact science. There are also other alternatives to hiring a third full-time clerk; for example, clerks can work overtime or part-time help can be hired.

Despite some practical problems in applying step-variable cost concepts, an understanding of cost behavior of checkout clerks provides Dixie Fair's management with information needed for planning costs as well as for planning for the required number of employees for a particular period of time.

Mixed Cost

A **mixed cost,** often called a *semivariable cost,* contains both fixed and variable elements. An example is the cost of electricity. Most businesses use a certain amount of electricity even when they are not open. For example, many stores keep lights on at night and the air conditioner running in summer even when they are closed. Thus, regardless of activity, a certain amount of electricity expense is incurred. This is a fixed cost. When a store is open or when a factory is operating, electricity expense increases. More lights are on; more machines are running; therefore, operating requires more electricity than not operating. The electricity expense incurred by these increased operations is variable. Consequently, electricity represents a mixed cost.

You might wonder at this point how mixed cost behavior affects the managerial functions of planning and control. The bill received from the power company is not classified according to fixed and variable; it merely shows the number of kilowatt hours used and the total cost. Management must plan for and control electricity usage in order to control cost. However, to do this, management must be aware of the cost behavior of electricity.

Exhibit 2.4 illustrates a mixed cost—the electricity expense of one of the Dixie Fair Food Stores. The graph shows a fixed monthly cost of $300 per month, at the point where the variable cost line crosses the vertical axis. The cost increases at a variable rate of $5 per hour the store is open.

As the dotted line shows, if the store is open 300 hours per month, total cost is $1,800. This can be proven mathematically as follows:

$$\$300 + \$5 \text{ per Hour (300 Hours)} = \$300 + \$1,500$$
$$= \$1,800$$

Another example of a mixed cost is repairs and maintenance. If a business operates a fleet of trucks, it incurs certain costs just to keep the vehicles in operating condition, much as an individual who operates an automobile

Exhibit 2.4 Mixed Cost

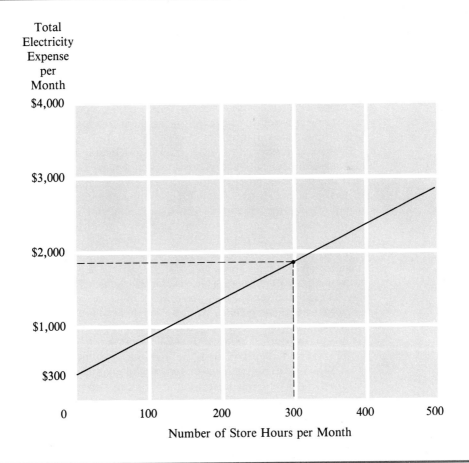

incurs costs for periodic lubrication, oil change, and tune-ups. The more the vehicles are operated, the greater the maintenance expense, just as an individual's automobile requires more repairs as it is used more. In just the same way, the operation of machinery in factories results in a mixed cost for repairs and maintenance.

Many costs are mixed. Management therefore has the problem of being able to separate the fixed element of the cost from the variable element for planning and controlling purposes. There are several methods for doing this. None of them is perfect; but if used appropriately, they generally provide satisfactory results. Three ways to accomplish the separation are: the scatter chart method, the high-low points method, and the method of least squares.

Scatter Chart Method

The **scatter chart method** involves estimating the fixed and variable elements of a mixed cost by a visual process. It is sometimes called the *visual-fit method.* The accountant must first determine the appropriate base against which to measure the variable cost. To do this, he or she assumes a base that appears to be the one causing the variable element of the mixed cost. Historical cost data is used to plot cost information about the mixed cost and the base against which it is assumed the variable element varies. This data is plotted on a **scatter chart,** often called a *scatter graph.* To illustrate the application of the scatter chart method, assume that the Deluxe Delivery Service is attempting to predict the amount of repairs and maintenance expense it will incur next year. It realizes that repairs and maintenance expense is a mixed cost; but it is uncertain as to what amount is fixed and what amount is variable.

Deluxe Delivery Service uses trucks to deliver packages within a city. Management believes that repairs and maintenance expense varies either in relation to the number of miles driven or in relation to the number of deliveries made. Historical data for last year is presented in Exhibit 2.5. This exhibit shows the amount of repairs and maintenance expense that has been incurred during each of the last twelve months, along with the total number of miles driven and the total number of deliveries made.

From this data, two scatter charts are constructed. On one, repairs and maintenance expense is plotted on the vertical axis against total miles driven. On the other, the expense is plotted against total number of deliveries. These scatter charts are shown as Exhibits 2.6 and 2.7.

Looking at the two charts, you can see that both indicate some relationship between the base activity and the repairs and maintenance expense. However, the dots in Exhibit 2.6 more clearly show a straight-line relationship, similar to a variable cost line. Exhibit 2.7 shows that although there may be some correlation between repairs and maintenance expense and the number of deliveries made, the dots are considerably more scattered than in Exhibit 2.6. Thus, management can conclude that total miles driven is the more appropriate base against which to measure the variable element of repairs and maintenance expense.

The procedure of using the scatter chart to estimate the amount of the fixed cost element and the variable rate is shown in Exhibit 2.8.

Exhibit 2.5 Data for Deluxe Delivery Service

Month	Total Repairs and Maintenance Expense	Number of Miles	Number of Deliveries
January	$410	2,000	50
February	375	1,500	100
March	430	2,500	120
April	450	3,200	160
May	495	4,000	150
June	490	3,800	175
July	500	4,200	200
August	460	3,000	100
September	470	3,500	140
October	435	2,600	200
November	480	3,700	75
December	570	5,400	250

A straight line is visually fitted through the clusters of dots on the scatter chart. The idea is to come as close to all the dots as possible. Since this is only a visual estimation—an "eyeballing" process—individuals will determine different lines. The point at which the straight line intersects the vertical axis represents fixed cost, in this case, $280 per month. The slope of the straight line—that is, the amount of increase on the vertical axis resulting from an increase on the horizontal axis—represents the variable rate.

The dotted lines in this exhibit show that, as the number of miles increases from 0 to 2,000, total repairs and maintenance expense increases from $280 to $390. Thus, an increase of 2,000 miles causes an increase in cost of $110. The variable rate therefore is $.055 per mile ($110 ÷ 2,000 miles).

Since the scatter chart method requires visual estimation, the results are not always completely reliable. Consequently, in some situations, the accountant may believe that the scatter chart method is not the best one to use to determine the fixed and variable elements of the mixed cost. In these cases, the scatter chart can be used to determine whether a straight-line relationship, or correlation, exists between the variable element of the mixed cost and the activity against which it is assumed the variable element varies; this was done in Exhibits 2.6 and 2.7. The accountant, having determined the appropriate base against which to measure the variable cost, can then use either the high-low points method or the method of least squares to determine more accurately the amount of fixed cost and variable cost within the mixed cost.

Exhibit 2.6 Scatter Chart–Miles as Base

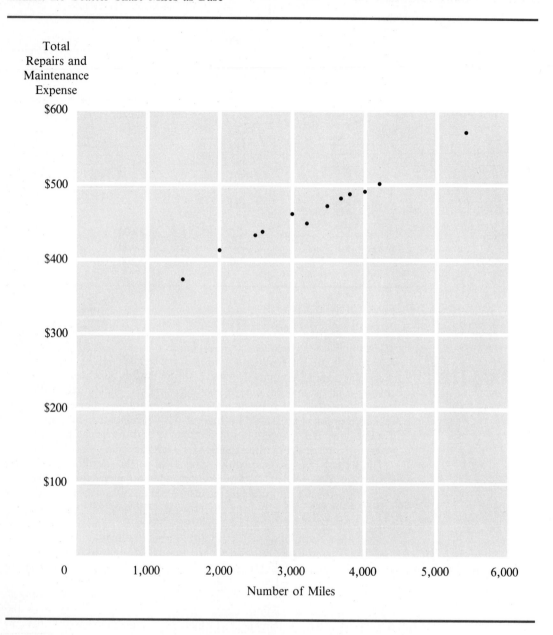

The **high-low points method** is a relatively simple method for determining the amount of the fixed element and the variable element of a mixed cost. It is not completely reliable; but in some cases it provides a better estimation than the scatter chart method. To use it, the appropriate base should already have been determined with a scatter chart. Once this has been done,

Exhibit 2.7 Scatter Chart–Deliveries as Base

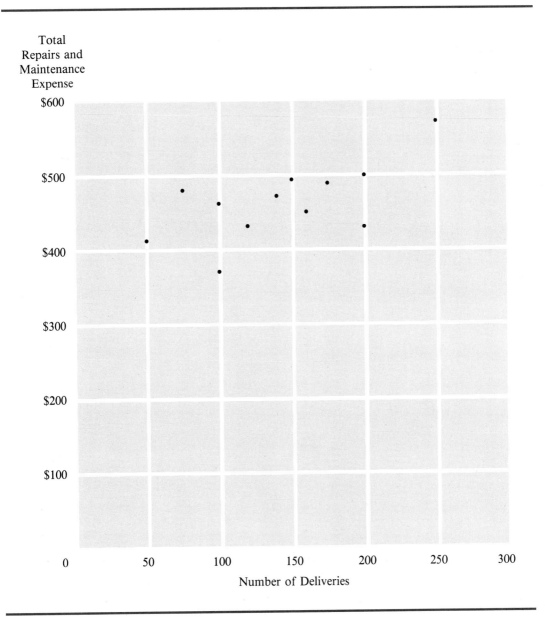

the high-low points method merely compares the amount of change in cost and in activity between the high and low points of activity, based on historical data.

To apply this method in our example of the Deluxe Delivery Service, first determine the high and low points of activity. From Exhibit 2.5, note that

Exhibit 2.8 Scatter Chart–Estimating Process

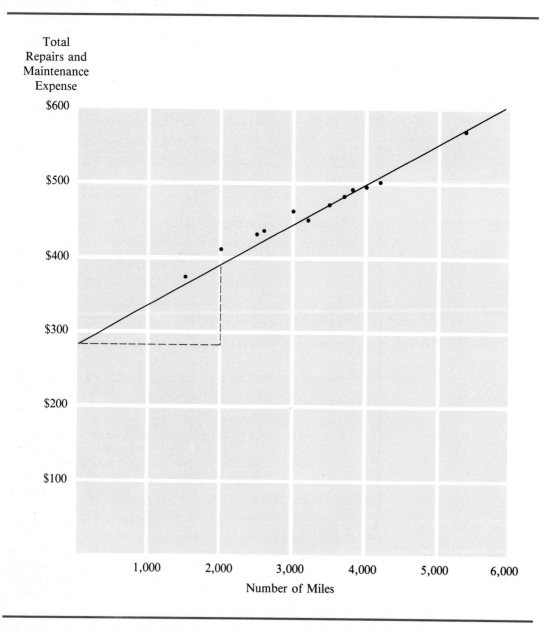

Total Repairs and Maintenance Expense

Number of Miles

the high point of activity was December, in which 5,400 miles were driven at a cost of $570. The low point of activity was February, with 1,500 miles and a cost of $375. The difference between these two periods in both miles and costs is calculated as follows:

Month	Number of Miles	Total Cost
December (High)	5,400	$570
February (Low)	1,500	375
Difference	3,900	$195

As you can see, with a difference of 3,900 miles there is a difference in total cost of $195. The cost per mile is determined by dividing $195 by 3,900 miles as follows:

$$\frac{\$195}{3,900 \text{ Miles}} = \$.05 \text{ per Mile}$$

That means every mile driven results in a repair and maintenance cost of $.05. That is the variable rate.

Now you can determine the fixed element of the mixed cost. In December, the high point of activity, total repairs and maintenance expense was $570. Knowing this, and knowing the variable rate is $.05 per mile, you can determine the fixed cost as follows:

Total Cost = Fixed Cost + Variable Cost
$570 = Fixed Cost + ($.05 × 5,400 Miles)
$570 = Fixed Cost + $270
Fixed Cost = $570 − $270
Fixed Cost = $300 per Month

You can determine the fixed cost by inserting the variable rate for either the high or the low month into the equation. Here, we used December. However, if you use February to determine the fixed cost, you will obtain the same answer.

Strictly speaking, the high-low points method is accurate only at the points used in the calculations. Applying the method assumes that all points lie on a straight line between the high and low points. That is not always a valid assumption. A scatter chart will show whether there is sufficient linearity between the high and low points for use of the high-low points method to be valid.

The high-low points method assumes a mixed cost can be divided into specific fixed and variable elements. For estimating purposes, this assumption works well in practice. You should realize, however, that it is merely an estimate. In our example, fixed cost is not necessarily exactly $300 per month; nor is variable cost necessarily exactly $.05 per mile. However, if management believes that these figures are realistic, it can plan for the amount of repairs and maintenance expense expected next year. For example, if the company expects to drive 80,000 miles next year, the expected repairs and maintenance expense is determined as follows:

Fixed Cost: $300 per Month × 12 Months = $3,600
Variable Cost: $.05 per Mile × 80,000 Miles = 4,000
     Total Cost $7,600

Next year's estimate is based on past costs. If costs are expected to rise, the accountant should attempt to estimate the expected increase in costs and adjust the figures accordingly.

The data used in this example were from the past year. In some cases, management may want to go back several years or maybe only several months. One difficulty in going back over longer periods of time is that costs incurred in prior years are normally lower than current costs. Therefore, a cost based on a five-year average probably does not accurately represent what the cost will be next year. In these cases, it is important to adjust the amounts derived for anticipated increases in costs.

**Method of
Least Squares**

A third technique for determining the fixed and variable elements of a mixed cost is the **method of least squares,** a statistical technique that provides a straight-line formula for the mixed cost. Basically, it attempts to find a straight line that represents the observed cost behavior better than any other straight line. The application of the least squares method used to be cumbersome, but recent advances in hand calculators and the availability of the computer makes the use of this statistical technique much easier.

The appendix to this chapter applies the least squares method to the Deluxe Delivery Service example. When this method is used, fixed cost is $310 per month and the variable rate is $.0469 per mile. The least squares method provides the most reliable representation of these costs.

A summary of the results of each method is shown below:

	Variable Rate	Fixed Cost
Scatter Chart	$.055	$280
High-Low Points	.05	300
Least Squares	.0469	310

You can see that the amounts calculated with the least squares method differ from those calculated with the high-low points method. The fixed cost is a little higher, and the variable rate is a little lower. For the relatively small amounts in this example, management might still decide to use the high-low points method. However, in situations involving millions of dollars, the use of the more reliable method of least squares is warranted.

There is also a difference in results between the method of least squares and the scatter chart method. That is not unusual. The scatter chart method is strictly an "eyeballing" process, and its use to separate a mixed cost into its fixed and variable elements is not always reliable.

The least squares illustration in the appendix again shows the other use of the scatter chart. The scatter chart shows whether a straight-line relationship exists between the variable element of the mixed cost and the base against which it is assumed the variable element varies. If a scatter chart shows that no such straight-line relationship exists, one does not waste time going through the mathematics of the method of least squares using an inappropriate base. However, when a straight-line relationship is indicated by the scatter chart (as in Exhibit 2.6), the method of least squares provides the most accurate determination of the fixed and variable elements.

A word of caution is in order. Although the method of least squares is more reliable than the other methods, it is only as good as the data used. If a scatter chart clearly indicates the lack of a straight-line relationship, forcing the numbers into the least squares equation will provide meaningless—or worse, misleading—results. If the scatter chart shows a weak correlation (such as in Exhibit 2.7), the method of least squares can still be used; but the amounts derived are not as accurate as they might appear to be.

Furthermore, the relationship established through a least squares analysis should be consistent with common-sense judgment. For example, a scatter chart may show a correlation between maintenance cost and the length of employees' coffee breaks; and you can use the least squares method to arrive at the numbers. But common sense tells you that this is not a sound basis for estimating future maintenance costs.

In summary, all methods illustrated can be useful provided that management understands the limitations of data and does not place unwarranted faith in their use.

Summary	In order to accomplish the managerial function of planning and controlling costs, management must understand how costs behave. Costs are generally classified into two primary categories: variable and fixed. A fixed cost remains constant within a relevant range of activity. A variable cost changes in total in proportion to some change in a particular activity.

In addition to fixed and variable costs, there are other cost behavior patterns, the two primary ones being step-variable cost and mixed cost. A step-variable cost changes in relation to changes in an activity, but not in direct proportion. A mixed cost contains both fixed and variable elements.

For planning and controlling purposes, management must be able to determine the fixed and variable elements of a mixed cost. This can be done by use of the scatter chart method, the high-low points method, or the method of least squares.

The scatter chart can be used to estimate the fixed and variable elements of a mixed cost; but it is also used to determine whether a relationship exists between the variable element and the base against which it is assumed the variable element varies. The high-low points method is a relatively simple but not highly accurate method of determining the fixed and variable elements of a mixed cost. The method of least squares is the most reliable method for dividing a mixed cost into its fixed and variable elements, because it uses statistical concepts in its application.

Knowledge of cost behavior is important in many areas of managerial accounting. Cost behavior concepts will be applied throughout this text. Therefore, it is important that you understand them.

Appendix: Applying the Method of Least Squares	The **method of least squares** is a method for determining the fixed and variable elements of a mixed cost, based on the statistical concepts of regression analysis. A discussion of these statistical concepts is beyond

the scope of this text; but the mathematical application is illustrated in this appendix.

As illustrated in this chapter's discussion of the scatter chart, we are attempting to determine a straight line that represents the mixed cost. The mathematical equation for a straight line is:

$$y = a + bx$$

The total cost is y; a is the fixed cost; b is the variable rate; and x is the activity that varies. In this example, x is miles. The straight line y is determined by solving the following simultaneous equations:

1. $\Sigma xy = a\Sigma x + b\Sigma x^2$
2. $\Sigma y = na + b\Sigma x$

In these equations, y represents the total mixed cost; Σ means summation; and n is the number of observations. In this example, an observation is made for each month's data. Thus, we have twelve observations based on the data generated for twelve months.

The data to be used in solving the simultaneous equations are based on the data for Deluxe Delivery Service in Exhibit 2.5; they are shown in Exhibit 2.9. The amounts to be used for the items in the equations are:

$$\Sigma x = 39,400 \qquad \Sigma xy = \$18,849,500 \qquad n = 12$$
$$\Sigma y = \$5,565 \qquad \Sigma x^2 = 141,680,000$$

Exhibit 2.9 Data for Method of Least Squares

Month	Number of Miles x	Total Repairs and Maintenance Expense y	xy	x^2
January	2,000	$ 410	$ 820,000	4,000,000
February	1,500	375	562,500	2,250,000
March	2,500	430	1,075,000	6,250,000
April	3,200	450	1,440,000	10,240,000
May	4,000	495	1,980,000	16,000,000
June	3,800	490	1,862,000	14,440,000
July	4,200	500	2,100,000	17,640,000
August	3,000	460	1,380,000	9,000,000
September	3,500	470	1,645,000	12,250,000
October	2,600	435	1,131,000	6,760,000
November........	3,700	480	1,776,000	13,690,000
December........	5,400	570	3,078,000	29,160,000
Σ	39,400	$5,565	$18,849,500	141,680,000

The fixed cost a and the variable rate b are the unknowns for which we are solving. Substituting the above data in the two equations results in the following:

1. $\$18,849,500 = 39,400a + 141,680,000b$
2. $\$ \quad 5,565 = \quad 12a + \quad 39,400b$

In order to solve the equations, we must eliminate one of the unknowns through subtraction. We can do this by multipling Equation 1 by 3 and Equation 2 by 9,850. This gives the following results:

1. $\$56,548,500 = 118,200a + 425,040,000b$
2. $\underline{\$54,815,250 = 118,200a + 388,090,000b}$
   $\$ \ 1,733,250 = \qquad\quad 36,950,000b$

Therefore:

$$b = \frac{\$1,733,250}{36,950,000}$$

$$b = \$.0469 \text{ per Mile}$$

Substituting \$.0469 for b in the original Equation 2, we determine the fixed cost as follows:

$$\$5,565 = 12a + 39,400 \ (\$.0469)$$
$$12a = \$5,565 - \$1,848^a$$
$$12a = \$3,717$$
$$a = \frac{\$3,717}{12}$$
$$a = \$310 \text{ per Month}^a$$

[a] Rounded to the nearest dollar.

In summary, the fixed cost is \$310 per month; and the variable rate is \$.0469 per mile.

Review Problem	**Problem**

Operating expenses for Riston Company for 19X2 are shown below:

Salaries	$60,000
Advertising	12,000
Supplies	5,220
Utilities	8,000

In predicting the costs for 19X3, the controller has determined that salaries are fixed at \$5,000 per month and advertising at \$1,000 per month. Supplies is a variable cost that varies in relation to units sold. Utilities appears to be a mixed cost; its variable portion varies in relation to the number of hours the firm is open. Data for the four quarters of last year are shown below:

Quarter	Hours Open	Utilities	Units Sold	Supplies
1st	750	$1,100	5,000	$150
2nd	800	1,140	8,000	240
3rd	600	980	4,000	120
4th	1,000	1,300	12,000	360

During the first quarter of 19X3, the firm expects to sell 7,500 units and to be open 780 hours.

Required:

Assuming no change in fixed costs or variable rates, determine the total expected cost for each operating expense for the first quarter of 19X3.

Solution

Salaries:

$$3 \text{ Months} \times \$5,000 \text{ per Month} = \$15,000$$

Advertising:

$$3 \text{ Months} \times \$1,000 \text{ per Month} = \$3,000$$

Supplies:

$$\frac{\$5,220}{29,000 \text{ Units Sold}^a} = \$.18 \text{ per Unit}$$

$$7,500 \text{ Units} \times \$.18 \text{ per Unit} = \$1,350$$

^{a} 5,000 + 8,000 + 4,000 + 12,000 = 29,000

Utilities: To determine the expected cost for utilities, it is necessary to use the high-low points method to determine the variable rate and fixed cost per quarter.

Quarter	Hours Open	Total Cost
4th (High)	1,000	$1,300
3rd (Low)	600	980
Difference	400	$ 320

$$\text{Variable Rate} = \frac{\$320}{400 \text{ Hours}} = \$.80 \text{ per Hour}$$

$$\text{Total Cost} = \text{Fixed Cost} + \text{Variable Cost}$$
$$\$1,300 = \text{Fixed Cost} + (\$.80 \times 1,000 \text{ Hours})$$
$$\$1,300 = \text{Fixed Cost} + \$800$$
$$\text{Fixed Cost} = \$1,300 - \$800$$
$$\text{Fixed Cost} = \$500 \text{ per Quarter}$$

Knowing the variable rate and fixed cost per quarter, we can calculate the expected utilities cost for the first quarter of 19X3 as follows:

Fixed cost: $ 500
Variable Cost: $.80 per Hour × 780 Hours =   624
     Total Cost $1,124

It is also possible to arrive at total cost by merely substituting the variable rate and fixed cost in the total cost equation as follows:

$$\text{Total Cost} = \$500 + (\$.80 \times 780 \text{ Hours})$$
$$= \$500 + \$624$$
$$= \$1,124$$

Questions

2-1 Distinguish between the terms *cost* and *expense*.

2-2 How can it be said that all expenses are costs, but not all costs are expenses?

2-3 Why does management need to know anything about cost behavior?

2-4 Assume that in October management plans for November's electricity expense to be $400. The actual November expense turns out to be $550. How can the expense be controlled when it has already been incurred?

2-5 Why should management be concerned with separating a mixed cost into its fixed and variable elements?

2-6 Define the following cost behavior patterns:
    a. Variable cost.
    b. Fixed cost.
    c. Step-variable cost.
    d. Mixed cost.

2-7. An individual was heard to say, "I don't know why they call it step-variable; it looks more like step-fixed to me." Comment.

2-8 If fixed costs do not change, how can they be controlled?

2-9 What is the difference between a committed fixed cost and a discretionary fixed cost?

2-10 "The term *discretionary cost* implies that the cost can be incurred or not incurred based on the judgment of management; therefore, a discretionary cost is an optional cost." Comment on the validity of this statement.

2-11 Name the three methods that can be used to separate a mixed cost into its fixed and variable elements.

2-12 How can a scatter chart be used?

2-13 What is the primary disadvantage in using a scatter chart to separate a mixed cost into its fixed and variable elements?

2-14 What is the primary disadvantage in using the high-low points method to separate a mixed cost into its fixed and variable elements?

2-15 Which is the best method for separating a mixed cost into its fixed and variable elements. Why?

2-16 The scatter charts for the Deluxe Delivery Service (Exhibits 2.6 and 2.7) show that number of miles is the better base. Why might you have expected this to be true?

2-17 Cost Behavior Identification Select the statement below that correctly describes the following graph:

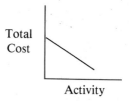

1. The graph represents a fixed cost.
2. An increase in activity reduces total cost.
3. An increase in activity reduces unit cost.
4. The graph represents a variable cost.

2-18 Understanding Fixed Costs Consider the following information:

Number of Units Produced	Fixed Cost
0– 25,000	$35,000
25,001– 50,000	65,000
50,001– 75,000	85,000
75,001–100,000	95,000

a. If 40,000 units are produced, what is the amount of fixed cost?
b. What is the relevant range for a fixed cost of $95,000?
c. Notice that the increases in fixed cost from range to range are not equal. How do you explain that?

2-19 Cost Behavior Identification Identify the cost behavior patterns illustrated by the following graphs:

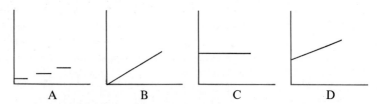

2-20 Distinguishing Fixed Costs Identify the following fixed costs as either committed or discretionary:
a. Salary of the vice-president for manufacturing.
b. Television commercials for a new product.
c. Depreciation on office building.

d. Salary of one researcher on a staff of 100 researchers.

e. Repairs and maintenance expense.

2–21 Scatter Chart Selection Which of the following scatter charts is the appropriate one to use in determining the base against which to measure the variable element of the mixed cost?

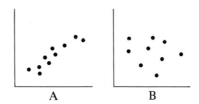

A   B

2–22 High-Low Points Method A company has determined the high and low points of yearly activity and cost for one of its mixed costs as follows:

	Total Activity (Hours)	Total Cost
High Month	20,000	$55,000
Low Month	4,000	15,000

Determine the fixed cost per month and the variable rate.

2–23 High-Low Points Method Refer to Exercise 2–22. Assume that the solution was $3,000 per month and $4 per hour. The company expects next year's activity to be 150,000 hours.

a. Determine next year's expected total cost for the company.

b. Draw a graph that represents the cost determined in part a.

2–24 High-Low Points Method Sam's Supermarket considers electricity a mixed cost. By using a scatter chart, Sam has determined that there is a relationship between electricity expense and the number of hours per month the store is open. During the past year, in the month that the store was open 500 hours, electricity expense totaled $2,100. In the month that it was open 250 hours, electricity expense totaled $1,350. What fixed monthly cost and hourly rate should Sam use to estimate electricity expense for the upcoming year?

2–25 High-Low Points Method Refer to Exercise 2–24. Assume that the solution was $800 per month and $5 per hour. Sam expects to be open a total of 5,000 hours in the upcoming year.

a. Determine next year's expected electricity expense.

b. Draw a graph that represents next year's expected electricity expense.

2–26 High-Low Points Method Last year, total operating expenses for Batsnip, Inc., were $325,000 in February, when sales were $500,000, the lowest for the year. They were $500,000 in December, when sales were $1,000,000, the highest for the year. Determine (1) variable operating expenses as a percentage of total sales and (2) fixed operating expenses per month.

Problems

2-27 High-Low Points Method E–Z Rider Mower Company has been analyzing its past experience with one of its mixed costs. Results for the past two years are as follows:

19X4, by Quarter	Total Number of Mowers Produced	Total Cost
1st	50,000	$ 450,000
2nd	35,000	340,000
3rd	20,000	200,000
4th	15,000	170,000
Total	120,000	$1,160,000

19X5, by Quarter		
1st	60,000	$ 530,000
2nd	40,000	400,000
3rd	30,000	310,000
4th	20,000	180,000
Total	150,000	$1,420,000

Required:

a. Based on the data for 19X4 and 19X5, use the high-low points method to determine the expected fixed cost per quarter and the variable rate per unit produced for 19X6.

b. If the company expects to produce 180,000 mowers in 19X6, what is the total expected cost?

c. Assume that the data for the fourth quarter of 19X5 had been $200,000 and 25,000 units. Would this have affected the answer you determined in part a? Why or why not?

2-28 Least Squares Method (*Appendix*) Refer to Problem 2–27.
Required:

Use the method of least squares to determine the expected fixed cost per quarter and the variable rate per unit produced.

2-29 Scatter Chart and High-Low Points Method Big Burst Balloon Company frequently must hire temporary secretarial help and also pay its regular secretaries overtime. Management believes that the need for additional secretarial help is based on either total sales or the total number of employee hours worked. Data from last year's records are shown below:

Month	Total Secretarial Expense	Total Sales	Total Number of Employee Hours
January	$14,000	$100,000	10,000
February	15,000	130,000	12,000
March	12,000	80,000	14,000
April	15,000	150,000	20,000

May	19,000	200,000	15,000
June	20,000	250,000	18,000
July	22,000	300,000	30,000
August	20,000	240,000	30,000
September	17,000	180,000	28,000
October	16,000	160,000	30,000
November	14,000	110,000	25,000
December	13,000	90,000	20,000

Required:
  a. Prepare two scatter charts to determine which activity—total sales or total number of employee hours—is the appropriate base against which to measure the variable element of total secretarial expense.
  b. Using the appropriate scatter chart prepared in part a, visually estimate the straight line that represents total cost. Draw this line and estimate the fixed cost and variable rate.
  c. Using the base determined in part a, use the high-low points method to calculate the variable rate and the fixed cost per month.

2–30 Least Squares Method (*Appendix*) Refer to Problem 2–29.
Required:
  Use the method of least squares to determine the fixed and variable elements of total secretarial expense. Use only the more appropriate base for these calculations.

2–31 Least Squares Method (*Appendix*) Refer to Exhibit 2.5, "Data for Deluxe Delivery Service."
Required:
  a. Using the number of deliveries as the base activity, use the method of least squares to determine the fixed and variable elements of total repairs and maintenance expense.
  b. Why does your answer differ from that obtained in the appendix, where number of miles was used as the base? Which answer do you think is more reliable? Why?

2–32 Scatter Chart and High-Low Points Method Merciful Arms Hospital installed a new body scanner last year. In trying to estimate the current year's expected cost of operating and maintaining the scanner, the hospital's controller has been reviewing cost and use data for each of the past four quarters, as shown below:

Quarter	Number of Patients	Number of Hours Used	Total Cost
1st	100	75	$10,750
2nd	350	200	12,500
3rd	400	550	15,000
4th	250	300	13,000

The controller feels confident that the cost of operating the scanner is a mixed cost.

Required:

a. Prepare two scatter charts to determine which activity—number of patients or number of hours used—is the appropriate base against which to measure the variable element of the total cost.

b. Using the appropriate scatter chart prepared in part a, visually estimate the straight line that represents total cost. Draw this line and estimate the fixed cost and variable rate.

c. Using the base determined in part a, use the high-low points method to calculate the variable rate and fixed cost per quarter.

d. The controller estimates that 1,600 patients will use the scanner in the current year. This will require 1,400 hours of scan time. Calculate expected total cost for the current year.

2-33 Least Squares Method (*Appendix*) Refer to Problem 2-32.
Required:

a. Use the method of least squares to determine the fixed and variable elements of total cost. Use only the more appropriate base for these calculations.

b. The controller estimates that 1,600 patients will use the scanner in the current year. This will require 1,400 hours of scan time. Calculate expected total cost for the current year.

2-34 High-Low Points Method Last year's operating expenses for Sizzlin Sales Company are shown below:

F	Salaries	$100,000
V	Sales Commissions	50,000
M	Repairs and Maintenance	61,800
F	Power	36,000
M	Supplies	18,600

In trying to predict costs for the current year, the controller has determined that salaries and power are fixed and sales commissions are variable. Repairs and maintenance and supplies appear to be mixed costs; their variable elements vary in relation to units sold. Data for the four quarters of last year are shown below:

Quarter	Repairs and Maintenance	Supplies	Units Sold
1st	$11,000	$3,500	30,000
2nd	16,500	5,200	60,000
3rd	13,300	3,900	40,000
4th	21,000	6,000	80,000

Required:

a. Use the high-low points method to determine the fixed and variable elements of repairs and maintenance expense and supplies expense.

b. Assume the firm expects to sell 250,000 units in the current year. Determine the total expected repairs and maintenance expense and supplies expense.

2-35 Least Squares Method (*Appendix*) Refer to Problem 2-34.

Required:

a. Use the method of least squares to determine the fixed and variable elements of repairs and maintenance expense and supplies expense.

b. Assume the firm expects to sell 250,000 units in the current year. Determine the total expected repairs and maintenance expense and supplies expense.

2–36 Cost Behavior Identification The controller for Krispy Cereal Company has been analyzing the cost behavior of several of the company's costs, as described below.

a. The company puts a toy that costs $.07 in each box of cereal. Sales are not expected to exceed 50,000 boxes a month.

b. The firm pays rent of $3,000 a month for a building in which it can manufacture up to 50,000 boxes of cereal a month.

c. Accounts receivable clerks are paid $750 a month. One clerk is needed for each 10,000 boxes sold per month.

d. The cost of office supplies seems to vary with sales. Yet, last year when production was stopped for two weeks, office supplies were still used. Analysis of last year's data shows that in one month, when 45,000 boxes were sold, office supplies expense totaled $1,500. In another month, when only 15,000 boxes were sold, office supplies expense totaled $600.

Required:

For each lettered item above, identify the type of cost behavior pattern described by the data. Draw a graph for each item described.

2–37 Cost Behavior Identification On the graphs below, the vertical axes represent *total* dollars of cost and the horizontal axes represent activity. In each case, the zero point is at the intersection of the two axes. Parts a–j below the graphs describe various cost data. For each description, select the graph that matches the data. Some graphs may be used more than once; some may not be used at all.

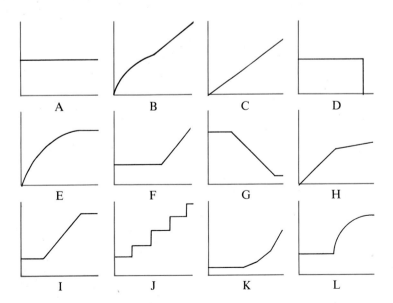

a. Depreciation of equipment, where the amount of depreciation charged is computed by the units-of-production method.

b. Electricity bill—a flat fixed charge plus a variable cost after a certain number of kilowatt hours is used.

c. City water bill, computed as follows:

First 1,000,000 Gallons or Less:	$1,000 Flat Fee
Next 10,000 Gallons:	$.003 per Gallon Used
Next 10,000 Gallons:	$.006 per Gallon Used
Next 10,000 Gallons:	$.009 per Gallon Used

d. Cost of lubricant for machines, where cost per unit decreases with each pound of lubricant used (for example, if one pound is used, the cost is $10.00; if two pounds are used, the cost is $19.98; if three pounds are used, the cost is $29.94; the minimum cost per pound is $9.25).

e. Depreciation of equipment, where the amount is computed by the straight-line method.

f. Rent on a factory building donated by the city, where the agreement calls for a fixed fee payment unless 200,000 employee-hours are worked, in which case no rent need be paid.

g. Salaries of repair personnel, where one such employee is needed for every 1,000 machine hours or less (that is, 0 to 1,000 hours requires one, 1,001 to 2,000 hours requires two, and so on).

h. A repair service contract that requires a minimum payment of $300 per month plus $50 per call for each service call over five per month.

i. A minimum salary for salespersons of $5,000 per year, plus a 10% commission on sales after $10,000 of sales have been achieved, with a maximum salary of $20,000 per year.

j. Rent on a factory building donated by the county, where an agreement calls for rent of $100,000 less $1 for each hour worked in excess of 200,000 hours; but a minimum rental payment of $20,000 must be paid.

Required:

Match each lettered cost description with the graph that shows the cost described. (AICPA adapted)

Chapter 3   Accounting for Manufacturing Costs

Learning Objectives

The purpose of this chapter is to introduce you to the procedures for accounting for manufacturing costs. The chapter defines some cost accounting terminology and illustrates how manufacturing costs are accumulated. Studying this chapter will enable you to:

1. Explain the differences between inventory and cost of goods sold for a merchandising firm and a manufacturing firm.
2. Define certain cost accounting terms.
3. Distinguish between product costs and period costs.
4. Journalize and post transactions of the cost accounting cycle.
5. Calculate factory overhead rates.
6. Prepare a schedule of cost of goods manufactured.

Chapter Topics

The major topics included in this chapter are:

Inventory and Cost of Goods Sold for a Merchandising Firm
Inventory for a Manufacturing Firm
Description of Manufacturing Costs
Product Costs and Period Costs
Accounting for Manufacturing Costs
Cost Accounting Cycle
Accounting for Variable Factory Overhead
Accounting for Fixed Factory Overhead
Accounting for Underapplied and Overapplied Overhead
Cost of Goods Manufactured

In a financial accounting course, emphasis usually centers on merchandising firms—business firms that buy and resell merchandise. The study of managerial accounting includes applications to both merchandising firms and manufacturing firms.

The basic difference between a merchandising firm and a manufacturing firm is that, while a merchandising firm buys a product that it later sells, the manufacturer buys certain types of materials and converts them into a product that it then sells. This additional function, manufacturing, requires a more complex accounting system than that used by a merchandising firm.

Manufacturing accounting is frequently referred to as **cost accounting,** because it places much emphasis on the development of manufacturing costs, that is, the cost of manufacturing products. Since managerial accounting is important to a manufacturing firm, it is necessary for the managerial accounting student to understand cost accounting terminology and the cost accounting process.

Inventory and Cost of Goods Sold for a Merchandising Firm

A major difference in accounting between a manufacturing firm and a merchandising firm is the method used to account for inventory and cost of goods sold. First, we will briefly review accounting for these two items for a merchandising firm.

Inventory (frequently called *merchandise inventory*) for a merchandising firm consists of items of merchandise that the business has purchased for resale. These items are in the same form when the business sells them as they were when it purchased them. For example, a clothing store buys shirts and sells them without changing them in any way. In some businesses, items may require some preparation before they are sold. For example, a new car dealer usually must add some accessories, wash the car, and service it. Nevertheless, the new car dealer is selling essentially the same car that was purchased.

Cost of goods sold represents the cost of merchandise the firm has bought and subsequently sold. On the income statement, cost of goods sold is shown as follows:

Inventory, January 1, 19X1	$150,000
Purchases	800,000
Cost of Goods Available for Sale	$950,000
Less: Inventory, December 31, 19X1	220,000
Cost of Goods Sold	$730,000

Inventory for a Manufacturing Firm

Unlike a merchandising firm, which has only one type of inventory, the manufacturer must purchase materials to be converted into the finished product through the manufacturing process. Consequently there are three types of inventory in a manufacturing firm: (1) raw materials inventory, (2) work-in-process inventory, and (3) finished goods inventory.

Raw Materials Inventory

Raw materials represent the items the manufacturer has purchased to use in producing a product. For example, an automobile manufacturer purchases steel, tires, glass, and other items that go into automobiles. The furniture manufacturer buys lumber, upholstery, paint, nails, glue, and other items to use in producing furniture. Any item used in the production process is raw material. The amount of raw materials on hand at any point is **raw materials inventory.**

The raw materials inventory account is a control account. The balance of the account at any point represents the total cost of raw materials on hand. Subsidiary accounts are used to keep a record of each individual item of raw material.

Raw material is further divided between direct material and indirect material. **Direct material** becomes an integral part of the final product. In the automobile manufacturing example, steel, tires, and glass are direct materials. For the furniture manufacturer, lumber and upholstery are direct materials.

Indirect material is used in the manufacturing process but does not become a part of the final product. These materials are often called supplies. Examples of indirect material are janitorial supplies for the factory, grease for the machinery, and light bulbs for the plant. In furniture manufacturing, sandpaper is indirect material. It is used in the process of manufacturing furniture, but it does not become a part of the final product. Often, minor items that become a part of the product, such as screws, nails, and bolts, are accounted for as indirect material. It is normally more practical and less expensive to account for such minor items in this way.

Work-in-Process Inventory

The conversion of raw materials into the final product takes some period of time. At any point in time, there will normally be raw materials at various stages of production. The started but unfinished production is called **work in process.** For example, the production of an automobile is work in process when steel has been molded into the body of the automobile but doors, glass, tires, and the other parts of the car have not been put on. The cost of unfinished production is **work-in-process inventory.** Work-in-process inventory includes not only the cost of the raw materials used but also all other manufacturing costs that are considered a part of the product, such as the wages for individuals who have worked in production, electricity used to run the machines, the heat for the plant, and janitorial services. In summary, any manufacturing cost used to get the product to a partially completed state is included in work-in-process inventory.

Finished Goods Inventory

Finished goods consist of the completed manufactured items the manufacturer has produced for sale to customers. The **finished goods inventory** account represents the cost of completed but unsold products. It is similar to merchandise inventory for the merchandising firm. Finished goods that have been sold during the period are reflected in cost of goods sold on the income statement. Raw materials inventory, work-in-process inventory, and finished goods inventory on hand at the balance sheet date are shown as assets on the balance sheet.

Description of Manufacturing Costs

Cost of goods sold for a merchandising firm is based on the cost of purchases and on increases or decreases in merchandise inventory. As previously illustrated, we can compute cost of goods sold by considering beginning and ending inventory in relation to purchases. The manufacturing firm does not sell what it purchases; it sells what it produces. Therefore, its cost of goods sold is based on cost of goods manufactured. **Cost of goods manufactured** is the manufacturing cost assigned to goods that were completed during a particular accounting period. In this respect, cost of goods manufactured for a manufacturing firm is similar to purchases for a merchandising firm. Three types of manufacturing costs combine to result in cost of goods manufactured: (1) direct material, (2) direct labor, and (3) factory overhead.

Direct Material

Variable Cost.

As stated earlier, **direct material** is raw material that becomes an integral part of the finished product. For accounting purposes, it is important to separate direct material from indirect material.

Direct material is always a variable cost. The use of direct material varies in direct proportion to the amount of the finished goods produced; therefore, direct material cost is directly proportional to production. For example, if production of a man's shirt requires one square yard of material at $3 per yard, production of 1,000 shirts results in use of 1,000 square yards of raw material and a direct material cost of $3,000.

Direct Labor

Direct labor is the cost of wages for the individuals who work on a specific product. For example, the cost of wages for individuals who operate the sewing machines in the manufacture of shirts is direct labor. In the manufacture of furniture, the individuals who cut lumber to the proper sizes are performing direct labor.

It is generally assumed that direct labor varies in proportion to the number of units produced. Thus, direct labor is usually considered a variable cost. In the discussion, examples, and problems in this text, direct labor is always considered variable. However, as a practical matter, some companies' contracts with workers require a minimum guaranteed annual wage, regardless of the amount worked. In these situations, the accountant must determine the appropriate manner for accounting for direct labor costs. It may be a mixed cost rather than a variable cost.

When direct material and direct labor are added together, the resultant total is called **prime cost.**

Factory Overhead

Any manufacturing cost that is not direct material or direct labor is **factory overhead.** It is not possible to list every item that may be a part of factory overhead, but some examples are shown below. Note that factory overhead is classified as either fixed or variable.

Examples of Fixed Factory Overhead Costs

Depreciation on Machinery and Equipment

Depreciation on Factory Building

Depreciation on Raw Materials Warehouse

Depreciation on Finished Goods Warehouse

Taxes on Plant and Equipment

Insurance on Plant and Equipment

Salaries for Upper-Level Production Managers

Examples of Variable Factory Overhead Costs

Electricity, Heating, and Water

Indirect Material

Indirect Labor

Indirect labor, in contrast to direct labor, is the cost of wages paid to individuals who work in the manufacturing process but who do not work directly on a specific product. For example, wages paid to supply clerks, custodians, and plant guards are considered indirect labor.

The salaries of factory supervisors, a lower-level management position, are considered variable costs (indirect labor). Salaries for upper-level production managers are generally considered fixed costs.

As suggested in Chapter 2, the classification of costs into fixed and variable may not be as easy as it appears here. The costs listed above as variable overhead may, for some firms, be step-variable, mixed, or even fixed costs, depending on the actual cost behavior in that firm. This is especially true of indirect labor. For example, if the number of supply clerks increases as certain stages of production increase, the cost for supply clerks is step-variable. However, if the number of supply clerks remains constant regardless of the amount of production, the cost for supply clerks is fixed.

The exact classification between fixed and variable depends upon the manner in which the cost behaves. Accountants must study cost behavior patterns in order to properly classify them. It is important to realize that factory overhead may be variable, fixed, or some combination of the two. The illustrations and problems in this text will distinguish between fixed and variable factory overhead. Unless otherwise stated, this text treats factory overhead as fixed or variable according to the classifications shown in the list above.

Although this text uses the term *factory overhead,* you should be familiar with other terms often used in other texts, articles, financial statements, or by specific business enterprises. Frequently used terms are: *manufacturing overhead, manufacturing burden, factory burden,* and *indirect manufacturing cost.*

The combination of direct labor and factory overhead is called **conversion cost** because these costs are incurred in the conversion of direct material into finished product.

Product Costs and Period Costs

The major cost classifications on the income statement of a merchandising firm are cost of goods sold and operating expenses. Operating expenses consist of two primary classifications: selling expenses and administrative expenses. Selling and administrative expenses are **period costs**—expired costs incurred during a specific accounting period that are considered to benefit the firm for that period. They are deducted as expenses on the income statement in the calculation of net income. The treatment of selling and administrative expenses for a manufacturing firm does not differ from their treatment for a merchandising firm.

As previously mentioned, the manufacturing firm has another major classification of cost not found in a merchandising firm—manufacturing cost. Manufacturing costs that are considered to attach to the product are called **product costs.** Until sold, product costs are assets classified as raw materials inventory, work-in-process inventory, or finished goods inventory. At the time finished goods are sold, the product cost (an asset) becomes an expense (cost of goods sold).

Direct material, direct labor, and variable factory overhead are always considered product costs. Fixed factory overhead may be treated as either a product cost or a period cost; there are two schools of thought on this matter.

One school maintains that all the manufacturing costs are incurred to produce a product. Thus, fixed factory overhead should be included as a product cost. The other school maintains that fixed factory overhead is a period cost because it represents the cost of maintaining and operating the manufacturing plant and benefits the period in which it is incurred. Since the cost does not vary with production, it does not attach to the product and is not logically considered a product cost.

At the present time, under generally accepted accounting principles, fixed factory overhead is accounted for as product cost for external reporting. Certain internal management decisions, however, are better made by considering fixed factory overhead as a period cost. Thus, this cost can be treated as a period cost for internal purposes and a product cost for external purposes. Chapter 4 provides further discussion of this point.

Accounting for Manufacturing Costs

Accounting for manufacturing costs requires that the flow of costs match the manufacturing process. Raw materials enter the production process and direct labor and factory overhead convert the raw materials into finished goods.

If fixed factory overhead is accounted for as a product cost, the accounting process is called **absorption costing,** because fixed factory overhead is absorbed into the cost of the product. If fixed factory overhead is treated as a period cost, the costing process is referred to as **variable costing,** because only the variable manufacturing costs are included as a part of the cost of the product. Variable costing is frequently referred to as *direct costing.* Chapter 4 discusses variable costing more thoroughly. This chapter provides a relatively simple example of an absorption costing system so that you can see how it works.

The flow of product cost through work in process, finished goods, and ultimately to cost of goods sold on the income statement is illustrated for absorption costing in Exhibit 3.1.

Exhibit 3.1 Cost Flow–Absorption Costing

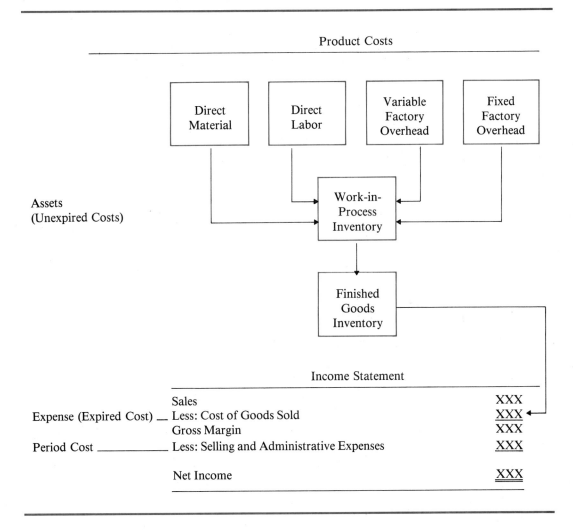

Cost Accounting Cycle

Accounting for the flow of manufacturing costs from initial incurrence to ultimate disposition as cost of goods sold is called the **cost accounting cycle.**

To illustrate this process, we will use the example of the Fabulous Furniture Manufacturing Company. The entries are numbered, rather than dated. Accounting for factory overhead is more complex than illustrated here. This example illustrates an **actual cost system** to record factory overhead; this is the simplest way, but not always the most practical.

1) Raw materials (direct and indirect) costing $30,000 were purchased on account.

Raw Materials Inventory	30,000	
Accounts Payable		30,000

Most manufacturing firms use the perpetual inventory method to account for raw materials. A firm must know at any time how many units of each type of raw material are in stock. The raw materials inventory account is a control account; there are subsidiary accounts for each type of inventory item. For example, if Entry 1 were a purchase of twenty-five different types of material, twenty-five subsidiary accounts would be needed. Each would be increased by the cost of the material for the account. The sum of entries to all twenty-five accounts would equal $30,000.

2) Lumber and upholstery materials (direct materials) costing $10,000 were put into the production process for the manufacture of chairs.

Work-in-Process Inventory	10,000	
Raw Materials Inventory		10,000

Since the raw materials inventory account is a control account, it is necessary for the specific subsidiary accounts for lumber and upholstery to be reduced by the costs of those items put into production.

3) Direct labor costs of $28,000 were incurred.

Work-in-Process Inventory	28,000	
Accrued Payroll		28,000

Direct labor is charged to the manufacturing process as a debit to work-in-process inventory. Depending on the size and complexity of the business, direct labor costs could be debited to an account called "direct labor," which would periodically be transferred to work-in-process inventory.

The credit depends on the type of payroll system the firm uses. For our purposes, we merely credit accrued payroll, which is a liability account. We ignore payroll deductions and the payment of payroll in this illustration.

It is important to note the difference in accounting for manufacturing labor costs versus accounting for salaries and wages that are selling and administrative expenses. Manufacturing labor costs are product costs. As such, they are not expenses of the period, but rather are assets. In this case, direct labor has been used in creation of a partially completed product. The asset is work-in-process inventory, an unexpired cost. Salaries and wages that are selling and administrative expenses are period costs. In those situations, the debit is made to salary expense or wages expense at the time the cost is incurred. Payroll manufacturing costs do not become expenses until the finished product is sold. At that time, the payroll costs, along with other manufacturing costs, become cost of goods sold expense.

4) The following variable factory overhead costs were incurred:

Power	$ 3,000
Indirect labor	11,500
Indirect material	
(sandpaper, screws, lightbulbs, janitorial supplies, repair parts)	1,500
Total	$16,000

Work-in-Process Inventory	16,000	
Utilities Payable		3,000
Accrued Payroll		11,500
Raw Materials Inventory		1,500

Since we are using an actual cost system, variable factory overhead costs are debited to work-in-process inventory as they are incurred. The credits depend on the individual cost items. In this case, utilities payable represents a liability to the utility company. Accrued payroll is similar to the credit for direct labor in Entry 3; it represents a liability to employees.

As with direct material, the company should maintain separate accounts for each type of item of indirect material. This is important for keeping track of how many are on hand, knowing when to order, and maintaining cost control. For example, the company is interested in knowing its repairs and maintenance expense. Therefore, it must keep accurate accounting records of the amount of supply parts used. In addition, indirect labor costs are also accounted for by type of cost. The company wants to know how much it is spending for plant guards, repair mechanics, and the other specific items of labor costs. Thus, using the natural classifications of costs (as discussed in Chapter 2) is necessary for cost control.

Note that costs incurred in Entry 4 are recorded as an asset, work-in-process inventory. Like direct materials and direct labor, overhead costs do not become expenses until the asset, finished goods inventory, is sold.

5) The following fixed factory overhead costs were incurred:

Managers' salaries	$3,500
Depreciation on equipment	1,500
Rent on factory building	3,000
Total	$8,000

Work-in-Process Inventory	8,000
Accrued Payroll	3,500
Accumulated Depreciation—Equipment	1,500
Rent Payable	3,000

This entry treats fixed factory overhead costs as product costs, using absorption costing. As product costs, they do not become expenses until the product is sold. The debit is made to work-in-process inventory and the credits to the respective liability accounts for salaries and rent and to accumulated depreciation.

6) The company completed chairs costing $50,000. The chairs were transferred from the factory to the finished goods warehouse.

Finished Goods Inventory	50,000	
Work-in-Process Inventory		50,000

Since the chairs have been completed and have been physically transferred from the manufacturing process to the finished goods warehouse, it is necessary to transfer the cost also. Under absorption costing, in which all manufacturing costs are charged to work in process, $50,000 is transferred to finished goods inventory by the debit and taken from work-in-process inventory by the credit.

Exhibit 3.2 Cost Accounting Cycle–Absorption Costing

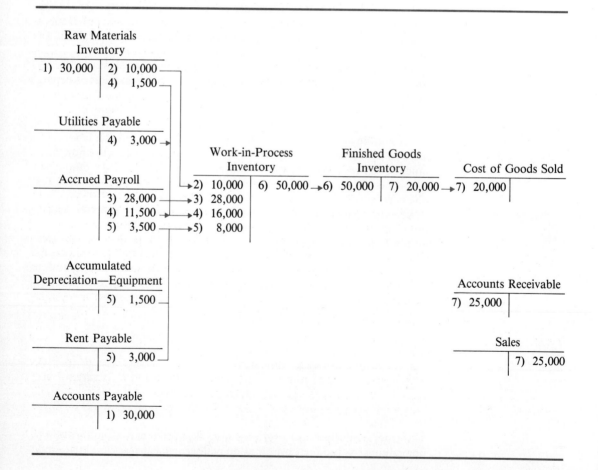

The final step in the cost accounting cycle is the sale of merchandise that has been manufactured.

7) Chairs costing $20,000 were sold on account for $25,000.

Cost of Goods Sold	20,000	
Finished Goods Inventory		20,000
Accounts Receivable	25,000	
Sales		25,000

It is at this point that the unexpired cost becomes an expired cost. The asset, in this case chairs costing $20,000, is no longer in inventory; it has been sold. The entry debits the expense account cost of goods sold and credits finished goods inventory. The asset has become an expense. The sale is recorded by a debit to accounts receivable and a credit to sales. The $5,000 difference between sales and cost of goods sold is the gross margin on this sale. It will be reflected on the income statement as part of total gross margin.

The postings to the individual ledger accounts shown in Exhibit 3.2 illustrate the flow of costs through the cost accounting cycle. Study the flow of costs carefully. You should understand how manufacturing costs are recorded as assets that later become an expense—cost of goods sold. If financial statements were prepared at the end of these particular transactions, the income statement would include $20,000 cost of goods sold expense. If a balance sheet were prepared, raw materials inventory would show a balance of $18,500; work-in-process inventory, $12,000; and finished goods inventory, $30,000.

Accounting for Variable Factory Overhead

The previous illustration assumed an actual cost system in which overhead costs were charged to work-in-process inventory as they were incurred. In most large companies, this system is not practical. Management requires timely—weekly or even daily—information on production costs.

Direct material and direct labor are incurred as an item is produced. Factory overhead, however, cannot be matched to the product so easily on a day-to-day basis. As a result, the accounting system must be designed to allow for recording factory overhead as it is actually incurred and for applying, or charging, factory overhead to work-in-process inventory at a predetermined, estimated overhead rate on a timely basis, such as weekly.

Variable Factory Overhead Incurred

A system under which direct material and direct labor are charged to work-in-process inventory at actual costs and factory overhead is charged at a predetermined rate is called an **actual/normal cost system.** The "normal" denotes that factory overhead is charged as though it occurred at an average rate, based on normal activity.

An actual/normal cost system requires that variable factory overhead be *debited* to an account called **variable factory overhead** as it is actually incurred. To illustrate, Entry 4 for the Fabulous Furniture Manufacturing Company would appear under an actual/normal cost system as follows:

4) Variable Factory Overhead	16,000	
Utilities Payable		3,000
Accrued Payroll		11,500
Raw Materials Inventory		1,500

After posting, the ledger account appears as follows:

Variable Factory Overhead

4) 16,000

Note that, in contrast with its treatment in the actual cost system, variable factory overhead is not charged to work-in-process inventory at the time it is incurred. Rather, the cost is accumulated on the debit side of the account, as shown above.

Variable Factory Overhead Applied

By definition, variable factory overhead varies in relation to some particular activity. However, the exact amount of cost is not usually known as it is incurred. For example, management usually does not know the exact amount of power cost from day to day or even from week to week. Although one can estimate the amount of indirect labor from day to day, the amount of cost actually incurred usually is not known until the end of the pay period—for example, at the end of two weeks.

In order that the appropriate amount of factory overhead can be charged to the product as it is produced, overhead costs are estimated prior to production, based on normal yearly activity. The estimated overhead, rather than the actual overhead, is charged to work-in-process inventory as manufacturing takes place. This procedure is referred to as **application of factory overhead.** It also provides management with current and timely information regarding product costs.

In order to apply factory overhead to work-in-process inventory, the company uses a predetermined overhead rate. The company uses an activity that it assumes variable overhead varies in relation to. The activity may be direct labor hours (DLH) worked, direct labor cost incurred (often called direct labor dollars), machine hours used, or number of units produced.

Fabulous Furniture Manufacturing Company uses direct labor hours worked as the base for applying factory overhead. This year, the company expects to incur variable factory overhead of $160,000 and use 40,000 hours of direct labor to produce its products. On this basis, the variable factory overhead rate is calculated as $4 per direct labor hour ($160,000 ÷ 40,000 DLH). To apply variable factory overhead costs to work-in-process inventory, the company makes periodic entries based on the number of direct labor hours worked.

During the current month, the Fabulous Furniture Manufacturing Company worked the following number of direct labor hours each week:

Week	DLH
1	800
2	1,200
3	1,300
4	900

= 3200
= 4800
= 5200
= 3600

The amount of factory overhead applied each week is determined by multiplying the overhead rate by the number of direct labor hours—$3,200 for Week 1 ($4 × 800 DLH). The entry to apply variable factory overhead at the end of Week 1 is as follows:

4A)	Work-in-Process Inventory	3,200	
	Variable Factory Overhead		3,200

A similar entry is made each week, the amount being based on the number of direct labor hours worked. The debit to work-in-process inventory is the same as that used in the actual cost system. However, instead of charging work-in-process inventory with the actual overhead incurred (which may not be known at the end of Week 1), we charge it with an estimated amount. This estimated amount is *credited* to variable factory overhead.

Assume that entries were made at the end of Weeks 2, 3, and 4. The ledger account for variable factory overhead, after posting all entries, now appears as follows:

Variable Factory Overhead

4) 16,000	4A)	3,200
	4B)	4,800
	4C)	5,200
	4D)	3,600
		16,800

Notice that the amount of variable factory overhead applied is $16,800, whereas the actual amount incurred is only $16,000. Accounting for this difference is illustrated in a later section.

Accounting for Fixed Factory Overhead

Accounting for fixed factory overhead under absorption costing is similar to accounting for variable factory overhead. We are concerned with fixed factory overhead incurred and fixed factory overhead applied.

Fixed Factory Overhead Incurred

Actual fixed factory overhead costs are *debited* to an account called **fixed factory overhead.** The actual costs were shown earlier to be $8,000. Most likely, they were recorded on the last day of the month.

The journal entry to record these costs is as follows:

5) Fixed Factory Overhead	8,000	
Accrued Payroll		3,500
Accumulated Depreciation—Equipment		1,500
Rent Payable		3,000

After the above entry has been posted, the ledger account for fixed factory overhead appears as follows:

Fixed Factory Overhead

5) 8,000	

Fixed Factory Overhead Applied

Ideally, a firm would wait until the end of the year, when all its costs would be known, before making any decisions regarding product pricing and other similar selling decisions. Practically, this is not possible. Furthermore, the manufacturing process should be charged with appropriate overhead costs on a timely basis. Therefore, under absorption costing, even though fixed overhead costs are not incurred in a variable fashion, they are applied (charged) to work in process on the basis of some activity. As with variable overhead, the activity may be direct labor hours, direct labor cost, machine hours, or units of production. In this example, we apply fixed factory overhead on the basis of direct labor hours.

A fixed factory overhead rate must first be determined. As previously mentioned, this year's production is expected to require 40,000 direct labor hours; and the company expects to incur total fixed factory overhead costs of $70,000. The fixed factory overhead rate, therefore, is $1.75 per direct labor hour ($70,000 ÷ 40,000 DLH).

The number of direct labor hours worked in the current month was shown earlier to be: Week 1, 800; Week 2, 1,200; Week 3, 1,300; and Week 4, 900. At the end of Week 1, fixed factory overhead of $1,400 ($1.75 × 800 DLH) is applied to work-in-process inventory as follows:

5A) Work-in-Process Inventory	1,400	
Fixed Factory Overhead		1,400

The fixed factory overhead account is similar to the variable factory overhead account. The debits represent actual costs incurred; the credits are the amounts applied. After entries for each week have been posted, the ledger account appears as follows:

Fixed Factory Overhead

5) 8,000	5A) 1,400
	5B) 2,100
	5C) 2,275
	5D) 1,575
	7,350

The amount of each credit was determined by multiplying $1.75 by the number of direct labor hours each week. Note that the actual fixed factory overhead incurred is $8,000. The amount applied to work in process, however, is only $7,350. Accounting for this difference of $650 is shown below.

Combined Overhead Rate

In this example, we used a variable overhead rate of $4.00 per direct labor hour and a fixed overhead rate of $1.75 per direct labor hour. It is possible to combine variable and fixed rates and use a single rate in applying overhead. In this case, it would be $5.75 per direct labor hour. A combined rate is useful for attempting to estimate total overhead costs for a period. However, management must be aware of cost behavior patterns, because certain decisions rely on the nature of cost behavior. Thus, using a separate rate for variable and fixed factory overhead and accumulating these costs in separate accounts often makes it easier to obtain data needed for internal decision making.

Accounting for Underapplied and Overapplied Overhead

Actual overhead incurred seldom (if ever) equals the amount of overhead applied in a particular year. If factory overhead applied is less than factory overhead incurred, the difference is called **underapplied overhead,** which is indicated by a debit balance in the factory overhead account. That means the actual overhead costs incurred were more than the amount charged to (absorbed by) the manufacturing process during the year.

If overhead applied is greater than overhead incurred, the difference is called **overapplied overhead,** which results in a credit balance in the factory overhead account. That means the amount of overhead charged to the manufacturing process was greater than the amount incurred.

Normally, a firm waits until the end of the year to account for any differences between incurred and applied overhead. This illustration will show how that is handled, assuming it is done at the end of the month.

The overhead accounts used in the example are shown below:

Variable Factory Overhead		Fixed Factory Overhead	
4) 16,000	4A) 3,200	5) 8,000	5A) 1,400
	4B) 4,800		5B) 2,100
	4C) 5,200		5C) 2,275
	4D) 3,600		5D) 1,575
	16,800		7,350

Variable factory overhead incurred was $16,000, but the amount applied was $16,800. The amount applied was $800 greater than the amount incurred; therefore, variable factory overhead was overapplied by $800. This means that the estimated amount of overhead charged to the manufacturing process was greater than the amount incurred.

Fixed factory overhead incurred was $8,000, but the amount applied was only $7,350. Since the amount applied is $650 less than the amount incurred, fixed factory overhead is underapplied by $650. In this case, less fixed overhead was charged to the manufacturing process than was incurred.

Overhead accounts must be closed out at the end of the accounting period, and the difference between overhead incurred and overhead applied must be disposed of. That is done either by adjusting cost of goods sold or by allocating to several accounts.

Adjusting Cost of Goods Sold

Differences in the overhead accounts are most easily and most frequently disposed of by adjustment of cost of goods sold. When the amount of underapplied or overapplied overhead is insignificant, this is the most practical thing to do. The entries are as follows:

8)	Variable Factory Overhead	800	
	Cost of Goods Sold		800
9)	Cost of Goods Sold	650	
	Fixed Factory Overhead		650

It is important to understand the nature of these entries. Since too much variable overhead has been charged to the manufacturing process, the entry credits cost of goods sold for $800. By this entry, the overcharge of $800 is taken out of cost of goods sold. The variable overhead account now has a zero balance and is ready for the next period's entries.

Fixed factory overhead was underapplied. By the entry shown above, the $650, which had not been charged to work-in-process inventory but which had been incurred, is now added to cost of goods sold. The fixed factory overhead account is also closed to a zero balance. Cost of goods sold now has a balance of $19,850. The ledger accounts after these entries appear below.

Variable Factory Overhead			Fixed Factory Overhead	
4) 16,000	4A) 3,200		5) 8,000	5A) 1,400
8) 800	4B) 4,800			5B) 2,100
16,800	4C) 5,200			5C) 2,275
	4D) 3,600			5D) 1,575
	16,800			7,350
				9) 650
				8,000

Cost of Goods Sold	
7) 20,000	8) 800
9) 650	
20,650	

Allocating to Accounts   As long as the underapplied or overapplied amount is not significant, an adjustment to cost of goods sold is the most practical thing to do. However, unless a firm has sold all of the product it has manufactured, the adjustment to cost of goods sold is not theoretically correct.

Overhead costs are charged to work-in-process inventory. These amounts are transferred to finished goods inventory, then to cost of goods sold. If there are balances in the inventory accounts, any underapplied or overapplied overhead should be allocated on the basis of the amount charged to the account during the period and still remaining in the account at the end of the period.

For example, assume that a company determines that it has underapplied fixed factory overhead by $100,000. Total overhead incurred was $600,000. The balance of each of the affected accounts and the amount of the current period's fixed overhead in each account is shown as follows:

	Account Balance	Amount of Applied Overhead
Work-in-Process Inventory	$ 200,000	$ 50,000
Finished Goods Inventory	500,000	200,000
Cost of Goods Sold	1,300,000	250,000
Total	$2,000,000	$500,000

In this case, $100,000 of underapplied fixed overhead is a significant amount. To merely add it to cost of goods sold would distort the income statement and the balance sheet. The $100,000 should be allocated to each of the accounts as follows;

Work-in-Process Inventory: $\dfrac{\$50,000}{\$500,000} \times \$100,000 = \$\ 10,000$

Finished Goods Inventory: $\dfrac{\$200,000}{\$500,000} \times \$100,000 = \quad 40,000$

Cost of Goods Sold: $\dfrac{\$250,000}{\$500,000} \times \$100,000 = \quad 50,000$

Total Underapplied Overhead: $\qquad\qquad \$100,000$

The entry to record this adjustment is as follows:

Work-in-Process Inventory	10,000	
Finished Goods Inventory	40,000	
Cost of Goods Sold	50,000	
Fixed Factory Overhead		100,000

To analyze each account and determine the amount of fixed overhead in the account balance may be time consuming. Therefore, this allocation process is used only when the amount of underapplied or overapplied overhead is significant enough to distort the financial statements.

It is possible to allocate overhead on the basis of the account balance. This process is easier, but not as accurate, because the amount of applied overhead in each account may not be in the same proportion as the amount of direct material and direct labor. In the above example, the $100,000 would be allocated based on the proportion of each account balance to the total $2,000,000. This results in the following adjustment:

$$\text{Work-in-Process Inventory:} \quad \frac{\$200,000}{\$2,000,000} \times \$100,000 = \$\ 10,000$$

$$\text{Finished Goods Inventory:} \quad \frac{\$500,000}{\$2,000,000} \times \$100,000 = \quad 25,000$$

$$\text{Cost of Goods Sold:} \quad \frac{\$1,300,000}{\$2,000,000} \times \$100,000 = \quad 65,000$$

$$\text{Total Underapplied Overhead:} \qquad\qquad\qquad \underline{\$100,000}$$

In this case, this method provides significantly different adjustments to finished goods inventory and cost of goods sold.

Cost of Goods Manufactured

At the end of an accounting period, a firm prepares a **schedule of cost of goods manufactured** before preparing the income statement. This schedule shows all manufacturing costs for the year. A schedule for the Fabulous Furniture Manufacturing Company, assuming it uses an actual cost system, is shown in Exhibit 3.3.

If work-in-process inventory has a beginning balance (as it usually will), it is shown first. To it is added the total amount of direct material, direct labor,

Exhibit 3.3 Schedule of Cost of Goods Manufactured

Fabulous Furniture Manufacturing Company Schedule of Cost of Goods Manufactured for the Year Ended December 31, 19X2		
Work-in-Process Inventory, January 1, 19X2		$ 32,000
Direct Material:		
Inventory, January 1, 19X2	$ 35,000	
Purchases	240,000	
Cost of Direct Material Available for Use	$275,000	
Less: Inventory, December 31, 19X2	20,000	
Direct Material Used	$255,000	
Direct Labor	320,000	
Variable Factory Overhead	165,000	
Fixed Factory Overhead	72,000	
Total Manufacturing Costs Charged to Production This Year		812,000
Total Manufacturing Costs for the Year		$844,000
Less: Work-in-Process Inventory, December 31, 19X2		72,000
Cost of Goods Manufactured		$772,000

Exhibit 3.4 Partial Income Statement

Fabulous Furniture Manufacturing Company		
Partial Income Statement		
for the Year Ended December 31, 19X2		
Sales		$975,000
Cost of Goods Sold:		
Finished Goods Inventory, January 1, 19X2	$ 55,000	
Cost of Goods Manufactured	772,000	
Cost of Goods Available for Sale	$827,000	
Less: Finished Goods Inventory, December 31, 19X2	115,000	
Cost of Goods Sold		712,000
Gross Margin		$263,000

and factory overhead that has been charged to the production process. These are the amounts that were debited to work-in-process inventory during the year. In this example, this total is $812,000.

It is necessary to show only the amount of direct material used. With a perpetual inventory system, this figure is readily available. However, Exhibit 3.3 illustrates the computation of the amount used, because it is often shown. Note that this is only *direct* material, not total raw materials, which would include indirect material.

Beginning work-in-process inventory plus current production costs equals total manufacturing costs for the year. Here, it is $844,000. By subtracting the work-in-process inventory balance at the end of the year, $72,000, you can determine the cost of goods manufactured for the year, $772,000. If you understand the logic of the calculation, it is not necessary to memorize the format. In fact, you will often see other formats; but the final result will be the same.

Cost of goods manufactured is used to determine cost of goods sold. A partial income statement is shown in Exhibit 3.4.

Notice that calculating cost of goods sold for a manufacturing firm is similar to calculating it for a merchandising firm. The primary difference is that cost of goods manufactured, rather than purchases, is used.

Summary

Cost accounting is a system of cost accumulation for a manufacturing firm. Accounting for a manufacturing firm differs from that for a merchandising firm in that a manufacturer requires a more complex accounting system to account for the manufacturing function.

The manufacturing firm has three types of inventory: (1) raw materials inventory, (2) work-in-process inventory, and (3) finished goods inventory. Raw materials inventory represents items used in the production process.

They may be either direct materials or indirect materials. Work-in-process inventory is the amount of partially completed production. Finished goods inventory represents completed manufactured items that the firm will sell to its customers; it is similar to merchandise inventory for a merchandising firm.

There are three types of manufacturing costs: (1) direct material, (2) direct labor, and (3) factory overhead. Direct material is raw material that becomes a part of the finished product. Direct labor is the cost of wages for factory workers who work on specific products. Both direct material and direct labor are variable costs. Factory overhead is any manufacturing cost that is not direct material or direct labor; it may be either variable or fixed. The combination of these three manufacturing costs, plus beginning work-in-process inventory and less ending work-in-process inventory, results in cost of goods manufactured. Cost of goods manufactured is similar to purchases for a merchandising firm. It is used to determine cost of goods sold on the income statement.

The manufacturing firm must distinguish between product costs and period costs. Period costs are incurred during the accounting period and benefit only that period; selling and administrative expenses are examples of period costs. They are shown as expenses for the period on the income statement.

Product costs are assigned to the finished product; they include direct material, direct labor, and variable factory overhead. Under absorption costing, fixed manufacturing overhead is assumed to be absorbed into the cost of the product and is thus considered a product cost.

The cost accumulation process for absorption costing with an actual cost system and with an actual/normal cost system was illustrated in this chapter. This illustration and the related exhibits should be reviewed as part of your summary.

When manufacturing costs are accounted for under an actual/normal system, direct material and direct labor are charged to work-in-process inventory at their actual amounts as incurred. However, variable and fixed factory overhead are applied (charged) to work-in-process inventory at a predetermined rate. The actual factory overhead costs incurred are also accumulated. At the end of the accounting period, any difference between factory overhead applied and incurred is adjusted to cost of goods sold. If the difference is significant, it should instead be allocated among work-in-process inventory, finished goods inventory, and cost of goods sold.

Review Problem   Below are several ledger accounts for Milton Manufacturing Company as of July 31, 19X4.

Work-in-Process Inventory	Finished Goods Inventory	Cost of Goods Sold
60,000	25,000	95,000

Variable Factory Overhead		Fixed Factory Overhead	
2,000	1,800	3,500	4,000

The following transactions occurred on July 31:

1. Product with a cost of $48,000 was completed and transferred to finished goods.

2. Product with a cost of $35,000 was sold.

3. Cost of goods sold was adjusted for the amount of underapplied or overapplied factory overhead.

Required:

a. Post the above transactions directly to the appropriate ledger accounts.

b. Determine the balance of each ledger account.

Solution

a.

Work-in-Process Inventory		Finished Goods Inventory		Cost of Goods Sold	
60,000	1) 48,000	25,000	2) 35,000	95,000	3) 300
		1) 48,000		2) 35,000	

Variable Factory Overhead		Fixed Factory Overhead	
2,000	1,800	3,500	4,000
	3) 200	3) 500	
	2,000	4,000	

Note that cost of goods sold was adjusted with one entry, with the net overapplied overhead credited to cost of goods sold. It is also correct to use two entries by which cost of goods sold is debited for $200 (underapplied variable factory overhead) and credited for $500 (overapplied fixed factory overhead).

b. Work-in-Process Inventory: $60,000 − $48,000   = $12,000
Finished Goods Inventory: $25,000 + $48,000 − $35,000 = $38,000
Cost of Goods Sold: $95,000 + $35,000 − $300   = $129,700

The two overhead accounts have been closed out and have zero balances.

Questions

3-1 What is the difference between inventory for a merchandising firm and inventory for a manufacturing firm?

3-2 What is the difference between cost of goods sold for a merchandising firm and cost of goods sold for a manufacturing firm?

3-3 What is cost accounting?

3-4 What is the difference between direct material and indirect material? Give an example of each.

3-5 What is the difference between direct labor and indirect labor? Give an example of each.

3-6 What is factory overhead? Give an example.

3-7 How can indirect material be both a raw materials cost and a factory overhead cost?

3-8 Can prime cost be added to conversion cost to determine total manufacturing cost? Explain.

3-9 What is the difference between a product cost and a period cost?

3-10 "Since delivery trucks are used to deliver the product, depreciation on delivery trucks is a product cost." Comment on the validity of this statement.

3-11 The vice-president of sales and the vice-president of manufacturing are arguing about whether their salaries are product costs or period costs. How would you settle the argument?

3-12 Since fixed factory overhead does not vary, what is the justification for applying it at a predetermined rate, which makes the fixed cost appear to vary?

3-13 Assume that a company's normal activity is 20,000 direct labor hours a year. If expected variable factory overhead is $50,000 and expected fixed factory overhead is $100,000, determine the factory overhead application rates.

3-14 If the debits to fixed factory overhead total $33,500 and the credits total $33,300, what does the difference represent?

3-15 What is the usual entry to dispose of an overapplied amount of variable factory overhead?

3-16 What does it mean to say that fixed factory overhead has been overapplied by $500?

3-17 If cost of goods sold of $10,000 is to be adjusted for a $300 underapplication of variable factory overhead, what is the amount of cost of goods sold after the adjustment? Explain.

3-18 Can cost of goods manufactured and cost of goods sold ever be the same? Explain.

Exercises

3-19 Product Costs and Period Costs Indicate which of the following costs are product costs and which are period costs:
  a. Rent on office building.
  b. Wages of plant guard.
  c. Freight costs of shipping finished goods to distribution points.
  d. President's salary.

e. Sweeping compound for factory.

f. Depreciation on typewriter used by factory supply clerks.

g. Depreciation on typewriter used by sales clerk.

h. Cost of painting factory superintendent's office.

3-20 Raw Material Journal Entries; Actual Cost System Ace Manufacturing Company purchased raw materials on account on March 1, 19X2, for $40,000. On March 2, direct materials costing $15,000 were placed into production, and manufacturing supplies costing $1,500 were drawn from inventory for use in the factory. Prepare journal entries to record these transactions. Assume an actual cost system.

3-21 Direct Labor and Indirect Labor Journal Entries; Actual Cost System For the week ending July 26, 19X0, Buildrite Construction Company incurred direct labor costs of $20,000 and indirect labor costs of $2,500. Prepare the journal entry to record these transactions on an actual cost system.

3-22 Factory Overhead Journal Entry; Actual Cost System The Rally Company incurred the following factory overhead costs during the month of October 19X1:

Indirect Material	$ 2,000
Indirect Labor	5,000
Depreciation on Factory Equipment	8,000
Rent on Factory Building	10,000
Factory Managers' Salaries	20,000

Prepare the journal entry to record these costs on an actual cost system as of October 31, 19X1.

3-23 Direct Material and Direct Labor Journal Entry Potter Corporation used direct materials costing $25,000 and incurred direct labor costs of $45,000 in its manufacturing process for the week ending January 9, 19X1. Prepare the journal entry to record these transactions.

3-24 Material, Labor, and Overhead Journal Entry; Actual Cost System A company incurred the following costs in its manufacturing process for the month ending June 30, 19X1:

Direct Material	$40,000
Indirect Material	24,000
Direct Labor	60,000
Indirect Labor	30,000
Depreciation of Factory and Equipment	10,000
Factory Managers' Salaries	25,000

Prepare a journal entry to record these costs on an actual cost system as of June 30, 19X1.

3-25 Completion and Sale of Product Journal Entries The Dawson Rubber Band Company completed production on rubber bands costing $65,000 during August 19X2. During August, it sold rubber bands on account for $35,000. The rubber bands sold cost $20,000 to manufacture. Prepare journal entries to record these transactions as of August 31, 19X2.

3-26 Completion and Sale of Product Journal Entries Happy Tot Toy Company began business on January 1, 19X3. During the year, it incurred production costs of $600,000 and completed manufacture of toys costing $450,000. It sold toys costing $400,000 for $560,000.

a. Prepare journal entries as of December 31, 19X3, to record the transfer of completed toys to finished goods and to record the sales for the year.

b. Determine the balance of the work-in-process inventory account and the finished goods inventory account as of December 31, 19X3.

3-27 Completion and Sale of Product Journal Entries The Miker Manufacturing Company had a balance of $120,000 in the work-in-process inventory account and a balance of $250,000 in the finished goods inventory account as of March 31, 19X2. On April 1, $80,000 of product was completed and transferred to the finished goods warehouse. On that same date, finished product costing $175,000 was sold on account for $220,000.

a. Prepare journal entries to record April transactions.

b. Determine the balance of work-in-process inventory and finished goods inventory after giving consideration to the entries in part **a**.

3-28 Overhead Rate Calculation Normal activity for the Whiz-Bang Firecracker Company is 60,000 direct labor hours. Management predicts that variable factory overhead next year will total $75,000 and fixed factory overhead will total $45,000. Calculate the variable and fixed factory overhead rates for next year.

3-29 Overhead Rate Calculation Determine the variable and fixed factory overhead rates under the conditions of parts **a, b,** and **c** below. Assume that the total variable factory overhead for the year is estimated to be $200,000 and the total fixed factory overhead is estimated to be $350,000. The basis for application is:

a. 100,000 direct labor hours.

b. 50,000 machine hours.

c. $1,000,000 direct labor cost.

3-30 Overhead Rate Calculation and Journal Entry In 19X4, the Wilshire Woolen Company used 200,000 direct labor hours and incurred variable factory overhead of $150,000. The company used this information as a basis for determining the variable factory overhead rate for 19X5.

a. What is the rate for 19X5?

b. Assume that 10,000 direct labor hours were worked during January, 19X5. Prepare the journal entry to record the application of variable factory overhead for January.

3-31 Overhead Journal Entries; Adjusting Cost of Goods Sold The following information applied to Braker Corporation for the month ended June 30, 19X1:

	Overhead Rate (per DLH)	Overhead Incurred
Variable	$1.10	$ 4,950
Fixed	2.50	12,820

The number of direct labor hours for June totaled 5,000.

a. Prepare journal entries to record the applied and incurred factory overhead for June. (Note: Credit "various accounts" in recording the incurred overhead.)

b. Prepare journal entries to adjust cost of goods sold as of June 30 for the amount of underapplied or overapplied overhead.

3–32 Overhead Journal Entries; Adjusting Cost of Goods Sold For the year ending December 31, 19X6, Risor Corporation incurred variable factory overhead totaling $93,000 and fixed factory overhead totaling $218,000. The company applied variable overhead on the basis of 30% of direct labor cost and fixed overhead on the basis of 75% of direct labor cost. Direct labor ` cost for the year totaled $300,000.

a. Prepare journal entries as of December 31, 19X6, to record the applied and incurred factory overhead for the year. (Note: Credit "various accounts" in recording the incurred overhead.)

b. Prepare journal entries to adjust cost of goods sold as of December 31 for the amount of underapplied or overapplied overhead.

3–33 Adjusting Cost of Goods Sold; Allocating Underapplied or Overapplied Overhead Ding Dong Bell Company incurred fixed factory overhead in 19X3 totaling $200,000. However, it only applied $150,000. The amount of fixed factory overhead applied in 19X3 and remaining in the accounts as of December 31 is as follows:

Work-in-Process Inventory	$ 30,000
Finished Goods Inventory	45,000
Cost of Goods Sold	75,000
Total	$150,000

a. Prepare the journal entry as of December 31, 19X3, to adjust cost of goods sold for the amount of underapplied or overapplied fixed factory overhead.

b. Prepare the journal entry as of December 31, 19X3, to allocate the amount of underapplied or overapplied fixed factory overhead to the appropriate accounts.

3–34 Adjusting Cost of Goods Sold The balances of selected ledger accounts for the Laden Company as of December 31, 19X2, are as follows:

Variable Factory Overhead	$3,000 Credit
Fixed Factory Overhead	$5,000 Debit
Cost of Goods Sold	$290,000

a. Prepare journal entries as of December 31, 19X2, to adjust cost of goods sold for the amount of underapplied or overapplied factory overhead.

b. Determine the amount of cost of goods sold after considering the entries in part **a.**

Problems

3–35 Journal Entries; Actual Cost System Transactions for Berrington Corporation for October 19X1 are shown below:

Oct. 1 Purchased raw materials costing $80,000 on account.
2 Placed direct materials costing $30,000 into the production process.

15 Direct labor costs of $50,000 for October 1–15 were incurred.
15 Indirect material used for October 1–15 totaled $10,000.
15 Indirect labor costs for October 1–15 totaled $20,000.
16 Paid for raw materials purchased on October 1.
17 Purchased raw materials costing $35,000 on account.
20 Paid payroll accrued on October 15.
31 Direct labor costs of $40,000 for October 16–31 were incurred.
31 Indirect material used for October 16–31 totaled $8,000.
31 Indirect labor costs for October 16–31 totaled $15,000.
31 Factory utility costs of $2,000 for October were accrued.
31 Depreciation on factory plant and equipment for October totaled $5,000.
31 Factory manager's salaries of $7,000 for October were paid.
31 Finished product costing $150,000 was completed during October.
31 Finished goods costing $120.000 were sold on account for $160,000.

Required:
Prepare journal entries to record the October transactions on an actual cost system.

3-36 Journal Entries; Actual Cost System Transactions for Hopner Manufacturing Company for September 19X2, its first month of operation, are shown below.

1) Raw materials purchased on account totaled $35,000.
2) Direct material used in production totaled $20,000.
3) Direct labor for the month totaled $45,000.
4) Variable factory overhead costs were incurred as follows:

Utilities	$ 2,500
Indirect Material	4,000
Indirect Labor	10,000

5) Fixed factory overhead costs were incurred as follows:

Managers' Salaries	$5,000
Depreciation on Factory and Equipment	1,500

6) Raw materials purchased in item 1 were paid for.
7) Salaries accrued in items 3, 4, and 5 were paid.
8) Product costing $70,000 was completed.
9) Finished goods costing $50,000 were sold on account for $75,000.

Required:
a. Prepare journal entries to record the September transactions on an actual cost system.
b. Determine the balance of each of the following accounts as of September 30, 19X2; 1. Raw materials inventory; 2. Work in process inventory; 3. Finished goods inventory. (*Note:* It is *not* necessary to prepare ledger accounts and post to each account to determine the balances, but you may wish to do so.)

3-37 Overhead Rate Calculation; Adjusting Cost of Goods Sold The Mason Machine Company applies variable factory overhead on the basis of machine hours and fixed factory overhead on the basis of direct labor hours. For 19X1, the company expected variable factory overhead to total $80,000 and fixed factory overhead to total $150,000. Expected machine hours were 160,000 and direct labor hours were 200,000. Actual results for 19X1 were as follows:

Variable Factory Overhead Incurred	$85,000
Fixed Factory Overhead Incurred	$152,000
Actual Machine Hours	175,000 Hours
Actual Direct Labor Hours	190,000 Hours

Required:

a. Determine the variable factory overhead rate and the fixed factory overhead rate for 19X1.

b. Prepare journal entries as of December 31, 19X1, to adjust cost of goods sold for the amount of underapplied or overapplied factory overhead.

3–38 Posting Transactions to Ledger Account Below is data for one month of manufacturing operations for Harry's Hat Company:

1) Raw materials purchased, $44,000.

2) Direct labor hours worked, 10,000 at $5 per hour. $50 000

3) Direct materials used, $30,000.

4) Indirect material used, $5,000.

5) Indirect labor costs incurred, $20,000.

6) Other variable factory overhead costs incurred, $14,500. (Credit accounts payable).

7) Fixed factory overhead costs incurred, $32,000. (Credit accrued payroll for $20,000 and accounts payable for $12,000.)

8) Variable factory overhead was applied on the basis of $4 per direct labor hour.

9) Fixed factory overhead was applied on the basis of $3 per direct labor hour.

10) Ten thousand units of product were manufactured. There was no beginning or ending work-in-process inventory. *all finished – nothing in between*

11) Sales for the month totaled 8,000 units at $20 per unit.

12) Cost of goods sold was adjusted for the amount of underapplied or overapplied factory overhead.

The following account titles are used by the company:

Raw Materials Inventory	Variable Factory Overhead
Work-in-Process Inventory	Fixed Factory Overhead
Finished Goods Inventory	Accounts Payable
Cost of Goods Sold	Accrued Payroll
Sales	Accounts Receivable

Required:

a. Prepare ledger accounts for each of the above account titles.

b. Post the data (items 1 through 12) directly to ledger accounts. (Note: It is not necessary to prepare journal entries.)

c. Determine the balance of each ledger account after posting.

3–39 Preparing and Posting Entries; Adjusting Cost of Good Sold On December 31, 19X8, the balance sheet for Miller Manufacturing Company included the following items:

Raw Materials Inventory $15,000
Work-in-Process Inventory 20,000
Finished Goods Inventory 35,000

Factory overhead rates are $2.00 per DLH for variable and $2.50 per DLH for fixed. Transactions for January 19X9, are shown below:

1) Raw materials purchased on account totaled $23,000. *C- Raw Mtl, D - Accts Pay*

2) Direct material used in production totaled $18,000. *D - WIP Inv, C - Inv Raw Mtl*

3) Direct labor for the month totaled $30,000 for 4,000 direct labor hours. *D - WIP Inv. C - Wages Payable or Accrued Payroll*

4) Variable factory overhead costs were incurred as follows:

D - Variable Factory Overhead. 8600
C -

Utilities	$1,500 *C - Util Payable.*
Indirect Material	3,000 *C - Raw Mtl. Inv.*
Indirect Labor	4,100 *C - Accrued Payroll*

8,600

5) Fixed factory overhead costs were incurred as follows:

D - Fixed Fac. OH 9200

Managers' Salaries	$4,200 *C Accrued Payr*
Depreciation on Equipment	2,000 *C Accum Depr on Equip*
Rent on Factory	3,000 *C Rents Payable*

6) Variable and fixed factory overhead were applied. *$2 $2.50 + $4.50 x (4000) Dir Lab hrs = $18000 - D-WIP*

FFOH - C - 10000
VFOH - C - 8000

7) Raw materials purchased in item 1 were paid for. *D - Accts Pay C - Cash*

8) Salaries accrued in items 3, 4, and 5 were paid. *C - 38300 - Cash*

9) Rent accrued in item 5 was paid. *3000 C - Cash, D - Rent*

10) Product costing $65,000 was completed. *D - Fin good Inv. C - WIP Inv*

11) Finished goods costing $85,000 were sold on account for $110,000.

Required:

a. Prepare journal entries to record the January transactions.

b. Post the journal entries to ledger accounts and determine the balance of the inventory accounts.

c. Prepare journal entries to adjust cost of goods sold for the amount of underapplied or overapplied factory overhead. (Do not post.)

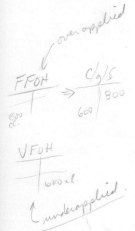

3-40 Preparing and Posting Entries; Adjusting Cost of Goods Sold The Anderson Company began July 19X2 with the following account balances:

Raw Materials Inventory $ 70,000
Work-in-Process Inventory 50,000
Finished Goods Inventory 100,000

Factory overhead rates are $1.50 per DLH for variable and $.70 per DLH for fixed. Transactions for July were as follows:

July 1 Product costing $30,000 was completed.

5 Placed direct material costing $40,000 into production.

10 Purchased raw materials costing $25,000 on account.

15 Direct labor costs of $65,000 (13,000 DLH) for the period July 1–15 were incurred.

15 Variable and fixed factory overhead were applied.

15 Indirect material used for the period July 1–15 totaled $6,000.

15 Indirect labor costs for the period July 1–15 totaled $12,000.

20 Sold finished goods costing $85,000 on account for $110,000.

20 Paid payroll accrued on July 15.

20 Paid for raw materials purchased on July 10.

25 Product costing $170,000 was completed.

27 Purchased raw materials costing $35,000 on account.

29 Started direct material costing $50,000 into production.

30 Received payment for goods sold on July 20.

30 Sold finished goods costing $140,000 on account for $200,000.

31 Direct labor costs of $50,000 (10,000 DLH) for the period July 16–31 were incurred.

31 Variable and fixed overhead were applied.

31 Indirect material used for the period July 16–31 totaled $4,000.

31 Indirect labor costs for the period July 16–31 totaled $8,000.

31 The following additional factory overhead costs were incurred in July:

Utilities (Not Paid)	$ 5,000
Managers' Salaries (Paid)	10,000
Depreciation on Plant and Equipment	6,000

Required:

a. Prepare journal entries to record the July transactions.

b. Post the journal entries to ledger accounts and determine the balance of the inventory accounts.

c. Prepare journal entries to adjust cost of goods sold for the amount of underapplied or overapplied overhead. (Do not post.)

3–41 Incomplete Ledger Accounts Below are incomplete ledger accounts for a manufacturing company. Not all of the company's accounts are shown. The company uses a combined factory overhead rate and applies overhead at a rate of 60% of direct labor cost.

Raw Materials Inventory

1/1	Balance 12,000	(b)	
	(a)	3,000	
1/31	Balance 14,000		

Work-in-Process Inventory

1/1	Balance 10,000	(e)	
	35,000		
	(c)		
	(d)		
1/31	Balance 25,000		

Finished Goods Inventory

(f)	80,000

Factory Overhead

(g)	30,000
	2,000

Cost of Goods Sold

80,000	
2,000	

Required:

Determine the correct amount of each lettered item in the ledger accounts. There were no beginning balances except as noted in the accounts. (Note: You will not be able to solve these in letter order. For example, you need to find amount b before you can find amount a.)

3–42 Schedule of Cost of Goods Manufactured Below is information for the year ended December 31, 19X3, for the E–Z Rest Mattress Company:

Direct Labor	$75,000
Direct Material Inventory, January 1, 19X3	20,000
Direct Material Inventory, December 31, 19X3	35,000
Direct Material Purchases	50,000
Finished Goods Inventory, January 1, 19X3	90,000
Finished Goods Inventory, December 31, 19X3	125,000
Fixed Factory Overhead	40,000
Variable Factory Overhead	60,000
Work-in-Process Inventory, January 1, 19X3	30,000
Work-in-Process Inventory, December 31, 19X3	45,000

Required:
a. Prepare a schedule of cost of goods manufactured for the year ended December 31, 19X3. Assume an actual cost system.

b. Was cost of goods sold equal to, more than, or less than cost of goods manufactured this year? Explain. (Answer this question without determining the actual cost of goods sold.)

c. Determine the amount of cost of goods sold.

3-43 Determining Amounts from Given Data Information from the records of the Bouncing Ball Manufacturing Company for the year ended December 31, 19X2, is shown below:

Sales	$50,000
Finished Goods Inventory, January 1, 19X2	12,000
Finished Goods Inventory, December 31, 19X2	8,000
Direct Labor	25,000
Direct Material Purchases	20,000
Variable Factory Overhead	15,000
Fixed Factory Overhead	20,000
Work-in-Process Inventory, January 1, 19X2	10,000
Selling and Administrative Expenses	16,000
Net Income	5,000

Conversion costs account for 75% of total manufacturing costs incurred during the period. The firm uses an actual cost system.
Required:
Determine the following amounts for the year ended December 31, 19X2:

a. Prime cost.
b. Cost of goods sold.
c. Cost of goods manufactured.
d. Work-in-process inventory, December 31, 19X2.

3-44 Determining Sales from Given Data Cathy's Calculator Company requires 10 numbered buttons for every hand calculator produced. During June 19X0, 350,000 buttons were purchased. Information regarding inventories is shown below:

	June 1, 19X0	June 30, 19X0
Buttons	40,000	75,000
Calculators	35,000	15,000
Work in Process	0	0

Required:

Determine the number of calculators sold in June.

3-45 Determining Amounts from Given Data The following information relates to the Wilson Watch Company for the year ended June 30, 19X4:

	July 1, 19X3	June 30, 19X4
Raw Materials Inventory		
(All Direct Material)	$ 40,000	$ 50,000
Work-in-Process Inventory	95,000	65,000
Finished Goods Inventory	200,000	150,000

In addition, the following information is available:

Direct Material Used	$180,000
Variable Factory Overhead Incurred	50,000
Fixed Factory Overhead Incurred	75,000
Total Manufacturing Costs for the Year	500,000
Cost of Goods Available for Sale	635,000

goes into WIP

The firm uses an actual cost system.

Required:

Determine the following:

a. Direct material purchases. *180 000 + (50 000 - 40000) = 190 000*

b. Direct labor cost. *≈ 100 000*

c. Cost of goods sold. *≈ 635000 - 150 000, = 485 000*

d. Cost of goods manufactured. *= 485000 + (150 000 - 200000) = 435 000*

b)
Total MFG Cost/yr =
Begin WIP Inv + Direct Mtl +
Direct Lab + Fac O.H. Var & FIX
500000 = 95000 + 180 000
+ Dir. Lab + 125000

c) goods avail for sale -
ending finished goods inv.
= cost of good sold.

3-46 Schedule of Cost of Goods Manufactured The Wanda Walker Company manufactures a single product. Information for the month ended June 30, 19X1, is given below:

Sales	20,000 Units at $15 per Unit
Production	16,000 Units
Direct Material Inventory, June 1	7,000 Units at $3 Each
Direct Material Purchases	18,000 Units at $4 Each
Work-in-Process Inventory, June 1	4,000 Units at a Total Cost of $28,000
Work-in-Process Inventory, June 30	3,000 Units at a Total Cost of $25,000

A review of the company's ledger accounts reveals the following additional information:

Salespersons' Salaries and Commissions	$40,000
Direct Labor	60,000
Indirect Labor	20,000
Factory Managers' Salaries	6,000
Office Salaries	15,000
Utilities for Office Building (Variable)	5,000
Utilities for Factory (Variable)	8,000
Depreciation on Factory Plant and Equipment	7,000
Depreciation on Office Building and Equipment	4,000
Depreciation on Delivery Truck	1,000
Other Variable Factory Overhead	3,000
Other Office Expenses	4,000

The company uses an actual cost system and the first-in, first-out method for valuing inventories.

Required:

Prepare a schedule of cost of goods manufactured for the month ended June 30, 19X1.

3–47 Determining Amounts after Fire Loss Combust Oil Company had a fire on February 28, 19X2, two months into its fiscal year. The company's work-in-process inventory was completely destroyed. You have been asked to help determine the amount of work-in-process inventory at the time of the fire, in order that the company can file a claim with the insurance company. Inventories as of January 1, 19X2, were as follows:

Direct Material Inventory	$35,000
Work-in-Process Inventory	17,000
Finished Goods Inventory	40,000

A physical inventory on March 1 showed direct material inventory as $10,000 and finished goods inventory as $45,000. The general ledger shows that during January and February the company purchased direct material costing $40,000 and incurred direct labor costs of $62,000. Factory overhead costs for the two months totaled $28,000. Sales totaled $210,000; gross margin normally averages 40% of sales.

Required:

  a. Determine the cost of goods sold.

  b. Determine the cost of goods manufactured.

  c. Determine the amount of work-in-process inventory lost in the fire.

(*Note:* It is not necessary to prepare a formal schedule of cost of goods manufactured, but it may be helpful to do so.)

Chapter 4   Contribution Approach to Decision Making

Learning Objectives

The purpose of this chapter is to describe how the contribution approach income statement aids in management decision making for both manufacturing and merchandising firms. Studying this chapter will enable you to:
1. Define contribution approach terminology.
2. Journalize and post transactions of the cost accounting cycle under variable costing.
3. Prepare a contribution approach income statement for a manufacturing firm and a merchandising firm.
4. Describe the arguments for and against absorption costing and variable costing.
5. Apply contribution approach concepts to decision-making situations.
6. Explain how absorption costing and variable costing affect net income and inventory valuation.
7. Determine the difference in net income between absorption costing and variable costing. (Appendix)

Chapter Topics

The major topics included in this chapter are:

Description of Variable Costing
Cost Accounting Cycle
Contribution Approach Income Statement
Absorption Costing versus Variable Costing
Merchandising Firms and the Contribution Approach Income Statement
Decision-Making Applications
Appendix: The Effect of Absorption Costing and Variable Costing on Net Income

As described in Chapter 3, generally accepted accounting principles require that, for external reporting, fixed factory overhead be accounted for under absorption costing and included as a product cost. Internal decision making, however, often calls for data to be presented in a different manner. This chapter describes a method called the contribution approach to decision making, which is based on the concept of variable costing.

Description of Variable Costing

Variable costing is a cost accounting method under which only variable manufacturing costs are included as product costs. Fixed factory overhead is treated as a period cost. Variable costing is often called *direct costing*. However, because the term *direct cost* has another meaning (described in later chapters) and because *variable costing* is more descriptive of the concept, *variable costing* is the term used in this text.

The primary usefulness of variable costing is in its ability to provide information for internal decision making. Some decision-making applications are presented in this chapter; others appear throughout the subsequent chapters.

An understanding of variable costing can best be obtained through example. The next section shows how variable costing is applied to the cost accounting cycle. That is followed by an illustration of a contribution approach income statement prepared under variable costing.

Cost Accounting Cycle

A simple illustration of the cost accounting cycle using absorption costing was provided in Chapter 3. As previously discussed, absorption costing treats fixed factory overhead as a product cost; but variable costing treats fixed factory overhead as a period cost.

The flow of product cost through work in process, finished goods, and ultimately to cost of goods sold on the income statement is illustrated for variable costing in Exhibit 4.1. You may wish to compare this exhibit with Exhibit 3.1, which illustrates cost flow for absorption costing. Note that fixed factory overhead is shown in Exhibit 4.1 as an expense—a period cost—on the income statement.

You have probably noticed that the format of the income statement differs from that shown for absorption costing in Exhibit 3.1. This type of income statement is discussed in the next section of this chapter.

In order to contrast absorption costing with variable costing, the illustration from Chapter 3 for the Fabulous Furniture Manufacturing Company is repeated here using an actual cost system, assuming variable costing. The first four transactions and entries are the same under both absorption and variable costing and are repeated below without additional comment. (You may wish to refer to Chapter 3 for the discussion of these entries.) Entries 5 through 7 differ under variable costing; the difference is discussed with each entry.

1) Raw materials (direct and indirect) costing $30,000 were purchased on account.

Raw Materials Inventory	30,000	
Accounts Payable		30,000

Exhibit 4.1 Cost Flow–Variable Costing

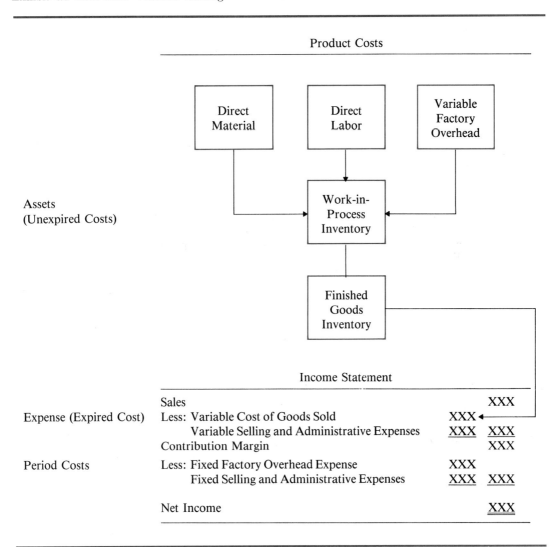

Product Costs

Assets
(Unexpired Costs)

Income Statement

Sales		XXX
Less: Variable Cost of Goods Sold	XXX	
Variable Selling and Administrative Expenses	XXX	XXX
Contribution Margin		XXX
Less: Fixed Factory Overhead Expense	XXX	
Fixed Selling and Administrative Expenses	XXX	XXX
Net Income		XXX

Expense (Expired Cost)

Period Costs

2) Lumber and upholstery material (direct material) costing $10,000 were put into the production process for the manufacture of chairs.

Work-in-Process Inventory   10,000
  Raw Materials Inventory   10,000

3) Direct labor costs of $28,000 were incurred.

Work-in-Process Inventory   28,000
  Accrued Payroll   28,000

4) The following variable factory overhead costs were incurred:

Power	$ 3,000
Indirect Labor	11,500
Indirect Material	
(Sandpaper, Screws, Lightbulbs, Repair Parts)	1,500
	$16,000

Work-in-Process Inventory	16,000	
Utilities Payable		3,000
Accrued Payroll		11,500
Raw Materials Inventory		1,500

5) The following fixed factory overhead costs were incurred:

Managers' Salaries	$3,500
Depreciation on Equipment	1,500
Rent on Factory Building	3,000
	$8,000

Fixed Factory Overhead Expense	8,000	
Accrued Payroll		3,500
Accumulated Depreciation—Equipment		1,500
Rent Payable		3,000

Notice that the credits in Entry 5 above are the same as they were for Entry 5 in Chapter 3. Under variable costing, however, fixed factory overhead is a period cost. Therefore, the debit is to an expense account that will be reflected in arriving at net income on the income statement for the period. The debit is the sum of all three costs. The company would maintain subsidiary accounts for the natural classifications of the fixed factory overhead costs in order to keep track of and control each of the individual costs.

6) The company completed chairs with a variable manufacturing cost of $45,000. The chairs were transferred from the factory to the finished goods warehouse.

Finished Goods Inventory	45,000	
Work-in-Process Inventory		45,000

Since no fixed factory overhead is included in work-in-process inventory under variable costing, only the appropriate amount of variable cost is transferred to finished goods inventory. It is stated as $45,000.

7) Chairs with variable manufacturing cost of $18,000 were sold on account for $25,000.

Cost of Goods Sold	18,000	
Finished Goods Inventory		18,000
Accounts Receivable	25,000	
Sales		25,000

The difference between this entry and the one for absorption costing in Chapter 3 is that here finished goods inventory does not include any fixed factory overhead; therefore, neither does cost of goods sold. In other words, cost of goods sold under variable costing is actually the variable cost of goods sold.

Exhibit 4.2 shows postings to the individual ledger accounts in order to illustrate the flow of costs through the cost accounting cycle. Under variable costing, the income statement would show cost of goods sold as $18,000 and fixed factory overhead expense as $8,000. If a balance sheet were prepared, raw materials inventory would show a balance of $18,500; work-in-process inventory, $9,000; and finished goods inventory, $27,000.

Exhibit 4.2 Costing Accounting Cycle–Variable Costing

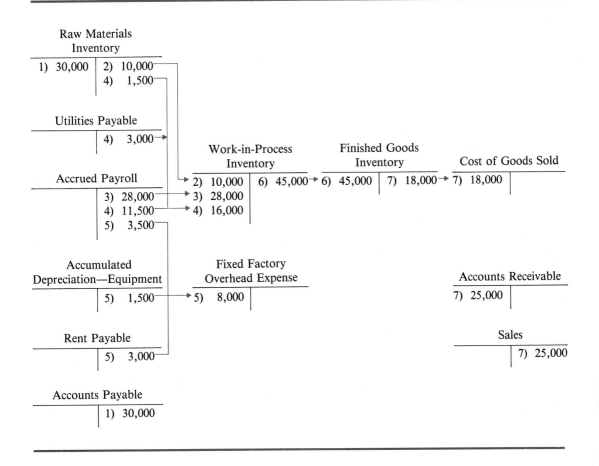

Contribution Approach Income Statement

Format

Exhibit 4.1 illustrates the format for an income statement prepared under variable costing. This statement, referred to as a **contribution approach income statement,** shows expenses according to cost behavior. They are classified as variable or fixed.

This chapter is concerned only with the income statement for the firm as a whole; and it will use the format shown in Exhibit 4.1. However, subsequent chapters are concerned with reporting by segments of the firm. In these cases, the contribution approach income statement requires that fixed costs be separated according to the traceability of such costs to the segments. This procedure is illustrated later.

The contribution approach income statement uses a format in which variable costs are subtracted from sales to arrive at contribution margin and fixed costs are subtracted from contribution margin to arrive at net income. Thus, mathematically, **contribution margin** is the difference between sales and variable costs. Conceptually, *contribution margin* represents an amount available to cover fixed costs for the period and provide a profit, or net income. It can be considered on both a total and a unit basis. Exhibit 4.1 showed the contribution approach income statement without numbers. A simple illustration of both the total basis and the unit basis is shown below:

	Total	**Unit (2,000 Units)**
Sales	$10,000	$5.00
Variable Costs[a]	6,000	3.00
Contribution Margin	$ 4,000	$2.00
Fixed Costs[a]	3,000	1.50
Net Income[b]	$ 1,000	$ .50

Although the illustration above is fairly easy to understand, a word of warning is in order. Fixed cost per unit and net income per unit can be misleading figures. Fixed cost, as you know, remains constant over a relevant range. Thus, although fixed cost per unit is a valid "after the fact" figure, its use for planning and control can be misleading. In this case, if 2,000 units are sold, then fixed cost per unit is, in fact, $1.50. However, if 1,500 units are sold, fixed cost per unit is $2 ($3,000 ÷ 1,500 units). If even fewer units are sold, fixed cost per unit increases more. Thus, one should be careful when looking at unit figures that include fixed cost per unit. This will be discussed more fully in later chapters.

The Fabulous Furniture Manufacturing Company example from Chapter 3 will help provide a more detailed illustration of the contribution approach income statement. To illustrate the income statement under variable

---

[a]The meanings of *cost* and *expense* were discussed in Chapter 2. For consistency throughout the text, contribution approach income statements will use the terms *variable cost* and *fixed cost*. Within the context of an income statement, this means the "cost of the period," which is an expense.
[b]Corporations must also deduct income tax expense on the income statement. However, the examples and problems in this text will ignore income taxes, unless they are relevant to the problem, in order to concentrate on the relevant concepts being discussed. Realistically, income taxes are almost always a consideration. Chapter 11 illustrates income tax considerations in capital budgeting.

Exhibit 4.3 Absorption Costing Income Statement

Fabulous Furniture Manufacturing Company
Income Statement
for the Year Ended December 31, 19X2

Sales		$975,000
Cost of Goods Sold:		
Finished Goods Inventory, January 1, 19X2	$ 55,000	
Costs of Goods Manufactured	772,000	
Cost of Goods Available for Sale	$827,000	
Less: Finished Goods Inventory, December 31, 19X2	115,000	
Cost of Goods Sold		712,000
Gross Margin		$263,000
Selling and Administrative Expenses		180,000
Net Income		$ 83,000

costing, we will compare it with the absorption costing income statement. Exhibit 3.4 provided a partial income statement for the Fabulous Furniture Manufacturing Company. Exhibit 4.3 shows the income statement under absorption costing using the information from Exhibit 3.4 and including selling and administrative expenses (which were not shown in Chapter 3).

To prepare a contribution approach income statement, we must prepare a schedule of cost of goods manufactured under variable costing. We must also know the amount of variable cost in finished goods inventory, as well as the amount of variable and fixed selling and administrative expenses.

From Exhibit 3.3, we know that fixed factory overhead charged to production in 19X2 totaled $72,000. However, Chapter 3 did not tell how much fixed factory overhead was included in work-in-process inventory at the beginning and end of the year. This information is provided below:

	Total	Fixed Factory Overhead	Variable Costs
Work-in-Process Inventory:			
January 1, 19X2	$32,000	$10,000	$22,000
December 31,19X2	72,000	16,000	56,000

With the information provided above, we can prepare a schedule of cost of goods manufactured under variable costing, as shown in Exhibit 4.4.

It is assumed that variable costs included in beginning and ending finished goods inventory totaled $50,000 and $103,000, respectively. The only other information needed is the breakdown between variable and fixed for selling and administrative expenses. The total for these expenses was shown to be $180,000 in Exhibit 4.3. We will assume that the variable portion of this amount is $78,000 and the fixed portion is $102,000. A contribution approach income statement is shown as Exhibit 4.5.

Exhibit 4.4 Schedule of Variable Cost of Goods Manufactured

Fabulous Furniture Manufacturing Company
Schedule of Variable Cost of Goods Manufactured
for the Year Ended December 31, 19X2

Work-in-Process Inventory, January 1, 19X2		$ 22,000
Direct Material Used	$255,000	
Direct Labor	320,000	
Variable Factory Overhead	165,000	
Total Manufacturing Costs Charged to Production This Year		740,000
Total Manufacturing Costs for the Year		$762,000
Less: Work-in-Process Inventory, December 31, 19X2		56,000
Cost of Goods Manufactured		$706,000

Comparison with Traditional Income Statement

Notice that net income under variable costing in this example is only $70,000, compared with $83,000 under absorption costing (Exhibit 4.3). We must analyze the statements to determine exactly why this $13,000 difference in net income arises.

The only difference between variable costing and absorption costing is

Exhibit 4.5 Contribution Approach Income Statement–Manufacturing Firm

Fabulous Furniture Manufacturing Company
Income Statement
for the Year Ended December 31, 19X2

Sales			$975,000
Variable Costs:			
Cost of Goods Sold:			
Finished Goods Inventory, January 1, 19X2	$ 50,000		
Cost of Goods Manufactured	706,000		
Cost of Goods Available for Sale	$756,000		
Less: Finished Goods Inventory, December 31, 19X2	103,000		
Cost of Goods Sold		$653,000	
Selling and Administrative Expenses		78,000	
Total Variable Costs			731,000
Contribution Margin			$244,000
Fixed Costs:			
Fixed Factory Overhead Expense		$ 72,000	
Selling and Administrative Expenses		102,000	
Total Fixed Costs			174,000
Net Income			$ 70,000

the way in which fixed factory overhead is treated. Under variable costing, it is a period cost; under absorption costing, it is a product cost. In Exhibit 3.3, fixed factory overhead for the year was shown to be $72,000. This amount has been subtracted as fixed factory overhead to arrive at net income under variable costing in Exhibit 4.5. But where is the $72,000 under absorption costing? It is a product cost connected with cost of goods manufactured and, in turn, related to cost of goods sold and inventories.

Compare the cost of goods sold section in Exhibit 4.3 with that in Exhibit 4.5. The differences in each item represent fixed factory overhead. These differences are highlighted in Exhibit 4.6.

Immediately, we can see that cost of goods sold under absorption includes $59,000 of fixed factory overhead. That tells us that the reason net income is $13,000 higher under absorption is because the amount of fixed factory overhead included as an expense under absorption was only $59,000 rather than $72,000. However, since $72,000 of fixed factory overhead cost was incurred, the next question is, "Where is the additional $13,000 under absorption?"

Examine the inventory figures. Notice that finished goods inventory increased from $55,000 on January 1 to $115,000 on December 31. Since the amount of finished goods inventory increased, the amount of fixed factory overhead included in finished goods inventory also increased. From Exhibit 4.6, you can see that the amount of fixed factory overhead in finished goods inventory carried into this period from the last period is $5,000. The amount of fixed factory overhead in finished goods inventory at the end of this period is $12,000. Thus, an additional $7,000 of fixed factory overhead is included as an asset because of the increase in finished goods inventory. That provides $7,000 of the $13,000 we are looking for.

Where is the rest? If you refer back to the illustration of work-in-process inventory on page 85, you will find the other $6,000. Note that work-in-process inventory increased from January 1 to December 31. Included in the work-in-process inventory on January 1 was $10,000 of fixed factory overhead; included in the work-in-process inventory on December 31 was $16,000 of fixed factory overhead. Thus, the increase in work-in-process inventory includes an increase of $6,000 of fixed factory overhead.

Exhibit 4.6 Comparison of Cost of Goods Sold Section

	Absorption	Variable	Fixed Factory Overhead
Finished Goods Inventory, January 1, 19X2	$ 55,000	$ 50,000	$ 5,000
Cost of Goods Manufactured	772,000	706,000	66,000
Cost of Goods Available for Sale	$827,000	$756,000	$71,000
Less: Finished Goods Inventory, December 31, 19X2	115,000	103,000	12,000
Cost of Goods Sold	$712,000	$653,000	$59,000

Exhibit 4.7 Disposition of Fixed Factory Overhead

	Absorption	Variable
Charged as an Expense	$59,000	$72,000
Increase in Work-in-Process Inventory	7,000	—
Increase in Finished Goods Inventory	6,000	—
Total Fixed Factory Overhead This Year	$72,000	$72,000

Exhibit 4.7 summarizes the preceding discussion insofar as accounting for the disposition of the $72,000 of fixed factory overhead under variable costing and absorption costing.

In summary, variable costing charged the entire $72,000 as an expense of the period. Absorption costing allocated the $72,000 to all units produced during the period; and only the amount charged to the units sold, $59,000, was charged to the current period. The additional $13,000 of fixed factory overhead was charged to inventory accounts and at present is shown as an asset. Thus, the difference of $13,000 in net income exists because more fixed factory overhead was charged against revenue this period under variable costing than under absorption costing.

From the preceding discussion, you can see that under absorption costing net income is affected by changes in inventory. In this example, inventory increased; and as a result, part of the fixed factory overhead under absorption went into ending inventory. On the other hand, if inventory decreases, then part of the prior period's fixed factory overhead in inventory becomes an expense of the current period. In this situation, net income under absorption costing is less than it would be under variable costing. The difference in the net income amounts produced by the two methods is discussed more fully in the appendix to this chapter.

Note also that the inventory figure under absorption costing is higher than under variable costing. It will always be higher because it includes fixed factory overhead, whereas the inventory figure under variable costing does not.

Absorption Costing versus Variable Costing

Accounting literature contains considerable discussion of variable costing and absorption costing. Most writings are phrased in a controversial tone, with emphasis on which costing method is better. Thus, it is useful to examine the features of absorption costing and variable costing from both a theoretical and a practical viewpoint.

Theoretical Considerations

The proponents of absorption costing maintain that all manufacturing costs are product costs. The theory is that fixed factory overhead is as much a part of the cost of the product as are direct material, direct labor, and variable factory overhead. Since the costs that comprise fixed factory overhead are as important to the creation of the product as the variable costs, it is entirely proper to defer these costs as charges to revenue until the product is sold. Since fixed factory overhead costs benefit the period in which the product is sold, it is only appropriate that they be deducted from the revenue of that period.

Proponents of variable costing argue that fixed factory overhead is a period cost. Their argument is that a manufacturing business requires certain plant capacity in order to produce a product. Thus, the fixed factory overhead costs are those costs necessary to maintain and operate a manufacturing plant. They are a part of the cost of being in business, just as the fixed selling and administrative expenses are. Fixed factory overhead costs offer no future benefit because they must be incurred year after year, regardless of whether anything is produced. Since the costs do not depend on any specific production, it is erroneous to consider that they attach to the product in the way that variable costs do.

Furthermore, variable costing avoids distortions in net income created by changes in production. The validity of this argument is demonstrated in the appendix to this chapter. A summary of the example used in the appendix is shown in Exhibit 4.8.

Exhibit 4.8 Comparison of Net Income–Absorption versus Variable

	Year 1	Year 2	Year 3
Absorption	$44,000	$24,000	$28,000
Variable	$28,000	$28,000	28,000

Sales totaled 12,000 units each year; yet, net income varied considerably from year to year under absorption costing. On the other hand, net income was the same each year under variable costing. The difference in net income from year to year under absorption costing is caused by the change in inventory levels and by the amount of fixed costs included in inventory.

Proponents of variable costing claim that net income should not fluctuate solely as a result of a fluctuation in production. Under absorption costing, it is possible to manipulate the net income figure by either increasing or decreasing production in any one year. On the other hand, variable costing provides a net income figure that is not affected by changes in inventory levels.

Finally, variable costing is useful for internal decision making by management. Absorption costing, when used for internal decisions, is often misleading and may result in faulty decisions.

The fluctuating net income argument is countered by proponents of absorption costing, who say that variable costing provides an artificial equalizing of net income and that changing of inventory levels should affect net income. Furthermore, over the long run, if everything produced is sold, total net income (over the years) will be the same under both costing systems. They also argue that although it is true that a firm could increase net income by producing *ad infinitum,* it is not practical for the firm to do so. There is a limit to the amount it can produce; and production without sales would also increase inventory storage costs, which would reduce net income. Consequently, proponents of absorption costing believe that income fluctuations caused by inventory fluctuations are minimal and temporary.

**Practical
Considerations**

The issues of absorption costing and variable costing need not be viewed in a controversial framework. Instead of choosing either absorption costing *or* variable costing, the firm can use absorption costing *and* variable costing to meet specific needs and purposes. Absorption costing must be used for external financial reporting and income tax determination. Nevertheless, variable costing has internal uses that provide management with information necessary for decision making. Although you will seldom (if ever) find a cost system designed solely on a variable costing basis, the concepts of variable costing are used in many decision-making situations.

Merchandising Firms and the Contribution Approach Income Statement

In its strictest sense, variable costing is applicable only to manufacturing firms. However, variable costing is both a method of inventory costing and a method of reporting costs. As a result, the concepts of variable costing, specifically the contribution approach income statement, are applicable to merchandising firms as well as manufacturing firms.

A contribution approach income statement for a merchandising firm is similar to one for a manufacturing firm. Items on the income statement are classified according to cost behavior. Variable costs are subtracted from revenue to determine contribution margin, and fixed costs are subtracted from contribution margin to arrive at net income. An example of such an income statement is shown as Exhibit 4.9.

This exhibit uses the Fantastic Furniture Sales Company. Costs are classified according to cost behavior. Cost of goods sold, selling expenses, and administrative expenses are shown on the income statement; but they are broken down according to whether they are variable or fixed.

A contribution margin of $300,000 indicates the amount available to cover fixed costs and provide a profit at the sales level of $1,200,000. In this case, fixed costs of $250,000 are met by the contribution margin, leaving a net income of $50,000.

Variable costs and contribution margin are also viewed in relation to sales. The **variable cost ratio** is variable cost as a percentage of sales. In this case, it is 75 percent ($900,000 ÷ $1,200,000).

Contribution margin as a percentage of sales is called the **contribution margin ratio.** The contribution margin ratio in this example is 25 percent ($300,000 ÷ $1,200,000). This ratio indicates what percentage of each dollar is available to cover fixed costs and provide net income. Thus, every dollar of sales provides 25¢ towards the fixed cost and the profit. Do not confuse

Exhibit 4.9 Contribution Approach Income Statement–Merchandising Firm

Fantastic Furniture Sales Company
Income Statement
for the Year Ended December 31, 19X2

Sales			$1,200,000
Variable Costs:			
Cost of Goods Sold:			
Inventory, January 1, 19X2	$200,000		
Purchases	650,000		
Cost of Goods Available for Sale	$850,000		
Less: Inventory, December 31, 19X2	150,000		
Cost of Goods Sold		$700,000	
Selling and Administrative Expenses		200,000	
Total Variable Costs			900,000
Contribution Margin			$ 300,000
Fixed Costs:			
Selling and Administrative Expenses			250,000
Net Income			$ 50,000

the contribution margin ratio with the gross margin percentage. On the traditional income statement, gross margin is the difference between sales and cost of goods sold. Gross margin is an amount to cover selling and administrative expenses. But selling and administrative expenses on the traditional income statement are not classified according to cost behavior.

Decision-Making Applications

The usefulness of the contribution approach income statement will become apparent in later chapters. However, in order to provide some insight as to how it can be used in decision making, two applications are presented in this section—one for a merchandising firm, the other for a manufacturing firm.

Merchandising Firm

The management of the Fantastic Furniture Sales Company is considering spending an additional $50,000 on advertising next year to increase sales. Management wonders how this increase in advertising expense would affect net income. By looking at the contribution approach income statement (Exhibit 4.9), you can tell immediately that if the increase in advertising failed to increase sales, then net income next year would be zero. This, of course, assumes that other costs and cost relationships remain the same as they were last year—the usual assumption in such situations. If it is known that the variable cost ratio or the contribution margin ratio will change or that other fixed costs will change, then the anticipated relationships should be used for the analysis.

Naturally, if sales fail to increase with an increase in advertising expense, then the advertising campaign has failed. The next question is: "By how much must sales increase in order that we not lose money on the advertising expenditure?" Since we know the contribution margin ratio is 25 percent, we know that every dollar of increased sales provides $.25 to cover fixed costs. Thus, the question is really: "How many $.25 contributions are needed to cover an additional $50,000 of fixed costs?"

You can answer this question by dividing the contribution margin ratio into the planned increase in advertising expense. The result is $200,000 ($50,000 ÷ .25). You can prove the validity of this computation by multiplying the variable cost ratio of 75 percent by the required increase in sales, $200,000. This results in $150,000 of variable costs. Thus, an additional $200,000 of sales will result in an additional $150,000 of variable costs, leaving an additional contribution margin of $50,000, enough to cover the increased advertising expense.

That means that in order for the advertising campaign to be worthwhile (that is, for it to increase net income above its current $50,000), sales must increase by more than $200,000. Every increase of $1 above $200,000 will increase net income by 25 percent or $.25. Thus, an increase in sales of $300,000 will increase net income by $25,000 [($300,000 − $200,000) × 25%].

The calculation above does not indicate whether the advertising campaign should be undertaken. It merely provides management with information as to what is required of the advertising campaign from a financial viewpoint. Managers must make the decision; they must consider whether they think the advertising campaign will result in additional sales in excess of $200,000. If they think it will, then they will probably decide to increase advertising; if they think it will not, then they will not increase advertising.

Manufacturing Firm

In the following example, a firm selling 10,000 units of a product at $10 per unit is losing $5,000 per year, as illustrated by both the traditional approach and the contribution approach in Exhibit 4.10.

The exhibit presents this information on both a total and a unit basis. (For simplicity, it is assumed that there are no beginning or ending inventories.) A proposal has been made to management to reduce the selling price. The assumption is that if the selling price is reduced the $9 per unit, sales will double—that is, increase from 10,000 units to 20,000 units. It is assumed that the firm can sell 20,000 units without increasing total fixed cost. Analyzing Exhibit 4.10 from the traditional approach, one might conclude that since the company is already losing $.50 per unit, cutting the selling price by $1.00 would increase losses even more. It appears to reduce gross margin per unit to zero; and therefore, the company would lose $1.50 on every unit sold.

This is the faulty reasoning that results from lack of care in analyzing fixed costs per unit. By definition, fixed costs do not change within a relevant range; and it has been assumed here that total fixed costs will not change. The prospect of increased sales should be analyzed by use of the contribution approach.

Exhibit 4.10 Comparison of Traditional Approach with Contribution Approach

Traditional Approach

	Total	Unit
Sales (10,000 Units)...............................	$100,000	$10.00
Cost of Goods Sold	90,000	9.00
Gross Margin	$ 10,000	$ 1.00
Selling and Administrative Expenses	15,000	1.50
Net Loss...........................	$(5,000)	$(.50)

Contribution Appoach

		Total		Unit
Sales (10,000 Units)........................		$100,000		$10.00
Variable Costs:				
Variable Cost of Goods Sold...................	$60,000		$6.00	
Selling and Administrative Expenses...............	5,000	65,000	.50	6.50
Contribution Margin........................		$ 35,000		$ 3.50
Fixed Costs:				
Fixed Factory Overhead Expense................	$30,000			
Selling and Administrative Expenses...............	10,000	40,000		
Net Loss............................		$(5,000)		

Looking at Exhibit 4.10, you can see that current sales provide a contribution margin of $35,000. That is not enough to cover the fixed costs of $40,000. Notice that the unit information under the contribution approach is shown only for sales and variable costs. Normally, we do not show fixed cost per unit under the contribution approach because of the misleading nature of this figure for decision-making purposes of this type.

Using the contribution approach, Exhibit 4.11 analyzes the proposed change in selling price and number of units sold. As you can see, rather than increasing the net loss, the proposed changes will in fact result in a net income of $10,000. The reason is that fixed costs remain at $40,000. However, the contribution margin has increased from $35,000 to $50,000, an increase of $15,000. This increase in contribution margin eliminates the $5,000 net loss and provides $10,000 for net income. Notice that the increase in volume (10,000 units to 20,000 units) more than offsets the decrease in the unit contribution margin ($2.50 compared with $3.50).

A word of caution is necessary here. Any analysis based on estimates of the future is subject to error. The conclusions from such analysis are only as valid as the estimates are accurate. This is a problem managers must face every day. In this example, the proposed results depend heavily on the assumption that a $1 price reduction will double sales volume with no

Exhibit 4.11 Proposed Changes Using Contribution Approach

		Total		**Unit**
Sales (20,000 Units)		$180,000		$9.00
Variable Costs:				
Variable Cost of Goods Sold	$120,000		$6.00	
Selling and Administrative Expenses	10,000	130,000	.50	6.50
Contribution Margin		$ 50,000		$2.50
Fixed Costs:				
Fixed Factory Overhead Expense	$ 30,000			
Selling and Administrative Expenses	10,000	40,000		
Net Income		$ 10,000		

increase in total fixed cost. If the assumption proves valid, you can see that the contribution approach has been more useful to management than the traditional approach.

In the examples used in this text, as in decisions made for everyday problems, assumptions will be used. Remember that the final decision to be made by a manager must also depend on analysis of the validity of the assumptions, along with the recommendations of the management accountant.

Summary

Variable costing treats fixed factory overhead as a period cost. The total amount of fixed factory overhead incurred during an accounting period is deducted on the income statement as an expense of the period. This differs from the treatment of fixed factory overhead under absorption costing, which charges fixed factory overhead as a product cost. As such, it is deducted on income statements only as a part of cost of goods sold when the applicable product is sold.

Variable costing involves use of the contribution approach income statement. An income statement with this format subtracts variable costs from sales to arrive at contribution margin and fixed costs from contribution margin to determine net income. Contribution margin represents an amount available to cover fixed costs and provide profit, or net income. Thus, the contribution approach income statement classifies cost according to cost behavior. The contribution approach income statement can be used by both manufacturing firms and merchandising firms.

For manufacturing firms, net income determined by use of absorption costing may differ significantly from net income determined by use of variable costing. The difference arises because of the way fixed factory overhead is treated. The chapter provided one illustration of this point; the appendix examines it more thoroughly.

Considerable controversy has been generated in the accounting profession over the years as to whether absorption costing or variable costing is the more appropriate method. There are theoretical arguments for and against both positions. However, from a practical viewpoint, there is really no controversy. At the present time, absorption costing must be used for external financial reporting and for income tax determination. Variable costing is generally more useful for internal decision making. The accounting system of a firm can be designed to provide information that meets the needs of external financial reporting on an absorption costing basis and meets the needs for management decision making on a variable costing basis.

Appendix: The Effect of Absorption Costing and Variable Costing on Net Income

This appendix illustrates how net income is affected by the type of costing used, depending on the relationship between sales and production. In order to simplify the illustration, it is assumed that there are no changes in work-in-process inventory amounts. Thus, all inventory changes are in finished goods inventory. Results depend on whether a firm uses the last-in, first-out (LIFO) or the first-in, first-out (FIFO) method of inventory valuation.

Use of LIFO

Production Exceeds Sales

This example assumes a variable cost of production of $8 per unit and a selling price of $15 per unit. Variable selling and administrative expenses total $.50 per unit sold. It is assumed that neither the selling price nor the variable costs per unit will change from one year to the next. In this example, fixed selling and administrative expenses total $10,000 per year and fixed factory overhead totals $40,000 per year. Sales for Year 1 total 12,000 units, and 20,000 units are produced. This is the first year of operation; so there is no beginning inventory. The results are shown in Exhibit 4.12.

The exhibit shows that net income under absorption costing is $16,000 higher than it is under variable costing. This difference is explained by the fact that fixed factory overhead of $40,000 is charged as a period cost under variable costing. Under absorption costing, however, the $40,000 is shown as a product cost. Since 20,000 units were produced, the fixed cost per unit is $2 ($40,000 ÷ 20,000 units).

The ending inventory of $80,000 (8,000 units) contains $16,000 of fixed factory overhead (8,000 units × $2 per unit). In effect, $16,000 of the $40,000 of fixed factory overhead has been deferred by being placed in inventory. This accounts for the difference in net income between the two methods.

Sales Exceed Production

In Year 2, we again assume sales of 12,000 units; but production is only 10,000 units. The results are shown in Exhibit 4.13.

Net income under variable costing is exactly the same as it was in Year

Exhibit 4.12 Year 1–Production Exceeds Sales

Absorption Costing			
Sales (12,000 Units × $15)			$180,000
Cost of Goods Sold:			
Cost of Goods Manufactured—			
Variable (20,000 × $8)	$160,000		
Fixed	40,000		
Cost of Goods Available for Sale		$200,000	
Less: Ending Inventory			
(8,000 × $10)[a]		80,000	
Cost of Goods Sold			120,000
Gross Margin			$ 60,000
Selling and Administrative Expenses			16,000
Net Income			$ 44,000

Variable Costing			
Sales (12,000 Units × $15)			$180,000
Cost of Goods Sold:			
Cost of Goods Manufactured—Variable (20,000 × $8)	$160,000		
Cost of Goods Available for Sale	$160,000		
Less: Ending Inventory (8,000 × $8)	64,000		
Cost of Goods Sold		$96,000	
Variable Selling and Administrative Expenses (12,000 × $.50)		6,000	
Total Variable Costs			102,000
Contribution Margin			$ 78,000
Fixed Costs:			
Fixed Factory Overhead Expense	$40,000		
Selling and Administrative Expenses	10,000		
Total Fixed Costs			50,000
Net Income			$ 28,000

[a] $\dfrac{\$200{,}000 \text{ Cost of Goods Manufactured}}{20{,}000 \text{ Units Produced}} = \$10$ per unit.

1. Since sales have not changed, cost of goods sold is still the variable cost of $8 per unit, which totals $96,000. Naturally, fixed factory overhead expense of $40,000 is the same as in Year 1.

Under absorption costing, net income is only $24,000, compared with $28,000 under variable costing. Since we are assuming the LIFO basis of inventory valuation, the entire production of 10,000 units is assumed to be sold in the period of production. From Exhibit 4.13, you can see that this totals $120,000. In addition, 2,000 units from beginning inventory are also included as part of cost of goods sold. In this case, the entire fixed factory

Exhibit 4.13 Year 2–Sales Exceed Production

Absorption Costing			
Sales (12,000 Units × $15)			$180,000
Cost of Goods Sold:			
Beginning Inventory		$ 80,000	
Cost of Goods Manufactured—			
Variable (10,000 × $8)	$ 80,000		
Fixed.......................	40,000	120,000	
Cost of Goods Available for Sale.............		$200,000	
Less: Ending Inventory (6,000 × $10)ᵃ		60,000	
Cost of Goods Sold.............................			140,000
Gross Margin			$ 40,000
Selling and Administrative Expenses			16,000
Net Income........................			$ 24,000

Variable Costing			
Sales (12,000 Units × $15)			$180,000
Cost of Goods Sold:			
Beginning Inventory	$ 64,000		
Cost of Goods Manufactured—Variable (10,000 × $8)	$ 80,000		
Cost of Goods Available for Sale....................	$144,000		
Less: Ending Inventory (6,000 × $8)...................	48,000		
Cost of Goods Sold		96,000	
Variable Selling and Administrative Expenses (12,000 × $.50)		6,000	
Total Variable Costs			102,000
Contribution Margin.......................			$ 78,000
Fixed Costs:			
Fixed Factory Overhead Expense....................		$40,000	
Selling and Administrative Expenses..................		10,000	
Total Fixed Costs.......................			50,000
Net Income........................			$ 28,000

ᵃSince LIFO is being used, ending inventory consists of 6,000 units that were in beginning inventory at a cost of $10 each.

overhead of $40,000 for Year 2 was charged as part of goods sold, because the entire 10,000 units produced this period were sold. In addition, 2,000 units of beginning inventory, which included $4,000 of fixed factory overhead (2,000 units × $2 per unit), are also charged against the revenue of this period. The $4,000 difference in net income between absorption costing and variable costing is caused by the $4,000 of fixed factory overhead that was in beginning inventory and is now being charged against revenue for the period.

As a result, under LIFO, when sales exceed production, you can expect net income under absorption to be less than it is under variable. This is logical, because under variable only the fixed factory overhead for the period is charged against revenue; but under absorption, all the fixed factory overhead for the period, plus some of the fixed factory overhead from a previous period, is charged against revenue.

Exhibit 4.14 Year 3–Production Equals Sales

Absorption Costing			
Sales (12,000 Units × $15)			$180,000
Cost of Goods Sold:			
Beginning Inventory		$ 60,000	
Cost of Goods Manufactured—			
Variable (12,000 × $8)	$ 96,000		
Fixed.	40,000	136,000	
Cost of Goods Available for Sale.		$196,000	
Less: Ending Inventory (6,000 × $10)ᵃ		60,000	
Cost of Goods Sold			136,000
Gross Margin			$ 44,000
Selling and Administrative Expenses			16,000
Net Income.			$ 28,000

Variable Costing			
Sales (12,000 Units × $15)			$180,000
Cost of Goods Sold:			
Beginning Inventory	$ 48,000		
Cost of Goods Manufactured—Variable (12,000 × $8)	$ 96,000		
Cost of Goods Available for Sale.	$144,000		
Less: Ending Inventory (6,000 × $8).	48,000		
Cost of Goods Sold		96,000	
Variable Selling and Administrative Expenses (12,000 × $.50)		6,000	
Total Variable Expenses			102,000
Contribution Margin.			$ 78,000
Fixed Costs:			
Fixed Factory Overhead Expense.		$40,000	
Selling and Administrative Expenses.		10,000	
Total Fixed Costs.			50,000
Net Income.			$ 28,000

ᵃSince LIFO is being used, and since production equals sales, ending inventory is the same as beginning inventory.

Production Equals Sales

When production and sales are equal, net income is the same under absorption costing and variable costing. This situation is shown in Exhibit 4.14.

The reason net income is the same is because the entire production for the period is sold. Thus, the $40,000 of fixed factory overhead that has been charged as a product cost under absorption is included in cost of goods sold. Naturally, this $40,000 is shown as a period cost under variable costing. Since there was no change in inventory, any fixed factory overhead in beginning inventory remains in beginning inventory.

A summary of the effect on net income of using absorption costing and variable costing under LIFO is shown in Exhibit 4.15.

Exhibit 4.15 Summary of Effect on Net Income

Production	Net Income
Production Exceeds Sales	Higher under Absorption
Sales Exceed Production	Higher under Variable
Production Equals Sales	No Difference

Use of FIFO

A comparison of absorption costing with variable costing when FIFO is used will not necessarily yield the same results as a comparison using LIFO. A discussion of why this is so is beyond the scope of this text. At this point, it is sufficient to point out that it is not possible to make a definitive statement as to the difference in the effect on net income between variable costing and absorption costing if the firm is using the FIFO method.

Review Problem

Problem

An income statement for Cantra Corporation's first year of operation appears below. It was prepared under absorption costing.

Cantra Corporation
Income Statement
for the Year Ended December 31, 19X5

Sales	$96,000
Cost of Goods Sold	60,000
Gross Margin	$36,000
Selling and Administrative Expenses	22,000
Net Income	$14,000

The company produced 10,000 units and sold 8,000 units. Fixed factory overhead for the year totaled $50,000 and was applied to the 10,000 units produced. Selling and administrative expenses includes $10,000 of fixed costs.

Required:

a. Determine the amount of fixed factory overhead per unit.

b. Determine the total variable cost of goods sold for the year.

c. Prepare a contribution approach income statement for the year ended December 31, 19X5.

d. Explain the difference in net income between absorption costing and variable costing.

Solution

a. $\dfrac{\$50,000}{10,000 \text{ Units}} = \$5 \text{ per Unit}$

b. $60,000 Total Cost of Goods Sold
 $-40,000$ Fixed Costs in Cost of Goods Sold ($5 × 8,000 Units)
 $20,000 Variable Cost of Goods Sold

c.
Cantra Corporation
Income Statement
for the Year Ended December 31, 19X5

Sales		$96,000
Variable Costs:		
Cost of Goods Sold	$20,000	
Selling and Administrative Expenses[a]	12,000	
Total Variable Costs		32,000
Contribution Margin		$64,000
Fixed Costs:		
Fixed Factory Overhead Expense	$50,000	
Selling and Administrative Expenses	10,000	
Total Fixed Costs		60,000
Net Income		$ 4,000

[a] $22,000 Total Selling and Administrative Expenses
 $-10,000$ Fixed Selling and Administrative Expenses
 $12,000 Variable Selling and Administrative Expenses

d. The difference in net income, $10,000, between absorption costing and variable costing is explained by the fact that, under absorption costing, the 2,000 units (10,000 − 8,000) that went into ending inventory included fixed factory overhead of $10,000 ($5 per unit × 2,000 units). Under variable costing, all fixed factory overhead, $50,000, was subtracted on the income statement in arriving at net income.

Questions

4-1 What is variable costing?

4-2 What is meant by *contribution margin*? How does it differ from gross margin?

4-3 Is cost of goods sold a variable cost? Explain.

4-4 Refer to Exhibit 4.5. Calculate the variable cost ratio and the contribution margin ratio.

4-5 How does the recording process for the cost accounting cycle under variable costing differ from that under absorption costing?

4-6 "Regardless of changes in production, inventory will always be valued higher under absorption costing than under variable costing." Do you agree with this statement? Explain.

4-7 What are the primary arguments in favor of absorption costing?

4-8 What are the primary arguments in favor of variable costing?

4-9 Since variable costing is considered a product costing technique, how is it applicable to merchandising firms?

4-10 Since fixed cost per unit decreases with increased production, should a manufacturing firm produce as much as possible in order to lower the cost per unit as low as possible, and therefore increase profits? Explain.

4-11 Since fixed cost is a cost of doing business, why does it appear to be ignored when variable costing concepts are applied in decision-making situations?

4-12 (*Appendix*) Assume that a firm uses the LIFO method of inventory valuation. Tell whether net income under absorption costing will be greater than, less than, or equal to net income under variable costing when:
   a. Production exceeds sales.
   b. Sales exceed production.
   c. Production equals sales.

4-13 (*Appendix*) Refer to Question 4–12. Explain the reason for the differences under parts a, b, and c.

4-14 (*Appendix*) "In order to show a continually increasing net income, a firm should use absorption costing and always produce more than it sells." Discuss the validity of this statement.

Exercises

4-15 Journal Entries; Actual Cost System; Variable Costing A company incurred the following costs in its manufacturing process for the month ending September 30, 19X0:

Direct Material	$50,000
Indirect Material	15,000
Direct Labor	75,000
Indirect Labor	25,000
Depreciation of Factory and Equipment	5,000
Factory Managers' Salaries	10,000

Prepare the journal entries to record these costs as of September 30, 19X0, on an actual cost system, under variable costing.

4-16 Journal Entries; Actual Cost System; Variable Costing Krinkle Krumpet Factory completed production on 50,000 crumpets with a variable cost of $200,000 during March 19X1. In addition, the company incurred fixed factory overhead of $75,000. During March, it sold 20,000 crumpets on account for $160,000. The sold crumpets had a variable manufacturing cost of $80,000. Prepare journal entries to record the transfer of costs to finished goods inventory and to record the sale of crumpets, under variable costing, as of March 31, 19X1. Assume an actual cost system.

4-17 Journal Entries; Variable Costing For internal purposes, Harlow Manufacturing Company uses variable costing. On January 31, 19X2, work-in-process inventory had a balance of $150,000 and finished goods inventory had a balance of $180,000. On February 1, product costing $70,000 was completed and transferred to the finished goods warehouse. On that same date, finished goods costing $200,000 were sold on account for $280,000.

a. Prepare journal entries to record these transactions.

b. Determine the balance of the work-in-process inventory account and the finished goods inventory account after giving consideration to the entries in part a.

4-18 Contribution Margin Approach Income Statement Vinson's Variety Store has presented you with the following information for the year ended December 31, 19X2.

Sales	$400,000
Inventory, January 1, 19X2	40,000
Inventory, December 31, 19X2	65,000
Purchases	300,000
Selling Expenses	80,000
Administrative Expenses	50,000

Further examination reveals that $20,000 of the selling expenses and $40,000 of the administrative expenses were fixed. Prepare an income statement for the year ended December 31, 19X2, using the contribution margin approach.

4-19 Contribution Margin Approach Income Statement Amabala, Inc., provides the following information regarding operations for the year ended December 31, 19X4:

Sales	$1,200,000
Finished Goods Inventory, January 1, 19X4	100,000
Finished Goods Inventory, December 31, 19X4	60,000
Variable Cost of Goods Manufactured	500,000
Selling Expenses	200,000
Administrative Expenses	150,000
Fixed Factory Overhead	100,000

Finished goods inventory includes only variable costs. Selling and administrative expenses included $40,000 and $120,000 of fixed costs, respectively. Prepare an income statement for the year ended December 31, 19X4, using the contribution margin approach.

4-20 Calculating Income Statement Items; Determining Expected Net Income Sellco Sales Company sold 50,000 units of its product for $3 per unit in 19X2. Its variable costs per unit were $1.80; its fixed costs per unit, $.50.

a. Determine the amount of net income for 19X2.

b. Determine the amount of contribution margin for 19X2.

c. Determine the amount of fixed costs for 19X2.

d. The company is considering a proposal to increase sales by 10,000 units by increasing advertising by $5,000 in 19X3. Assuming no change in other fixed costs, determine the amount of expected net income for 19X3 under the proposal.

4-21 Determining Expected Net Income The Noof Company sells a product that provides a contribution margin ratio of 30%. How will net income be affected by a proposal that is expected to increase sales by $20,000 and increase fixed costs by $8,000?

4-22 Determining Required Sales Douglas Williams is considering preparing and selling hot dogs at the local football stadium. To do this, he will incur fixed costs of $300 for the season. Each hot dog sells for $.75 and has a variable cost of $.50. How many hot dogs must he sell in order to avoid losing money on this venture?

4-23 Net Income; Absorption Costing and Variable Costing (*Appendix*) A company produced 120,000 units and sold 100,000 units of product in 19X3. Fixed factory overhead for the year totaled $240,000. The company uses the LIFO method of inventory valuation. Under which type of costing, absorption or variable, will net income be greater? By how much?

4-24 Net Income; Absorption Costing and Variable Costing (*Appendix*) A company produced 80,000 units and sold 90,000 units of product in 19X5. Fixed factory overhead for the year totaled $100,000. Production and fixed factory overhead were the same in 19X5 as they were in 19X4. The company uses the LIFO method of inventory valuation. Under which type of costing, absorption or variable, will net income be greater? By how much?

4-25 Net Income; Variable Costing; Two Years (*Appendix*) Abvar Company incurred fixed factory overhead of $50,000 in both 19X1 and 19X2. Unit sales and production for each year were as follows:

	19X2	19X1
Sales	230,000	200,000
Production	200,000	250,000

Net income under absorption costing was $33,000 in 19X1 and $40,000 in 19X2. The company uses the LIFO method of inventory valuation. Determine the amount of net income under variable costing for 19X1 and 19X2.

4-26 Net Income; Absorption Costing; Two Years (*Appendix*) Varab Company computes its net income on a variable costing basis for internal purposes. For 19X3, this amount was $65,000; for 19X4, $82,000. Unit sales and production for each year were as follows:

	19X4	19X3
Sales	75,000	50,000
Production	72,000	60,000

Fixed factory overhead was $90,000 each year. The company uses the LIFO method of inventory valuation. Determine the amount of net income under absorption costing for 19X3 and 19X4.

Problems

4-27 Journal Entries; Actual Cost System; Variable Costing Transactions for Falcon Manufacturing Company for April 19X2, its first month of operation, are shown below. The firm uses an actual cost system.

1) Raw materials purchased on account totaled $80,000.

2) Direct material used in production totaled $60,000.

3) Direct labor for the month totaled $110,000.

4) Variable factory overhead costs were incurred as follows:

Utilities	$ 4,500
Indirect Material	10,000
Indirect Labor	18,000

5) Fixed factory overhead costs were incurred as follows:

Managers' Salaries	$12,000
Depreciation on Equipment	2,500
Rent on Factory	3,000

6) Raw materials purchased in item 1 were paid for.

7) Salaries and rent accrued in items 3, and 4, and 5 were paid.

8) Finished product costing $145,000 was completed.

9) Finished goods costing $90,000 were sold on account for $155,000.

Required:

a. Prepare journal entries to record the April transactions, assuming the use of variable costing.

b. Without posting to ledger accounts, determine the balance of the following accounts as of April 30, 19X2:

1) Raw materials inventory.

2) Work-in-process inventory.

3) Finished goods inventory.

4-28 Journal Entries; Actual Cost System; Variable Costing On December 31, 19X0, the balance sheet for Aksala Manufacturing Company included the following items:

Raw Materials Inventory	$32,000
Work-in-Process Inventory	60,000
Finished Goods Inventory	85,000

Transactions for January 19X0 are shown below. The firm uses an actual cost system.

1) Raw materials purchased on account totaled $40,000.

2) Direct material used in production totaled $55,000.

3) Direct labor for the month totaled $70,000.

4) Variable factory overhead costs were incurred as follows:

Utilities	$3,400
Indirect Material	5,000
Indirect Labor	7,600

5) Fixed factory overhead costs were incurred as follows:

| Managers' Salaries | $7,500 |
| Depreciation on Plant and Equipment | 8,000 |

6) Raw materials purchased in item 1 were paid for.

7) Salaries accrued in items 3, 4, and 5 were paid.

8) Finished product costing $115,000 was completed.

9) Finished goods costing $180,000 were sold on account for $245,000.

Required

a. Prepare journal entries to record the January transactions, assuming the use of variable costing.

b. Post the journal entries to ledger accounts and determine the balance of the inventory accounts.

4–29 Contribution Approach Income Statement Information from the records of the Rolling Wheels Auto Parts Company for the year ended December 31, 19X6, is shown below:

Sales	$465,000
Sales Returns and Allowances	15,000
Sales Commissions	45,000
Sales Salaries Expense	60,000
Inventory, January 1, 19X6	55,000
Inventory, December 31, 19X6	20,000
Purchases	180,000
Office Salaries Expense	25,000
Rent Expense	10,500
Office Supplies Expense	3,600
Store Supplies Expense	3,000
Utilities Expense	5,000
Postage Expense	500
Insurance Expense	2,000
Depreciation Expense	2,400

Sales commissions, store supplies expense, and postage expense are variable costs. Rent expense is $500 per month plus 1% of net sales. All other expenses are fixed.

The variable portion of rent expense and 50% of utilities expense, insurance expense, and depreciation expense are considered selling expenses. Sales commissions, sales salaries, and store supplies are also selling expenses. The remaining expenses are administrative.

Required:

Prepare a contribution approach income statement. Show the selling and administrative expenses by natural classification.

4–30 Contribution Approach Income Statement Information from the records of the Little Tyke Toy Company for the year ended December 31, 19X5, is shown below:

Sales	$950,000
Direct Materials Inventory, January 1, 19X5	25,000
Direct Materials Inventory, December 31, 19X5	35,000
Direct Materials Purchases	160,000
Indirect Material Used	42,000
Direct Labor	200,000
Rent on Factory	48,000
Indirect Labor	60,000
Other Variable Factory Overhead	30,000
Other Fixed Factory Overhead	62,000
Variable Selling Expenses	65,000
Fixed Selling Expenses	100,000
Variable Administrative Expenses	20,000
Fixed Administrative Expenses	85,000
Work-in-Process Inventory, January 1, 19X5	68,000
Work-in-Process Inventory, December 31, 19X5	95,000
Finished Goods Inventory, January 1, 19X5	140,000
Finished Goods Inventory, December 31, 19X5	115,000

Required:

a. Prepare a schedule of variable cost of goods manufactured for the year ended December 31, 19X5. (Work-in-process inventory includes only variable costs.)

b. Prepare a contribution approach income statement for the year ended December 31, 19X5. (Finished goods inventory includes only variable costs.)

4-31 Contribution Approach Income Statement An income statement for Fancy Pants Company's first year of operation appears below. It was prepared under absorption costing.

Fancy Pants Company
Income Statement
for the Year Ended December 31, 19X2

Sales	$220,000
Cost of Goods Sold	150,000
Gross Margin	$ 70,000
Selling and Administrative Expenses	50,000
Net Income	$ 20,000

The company produced 25,000 units and sold 20,000 units. Fixed factory overhead for the year totaled $75,000 and was applied to the 25,000 units produced. Selling and administrative expenses includes $28,000 of fixed costs.

Required:

a. Determine the amount of fixed overhead per unit.

b. Determine the total variable cost of goods sold for the year.

c. Prepare a contribution approach income statement for the year ended December 31, 19X2.

4-32 Contribution Approach Income Statement An income statement prepared under absorption costing for Harrison Hat Company appears below. The company uses the LIFO method of inventory valuation.

Harrison Hat Company
Income Statement
for the Year Ended December 31, 19X2

Sales	$350,000
Cost of Goods Sold	210,000
Gross Margin	$140,000
Selling and Administrative Expenses	100,000
Net Income	$ 40,000

The company began the year with 15,000 units in finished goods inventory, produced 45,000 units, and sold 52,000 units. In 19X1, production totaled 60,000 units. In each of the years 19X1 and 19X2, fixed factory overhead totaled $90,000 and was applied to units produced. Variable selling and administrative expenses are 10% of sales.

Required:
a. Determine the amount of fixed factory overhead per unit each year.
b. Determine the total variable cost of goods sold for 19X2.
c. Prepare a contribution approach income statement for the year ended December 31, 19X2.

4-33 Income Statement under Absorption Costing and Variable Costing
Tremble Corporation manufactures a single product. Information regarding operations for the year ended December 31, 19X4, is as follows:

Selling Price per Unit:	$25
Variable Manufacturing Costs per Unit:	$15
Variable Selling and Administrative Expenses per Unit:	$5
Total Fixed Factory Overhead:	$30,000
Total Fixed Selling and Administrative Expenses:	$10,000
Beginning Inventory (Absorption Basis)	$128,000

The company began the year with 8,000 units in finished goods inventory, produced 40,000 units, and sold 45,000. Variable manufacturing costs in beginning inventory were $15 per unit. The company uses the LIFO method of inventory valuation.

Required:
Prepare an income statement for the year ended December 31, 19X4, under:
a. Absorption costing.
b. Variable costing.

4-34 Income Statement under Absorption Costing and Variable Costing
Adaven Corporation, which had no beginning finished goods inventory, provided the following information for the year ended December 31, 19X5:

	Dollars	Units
Sales	$300,000	30,000
Variable Manufacturing Costs	180,000	40,000
Fixed Factory Overhead	50,000	
Variable Selling and Administrative Expenses	15,000	
Fixed Selling and Administrative Expenses	20,000	

Required:
Prepare an income statement for the year ended December 31, 19X5, under:
a. Absorption costing.
b. Variable costing.

4-35 Determining Net Income after Product Line Is Dropped An income statement for Honest Harry's Auto Sales for the month ended March 31, 19X5, is shown below:

Honest Harry's Auto Sales
Income Statement
for the Month Ended March 31, 19X5

Sales	$350,000
Cost of Goods Sold	210,000
Gross Margin	$140,000
Selling and Administrative Expenses	136,500
Net Income	$ 3,500

Cost of goods sold is entirely variable, consisting of the amount Harry pays the manufacturer for each car. Harry pays his salespeople a 20% commission on each car sold. Variable administrative expenses are 5% of sales. Fixed costs total $49,000 per month.

In March, 70 cars at prices ranging from $4,000 to $6,000 were sold. Cost of goods sold as a percentage of sales is the same for all models. Included in the total of 70 cars were 20 cars that sell for $4,000 each. Harry has done some unit analysis of the $4,000 cars as follows:

Sales Price		$4,000
Cost of Goods Sold		2,400
Gross Margin		$1,600
Variable Selling and Administrative Expenses	$1,000	
Fixed Selling and Administrative Expenses[a]	700	1,700
Net Loss per Car		$ (100)

Based on this analysis, Harry is considering dropping the $4,000 car because it is losing money. He figures he will increase net income in April by $2,000 (20 cars × $100) by this action.

---

[a] $\frac{\$49,000}{70 \text{ cars}} = \$700$ per Car

Required:

a. Assuming that Harry quits selling the $4,000 car and that the sales, unit variable costs, and total fixed costs for the other 50 cars are the same in April as they were in March, determine the amount of net income for April.

b. Assuming that Harry is not happy with the results in April (as determined above), how do you explain the difference between his expectations and the results?

4-36 Determining Effect of Proposed Promotion on Net Income The income statement for Lossco Manufacturing Company for the year ended December 31, 19X8, is shown below. The company had no beginning or ending inventories and produces a single product.

Lossco Manufacturing Company
Income Statement
for the Year Ended December 31, 19X8

Sales (10,000 Units)	$300,000
Cost of Goods Sold	310,000
Gross Margin	$(10,000)
Selling and Administrative Expenses	55,000
Net Loss	$(65,000)

The company's management is distressed over these results and is considering ways to improve the company's profit picture. A proposal has been made that the company conduct a sweepstakes contest in 19X9. Prizes totaling $50,000 would be awarded. The cost of promoting and conducting the contest is estimated at $20,000. Although no purchase would be required for a person to participate in the contest, the marketing manager estimates that unit sales would double from what they were in 19X8 because of the advertising and publicity associated with the contest. No increase in sales price is anticipated.

You have been asked to provide management with an analysis of the effect of the contest on net income. Your review of the accounting records reveals that fixed factory overhead was $100,000 and fixed selling and administrative expenses were $40,000 in 19X8. No change in either of these items, except for the sweepstakes cost, is expected in 19X9. You also are told that variable costs per unit are not expected to change and that the company wants no ending inventory.

Required:

a. Determine the amount of net income for 19X9 if the sweepstakes proposal is accepted. (A formal income statement is not required.)

b. Do you recommend that the proposal be accepted? Explain your answer.

4-37 Net Income; Variable Costing; Differences between Variable and Absorption Costing (*Appendix*) Comparative income statements under absorption costing for the Rubber Duck Company appear below. The company uses the LIFO method of inventory valuation.

Rubber Duck Company
Comparative Income Statements
for the Years Ended December 31, 19X1 and 19X2

	19X2	19X1
Sales	$175,000	$200,000
Cost of Goods Sold	122,000	138,000
Gross Margin	$ 53,000	$ 62,000
Selling and Administrative Expenses	35,000	40,000
Net Income	$ 18,000	$ 22,000
Additional Information		
Sales in Units:	44,000	50,000
Production in Units:	40,000	80,000
Beginning Inventory in Units:	30,000	0
Fixed Factory Overhead:	$60,000	$60,000

Required:

a. Determine the amount of net income under variable costing for 19X1. (A formal income statement is not required.) Explain why it differs from the amount shown for absorption costing.

b. Determine the amount of net income under variable costing for 19X2. (A formal income statement is not required.) Explain why it differs from the amount shown for absorption costing.

4-38 Net Income; Variable Costing; Differences between Variable and Absorption Costing (*Appendix*) Comparative income statements under absorption costing for the Bellweather Barometer Company appear below. The company uses the LIFO method of inventory valuation.

Bellweather Barometer Company
Comparative Income Statements
for the Years Ended December 31, 19X2 and 19X3

	19X3	19X2
Sales	$50,000	$50,000
Cost of Goods Sold	35,000	40,000
Gross Margin	$15,000	$10,000
Selling and Administrative Expenses	8,000	8,000
Net Income	$ 7,000	$ 2,000
Additional Information		
Sales in Units:	5,000	5,000
Production in Units:	10,000	5,000
Fixed Factory Overhead:	$10,000	$10,000

Required:

a. Explain why net income increased by $5,000 with no change in units sold.

b. Determine the amount of net income in 19X3 under variable costing. (A formal income statement is not required.)

c. Explain the difference in net income between absorption costing and variable costing in 19X3.

d. Determine the amount of net income under variable costing in 19X2.

4–39 Explaining Increases in Cost of Goods Sold; Absorption Costing (*Appendix*) Comparative income statements under absorption costing for the Rialto Ringer Company appear below.

Rialto Ringer Company
Comparative Income Statements
for the Years Ended December 31, 19X6 and 19X7

	19X7	19X6
Sales	$650,000	$650,000
Cost of Goods Sold	611,000	520,000
Gross Margin	$ 39,000	$130,000
Selling and Administrative Expenses	100,000	100,000
Net Income (Loss)	$(61,000)	$ 30,000
Additional Information		
Sales in Units:	65,000	65,000
Production in Units:	60,000	100,000

The president of the company, who is very upset over this year's loss, has told you, "We just began operations last year and made a modest profit of $30,000. Although sales didn't increase this year, we felt confident that net income would improve because we were able to reduce our fixed factory overhead by $29,000 in 19X7. I realize that the decline in net income was caused by the increase in cost of goods sold. But, with the same number of units being sold, I just don't understand how cost of goods sold could have gone up by $91,000. The statements must be in error."

Further examination by you reveals that fixed factory overhead was $300,000 in 19X6 and that the variable manufacturing costs per unit were the same in both years. The company uses the LIFO method of inventory valuation.

Required:

Prepare calculations that show why cost of goods sold increased by $91,000.

4–40 Income Statement under Absorption Costing and Variable Costing (*Appendix*) Management of Bicent Company uses the following unit costs for the single product it manufactures:

	Cost per Unit
Direct Material	$30.00
Direct Labor	19.00
Factory Overhead:	
Variable Cost	6.00
Fixed Cost (Based on 10,000 Units per Month)	5.00
Selling and Administrative:	
Variable Cost	4.00
Fixed Cost (Based on 10,000 Units per Month)	2.80

The selling price is $80 per unit. Fixed costs remain fixed within the relevant range of 4,000 to 16,000 units of production. The company uses the LIFO method of inventory valuation. Management has shown you the following data for the month ending June 30,19X2:

	Units
Beginning Inventory	2,000
Production	10,000
Available	12,000
Sales	7,500
Ending Inventory	4,500

Required:

a. Prepare income statements for June 19X2 under each of the following product-costing methods:

   1. Absorption costing.

   2. Variable costing.

b. Explain the reason for the difference in net income between absorption costing and variable costing, as determined in part a. (AICPA adapted)

Part Two

Managerial Accounting for Planning and Controlling

Chapter 5   Budgeting

Learning Objectives

The purpose of this chapter is to introduce you to concepts of budgeting for a business firm. The chapter describes the nature and purpose of budgeting and shows how to prepare a budget for a manufacturing firm. Studying the chapter will enable you to:

1. Define *budget*.
2. Describe the nature and purpose of budgeting.
3. Describe how budgeting helps management to plan and control business operations.
4. Describe how budgeting coordinates business activities.
5. Describe the nature of feedback.
6. Define *performance report*.
7. Describe the human relations factors of budgeting.
8. Prepare the schedules and budgeted statements leading to a master budget.
9. Describe how budgeted statements can be used by management.

Chapter Topics

The major topics included in this chapter are:

Description of Budgeting
Purpose of Budgets
The Master Budget
Importance of Human Relations
Budgeting for Nonmanufacturing Firms

Chapter 1 discussed the functions of management. Budgeting plays an important role in the ability of management to perform at least two of these functions—planning and controlling. A **budget** is a formal expression of planned operations expressed in financial terms.

It is important that management know what has happened in the past and where the business stands in the present. Financial statements, such as the income statement and the balance sheet, provide this information. It is equally important, however, that management know where the firm is headed. If the future does not look as good as management would like, it can take steps to try to change what appears on the horizon.

This look at the future is accomplished through budgeting. This chapter describes the budgeting process and illustrates how management uses the budget internally to plan and control business operations.

Description of Budgeting

Budgeting is the process of planning future operations and controlling operations by comparing actual results with planned expectations. A budget is the formal written plan used to communicate these expectations and serves as the basis for comparing them with results.

A budget is an internal document. It is used within the firm and normally is not distributed outside the firm. A budget is a forecast. It indicates management's expectations of what the firm plans to do and what the financial results of operations will be during the future period. The budget shows what each manager is expected to accomplish during the budget period.

Budgeting can be performed by business, government, and individuals.

Business Firms

The major purposes of the business budget are planning and controlling operations. These functions are discussed more fully later. Simply stated, the budget: (1) helps the firm to plan where it is going by presenting a formal structure; (2) identifies the person responsible for carrying out each step of the plan; and (3) helps insure adherence to the plan by pointing out deviations from it. Pointing out deviations allows management to focus attention on problem areas; this represents the control function. Theoretically, the firm does not need to prepare a budget. It can go blindly from day to day and month to month. But most likely this manner of operation will result in the firm's performance not being as good as it could be.

Government

You have probably read about budgets prepared by local, state, and federal governments. Budgets help government agencies to plan and control expenditures of public funds. These entities are required by law to prepare budgets. Theoretically, the budgets represent plans to best accomplish the goals of the agencies, given the resources available. Actually, they often represent political decisions to spend or not to spend certain amounts of money for particular programs. Government budgets represent not only the amount expected to be spent but also the maximum amount that legally can be spent.

While many of the concepts discussed in this chapter for business budgets also apply to governmental budgets, governmental budgeting is usually much more directed and controlled by law. Nevertheless, the principles of budgeting for business entities should, ideally, be applied to governmental budgeting, especially the idea of using limited resources in the best possible manner. The discussion in this chapter focuses on business budgets.

Individuals

Budgeting concepts are as applicable to individuals as they are to businesses. Budgeting is important to individuals because an individual's sources of funds are usually limited. It is important that individuals plan the use and control of their money as much as possible.

Most of us have heard of personal budgets. Perhaps you have been involved in the preparation of your own budget. For many individuals, financial management consists primarily of attempting to avoid writing checks for more than the amount in the bank. While this is an admirable goal, an individual should try to plan receipts and payments over a period of time, such as a year. In this way, the individual has some idea of what to expect and may also be able to make changes if the expectations are not favorable. Although this chapter focuses on business budgets, many of the concepts discussed apply to individuals as well.

Purpose of Budgets

Chapter 1 pointed out that, within certain constraints, the objective of a profit-oriented organization is to maximize profits. Budgeting helps a business firm achieve this objective. In fact, budgeting is often referred to as *profit planning*. As pointed out earlier, the primary purposes of budgeting are planning and controlling business operations. It is through these two functions that management achieves its profit goals.

Planning

In any endeavor—such as taking a trip, going Christmas shopping, or holding a meeting—the results are usually better if someone has planned ahead. In planning a trip, you decide where you want to go and find the best route to get there. A Christmas shopping plan provides ideas in advance of what to buy for whom. A meeting that has not been planned will most likely be disorganized, will probably take too long, and may not accomplish its objectives.

A budget forces business managers to plan ahead. For example, rather than waiting for sales to occur, the manager can take steps to attempt to insure that sales occur at the desired level. Furthermore, by knowing of a problem in advance, the manager can take steps to solve the problem before it becomes unmanageable. In short, budgeting requires managers to think formally about what they expect to happen. If these expectations are good, the managers can try to see that they come about. If the expectations are not good, the managers can try to see what can be done to change the undesirable expected results.

Budgeting does not eliminate problems nor insure profits. It merely allows management to be aware of problems in advance. As the saying goes, "Forewarned is forearmed." Or as a well-known lodging firm pointed out in its television commercials of several years ago, "The best surprise is no surprise." Budgeting helps reduce surprises.

Planning, as a part of budgeting, results in two additional advantages for a firm: It provides communication and coordination.

Communication A written budget communicates the firm's plans to managers. It serves as a link between the planning and controlling functions. A budget allows managers to know what is expected of them. Knowing expectations, they are better able to meet the goals of the firm.

A budget serves as a motivational device in that a manager will attempt to meet the expectations it sets. Since performance will be measured, to some extent, on the ability to meet stated goals, a manager is motivated to adhere to the budget. Future pay raises and promotions may also hinge, partially, on this factor. Without a budget to show what is expected, a manager is less motivated to control costs or operate efficiently. As a result, costs for the company as a whole may be more than they should be and more than they would have been if the firm had used a budget.

Coordination As part of planning business operations, budgeting provides coordination within the company. Managers of various divisions in a firm develop their individual plans. The plan of one division will certainly affect and be affected by the plans of other divisions. Thus, the budgets of the various divisions must be coordinated in order for management to arrive at an overall budget that will meet the firm's goals.

To illustrate, the purchasing department purchases raw materials. To know the amount of raw materials to purchase, this department must know how many units of finished goods are going to be produced as well as what level of raw materials inventory is desired. Thus, the budget for raw materials purchases must be coordinated with the production budget.

Production is based on sales, as well as on the desired ending inventory levels of finished goods. Therefore, the production manager must plan production based on the sales budget. Without such coordination, a production department may produce more items than are needed, increasing storage and inventory costs. On the other hand, it may produce too few units. The company is then unable to meet customer demand, and this results in lost sales and dissatisfied customers.

From this illustration, you can see the importance of budgeting as a means of coordinating business operations. Without a budget, there is no coordination. Each department operates without regard to what any other department is doing. This lack of coordination results in chaos and may eventually result in the firm's going out of business.

Controlling

The planning function of budgeting should be coupled with the controlling function. Preparing a budget is fine. But unless the results of operations are followed up and compared with the budget, the budgeting process is not nearly as effective as it could be.

Controlling is the process of comparing actual results with plans and taking corrective action, where necessary, when results differ significantly from the plan. Controlling, then, depends on planning—without a plan, there is no basis for comparing results and evaluating performance.

Feedback The concept of responsibility accounting was described in Chapter 1. The budgeting process provides one application of this concept. Managers are responsible for adhering to the goals set forth in their segments' budgets. The extent of compliance with budget goals is provided by feedback.

Feedback is the process of gathering data about actual operations, comparing the results against budgeted plans, and communicating exceptions to the managers responsible. Feedback is provided through a performance report.

Performance Report A **performance report** is a document that shows budgeted expectations, actual results, and deviations from the budget for some segment of the firm. A budget deviation is referred to as a **variance,** which may be favorable or unfavorable. For example, if expenses are higher than expected, an unfavorable variance results. If expenses are lower than expected, the variance is favorable.

It is unlikely that results will ever be exactly the same as expectations. Budgets are estimates. Therefore, some variance is expected. Management must decide how much of a variance will be considered significant. For example, a variance in excess of 5 percent of the amount budgeted may be significant in some situations. When variances exceed this allowable tolerance, management investigates the reasons for the variance to see if corrective action needs to be taken. This practice, under which management concentrates its time and effort in exceptional (or problem) situations, is referred to as **management by exception.**

An example of a performance report is shown in Exhibit 5.1. The exhibit shows that the assembly department was $750 over its budget for the month of March. Of more interest, however, are the individual variances. The only variance that appears to be significant is the $800 unfavorable variance for direct labor. The manager of the assembly department will want to know—and may be required to explain—why direct labor was 16 percent over budget ($800 ÷ $5,000). There may be some logical and reasonable explanation. For example, perhaps a union contract negotiated by top management included wages higher than originally planned for. That would not be the responsibility of the manager of the assembly department. Future budgets would have to take into consideration this higher wage rate. On the other hand, perhaps workers were inefficient and wasted time. That *would*

Exhibit 5.1 Performance Report

	Budget	Actual	Variance
Assembly Department **Performance Report** **for the Month Ended March 31, 19X2**			
Direct Material	$2,000	$2,020	$ 20 U
Direct Labor	5,000	5,800	800 U
Indirect Material	300	260	40 F
Utilities	500	470	30 F
Totals	$7,800	$8,550	$750 U

be the responsibility of the assembly department manager, who would have to do a better job of getting people to work efficiently.

From this brief illustration, you can see that an unfavorable variance does not necessarily mean that someone is not performing properly. Rather, it serves as a communication device to let managers know that some aspect of operations is not running according to plan. A manager who receives such information can ask the question, "Why is this happening?" The answer may be reasonable and acceptable, or it may not be. If it is not, steps can be taken to correct the cause of the unfavorable situation.

In many cases, the fault is that the budget was not realistic. That means that future budgets must be modified based on the feedback received. The budgeting process never really stops; it follows a cycle that includes preparing the budget, receiving results, comparing results with the budget, acting on the information resulting from the comparison, and revising future plans in a new budget—thus starting the cycle over again.

In summary, a comparison of results with the budget serves as a control technique for management. With budgeting control, management not only knows what is expected but also knows how well these expectations are being achieved. If results are not consistent with expectations, management can take action to correct the situation. Later chapters discuss the use of performance reports more fully in regard to budgeting, responsibility accounting, and the evaluation of managerial performance.

The Master Budget

A **master budget** (often called a *comprehensive budget*) represents a series of budgets for all activities of a firm for the budget period, generally one year. It normally is divided into shorter periods, such as quarters. The type and number of individual budgets included in the master budget depend on the nature of the firm.

In the pages that follow, a master budget is illustrated for Kamp Company for the year ended December 31, 19X3. The master budget is presented in a series of schedules as follows:

Schedule	Title
1	Sales Budget
2	Production Budget
3	Direct Materials Budget
4	Direct Labor Budget
5	Factory Overhead Budget
6	Variable Cost of Production Budget
7	Operating Expense Budget
8	Variable Cost of Goods Sold Budget
9	Budgeted Income Statement
10	Cash Receipts Budget
11	Cash Payments Budget
12	Cash Budget
13	Budgeted Balance Sheet

The illustration describes the preparation of each schedule. It allows you to see the interrelationship of the budgets and how one budget depends on another. This interdependence results in the coordination among elements of the firm described earlier.

Normally, a master budget also includes a **capital budget**—a long-range forecast of expenditures for property, plant, and equipment. To avoid unnecessary detail at this point, the master budget for Kamp Company does not include a capital budget. However, the illustration does describe those long-lived assets expected to be purchased during the next year. Capital budgeting is described fully in Chapter 11.

Some of the budgeted data for 19X3 is based on the balance sheet as of December 31, 19X2. This balance sheet is presented as Exhibit 5.2 to begin the illustration.

Exhibit 5.2 Balance Sheet as of the End of the Current Period

Kamp Company
Balance Sheet
December 31, 19X2

Current Assets:			
Cash		$ 6,800	
Accounts Receivable		80,000	
Direct Materials Inventory		32,400	
Finished Goods Inventory[a]		40,400	
Total Current Assets			$159,600
Property, Plant, and Equipment:			
Land		$ 50,000	
Building	$200,000		
Equipment	150,000		
Furniture and Fixtures	50,000		
	$400,000		
Less: Accumulated Depreciation	210,000	190,000	
Net Property, Plant, and Equipment			240,000
Total Assets			$399,600
Current Liabilities:			
Accounts Payable		$ 70,000	
Dividends Payable		20,000	
Notes Payable (Due March 1, 19X3)		100,000	
Total Liabilities			$190,000
Stockholders' Equity:			
Common Stock, $1 Par, 100,000 Shares Issued and Outstanding . .		$100,000	
Premium on Common Stock		50,000	
Retained Earnings		59,600	
Total Stockholders' Equity			$209,600
Total Liabilities and Stockholders' Equity			$399,600

[a]The company uses variable costing for internal purposes. Thus the finished goods inventory balance represents the variable cost of inventory.

Kamp Company is a manufacturing company. For the sake of simplicity, it is assumed to produce only one product, although realistically, most companies produce many products. Budgeting concepts for a multiproduct firm are the same as those shown here for a single-product firm. But there is more detail and the process is slightly more complicated. Budgeting for a merchandising firm also uses the concepts shown here. Once you master the concept of budgeting for a manufacturing firm, it is quite easy to adapt the concept to a merchandising concern.

Sales Budget

The sales budget is the foundation of the master budget. Almost every other item in the master budget is based, to some extent, on the sales budget. Errors in the sales budget automatically result in errors in most of the rest of the master budget.

The sales budget is based on the **sales forecast.** This forecast is the most important one the firm must make; unfortunately, it is also the most difficult. Many factors affect a firm's ability to predict sales. It must consider past sales, economic conditions, and competition. Although future sales will rarely be the same as past sales, past sales provide a starting point in looking at the future. A new firm has even more difficulty, because it has no past history to guide it.

Economic conditions relate to the national economy and the specific industry. Some industries, such as automobile manufacturers, are affected greatly by national economic conditions. Other industries, such as tobacco and utilities, are generally not affected by swings in the national economy.

Competition can certainly influence a company's ability to sell. A firm must know not only its own product but also its competitors' products. Trying to predict one's own sales also involves trying to determine how competition will affect them. The problems and uncertainties of sales forecasting are more complex than discussed here. But you can see that it involves more than just taking a guess.

The firm must first forecast the number of units to be sold. This amount is next converted into dollars, based on the selling price per unit ($20 per unit for the Kamp Company). Since we need to know the timing of cash flow from sales, we need to predict not only sales but also the division between cash sales and credit sales. The information regarding cash sales and credit collection is used in the cash budget. Based on its predictions, Kamp Company prepares the sales budget shown as Schedule 1.

Production Budget

The quantity to be produced is based on: (1) units on hand at the beginning of the period, (2) expected sales, and (3) desired inventory at the end of the period. Required production equals expected sales plus desired ending inventory less beginning inventory.

Kamp Company's ending inventory of finished goods as of December 31, 19X2, was 4,000 units. That becomes the beginning inventory on January 1, 19X3. Management wants the inventory at the end of each quarter to equal 20 percent of expected sales of the next quarter. There was no work-in-

Schedule 1

<table>
<tr><td colspan="6" align="center">**Kamp Company**
Sales Budget
for the Year Ended December 31, 19X3</td></tr>
<tr><td></td><td colspan="4" align="center">Quarter</td><td></td></tr>
<tr><td></td><td align="center">1st</td><td align="center">2nd</td><td align="center">3rd</td><td align="center">4th</td><td align="center">Total
for Year</td></tr>
<tr><td>Unit Sales. . . . .</td><td>20,000</td><td>11,000</td><td>22,000</td><td>35,000</td><td>88,000</td></tr>
<tr><td>Selling Price per Unit . . . .</td><td>×$20</td><td>×$20</td><td>×$20</td><td>×$20</td><td>×$20</td></tr>
<tr><td> Total Sales . . . .</td><td>$400,000</td><td>$220,000</td><td>$440,000</td><td>$700,000</td><td>$1,760,000</td></tr>
<tr><td>Cash Sales . . . .</td><td>$100,000</td><td>$ 60,000</td><td>$120,000</td><td>$200,000</td><td>$ 480,000</td></tr>
<tr><td>Credit Sales . . . .</td><td>300,000</td><td>160,000</td><td>320,000</td><td>500,000</td><td>1,280,000</td></tr>
<tr><td> Total Sales . . . .</td><td>$400,000</td><td>$220,000</td><td>$440,000</td><td>$700,000</td><td>$1,760,000</td></tr>
</table>

process inventory as of December 31, 19X2. Based on expected sales for the first quarter of 19X4, desired ending inventory for the fourth quarter of 19X3 is 6,000 units. The production budget is shown as Schedule 2. Note that it is shown only in units.

Schedule 2

<table>
<tr><td colspan="6" align="center">**Kamp Company**
Production Budget
for the Year Ended December 31, 19X3</td></tr>
<tr><td></td><td colspan="4" align="center">Quarter</td><td></td></tr>
<tr><td></td><td align="center">1st</td><td align="center">2nd</td><td align="center">3rd</td><td align="center">4th</td><td align="center">Total
for Year</td></tr>
<tr><td>Expected Sales. . . . .</td><td>20,000</td><td>11,000</td><td>22,000</td><td>35,000</td><td>88,000</td></tr>
<tr><td>Desired Ending Inventory[a] . . . .</td><td>2,200</td><td>4,400</td><td>7,000</td><td>6,000</td><td>6,000[c]</td></tr>
<tr><td>Total Needed. . . . .</td><td>22,200</td><td>15,400</td><td>29,000</td><td>41,000</td><td>94,000[d]</td></tr>
<tr><td>Less: Beginning Inventory[b] . . . .</td><td>4,000</td><td>2,200</td><td>4,400</td><td>7,000</td><td>4,000[c]</td></tr>
<tr><td> Required Production . . . .</td><td>18,200</td><td>13,200</td><td>24,600</td><td>34,000</td><td>90,000</td></tr>
</table>

[a] Twenty percent of next quarter's expected sales. Given for fourth quarter.

[b] Ending inventory of previous quarter becomes beginning inventory next quarter.

[c] These are inventory levels for the beginning and end of the year. They are not totals for the year.

[d] This is the total needed for the year. It is not the sum of each quarter because each quarter is affected by quarterly inventory levels.

You can now begin to see how the budget aids in the coordination of business activities. The production department now knows how much to produce each quarter. Based on the production budget, plans can be made for the purchase of direct materials.

Direct Materials Budget

The direct materials budget shows how much direct material must be purchased to meet the production requirements shown in the production budget. Each unit of Kamp Company's finished product requires three pounds of direct material at a cost of $2 per pound. Management wants the ending inventory of direct material each quarter to equal 30 percent of the amount of direct material needed for production in the next quarter. Ending inventory of direct material as of December 31, 19X2, totals 16,200 pounds. As with finished goods inventory, desired ending inventory for direct materials for the fourth quarter of 19X3, 18,000 pounds, is given. The direct materials inventory budget for Kamp Company appears as Schedule 3.

Schedule 3

Kamp Company
Direct Materials Budget
for the Year Ended December 31, 19X3

	Quarter				
	1st	2nd	3rd	4th	Total for Year
Required Production (Units of Finished Goods)[a]	18,200	13,200	24,600	34,000	90,000
Direct Material per Unit (in Pounds)	×3	×3	×3	×3	×3
Needed for Production	54,600	39,600	73,800	102,000	270,000
Desired Ending Inventory[b]	11,880	22,140	30,600	18,000	18,000[d]
Total Needed	66,480	61,740	104,400	120,000	288,000[e]
Less: Beginning Inventory[c]	16,200	11,880	22,140	30,600	16,200[d]
Required Purchases (in Pounds)	50,280	49,860	82,260	89,400	271,800
Cost per Pound	×$2	×$2	×$2	×$2	×$2
Cost of Required Purchases	$100,560	$99,720	$164,520	$178,800	$543,600

[a] From Schedule 2.

[b] Thirty percent of amount needed for production in next quarter. Given for fourth quarter.

[c] Ending inventory of previous quarter becomes beginning inventory of next quarter.

[d] These are inventory levels for the beginning and end of the year. They are totals for the year.

[e] This is the total needed for the year. It is not the sum of each quarter because each quarter is affected by quarterly inventory levels.

By knowing the amount of direct materials needed in advance, the company can plan for timely delivery. This prevents the helter-skelter activity that results when a firm runs out of material and must attempt to find a supplier at the last minute—a situation that may cost more as well. The cost information in the direct materials budget will be used in the cash budget.

Direct Labor Budget

The direct labor budget shows the cost of direct labor needed to meet the production budget. Kamp Company can produce two units of finished product per hour—that is, it uses thirty minutes, or .5 direct labor hours (DLH), per unit. Direct labor costs $6 per hour. The direct labor budget appears as Schedule 4.

Schedule 4

<table>
<tr><td colspan="6" align="center">**Kamp Company**
Direct Labor Budget
for the Year Ended December 31, 19X3</td></tr>
<tr><td></td><td colspan="5" align="center">Quarter</td></tr>
<tr><td></td><td>1st</td><td>2nd</td><td>3rd</td><td>4th</td><td>Total
for Year</td></tr>
<tr><td>Required Production[a] . . . .</td><td>18,200</td><td>13,200</td><td>24,600</td><td>34,000</td><td>90,000</td></tr>
<tr><td>Direct Labor Per Unit. . . . .</td><td>×0.5 DLH</td><td>×0.5 DLH</td><td>×0.5 DLH</td><td>×0.5 DLH</td><td>×0.5 DLH</td></tr>
<tr><td>Total Time Needed (DLH) . . . .</td><td>9,100</td><td>6,600</td><td>12,300</td><td>17,000</td><td>45,000</td></tr>
<tr><td>Cost per Hour . . .</td><td>×$6</td><td>×$6</td><td>×$6</td><td>×$6</td><td>×$6</td></tr>
<tr><td>Total Direct Labor Cost . . .</td><td>$54,600</td><td>$39,600</td><td>$73,800</td><td>$102,000</td><td>$270,000</td></tr>
</table>

[a]From Schedule 2.

This budget allows the company to determine in advance its need for employees. The company can schedule the necessary training for new employees before they are needed on the job. The situation is somewhat similar to that of direct material. Without a budget, the firm may find it needs additional employees at a critical time during production. But it may be unable to find them. Furthermore, production might be slowed because employees were not hired soon enough to be trained by the date needed. The cost data provided here is also used on the cash budget.

This illustration assumes that all direct labor employees are paid the same rate. In practice, of course, different employees are paid different rates depending on the type of job and the employee's skill and experience.

Factory Overhead Budget

Factory overhead costs should be shown according to cost behavior. The Kamp Company uses variable costing for internal purposes and develops only a variable factory overhead rate for applying overhead to production. Under variable costing, fixed factory overhead is shown as a period expense on the income statement. The factory overhead budget is shown as Schedule 5.

Schedule 5

Kamp Company
Factory Overhead Budget
for the Year Ended December 31, 19X3

	Quarter				Total for Year
	1st	2nd	3rd	4th	
Variable:					
Indirect Labor	$10,000	$ 7,000	$12,000	$15,000	$ 44,000
Indirect Material	5,000	3,000	8,000	10,000	26,000
Utilities	6,000	4,000	8,000	11,000	29,000
Total Variable	$21,000	$14,000	$28,000	$36,000	$ 99,000
Fixed:					
Managers' Salaries	$10,000	$10,000	$12,000	$12,000	$ 44,000
Insurance	3,000	3,000	3,000	3,000	12,000
Property Taxes	2,000	2,000	2,000	2,000	8,000
Depreciation	4,000	5,000	5,000	5,000	19,000
Total Fixed	$19,000	$20,000	$22,000	$22,000	$ 83,000
Total Factory Overhead	$40,000	$34,000	$50,000	$58,000	$182,000

The increase in managers' salaries beginning in the third quarter results from anticipated raises to be effective July 1. The company plans to buy new machinery costing $40,000 on April 1. This causes the increase in depreciation expense shown for the second, third, and fourth quarters.

Variable factory overhead is assumed to vary in relation to direct labor hours. The variable factory overhead rate is calculated as follows:

$$\frac{\$99,000}{45,000 \text{ DLH}} = \$2.20 \text{ per DLH}$$

The total number of direct labor hours, 45,000, comes from Schedule 4. Total variable cost, $99,000, is from Schedule 5.

Variable Cost of Production Budget

The variable cost of production budget shows the variable production costs required to meet the production budget. It is based on the unit costs multiplied by the number of units produced. In effect, it is the variable cost of goods manufactured. The unit variable cost of production is also used to determine the variable cost of goods sold for the budgeted income statement. In addition, it is used to determine the inventory value of finished goods inventory for the budgeted balance sheet. As previously mentioned, fixed factory overhead costs are deducted on the budgeted income statement for Kamp Company as period costs. The variable cost of production budget is shown as Schedule 6.

Schedule 6

Kamp Company
Variable Cost of Production Budget
for the Year Ended December 31, 19X3

	Quarter				Total for Year
	1st	2nd	3rd	4th	
Required Production[a]	18,200	13,200	24,600	34,000	90,000
Cost per Unit[b]	×$10.10	×$10.10	×$10.10	×$10.10	×$10.10
Total	$183,820	$133,320	$248,460	$343,400	$909,000

[a] From Schedule 2.

[b] Unit cost calculations:

Direct Material:	3 Pounds per Unit × $2 per Pound =	$ 6.00
Direct Labor:	.5 DLH per Unit × $6 per DLH =	3.00
Factory Overhead:	.5 DLH per Unit × $2.20 per DLH =	1.10
Total Unit Cost:		$10.10

Operating Expense Budget

The operating expense budget shows expected costs to be incurred for selling and administrative expenses. These, of course, are nonmanufacturing expenses. Information from this budget is used for the budgeted income statement and the cash budget.

Since depreciation expense does not involve an outlay of cash, the amount to be shown on the cash budget for operating expenses should not include depreciation. Therefore, selling expense depreciation of $500 per quarter and administrative expense depreciation of $800 per quarter (a total of $1,300 per quarter) is subtracted from total operating expenses in determining the amount of operating expenses to be shown on the cash budget. The operating expense budget is divided into two parts for Kamp Company—Part I for the budgeted income statement and Part II for the cash budget. It is shown as Schedule 7.

Variable Cost of Goods Sold Budget

At this point, the budgeted income statement requires only one more schedule before it can be prepared—the variable cost of goods sold budget. It is shown as Schedule 8.

Schedule 7

Kamp Company
Operating Expense Budget
for the Year Ended December 31, 19X3

	Quarter				Total for Year
	1st	2nd	3rd	4th	
Part I					
Variable Selling Expenses:					
Sales Commissions	$20,000	$11,000	$22,000	$35,000	$ 88,000
Packaging	2,000	1,000	2,000	3,000	8,000
Total	$22,000	$12,000	$24,000	$38,000	$ 96,000
Variable Administrative Expenses:					
Office Supplies	$ 500	$ 800	$ 1,500	$ 2,000	$ 4,800
Total Variable Operating Expenses . . .	$22,500	$12,800	$25,500	$40,000	$100,800
Fixed Selling Expenses:					
Sales Salaries	$20,000	$20,000	$20,000	$20,000	$ 80,000
Depreciation.	500	500	500	500	2,000
Total	$20,500	$20,500	$20,500	$20,500	$ 82,000
Fixed Administrative Expenses:					
Salaries	$50,000	$50,000	$50,000	$50,000	$200,000
Insurance	1,500	1,500	1,500	1,500	6,000
Property Taxes	1,000	1,000	1,000	1,000	4,000
Utilities	2,200	2,200	2,200	2,200	8,800
Depreciation.	800	800	800	800	3,200
Total	$55,500	$55,500	$55,500	$55,500	$222,000
Total Fixed Operating Expenses	$76,000	$76,000	$76,000	$76,000	$304,000
Part II					
Total Variable Operating Expenses	$22,500	$12,800	$ 25,500	$ 40,000	$100,800
Total Fixed Operating Expenses	76,000	76,000	76,000	76,000	304,000
Total Operating Expenses	$98,500	$88,800	$101,500	$116,000	$404,800
Less: Depreciation	1,300	1,300	1,300	1,300	5,200
Total Cash Operating Expenses	$97,200	$87,500	$100,200	$114,700	$399,600

Budgeted Income Statement

The budgeted income statement, prepared on a variable costing basis for internal purposes, is shown as Schedule 9.

The budgeted income statement does not reflect interest income or interest expense that may result from short-term investments or borrowing. These amounts are not known until the cash budget is prepared. As a practical matter, however, the net amount of interest income or expense,

Schedule 8

Kamp Company
Variable Cost of Goods Sold Budget
for the Year Ended December 31, 19X3

	Quarter				Total for Year
	1st	2nd	3rd	4th	
Unit Sales (Schedule 1)	20,000	11,000	22,000	35,000	88,000
Variable Unit Cost of Production (Schedule 6)	×$10.10	×$10.10	×$10.10	×$10.10	×$10.10
Variable Cost of Goods Sold	$202,000	$111,100	$222,200	$353,500	$888,800

based on the cash budget, is not expected to be material enough to affect management's judgment concerning the budgeted income statement. If necessary, adjustments to budgeted net income can be made after the cash budget is prepared.

Schedule 9

Kamp Company
Budgeted Income Statement
for the Year Ended December 31, 19X3

	Quarter				Total for Year
	1st	2nd	3rd	4th	
Sales (Schedule 1)	$400,000	$220,000	$440,000	$700,000	$1,760,000
Variable Costs:					
Cost of Goods Sold (Schedule 8)	$202,000	$111,100	$222,200	$353,500	$ 888,800
Operating Expenses (Schedule 7)	22,500	12,800	25,500	40,000	100,800
Total Variable Costs	$224,500	$123,900	$247,700	$393,500	989,600
Contribution Margin	$175,500	$ 96,100	$192,300	$306,500	$ 770,400
Fixed Costs:					
Factory Overhead (Schedule 5)	19,000	$ 20,000	$ 22,000	$ 22,000	$ 83,000
Operating Expenses (Schedule 7)	76,000	76,000	76,000	76,000	304,000
Total Fixed Costs	$ 95,000	$ 96,000	$ 98,000	$ 98,000	$ 387,000
Income before Taxes	$ 80,500	$ 100	$ 94,300	$208,500	$ 383,400
Income Tax Expense[a]					160,000
Net Income					$ 223,400

[a] Variable costing cannot be used for determining income tax expense. Therefore, Kamp Company has estimated its income tax expense for the year under absorption costing as $160,000.

For this illustration, management of Kamp Company is satisfied with the anticipated results. If, however, management felt that the projected net income was inadequate, it could examine the budget to determine what could be done to improve results. For example, the possibility of increasing advertising to stimulate sales might be considered. While the budget should already reflect only reasonable and necessary expenses, they might be examined again. Perhaps there are areas in which expenses can be reduced.

In summary, the budgeted income statement allows management to look into the future. If management does not like what it sees, perhaps steps can be taken to change what is expected to happen. Perhaps no changes can be made. But at least management knows what to expect, which is far better than operating in the dark with no idea of what might happen.

Cash Budget

The cash budget is usually the most important budget the firm prepares. Regardless of what net income might be, the firm must have cash on a current basis to pay its employees and suppliers and to meet its other cash needs.

Conceptually, the cash budget is quite simple. It shows how much cash is expected to come in and how much cash is expected to go out. The difference between expected inflow and outflow represents an expected excess or deficiency in cash flow. If the firm expects an excess, it can make plans to invest it until it is needed. If a deficiency is anticipated, plans can be made for short-term borrowing.

In practice, preparing the cash budget is difficult, because it relies on several forecasts of cash flow from various sources. We will examine each of these forecasts for the Kamp Company.

Cash Receipts Budget The Kamp Company receives cash from cash sales, collection of receivables, and other miscellaneous sources. The expected cash sales are shown in Schedule 1. The amount to be collected from receivables is based on credit sales and the pattern of collections. Kamp Company normally collects 80 percent of its credit sales in the quarter the merchandise is sold and 20 percent in the following quarter. The company seldom has any problem collecting its accounts receivable. Therefore, bad debts are considered negligible. The only miscellaneous cash receipt expected is $2,000 from the sale of old machinery on April 1. The machine's original cost was $20,000, and accumulated depreciation amounts to $18,000. Therefore, its book value is $2,000; so there is no gain or loss to be considered on the budgeted income statement. Exhibit 5.2 shows an accounts receivable balance of $80,000 as of December 31, 19X2. The entire amount is expected to be collected in the first quarter of 19X3.

The cash receipts budget is shown as Schedule 10.

Cash Payments Budget Budgeted cash payments represent the amount of cash expected to flow from the firm. The term *cash disbursements* is often used for these payments.

A major outflow of cash for Kamp Company is payment for direct materials, which are paid for in the quarter following the quarter in which they

Schedule 10

Kamp Company
Cash Receipts Budget
for the Year Ended December 31, 19X3

	Quarter				Total for Year
	1st	2nd	3rd	4th	
Credit Sales[a]	$300,000	$160,000	$320,000	$500,000	$1,280,000
Collected in Current Quarter (%)	×.80	×.80	×.80	×.80	
Current Quarter Collections	$240,000	$128,000	$256,000	$400,000	
20% of Last Quarter's Sales	80,000[b]	60,000	32,000	64,000	
Collection of Accounts Receivable	$320,000	$188,000	$288,000	$464,000	$1,260,000
Cash Sales[a]	100,000	60,000	120,000	200,000	480,000
Miscellaneous Cash Receipts[c]		2,000			2,000
Total Cash Receipts	$420,000	$250,000	$408,000	$664,000	$1,742,000

[a] From Schedule 1.

[b] Accounts receivable as of December 31, 19X2.

[c] From sale of old machinery on April 1.

were purchased. Exhibit 5.2 shows accounts payable at the end of 19X2 as $70,000. This amount is to be paid in the first quarter of 19X3. Other cash payments are made on a regular basis for direct labor, factory overhead items (including indirect material), and operating expenses. For the latter two items, it is important to remember that depreciation expense does not use cash. Therefore, amounts budgeted for depreciation should not be included in the budget of cash payments.

Several other cash payments are expected to be made in 19X3. One is a payment of $40,000 on April 1 for the purchase of a new machine. In addition, the balance sheet for December 31, 19X2 (Exhibit 5.2), shows that notes payable of $100,000 are due on March 1, 19X3. This represents a cash payment for the first quarter. Another major cash payment is for income taxes; Kamp Company will pay 25 percent of the total amount due for the year each quarter. Finally, the dividend payable of $20,000 as of December 31, 19X2 (Exhibit 5.2) will be paid in the first quarter. The board of directors also expects to declare dividends of $.25 per share in each quarter of 19X3, to be paid in the following quarter. Each dividend payment is $25,000 ($.25 × 100,000 shares).

The cash payments budget is shown as Schedule 11.

Format for Cash Budget The format for the cash budget varies among firms. Generally, it shows total cash available, total cash required, cash excess or deficiency, financing for short-term investing or borrowing, and the ending cash balance after financing.

Schedule 11

**Cash Payments Budget
for the Year Ended December 31, 19X3**

	Quarter				
	1st	2nd	3rd	4th	Total for Year
Payment of Raw Material Purchases[a]	$ 70,000	$100,560	$ 99,720	$164,520	$ 434,800
Direct Labor[b]	54,600	39,600	73,800	102,000	270,000
Factory Overhead[c]	36,000	29,000	45,000	53,000	163,000
Operating Expenses[d]	97,200	87,500	100,200	114,700	399,600
Purchase of New Machine[e]		40,000			40,000
Payment of Notes[e]	100,000				100,000
Payment of Income Taxes[f]	40,000	40,000	40,000	40,000	160,000
Payment of Dividends[e]	20,000	25,000	25,000	25,000	95,000
Total Cash Payments	$417,800	$361,660	$383,720	$499,220	$1,662,400

[a] First quarter accounts payable, Exhibit 5.2, $70,000; second, third, and fourth quarters, Schedule 3, payment made in quarter following quarter of purchase.

[b] Schedule 4.

[c] Schedule 5, total for each quarter, less $4,000 depreciation in first quarter and $5,000 depreciation in second, third, and fourth quarters.

[d] Schedule 7.

[e] Information provided on page 131.

[f] Schedule 9: $160,000 ÷ 4 = $40,000 per quarter.

Cash available is the beginning cash balance plus cash receipts. This amount is not the same as cash receipts because the firm will have a cash balance at the beginning of each quarter that is part of cash available. The balance sheet as of December 31, 19X2 (Exhibit 5.2), shows the beginning cash balance for Kamp Company as $6,800.

Cash required is the minimum cash balance plus cash payments. This amount is not the same as cash payments. It is important to plan to keep some minimum amount of cash on hand. During each quarter, the timing of cash inflow does not coincide exactly with the timing of cash outflow. To avoid running out of cash, Kamp Company attempts to maintain a minimum cash balance of $5,000.

Cash excess or deficiency is the difference between cash available and cash required. This item tells the firm whether it has cash that can be used for short-term investments until it is needed or whether short-term borrowing will be necessary.

A firm may invest the exact amount available or borrow the exact amount needed for the appropriate time period. However, in order to keep the illustration from getting too complicated, it is assumed that Kamp Company borrows, invests, repays loans, and disinvests in multiples of $1,000. Investments or loans are assumed to take place on the *first* day of the quarter of cash excess or deficiency. Disinvestments are assumed to take place on the *first* day of the quarter in which an amount is disinvested. Loan repayments are assumed to take place on the *last* day of the quarter in which a loan is repaid. This is illustrated and explained with Kamp Company's cash budget.

Investments earn interest at an annual rate of 6 percent, which is .5 percent per month. Interest expense on loans is 12 percent per year, which is 1 percent per month. Interest earned is assumed to be received at the time any amount of investment is disinvested and is calculated only on the amount being disinvested. Interest expense is assumed to be paid at the time any amount of the loan is repaid; it is calculated only on the amount of repayment. The company wishes to pay off loans as quickly as possible. The cash budget is shown as Schedule 12.

Although Kamp Company will have excess cash for the year, it expects a large cash deficiency in the second quarter. Anticipating this deficiency allows management to take steps in advance to cover it. With its budget, it can show the bank when and why it will need a loan. Just as importantly, it can show when and how the loan will be repaid. Thus, all loan arrangements can be made *before* the cash is needed. When it is needed, the company can merely phone the bank and ask to have its bank account increased by the amount of the loan.

Without a budget to show management what to expect, the cash deficiency could be a catastrophe. The company would run out of cash unexpectedly and would then need to try to borrow in a hurry. Perhaps funds would be unavailable. Even if funds were available, the interest rate might be unfavorable.

The cash budget shows that the company can plan to have $72,000 in short-term investments at the end of 19X3. In preparing its 19X4 budget, management might want to consider committing some of this amount to long-term investment, if it is not all needed for 19X4 operations.

Budgeted Balance Sheet

The last budget to prepare is the budgeted balance sheet, which shows what the balance sheet is expected to look like at the end of the year. To prepare it, changes expected to take place during the year are added to or subtracted from the balance sheet items as they appeared at the beginning of the year. The balance sheet as of December 31, 19X2, was presented as Exhibit 5.2. The budgeted balance sheet is shown as Schedule 13; for each item, a note is provided to explain how the amount was determined.

The budgeted balance sheet is generally not as useful as the budgeted income statement and the cash budget. Nevertheless, it does allow management to see what the balance sheet is expected to look like next year. From this estimate, possible problems may be seen that can be corrected.

With the complete set of budgets, you should be able to see how management is able to plan business activities for the coming year. It is unlikely that everything will go according to plan. But at least management can ask questions when things do not go according to plan and change the plan

Schedule 12

Kamp Company
Cash Budget
for the Year Ended December 31, 19X3

	1st	2nd	3rd	4th	Total for Year
			Quarter		
Cash Available:					
Beginning Cash Balance	$ 6,800	$ 5,000	$ 5,400	$ 5,300	$ 6,800[d]
Cash Receipts (Schedule 10)	420,000	250,000	408,000	664,000	1,742,000
Total Cash Available	$426,800	$255,000	$413,400	$669,300	$1,748,800[e]
Cash Required:					
Minimum Balance	$ 5,000	$ 5,000	$ 5,000	$ 5,000	$ 5,000[d]
Cash Payments (Schedule 11)	417,800	361,660	383,720	499,220	1,662,400
Total Cash Required	$422,800	$366,660	$388,720	$504,220	$1,667,400[e]
Cash Excess (Deficiency)	$ 4,000	$(111,660)	$ 24,680	$165,080	$ 81,400[f]
Short-Term Financing:					
Investment	$ 4,000			$ 72,000	
Disinvestment		$ 4,000			
Interest Earned		60			$ 60
Borrowed		108,000			
Repaid			$ 23,000	$ 85,000	
Interest Expense			1,380	7,650	9,030
Total Financing	$ 4,000	$112,060[a]	$ 24,380[b]	$164,650[c]	
Ending Cash Balance:					
Minimum	$ 5,000	$ 5,000	$ 5,000	$ 5,000	
Excess after Financing		400	300	430	
Ending Balance	$ 5,000	$ 5,400[a]	$ 5,300[b]	$ 5,430[c]	

[a] To help meet the cash deficiency, the $4,000 invested at the beginning of the first quarter is disinvested at the beginning of the second quarter. Interest earned is $60 ($4,000 × .005 × 3 months). Subtracting $4,060 from the deficiency of $111,660 leaves a remaining deficiency of $107,600. Since borrowings must be in multiples of $1,000, $108,000 is borrowed. The difference of $400 ($112,060 total financing − $111,660 cash deficiency) increases the ending cash balance to $5,400.

[b] The cash excess of $24,680 is used to repay part of the loan. Loan principal repayments must be in multiples of $1,000. The interest on $24,000 is $1,440 ($24,000 × .01 × 6 months). Thus the firm cannot repay $24,000 without falling below the minimum balance of $5,000. That is why $23,000 is repaid. Interest is $1,380 ($23,000 × .01 × 6 months). The excess of $24,680 less the payment of principal and interest of $24,380 increases the ending cash balance to $5,300.

[c] With the large cash excess, the remaining loan balance of $85,000 ($108,000 − $23,000) is repaid. Interest is $7,650 ($85,000 × .01 × 9 months). The excess of $165,080, less the payment of principal and interest of $92,650, equals $72,430. Of this, $72,000 is invested and $430 is added to the cash balance, resulting in an ending cash balance of $5,430.

[d] These are beginning and minimum cash balances. They are not totals for the year.

[e] Because of the beginning and minimum cash balances, the amounts for each quarter do not add across to the total for the year.

[f] Because excess cash from financing was included in the beginning cash balance for the following quarter ($400 + $300 = $700), the amounts for each quarter do not add across to the cash excess for the year. It differs by $700. Also, because of interest earned ($60), interest expense ($9,030), and excess cash after financing in the fourth quarter ($430), the cash excess for the year ($81,400) exceeds the amount invested as of the end of the year ($72,000).

Schedule 13

Kamp Company
Budgeted Balance Sheet
December 31, 19X3

Current Assets:			
Cash (1)		$ 5,430	
Marketable Securities (2)		72,000	
Accounts Receivable (3)		100,000	
Direct Materials Inventory (4)		36,000	
Finished Goods Inventory (5)		60,600	
Total Current Assets			$274,030
Property, Plant, and Equipment:			
Land (6)		$ 50,000	
Building (6)	$200,000		
Equipment (7)	170,000		
Furniture and Fixtures (6)	50,000		
	$420,000		
Less: Accumulated Depreciation (8)	216,200	203,800	
Net Property, Plant, and Equipment			253,800
Total Assets			$527,830
Current Liabilities:			
Accounts Payable (9)		$178,800	
Dividends Payable (10)		25,000	
Total Liabilities			$203,800
Stockholders' Equity:			
Common Stock, $1 Par, 100,000 Shares, Issued and			
Outstanding (6)		$100,000	
Premium on Common Stock (6)		50,000	
Retained Earnings (11)		174,030	
Total Stockholders' Equity			324,030
Total Liabilities and Stockholders' Equity			$527,830

Explanations of balance sheet items:

(1) Schedule 12, ending cash balance, fourth quarter.

(2) Schedule 12, investment, fourth quarter.

(3) Schedule 10, fourth quarter, $500,000 credit sales − $400,000 collected in fourth quarter = $100,000 accounts receivable.

(4) Schedule 3, fourth quarter, desired ending inventory, 18,000 pounds × $2 per pound = $36,000.

(5) Schedule 2, fourth quarter, desired ending inventory, 6,000 units × $10.10 per unit = $60,600.

(6) No change from December 31, 19X2, Exhibit 5.2.

(7) $150,000 (Exhibit 5.2) − $20,000 (cost of old machine, as stated earlier) + $40,000 (cost of new machine, as stated earlier) = $170,000.

(8) $210,000 (Exhibit 5.2) − $18,000 (accumulated depreciation of old machine, as stated earlier) + $19,000 (Schedule 5) + $5,200 (Schedule 7) = $216,200.

(9) Schedule 3, purchased in fourth quarter, 19X3, to be paid in first quarter, 19X4.

(10) As stated earlier, dividend of $.25 per share to be declared in each quarter, to be paid in the following quarter.

(11) $59,600 (Exhibit 5.2) + $223,400 net income (Schedule 9) − $100,000 dividends declared (as stated earlier) + $60 interest earned (Schedule 12) − $9,030 interest expense (Schedule 12) = $174,030.
Note: Interest income and interest expense are normally shown on the income statement. However, as explained in the text, these amounts are not known until the cash budget is prepared. Therefore, for internal purposes, they can just be added and subtracted from retained earnings. This would *not* be an acceptable procedure for external reporting purposes.

when appropriate. Although the control function was not emphasized in the Kamp Company example, it will be illustrated more fully in subsequent chapters.

Importance of Human Relations

The budgeting process illustrated above might lead you to believe that budgeting merely involves plugging numbers into forms. It is important to remember that mechanical processes are only means to an end, and budgeting is no exception. Successful budgeting requires careful consideration of human factors.

Although budgeting has been described as a motivational device to help insure adherence to company goals, it has sometimes been used as a device to invoke fear. Often individuals are afraid to exceed their budgets. They are concerned about the consequences if they do. As a result, they sometimes consider budgets in a very negative manner. Managers look at budgets as a threat to their freedom to operate and their ability to make decisions. Such attitudes need not exist.

Behind every budget are people who must meet the goals of the organization as communicated through the budget. It is not enough to simply tell them, "Here is the budget; carry it out." It is important that employees understand why the budget is the way it is and how budgeting helps them. Sometimes an educational program is necessary. As we have seen, budgeting is a form of profit planning. Profits are the life-blood of any business. Without profits, there is no business—and hence, no employees. Therefore, it is important for employees to recognize that the budget helps the business prosper; and in so doing, helps the employees.

In order to gain better employee acceptance of a budget, it is a good idea to bring employees into the budget's preparation as much as possible. Studies have found that better results were usually obtained when employees participated in budget preparation. For example, the vice-president of marketing—rather than simply telling sales managers of various territories, "This is your budget; live with it"—should ask for their ideas and opinions in developing the budget. Sometimes they may think of things that the vice-president had not thought of. Furthermore, employees who understand the budget and feel that they played a part in its preparation are more likely to have a greater interest in attempting to meet its goals. In these cases, employees adhere to the budget because they *want* to, not just because they *have* to.

Many managers believe that budgets restrict their freedom. The fact is, the budget lets managers know just how much leeway they have. Restrictions are not caused by the budget. Restrictions are caused by a shortage of resources. Knowing the availability of resources, managers can plan their actions accordingly. The absence of a budget would not allow managers to spend more money. Instead, they would spend money while not knowing how much money was available to spend. With a budget, a manager gains the ability to plan to make expenditures in areas where they will do the most good.

In summary, top management must never forget that employees' attitudes toward budgeting can be positive or negative. Obviously, positive attitudes are much better for the business. It is therefore necessary for top management to foster the proper attitudes among employees in order to be more assured of achieving the goals of the budget.

Budgeting for Nonmanufacturing Firms

Budgeting is just as important for nonmanufacturing firms as for manufacturing firms; but normally, it is not as complex. Like that of the manufacturing firm, the master budget of the merchandising firm relies quite heavily on the sales forecast. Although merchandisers are not concerned with raw materials, direct labor, and factory overhead, they are concerned with purchases of merchandise. The amount of these purchases is related to expected sales, which affects payments for merchandise and accounts payable. Cash receipts depend on cash sales and the collection of receivables from credit sales. Preparing a budget of operating expenses is virtually the same for a merchandising firm as it is for a manufacturing firm.

In summary, a budget helps management of a merchandising firm to plan and control activities in much the same way as it helps management of a manufacturing firm. The procedures for budget preparation are also similar. However, because merchandisers are not involved in manufacturing activities, preparing the budget is usually easier for them than it is for manufacturers.

Summary

A budget is a formal expression of planned operations expressed in financial terms. The major purpose of a business budget is to help in planning and controlling operations. A budget forces managers to plan ahead so that problems can be anticipated. It helps in controlling business operations because it tells employees what is expected of them. They will be held responsible to explain deviations from the plan (budget) and will thus normally attempt to work within it.

Operating results for a segment of a business are reflected on a performance report, which shows the budget, actual results, and variances from the budget. Significant variances must be explained.

In all stages of budgeting, human relations must be considered. Employees must understand the reason for and the importance of the budget. For a budget to be truly effective, employee cooperation is necessary. Employee participation at the earliest possible stage in budget development is helpful. Company goals can be more easily attained if employees are a part of the budgeting process.

The master budget for Kamp Company illustrated the procedures for developing a budget. Studying that illustration will help you to understand the planning function of budgeting. As part of the summary, you should review the master budget for Kamp Company to insure that you understand the budgeting procedures used.

Review Problem

Problem

Johnson's, Inc., projects sales for the next 4 months as follows: January, $30,000; February, $50,000; March, $80,000; and April, $100,000. Cost of goods sold averages 70% of sales. The firm wants the ending inventory each month to equal 20% of the next month's sales. Forty percent of purchases are paid for in the month of purchase, and 60% in the month following purchase. Accounts payable as of December 31 amount to $25,000; and beginning inventory totals $4,200.

Required:

Prepare schedules for January, February, March, and the quarter showing:

a. Cost of required purchases.
b. Payment for purchases.

Solution

a.

	January	February	March	Total for Quarter
Expected Sales (at Cost)	$21,000	$35,000	$56,000	$112,000
Desired Ending Inventory	7,000	11,200	14,000	14,000
Total Needed	$28,000	$46,200	$70,000	$126,000
Less: Beginning Inventory	4,200	7,000	11,200	4,200
Required Purchases	$23,800	$39,200	$58,800	$121,800

Note that when calculating required purchases using dollar data (rather than unit data), we show all amounts at cost. Thus, we determine expected sales at cost by multiplying expected sales in dollars by the cost of goods sold percentage—in this case, 70%. Also, we determine desired ending inventory by multiplying 20% by the next month's expected sales at cost.

b.

	January	February	March	Total for Quarter
Paid for Current Month's Purchases:				
40% × $23,800	$ 9,520			
40% × $39,200		$15,680		
40% × $58,800			$23,520	
Paid for Last Month's Purchases:				
Accounts Payable, December 31	25,000			
60% × $23,800		14,280		
60% × $39,200			23,520	
Total Payments	$34,520	$29,960	$47,040	$111,520

In this case, the accounts payable balance as of December 31 represents unpaid purchases for December that are to be paid in January.

Questions

5-1 What is a budget?

5-2 What is the primary purpose of a budget?

5-3 A retail firm that had no budget recently ran out of a very popular product. How could a budget have helped prevent this problem?

5-4 The credit department of a retail store had a budget of $500 for office supplies in a recent month. The department actually spent $1,000 for office supplies that month, but nothing was said to the credit department manager about it. What purpose did the budget serve in this case? Explain.

5-5 A manufacturing firm recently forecast a 30% decrease in sales for the next year. During the year, inventories increased significantly although the sales forecast was right on target. Give one possible reason for this problem.

5-6 What is feedback?

5-7 What is a performance report and how is it used?

5-8 Is a significant unfavorable variance on a performance report a sign that the manager responsible has done a poor job? Explain.

5-9 "A favorable variance indicates good managerial performance." Comment on the validity of this statement.

5-10 What role does human relations play in budgeting?

5-11 Why is the sales forecast considered the cornerstone of the budgeting process?

5-12 A firm's cash budget projected that $100,000 of excess cash would be on hand at year end. Of what value is the budget to the firm in this case?

5-13 A firm expects record net income for the year. However, it expects a loss in the second quarter. How might the budgeted income statement provide stability to the firm's dividend policy in this situation?

5-14 A firm has bonds outstanding that require that its current assets always be at least twice its current liabilities. How might a budgeted balance sheet assist the firm in insuring that this requirement is met?

Exercises

5-15 Describing a Performance Report A partial performance report for a department is as follows:

	Budget	Actual	Variance
Direct Material	$20,000	$15,000	$5,000 F
Direct Labor	45,000	50,000	5,000 U
Totals	$65,000	$65,000	$ 0

Since the total variance is zero, the department manager believes that there is no problem. Do you agree? Explain.

5-16 Schedule of Accounts Receivable Collections Alton Corporation expects credit sales for next year as follows: first quarter, $40,000; second quarter, $80,000; third quarter, $140,000; fourth quarter, $200,000. Sales last quarter totaled $120,000. Seventy percent of credit sales are collected in the quarter of sale, and 30% in the following quarter. Prepare a schedule of accounts receivable collections for each quarter and for the year.

5-17 Schedule of Cash Receipts Riley Company has projected sales for next year as follows: first quarter, $200,000; second quarter, $450,000; third quarter, $300,000; fourth quarter, $500,000. Beginning accounts receivable total $100,000. Sixty percent of all sales are credit sales and are collected in the quarter following the quarter in which the sales were made. Bad debts are negligible. Prepare a schedule showing expected cash receipts for each quarter and for the year.

5-18 Schedule of Accounts Receivable Collections Blandon Company sells 80% of its merchandise on credit. Accounts are normally collected in the following pattern: 60% in the month following sale; 35% in the second month following sale; and 5% uncollectible. Total sales for November were $100,000; for December, $120,000. Budgeted sales for the next quarter are: January, $150,000; February, $80,000; March, $200,000. Prepare a schedule showing expected collection of accounts receivable for each month and for the first quarter.

5-19 Schedule of Accounts Receivable Collections Varsity Company is preparing its cash budget for the month of May. The following information on accounts receivable collections is available from Varsity's past collection experience:

Current Month's Sales	12%
Prior Month's Sales	75%
Sales Two Months prior to Current Month	6%
Sales Three Months prior to Current Month	4%
Cash Discounts Taken	2%
Doubtful Accounts	1%

Credit sales are as follows: May (estimated) $100,000; April, $90,000; March, $80,000; February, $95,000. Determine the estimated collections from accounts receivable for May. (AICPA adapted)

5-20 Schedule of Required Production Mighty Manufacturing Company produces a single product. Current finished goods inventory is 20,000 units; and the company expects unit sales next year as follows: first quarter, 80,000 units; second quarter, 60,000 units; third quarter, 75,000 units; fourth quarter, 100,000 units. Sales for the first quarter of the following year are expected to be 90,000 units. The firm wants ending inventory each quarter to equal 25% of next quarter's expected sales. Prepare a schedule of required production for each quarter and for the year.

5-21 Schedule of Required Production Malco, Inc., has 10,000 units of finished goods inventory as of December 31. Sales for the first 4 months of next year are projected as follows: January, 30,000 units; February, 40,000 units; March, 60,000 units; April, 50,000 units. The firm wants ending inventory each month to equal 30% of next month's sales. Prepare a schedule of required production for each month and for the quarter.

5-22 Schedule of Required Purchases Jeno Jeans Store has 1,000 pairs of jeans on hand as of December 31. Unit sales for the first 4 months of next year are projected as follows: January, 5,000 pairs; February, 7,000 pairs; March, 10,000 pairs; April, 6,000 pairs. The firm pays $8 a pair for the jeans and wants ending inventory each month to equal 20% of next month's sales. Prepare a schedule showing the required amount of dollar purchases for each month and for the quarter.

5-23 Schedule of Required Purchases Tryler Company anticipates credit sales for the first 4 months of next year as follows: January, $25,000; February, $35,000; March, $20,000; April, $30,000. Beginning inventory is $3,500. The cost of merchandise averages 70% of sales. The firm wants ending inventory to equal 20% of next month's expected sales. Prepare a schedule of required purchases for each quarter and for the year.

5-24 Determining Budgeted Cost of Goods Sold and Purchases The Zel Company, a wholesaler, budgeted the following sales for the indicated months of 19X1:

	June	July	August
Sales on Account	$1,500,000	$1,600,000	$1,700,000
Cash Sales	200,000	210,000	220,000
Total Sales	$1,700,000	$1,810,000	$1,920,000

All merchandise is marked up to sell at its invoice cost plus 25%. Merchandise inventories at the beginning of each month are at 30% of that month's projected cost of goods sold. For each lettered item below, select the correct answer. Show your calculations. (AICPA adapted)

a. The cost of goods sold for the month of June 19X1 is anticipated to be:
   1. $1,530,000.
   2. $1,402,500.
   3. $1,275,000.
   4. $1,190,000.
   5. None of the above.

b. Merchandise purchases for July 19X1 are anticipated to be:
   1. $1,605,500.
   2. $1,474,400.
   3. $1,448,000.
   4. $1,382,250.
   5. None of the above.

5-25 Schedule of Required Purchases Ronald's Clothing Store anticipates sales for the next year as follows: first quarter, $30,000; second quarter, $45,000; third quarter, $60,000; fourth quarter, $80,000. Sales for the first quarter of the following year are expected to total $40,000. The cost of merchandise averages 60% of sales. Ronald wants ending inventory each quarter to equal 30% of next quarter's expected sales. Prepare a schedule of required purchases for each quarter and for the year.

5-26 Schedule of Payments for Purchases Mayfield Company anticipates purchases for the next quarter as follows: January, $20,000; February, $40,000; March, $50,000. Purchases in December totaled $30,000. Forty percent of the amount purchased is paid for in the month of purchase, and 60% in the month following purchase. Prepare a schedule of payments for purchases for each month and for the next quarter.

5-27 Determining Cash Payments for Inventories Terry Company is preparing its cash budget for the month of April. The following information is available concerning its inventories:

Inventories at Beginning of April:	$90,000
Estimated Purchases for April:	$440,000
Estimated Cost of Goods Sold for April:	$450,000
Estimated Payments in April for Purchases in March:	$75,000
Estimated Payments in April for Purchases prior to March:	$20,000
Estimated Payments in April for Purchases in April:	75%

Determine the estimated cash payments for inventories in April. (AICPA adapted)

5-28 Determining Salaries and Commission Expense and Payments Sampson Sales Company pays each of its 5 salespersons a salary of $500 per month plus a commission of 10% of sales. The salary is paid in the month of sale and the commission is paid on the fifteenth day of the month following the month of sale. Sales for December totaled $100,000. Expected sales for the next quarter are: January, $80,000; February, $120,000; March, $150,000. For each of the three months and for the first quarter of next year, determine:
   a. Salaries and commissions expense.
   b. Payments for salaries and commissions.

Problems

5-29 Schedule of Cash Receipts Talbat Company has projected sales for the year as follows: first quarter, $40,000; second quarter, $30,000; third quarter, $50,000; fourth quarter, $80,000. Twenty percent of sales are cash sales, and 80% are credit sales. Credit sales are collected in the quarter following the quarter in which the sales were made. Beginning accounts receivable total $60,000. Bad debts are negligible.
Required:
   Prepare a schedule of cash receipts for each quarter and for the year.

5-30 Schedule of Cash Receipts Webber Corporation has projected sales for the first quarter of next year as follows: January, $100,000; February, $80,000; March, $120,000. Forty percent of sales are cash sales and 60% are credit sales. Ten percent of credit sales are collected in the month of sale, 60% in the month following sale, and 30% in the second month after sale. Bad debts are negligible. Sales in November totaled $150,000; in December, $200,000.

Required:

Prepare a schedule of cash receipts for each month and for the quarter.

5-31 Schedules of Direct Materials Purchases and Payment Bolton Company estimated next year's production of finished units as follows: first quarter, 40,000; second quarter, 55,000; third quarter, 45,000; and fourth quarter, 60,000.

Direct material costs $.60 per gallon, and 2 gallons are needed for each finished unit. The firm wants direct material ending inventory to equal 25% of the amount needed for next quarter's production. Beginning direct material inventory is 20,000 gallons, and fourth-quarter desired ending inventory is estimated to be 35,000 gallons. Direct material purchases are paid for in the quarter following the quarter of purchase. Accounts payable as of December 31 total $80,000.

Required:

Prepare the following schedules for each quarter and for the year:

a. Direct materials budget.

b. Payment for purchases.

5-32 Schedules of Production, Direct Materials Purchases and Payments Hopkins Manufacturing Company anticipates unit sales next year as follows: first quarter, 20,000; second quarter, 25,000; third quarter, 40,000; and fourth quarter, 30,000. Sales for the first quarter of the following year are expected to be 35,000 units.

Each unit produced requires 1/2 pound of direct material at a cost of $4 per pound. Management wants finished goods inventory to equal 30% of next quarter's sales and direct material ending inventory to equal 20% of that needed for next quarter's production. Desired ending inventory of direct material at the end of the fourth quarter is estimated to be 3,000 pounds.

Accounts payable are paid in the quarter following the quarter of purchase. Accounts payable on December 31 total $65,000. Inventory on December 31 totals 6,000 finished units and 2,150 pounds of direct material.

Required:

Prepare the following schedules for each quarter and for the year:

a. Production budget.

b. Direct materials budget.

c. Payment for purchases.

5-33 Schedules for Purchases and Payments Del's Discount Store's sales in November and December and its projected sales for the next 4 months are as follows: November, $150,000; December, $200,000; January, $120,000; February, $80,000; March, $100,000; April, $110,000.

Cost of goods sold averages 60% of sales. Del wants ending inventory each month to equal 30% of next month's sales. Eighty percent of purchases are paid for in the month following the month of purchase; 20%, in the second month following the month of purchase.

Required:

Prepare schedules for January, February, March, and the quarter showing:

a. Cost of required purchases.

b. Payment for purchases.

5-34 Determining Cash Budget Items Tomlinson Retail seeks your assistance to develop cash and other budget information for May, June, and July 19X3. At April 30, 19X3, the company had cash of $5,500, accounts receivable of $437,000, inventories of $309,400, and accounts payable of $133,055.

The budget is to be based on the following assumptions.

I. Sales

a. Each month's sales are billed on the last day of the month.

b. Customers are allowed a 3% discount if payment is made within 10 days after the billing date. Receivables are booked gross.

c. Sixty percent of the billings are collected within the discount period, 25% are collected by the end of the month, 9% are collected by the end of the second month, 6% prove uncollectible.

II. Purchases

a. Selling, general, and administrative expenses and 54% of all purchases of material are paid in the month of purchase; and the remainder of material purchases are paid for in the following month.

b. Each month's units of ending inventory equal 130% of the next month's units of sales.

c. The cost of each unit of inventory is $20.

d. Selling, general, and adminsitrative expenses, of which $2,000 represents depreciation, are equal to 15% of the current month's sales.

Actual and projected sales are as follows:

19X3	Dollars	Units
March	$354,000	11,800
April	363,000	12,100
May	357,000	11,900
June	342,000	11,400
July	360,000	12,000
August	366,000	12,200

Required:

Calculate the following budgeted items:

a. Budgeted cash disbursements during the month of June 19X3.

b. Budgeted cash collections during the month of May 19X3.

c. Budgeted number of units of inventory to be purchased during July 19X3. (AICPA adapted)

5-35 Determining Cash Budget Items The Dilly Company marks up all merchandise at 25% of gross purchase price. All purchases are made on account with terms of 1/10, n/60. Purchase discounts, which are recorded as miscellaneous income, are always taken. Normally, 60% of each month's purchases are paid for in the month of purchase, while the other 40% are paid during the first 10 days of the first month after purchase. Inventories of merchandise at the end of each month are kept at 30% of next month's projected cost of goods sold.

Terms for sales on account are 2/10, n/30. Cash sales are not subject to discount. Fifty percent of each month's sales on account are collected during the month of sale, 45% are collected in the succeeding month, and the remainder are usually uncollectible. Seventy percent of the collections in the month of sale are subject to discount, while 10% of the collections in the succeeding month are subject to discount.

Projected sales data for selected months follow:

	Sales on Account–Gross	Cash Sales
December	$1,900,000	$400,000
January	1,500,000	250,000
February	1,700,000	350,000
March	1,600,000	300,000

Required:

Calculate the following budgeted items:

a. Projected gross purchases for January

b. Projected inventory at the end of December.

c. Projected payments to suppliers during February.

d. Projected sales discounts to be taken by customers making remittances during February.

e. Projected total cash receipts from customers during February. (AICPA adapted)

5-36 Preparing Budgeted Income Statements Roberts Company was formed 5 years ago and has shown increasing profitability each year. Management desires a budgeted income statement for the year ending December 31, 19X3. The sales forecast for 19X3 is as follows: first quarter, $90,000; second quarter, $70,000; third quarter, $50,000; and fourth quarter, $40,000. Cost of goods sold averages 60% of sales.

The following operating expenses are anticipated: rent expense, $1,000 per month plus 2% of sales; commissions expense, $600 per month plus 15% of sales for each of 4 salespersons; depreciation, $300 per month; utilities, $500 per month; salaries, $5,000 per month; and other operating expenses, $1,500 per month. Income taxes are expected to be 30% of income before taxes.

The company has declared dividends each quarter since 19X0 on its 1,000 shares of common stock. Dividends last year were $.20 per share per quarter. The board of directors hopes to be able to increase the dividends in 19X3.

Required:

a. Prepare a budgeted income statement for each quarter and for the year. Separate expenses between variable and fixed.

b. Describe the significance of your budgeted income statement, and comment on actions management might take, based on the budget.

5-37 Preparing Monthly Cash Budgets Management of Kamp Company, whose master budget was illustrated in the chapter, desires more information regarding the expected cash deficiency in the second quarter. Accordingly, you have been asked to prepare a cash budget for April, May, and June in order that management can determine more closely when the need for additional cash will arise. Additional information is provided below:

	April	May	June
Cash Collections from Second Quarter's Credit Sales:	$20,000	$68,000	$40,000
Cash Collections from First Quarter's Credit Sales:	60%	30%	10%
Cash Sales:	$30,000	$20,000	$10,000
Payment for First Quarter's Direct Material Purchases:	50%	25%	25%
Required Production (Units):	6,000	4,000	3,200
Factory Overhead (Exclusive of Depreciation):	$12,000	$9,000	$8,000
Cash Operating Expenses:	$45,000	$25,000	$17,500

As noted in the chapter, the firm plans to sell old machinery for $2,000 on April 1 and purchase a new machine for $40,000 on that same date. Income taxes are paid on April 15 and dividends are paid on April 20.

Refer to the master budget illustration in the chapter for any other data you might need. For short-term financing, apply the same rules described in the chapter, but apply them on a monthly basis.

Required:

  a. For April, May, June, and the quarter, prepare:

    1. A cash receipts budget.

    2. A cash payments budget.

    3. A cash budget.

  b. Describe how the cash budget prepared in part a is more useful to management than the one shown in Schedule 12.

5-38 Preparing Various Budgets The Scarborough Corporation manufactures and sells Thingone and Thingtwo. In July 19X2, Scarborough's budget department gathered the following data in order to project sales and budget requirements for 19X3:

19X3 Projected Sales			Inventories (Units)	
Product	Units	Price	Expected 1/1/X3	Desired 12/31/X3
Thingone	60,000	$ 70	20,000	25,000
Thingtwo	40,000	100	8,000	9,000

Data regarding raw materials are as follows:

Raw Material	Unit	Used per Finished Unit Thingone	Thingtwo	Unit Cost	Inventories Expected 1/1/X3	Desired 12/31/X3
A	Pounds	4	5	$8	32,000 Pounds	36,000 Pounds
B	Pounds	2	3	$5	29,000 Pounds	32,000 Pounds
C	Each		1	$3	6,000 Each	7,000 Each

Projected direct labor requirements for 19X3 and rates are as follows:

Product	Hours per Unit	Rate per Hour
Thingone	2	$3
Thingtwo	3	4

Factory overhead is applied at the rate of $2 per direct labor hour.

Required:

Based upon the above projections and budget requirements for Thingone and Thingtwo, prepare the following budgets for 19X3:

a. Sales budget (in dollars).

b. Production budget (in units).

c. Raw materials purchase budget (in quantities).

d. Raw materials purchase budget (in dollars).

e. Direct labor budget (in dollars).

f. Budgeted finished goods inventory as of December 31, 19X3 (in dollars). (AICPA adapted)

Chapter 6   Flexible Budgets and Standard Costs

Learning Objectives

The purpose of this chapter is to describe and illustrate the use of flexible budgets and standard costs for a business firm. The chapter shows how flexible budgets and standard costs help management to control business operations. Studying this chapter will enable you to:
1. Compare a flexible budget with a static budget.
2. Prepare a flexible budget.
3. Explain why actual net income differs from budgeted net income, based on the flexible budget.
4. Calculate the net income variance and the sales variance.
5. Define *standard cost* and *standard cost system*.
6. Describe the process of setting standards.
7. Calculate variances for direct material, direct labor, and variable factory overhead.
8. Describe how standard costs help management to control business operations.

Chapter Topics

The major topics included in this chapter are:

Flexible Budgets
Standard Costs
Variance Analysis
Direct Material Variances
Direct Labor Variances
Variable Overhead Variances

In Chapter 5, Kamp Company budgeted net income for 19X3 as $223,400. At the end of 19X3, management would compare actual net income with this budgeted figure. If there was a significant difference, management would want to know why.

There are two basic reasons for actual net income to differ from budgeted net income: (1) total sales were more or less than expected; (2) costs were more or less than expected. This chapter illustrates how to determine the reasons for the company's variance in net income.

The chapter also explains and illustrates the use of standard costs with a flexible budget. It provides illustrations of cost variances from standard for direct material, direct labor, and variable overhead. Fixed cost variances are described in Chapter 7.

Flexible Budgets

The budget prepared for Kamp Company in Chapter 5 was a **static budget**—a budget prepared for only one level of activity. Kamp Company prepared a budget for sales of 88,000 units. When actual sales differ from budgeted sales, it is necessary to adjust the budget to relate expected costs to the achieved level of activity. A budget that allows for adjustments according to various levels of activity is called a flexible budget. Simply stated, then, a **flexible budget** is a budget or a series of budgets for different levels of activity.

Illustration of a Flexible Budget

To illustrate, assume that for October 19X5, Redd Company budgeted sales of 30,000 units at a selling price of $10 each and a variable cost of $6 each. Actual sales were only 28,000 units. Exhibit 6.1 shows that net income was $17,000 less than budgeted. Management wants to know why.

Looking at the exhibit, one is led to believe that the reduced sales caused net income to be reduced by $20,000. It would appear that variable costs were $5,000 less than expected, helping to offset the reduced sales. However, this appearance is misleading. In the illustration, the $5,000 favorable variance was derived by comparison of the actual costs for 28,000 units with the budgeted costs for 30,000 units. Such a comparison is totally inappropriate. Costs are expected to be lower if sales are lower. In fact, the firm can reduce variable costs to zero by selling nothing. In that case, the exhibit

Exhibit 6.1 Static Budget

<table>
<tr><td colspan="4" align="center">Redd Company
Income Statement
for the Month Ended October 31, 19X5</td></tr>
<tr><td></td><td align="center">Budget
(30,000 Units)</td><td align="center">Actual
(28,000 Units)</td><td align="center">Variance</td></tr>
<tr><td>Sales . . . .</td><td>$300,000</td><td>$280,000</td><td>$20,000 U</td></tr>
<tr><td>Variable Costs . . . .</td><td>180,000</td><td>175,000</td><td>5,000 F</td></tr>
<tr><td>Contribution Margin . . . . . .</td><td>$120,000</td><td>$105,000</td><td>$15,000 U</td></tr>
<tr><td>Fixed Costs . . . .</td><td>50,000</td><td>52,000</td><td>2,000 U</td></tr>
<tr><td>Net Income . . . .</td><td>$ 70,000</td><td>$ 53,000</td><td>$17,000 U</td></tr>
</table>

Exhibit 6.2 Flexible Budget

Redd Company
Income Statement
for the Month Ended October 31, 19X5

	Budget (28,000 Units)	Actual (28,000 Units)	Variance
Sales	$280,000	$280,000	—
Variable Costs	168,000	175,000	$7,000 U
Contribution Margin	$112,000	$105,000	$7,000 U
Fixed Costs	50,000	52,000	2,000 U
Net Income	$ 62,000	$ 53,000	$9,000 U

would show a favorable variable cost variance of $180,000. Does this mean a savings of $180,000 for the company? Certainly not! To see the real picture, it is necessary to prepare a flexible budget that shows total variable costs for 28,000 units rather than 30,000 units, at a variable cost per unit of $6. This is illustrated in Exhibit 6.2.

The exhibit shows that variable costs are not $5,000 favorable but $7,000 unfavorable. In other words, since the company sold only 28,000 units, variable costs should have been only $168,000 ($6 × 28,000 units). Instead, they were $175,000. Management would want a further analysis of the variable cost variances. These variances are discussed later in this chapter.

Fixed cost variances total $2,000 unfavorable. Notice that the budget for fixed costs is $50,000 in both the static budget and the flexible budget. By definition, fixed costs do not change within a relevant range. Assuming a relevant range of 0–50,000 units for Redd Company's fixed costs, these costs would be the same for both 28,000 units and 30,000 units of sales. Thus, within the relevant range, the flexible budget shows the same amount of fixed costs. However, outside the relevant range, the flexible budget would show different levels of fixed costs as well. A detailed analysis of specific items of fixed cost would reveal those costs that resulted in the $2,000 unfavorable variance. Fixed cost analysis is discussed in Chapter 7.

Net Income Variance

Refer to Exhibit 6.1. The exhibit shows actual net income was $17,000 less than budgeted net income. The difference between budgeted net income and actual net income is referred to as the **net income variance.** The flexible budget in Exhibit 6.2 revealed that $9,000 of that $17,000 was caused by variances in costs. Specifically, variable costs were $7,000 more than they should have been for the achieved level of activity, 28,000 units; and fixed costs were $2,000 more than they should have been. Although the flexible budget is used in order to analyze variable costs more closely, the fact that actual sales in units were less than budgeted also caused net income to be less than expected. This difference is referred to as the *sales variance*, sometimes called the *marketing variance*. The **sales variance** is the difference between budgeted units and actual units multiplied by the contribution margin per unit. The sales variance shows how much contribution margin was lost because budgeted sales were not achieved. It ignores variable cost variances, because these variances are analyzed separately.

In this case, the contribution margin is $4 per unit ($10 selling price − $6 variable cost). The sales variance is calculated as follows:

$$\text{Sales Variance} = (\text{Actual Unit Sales} - \text{Budgeted Unit Sales})$$
$$\times \text{ Contribution Margin per Unit}$$

$$\text{Sales Variance} = (28,000 \text{ Units} - 30,000 \text{ Units}) \times \$4 \text{ per Unit}$$
$$= -2,000 \text{ Units} \times \$4 \text{ per Unit}$$
$$= -\$8,000 \text{ U}$$

The calculation above shows that because sales were 2,000 units less than expected, net income was $8,000 less than expected, resulting in an unfavorable sales variance. If actual sales exceeds budgeted sales, the sales variance is favorable—net income is more than expected—by the amount of the sales variance. We can now summarize the $17,000 unfavorable variance in net income shown in Exhibit 6.1 as follows:

Sales Variance	$ 8,000 U
Variable Cost Variances	7,000 U
Fixed Cost Variances	2,000 U
Net Income Variance	$17,000 U

In summary, the company failed to achieve its budgeted net income of $70,000 because lost sales (in terms of units it had expected to sell but didn't) resulted in an $8,000 decrease in expected net income; variable cost variances resulted in a $7,000 decrease in expected net income; and fixed cost variances resulted in a $2,000 decrease in expected net income. Management can now analyze the details of these variances to determine more specific reasons why they occurred.

Preparation of a Flexible Budget

As explained above, a flexible budget adjusts budgeted costs to the level of activity achieved. To adjust costs, we need to know the manner in which costs vary with levels of activity. Specifically, we need to know the standard variable cost per unit of product (or per unit of activity base with which total variable cost varies).

The following example further illustrates the concept of the flexible budget. Redd Company's variable factory overhead costs vary in relation to the number of units produced. Specifically, the following unit costs have been identified:

Indirect Labor	$.40
Indirect Material	.25
Utilities	.10
Total	$.75

The company expected to produce 40,000 units in November 19X5. However, only 35,000 units were produced. The static budget for 40,000 units is compared with the actual cost for 35,000 units in Exhibit 6.3 below. The exhibit also shows the appropriate fixed overhead costs.

There is a fallacy in the comparison shown in Exhibit 6.3. A $500 favorable variance is shown for indirect labor. However, the exhibit is comparing the cost of indirect labor for 35,000 units with a budget for 40,000 units. The same problem exists in comparing the other two variable overhead items. The fixed cost comparison presents no problem; it is assumed the fixed costs are the same for both 35,000 and 40,000 units.

In order to properly compare the actual results with the budgeted expectations for the variable overhead items, it is necessary to prepare a flexible overhead budget for 35,000 units. Such a budget is prepared in Exhibit 6.4.

The flexible budget for variable overhead was calculated by multiplication of the unit cost for each item by 35,000 units. A totally different picture is presented. There are no favorable variances. Furthermore, the variance for indirect material is $2,250 unfavorable rather than $1,000 unfavorable. This comparison is more meaningful than that shown in Exhibit 6.3.

Flexible Budget Formula

A flexible budget formula can be prepared to allow management to determine expected factory overhead costs at any level of activity. For Redd Company, this formula is:

Flexible Budget Formula = $28,000 + $.75 per Unit

The "flex" in the flexible budget generally applies only to variable costs, since fixed costs remain constant within a relevant range. However, the

Exhibit 6.3 Performance Report–Static Budget

	Budget	Actual	Variance
Redd Company Factory Overhead Performance Report for the Month Ended November 30, 19X5			
Production (Units)	40,000	35,000	
Variable Costs:			
Indirect Labor	$16,000	$15,500	$ 500 F
Indirect Material	10,000	11,000	1,000 U
Utilities	4,000	3,950	50 F
Total Variable Costs	$30,000	$30,450	$ 450 U
Fixed Costs:			
Supervisors' Salaries	$15,000	$15,000	—
Property Taxes	11,000	11,500	$ 500 U
Depreciation.	2,000	2,100	100 U
Total Fixed Costs	$28,000	$28,600	$ 600 U
Total Factory Overhead	$58,000	$59,050	$1,050 U

Exhibit 6.4 Performance Report–Flexible Budget

Redd Company
Factory Overhead Performance Report
for the Month Ended November 30, 19X5

	Budget	Actual	Variance
Production (Units)	35,000	35,000	
Variable Costs:			
Indirect labor	$14,000	$15,500	$1,500 U
Indirect material	8,750	11,000	2,250 U
Utilities	3,500	3,950	450 U
Total Variable Costs	$26,250	$30,450	$4,200 U
Fixed Costs:			
Supervisors' salaries	$15,000	$15,000	$ —
Property taxes	11,000	11,500	500 U
Depreciation	2,000	2,100	100 U
Total Fixed Costs	$28,000	$28,600	$ 600 U
Total Factory Overhead	$54,250	$59,050	$4,800 U

budget formula includes fixed costs, because with these data management can readily determine the expected total factory costs at any given level of activity. With the flexible budget formula, management can prepare a series of budgets in advance for a number of levels of activity. Management can also use the formula to determine, after the fact, the flexible budget amount, as we did to Exhibit 6.4. For example, if actual production was 38,200 units, the flexible budget amount would be determined as follows:

$$\text{Flexible Budget Formula} = \$28,000 + (\$.75 \times 38,200 \text{ Units})$$
$$= \$28,000 + \$28,650$$
$$= \$56,650$$

The formula above includes only overhead costs. It is also possible to develop a flexible budget formula for total production costs, as well as for each individual overhead cost element. A total flexible budget formula includes direct material and direct labor as well as variable and fixed overhead. For example, if Redd Company's unit variable costs are $1.75 for direct material and $2.00 for direct labor, then the total production flexible budget formula is $28,000 plus $4.50 per unit ($1.75 + $2.00 + $.75).

Standard Costs

In Chapter 5, direct materials for the Kamp Company were budgeted on the basis of three pounds of material's being used for every finished unit; and direct labor costs were budgeted on the basis of one-half hour's being taken to complete a finished unit at a direct labor cost of $6 per hour. Kamp Company used standard costs to budget its production costs. A **standard cost** is the expected cost of producing one unit. It is, in effect, a budget for one unit.

Standard costs help management to plan and control business operations. In the Kamp Company example, the standard variable cost per unit was $10.10. Standard prices for material and labor were used in arriving at the standard cost figure. Management used this figure in planning its production budget. Using standard costs enhances management control by making performance reports more informative. The performance report in Exhibit 5.1 showed only total variances for cost items. When deviations from standard costs are shown, variances can be explained more completely. As described later in the chapter, this helps management to control operations.

Standard Cost System

A **standard cost system** is an accounting system under which all manufacturing costs are charged to production at standard costs. This practice is in contrast to an **actual cost system,** which charges actual costs to production as they are incurred, or to an **actual/normal cost system,** which charges actual direct material and direct labor costs to production but charges variable and fixed factory overhead at a predetermined, or standard, rate.

Under a standard cost system, work-in-process inventory is charged for the standard costs of direct material and direct labor and for standard variable and fixed factory overhead. Differences between actual costs incurred and standard costs charged to production are recorded as variances in separate accounts. Chapter 7 describes the standard cost system more fully, and the appendix to Chapter 7 illustrates the debit and credit process.

Setting Standards

Setting standards is not an easy task. A firm may set ideal standards or currently attainable standards. **Ideal standards** can be achieved only with absolute peak performance and efficiency under perfect conditions. They do not allow for machine breakdowns, worker fatigue, worker absences, or any of the common problems that slow up production. In other words, ideal standards assume that everything and everybody is going to work perfectly. Such perfection occurs only rarely. Thus, ideal standards may never be achieved. Some managers feel that ideal standards should be used in order that employees always have something to strive for. On the other hand, ideal standards may tend to discourage rather than motivate employees; if they believe they can never achieve the standards set, they may not even try.

Currently attainable standards allow for the fact that some inefficiency is inescapable. These standards are set high enough to provide a goal for employees to seek, yet not so high as to be discouraging. As the name suggests, the standards can be attained with efficient performance. Inefficiency beyond that normally expected (for example, normal machine breakdown) will result in inability to achieve the standard. In other words, currently attainable standards are considered reasonable under the prevailing working conditions. It is normally better for a firm to use currently attainable standards than ideal standards.

For direct material, direct labor, and variable factory overhead, standards are set for both price and usage. The degree of difficulty in setting standards depends on the nature of the cost element.

Direct Material The **material price standard** is the amount the firm expects to pay for one unit of direct material. Material price standards are based on the expected future costs of the direct material. In the Kamp Company example of Chapter 5, the direct material cost standard was $2 per pound. Determination of the appropriate costs may rely to a large extent on past costs; however, it is important to try and predict future ones. That is sometimes difficult. In some instances, perhaps little price rise is expected. However, in recent years petroleum-based materials have increased in price dramatically. In 1979 and 1980, gold and silver prices rose to unprecedented levels in an extremely short period of time. Industries using these metals had difficulty in predicting prices a year in advance. Nevertheless, it is important to consider future expected price increases in setting direct material price standards, since the material price is used in budget preparation.

In most firms, a **purchasing agent** is responsible for buying raw materials for the company. This individual has the most knowledge of past prices and is usually responsible for determining material price standards. However, a purchasing agent may set the price standard higher than is reasonable in order to look good by buying at a lower than standard price. Therefore, no one individual should have sole responsibility for setting standards—the purchasing agent's standards should be reviewed by a higher authority.

The **material usage standard** is the quantity of material needed for each unit of finished product. Setting standards for material usage may be more difficult than setting standards for material prices. It depends on the manner in which the material is used, as well as the type of material. In the Kamp Company example, the material usage standard was three pounds of direct material for each finished unit produced. For a firm that has been in business a while, the usage standard is based on past performance. For a new firm, it may be necessary to get experience before the standard can be meaningful.

In many cases, engineering estimates are used to set material usage standards. Past experience must be analyzed carefully to determine whether adjustments are needed in the standard. For example, if it is found that more material is consistently needed than allowed for in the standard, the standard may be too low. Conversely, if the standard always exceeds the amount used, perhaps the standard is too high.

The combination of the direct material price standard and the direct material usage standard provides the direct material standard per finished unit. For Kamp Company, the standard cost of direct material per finished unit produced was $6 (three pounds per unit at $2 per pound).

Direct Labor The standard direct labor cost per finished unit produced is based on the standard cost of direct labor and the standard amount of time expected to be used in completing a finished unit. The "price" of direct labor is normally indicated as a rate per hour. Therefore, the **labor rate standard** is the expected direct labor cost per hour. The **labor efficiency standard** (often called the *labor usage standard*) is the number of hours of direct labor needed to complete one unit of finished product. Theoretically, labor is either efficient or inefficient in performing its job. If the labor usage standard is met or exceeded, direct labor is said to be efficient; if it is not met, direct labor is said to be inefficient. For Kamp Company, the direct labor rate standard was $6 per hour. The labor efficiency standard was thirty minutes, or one-half direct labor hour, per finished unit. Thus, the standard direct labor cost per finished unit was $3 ($6 per hour × .5 hours).

The direct labor rate standard is one of the easiest standards to set. Generally, there are wage contracts or a government minimum wage that apply to workers. Consequently, determining the appropriate standard to use for a particular employee is usually not too difficult. However, the standard rate used for charging work-in-process inventory normally is an average of wages for several skill levels. For example, in the manufacturing process, workers receive wages that range from the minimum wage for unskilled labor to a very high wage for certain skilled labor. In the Kamp Company example, the standard rate was $6 per hour. That most likely is an average rate for the several labor skills involved. As discussed later, this fact is significant for analysis of the rate variance.

The labor efficiency standard is probably the most difficult standard to set. How long it takes to do a job varies depending on the job and the individuals. Furthermore, if workers know they are being observed so that management can set a standard, they may purposely work more slowly in order to have a lower one.

Engineering studies, such as time and motion observations, are frequently used in determining labor standards. Despite the difficulties, it is important to set such efficiency standards. Direct labor cost is a major element of product cost; its control is necessary. As with all standards, careful review of actual costs is required so that adjustments to the standard can be made as appropriate.

Variable Overhead Chapter 3 described the process of applying factory overhead. The factory overhead rate is based on the estimated total amount of overhead, as well as on the total estimated activity. The overhead rate, in effect, is a type of standard. It s based on the budgeted amounts for the various overhead items, such as power, indirect labor, and indirect materials.

To set standards for variable overhead items requires analysis of the individual costs. A budget is prepared for each cost, and the costs are combined to determine the total budgeted overhead used in the application rate. Discussion of the elements of variable overhead, as well as the discussion of fixed overhead, is presented in Chapter 7.

Variance Analysis

To illustrate how standard costs are used in analyzing variances, an example is presented below for Redd Company. For the current year, 19X6, Redd is applying variable factory overhead on the basis of direct labor hours rather than units produced. The overhead cost per unit is also higher ($1.00 versus $.75) than it was in 19X5. Standard variable costs are as follows:

	Unit Cost
Direct Material ($2\frac{1}{2}$ Pounds per Unit at $.70 per Pound):	$1.75
Direct Labor ($\frac{1}{4}$ Hour per Unit at $8 per Hour):	2.00
Factory Overhead ($\frac{1}{4}$ Hour per Unit at $4 per DLH):	1.00
Total Standard Variable Cost per Unit:	$4.75

For January 19X6, Redd Company budgeted production of 12,000 units. However, only 10,000 units were produced. A performance report based on a flexible budget of 10,000 units is shown as Exhibit 6.5.

Exhibit 6.5 Variance Analysis

<table>
<tr><td colspan="4" align="center">Redd Company
Performance Report
for the Month Ended January 31, 19X6</td></tr>
<tr><td></td><td>Budget</td><td>Actual</td><td>Variance</td></tr>
<tr><td>Direct Material . . . .</td><td>$17,500</td><td>$16,900</td><td>$ 600 F</td></tr>
<tr><td>Direct Labor . . . .</td><td>20,000</td><td>21,735</td><td>1,735 U</td></tr>
<tr><td>Variable Factory Overhead. . . . .</td><td>10,000</td><td>11,200</td><td>1,200 U</td></tr>
<tr><td>Totals . . . .</td><td>$47,500</td><td>$49,835</td><td>$2,335 U</td></tr>
</table>

The budgeted amounts in the performance report are based on the standard variable costs per unit multiplied by 10,000 units. From the performance report, you can see that the total variable cost variance for January was unfavorable by $2,335. The performance report also shows the total cost variance for each individual variable cost. However, the report provides no indication of possible causes for the reported variances. More specific information is desired regarding the reasons for the cost variances. The following sections show ways to obtain more information by analyzing the variances.

Direct Material Variances

Exhibit 6.5 shows the total direct material variance as $600 favorable. At first glance, that might appear to be good. However, the total cost of direct material is based on both the cost per unit and the number of units used. Therefore, the total direct material variance is divided into a *material price variance* and a *material usage variance*. In producing 10,000 finished units, Redd Company purchased and used 26,000 pounds of direct material at $.65 per pound. With this information, we can calculate the material price variance and the material usage variance.

Material Price Variance

The **material price variance** is the difference between the actual quantity purchased at the actual price and the actual quantity purchased at the standard price. It represents the difference between how much was paid and how much should have been paid for the material purchased. It is analyzed as shown in Exhibit 6.6.

The exhibit shows the material price variance to be $1,300 favorable. The company purchased 26,000 pounds of direct material. At a standard price of $.70 per pound, this should have cost $18,200. However, since the company paid only $.65 per pound, the actual total cost was $16,900. The $1,300 favorable variance means the company paid $1,300 less than expected for the direct material purchased. Another way of calculating the material price variance in this situation is to recognize that the company paid $.05 per pound less than standard. Since it bought 26,000 pounds, it paid $1,300 less than expected (26,000 pounds × $.05 per pound).

Remember that the designation of variances as favorable or unfavorable does not necessarily mean the variances are good or bad; it merely indicates mathematically a deviation from the budget. Whether a variance is good or bad depends upon the reasons for its existence. In this case, the $1,300 savings in direct material may have resulted from smart buying by the purchasing agent. If so, than the $1,300 can be regarded as a good sign. On the other hand, if the savings resulted from the purchase of inferior-quality material, the favorable variance may be misleading. Buying lower-quality material may result in excess waste or a poor-quality product. Excess waste will show up in the material usage variance. A poor-quality product may show up in examination or testing of the product or in reduced sales at some later date. Variance analysis provides management with a means of knowing whether results conform with the plan. When there are significant deviations from the plan, management can ask the individuals responsible for the reasons; it is these reasons that determine whether the variances are good or bad.

Material price variances are the responsibility of the purchasing agent, who buys the material and has the best knowledge as to the appropriate price to pay. An unfavorable price variance does not mean that the purchasing agent has not done the job properly; there may have been unex-

Exhibit 6.6 Material Price Variance

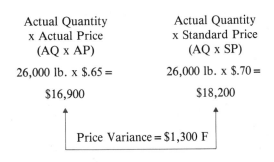

Actual Quantity x Actual Price (AQ x AP)	Actual Quantity x Standard Price (AQ x SP)
26,000 lb. x $.65 =	26,000 lb. x $.70 =
$16,900	$18,200

Price Variance = $1,300 F

pected price increases that were unavoidable. However, one purpose of variance analysis is to allow management to ask questions of individuals who are most likely to have the answers. In the case of material prices, this person is the purchasing agent.

Material Usage Variance

The **material usage variance** is the difference between the amount of direct material used and the amount that should have been used for the quantity of finished units produced, based on the standard price. It is often called the *material quantity variance* or *material efficiency variance*. The material usage variance for Redd Company is shown in Exhibit 6.7.

Redd Company produced 10,000 units in January. Since the material standard is two and one-half pounds per finished unit, the firm should have used 25,000 pounds (10,000 units $\times$ $2\frac{1}{2}$ pounds per unit). This quantity—25,000 pounds—is referred to as the **standard quantity allowed for the flexible budget.** Since the standard price of direct material is $.70 per pound, the flexible budget for direct material is $17,500 (25,000 pounds $\times$ $.70 per pound). The company used 26,000 pounds. At a standard cost of $.70 per pound, the total cost is $18,200. The difference between $18,200 and $17,500 is the $700 unfavorable material usage variance.

In this case, an easy way to compute the usage variance is to consider that the firm used 26,000 pounds instead of the 25,000 pounds it should have used—1,000 pounds more than the standard quantity allowed by the flexible budget. At a standard price of $.70 per pound, that amounts to an unfavorable material usage variance of $700.

You might ask why the actual quantity is multiplied by the *standard price,* rather than the *actual price* of $.65 per pound. Remember, the purchasing agent has responsibility for the purchase price. The production foreman has no control or responsibility for prices. Using the actual price to calculate the usage variance would mean that the production foreman would be affected by the performance of the purchasing agent. Therefore, the usage variance is based on the standard price rather than the actual price.

Exhibit 6.7 Material Usage Variance

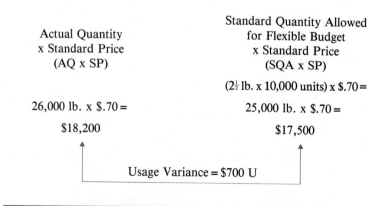

Actual Quantity
x Standard Price
(AQ x SP)

Standard Quantity Allowed
for Flexible Budget
x Standard Price
(SQA x SP)

$(2\frac{1}{2}$ lb. x 10,000 units) x $.70 =

26,000 lb. x $.70 =

$18,200

25,000 lb. x $.70 =

$17,500

Usage Variance = $700 U

As with the material price variance, designation of favorable or unfavorable does not mean good or bad, as such. The $700 unfavorable variance means that cost was $700 more than budgeted because of the amount of material used. Management may want to know why. It may be that there was waste and inefficiency in the production process. If so, the production foreman is responsible. However, it may also be that the material used was of poor quality or that a machine malfunction created an excess usage of material. Further, there is always the possiblity that the standard is inappropriate. Once again, the point is that the variance indicates the difference between actual results and budgeted plans. If this difference is considered significant, management can ask the responsible individual to explain the reason for the difference.

Total Material Variance

Exhibit 6.8 presents the total material variance with the breakdown between the material price variance and the material usage variance. The exhibit shows that the $600 favorable total variance results from the combination of the $1,300 favorable price variance and the $700 unfavorable usage variance. Thus, the $600 favorable variance shown in the performance report of Exhibit 6.5 must be analyzed according to price and usage in order for it to be meaningful. With the total variance broken down as shown in Exhibit 6.8, management is in a better position to ask questions and to determine the reasons for the deviations from the budget.

This illustration assumed that production used all the material purchased. As a practical matter, this probably seldom occurs. Purchasing is a separate function from production. The amount of material purchased is based on the amount of production anticipated. However, the amount purchased also depends on the desired inventory levels, the time it takes to receive the material, and the amount desired as a safety level. As a result, a firm often does not compute a total material variance; rather, it computes a

Exhibit 6.8 Total Material Variance

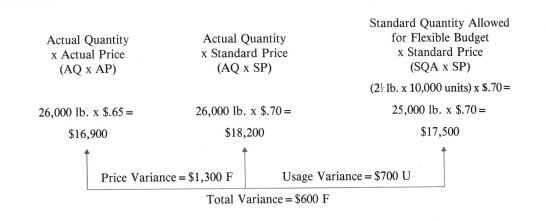

Actual Quantity x Actual Price (AQ x AP)	Actual Quantity x Standard Price (AQ x SP)	Standard Quantity Allowed for Flexible Budget x Standard Price (SQA x SP)
		$(2\frac{1}{2}$ lb. x 10,000 units) x $.70 =$
26,000 lb. x $.65 =	26,000 lb. x $.70 =	25,000 lb. x $.70 =
$16,900	$18,200	$17,500

Price Variance = $1,300 F   Usage Variance = $700 U

Total Variance = $600 F

price variance based on purchases and a usage variance based on production. This practice is also desirable when the firm wants to isolate the price variance at the earliest possible moment—at the time material is purchased—rather than at the time material is used.

To illustrate, assume that in February 19X6, Redd Company purchased 40,000 pounds of direct material at $.72 per pound. It produced 12,000 finished units using 31,200 pounds of direct material. The material price variance and material usage variance for this situation are illustrated in Exhibit 6.9.

Exhibit 6.9 Material Price and Usage Variance without Total Variance

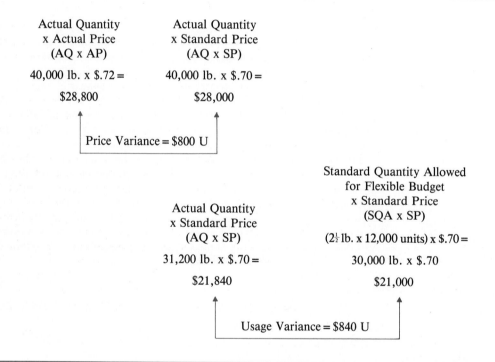

In this case, the price variance for the 40,000 pounds purchased is $800 unfavorable. The usage variance, however, is based on the 31,200 pounds actually used compared with the 30,000 pounds that should have been used for the flexible budget of 12,000 finished units. This variance is $840 unfavorable. It is inappropriate to compare the purchase of 40,000 pounds with the usage of 31,200 pounds in the flexible budget. As a result, no total variance is calculated; but none is needed. The purpose of all variance analysis is to provide management with information regarding deviations from the budget. In this case, there are two distinct operations—purchasing and production. The amount purchased does not relate to the amount used in this period. Therefore, a total variance would not provide a meaningful figure. The individual price variance and usage variance provide management with the data needed for further inquiry.

Direct Labor Variances

Direct labor for Redd Company totaled 2,700 hours at $8.05 per hour. This represented a total cost of $21,735 and resulted in an unfavorable total direct labor variance of $1,735, as shown in Exhibit 6.5. As with the direct material variance, it is necessary to divide the direct labor variance into two parts—the *labor rate variance* and the *labor efficiency variance*.

Labor Rate Variance

The **labor rate variance** is the difference between the actual labor rate and the budgeted labor rate, multiplied by the number of actual hours worked. The labor rate variance for Redd Company is shown in Exhibit 6.10 to be $135 unfavorable.

Another way of looking at it is to consider that the company worked 2,700 hours and paid a rate $.05 per hour above standard, resulting in an unfavorable variance of $135 (2,700 hours × $.05 per hour). The exhibit shows the actual rate, $8.05 per hour. If the amount of total wages paid is known, it is not necessary to know the actual rate to compute the variance. The rate variance is the difference between the total actual cost of direct labor and the cost that should have been incurred, based on the actual hours and the standard rate. For example, if the total direct labor cost for Redd Company had been $22,000, the rate variance would have been $400 unfavorable ($22,000 − $21,600). This result reflects an actual direct labor rate of $8.148 ($22,000 ÷ 2,700 hours). The actual direct labor rate does not necessarily represent the rate paid to any individual. As previously discussed, the labor rate standard is usually an average rate for a number of different job skills. Therefore, the actual rate is usualy the average paid to all workers.

One does not expect significant variances in the labor rate, because the labor rate standard is normally based on minimum wage laws and contracts.

Exhibit 6.10 Labor Rate Variance

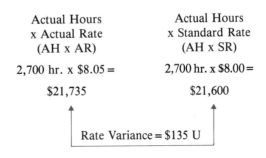

Actual Hours x Actual Rate (AH x AR)	Actual Hours x Standard Rate (AH x SR)
2,700 hr. x $8.05 =	2,700 hr. x $8.00 =
$21,735	$21,600

Rate Variance = $135 U

A rate variance may arise because of pay raises that were not anticipated when the budget was prepared.

A significant rate variance may be caused by the use of workers paid at a higher-skilled rate than the job requires. The production foreman is responsible for this variance. It may have arisen because of a shortage of workers with the needed skill—perhaps some workers were ill or perhaps management had not been able to hire enough workers with the needed skill. In order to get the job done, then, it may have been necessary to shift workers from one job to another. In this case, the production foreman may not have been at fault. On the other hand, the variance may have resulted from poor scheduling by the foreman, which created a need to shift workers that would not have existed under proper scheduling.

Another possible reason for an unfavorable rate variance is overtime. If overtime that had not been budgeted is paid to complete a job, the production foreman must be able to explain it.[1] Again, it may not be the foreman's fault. Outside factors may have required an earlier completion than expected; or a rush order may have required overtime. In these instances, the production foreman can easily explain the variance satisfactorily. In other instances, management may wish to question the sales manager regarding orders that have resulted in increased costs. The overtime may have resulted, however, because the workers did not work efficiently. The production foreman is responsible for this situation. In addition, inefficient use of time will also be reflected in the direct labor efficiency variance, as described below.

Labor Efficiency Variance

The **labor efficiency variance** (also called the *labor usage variance*) is the difference between the actual number of hours worked and the standard number of hours allowed in the flexible budget, multiplied by the standard rate. The labor efficiency variance measures the cost of the difference in how long it took to do the job and how long it should have taken to do the job. The cost of the difference in hours is measured at the standard rate. If the job took longer than it should have, then direct labor is said to have been inefficient. If the job took less time than it should have, then direct labor is said to have been efficient. The labor efficiency variance for Redd Company is shown in Exhibit 6.11.

Production in January took 2,700 hours. At a standard rate of $8 per hour, that amounts to a cost of $21,600. The standard for direct labor usage is one-fourth hour per unit. Since 10,000 units were completed, production should have taken 2,500 hours, at $8 per hour, and have cost $20,000. The difference is $1,600 unfavorable, as shown in the exhibit. Another way to find the variance is to consider that the job actually took 2,700 hours, when it should have taken 2,500 hours. Thus, direct labor was 200 hours inefficient. At a cost of $8 per hour, that represents an unfavorable efficiency variance of $1,600.

---

[1]Budgeted overtime is usually charged as factory overhead rather than direct labor so that a particular job is not penalized with extra costs simply because of when it is scheduled for production. Charging budgeted overtime to factory overhead allows these extra costs to be shared by all jobs.

Exhibit 6.11 Labor Efficiency Variance

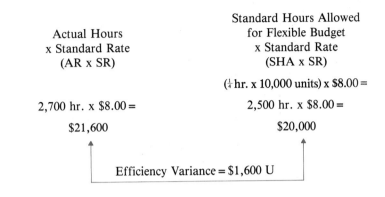

Actual Hours x Standard Rate (AR x SR)	Standard Hours Allowed for Flexible Budget x Standard Rate (SHA x SR)
	($\frac{1}{4}$ hr. x 10,000 units) x $8.00 =
2,700 hr. x $8.00 =	2,500 hr. x $8.00 =
$21,600	$20,000

Efficiency Variance = $1,600 U

As previously discussed, the labor efficiency standard is generally the most difficult standard to set. Consequently, the reason for the efficiency variance is sometimes the most difficult to determine. Again, the production foreman is responsible for the variance and must be able to explain it. Perhaps a machine breakdown resulted in wasted labor time. Machine breakdowns are normal, so this explanation may be satisfactory. On the other hand, too many machine breakdowns may indicate that maintenance procedures are not being properly applied. Of course, workers may have taken longer to do the job than they should have; that is a problem the production foreman must deal with. As always, one possible explanation for the variance is that the standard is inappropriate. Standards must be monitored to insure their validity. Over a period of time, management can determine whether a continually favorable or unfavorable variance is the result of inappropriate standards.

Total Labor Variance   The total unfavorable labor variance of $1,735 for Redd Company presented in Exhibit 6.5 consists of a rate variance that is $135 unfavorable and an efficiency variance that is $1,600 unfavorable. This relationship is shown in Exhibit 6.12.

It is important for management to divide the total variance into the rate variance and the efficiency variance. A number of factors affect the total variance, and only by calculating separate variances for rate and efficiency can management begin to determine what these factors are. As previously discussed, calling a variance favorable or unfavorable does not mean it is good or bad. The variances serve as a means of communicating to management deviations from the plan. By analyzing variances separately according to rate and efficiency, management can determine whether more attention is needed.

Exhibit 6.12 Total Labor Variance

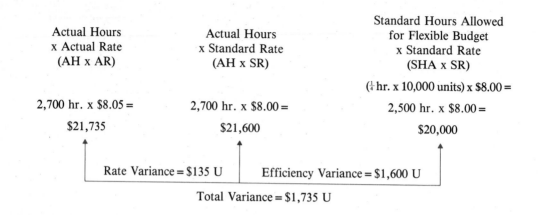

Total Variance = $1,735 U

Variable Overhead Variances

Variable overhead consists of a number of items, such as indirect material, indirect labor, maintenance, and utilities. To properly analyze these costs, it is necessary to have information on each specific one. Chapter 7 discusses specific classifications of variable overhead. This section discusses all variable overhead items as one cost for purposes of analysis. The Redd Company variable factory overhead standard is $4 per direct labor hour.

Overhead Spending Variance

The **overhead spending variance** is the difference between the actual variable cost incurred and the cost that should have been incurred, based on the actual hours worked at the standard rate. The spending variance for Redd Company is shown in Exhibit 6.13.

Redd Company actually spent $11,200 on variable overhead items. Since the company worked 2,700 direct labor hours, it should have spent $10,800 on variable overhead (2,700 hours × $4 per hour). This difference resulted in a $400 unfavorable spending variance. It is important to understand that nothing and no one was paid that $4 per hour; it represents a predetermined overhead rate based on the total expected overhead cost incurred and the total expected activity (in this case direct labor hours).

Notice in Exhibit 6.13 that the actual overhead rate is not shown. That is because the total cost incurred is not the product of the actual rate and the hours worked. The company incurred costs for such items as indirect labor, indirect material, and other variable items. The total cost of these items in January was $11,200. The actual overhead rate can be computed as $4.148 per hour ($11,200 ÷ 2,700 hours). This rate is not shown in Exhibit 6.13 because it is not used to determine actual cost incurred. Rather, the actual

Exhibit 6.13 Overhead Spending Variance

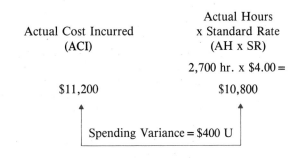

cost incurred is used to determine the actual rate. There is no particular significance in the actual rate; but it may be calculated in order that it can be compared with the standard rate. If the actual rate is consistently above or below the standard rate, management may want to look more closely at how it calculates the standard rate to see whether or not it should be revised. However, this analysis should concentrate on analyzing each component of variable overhead to determine the reasons for variances of each item. Responsibility for the spending variance depends on the specific cost elements of variable overhead. As previously mentioned, this matter is discussed in Chapter 7.

The $10,800 amount shown in Exhibit 6.13 indicates that since 2,700 direct labor hours were worked, the firm should have spent $10,800 in overhead. The fact that production took 2,700 hours, rather than the 2,500 hours it should have taken, is analyzed as the overhead efficiency variance.

Overhead Efficiency Variance

The **overhead efficiency variance** is the difference between the cost of overhead for the actual hours worked and the cost of overhead for the number of hours that should have been worked, based on the standard rate. The overhead efficiency variance for Redd Company is shown in Exhibit 6.14.

Since direct labor hours are used as the basis for applying variable overhead, a direct relationship exists between the overhead efficiency variance and the direct labor efficiency variance. The flexible budget for 10,000 units allows 2,500 direct labor hours. The overhead rate is $4 per direct labor hour. Therefore, the flexible budget for 10,000 units shows a cost of $10,000 as shown in Exhibit 6.14. Since the company actually spent 2,700 hours in doing the work, however, overhead costs were increased to $10,800. In other words, because direct labor was 200 hours inefficient, overhead cost increased by $800 (200 hours × $4 per hour).

It is important to realize that overhead itself is not efficient or inefficient. But if overhead varies in relation to direct labor hours, then using more direct labor hours requires the use of more variable overhead items. This

Exhibit 6.14 Overhead Efficiency Variance

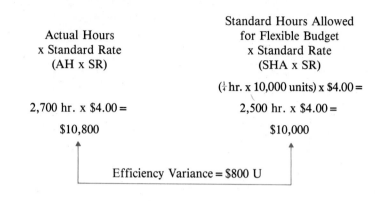

Actual Hours x Standard Rate (AH x SR)	Standard Hours Allowed for Flexible Budget x Standard Rate (SHA x SR)
	($\frac{1}{4}$ hr. x 10,000 units) x $4.00 =
2,700 hr. x $4.00 =	2,500 hr. x $4.00 =
$10,800	$10,000

Efficiency Variance = $800 U

naturally increases the cost of variable overhead. If the direct labor effi-ciency variance had been favorable, the overhead efficiency variance would also have been favorable. Both the direct labor efficiency variance and the overhead efficiency variance are based on the difference between actual direct labor hours and standard direct labor hours allowed in the flexible budget. When both are based on direct labor hours, there will always be a direct relationship between these two variances.

In determining the reasons for the overhead efficiency variance, manage-ment need only look at the reasons for the labor efficiency variance. What-ever caused inefficiency in direct labor resulted in the additional use of overhead items. Therefore, the production foreman is also responsible for the overhead efficiency variance.

Total Variable Overhead Variance

The total variable overhead variance for Redd Company is shown in Ex-hibit 6.5 to be $1,200 unfavorable. The variance is divided between the spending variance and the efficiency variance as shown in Exhibit 6.15.

The total variance of $1,200 unfavorable comprises a $400 unfavorable spending variance and an $800 unfavorable efficiency variance. It is impor-tant to understand the nature of these variances. As described above, the efficiency variance represents additional overhead cost incurred because more direct labor hours were worked than should have been worked, based on the flexible budget. In this case, the company worked 2,700 hours when it should have worked only 2,500 hours, causing an $800 increase in direct labor cost. Given, however, that the company actually worked 2,700 hours, variable overhead should have cost only $10,800. The additional $400 spent means the company spent more for overhead items than it should have for

Exhibit 6.15 Total Variable Overhead Variance

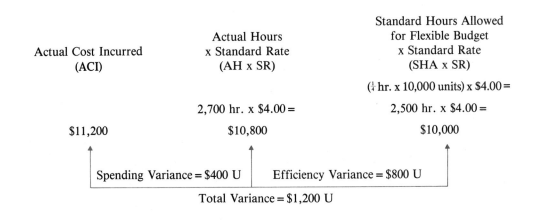

Actual Cost Incurred (ACI)	Actual Hours x Standard Rate (AH x SR)	Standard Hours Allowed for Flexible Budget x Standard Rate (SHA x SR)
		($\frac{1}{4}$ hr. x 10,000 units) x $4.00 =
	2,700 hr. x $4.00 =	2,500 hr. x $4.00 =
$11,200	$10,800	$10,000

Spending Variance = $400 U   Efficiency Variance = $800 U

Total Variance = $1,200 U

the number of hours worked. As previously mentioned, management needs to analyze individual items of overhead to determine their significance and to pinpoint responsibility.

Summary of Variance Calculations for Variable Costs

Total variances for direct material, direct labor, and variable overhead are the differences between actual costs incurred and the costs that should have been incurred, based on the flexible budget. In order that management can properly control costs, it must have detailed information regarding variances. This chapter has shown how the total variances for the variable manufacturing costs can be divided into two other variances. Exhibit 6.16 summarizes the manner in which these variances are calculated.

As described in the chapter, there are often short cuts in calculating the variances. For example, the material price variance is simply the difference between the actual price and the standard price, multiplied by the quantity purchased. The labor efficiency variance is the difference between the number of hours that should have been worked and the number of hours that were worked, multiplied by the standard rate. If you understand the nature and meaning of the variances, calculating them presents no problem, and memorizing formulas is unnecessary. The only purpose in variance calculations is to provide management with information that can be used to help control costs.

Exhibit 6.16 Variance Calculation Summary

Material Price Variance

(Actual Quantity × Actual Price) − (Actual Quantity × Standard Price)
$$(AQ \times AP) - (AQ \times SP)$$

Material Usage Variance

(Actual Quantity × Standard Price) − (Standard Quantity Allowed for Flexible Budget × Standard Price)
$$(AQ \times SP) - (SQA \times SP)$$

Labor Rate Variance

(Actual Hours × Actual Rate) − (Actual Hours × Standard Rate)
$$(AH \times AR) - (AH \times SR)$$

Labor Efficiency Variance

(Actual Hours × Standard Rate) − (Standard Hours Allowed for Flexible Budget × Standard Rate)
$$(AH \times SR) - (SHA \times SR)$$

Overhead Spending Variance

Actual Cost Incurred − (Actual Hours × Standard Rate)
$$ACI - (AH \times SR)$$

Overhead Efficiency Variance

(Actual Hours × Standard Rate) − (Standard Hours Allowed for Flexible Budget × Standard Rate)
$$(AH \times SR) - (SHA \times SR)$$

Summary

When actual net income differs from budgeted net income, management is interested in knowing why. The two basic reasons are that: (1) sales were more or less than budgeted, and (2) costs were more or less than budgeted. The sales variance is the difference between the actual sales and the budgeted sales in units, multiplied by the contribution margin per unit. If actual unit sales were more than budgeted, net income was increased directly by the increase in contribution margin. If unit sales were less than budgeted, the decreased contribution margin resulted in a direct reduction of net income.

Costs have a direct effect on net income. In order for management to control costs, it must be able to analyze the reasons for deviations from the budget. To analyze variable cost variances properly, it is necessary to prepare a flexible budget—a budget based on various levels of activity. With a flexible budget, actual variable costs are compared with expected variable costs for actual production.

A standard cost is the expected cost of producing one unit. A budget is prepared on the basis of standard costs. Standard costs are developed for direct material, direct labor, and variable overhead. Setting standards for each item is usually a difficult task. Once standards have been set, it is necessary to review them frequently to insure they are appropriate.

At the end of a period, actual costs incurred are compared with the amounts shown in the flexible budget, which is based on standard costs. The material, labor, and overhead variances are broken down into material price and material usage variances, labor rate and labor efficiency variances, and overhead spending and overhead efficiency variances. The analysis of these variances provides management with information that enables it to control costs. Individuals responsible for costs must be able to adequately explain the reasons for significant variances. Depending on the reasons given, management can take steps to reduce the possibility of significant budget variances in the future.

Review Problem

Problem

Belton Company uses a standard cost system with standards as follows:

Material: $2.30 per gallon and $1\frac{1}{2}$ gallons per finished unit.
Labor: $7.50 per hour and 2 hours per finished unit.
Variable overhead: $1.80 per DLH.

During January, the firm purchased 20,000 gallons of direct material at $2.40 per gallon. It used 16,000 gallons in producing 11,000 finished units. This production required 22,300 hours of direct labor at a total cost of $168,000. Actual variable overhead costs totaled $40,000.

Required:

Calculate the following variances:

   a. Material price and material usage variances.
   b. Labor rate, labor efficiency, and total labor variances.
   c. Overhead spending, overhead efficiency, and total variable overhead variances.

Solution

   a. Since the quantity used differs from the quantity purchased, we do not calculate a total material variance. Therefore, the price variance and the usage variance are calculated as shown below:

AQ x AP	AQ x SP
20,000 gal. x $2.40 =	20,000 gal. x $2.30 =
$48,000	$46,000

Price Variance = $2,000 U

AQ x SP	SQA x SP
	($1\frac{1}{2}$ gal. x 11,000 units) x $2.30 =
16,000 gal. x $2.30 =	16,500 gal. x $2.30 =
$36,800	$37,950

Usage Variance = $1,150 F

b. The actual labor rate is not given. However, it is not needed. The labor rate variance can be calculated based on the actual cost incurred for labor, as shown below:

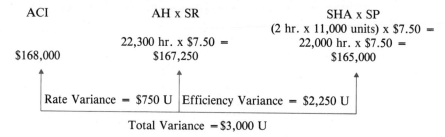

ACI

$168,000

AH x SR

22,300 hr. x $7.50 =
$167,250

SHA x SP
(2 hr. x 11,000 units) x $7.50 =
22,000 hr. x $7.50 =
$165,000

Rate Variance = $750 U | Efficiency Variance = $2,250 U

Total Variance = $3,000 U

c. The variable overhead variances are calculated as shown below:

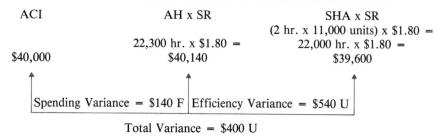

ACI

$40,000

AH x SR

22,300 hr. x $1.80 =
$40,140

SHA x SR
(2 hr. x 11,000 units) x $1.80 =
22,000 hr. x $1.80 =
$39,600

Spending Variance = $140 F | Efficiency Variance = $540 U

Total Variance = $400 U

Questions

6-1 What is the difference between a static budget and a flexible budget?

6-2 Janson Company expected total variable costs of $10,000 for budgeted production of 2,000 units. It only produced 1,500 units. What should variable costs be, based on the flexible budget?

6-3 The manager of Cole Company recently prepared an income statement in which she compared actual results from sales of 125,000 units against a budget for 150,000 units. She could not understand why all variable cost variances were favorable, yet net income was significantly less than budgeted. Explain why this could be so.

6-4 What is a sales variance? What information does it provide management?

6-5 If the sales variance is favorable, must the net income variance also be favorable?

6-6 Define *standard cost* and *standard cost system*. How are standard costs used in budgeting?

6-7 Distinguish between ideal standards and currently attainable standards. Which are normally better to use? Why?

6-8 What do you think is meant by the terms *loose standards* and *tight standards?*

6-9 Which standard is probably the most difficult to set? Why?

6-10 The material price variance at Kerr Company is consistently favorable. Does that indicate that the purchasing agent is doing a good job in buying? Explain.

6-11 The foreman of a manufacturing department had a significantly high favorable labor rate variance. When questioned about it, the foreman replied that because of a shortage of skilled labor, he hired unskilled workers and saved the company money. Does the favorable variance indicate good performance in this case? Explain.

6-12 The manager of a large division of a company never questions his department foreman about variances as long as the total departmental variance is within limits. Is this a good policy? Explain.

6-13 What is the significance of the overhead efficiency variance? How can overhead be efficient or inefficient?

6-14 How does a standard cost system help control costs? After all, even if the variances are unfavorable, the costs have already been incurred; and the firm can't get that money back.

Exercises

6-15 Preparing a Flexible Budget Manry Company has prepared the following budget based on expected sales of 50,000 units:

Sales	$250,000
Variable Costs	175,000
Contribution Margin	$ 75,000
Fixed Costs	40,000
Net Income	$ 35,000

Actual sales totaled 55,000 units. Prepare a flexible budget.

6-16 Preparing a Flexible Budget Wilton Company prepared a production budget for 45,000 units as follows:

	Unit Cost	Budget
Direct Material	$2.50	$112,500
Direct Labor	4.00	180,000
Variable Factory Overhead	1.50	67,500
Fixed Factory Overhead	—	100,000
Total Manufacturing Costs		$460,000

Only 38,000 units were produced. Prepare a flexible budget for this production.

6-17 Sales Variance; Net Income Variance Helm Company budgeted sales of 20,000 units with a contribution margin of $3 per unit. The company actually sold 18,500 units. Cost variances were $2,500 unfavorable for variable costs and $1,000 favorable for fixed costs.
   a. Determine the sales variance.
   b. Determine the net income variance.

6-18 Explaining Net Income Variance Ajax Company budgeted net income for the year at $30,000. Actual net income was $28,000. The firm's owner does not understand this, because actual sales of 12,000 units exceeded budgeted sales by 2,000 units. The selling price is $10.00 per unit; standard variable costs are $6.50 per unit; and actual variable costs were $7.00 per unit. Actual fixed costs exceeded budgeted fixed costs by $3,000. Prepare calculations to explain the $2,000 unfavorable variance in net income.

6-19 Explaining Net Income Variance Grady Company budgeted sales at $500,000 and net income at $50,000. The standard variable cost ratio is 70% and fixed costs were expected to be $100,000. Actual sales were $450,000, and net income was $20,000. Variable cost variances totaled $10,000 unfavorable; actual fixed costs were $105,000. Prepare calculations to explain the $30,000 unfavorable variance in net income.

6-20 Explaining Net Income Variance The president of Cramer Company is examining the following income statement for the recently ended year:

	Budget (75,000 Units)	Actual (80,000 Units)	Variance
Sales	$600,000	$640,000	$40,000 F
Variable Costs	450,000	464,000	14,000 U
Contribution Margin	$150,000	$176,000	$26,000 F
Fixed Costs	60,000	57,000	3,000 F
Net Income	$ 90,000	$119,000	$29,000 F

The president, although pleased that actual net income was $29,000 more than budgeted, has criticized managers for letting variable costs get out of control. Is this criticism justified? Prepare calculations to support your answer.

6-21 Material Variances Standard material costs and usage for Kelly Company are $1.50 per gallon and 3 gallons per finished unit. In a recent month, the company purchased and used 26,200 gallons at a cost of $1.40 per gallon to produce 8,000 finished units. Determine the following:
  a. Material price variance.
  b. Material usage variance.
  c. Total material variance.

6-22 Material Variances Blannery Corporation purchased 3,000 pounds of direct material at $2.35 per pound. It used 2,200 pounds in manufacturing 4,600 finished units. Standard material cost is $2.25 per pound; standard material usage is 1/2 pound per finished unit. Determine the following:
  a. Material price variance.
  b. Material usage variance.

6-23 Labor Variances Standard direct labor costs for Stanley Company are $6 per hour. The labor efficiency standard is 2 hours per finished unit. In a recent month, the company completed 4,500 units using 8,800 direct labor hours at a cost of $6.10 per hour. Determine the following:
  a. Labor rate variance.
  b. Labor efficiency variance.
  c. Total labor variance.

6-24 Variable Overhead Variances Drake Company applies variable factory overhead on the basis of $.50 per direct labor hour. The labor efficiency standard is 3 hours per finished unit. Last month, the firm completed 7,000 units while using 22,000 direct labor hours. Actual variable factory overhead costs incurred totaled $12,500. Determine the following:

    a. Overhead spending variance.
    b. Overhead efficiency variance.
    c. Total variable overhead variance.

6-25 Labor and Variable Overhead Variances Hatfield Corporation uses a standard cost system. Standard direct labor costs are $7.50 per hour, with an efficiency standard of 1/4 hour per finished unit. Variable factory overhead is applied at the rate of $3 per direct labor hour. In March, the company produced 6,000 finished units while using 1,600 direct labor hours at a total cost of $12,480. Actual variable factory overhead costs incurred totaled $4,500. Determine the following:

    a. Labor rate variance.
    b. Labor efficiency variance.
    c. Total labor variance.
    d. Overhead spending variance.
    e. Overhead efficiency variance.
    f. Total variable overhead variance.

6-26 Material and Labor Variances Standard cost data relative to direct material and direct labor for Lion Company are as follows:

Material		**Labor**	
Actual Quantity Used (Pounds):	20,000	Actual Hours:	20,000
Actual Cost:	$40,000	Standard Hours Allowed:	21,000
Standard Price per Pound:	$2.10	Rate Variance:	$3,000 U
Usage Variance:	$3,000 F	Actual Labor Cost:	$126,000

    Determine the following:

    a. Material price variance.
    b. Labor efficiency variance. (AICPA adapted)

6-27 Calculating Data from Variances Standard cost data relative to direct material and direct labor for Westcott Company are as follows:

Material		**Labor**	
Standard Price Each:	$3.60	Standard Rate:	$3.75
Actual Quantity Purchased:	1,600	Actual Rate:	$3.50
Standard Quantity Allowed for		Standard Hours Allowed for	
Actual Production:	1,450	Actual Production:	10,000
Price Variance:	$240 F	Efficiency Variance:	$4,200 U

    Determine the following:

    a. Actual purchase price per unit.
    b. Number of actual hours worked. (AICPA adapted)

Problems

6-28 Preparing a Flexible Budget A production performance report for Jambo Corporation is shown below.

Jambo Corporation
Production Performance Report
for the Month Ended June 30, 19X4

	Budget	Actual	Variance
Production (Units)	50,000	44,000	
Variable Costs:			
Direct Material	$100,000	$ 90,000	$10,000 F
Direct Labor	250,000	230,000	20,000 F
Factory Overhead:			
Indirect Labor	25,000	21,000	4,000 F
Indirect Material	20,000	17,000	3,000 F
Maintenance	15,000	15,000	—
Utilities	12,500	12,000	500 F
Total Variable Costs	$422,500	$385,000	$37,500 F
Fixed Costs:			
Supervisors' Salaries	$ 12,500	$ 12,500	$ —
Property Taxes	2,000	2,200	200 U
Depreciation	5,000	5,100	100 U
Insurance	1,000	1,000	—
Total Fixed Costs	$ 20,500	$ 20,800	$ 300 U
Total Production Costs	$443,000	$405,800	$37,200 F

The manufacturing vice-president is quite pleased with the results; except for some minor unfavorable fixed cost variances, the variances are all favorable. However, the president of the firm feels that somehow the report is misleading, but he's not sure why.

Required:

a. Prepare a flexible budget based on actual production.

b. Based on the flexible budget you prepared in part a, is the president's concern justified? Explain.

c. Develop the flexible budget formula for total production costs.

d. If the firm expects to produce 60,000 units next month, what is its expected total production cost?

6-29 Preparing a Flexible Budget; Explaining Net Income Variance Dixon Company sells its product for $3 per unit. Variable cost per unit is $2. A recent income statement, with the budget, is shown below:

Dixon Company
Income Statement
for the Year Ended December 31, 19X8

	Budget (250,000 Units)	Actual (200,000 Units)	Variance
Sales	$750,000	$600,000	$150,000 U
Variable Costs	500,000	450,000	50,000 F
Contribution Margin	$250,000	$150,000	$100,000 U
Fixed Costs	100,000	100,000	—
Net Income	$150,000	$ 50,000	$100,000 U

Required:
   a. What is wrong with the data as presented above?
   b. Prepare an income statement based on the flexible budget.
   c. Calculate the sales variance.
   d. Prepare calculations that explain the $100,000 unfavorable net income variance.

6–30 Determining and Explaining Net Income Variance Unit standard costs for Praxton Company are as follows: direct material, $.35; direct labor, $.50; variable factory overhead, $.25; variable selling and administrative, $.40. Fixed costs are budgeted at $10,000 per month. Selling price is $2 per unit.

Last month, the firm budgeted sales at 35,000 units but actually produced and sold 40,000 units. Actual costs were as follows: direct material, $15,500; direct labor, $22,000; variable factory overhead, $9,500; variable selling and administrative, $16,000; fixed costs, $11,500.

Required:
   a. Determine the difference between budgeted net income and actual net income. (*Note:* No formal budget or income statement is required.)
   b. Prepare calculations to explain the difference determined in part a.

6–31 Calculating Standard Cost Variances; Explaining Net Income Variance Natson Manufacturing Company budgeted sales for the past year at 300,000 units and net income at $230,000. Selling price per unit is $4.00, and standard variable cost per unit is $2.40. Fixed costs were budgeted at $250,000.

Management is extremely disappointed that actual net income was only $118,000. Production and sales totaled 280,000 units. The total direct material variance was $.10 per unit unfavorable. The direct labor efficiency standard is 1/4 hour per finished unit. Production required 72,000 hours. The standard direct labor rate of $5 per hour was actually paid.

Variable overhead is applied at the rate of $1.50 per direct labor hour. The spending variance was $1,000 favorable. Fixed factory overhead totaled $2,000 less than expected. Variable selling and administrative expenses were $.15 per unit unfavorable. There were no variances in fixed selling and administrative expenses.

Required:
Prepare calculations to explain to management why net income was $112,000 less than budgeted.

6–32 Calculating Standard Cost Variances Bronson Manufacturing Company uses a standard cost system with standards as follows:

   Material: $1.50 per pound and 2 pounds per finished unit.
   Labor: $8 per hour and 3 hours per finished unit.
   Variable overhead: $2 per DLH.

In a recent month, the firm purchased and used 64,000 pounds of direct material at $1.65 per pound while producing 33,000 finished units. Production required 102,500 hours of direct labor at $8.20 per hour. Actual variable overhead costs totaled $202,000.

Required:
Calculate the following variances:

a. Material price, material usage, and total material variances.

b. Labor rate, labor efficiency, and total labor variances.

c. Overhead spending, overhead efficiency, and total variable overhead variances.

6-33 Calculating Standard Cost Variances Wilson Manufacturing Company purchased 8,000 pounds of direct material for $10,500. The material price standard is $1.25 per pound; and the material usage standard is $1\frac{1}{2}$ pounds per finished unit. The company produced 3,000 finished units while using 4,700 pounds of direct material. Production required 4,650 direct labor hours at a total direct labor cost of $35,000.

The standard labor rate is $7.50 per hour, and $1\frac{1}{4}$ hours are allowed per finished unit. Variable overhead is applied at the rate of $3 per direct labor hour. Actual variable overhead costs totaled $13,600.

Required:
Calculate the following variances:

a. Material price and material usage. } PRIME COST VARIAN·

b. Labor rate and labor efficiency.

c. Overhead spending and overhead efficiency.   always VOF

6-34 Calculating and Explaining Standard Cost Variances The president of Travis Company is extremely upset over the following performance report:

Travis Company
Performance Report
for the Month Ended October 31, 19X1

	Budget	Actual	Variance
Direct Material	$40,500	$49,000	$ 8,500 U
Direct Labor	12,000	14,280	2,280 U
Variable Factory Overhead	6,000	7,000	1,000 U
Totals	$58,500	$70,280	$11,780 U

The president has demanded an explanation from the manufacturing vice-president for this "utterly poor performance."

Upon close investigation, the vice-president determined several facts. Although the standard price of material is $4.50 per pound, the purchasing agent forgot to order it in time from the regular supplier and was forced to buy from another source at a price $.50 per pound higher than standard.

The production foreman said he had a difficult time with the material. Much of it was of inferior quality and had to be discarded. Some of the poor material was put into process and jammed up the machines. He figures he used 10% more material than he should have because of these problems and wasted 150 direct labor hours because of machine down-time.

The material usage standard is 2 pounds per finished unit; but it took 9,800 pounds to produce 4,500 finished units. The labor standard allows 1/3 hour per finished unit. This time it took 1,700 hours. Although the direct labor standard rate is $8 per hour, the workers were granted a 5% raise, effective October 1. Someone forgot to include it in the budget.

Variable factory overhead is applied at the rate of $4 per direct labor hour. Total variable factory overhead cost was $7,000.

Required:

  a. Calculate the following variances:

    1. Material price, material usage, and total material variances.

    2. Labor rate, labor efficiency, and total labor variances.

    3. Overhead spending, overhead efficiency, and total variable overhead variances.

  b. As manufacturing vice-president, how would you reply to the president regarding each of the variances calculated in part a?

6–35 Calculating Standard Cost Variances Milnew Manufacturing Company manufactures one product with standard costs as follows:

Direct Material (20 Yards at $.90 per Yard):	$18
Direct Labor (4 Hours at $6 per Hour):	24
Total Factory Overhead (Applied at the rate of $5 per hour; the ratio of variable costs to fixed costs is 3:1.):	20
Variable Selling and Administrative Expenses:	12
Fixed Selling and Administrative Expenses:	7
Total Unit Cost:	$81

The standards are based on a "normal" activity of 2,400 direct labor hours. Actual activity for last month was as follows:

Direct Material Purchased (18,000 Yards at $.92 per Yard):	$16,560
Direct Material Used (in Yards):	9,500
Direct Labor (2,100 Hours at $6.10 per Hour):	$12,810
Total Factory Overhead Incurred:	$11,100

There was no fixed factory overhead variance. The company actually produced 500 finished units.

Required:

  a. Compute the standard variable factory overhead rate.

  b. Compute the following variances:

    1. Material price and material usage variances.

    2. Labor rate, labor efficiency, and total labor variances.

    3. Overhead spending, overhead efficiency, and total variable overhead variances. (AICPA adapted)

6–36 Calculating Standard Cost Variances Eastern Company manufactures special electrical equipment and parts, using a standard cost system for each product. A special transformer is manufactured in the transformer department. Production volume is measured by direct labor hours in this department, and a flexible budget system is used to plan and control department overhead.

  Standard production costs for the transformer are shown below:

Direct Material:	
Iron (5 Sheets at $2 per Sheet):	$10
Copper (3 Spools at $3 per Spool):	9
Direct Labor (4 Hours at $7 per Hour):	28
Variable Overhead (4 Hours at $3 per Hour):	12
Fixed Overhead (4 Hours at $2 per Hour):	8
Total:	$67

Overhead rates are based on normal monthly production of 4,000 direct labor hours. Variable overhead costs are expected to vary on the basis of direct labor hours.

During October, 800 transformers were produced. This number was below expectations, because a work stoppage occurred during contract negotiations with the labor force. Once the contract was settled, the department scheduled overtime in an attempt to catch up to expected production levels.

The following costs were incurred in October:

Direct Material:

Iron:	Purchased 5,000 sheets at $2; used 3,900 sheets.
Copper:	Purchased 2,200 spools at $3.10; used 2,600 spools.

Direct Labor:

Regular Time:	2,000 hours at $7 per hour; 1,400 hours at $7.20 per hour.
Overtime:	600 of the 1,400 hours were subject to overtime premium. Total overtime premium of $2,160 is included in variable overhead in accordance with company accounting practices.
Variable Overhead:	$10,000
Fixed Overhead:	$8,800

Required:
Calculate the following variances:
  a. Total material usage variance.
  b. Labor rate variance.
  c. Variable overhead spending variance.
  d. Variable overhead efficiency variance. (CMA adapted)

6-37 Calculating Standard Cost Variances The Groomer Company manufactures two products, Florimene and Glyoxide, used in the plastics industry. The company uses a flexible budget in its standard cost system to develop variances. Selected data follow:

	Florimene	Glyoxide
Data on Standard Costs		
Raw Material per Unit	3 Pounds at $1 per Pound	4 Pounds at $1.10 per Pound
Direct Labor per Unit	5 Hours at $2 per Hour	6 Hours at $2.50 per Hour
Variable Factory Overhead per Unit	$3.20 per DLH	$3.50 per DLH
Fixed Factory Overhead per Month	$20,700	$26,520
Normal Activity per Month	5,750 DLH	7,800 DLH
Units Produced in September	1,000	1,200
Cost Incurred for September:		
Raw Material	3,100 Pounds at $.90 per Pound	4,700 Pounds at $1.15 per Pound

ACTUALS (handwritten annotation pointing to Units Produced, Cost Incurred, and Raw Material rows)

Direct Labor	4,900 Hours at	7,400 Hours at
	$1.95 per Hour	$2.55 per Hour
Variable Factory Overhead	$16,170	$25,234
Fixed Factory Overhead	$20,930	$26,400

Required:

For each product, calculate the following variances:

  a. Material price and material usage.

  b. Labor rate and labor efficiency.

  c. Variable overhead spending and efficiency. (AICPA adapted)

6-38 Explaining Labor Variances The Clark Company has a contract with a labor union that guarantees a minimum wage of $500 per month to each direct labor employee having at least 12 years of service. One hundred employees currently qualify for coverage. All direct labor employees are paid $5 per hour.

The direct labor budget for 19X5 was based on the annual usage of 400,000 hours of direct labor at $5, or a total of $2,000,000. Of this amount, $50,000 (100 employees × $500) per month (or $600,000 for the year) was regarded as fixed. Thus, the budget for any given month was determined by the following formula:

$50,000 + ($3.50 × Direct Labor Hours Worked)

Data on performance for the first three months of 19X5 follow:

	January	February	March
Direct Labor Hours Worked:	22,000	32,000	42,000
Direct Labor Costs Budgeted:	$127,000	$162,000	$197,000
Direct Labor Costs Incurred:	$110,000	$160,000	$210,000
Variance:	$17,000 F	$2,000 F	$13,000 U

The factory manager was perplexed by the results, which showed favorable variances when production was low and unfavorable variances when production was high, because he believed his control over labor costs was consistently good.

Required:

  a. Why did the variances arise? Explain and illustrate using amounts and graphs as necessary.

  b. Does this direct labor budget provide a basis for controlling direct labor costs? Explain, indicating changes that might be made to improve control over direct labor cost and to facilitate performance evaluation of direct labor employees. (AICPA adapted)

Chapter 7   Overhead Analysis

Learning Objectives

The purpose of this chapter is to expand upon the subject of variance analysis for factory overhead. The chapter describes variable factory overhead in detail and also illustrates variance analysis for fixed factory overhead. The appendix shows journal entires for a standard cost system. Studying the chapter will enable you to:

1. Analyze the details of variable overhead variances.
2. Apply variable overhead analysis to bases other than direct labor hours.
3. Calculate the variable overhead variances.
4. Describe fixed factory overhead as a standard cost.
5. Describe the fixed factory overhead variances.
6. Calculate the fixed factory overhead variances.
7. Describe how a standard cost system is used.
8. Prepare journal entries using a standard cost system. (Appendix)
9. Prepare an income statement on the basis of standard cost. (Appendix)

Chapter Topics

The major topics included in this chapter are:

Variable Factory Overhead
Fixed Factory Overhead
Standard Cost System
Appendix: Record Keeping for a Standard Cost System

Chapter 6 illustrated the calculation of variable factory overhead variances on a total basis. This chapter considers the individual items that may comprise variable factory overhead. It also illustrates the use of bases other than direct labor hours for the application of variable overhead.

Fixed factory overhead presents special problems. Fixed overhead is applied to production as though it were a variable cost. Of course, it is not a variable cost. This chapter illustrates the computation of fixed overhead variances and considers the problems in applying fixed factory overhead as a standard cost.

A standard cost was defined in Chapter 6 as the budget of one unit. A standard cost system is used to charge standard cost into the manufacturing process. Through the double entry process, variances are isolated for later analysis. This chapter describes the standard cost system and the appendix illustrates its application.

Variable Factory Overhead

The Hadd Company uses a standard cost system in its manufacturing operations. Variable factory overhead is applied at the rate of $1.50 per direct labor hour. This rate consists of three overhead items as follows:

	Per DLH
Supplies	$ .30
Power	.70
Maintenance	.50
Total	$1.50

The firm determined the rate for each item by estimating the total amount expected to be spent on each item and dividing that by the total direct labor hours expected for the year. In this example, the standard for direct labor is two direct labor hours per unit. In its most recent month, Hadd Company budgeted production of 25,000 units but produced only 22,000 units. It used 45,000 direct labor hours, incurring a total variable overhead cost of $70,200. The variable overhead variances are shown in Exhibit 7.1.

Although the company budgeted for 25,000 units, the flexible budget for overhead must be based on actual production of 22,000 units. Since standard hours allowed is two hours per unit, the flexible budget for 22,000 units

Exhibit 7.1 Variable Overhead Variances

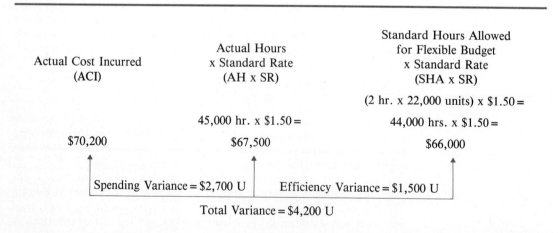

is 44,000 hours. At a standard overhead rate of $1.50 per hour, the flexible budget for variable overhead is $66,000. Since the total cost was $70,200, the total variance was $4,200 unfavorable. Using the techniques shown in Chapter 6, the exhibit illustrates a $1,500 unfavorable efficiency variance and a $2,700 unfavorable spending variance.

Efficiency Variance

The efficiency variance is calculated as shown in Chapter 6. In short, the flexible budget required 44,000 direct labor hours. The company used 45,000 direct labor hours. Therefore, it was 1,000 hours inefficient. At a variable overhead rate of $1.50 per hour, the efficiency variance is $1,500 unfavorable (1,000 hours × $1.50). As discussed in Chapter 6, overhead in itself is not inefficient. The overhead rate in this case is based on direct labor hours. Since the direct labor hours exceeded budget, more overhead costs were incurred than budgeted. In effect, the inefficiency of direct labor resulted in an unfavorable efficiency variance for variable overhead.

$= ACI$ for VOH items $- (AH \times Std\ OH\ rate)$

Spending Variance

The spending variance is the difference between the actual cost incurred for variable overhead items and the cost that should have been incurred, based on the actual number of hours, at the standard overhead rate. Exhibit 7.1 shows that the company spent $70,200 for various items included in variable overhead. Based on the fact that direct labor hours totaled 45,000, the company should have incurred a total variable overhead cost of $67,500. (It is already recognized that $1,500 more was spent than should have been because of inefficiency in direct labor.) Instead, it spent $70,200, resulting in a $2,700 unfavorable spending variance. At this point, management needs more detailed information regarding each of the three overhead items so that it can determine what problems exist relative to variable overhead and discuss these problems with the individuals responsible. The accounting system is designed to accumulate data on each item. A performance report for each is shown in Exhibit 7.2.

The flexible budget amount for 45,000 hours is derived by multiplication of the rate shown in the exhibit for each item by 45,000 hours. The $2,700 unfavorable spending variance is more meaningful when analyzed in relation to each item. Spending for supplies was $300 less than budgeted for 45,000 hours. However, the other two items, power and maintenance, exceeded the flexible budget by $1,800 and $1,200, respectively. The manager

Exhibit 7.2 Variable Overhead Analysis

	Rate	Budget (45,000 Hours)	Actual	Variance
Supplies	$ .30	$13,500	$13,200	$ 300 F
Power	.70	31,500	33,300	1,800 U
Maintenance	.50	22,500	23,700	1,200 U
Totals	$1.50	$67,500	$70,200	$2,700 U

responsible should analyze the power and maintenance variances to determine why they occurred. Perhaps utility rates were increased by the power company after the overhead rate of $.70 per hour had been calculated. If so, the variance can be explained simply by the increase in utility rates; and nothing can be done about it. Management should consider revising the overhead rate for power in that event. On the other hand, a primary reason for an unfavorable variance in power is that power is being wasted. If the power cost for the entire factory is being considered (as assumed in this example), determining the responsibility for wasted power is somewhat difficult. If it is possible to look at power usage by department, then the foreman of each department can be held responsible for power usage and should be able to explain any excess usage. If the reason for the variance is wasted power, management might want to emphasize the need to conserve energy and institute programs to try to meet its goal of energy conservation.

The maintenance variance of $1,200 unfavorable should be analyzed to determine why it occurred. Again, the overhead rate may not be appropriate and may need to be revised. However, the variance may have been caused by an excessive number of machine breakdowns. If so, management will want to look into the causes for them. Some breakdowns are expected; but a good maintenance program should preclude excessive breakdowns. If maintenance is not being conducted on a timely basis, breakdowns may occur more frequently than they should. If so, the individual responsible needs to explain why regular maintenance is not being conducted.

From the above discussion, you can see how foremen and their superiors can use the individual overhead variances to determine reasons for their occurrence. This process is one way of controlling overhead costs. The example used only three items for simplicity. However, variable overhead consists of a number of items; and it is necessary to prepare performance reports showing details of each. Only in this way can overhead costs be controlled on a company-wide basis.

Use of Base Other Than Direct Labor Hours

Previous examples have used direct labor hours as the base for applying variable overhead. As described in Chapter 2, management must determine the appropriate base against which to measure variable cost; Chapter 2 illustrated how this is done. Management often chooses **direct labor hours** to be the base, because it is natural to assume that the greater the number of hours required for production, the higher the overhead cost incurred. The use of **direct labor dollars** (often called *direct labor cost*) as the base will yield similar results to use of direct labor hours, because total direct labor dollars are based on direct labor hours. Overhead may also be applied on the basis of **machine hours** or on the basis of **units produced.**

It is possible to use more than one base. For example, a company may use direct labor hours for indirect material and indirect labor and use machine hours for power and maintenance costs. Whether to use more than one base depends on the expected results; if they do not differ significantly, it is usually more practical to use only one base. The primary concern in choosing the appropriate base is cost control. The base that best provides management with information that leads to better cost control is the one that should be used.

Machine Hours As mentioned above, machine hours are sometimes used as the base when utilities and maintenance represent a major portion of variable overhead cost. A strong relationship usually exists between machine hour usage and utilities and maintenance costs.

To illustrate, assume that Valley Company uses machine hours as a base for applying variable factory overhead. The variable rate is $.40 per machine hour, and it takes one-half machine hour to finish one unit. In a recent month, the company produced 20,000 finished units. The variable overhead variances, based on a flexible budget of 20,000 finished units, are shown in Exhibit 7.3.

The method of calculation in the exhibit does not differ from that used when direct labor hours are used as the base. The interpretation is also the same. In this case, the company produced 20,000 units. At a standard rate of one-half hour per unit at $.40 per hour, the company should have used 10,000 machine hours at a cost of $4,000; but it actually used 9,500 hours. Therefore, there is a favorable efficiency variance of 500 hours. At $.40 per hour, this results in a favorable variance of $200. As with direct labor hours, the overhead items themselves are not efficient. Rather, because it took less time than expected to produce 20,000 units, the amount of overhead cost at the standard rate was correspondingly less.

The spending variance is $500 unfavorable. Since the company required only 9,500 hours to produce 20,000 units, it should have spent only $3,800. Instead, it spent $4,300. The possible reasons for this spending variance are similar to those enumerated in the discussion of direct labor as base. The overhead items themselves may have cost more than originally expected. In addition, there may have been waste in the use of overhead items, such as power. As previously described, management can obtain detailed analysis of the spending variance by each item if necessary.

Units Variable factory overhead may be applied on the basis of units produced. Under this method, overhead costs are not related to either direct

Exhibit 7.3 Machine Hours as Base

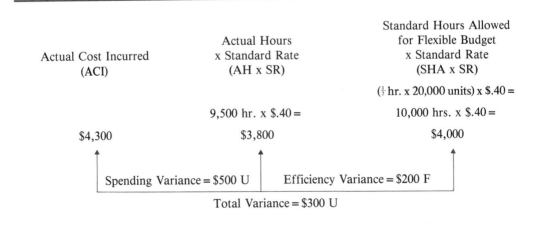

Actual Cost Incurred (ACI)	Actual Hours x Standard Rate (AH x SR)	Standard Hours Allowed for Flexible Budget x Standard Rate (SHA x SR)
		($\frac{1}{2}$ hr. x 20,000 units) x $.40 =
	9,500 hr. x $.40 =	10,000 hrs. x $.40 =
$4,300	$3,800	$4,000

Spending Variance = $500 U Efficiency Variance = $200 F

Total Variance = $300 U

labor hours or machine hours. That means there is no efficiency variance, only a spending variance.

The procedure for using units produced as base is illustrated by the example of the Madden Company, which applies overhead at the rate of $.75 per finished unit. In a recent month, the company budgeted for 10,000 units of production but produced only 8,000 units, incurring overhead costs of $6,350. As before, a flexible budget for 8,000 units must be prepared. For overhead, we compute variances as shown in Exhibit 7.4.

Exhibit 7.4 Units as Base

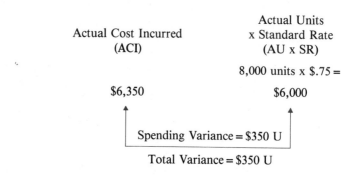

Since the company produced 8,000 units, the overhead should have cost $6,000. Instead, actual overhead cost $6,350, resulting in an unfavorable spending variance of $350. This amount is also the total variance, since there is no efficiency variance. Remember that in the previous illustrations, the variable overhead efficiency variances resulted from the fact that more overhead was required because either direct labor or machine usage was inefficient—that is, more labor hours or machine hours were used than budgeted. That is not true in this case. Overhead cost is incurred because a unit is produced. Therefore, there is nothing to be efficient or inefficient. An efficiency variance for direct labor may still be computed; but under the assumption used in Exhibit 7.4, it does not affect the amount of overhead required.

Fixed Factory Overhead

Fixed factory overhead presents special problems in a standard cost system. As previously described, a predetermined overhead rate is calculated, based on the total expected fixed factory overhead and the total expected activity for the year. This fixed overhead rate is then applied to production during the year. The rate is merely an estimate of the amount of overhead being incurred as the items are being produced. At the end of the year, the firm accounts for any difference between actual overhead costs incurred and overhead applied by either adjusting cost of goods sold or prorating the difference among the appropriate balances in the manufacturing accounts. The problem, however, is that fixed factory overhead is applied as though it were a variable cost. Of course, it is not variable. This results in difficulties when the firm tries to analyze variances from standard. It is necessary, then, to consider the nature of fixed overhead in analyzing fixed overhead variances.

Fixed Overhead as a Standard Cost

As previously defined, standard cost represents the budgeted cost for one unit. For variable costs, the standard cost concept works well, because the unit cost does not change as production increases or decreases. When fixed overhead is considered as a standard cost, however, a problem arises in that the fixed overhead per unit is only applicable for one specific volume of activity. For example, assume that Holley Company expects to spend $450,000 for fixed overhead next year. It anticipates using 150,000 direct labor hours in producing 75,000 finished units. The fixed overhead rate is determined to be:

$$\frac{\$450,000}{150,000 \text{ DLH}} = \$3 \text{ per DLH}$$

In this case, the standard fixed overhead is $3 per direct labor hour. Since two direct labor hours are required to produce one finished unit (150,000 hours ÷ 75,000 units), the standard fixed overhead per unit is $6. This figure is only applicable if the company produces exactly 75,000 units and if total fixed overhead is $450,000. If more units are produced, fixed overhead cost per unit decreases. If fewer than 75,000 units are produced, fixed overhead cost per unit increases. Furthermore, if actual fixed overhead cost is more or less than $450,000, unit cost will differ from $6.

Nevertheless, for product costing, as well as for control purposes, fixed overhead must be calculated as a standard cost; and the problems arising when more or less is produced than budgeted must be considered in the variance analysis. Because of these considerations, the significance of fixed overhead variances differs from that of variable overhead variances. Management must clearly understand their significance in order to make proper decisions regarding cost control.

Fixed Overhead Budget Variance

As mentioned above, Holley Company budgeted $450,000 for fixed overhead for the current year. At the end of the year, the company had actually spent $455,000. An analysis of this difference is shown in Exhibit 7.5.

The **budget variance** is the difference between actual cost incurred and budgeted fixed overhead cost. In this case, there is an unfavorable difference of $5,000. This variance is similar to the spending variance for variable overhead; it is the difference between the amount actually spent and the amount that should have been spent. The budgeted amount of $450,000 is sometimes called the *flexible budget amount*, because it represents the amount budgeted for actual units produced. It would, of course, represent

Exhibit 7.5 Fixed Overhead Budget Variance

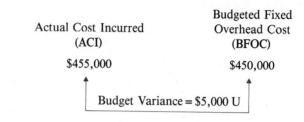

Actual Cost Incurred
(ACI)

$455,000

Budgeted Fixed
Overhead Cost
(BFOC)

$450,000

Budget Variance = $5,000 U

the budget for a range of production. If the budget variance is considered significant, management is interested in knowing why it occurred.

Generally, the budget variance should not be significant. By definition, fixed costs are not expected to change within a relevant range. Therefore, they can usually be predicted fairly accurately. As with the variable overhead spending variance, the managers responsible can compare the actual cost incurred with the budgeted cost for each individual item.

or std. volume variance = BFOH − FOH cost applied to WIP

Fixed Overhead Volume Variance

The **volume variance** is the difference between the budgeted fixed overhead cost and the amount of fixed overhead cost applied to work-in-process inventory. It is caused solely by a difference between actual activity and budgeted activity. You will find a volume variance only under absorption costing. Variable costing includes all fixed overhead on the income statement as a period cost. Therefore, under variable costing, only a budget variance will exist. On the other hand, under absorption costing, fixed overhead is applied to production. A volume variance arises when actual production differs from budgeted production. In that case, the amount of fixed overhead applied does not equal the amount budgeted.

It is important to understand the nature and reason for the volume variance. In the Holley Company example, expected production was 75,000 units. At two direct labor hours per unit, this production level would have required 150,000 direct labor hours. With a fixed overhead application rate of $3 per DLH, budgeted fixed overhead would have been fully absorbed if actual units produced had been as expected—75,000 units. However, assume only 70,000 units were produced. Standard direct labor hours allowed to produce this quantity is 140,000. Consequently, the total amount of fixed overhead applied to units produced during the period is $420,000. This calculation is illustrated in Exhibit 7.6.

In the exhibit, notice that fixed overhead was applied on 140,000 direct labor hours, resulting in a total application of $420,000. Budgeted fixed overhead was $450,000. Based on the budget alone, overhead has been underapplied by $30,000. This difference is the volume variance. The designation of unfavorable is somewhat misleading. It does not mean that the

Exhibit 7.6 Fixed Overhead Volume Variance

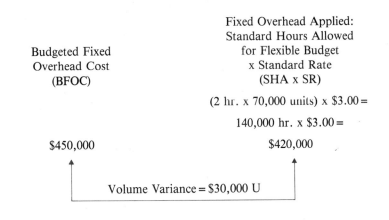

	Fixed Overhead Applied:
Budgeted Fixed Overhead Cost (BFOC)	Standard Hours Allowed for Flexible Budget x Standard Rate (SHA x SR)
	(2 hr. x 70,000 units) x $3.00 =
	140,000 hr. x $3.00 =
$450,000	$420,000

Volume Variance = $30,000 U

firm spent $30,000 more than it should have. Overspending or underspending is accounted for with the budget variance. Rather, it means that $30,000 of budgeted cost was not absorbed into the product. The unfavorable designation indicates the mathematical difference between the amount budgeted and the amount applied. It also indicates an underutilization of facilities—that is, planned production was to use 75,000 hours, but only 70,000 hours were used.

It is important to understand the use of the flexible budget term in the calculation above. Remember that fixed overhead does not in fact increase or decrease based on changes in activity. However, fixed overhead is applied on the basis of standard hours allowed for the flexible budget. In other words, fixed overhead applied is based on direct labor hours allowed for units produced; and the number of direct labor hours allowed is based on the standard. Therefore, the flexible budget enters into the calculation of the volume variance simply because the overhead application is based on a variable item, direct labor hours, while the total budgeted fixed overhead does not vary with direct labor hours.

Assume that the Holley Company had the budget previously described but actually produced 77,000 units. The fixed overhead volume variance in this instance is calculated as shown in Exhibit 7.7.

Since the company produced 77,000 units, standard hours allowed total 154,000. That means fixed overhead was applied to 154,000 hours—at $3 per hour, an application of $462,000. The budget for fixed overhead is only $450,000. This overapplication results in a favorable volume variance of $12,000. The favorable designation does not mean that less money was spent than budgeted. Again, it is a mathematical designation indicating that the amount applied was $12,000 more than the budget. It also indicates that the use of facilities exceeded expectations—77,000 units rather than 75,000 units were produced.

Exhibit 7.7 Favorable Fixed Overhead Volume Variance

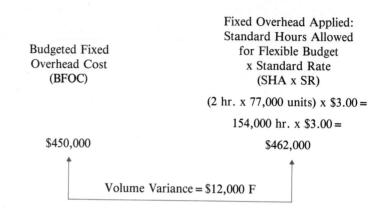

Budgeted Fixed
Overhead Cost
(BFOC)

Fixed Overhead Applied:
Standard Hours Allowed
for Flexible Budget
x Standard Rate
(SHA x SR)

(2 hr. x 77,000 units) x \$3.00 =

154,000 hr. x \$3.00 =

\$450,000

\$462,000

Volume Variance = \$12,000 F

Another way to compute the volume variance is to determine the difference in budgeted activity and activity allowed for the flexible budget and multiply this difference by the fixed overhead rate. For example, in Exhibit 7.6, the budget was for 150,000 direct labor hours; standard hours allowed for the flexible budget totaled 140,000 direct labor hours. The underapplication of 10,000 hours, at \$3 per hour, resulted in an unfavorable volume variance of \$30,000. In Exhibit 7.7, the 154,000 hours allowed for the flexible budget exceeded the budgeted activity of 150,000 hours by 4,000 hours. At \$3 per direct labor hour, this difference represents a volume variance that is \$12,000 favorable. Again, the variance is favorable because the amount applied exceeds the amount of the budget.

Fixed Overhead Total Variance

The fixed overhead total variance is the difference between actual cost incurred and the amount of fixed overhead applied. This situation is illustrated in Exhibit 7.8.   *applied at actual volume.*

The company incurred fixed overhead cost of \$455,000. Because fixed overhead is applied on the basis of standard direct labor hours allowed for the flexible budget production of 70,000 units, only \$420,000 of fixed overhead was applied. The total variance of \$35,000 represents the underapplied overhead. As in previous examples, the unfavorable designation indicates that more cost was incurred than was charged to the product; it does not necessarily mean that excess costs were incurred. Excess costs incurred over the budgeted amount are represented by the \$5,000 unfavorable budget variance. The additional \$30,000 unfavorable variance is the volume variance, which is due strictly to the difference between the budgeted cost and the applied cost.

Thus, the underapplied overhead of \$35,000 results from two factors: (1) the company did not produce as many units as it expected, and (2) the

Exhibit 7.8 Fixed Overhead Total Variance

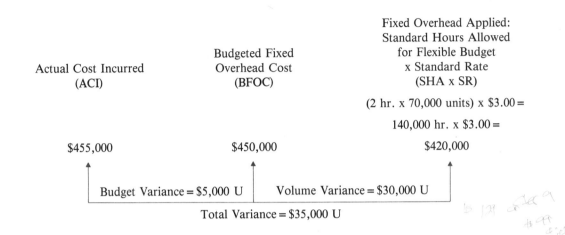

Actual Cost Incurred (ACI)	Budgeted Fixed Overhead Cost (BFOC)	Fixed Overhead Applied: Standard Hours Allowed for Flexible Budget x Standard Rate (SHA x SR)
		(2 hr. x 70,000 units) x $3.00 =
		140,000 hr. x $3.00 =
$455,000	$450,000	$420,000

Budget Variance = $5,000 U   Volume Variance = $30,000 U

Total Variance = $35,000 U

company spent more than it budgeted. For cost control purposes, only the budget variance is significant. The volume variance is related more to production and marketing control. Management is interested in knowing why less was produced than budgeted as well as in the effect of this underproduction on profit; but these matters are not relevant to underspending or overspending on the amount produced.

Standard Cost System

A **standard cost system** was defined in Chapter 6 as a system under which manufacturing costs are charged to production at standard cost. This chapter describes the standard cost system more fully and illustrates how it is used.

To differentiate the standard cost system from other types of systems, consider what you have learned so far. An **actual cost system** charges all manufacturing costs—direct material, direct labor, and variable and fixed factory overhead—to work-in-process inventory as the actual costs are incurred. Such a cost system often encounters problems with overhead costs, because fixed costs are generally incurred in lumps and some variable overhead costs may not be known until some time later than needed. As a result, the firm does not have timely cost information on products, which makes it difficult to determine a product's unit cost at a point in time.

The **actual/normal cost system** charges direct material and direct labor to work-in-process inventory at actual costs and charges variable and fixed overhead at a predetermined overhead rate that is based on the budgeted overhead and a budgeted activity, such as direct labor hours. This system has an advantage over the actual cost system in that overhead is charged to work in process on a timely basis. While the actual overhead incurred for the year will normally differ from the amount budgeted, the difference between the two can be adjusted to cost of goods sold or to the inventory accounts at the end of the year.

The difficulty with the actual/normal cost system is that it does not provide management with data for controlling costs. The **standard cost system** is helpful in that it charges all manufacturing costs to work in process at a standard amount, which represents the expected cost for one unit. Through the use of variance analysis, management can determine deviations from standard. Significant variances indicate the possibility that problems exist.

The standard cost system does have some difficulty with fixed overhead analysis. However, as long as management understands the nature of the fixed overhead variances, it should have no problems in using a standard cost for fixed overhead. Thus, management can arrive at a single unit cost figure that should be incurred in the production process. If actual costs are different from this expected amount, adjustments may be needed.

Another advantage of the standard cost system is that it makes inventory calculations easier. It is not necessary to use FIFO, LIFO, or weighted-average inventory systems; rather, all units are inventoried at standard cost. A single figure can therefore be used. At the end of the accounting period, it is necessary only to count the number of physical units and multiply by the standard cost per unit. Differences between standard and actual cost are accounted for as variances, as previously described.

The standard cost system can be included as a part of the double entry system. In this case, the variances are isolated in separate accounts. An illustration applying the standard cost system to the double entry process is provided in the appendix to this chapter.

Summary

A meaningful analysis of variable overhead variances requires that the total overhead cost be detailed according to individual items. Only in this way can management determine which overhead costs are under control and which need more attention.

The variable overhead efficiency variance can be based on direct labor hours, direct labor dollars (direct labor cost), or machine hours. This variance is a direct result of efficiency or inefficiency in direct labor or use of machinery. When units are used as a base for applying variable overhead, there is no variable overhead efficiency variance.

The variable overhead spending variance is the result of the firm's having spent more or less on overhead items than allowed on the basis of actual units of input, such as direct labor hours. Management is interested in a detailed analysis of the spending variance so that it can see those specific items that may be problem areas.

Under absorption costing, the fixed overhead total variance consists of a budget variance and a volume variance. The total variance represents the difference between fixed overhead budgeted and fixed overhead applied. An unfavorable volume variance does not represent more cost's having been incurred than should have been; nor does a favorable volume variance represent a reduction in cost. Rather, the volume variance represents the difference between the amount budgeted and the amount of cost charged to work-in-process inventory (through the application process).

A standard cost system is a means for charging production with standard costs. Work-in-process inventory is charged for the standard cost of direct material and direct labor. In addition, the variable and fixed overhead application rates are used to determine the overhead charge to work-in-process inventory. The rates are multiplied by the standard hours allowed for the flexible budget. Any variances from standard for material, labor, or overhead are isolated. The appendix to this chapter illustrates the procedures for using a standard cost system, including the recording of variances in separate accounts.

Appendix: Record Keeping for a Standard Cost System	The chapter described a standard cost system. This appendix illustrates the record-keeping process by which manufacturing costs are charged to production at standard. The illustration uses a hypothetical example of the Wiggins Company, whose standard costs are as follows:

	Unit Cost
Direct Material (2 Pounds per Unit at $.60 per Pound):	$1.20
Direct Labor (1/2 Hour per Unit at $7 per Hour):	3.50
Variable Factory Overhead (1/2 Hour per Unit at $.80 per Hour):	.40
Total Variable Cost per Unit:	$5.10
Fixed Factory Overhead (1/2 Hour per Unit at $2 per Hour):	1.00
Total Standard Cost per Unit:	$6.10

The fixed factory overhead rate of $2 per hour is based on the company's estimate of $50,000 of total fixed factory overhead and 25,000 direct labor hours ($50,000 ÷ 25,000 DLH = $2 per DLH). To illustrate the system, the appendix presents a series of summary entries for the year along with explanations. Although the company's master budget had predicted sales of 50,000 units, the company produced and sold only 46,000 units.

Entry 1: Purchase of Raw Material The company purchased 110,000 pounds of raw materials at $.63 per pound. The entry is:

Raw Materials Inventory	66,000	
Material Price Variance	3,300	
Accounts Payable		69,300

The variance calculation is:

110,000	Pounds Purchased
×$.03	Cost per Pound above Standard
$3,300	U

Notice that raw materials inventory is debited for $66,000, the total standard cost of material purchased (110,000 pounds × $.60). The material price variance of $3,300 is shown as a debit. In effect, the actual cost of $69,300 exceeded the standard cost of $66,000 by $3,300. The debit to material price variance reflects this increase in cost. The credit of $69,300 to accounts payable represents the actual cost of the amount purchased, and therefore the amount owed (110,000 pounds × $.63).

Entry 2: Use of Direct Material In producing 46,000 finished units, the company actually used 91,500 pounds of direct material. The standard quantity allowed for the flexible budget is 92,000 pounds (46,000 units × 2 pounds per unit). The entry is:

Work-in-Process Inventory	55,200	
Material Usage Variance		300
Raw Materials Inventory		54,900

The variance calculation is:

92,000	Pounds Standard Quantity Allowed
91,500	Pounds Actually Used
500	Pounds Used under Standard
×$.60	Standard Price
$300.00	F

The debit to work-in-process inventory is for $55,200, the standard cost of the standard quantity allowed for 46,000 units (92,000 pounds × $.60). The credit to material usage variance represents a reduction in cost because the amount used was less than required by standard. The credit to raw materials inventory represents the standard cost of the actual pounds of raw material taken from the inventory (91,500 pounds × $.60 per pound).

Entry 3: Incurrence of Direct Labor Costs The company used 23,500 direct labor hours at a cost of $165,000 in producing 46,000 finished units. The entry is:

Work-in-Process Inventory	161,000	
Labor Efficiency Variance	3,500	
Labor Rate Variance	500	
Accrued Payroll		165,000

The variance calculations are:

Labor Efficiency

23,500	Actual Hours
23,000	Standard Hours Allowed
500	Hours over Standard Hours Allowed
×$7	Standard Rate per Hour
$3,500	U

Labor Rate

$165,000	Actual Cost Incurred
164,500	Actual Hours × Standard Rate (23,500 Hours × $7)
$ 500	U

Work-in-process inventory is debited for the standard cost of direct labor based on the standard hours allowed for 46,000 units—23,000 hours (1/2 hour per unit × 46,000 units). At a standard cost of $7 per hour, the debit totals $161,000 (23,000 hours × $7 per hour). The amount actually paid to workers is shown as a credit to accrued payroll for $165,000. In this case, both labor variances are unfavorable, so they are shown as debits. In effect, this increases the direct labor cost over the amount recorded at standard. If either of the labor variances had been favorable, it would be shown as a credit in the entry.

Entry 4: Application of Variable Overhead The variable factory overhead application rate is $.80 per hour. Under a standard cost system, variable factory overhead is charged to work in process on the basis of the standard hours allowed for the flexible budget. As described above, 23,000 standard direct labor hours are allowed for 46,000 units. The entry is:

Work-in-Process Inventory	18,400	
Variable Factory Overhead		18,400

Work-in-Process Inventory is debited for $18,400, the standard cost of variable factory overhead (23,000 DLH × $.80 per hour). The credit to variable factory overhead is for the same amount.

Entry 5: Incurrence of Variable Overhead During the year, the company incurred the following variable factory overhead costs: indirect material, $4,000; utilities, $3,150; indirect labor, $11,500. The entry is:

Variable Factory Overhead	18,650	
Raw Materials Inventory		4,000
Utilities Payable		3,150
Accrued Payroll		11,500

The debit to variable factory overhead for $18,650 is for the actual costs incurred. The credits represent the individual cost items.

Entries 4 and 5 represent the typical entries for applying and incurring variable overhead costs. After making Entries 4 and 5, you can compute the total underapplied or overapplied variable overhead as follows:

$18,650	Actual Cost Incurred
18,400	Applied
$ 250	U (Underapplied)

The $250 underapplied overhead represents the total variable overhead variance and is $250 unfavorable. Under a standard cost system, we want to determine the specific elements of the underapplication and record the appropriate variances. That is done in the next entry.

Entry 6: Recognition of Variable Overhead Variances Since variable factory overhead is applied on the basis of direct labor hours, the information given for Entry 3 provides the basis for calculating the variable overhead variances. These variances are recorded, and the variable factory overhead account is closed out. The entry is:

Variable Overhead Efficiency Variance   400
    Variable Overhead Spending Variance   150
    Variable Factory Overhead   250

The variance calculations are:

Overhead Efficiency

23,500	Actual Hours
23,000	Standard Hours Allowed
500	Hours over Standard Hours Allowed
×$.80	Standard Rate per Hour
$400	U

Spending

$18,650	Actual Cost Incurred
18,800	Actual Hours × Standard Rate (23,500 Hours × $.80)
$ 150	F

If a standard cost system were not used, the difference between variable factory overhead applied and variable factory overhead incurred would be adjusted directly to cost of goods sold, as was done in Chapter 3. Here, however, we calculate the overhead efficiency variance and the overhead spending variance separately and record them. The overhead efficiency variance is unfavorable—overhead costs were increased because of this variance. It is reflected as a debit. The variable overhead spending variance is favorable; so it represents a reduction in overhead costs and is recorded as a credit. In a later entry, these variances will be closed to cost of goods sold.

Entry 7: Application of Fixed Overhead Fixed factory overhead is applied at the rate of $2 per direct labor hour. Since we are using a standard cost system, fixed overhead is applied on the basis of standard hours allowed for the flexible budget. This was shown earlier as 23,000 direct labor hours. The entry is:

Work-in-Process Inventory   46,000
        Fixed Factory Overhead   46,000

The debit to work-in-process inventory is $46,000 (23,000 hours × $2 per hour). This entry is the typical one for applying fixed factory overhead, whether or not a standard cost system is being used.

Entry 8: Incurrence of Fixed Overhead The company incurred fixed factory overhead costs as follows: depreciation on plant and equipment, $12,000; supervisors' and managers' salaries, $40,000. The entry is:

Fixed Factory Overhead   52,000
        Accumulated Depreciation   12,000
        Accrued Payroll   40,000

This is a typical entry for recording the actual fixed overhead costs incurred.

At this point, the amount of fixed overhead costs underapplied or overapplied can be determined as follows:

$52,000   Actual Cost Incurred
 46,000   Applied
$ 6,000   U (Underapplied)

Under a standard cost system, the $6,000 underapplied fixed factory over-
head represents the total fixed factory overhead variance of $6,000 unfavor-
able.

Entry 9: Recognition of Fixed Overhead Variances Based on the data given,
the volume variance and budget variance can be calculated and recorded.
The entry is:

Fixed Overhead Volume Variance   4,000
Fixed Overhead Budget Variance   2,000
    Fixed Factory Overhead   6,000

The variance calculations are:

Volume
   $50,000   Budgeted Fixed Overhead
    46,000   Applied
   $ 4,000   U

Budget
   $52,000   Actual Cost Incurred
    50,000   Budgeted Fixed Overhead
   $ 2,000   U

If a standard cost system had not been used, the difference between fixed
overhead applied and fixed overhead incurred would have been shown as a
debit to cost of goods sold. Under a standard cost system, however, we wish
to know the components of the total underapplication. They are calculated
above as a $4,000 volume variance and a $2,000 budget variance. These
amounts are recorded as debits, because they represent increases in total
cost over the amount applied. They will be closed to cost of goods sold in a
later entry.

Entry 10: Transfer of Completed Units As previously mentioned, the company sold 46,000 units. The entry to transfer the cost of units completed
from work-in-process inventory to finished goods inventory is:

Finished Goods Inventory   280,600
    Work-in-Process Inventory   280,600

The manufacturing costs charged to work-in-process inventory have all been
at standard. Therefore, the cost of finished goods transferred out of work-
in-process inventory must also be at standard. The standard cost per finished unit is $6.10. The total cost of goods transferred from work-in-process
inventory is $280,600 (46,000 units × $6.10 per unit).

Entry 11: Sale of Product The selling price per unit is $10. Entry 11 records
the sale of 46,000 finished goods for $460,000. An entry is also needed to
record cost of goods sold. The entries are:

Cost of Goods Sold	280,600	
Finished Goods Inventory		280,600
Accounts Receivable	460,000	
Sales		460,000

Cost of goods sold is debited for $280,600, the standard cost of finished goods that have been sold (46,000 units × $6.10 per unit); and finished goods inventory is credited for the same amount. Accounts receivable is debited for $460,000, and sales is credited. Instead of two separate entries, the data above could be recorded in one compound entry.

Entry 12: Closing Out of Variances The variances from standard may be either allocated to appropriate accounts or adjusted to cost of goods sold. Unless the amount is significant and would distort the financial statements, the usual procedure is to adjust the variances to cost of goods sold. In effect, the variance accounts are closed out. Therefore, variances with debit balances are credited for their balance and variances with credit balances are debited for their balance. The entry is:

Cost of Goods Sold	13,250	
Material Usage Variance	300	
Variable Overhead Spending Variance	150	
Material Price Variance		3,300
Labor Efficiency Variance		3,500
Labor Rate Variance		500
Variable Overhead Efficiency Variance		400
Fixed Overhead Volume Variance		4,000
Fixed Overhead Budget Variance		2,000

There were only two favorable variances—material usage and variable overhead spending. They totaled $450. The unfavorable variances totaled $13,700. Therefore, cost of goods sold is debited (increased) by the net unfavorable variance of $13,250 ($13,700 − $450).

For external reporting purposes, variances are not shown on the income statement. The net variance is adjusted to cost of goods sold. Therefore, cost of goods sold on the income statement reflects the total cost of goods sold, including any adjustment for variances. Internally, management prepares income statements using the contribution margin approach and variable costing. On these internal statements, the net variance is shown so that management can see the total effect of deviations from standard. The individual variance calculations are reflected in performance reports. For Wiggins Company, a contribution approach income statement for the year ended 19X6 is shown as Exhibit 7.9.

Notice that variable cost of goods sold has been increased by the net unfavorable variable cost variances of $7,250. Fixed costs have been increased by the net unfavorable fixed overhead of $6,000. Thus, the income statement reflects the actual costs incurred by the company but indicates to management how these actual costs differed from standard.

Another interesting point is that the company has used absorption costing for recording its costs and therefore has the appropriate information to prepare the income statement on an absorption costing basis for external purposes. Yet, the accounting system has also provided data so that an income

Exhibit 7.9 Income Statement Based on Standard Costs

Wiggins Company
Income Statement
for the Year Ended December 31, 19X6

Sales			$460,000
Variable Costs:			
Cost of Goods Sold (at Variable Standard Cost)	$234,600[a]		
Add: Net Unfavorable Variable Cost Variances.	7,250[b]		
Cost of Goods Sold		$241,850	
Selling and Administrative Expenses		69,000	
Total Variable Costs.			310,850
Contribution Margin			$149,150
Fixed Costs:			
Factory Overhead (at Standard)	$ 46,000		
Add: Net Unfavorable Fixed Overhead Variances	6,000[c]		
Total Factory Overhead		$ 52,000	
Selling and Administrative Expenses		80,000	
Total Fixed Costs			132,000
Net Income			$ 17,150

[a]$5.10 per unit × 46,000 units = $234,600.
[b]Variable Cost Variances:

Unfavorable:			
Material Price Variance		$3,300	
Labor Efficiency Variance		3,500	
Labor Rate Variance		500	
Overhead Efficiency Variance		400	
Total Unfavorable			$7,700
Favorable:			
Material Usage Variance		$ 300	
Overhead Spending Variance		150	
Total Favorable			450
Net Unfavorable Variances			$7,250

[c]Fixed Cost Variances (All Unfavorable):

Volume Variance		$4,000	
Budget Variance		2,000	
Net Unfavorable Variances		$6,000	

statement using a variable costing basis can be easily prepared. This point illustrates that no conflict need be involved in using absorption costing for external purposes and variable costing for internal purposes.

Review Problem

Problem
Travis Manufacturing Company budgeted production of 40,000 units for June. Actual production totaled 42,000 units and required 21,350 direct labor hours. One-half hour per finished unit is the standard allowed. Fixed

factory overhead was budgeted at $50,000. Overhead application rates per direct labor hour were $2.50 (fixed) and $.90 (variable). Actual overhead costs incurred were $51,500 (fixed) and $19,300 (variable).

Required:
Calculate the following variances:
a. Efficiency, spending, and total variable overhead variances.
b. Budget, volume, and total fixed overhead variances.

Solution
a.

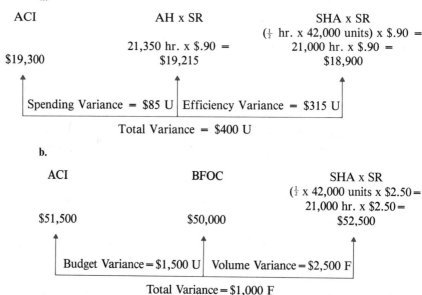

ACI	AH x SR	SHA x SR
		($\frac{1}{2}$ hr. x 42,000 units) x $.90 =
	21,350 hr. x $.90 =	21,000 hr. x $.90 =
$19,300	$19,215	$18,900

Spending Variance = $85 U   Efficiency Variance = $315 U

Total Variance = $400 U

b.

ACI	BFOC	SHA x SR
		($\frac{1}{2}$ x 42,000 units x $2.50 =
		21,000 hr. x $2.50 =
$51,500	$50,000	$52,500

Budget Variance = $1,500 U   Volume Variance = $2,500 F

Total Variance = $1,000 F

Questions

7-1 Why is it important to analyze individual items of variable factory overhead?

7-2 A portion of a departmental performance report for variable overhead prepared on a flexible budget basis is shown below:

	Budget	**Actual**	**Variance**
Maintenance	$10,000	$ 5,000	$5,000 F
Utilities	10,000	15,000	5,000 U

The foreman was heard to say, "Everything else was within 1% or 2% of budget, and the maintenance and utilities variances offset each other. So there's no problem." Do you agree with that statement? Explain.

7-3 Name four bases that can be used for applying variable factory overhead.

7-4 In a highly automated manufacturing company, what is probably the most appropriate base to use in applying variable overhead? Why?

7-5 Since an unfavorable material usage variance indicates possible waste in the use of direct material, and since an unfavorable labor efficiency variance indicates possible waste in the use of direct labor, why doesn't an unfavorable variable overhead efficiency variance indicate possible waste in the use of overhead items? Where is such waste indicated? Explain.

7-6 Explain why there is no variable overhead efficiency variance when units are used as the basis for applying variable overhead.

7-7 Why is fixed overhead a problem in a standard cost system?

7-8 Which fixed overhead variance reflects that more was spent on fixed overhead items than was planned?

7-9 A manufacturing division foreman, upon looking at a performance report that showed a $40,000 unfavorable fixed overhead volume variance, was heard to say, "This is outrageous! This overspending has got to stop!" Comment.

7-10 Why is there no fixed overhead volume variance when variable costing is used?

7-11 If a firm consistently has a significant unfavorable fixed overhead volume variance, would it be appropriate to increase the fixed overhead application rate? Explain.

7-12 How does a standard cost system differ from an actual/normal cost system? How are they similar?

7-13 How does a standard cost system make the journal entry process for cost accounting easier?

7-14 How does a standard cost system help in taking a physical inventory?

Exercises

7-15 Variable Overhead Variances Clark Company developed the following variable overhead budget for expected production requiring 30,000 direct labor hours:

Indirect Material	$13,500
Indirect Labor	15,000
Utilities	6,000

Standard hours allowed for actual production were 38,000 direct labor hours. Actual costs were: indirect material, $18,000; indirect labor, $20,500; and utilities, $8,000. Determine the variable overhead variances, based on the flexible budget.

7-16 Variable Overhead Variances; Preparing Performance Reports Thompson Tent Company applies variable overhead at the following rates per direct labor hour:

Supplies	$ .85
Indirect Labor	1.00
Power	.40
Total	$2.25

The standard direct labor efficiency standard is 1 1/2 hours per tent. In March, the company produced 10,000 tents using 16,000 direct labor hours. Actual variable overhead costs were: supplies, $14,000; indirect labor, $15,850; and power, $5,800.

    a. Calculate the spending variance, efficiency variance, and total variable overhead variance.

    b. Prepare a performance report for variable overhead, based on the flexible budget.

7-17 Variable Overhead Variances Tamber Manufacturing Company applies variable factory overhead at the rate of $3.50 per machine hour. Last month, production required 3,450 machine hours, when the standard hours allowed were 3,600 machine hours. Total variable overhead cost was $12,400. Calculate the following:

    a. Spending variance.

    b. Efficiency variance.

    c. Total variable overhead variance.

7-18 Variable Overhead Variances Madison Mop and Broom Company applies variable factory overhead at the rate of $1.75 per mop or broom. Last month, the company made 300 mops and 500 brooms. Total variable overhead was $1,550. Calculate all appropriate variable overhead variances.

7-19 Fixed Overhead Variances Barbara's Beauty Products Company applies fixed factory overhead at the rate of $4 per direct labor hour. The fixed overhead budget is $50,000 per month. The standard hours allowed for direct labor is $\frac{1}{2}$ hour per finished unit. Last month, the company produced 23,000 units, incurring fixed factory overhead costs of $48,500. Calculate the following fixed overhead variances:

    a. Budget variance.

    b. Volume variance.

    c. Total variance.

7-20 Fixed Overhead Variances Zingle Corporation budgeted fixed factory overhead in October at $80,000. It planned to produce 20,000 units but only produced 18,600. Fixed overhead is applied at the rate of $2 per direct labor hour; and the labor efficiency standard requires 2 hours per finished unit. Actual fixed overhead costs totaled $82,500. Calculate the fixed overhead:

    a. Budget variance.

    b. Volume variance.

    c. Total variance.

7-21 Fixed Overhead Variances Benson Book Company incurred $218,000 of fixed overhead costs in the first quarter of the year. It produced 155,000 books—5,000 more than budgeted. The fixed overhead application rate is $1.50 per book. Calculate the following fixed overhead variances:

    a. Budget variance.

    b. Volume variance.

    c. Total variance.

7-22 Variable and Fixed Overhead Variances Information on Fire Company's overhead costs is as follows:

Actual Variable Overhead:	$73,000
Actual Fixed Overhead:	$17,000
Standard Hours Allowed for Actual Production:	32,000
Standard Variable Overhead Rate per Direct Labor Hour:	$2.50
Standard Fixed Overhead Rate per Direct Labor Hour:	$.50

Calculate the *total* overhead variance, to include variable and fixed. (AICPA adapted)

7-23 Volume Variance Information on Ripley Company's overhead costs for the January 19X1 production activity is as follows:

Budgeted Fixed Overhead:	$75,000
Standard Fixed Overhead Rate per Direct Labor Hour:	$3
Standard Variable Overhead Rate per Direct Labor Hour:	$6
Standard Direct Labor Hours Allowed for Actual Production:	24,000
Actual Total Overhead Incurred:	$220,000

Ripley has a standard absorption and flexible budgeting system. Calculate the volume variance for January 19X1. (AICPA adapted)

7-24 Variable and Fixed Overhead Variances Strope Company budgeted fixed factory overhead cost at $50,000 a month. Fixed factory overhead is applied at the rate of $2 per direct labor hour, and variable at $3 per direct labor hour. Standard direct labor hours allowed for July production were 18,000. The variable overhead spending variance was $2,000 favorable, with actual variable overhead costs of $67,000 incurred. Actual fixed overhead costs totaled $51,000. Calculate the following:

a. Fixed overhead budget variance.

b. Fixed overhead volume variance.

c. Variable overhead efficiency variance.

7-25 Calculating Data from Variances The following information relates to a given department of Herman Company for the fourth quarter of its most recently ended year:

Actual Total Overhead (Fixed and Variable):	$178,500
Overhead Budget Formula:	$110,000 + $.50 per Hour
Total (Combined) Overhead Application Rate:	$1.50 per Hour
Budget and Spending Variances (Combined):	$8,000 U
Volume Variance:	$5,000 U

a. Calculate the standard hours allowed for finished units completed in this department during the quarter.

b. Calculate the actual hours worked in this department during the quarter. (AICPA adapted)

7-26 Standard Cost System Journal Entries (*Appendix*) On March 1, Kay Company purchased 5,000 gallons of raw materials on account for $12,750 and used 3,500 gallons in producing 6,700 finished units. The material standards are $2.50 per gallon for price and 1/2 gallon per finished unit for usage. Prepare journal entries to record these transactions.

7-27 Standard Cost System Journal Entries (*Appendix*) Wilbur Company used 15,400 direct labor hours at a cost of $94,000 in producing 62,000 finished units. The labor standards are $6 per hour for rate and 1/4 hour per finished unit for efficiency. Prepare journal entries to record these transactions. Use April 30 as the date.

7-28 Standard Cost System Journal Entries (*Appendix*) Rocky Company applies variable factory overhead at the rate of $1.20 per direct labor hour and fixed factory overhead at the rate of $.50 per direct labor hour. In June, standard hours allowed for production totaled 41,000; actual hours totaled 42,000. The total overhead variances were $2,800 unfavorable (variable) and $1,200 unfavorable (fixed). Budgeted fixed overhead was $20,000. Prepare journal entries to record these transactions, including the variances. Use June 30 as the date. (*Note:* Credit "various accounts" in recording overhead costs incurred.)

Problems

7-29 Variable and Fixed Overhead Variances Saturn Manufacturing Company budgeted 25,000 units for March but produced only 23,500 units, using 72,000 direct labor hours. Fixed factory overhead was budgeted at $225,000 and applied at the rate of $3.00 per hour; and variable factory overhead was applied at the rate of $1.50 per hour. Standard hours allowed were 3 per finished unit. Total actual costs incurred were $220,000 (fixed) and $110,000 (variable).

Required:
   Calculate the following overhead variances:
   a. Spending.
   b. Efficiency.
   c. Budget.
   d. Volume.

7-30 Variable and Fixed Overhead Variances Bow Wow Dog Food Company planned production of 100,000 cases of dog food in October. Standard time allowed is one-half hour per case; and overhead is applied on the basis of direct labor hours. Fixed overhead for October was budgeted at $150,000 and variable overhead at $25,000. The company produced 95,000 cases in 48,000 hours at a total overhead cost of $175,000. There was no budget variance.

Required:
   Calculate the following overhead variances:
   a. Spending.
   b. Efficiency.
   c. Volume.

7-31 Variable and Fixed Overhead Variances Choo-Choo Spike and Rail Manufacturing Company has developed the following standard costs for its railroad spikes:

$$\text{Variable: } \$2 \text{ per Hour} \times \frac{1}{4} \text{ Hour per Unit} = \$.50$$

$$\text{Fixed: } \quad \$5 \text{ per Hour} \times \frac{1}{4} \text{ Hour per Unit} = \$1.25$$

Normal monthly volume is 20,000 spikes. In April, 22,000 spikes were produced in 5,300 hours at a total overhead cost of $36,300, of which $11,500 was variable.

Required:

Calculate the following overhead variances:

a. Spending.

b. Efficiency.

c. Budget.

d. Volume.

7–32 Variable and Fixed Overhead Variances The Generator Division of Machine Specialty Corporation has a budgeted output of 1,000 generators per month. Fixed factory overhead is budgeted at $600,000 per year and is applied on the basis of units produced. There are 2 types of variable overhead, both based on annual budgeted output. One type of variable overhead is budgeted at $420,000 for the year and applied on the basis of units produced, while the other is budgeted at $240,000 for the year and applied on the basis of machine hours. The standard allowance for machine hours is 4 per unit produced.

During June, the division produced 930 generators, using 3,800 machine hours. Fixed overhead was $52,000. Unit-based variable overhead totaled $33,000; and machine-hour-based variable overhead totaled $18,700.

Required:

Calculate all appropriate overhead variances for June.

7–33 Variable and Fixed Overhead Variances Air, Inc., uses a standard cost system. Overhead cost information for Product CX for the month of October is as follows:

Total Actual Overhead Incurred:	$12,600
Fixed Overhead Budgeted:	$3,300
Total Variable Overhead Incurred:	$9,000
Total Standard Overhead Rate per Direct Labor Hour:	$4
Variable Overhead Rate per Direct Labor Hour:	$3
Variable Overhead Efficiency Variance:	$600 F
Standard Hours Allowed for Actual Production:	3,500

Required:

Calculate the following:

a. Budget variance.

b. Volume variance.

c. Actual hours worked.

d. Spending variance. (AICPA adapted)

7–34 Calculating All Standard Cost Variances Monroe Manufacturing Company budgeted production of 5,000 units in January but actually produced 5,200. Standard costs are as follows:

Direct material: 3 pounds per unit at $2 per pound.
Direct labor: 1 1/2 hours per unit at $6 per hour.
Variable factory overhead: $3 per direct labor hour.
Fixed factory overhead: $15,000 per month.

In January, production required 16,000 pounds of direct material that had been purchased for $2.15 per pound. The firm used 8,000 direct labor hours at a total cost of $46,500. Actual variable totaled $24,800, and fixed totaled $16,000.

Required:

Calculate all appropriate standard cost variances for January.

7-35 Calculating All Standard Cost Variances Drydaze Umbrella Company budgets production at 20,000 umbrellas per month. In August, however, it produced only 18,000. Standard unit costs are as follows:

Direct Material (1 1/2 Square Yards of Cloth at $2.50 per Yard):	$ 3.75
Direct Material (1 2-1/2-Foot Piece of Metal at $1.40 per Foot):	3.50
Direct Labor (1/4 Hour per Umbrella at $8 per Hour):	2.00
Variable Overhead (1/4 Hour per Umbrella at $3 per Hour):	.75
Fixed Overhead (1/4 Hour per Umbrella at $2 per Hour):	.50
Total Unit Cost:	$10.50

In August, the company purchased and used 28,300 yards of cloth at a cost of $2.45 per yard and 44,500 feet of metal at a cost of $1.50 per foot. Production required 4,700 direct labor hours at a total cost of $38,000. Total actual overhead costs were $14,000 for variable and $10,300 for fixed.

Required:

Calculate all appropriate standard cost variances for August.

7-36 Supplying Missing Data Overhead data for 3 independent cases is provided below, with unknown amounts indicated by letters.

	Case A	Case B	Case C
Budgeted Activity in Direct Labor Hours	5,000	i	q
Standard Hours Allowed for Finished Production	a	9,500	1,050
Actual Hours Worked	4,500	j	r
Variable Overhead Rate per Direct Labor Hour	$.40	k	$.20
Variable Overhead Applied	b	$19,000	s
Fixed Overhead Applied	c	l	t
Budgeted Fixed Overhead Cost	d	$5,000	$600
Variable Overhead Spending Variance	$200 U	m	$30 U
Variable Overhead Efficiency Variance	$40 F	$600 U	u
Total Variable Overhead Variance	e	$500 U	$40 U
Fixed Overhead Budget Variance	f	0	$20 F
Fixed Overhead Volume Variance	$600 U	n	$30 F
Total Fixed Overhead Variance	g	$250 U	v
Actual Variable Overhead Cost Incurred	h	o	w
Actual Fixed Overhead Cost Incurred	$7,200	p	x

Required:

Supply the missing data for each case.

7-37 Calculating All Standard Cost Variances The Carberg Corporation manufactures and sells a single product and uses a standard cost system. The standard cost per unit of product is shown below:

Direct Material (1 Pound Plastic at $2 per Pound): $ 2.00
Direct Labor (1.6 Hours at $4 per Hour):   6.40
Variable Overhead Cost: 3.00
Fixed Overhead Cost: 1.45
$12.85

The overhead cost per unit was calculated from the following annual over-head cost budget for a 60,000-unit volume:

Variable Overhead Cost:
    Indirect Labor (30,000 Hours at $4 per Hour): $120,000
    Supplies—Oil (60,000 Gallons at $.50 per Gallon):   30,000
    Allocated Variable Service Department Costs: 30,000
        Total Variable Overhead Cost: $180,000

Fixed Overhead Cost:
    Supervision: $ 27,000
    Depreciation: 45,000
    Other Fixed Costs: 15,000
        Total Fixed Overhead Cost: $ 87,000
Total Budged Annual Overhead Cost at 60,000 Units: $267,000

The charges to the manufacturing department for November, when 5,000 units were produced, are given below:

Direct Material (5,300 Pounds at $2 per Pound): $10,600
Direct Labor (8,200 Hours at $4.10 per Hour):   33,620
Indirect Labor (2,400 Hours at $4.10 per Hour):   9,840
Supplies—Oil (6,000 Gallons at $.55 per Gallon):   3,300
Allocated Variable Service Department Costs: 3,200
Supervision: 2,475
Depreciation: 3,750
Other: 1,250
    Total: $68,035

The purchasing department normally buys about the same quantity as is used in production during a month. In November, 5,200 pounds were purchased at a price of $2.10 per pound.

Required:
    Calculate the following variances from standard costs:
    a. Material price.
    b. Material usage.
    c. Direct labor rate.
    d. Direct labor efficiency.
    e. Spending.
    f. Budget.
    g. Volume. (CMA adapted)

7–38 Calculating Data from Standard Cost Variances On May 1, Bovar Company began the manufacturing of a new mechanical device known as

"Dandy." The company installed a standard cost system to be used in accounting for manufacturing costs. The standard costs for a unit of Dandy are as follows:

Raw Materials (6 Pounds at $1 per Pound):	$ 6
Direct Labor (1 Hour at $4 per Hour):	4
Overhead (Combined) (75% of Direct Labor Cost):	3
	$13

The following data were obtained from Bovar's records for the month of May:

Units of Dandy Produced:	4,000
Units of Dandy Sold:	2,500
Sales and Cost Data:	
Sales	$50,000
Purchases (26,000 Pounds)	27,300
Material Price Variance	1,300 U
Material Quantity Variance	1,000 U
Direct Labor Rate Variance	760 U
Direct Labor Efficiency Variance	800 F
Manufacturing Overhead Total Variance	500 U

The amount shown above for material price variance is applicable to raw material purchased during May.

Required:

Compute each of the following for Bovar for the month of May:

a. Standard quantity of raw materials allowed (in pounds).
b. Actual quantity of raw materials used (in pounds).
c. Standard hours allowed.
d. Actual hours worked.
e. Actual direct labor rate.
f. Actual total overhead. (AICPA adapted)

7-39 Calculating All Standard Cost Variances The Bronson Company manufactures a fuel additive that has a stable selling price of $40 per drum. Since losing a government contract, the company has been producing and selling 80,000 drums per month, 50% of normal capacity. Management expects to increase production to 140,000 drums in the coming fiscal year.

In connection with your examination of the financial statements of the Bronson Company for the year ended September 30, 19X4, you have been asked to review some computations made by Bronson's cost accountant. Your working papers disclose the following about the company's operations:

1. Standard costs per drum of product manufactured:

Materials: 8 Gallons Miracle Mix:	$16
1 Empty Drum:	1
	$17

Direct Labor—1 hour:	$5
Factory Overhead:	$6

2. Costs and expenses during September 19X4:

Miracle mix: 500,000 gallons purchased at a cost of $950,000; 650,000 gallons used.
Empty drums: 94,000 purchased at a cost of $94,000; 80,000 used.
Direct labor: 82,000 hours worked at a cost of $414,100.
Factory Overhead:

Depreciation of Building and Machinery (Fixed)	$210,000
Supervision and Indirect Labor (Semivariable)	460,000
Other Factory Overhead (Variable)	98,000
	$768,000

3. "Other factory overhead" was the only actual overhead cost that varied from the overhead budget for the September level of production; actual other factory overhead was $98,000, and the budgeted amount was $90,000.

Required:
Calculate the following variances:
a. Material price variance.
b. Material usage variance.
c. Labor rate variance.
d. Labor efficiency variance.
e. Combined budget and spending variance.
f. Volume variance. (AICPA adapted)

7–40 Standard Cost System Journal Entries and Income Statement (*Appendix*) Zimbo Company charges manufacturing costs to production at standard. Standard costs are as follows:

Direct Material (1/2 Gallon per Unit at $4 per Gallon):	$ 2.00
Direct Labor (1 Hour per Unit at $7.50 per Hour):	7.50
Variable Overhead (1 Hour per Unit at $2 per Hour):	2.00
Fixed Overhead (1 Hour per Unit at $.50 per Hour):	.50
Total Standard Cost per Unit:	$12.00

The fixed overhead rate of $.50 per hour is based on the company's estimate of $100,000 of total fixed factory overhead for the year and 200,000 direct labor hours. For 19X3, the master budget showed sales of 200,000 units. However, actual sales and production totaled 215,000 units. The following summary transactions occurred in 19X3:
1) Purchased 120,000 gallons of direct material at $4.08 per gallon on account.
2) Used 106,000 gallons of direct material in production.
3) Used 214,600 direct labor hours in production at a total cost of $1,620,000.
4) Applied variable factory overhead.
5) Incurred variable overhead as follows: Indirect material, $140,000; utilities, $100,000; indirect labor, $200,000.
6) Applied fixed factory overhead.
7) Incurred fixed overhead as follows: depreciation on plant and equipment, $40,000; supervisors' and managers' salaries, $65,000.
8) Recorded variable overhead variances.

9) Recorded fixed overhead variances.

10) Transferred finished product from work in process.

11) Recorded cost of goods sold. Recorded sales on account at $20 per unit.

Required:

a. Prepare journal entries to record the transactions above.

b. Assume variable selling and administrative expenses are $3 per unit and fixed selling and administrative expenses total $300,000 for the year. Prepare an income statement for the year ended December 31, 19X3, using the contribution margin approach. Show variances from standard cost.

Chapter 8   Responsibility Accounting and Performance Measurement

Learning Objectives

The purpose of this chapter is to provide you with an understanding of a system of responsibility accounting and to describe how managers' performance can be evaluated. The chapter also describes transfer pricing. Studying this chapter will enable you to:

1. Contrast a centralized firm with a decentralized firm.

2. Describe a responsibility accounting system.

3. Describe segment margin.

4. Distinguish among types of costs.

5. Describe the components of the return on investment calculation.

6. Calculate return on investment and residual income.

7. Distinguish among asset bases used in return on investment calculations.

8. Distinguish among transfer pricing techniques.

9. Calculate the effect of a particular transfer price on the income of a segment or of the firm.

10. Describe the human relations factors of performance evaluation.

Chapter Topics

The major topics included in this chapter are:

Centralization versus Decentralization
Responsibility Accounting
Measuring Segment Performance
Cost Terminology
Evaluation Techniques
Transfer Pricing
Goal Congruence, Motivation, and Human Relations

To this point, you have seen various techniques for gathering and reporting information internally. Previous chapters have discussed the importance of accounting information used by management to plan and control operations. The concept of responsibility accounting was mentioned briefly in previous chapters. In this chapter, we will look at this concept more closely. The chapter also focuses on specific ways in which the performance of management personnel can be evaluated. If a firm is to perform effectively, it must have a system by which managers who perform well are rewarded and managers who do not perform well are made aware of their deficiencies. This can be achieved by use of a system of responsibility accounting to highlight areas of good and poor performance.

The subject of transfer pricing also relates to managerial performance evaluation. The problems of transfer pricing, along with techniques that can be used in its application, are also considered in this chapter.

Centralization versus Decentralization

A **centralized** firm is one in which top management makes the decisions and middle and lower management merely follow them. In a highly centralized firm, middle and lower management have little authority; their primary responsibility is to follow the dictates of top management. In a **decentralized** firm, managers at the lower levels have more authority to make decisions regarding their particular operations. Therefore, they are responsible for the results of these decisions. There are degrees of centralization and decentralization, and most firms probably fall somewhere in the middle between highly centralized and highly decentralized.

A primary advantage of centralization is that it enables top management to be more sure that the goals of the company are adhered to. Also, lower-level managers who are not considered to be as competent as they should be pose a smaller risk when decisions are centralized.

Firms may consider a number of factors in determining whether to decentralize operations.[1] One major reason for decentralization is that it helps motivate lower-level managers. When given more authority, these managers feel more as if they were their own bosses (although, of course, they are not). Decentralized firms are often able to attract top managerial talent because operations are decentralized.

The degree of decentralization depends upon the individual firm. Several years ago, Sears, Roebuck and Company found it necessary to centralize certain operations that had been previously decentralized—the authority given individual store managers was greatly curtailed. It had been found that some managers were not acting in the best interests of the company. There was a lack of goal congruence, a topic described later in this chapter. For example, store managers often would not install budget apparel shop merchandise, because it offered smaller profit margins, even though budget departments were in line with the parent company's objectives. In some cases, the corporate buyer bought merchandise that was then rejected by store managers because its profit margin was too low. Yet, it would have been in the best interests of the overall company to sell the merchandise. These and other problems resulted in a tightening of the reins of store managers.[2]

[1]See Richard M. Hodgetts, *Management: Theory, Process, and Practice,* 3rd ed. (Hinsdale, Ill.: The Dryden Press, 1981), pp. 118–121.
[2]David M. Elsner, "Retailer's Recovery," *Wall Street Journal,* August 9, 1977, p. 1.

Responsibility Accounting

Responsibility accounting is a system under which managers are given decision-making authority and responsibility for each activity occurring within a specific area of the company.[3] Under a system of responsibility accounting, managers are made responsible for the activities of segments. As described in Chapter 1, these segments may be called departments, branches, divisions, or some similar designation. There is no particular significance in the title used; it depends upon the firm. The important point is that the manager is responsible for a segment, which is referred to as a **responsibility center.**

There are generally three types of responsibility centers: cost centers, profit centers, and investment centers. A **cost center** is a responsibility center whose manager is responsible for costs incurred by the segment. Cost centers do not generate revenue directly. Primary examples of cost centers are the responsibility centers found in manufacturing. For example, the foreman of a factory's painting department is responsible for the amount of paint used, for the cost of labor used, and perhaps for some of the variable overhead costs incurred by the department. When actual costs of the department differ from budgeted costs, the foreman must explain significant variances, as described in Chapters 6 and 7.

A segment that generates revenue is usually designated as a profit center. A **profit center** is a responsibility center whose manager is responsible for the amount of profit earned. Profit-center managers are therefore responsible for both revenues and costs. For example, the manager of the appliance department of a department store is responsible for earning a profit on the appliances sold. The department store itself may be an investment center.

An **investment center** is a responsibility center whose manager is responsible for earning a rate of return on the segment's investment in assets. (The manner in which this rate of return is calculated is described later.) Major segments of companies are normally investment centers. For example, individual grocery stores of a retail grocery chain, individual department stores of a department store chain, and major divisions of an automobile manufacturing firm may be investment centers.

Investment centers differ from profit centers in that an investment center is evaluated on the basis of the rate of return earned on the assets invested in the segment, while a profit center is concerned only with the excess of revenue over expenses for the period. Where practical, it is better to designate a segment as an investment center rather than a profit center in order to increase the usefulness of responsibility accounting. A segment earning a larger amount of profit than another segment is not necessarily performing better, because it may be using more assets to earn its larger profit.

A system of responsibility accounting uses the **management by exception** concept, under which management concentrates its time and efforts in exceptional (or problem) situations. In other words, in evaluating performance, management is concerned only with significant deviations from the plan.

---

[3]You may wish to refer to the discussion of authority and responsibility that was presented in Chapter 1.

An application of responsibility accounting and the management by exception concept is illustrated for Dixie Fair Food Stores, Inc., the company discussed in Chapter 1. Selected performance reports from three levels of operations of Dixie Fair Food Stores are shown in Exhibit 8.1.

Exhibit 8.1 Responsibility Accounting System

Store Operations
Operating Income Performance Report
for the Month Ended May 31, 19X3

	Budget	Actual	Variance	Percent Variance
Alabama	$1,200,000	$1,250,000	$50,000 F	+4.2%
Louisiana	1,500,000	1,539,000	39,000 F	+2.6
Mississippi	1,000,000	980,000	20,000 U	−2.0
Totals	$3,700,000	$3,769,000	$69,000 F	+1.9

Louisiana Operations
Operating Income Performance Report
for the Month Ended May 31, 19X3

	Budget	Actual	Variance	Percent Variance
Baton Rouge	$ 300,000	$ 309,000	$ 9,000 F	+3.0%
New Orleans	950,000	995,000	45,000 F	+4.7
Shreveport	250,000	235,000	15,000 U	−6.0
Totals	$1,500,000	$1,539,000	$39,000 F	+2.6

Baton Rouge Area Operations
Operating Income Performance Report
for the Month Ended May 31, 19X3

	Budget	Actual	Variance	Percent Variance
Store Number 1	$ 50,000	$ 52,000	$ 2,000 F	+ 4.0%
Store Number 2	80,000	75,000	5,000 U	− 6.3
Store Number 3	40,000	39,000	1,000 U	− 2.5
Store Number 4	70,000	80,000	10,000 F	+14.3
Store Number 5	60,000	63,000	3,000 F	+ 5.0
Totals	$300,000	$309,000	$ 9,000 F	+ 3.0

The area operations manager for Baton Rouge receives operating income figures on each of the five stores in his area (bottom of exhibit). The firm believes that actual operating income should generally be within 5 percent of the budget. The performance report shows that Store 2 is 6.3 percent below the budget. The area operations manager may ask the manager of Store 2 for more details on operations, in an effort to determine why actual income is less than budgeted income by more than 5 percent. Each store manager would have received a performance report on his or her individual store. Therefore, the store managers should already be aware of the problems pointed out by the report. The store performance reports may have included detailed information regarding each of the departments.

Store 4 has exceeded the budget by 14.3 percent. This performance is probably regarded as favorable; nevertheless, the area operations manager will be interested in knowing how Store 4 has managed to outperform the other stores by as much as it has. It may be a sign of good, efficient management. Of course, it is always possible that the original budget for Store 4 was unrealistically low.

Typically, performance reports show the year-to-date information along with the current month's, to provide management with an understanding of how the segments are doing for the whole year. In some instances, unfavorable variances in one month may be more than offset by favorable variances in other months. Therefore, year-to-date information provides a perspective on operations throughout the whole year. Under the management by exception concept, the Baton Rouge area operations manager would probably not inquire too much into the operations of Stores 1, 3, and 5, since they fell within the 5-percent tolerance established by management.

The manager of Louisiana operations receives a performance report for all the area operations under his supervision. Exhibit 8.1 shows this performance report (middle of exhibit). Louisiana operations exceeded its operating income budget by 2.6 percent. In looking at the three areas, however, the manager notes that the Shreveport area failed to meet its budget by 6 percent. The Louisiana operations manager would naturally inquire more into the Shreveport area operations than operations of areas that have smaller deviations. This illustrates the meaning of the management by exception concept. Without a performance report, the area manager might spend equal time on all areas, which might mean wasting time on two areas and not spending enough time on the Shreveport area.

The vice-president of store operations receives a performance report (top of exhibit) showing that all states exceeded the budgeted operating income by 1.9 percent. Looking at the performance report, you can see that Alabama and Louisiana exceeded the budget by 4.2 percent and 2.6 percent, respectively, while Mississippi failed to meet the budget by 2 percent. In no instance was the variance more than 5 percent of the budget. Therefore, under management by exception, it appears that no area requires attention. Therefore, it is unlikely that the vice-president for store operations will inquire any more deeply into the operations of any of the states.

The president of the company receives a performance report (not shown) from the vice-president of store operations showing that stores have exceeded the profit goals by 1.9 percent. Since this is within the 5 percent range, it is unlikely that the president will make any specific inquiries into store operations. The president also receives performance reports from the other vice-presidents. The nature of these performance reports, however, differs from those received from the vice-president of store operations. The vice-president of finance and the vice-president of personnel have no revenue-producing activities; they most likely submit performance reports showing only budgeted costs and actual costs. Thus, they are responsibile for cost centers. The vice-president for transportation is probably also responsible for a cost center. However, the president is likely to require other information regarding transportation—for example, the effectiveness of transportation management, which may be measured in terms of on-time deliveries. The vice-president for purchasing is most likely responsible for insuring that the appropriate types of products are purchased at the appropriate time so that stores have what they need to sell. Purchasing and transportation must be coordinated in order to insure timely delivery of products to stores. Problems with either transportation or purchasing may be reflected in the individual store variances. For example, if a particular store has difficulty in obtaining the products it needs on a timely basis, its sales may decline. This situation might explain an operating income variance of a particular store.

The responsibility accounting system presented in Exhibit 8.1 shows only operating income performance. However, performance reports may include more detail regarding revenues and costs as well. In some instances, the segments may be investment centers. Management might be interested in the total number of customers as well. The point is that under the concept of management by exception, management can require whatever information it needs in order to make decisions about operations and will look most closely at operations that significantly deviate from standards.

Measuring Segment Performance

Responsibility accounting requires a knowledge of how well a segment has performed. This section illustrates how segment data should be presented in order that meaningful decisions regarding segment performance can be made. Our concern here is with the use of segment data for internal decision making. However, you should be aware that there is an external reporting requirement regarding segments.

External Reporting   *FASB Statement No. 14* requires that firms subject to FASB pronouncements provide certain segment information in external financial statements.[4] Because of this standard, users of these statements now have more information regarding operations of a firm. However, the segment information required by *FASB Statement No. 14* is much less detailed than that needed by management for making decisions about the internal operations of the firm. For example, *FASB Statement No. 14* requires industry segment information. General Motors considers itself to be in the transportation

---

[4]"Financial Reporting for Segments of a Business Enterprise," *Statement of Financial Accounting Standards No. 14* (Stamford, Conn.: Financial Accounting Standards Board, December 1976).

industry. Therefore, for external purposes, in its annual report to stockholders, GM presents all data regarding the transportation products it produces as a single amount. For internal purposes, however, General Motors needs information regarding each of its divisions, such as Chevrolet and Cadillac. Its internal needs for segment information are greater and require more detail than its requirements for external reporting.

Another problem with the FASB external reporting requirement is that, in arriving at segment profitability under the FASB statement, firms may allocate certain costs that should not be allocated for internal decision making. As described later in this chapter, such allocations tend to distort the real picture and may lead to erroneous decisions.

You should be aware of the external reporting requirement so that you can better understand information presented in financial statements. However, realize that there is no necessary relationship between the requirements for external reporting and the need for internal reporting. The information presented differs in type and in format between the two needs.

Cost Allocation

A manager's performance is evaluated to a large extent on the basis of comparison of costs incurred with costs budgeted. It is therefore important to determine the appropriate costs to be charged to the segments being measured. Problems often arise in this process because of the way costs are allocated to segments.

Chapter 14 describes means for allocating costs to production, as required under generally accepted accounting principles. Furthermore, many defense contractors are required by law to allocated certain costs to segments. However, as discussed below, a problem arises when the results of these allocation procedures are used internally to arrive at costs that are used as a basis for evaluating management performance.

Segment Margin

One means of measuring a segment's performance is to determine its profitability based on **segment margin**—the difference between the segment's revenue and its direct costs. Segment margin represents the amount of income that has been earned by the particular segment. An illustration of segment performance based on this margin is shown for Savemore Stores in Exhibit 8.2.

If the president of Savemore Stores considers each branch a profit center, segment performance is measured by the amount of segment margin produced by each branch. Rate of return on sales might also be considered. Branch A has a rate of return on sales of 8.3 percent ($25,000 ÷ $300,000), and Branch B has a rate of return on sales of 8.8 percent ($35,000 ÷ $400,000). The method for evaluating the branches as investment centers is described later.

At this point, it is important to understand how segment margin is calculated. The amount of segment margin, whether looked at in total or as a percentage of sales, has a direct effect on the evaluation of performance. In determining segment margin, we subtract only those costs incurred directly for the benefit of each branch. Notice that home office expenses are not allocated to each branch. Instead, they are subtracted from the total seg-

Exhibit 8.2 Segment Performance

Savemore Stores
Income Statement
for the Year Ended December 31, 19X3

	Branch A	Branch B	Company Total
Sales	$ 300,000	$ 400,000	$ 700,000
Cost of Goods Sold	(180,000)	(250,000)	(430,000)
Variable Selling and Administrative Expenses	(30,000)	(35,000)	(65,000)
Contribution Margin.	$ 90,000	$ 115,000	$ 205,000
Fixed Selling and Administrative Expenses	(65,000)	(80,000)	(145,000)
Segment Margin	$ 25,000	$ 35,000	$ 60,000
Home Office Expenses			(21,000)
Net Income.			$ 39,000

ment margin of $60,000. Frequently, home office expenses are allocated to branches, based on sales. If home office expenses were allocated on that basis in this case, each branch would be charged as follows:

$$\text{Branch A: } \frac{\$300,000}{\$700,000} \times \$21,000 = \$ 9,000$$

$$\text{Branch B: } \frac{\$400,000}{\$700,000} \times \$21,000 = \underline{\$12,000}$$

$$\text{Total} \qquad \qquad \qquad \qquad \underline{\underline{\$21,000}}$$

You can see immediately that Branch B's segment margin would be reduced by more than Branch A's simply because branch B had more sales. Yet, the $12,000 charged to Branch B is in no way related to the amount of sales of Branch B. Savemore incurred $21,000 of expenses in the operation of the company as a whole. Logically, that amount should not be allocated based on the amount of sales of either branch.

To further illustrate the fallacy of allocating home office expenses in evaluating segment performance, assume that next year Branch A's sales remain at $300,000 and Branch B's sales increase to $600,000. Home office expenses remain constant at $21,000. Under these assumptions, home office expenses would be allocated as follows:

$$\text{Branch A: } \frac{\$300,000}{\$900,000} \times \$21,000 = \$ 7,000$$

$$\text{Branch B: } \frac{\$600,000}{\$900,000} \times \$21,000 = \underline{\$14,000}$$

$$\text{Total} \qquad \qquad \qquad \qquad \underline{\underline{\$21,000}}$$

We must assume that making more sales is better than making fewer sales. However, Branch A, whose sales have remained constant, is charged with

$2,000 less home office expenses than previously. Branch B, which has sold more, is charged with $2,000 more. The manager of Branch B cannot be particularly pleased with this situation. From the point of view of motivation, then, it is not good policy.

Cost Terminology

Since the concepts of responsibility accounting and performance measurement are so dependent on costs, it is appropriate at this time to consider cost terminology so that cost terms can be understood as they are discussed in the remainder of this chapter and the text.

Variable and Fixed Costs

The concepts of variable and fixed costs, which relate to the manner in which costs behave, were discussed in Chapter 2. A **variable cost** is one that changes in total in direct proportion to changes in a specific activity. A **fixed cost** is one that does not change in total in relation to changes in a specific activity within a relevant range of time or activity. Modifications of variable and fixed costs include *mixed costs* and *step-variable costs*. Whether a cost is variable of fixed has nothing to do with whether it is direct or indirect, controllable or noncontrollable. These characteristics are described below.

Direct and Indirect Costs

A **cost objective** is anything for which a firm wishes to accumulate costs. In manufacturing, the ultimate cost objective is product cost. Under responsibility accounting, we want to measure performance for the various responsibility centers. Thus, the segments are cost objectives. A **direct cost** benefits a specific cost objective or is caused by the activities of a specific cost objective. It can be traced directly to that cost objective. An **indirect cost** benefits or is caused by the activities of more than one cost objective and cannot be traced to a specific cost objective. In Exhibit 8.2, cost of goods sold, variable selling and administrative expenses, and fixed selling and administrative expenses shown for Branch A and Branch B are direct costs of the segments—they are incurred because those segments exist. The $21,000 of home office expenses are direct costs for the company; but they are indirect costs for the branches. The $21,000 cannot be traced directly to Branch A or Branch B because it was not caused by or incurred specifically for the benefit of either branch.

Notice that the terms *direct* and *indirect* do not relate to cost behavior. Each branch incurred direct costs, some of which were variable and some of which were fixed. The home office expenses apparently were all fixed, because the firm did not subtract them in arriving at contribution margin. Two terms sometimes used to describe direct and indirect fixed costs are *separable fixed costs* and *common fixed costs*. A direct fixed cost of a segment is often called a **separable fixed cost.** This means that it is incurred solely because the segment exists. A fixed cost that is not a direct cost of a segment is often called a **common fixed cost.** In Exhibit 8.2, the $21,000 home office expense was a common fixed cost, because it was incurred for the benefit of all segments of the company, not any particular segment.

When segment performance is evaluated, segments should be charged only with their direct costs. The indirect costs of the segments should not be allocated to them. As previously discussed, there may be valid reasons for allocation of indirect costs for external purposes or for product costing purposes. But for internal decisions about segment performance, the allocation of the indirect costs, such as home office expenses, creates misleading impressions as to how well or how poorly a particular segment has done.

Controllable and Noncontrollable Costs

In evaluating management performance, it is important to distinguish between controllable and noncontrollable costs. A **controllable cost** is one that an individual manager has the ability to influence within a specified time period. A **noncontrollable cost** is one that an individual manager does not have the ability to influence within a specified time period. The concept of controllable and noncontrollable costs relates to the individual manager and the time period. For example, in Exhibit 8.2 the $21,000 of home office expenses is considered noncontrollable by the managers of Branch A and Branch B; thus, when these branches' performance is evaluated, the $21,000 should not be considered. However, someone must control the $21,000. Someone made decisions at some time that resulted in the incurrence of that cost. All costs are controllable by someone over some period of time. In evaluating management performance under a system of responsibility accounting, only those costs over which a particular manager has control should be charged to that manager.

Sometimes top managers tend to feel that all costs should be allocated to the segments. Their philosophy is that managers should be aware of all costs incurred by the company with the understanding that revenues must be sufficient to cover these costs; each segment must "carry its share of the load." Certainly all costs must be covered by revenues if the firm is to survive. The total segment margin from all segments must be sufficient to cover all home office expenses and other costs. However, if costs allocated to segments are not controllable by the segment managers, distorted results appear if the final figures are used as a basis for evaluating segment performance (as was illustrated above). Furthermore, charging noncontrollable costs to segment managers and then evaluating them on the results leads to poor morale. It may cause better managers to leave the company. Therefore, top management must be particularly leery of allocating costs to segment managers when these managers have no control over the costs.

It is important to realize that, as mentioned earlier, the concept of controllability and noncontrollability does not relate to cost behavior concepts of variable and fixed. It is true that a close relationship often exists between the controllability or noncontrollability of a cost and the directness and indirectness of the cost to a particular segment. Generally, the direct costs charged to a segment are controllable by its manager. But this is not necessarily so. For example, each individual store of a department store chain may be considered a segment. Depreciation on each store is a direct cost of that store. However, the individual store manager probably has no control over the amount of depreciation and probably had no decision-making authority as to the size of the store or the amount of cost incurred in its construction. So, although top management may often use the direct cost of a segment as a basis for evaluating its management's performance, they must insure that no managers are unfairly penalized for direct costs over which they had no control.

Summary of Cost Terminology

Previously described costs relate to responsibility accounting in the following manner:

Variable and Fixed: Cost Behavior
Direct and Indirect: Cost Objective
Controllable and Noncontrollable: Individual Manager

A single cost may fit into all these categories. For example, a sales commission is a variable cost, is a direct cost of the items sold, and is controllable by the sales manager. Direct labor represents a variable cost that is a direct cost of the product and is controllable by the department foreman. Indirect labor is normally considered a variable cost that is an indirect cost of the product and is noncontrollable by the department foreman (although it is controllable by someone). For example, custodial salaries for the factory represent indirect labor; they are a direct cost of the custodial department and controllable by the manager of that department. Home office expenses may be variable or fixed. They are indirect costs of a segment but direct costs of some cost objective within the home office. These expenses are noncontrollable by segment managers but are controllable by some manager within the home office.

To summarize, it is important to understand the nature of individual costs. You should understand the significance of a particular cost for internal decision making with regard to cost behavior, various cost objectives, and the individual manager.

Evaluation Techniques

The primary purpose of a responsibility accounting system is to determine how well or how poorly individual segment managers are doing. This determination is based on the type of responsibility center being considered. Managers of cost centers are responsible for controlling costs, which means they must insure that costs do not exceed the budget by a significant amount. Managers of profit centers are responsible for earning an acceptable profit, measured in terms of segment margin or rate of return on sales for the profit center.

The concepts of measuring segment performance in relation to manufacturing costs are, for the most part, described in Chapters 6 and 7. Lack of adherence to budgeted goals is measured by the variances described in those chapters. As pointed out there, deviations from the budgets do not in themselves represent poor performance. Rather, they are a means of pointing out that deviations have occurred and providing a basis for inquiring into the reasons for the lack of adherence to the budget. How well or how poorly a manager is doing depends upon the specific reasons for the variances.

Profit center measurement was described earlier in this chapter. It is based on the difference between sales and the identifiable direct costs of the segments, assuming these costs are controllable by the segment managers. At this point, we want to look at evaluation of investment centers, which also incorporate the concepts of cost centers and profit centers in the evaluation process.

Minimum Rate of Return

An investment center was previously defined as a responsibility center in which a manager is responsible for earning a rate of return on the segment's investment in assets. Top management establishes what is considered minimum acceptable performance. It may be called the minimum rate of return or the **minimum desired rate of return.** Many firms set the minimum rate of return at their **cost of capital,** which represents the interest rate that a firm must pay for its funds. A firm should not invest in a project that earns a rate of return less than the cost of the funds used for the investment. Therefore, cost of capital becomes the minimum rate of return. Firms may require a rate of return higher than the minimum for their investments. In this text, the desired or minimum rate of return or cost of capital will always be given in the examples and problems. The actual determination of this rate is not always so simple. Nevertheless, it is important for management to make this determination, because it is the basis upon which managerial performance will be evaluated.

Return on Investment

One way of evaluating management performance is to calculate the rate of return on investment for the segment; it is usually referred to as **return on investment (ROI).** The calculation for return on investment is:

$$\text{Return on Investment (ROI)} = \frac{\text{Income}}{\text{Investment}}$$

In the equation, *income* is the segment margin of the segment being measured. *Investment* is the amount of average assets used by the segment. The return on investment calculation can also be viewed as follows:

$$\text{ROI} = \frac{\text{Income}}{\text{Sales}} \times \frac{\text{Sales}}{\text{Investment}}$$

The calculation above breaks the return on investment calculation down into two components. Obviously, sales cancel out and you are left with the original calculation (income ÷ investment). But, rather than cancelling out sales, we want to analyze these two components.

The first component of the equation (income ÷ sales) is called the **return on sales** or sales margin; it may also be referred to as the *rate of return on sales.* It represents segment margin as a percentage of sales. The second component (sales ÷ investment) is referred to as the **investment turnover.** It is also called *asset turnover* or *capital turnover.* To improve return on investment, a segment can increase its return on sales, increase its investment turnover, or do both. A low return on sales requires a greater number of sales in order for profitability to be high. By the same token, a firm with a high investment turnover can accept a lower return on sales. Increasing sales will increase ROI, because it increases income. However, two other ways of improving return on investment are to reduce expenses, thereby increasing income, or to reduce investment. If a segment can reduce its investment in assets without reducing sales, its return on investment will increase. This encourages management not to have its funds invested in assets that are not productive.

To illustrate the return on investment concept, we will again use the Savemore Stores example. The average assets for Savemore Stores for the current period are as follows:

Branch A	$125,000
Branch B	300,000
Home Office	25,000
Total Average Assets	$450,000

With this information, return on investment for each branch and for the company as a whole can be calculated as shown in Exhibit 8.3.

Assume that management wants each branch to earn a minumum rate of return of 15 percent. An evaluation of management performance shows that Branch A has exceeded the desired rate of return and that Branch B has not met it. This does not automatically mean that the manager of Branch B is ineffective or not doing the job properly. Nevertheless, top management will want to look at Branch B's operations more closely to determine why the desired rate of return of 15 percent was not met.

Looking at the components of the rate of return calculation, you see that the return on sales is approximately the same for both branches (8.33 percent versus 8.75 percent). However, investment turnover for Branch B is significantly lower than for Branch A. This appears to be the reason for Branch B's lower rate of return. For every dollar of assets invested in Branch

Exhibit 8.3 Return on Investment

Branch A: $\text{ROI} = \dfrac{\$25,000}{\$300,000} \times \dfrac{\$300,000}{\$125,000} = \dfrac{\$25,000}{\$125,000} = 20\%$

OR

$\text{ROI} = 8.33\% \times 2.4 = 20\%$

Branch B: $\text{ROI} = \dfrac{\$35,000}{\$400,000} \times \dfrac{\$400,000}{\$300,000} = \dfrac{\$35,000}{\$300,000} = 11.7\%$

OR

$\text{ROI} = 8.75\% \times 1.33 = 11.7\%$

Company: $\text{ROI} = \dfrac{\$39,000}{\$700,000} \times \dfrac{\$700,000}{\$450,000} = \dfrac{\$39,000}{\$450,000} = 8.7\%$

OR

$\text{ROI} = 5.57\% \times 1.56 = 8.7\%$

A, the firm generates $2.40 of sales, on which it earns a return on sales of 8.33 percent. Branch B, however, only generates sales of $1.33 for every dollar invested in assets. Although its return on sales—8.75 percent—is slightly higher than Branch A's, its sales per dollar invested is just not high enough. The manager of Branch B will want to look closely at the assets invested to determine why it is not getting as much per dollar as Branch A. Possibly some assets could be disposed of, which would increase the rate of return.

Notice that the company's rate of return is only 8.7 percent. Since the home office expenses and assets are not allocated to each branch, the income generated by both branches is required to cover all company expenses and earn a return on investment on all company assets. This is one reason top management often allocates home office expenses and assets to each segment. It believes that this allocation makes the segment managers aware that they must cover all expenses and earn an adequate rate of return on all assets. Nevertheless, as emphasized earlier, if top management is interested in knowing how well an individual manager is performing, it must not allocate either home office expenses or home office assets to the segments. The problem of allocating home office assets is just as serious as that of allocating home office expenses. Allocating home office assets lowers the return on investment, creating the same morale problems with segment managers as allocating home office expenses.

Return on investment for the firm as a whole must meet the goals of top management. Therefore, the return on investment required by the operating segments must be high enough to provide an adequate rate of return for the firm as a whole. It is better to require a segment to earn a higher minimum rate of return than to make segment managers "aware" of their responsibilities by charging them with expenses and assets over which they have no control.

Residual Income

Residual income is the difference between actual income (segment margin) earned on an investment and the desired income on the investment as specified by minimum desired rate of return. It is calculated as follows:

$$\text{Residual Income (RI)} = \text{Income (Segment Margin)} \\ - (\text{Investment} \times \text{Minimum Desired Rate of Return})$$

Assume a segment has an investment in assets of $500,000 and the firm's minimum desired rate of return is 15 percent. The firm earns a segment margin of $95,000. Residual income is calculated as shown in Exhibit 8.4.

In effect, residual income is the excess earnings above the minimum desired rate of return. If the firm sets its minimum desired rate of return at its cost of capital, it must earn a return on investment that is at least equal to the cost of funds used in making the investment. Any amount of income earned above the cost of capital is profit to the firm. The more earned above the cost of capital, the better off the firm is. In short, a firm wants to maximize its residual income.

Residual income is often used as a substitute for or along with return on investment as a means of evaluating managerial performance. The problem with using return on investment as the sole criterion in evaluating perform-

Exhibit 8.4 Residual Income

Income (Segment Margin)		$95,000
Investment	$500,000	
Minimum Desired Rate of Return	×.15	
Minimum Desired Income		75,000
Residual Income		$20,000

ance is that it can cause managers to avoid investing in any project that might lower the rate of return. For example, assume a company with two divisions, East Division and West Division, currently has residual income and return on investment as shown in Exhibit 8.5.

For purposes of this illustration, assume that both divisions have been operating exactly the same in terms of performance. Each division now has an opportunity to invest $100,000 in a project that will yield a 17-percent rate of return. The firm's cost of capital (and minimum desired rate of return) is 15 percent. Therefore, investment in the project will be beneficial to the firm as a whole because the 17-percent rate of return exceeds the cost of capital. The manager of East Division decides to invest in the project. The manager of West Division decides not to make the investment. The results of these decisions are shown in Exhibit 8.6.

Notice that the return on investment for East Division has declined from 20 percent to 19 percent. If top management analyzes performance merely on the basis of return on investment, then it appears that East Division is not doing as well as West Division. Yet, looking at residual income, you can see that East Division earned $2,000 more on its investment above the cost of capital than did West Division. East Division, then, has actually performed better than West Division.

The use of residual income as a criterion in the evaluation of management performance helps to foster **goal congruency**—that is, to make the

Exhibit 8.5 Residual Income and ROI before Proposed Investment

	East Division		West Division	
Income.		$40,000		$40,000
Investment	$200,000		$200,000	
Minimum Desired Rate of Return	×.15		×.15	
Minimum Desired Income		30,000		30,000
Residual Income		$10,000		$10,000
Return on Investment		$\frac{\$40,000}{\$200,000} = 20\%$		$\frac{\$40,000}{\$200,000} = 20\%$

Exhibit 8.6 Residual Income and ROI after Proposed Investment

	East Division	West Division
Income.	$57,000	$40,000
Investment	$300,000	$200,000
Minimum Desired Rate of Return.	×.15	×.15
Minimum Desired Income	45,000	30,000
Residual Income	$12,000	$10,000
Return on Investment	$\frac{\$57,000}{\$300,000} = 19\%$	$\frac{\$40,000}{\$200,000} = 20\%$

goals of the segment managers conform with the goals of the company. The firm is interested in maximizing its income above the cost of capital. If the individual managers are measured only on the basis of return on investment, they will not necessarily maximize residual income. Thus, the manager's goal of maximizing return on investment and the firm's goal of maximizing income are incongruent. Using residual income in evaluating segment performance reduces this problem. Managers are judged not only on the return on their investment, but also on the amount of residual income. One problem arises when residual income is used, especially if it is the only measurement. A segment with a large investment in assets normally has a larger amount of residual income simply because it's bigger, not necessarily because it's better managed. Therefore, a firm should use residual income along with return on investment when it evaluates performance.

Asset Base

As previously discussed, the amount shown as investment in an ROI calculation affects the rate of return. Assets charged to a segment should include both current and noncurrent assets used by the segment. The amount used in the ROI calculation for current assets—such as cash, accounts receivable, and inventory—should be the amount of the assets under the control of the segment. The amount shown for property, plant, and equipment should also be based on those assets controlled by the segment; however, several approaches can be used in calculating the amount to be shown for property, plant, and equipment. Among the bases that may be used are book value, original cost, and replacement cost.

Book Value   The most common base for determining the amount of assets used in the ROI calculation is **book value.** Book value is used because it is readily available from accounting records. Using book value involves several problems, however. Book value depends upon the depreciation method used. If divisions do not use the same method of depreciation, investment bases will show different amounts for similar assets. This inconsistency distorts the comparison of return on investment among divisions.

To overcome this problem, top management can prescribe the method of depreciation to be used by the divisions so that similar assets are depreciated in a similar manner. Of course, top management's prescribing methods of depreciation results in more centralization, which may not be popular with segment managers.

Another problem with using book value is that a segment could show an increasing rate of return simply because book value was declining. For example, assume a segment invests in a machine costing $100,000 with an estimated four-year life and no salvage value. Straight-line depreciation is $25,000 per year. The ROI computation is based on the average book value for the year. If income remains constant each year at $20,000, the return on investment becomes absurd, as shown in Exhibit 8.7. The exhibit shows a return on investment of 22.9 percent in the first year, increasing to 160 percent in the fourth year. The decreasing book value causes an increased return on investment. Yet income remains constant.

There is an argument to counter this criticism, however. The assumption that income remains constant at $20,000 is probably unrealistic. As time passes, a machine usually requires more maintenance and becomes less efficient. Therefore, income will probably decrease because of increased maintenance costs and less efficient production. Nevertheless, the effect of declining book value on ROI is one factor that management should consider when using book value as the asset base on the ROI calculation.

Original Cost Another base that may be used in calculating return on investment is **original cost,** or **gross cost.** Some proponents of this approach argue that the use of original cost prevents the problem caused by using book value shown in Exhibit 8.7. The asset base remains constant. If income also remains constant, then return on investment does not change from year

Exhibit 8.7 Book Value as Asset Base

Year 1	Year 2	Year 3	Year 4
$\frac{\$20,000}{\$87,500} = 22.9\%$	$\frac{\$20,000}{\$62,500} = 32.0\%$	$\frac{\$20,000}{\$37,500} = 53.3\%$	$\frac{\$20,000}{\$12,500} = 160.0\%$

Average book value is calculated as follows:

	Year 1	Year 2	Year 3	Year 4
Book Value				
Beginning of Year	$100,000	$ 75,000	$50,000	$25,000
End of Year[a]	$ 75,000	$ 50,000	$25,000	$ 0
Average	$\frac{\$175,000}{2}$	$\frac{\$125,000}{2}$	$\frac{\$75,000}{2}$	$\frac{\$25,000}{2}$
	= $87,500	= $62,500	= $37,500	= $12,500

[a] Beginning of year less $25,000 depreciation.

to year. The problem with using original cost, however, is that it may cause management to avoid getting rid of older equipment because to replace it with new equipment would lower its rate of return. Of course, the older equipment is probably less efficient; and therefore income is not as great as it would be if newer equipment were used. Nevertheless, the fear of an instant reduction in return on investment because of a large investment in new equipment (which would probably be beneficial to the firm) may tend to discourage investments in modernizing particular segments. Furthermore, this method too can make comparison between segments misleading, because a segment using older equipment may show a higher rate of return than a segment using newer equipment. This situation will lead to morale problems for managers trying to update their plants.

Replacement Cost   The cost of replacing assets now in use with similar assets is **replacement cost.** Replacement cost is not the cost of replacing old assets with new assets. Rather, it is the current cost of an asset, less depreciation on its current cost. For example, if a firm has a five-year-old drill press of a particular type, replacement cost is the cost to purchase a similar drill press today, less five years' depreciation.

Replacement cost is considered by many to be the best basis for determining the asset amount to be used in the ROI calculation. Because it represents the current investment, using it allows ROI to reflect current investment and current income. The problem with using replacement cost, though, is determing what the replacement cost is. The amount is not shown in the accounting records and is not always easy to determine. Nevertheless, for external reporting, as described in Chapter 17, some firms are now required to show replacement costs of some assets as supplementary information to their financial statements. Consequently, it is quite likely that the use of replacement cost for internal measurement will become more common.

Summary of Asset Bases   Three approaches for determining the amount to be shown as assets have been discussed here. Each has advantages and disadvantages. The use of book value is currently the most common and is likely to remain so for a while. However, it is expected that the use of replacement cost will increase. The important point is that the base selected be applied consistently from segment to segment and year to year, because management performance is compared among segments annually. An inconsistent application of the asset base distorts the comparison. Consistency in the application of the asset base is more important than the actual selection of the base itself.

Transfer Pricing

In many firms, a product is transferred from one segment to another. To account for the transfer properly, a dollar amount must be recorded. There is often a question as to the dollar amount at which the transfer should be made. The dollar amount used in recording the transfer is referred to as the **transfer price.** This price is important because it has a direct effect on both the selling segment's and the buying segment's return on investment. Transfer price is typically based on cost, market price, variable cost, or a price negotiated between the segment managers. To some extent, the transfer price determination is based on the type of segment, the type of product, the type of firm, and the degree of decentralization within the firm.

Cost

Transfers between cost centers are typically based on cost. Normally, this should be standard cost and should include both variable and fixed costs. Since managers of cost centers are evaluated on their conformity to standard cost in the budget, the use of standard cost as a transfer price does not normally present any problems.

If a firm transfers actual costs, rather than standard costs, problems may develop. The transfer of actual costs provides no incentive for efficiency in the division transferring the costs, because if it incurs excess costs, it merely transfers them. In addition, the segment receiving the costs is unfairly charged with the cost of inefficiencies of the segment that transferred them. If the receiving segment is an investment center, then its rate of return is affected by the inefficiency of the cost center. For this reason, the use of standard costs, not actual costs, is encouraged when cost centers transfer costs.

Cost Plus Profit

If the selling segment is a profit or investment center, it will want to sell its product to the buying segment at some amount greater than cost. It will want to earn a profit on its sale that is in line with what is required to earn an adequate profit or rate of return for the segment. In some instances, the transfer price, and therefore the profit, may be based on the outside market price. If no outside market price exists, the question of how much above cost to charge is sometimes difficult to determine. If the selling segment sells other products, it may calculate its profit on the internal transfer in the same way it calculates its profit on the other products—a percentage of cost, for example. As described below, the transfer price may also be based on negotiations between the buying and selling segments.

Market Price

If there is an outside market for the product being transferred between segments of a firm, then that price often serves as the basis for the transfer price. Many times the outside market price is the ideal transfer price, because it is considered to be objectively determined—the amount was arrived at by factors outside the firm, and therefore no one within the firm was able to influence it. Market price is usually considered an ideal price to use for profit centers and investment centers.

Since investment centers are interested in maximizing their rate of return (or residual income), the selling segment wants to transfer the product to the buying segment at the highest possible price. By that same token, the buying segment wants to buy the product from the selling segment at the lowest possible price. Therefore, disputes often arise. Using the outside market price settles such disputes in many cases.

Often, a selling segment wants to price the transfer at its cost plus some amount of profit large enough to meet its rate of return objectives. If its costs are excessive, the buying segment may balk at the price. If the internal price is greater than the outside market price, one may question whether there is inefficiency within the selling segment and whether it should even be manufacturing the product being sold to the buying segment. If the selling segment is manufacturing a product similar to the one sold on the outside, it would seem that it could sell it at a price lower than the outside market price; after all, it does not incur selling costs when it sells within the firm.

In some instances, the selling segment may be able to sell its product to an outside customer. In such cases, it may decide that it is more profitable to sell on the outside than to sell to the inside segment. Other cases arise in which the buying segment has the opportunity to buy a product from an outside source at a price lower than it would have to pay the inside segment. Again, the manager of the buying segment would not want to lower the segment's rate of return by buying from the inside.

In most instances, it is to the company's benefit for transfers to remain internal. In other words, the company as a whole is better off if the selling segment sells to the inside and the buying segment buys from the inside. Whether this must be done depends on the degree of decentralization within the firm. In a truly decentralized firm, management of the various segments are free to buy on the inside or outside to best meet the goals of their segments, and managers of selling segments are free to sell on the inside or outside in accordance with their goals. This policy often leads to an incongruency of goals whereby managers transact with outside sources in order to meet segment goals when the company's long-range profit goals would be best served by their dealing internally with each other.

The extent to which top management should interfere in such transactions depends on how important they believe decentralization to be. As previously discussed, a decentralized firm is often able to attract good managerial talent because of its decentralization. To force managers to buy internally takes away some of their prerogatives, which may result in low morale. On the other hand, if a manager consistently makes decisions that are working to the long-range detriment of the firm, top management may feel a need to step in. Thus, a firm must often strike a happy medium between the goal of decentralization and the goal of profit maximization. Some managers will make mistakes; that is part of the learning process. But continued mistakes that prove costly to the firm probably should be stopped.

Variable Cost

There are times when variable cost is the best transfer price. This situation may occur when the selling segment has no other alternatives for selling its product but the buying segment has alternative sources for obtaining it. For example, assume that Division A can buy a particular part it needs for its product from an outside source for $10 apiece. It anticipates a need for 100,000 parts a year. Division B can manufacture the part with the following costs:

Variable	$ 7.00
Fixed	4.00[a]
Total	$11.00

The manager of Division B does not want to sell below $11 and would prefer to sell for more in order to earn a profit. However, the manager of Division A, who can buy the same product for $10 on the outside, is unwilling to pay more than that to buy internally. Any price between $7 and $10 would be an appropriate transfer price in this case. Any price $10 or below is equal to or better than the outside price. Any price above $7 provides Division B with some contribution towards fixed costs. If Division B has no other use for its fixed facilities, it could sell at a variable cost of $7 and not lose any more than it is going to lose anyway. Thus, in some short-run situations, an internal price may be set at the variable cost, just to keep facilities from becoming idle. Over the long run, all fixed costs must be covered. Therefore, if there are no other uses for the facilities, and if Division B cannot lower its costs, one might question whether it should be manufacturing this particular item.

Negotiated Price

Many times the actual transfer price is the result of negotiations between the buyer and seller segments. In the illustration above, if the market price is $10 and the variable cost is $7, the two managers may negotiate a price between $7 and $10. The manager of Division B may not like selling below the $11 total cost. However, if the company is truly decentralized, the manager of Division A will be unwilling to pay more than $10, the outside market price. In that instance, it would be to Division B's advantage to negotiate a price between $7 and $10.

If no agreement on an internal price can be arrived at, an impartial arbitrator may be used. Whether the decision of the arbitrator will be binding on each division depends again on the degree of centralization within the company. As previously discussed, in a truly decentralized firm, the managers of each segment have the authority to make their own decisions regarding these matters. On the other hand, if buying on the outside is not to the advantage of the company as a whole, top management may require an internal transfer and force the managers to arrive at some appropriate price.

Transfer Pricing Illustration

An illustration of transfer pricing is presented here to show how market price may affect the transfer price. Four different market prices are used. Division A of Maple Company is an investment center. It manufactures some products that are sold outside the firm; however, it also manufactures one product that is used only by Division B within the firm. Division B has requested 10,000 units from Division A for the current year. Division A has proposed a transfer price based on cost and profit as follows:

[a]$400,000 ÷ 100,000 Units

	Unit Price (Based on 10,000 Units)
Variable Cost	$3.00
Fixed Cost	1.25[a]
Total Cost	$4.25
Profit	.75
Transfer Price	$5.00

Market Price of $6 per Unit If the outside market price is $6 per unit, a transfer price of $5 presents no problem. The buying division cannot buy the product at a price less than the selling division's transfer price. The selling division makes the amount of profit it desires.

In this case, there is no question that it is to the company's benefit, as well as to each division's benefit, for Division B to purchase the product on the inside.

Market Price of $5 per Unit A market price of $5 should have the same result as a market price of $6. Buying on the outside offers no advantage to the buying division as long as it can buy on the inside at the same price. Obviously, it is to the advantage to the selling division to sell at $5, because that is the price it established as desirable.

Although the buying division will be indifferent, insofar as its rate of return is concerned, as to whether it buys on the inside or outside, the company as a whole benefits from an inside purchase. Looking at it from the company viewpoint, if 10,000 units are bought on the outside, the total cost to the company is $50,000. However, if these units are bought on the inside, the additional cost to the company is only $30,000 ($3 per unit × 10,000 units), assuming that the selling division has no other use for the facilities, which are resulting in a fixed cost of $1.25 per unit (or a total of $12,500). This $12,500 cost will be incurred regardless of whether the division buys on the inside or the outside.

Market Price of $4 per Unit If the outside market price is $4 per unit, the manager of Division B will be unwilling to pay $5 per unit to Division A. Assuming the firm is decentralized, Division B will buy from the outside unless Division A lowers its price. Division A may be unwilling to lower its price below $4.25, since if it did it would lose money. However, if Division B buys on the outside, then Division A will lose money anyway, because its fixed costs will not be covered at all. If Division A lowers its price to $4 per unit, it will cover its variable costs and have $1 per unit to help cover fixed costs.

Again, it is to the company's benefit for Division B to buy on the inside. The total cost on the outside is $40,000 ($4 per unit × 10,000 units). The variable cost of buying on the inside is $30,000, as calculated above. Since the fixed costs will be incurred anyway, the company is $10,000 better off if Division B buys from Division A. As previously mentioned, though, Divi-

[a]$12,500 ÷ 10,000 Units

sion B will be unwilling to buy at a price of $5. Here is where a lack of goal congruency may occur. The company benefits only if the transfer is made internally. In a truly decentralized firm, the division managers will either work out a price between themselves or Division B will buy on the outside. The second alternative will result in a $10,000 disadvantage to the firm as a whole. If top management feels that this $10,000 is significant, it may force Division B to buy on the inside at Division A's price (thus creating a morale problem for the Division B manager); or it may force Division A to lower its price to the outside price. Again, top management's role depends on the degree of centralization.

Market Price of $2.50 per Unit If the outside market price is $2.50 per unit, there is a definite problem in Division A. The $2.50 is less than Division A's variable cost. In this case, it is not only to Division B's benefit to buy on the outside but to the company's benefit as well. The total outside cost is $25,000 ($2.50 per unit × 10,000 units). As we know, the total variable cost of buying on the inside is $30,000. In other words, it costs the company $5,000 more in variable costs alone if the item is manufactured within the firm. In this instance, the item should definitely be bought on the outside. Further, management should look closely at Division A's costs for the item. If Division A cannot produce the item at a variable cost that is less than the outside price, then Division A probably should not be producing it.

Goal Congruence, Motivation, and Human Relations

Goal Congruence

The primary objective of a business enterprise is to earn a profit that represents an acceptable rate of return on the owners' investment. Within a firm, operating managers are responsible for earning an acceptable rate of return if the business is to achieve its profit objectives. Simply stated, we might say that the primary evaluation technique of managerial performance is to measure the return on investment earned by an investment center. Theoretically, the higher the rate of return, the better the performance by the manager.

However, as previously discussed, this is not always so. Individual managers might maximize their personal performance and therefore their individual goals while at the same time not maximizing the goals of the company as a whole. Therefore, a responsibility system should provide for goal congruence. **Goal congruence** is a concept under which the segment managers' goals are in conformity with the goals of the company as a whole. Lack of goal congruence was mentioned earlier in the chapter in connection with the budget apparel problems in Sears' stores. In further efforts to achieve goal congruence, Sears instituted a bonus plan that was based not only on an individual store manager's performance but also on the performance of all stores in his or her region. This policy was intended to insure that one store manager would not, for example, hoard air conditioners if another store in the area had run out and needed them quickly.[5]

[5]Elsner, "Retailer's Recovery."

Motivation

If managers are to perform well, they must be motivated. The responsibility accounting system is designed to indicate how well managers have performed. However, if managers believe that the system is unfair, it will not work. For example, as emphasized earlier, allocating costs to segments over which the segment managers have no control provides results that are not meaningful. If a manager's performance—and therefore, that manager's bonus, promotion, or raise—is based on such results, he or she is not likely to be happy with the company. This low morale tends to force better managers to look for jobs in companies with more enlightened top management.

In this same vein, budgets and goals set for managers must be realistic. If the goals set seem impossible to achieve, managers tend to become demoralized and not to put forth their best effort in trying to achieve them. It is important for managers to have positive attitudes about the budgets and the system under which they are evaluated. If the responsibility accounting system is not perceived by managers to be fair and objective, then it is quite likely that the time and effort spent in designing and implementing it has not been productive.

A firm must walk a fine line between goal congruence and motivation. Company goals must be achieved if the company is to survive. Thus, managers must adhere to company goals as they are satisfying their personal goals. Nevertheless, top management must insure that company goals are reasonable and realistic if they expect managers to work to achieve them.

Human Relations

The importance of human relations in the budgeting process was described in Chapter 5. Human relations are equally important in evaluating management performance. Of course, to a large extent, how well managers have performed is based on how well they have complied with the budget. As described in this chapter, however, evaluating management performance goes beyond just monitoring adherence to a budget.

If a firm is to achieve its long-range profit goals, it must motivate managers to perform well and must have a system of responsibility accounting whereby it can evaluate management performance. If a manager is doing a good job, both the manager and the firm will be glad to find it out. Unfortunately, not everyone always performs well. Managers who do not meet expectations must be told. No one likes to be criticized; and in dealing with people, tact and diplomacy are essential. In setting up the system, the firm must be sure it is fair, objective, and accepted by the individuals to whom it applies. As mentioned earlier, if managers believe the system is unfair, they will be demoralized and disgruntled and will not perform as well as they could. On the other hand, a responsibility system that fairly measures the performance of the managers will provide them with realistic goals and motivation for achieving them.

Common sense is essential in the application of a responsibility accounting system. As this chapter has shown, a system that evaluates managers on how well they have performed when they have been allocated noncontrollable costs and assets is not really a good system. People tend to be defensive when they are being rated, especially if they are being rated as having performed poorly. Management must insure it has taken every step to use common sense and install a fair, equitable, objective system of responsibility accounting.

Summary

Responsibility accounting is a system under which a manager is given decision-making authority and responsibility for each activity occurring within a specific area of the company. Managers are made responsible for cost centers, profit centers, or investment centers. The degree of authority given to a manager depends on the company's philosophy regarding centralization and decentralization.

A responsibility accounting system is used to help a firm evaluate how well managers are performing. Managers of cost centers are normally evaluated on how well the costs they have incurred conform to the budget. Managers of profit centers are evaluated on the basis of whether their segments have earned an adequate segment margin—the difference between the segment's revenue and direct costs. Managers of investment centers are measured by the rate of return on investment earned on the assets of the segment or by the amount of residual income earned by the investment center. In all cases of performance evaluation, managers should be charged only with those costs and assets over which they have control. A controllable cost is one that an individual manager has the ability to influence within a specified time period.

The asset base to be used in determining return on investment for an investment center may be book value, original cost, or replacement cost. Book value is most commonly used, although replacement cost will probably be used more in the future than it has been in the past.

Intracompany transfers of product require determination of a transfer price. This price may be based on cost, cost plus profit, variable cost, market price, or a negotiated price. Disputes often arise between buying and selling segments over the appropriate transfer price. Depending on the degree of centralization within a firm, top management may impose a transfer price in some situations. Problems of goal congruency are sometimes inherent in transfer pricing. Often the transfer price most beneficial to one segment or another is not the one most beneficial to the firm as a whole.

If a responsibility accounting system is to work properly, human relations must be considered. The numbers calculated to determine how well a person is doing have an effect on that person's life. It is vitally important, therefore, that any such system be fair and objective.

Review Problem

Problem

Below is a product-line income statement for 2 divisions of Ashley Company.

	Division A	Division B
Sales	$200,000	$400,000
Variable Costs	(120,000)	(240,000)
Contribution Margin	$ 80,000	$160,000
Division Fixed Costs	(30,000)	(85,000)
Corporate Fixed Costs	(20,000)	(40,000)
Net Income	$ 30,000	$ 35,000
Division Average Assets	$400,000	$550,000
Corporate Average Assets	100,000	200,000
Total Average Assets	$500,000	$750,000

Corporate fixed costs and assets are indirect costs of the segments and have been allocated on the basis of sales. The firm's cost of capital is 10%.

Required:

For each division, calculate the following:

a. Return on sales.

b. Investment turnover.

c. Return on investment.

d. Residual income.

Solution

In calculating items a–d it is important to use only the direct costs and assets of each division. Thus, it is necessary first to calculate each division's segment margin as follows:

	Division A	Division B
Contribution Margin	$80,000	$160,000
Division Fixed Costs	(30,000)	(85,000)
Segment Margin	$50,000	$ 75,000

a. Return on sales:

Division A: $\dfrac{\$50,000}{\$200,000} = 25\%$

Division B: $\dfrac{\$75,000}{\$400,000} = 18.8\%$

b. Investment turnover:

Division A: $\dfrac{\$200,000}{\$400,000} = .5$

Division B: $\dfrac{\$400,000}{\$550,000} = .73$

c. Return on investment:

Division A: $\dfrac{\$50,000}{\$400,000} = 12.5\%$

Division B: $\dfrac{\$75,000}{\$550,000} = 13.6\%$

d. Residual income:

Division A: $50,000 − ($400,000 × .10) =
$50,000 − $40,000 =
$10,000

Division B: $75,000 − ($550,000 × .10) =
$75,000 − $55,000 =
$20,000

Note that the format used in calculating residual income above differs from that shown in Exhibit 8.4. In the calculation above, the data were merely inserted into the residual income equation shown in the chapter. In working problems of this type, you can use either format.

Questions

8-1 What is the primary feature that distinguishes a centralized firm from a decentralized firm?

8-2 What is meant by *responsibility accounting*?

8-3 What is the difference between a cost center, a profit center, and an investment center?

8-4 What is meant by *management by exception*?

8-5 Define segment margin. How does it differ from contribution margin?

8-6 Why should allocated costs not be included when segment margin is determined?

8-7 Distinguish between controllable and noncontrollable costs.

8-8 What is a cost objective?

8-9 Distinguish between direct and indirect costs.

8-10 A firm's investment turnover is 3. What does that mean? Why does return on investment increase if investment turnover increases?

8-11 Why doesn't the average of the segments' return on investment equal the return on investment for the firm as a whole?

8-12 What are the advantages of using book value as the asset base in return on investment calculations? What are the disadvantages?

8-13 Which asset base provides the most realistic return on investment from year to year? Why? What is the primary problem with using this base?

8-14 Briefly describe the problems involved in determining transfer price.

8-15 Why is market price generally considered an ideal basis for a transfer price? What effect does the degree of decentralization have on the use of market price as the basis for the transfer price?

8-16 What is the relationship of goal congruence to performance evaluation?

8-17 What is the primary concern regarding human relations and performance evaluation?

Exercises

8-18 Division Evaluation. You are manager of the Plastic Parts Division of your company. You have received the following performance report from the departments in your division, all of which are cost centers:

Department Number	Budget	Actual	Variance
1	$ 35,000	$ 30,000	$ 5,000 F
2	60,000	62,000	2,000 U
3	20,000	30,000	10,000 U
4	85,000	88,000	3,000 U
Totals	$200,000	$210,000	$10,000 U

a. What is your evaluation of the division as a whole?
b. Under the management by exception concept, would you ask for more data or for explanations from any of the departments. If so, which ones? Why?

8-19 Distinguishing Types of Responsibility Centers. Indicate whether each of the following responsibility centers would be considered a cost center, a profit center, or an investment center.
  a. Painting department of an automobile manufacturing firm.
  b. Automobile division of an automobile manufacturing firm.
  c. Store #1576 of a national chain of supermarkets.
  d. Produce department of a grocery store.
  e. Custodial service of a department store.
  f. Beverage and bar operations of a restaurant.
  g. Laundry service of a hospital.
  h. X-ray service of a hospital.

8-20 Calculating Segment Margin. Calculate segment margin for each of the following independent companies:

	Company A		Company B	
	Branch 1	Branch 2	Branch 1	Branch 2
Costs of Goods Sold:	$25,000	$50,000	60%	40%
Home Office Expenses:	$10,000	$16,000	$ 5,000	$ 5,000
Units Sold:	—	—	4,000	2,800
Fixed Selling and Administrative Expenses:	$10,000	$15,000	$ 6,000	$15,000
Variable Selling and Administrative Expenses:	$ 5,000	$10,000	$3/Unit	$5/Unit
Sales:	$50,000	$80,000	$40,000	$70,000

8-21 Division Evaluation Partial performance reports for 2 divisions of the same company are presented below:

	Division A	Division B
Contribution Margin	$ 90,000	$45,000
Fixed Selling and Administrative Expenses	(50,000)	(15,000)
Home Office Expenses	(50,000)	(25,000)
Net Income (Loss)	$(10,000)	$ 5,000

Home office expenses are incurred for the company as a whole and are indirect costs of the divisions. They are allocated on the basis of contribution margin. The manager of Division A has been criticized because the division showed a loss. Do you think the criticism is justified? Explain.

8–22 Distinguishing Types of Cost Below are listed 10 items of cost at the Malcom Manufacturing Company. Across the top are listed the titles of several individuals employed by the company.

	Painting Department Foreman	Custodial Foreman	Vice-President of Sales	Credit Department Manager
a. Wages in Painting Department				
b. Cost of Paint Used				
c. Custodial Wages				
d. Cost of Sweeping Compound Used				
e. Cost of Repairs to Painting Machinery				
f. Salary of Manufacturing Vice-President				
g. Sales Commissions				
h. Cost of Uncollectible Accounts				
i. Depreciation on Factory Building				
j. Depreciation on Administrative Building				

Indicate the applicability of each cost to each individual as:
1. Direct.
2. Indirect.
3. Controllable.
4. Noncontrollable.
5. Not applicable.

For example, cost a, wages in painting department, is applicable to the painting department foreman as 1 (direct) and 3 (controllable); but to the custodial foreman, the vice-president of sales, and the credit department manager, it is 5 (not applicable).

8–23 Return on Investment Below are selected data for the Bingle Bangle Company and its 2 branches.

	Bingle Branch	Bangle Branch	Company Total
Sales	$200,000	$600,000	$800,000
Contribution Margin	80,000	250,000	330,000
Segment Margin	40,000	60,000	100,000
Home Office Expenses			60,000
Net Income			40,000
Average Investment	160,000	400,000	650,000

For each branch and for the company as a whole, determine the following:
  a. Return on sales.
  b. Investment turnover.
  c. Return on investment.

8-24 Return on Investment The Omega Company operates 2 divisions—
Beta and Gamma. Selected data from last year's results are shown below.

	Beta	Gamma	Company Total
Sales	$50,000	$150,000	$200,000
Variable Costs	35,000	105,000	140,000
Division Fixed Costs	10,000	25,000	35,000
Corporate Headquarters Fixed Costs (Allocated)	5,000	15,000	20,000
Average Assets	40,000	250,000	320,000

For each division and for the company as a whole, determine the following:
  a. Return on sales.
  b. Investment turnover.
  c. Return on investment.

8-25 Return on Investment Calculate return on sales, investment turnover,
and return on investment for each of the following independent segments:

	Segment 1	Segment 2	Segment 3	Segment 4	Segment 5
Sales	$25,000	$80,000	$65,000	$180,000	$100,000
Segment Margin	10,000	20,000	15,000	45,000	8,000
Net Income		10,000		20,000	
Average Assets	5,000	20,000	50,000	160,000	35,000

8-26 Return on Investment Eastern Division of National Corporation had
an average investment of $1,000,000 last year. Sales totaled $400,000. Variable costs were $200,000, and fixed costs were $100,000. Calculate the following:
  a. Return on sales.
  b. Investment turnover.
  c. Return on investment.

8-27 Return on Investment; Residual Income Apple Division of Tasty Fruit
Company earned $18,000 on an investment of $120,000. Banana Division
earned $25,000 on an investment of $140,000. The firm's minimum desired
rate of return is 12%. For each division, calculate the following:
  a. Return on investment.
  b. Residual income.

8-28 Return on Investment; Investment Evaluation Baker Division of ABC
Corporation currently earns $100,000 on an investment of $800,000. The
division has an opportunity to invest $200,000 with projected earnings of
$22,000. The firm's cost of capital is 10%.

a. Calculate Baker Division's current return on investment.

b. Should the division make the proposed investment? Why or why not?

c. As division manager, why might you be unwilling to make the investment?

8-29 Transfer Pricing Division A of the Green Company manufactures a product with the following unit costs:

Variable	$ 7
Fixed	3
Total Cost	$10
Profit	2
Selling Price	$12

It sells 100,000 units a year to Division B, its only customer. Division B has asked for a lower price, because it can now buy the same product from an outside supplier for $8 per unit. Division A has no other use for the facilities if it stops manufacturing the product.

Calculate the dollar advantage or disadvantage to the firm as a whole in terms of net income if Division B buys on the outside.

8-30 Transfer Pricing Mar Company has 2 decentralized divisions, X and Y. Division X has always purchased certain units from Division Y at $75 per unit. Because Division Y plans to raise the price to $100 per unit, Division X now wants to purchase these units from outside suppliers, who charge $75 per unit. Division Y's costs follow:

Y's Variable Costs per Unit:	$70
Y's Annual Fixed Costs:	$15,000
Y's Annual Unit Production for X:	1,000

If Division X buys from an outside supplier, the facilities Division Y uses to manufacture these units will remain idle. What would be the result if Mar forced Division X to accept a transfer price of $100 per unit?

a. It would be suboptimal for the company, because X should buy from outside suppliers at $75 per unit.

b. It would provide lower overall company net income than a transfer price of $75 per unit.

c. It would provide higher overall company net income than a transfer price of $75 per unit.

d. It would be more profitable for the company than allowing X to buy from outside suppliers at $75 per unit.

Provide calculations to support your answer. (AICPA adapted)

Problems

8-31 Return on Investment; Residual Income; Division Evaluation Below is an income statement for the most recently ended year for the Yard Products Company and its 2 divisions:

	Shovel	Hoe	Company Total
Sales	$1,000,000	$500,000	$1,500,000
Variable Costs	(600,000)	(300,000)	(900,000)
Contribution Margin	$ 400,000	$200,000	$ 600,000
Segment Fixed Costs	(200,000)	(75,000)	(275,000)
Corporate Fixed Costs	(140,000)	(70,000)	(210,000)
Net Income	$ 60,000	$ 55,000	$ 115,000
Segment Average Assets	$ 600,000	$300,000	$ 900,000
Corporate Average Assets	400,000	200,000	600,000
Total Average Assets	$1,000,000	$500,000	$1,500,000

The president of the company has severely criticized the manager of the Shovel Division for its dismal 6% return on investment, "which doesn't come close to the firm's 10% cost of capital." The manager of the Hoe Division was also criticized for an 11% return on investment, "which barely exceeds the cost of capital." Corporate fixed costs and assets are allocated to each division on the basis of sales.

Required:

  a. Show the calculations that the president used as the basis for the criticism.

  b. For each division and for the company as a whole, using appropriate data, calculate the following:

   1. Return on sales.

   2. Investment turnover.

   3. Return on investment.

  c. Calculate residual income for each division.

  d. In view of your answers to parts b and c, is the president's criticism justified?

8–32 Segment Margin; Return on Investment; Residual Income; Division Evaluation Data for the 2 divisions of Terry's Tree Processing Company are shown below:

	Pine	Oak
Sales	$180,000	$300,000
Variable Costs	100,000	165,000
Division Fixed Costs	40,000	75,000
Corporate Fixed Costs	25,000	25,000
Beginning Assets	200,000	320,000
Ending Assets	300,000	580,000
Corporate Average Assets	100,000	100,000

The corporate fixed costs and average assets were allocated equally between the divisions. The firm requires that each division earn a 15% return on investment.

Required:

  a. Calculate net income for the company as a whole.

b. Calculate the segment margin for each division.

c. For each division and for the company as a whole, calculate the following:

    1. Return on sales.

    2. Investment turnover.

    3. Return on investment.

d. Calculate residual income for each division.

e. Based on your answers to parts c and d, comment on the performance of each division.

8-33 New Product Evaluation; Return on Investment The Kitchenware Products Division of the Manymulti Products Corporation manufactures and sells a variety of kitchenware items. A budget for next year is as follows:

Sales		$220,000
Variable Cost of Goods Sold	$100,000	
Variable Selling and Administrative Expenses	50,000	150,000
Contribution Margin		$ 70,000
Fixed Selling and Administrative Expenses		50,000
Segment Margin		$ 20,000

Average assets for the period are expected to total $100,000. Corporate headquarters does not allocate indirect company costs or assets to the operating divisions. However, top management evaluates each division on its return on investment. There is fierce competition among division managers to constantly improve the ROI, because pay raises, bonuses, and promotions hinge on the results.

The vice-president of Kitchenware Products Division recently rejected a proposal to expand into a new product line. The new product would have doubled the division's segment margin, providing additional sales of $80,000 and increasing variable costs by $45,000 and fixed costs by $15,000. It would have required an additional investment in assets of about $125,000.

The cost of capital for the corporation is 15%, and corporate headquarters usually is able to provide the necessary funds to divisions for worthwhile investments.

Required:

a. Why do you think the new product line was rejected? Be specific. Show appropriate calculations.

b. Was this rejection in the best interest of the company as a whole? Explain.

c. What problems, if any, do you see with the current performance evaluation system of the corporation.

8-34 Return on Investment; Different Asset Bases Wright Company recently purchased new equipment at a cost of $20,000. The equipment has a 4-year life with no salvage value at the end of the 4 years. Income resulting from the new equipment and replacement cost at the end of each year are expected to be as follows:

Year	Income	Replacement Cost (Year-End)
1	$5,000	$22,000
2	5,000	23,500
3	4,000	24,000
4	3,000	25,000

Management is trying to decide on the best base to use for return on investment calculations.

Required:

a. Calculate return on investment for each year using the following asset bases:

1. Book value (using the straight-line method of depreciation).

2. Original cost.

3. Replacement cost (using the year-end amount).

b. Which base do you recommend? Why?

8–35 Return on Investment; Various Assumptions Reece Radio Company manufactures transistor radios that it sells for $10 each. Last year, sales totaled $2,000,000. Average assets are as follows:

Cash	$ 80,000
Accounts Receivable (Net)	600,000
Property, Plant, and Equipment (Net)	320,000
	$1,000,000

Net income last year was $60,000. Efforts are being made to try to improve return on investment. A proposal was made to increase the selling price by $.50 per unit. It is anticipated that this will have no effect on the number of units sold.

Required:

a. Calculate the following, based on last year's results:

1. Return on sales.

2. Investment turnover.

3. Return on investment.

b. What component of the ROI calculation is the proposed plan attempting to improve?

c. Assuming the price is increased by $.50 per unit, calculate:

1. Return on sales.

2. Investment turnover.

3. Return on investment.

d. Additional analysis reveals that increasing the price by $.50 per unit will result in a tremendous drop in units sold because of competitive pressures. Therefore, other steps are being considered. Specifically, management will attempt to speed up collection of receivables and reduce the average by $200,000. It is also believed that equipment averaging $100,000 in value can be disposed of with no effect on sales or costs. What component of the ROI calculation would these actions improve?

e. Assuming management takes the steps outlined in part d, calculate:

1. Return on sales.

   2. Investment turnover.

   3. Return on investment.

   f. Assume the selling price is increased by $.50 with no effect on the number of units sold and the steps outlined in part d are taken. Calculate the following:

   1. Return on sales.

   2. Investment turnover.

   3. Return on investment.

8-36 Various Plans to Improve ROI The manager of the Men's Slacks Division of the Kramer Clothing Company has been told to do something about the division's low return on investment. Mr. Kramer, the president, stated, "Your ROI does not even meet the company's 13% cost of capital. Either improve your ROI, or I'll hire a new manager." Unit data regarding the product are as follows:

	Per Unit	Percent of Selling Price
Selling Price	$25.00	100%
Variable Cost of Goods Sold	15.00	60
Variable Selling and Administrative Expenses	2.50	10
Contribution Margin	$ 7.50	30

Last year, the division sold 10,000 pairs of slacks and incurred fixed costs of $60,000. The outlook for next year is about the same. The division's average investment in assets is $150,000, comprised as follows:

Cash	$ 40,000
Inventory	50,000
Equipment (Net)	60,000
	$150,000

The division manager wants to improve the ROI as much as possible and must earn at least 13%, the firm's cost of capital.

Required:

   a. For last year, calculate the following:

   1. Return on sales.

   2. Investment turnover.

   3. Return on investment.

   b. To improve ROI, the manager is considering several plans:

   Plan A—Reduce cash by $20,000, inventory by $10,000, and equipment by $10,000.

   Plan B—Reduce variable costs by 5%.

   Plan C—Reduce fixed costs by $5,000.

   Plan D—Combine Plans A, B, and C.

For each plan, calculate the following:

   1. Return on sales.

   2. Investment turnover.

   3. Return on investment.

c. Assume that none of the plans is feasible. Costs and investment are currently at the minimum necessary to conduct operations. The manager is considering reducing selling price by 10% in an effort to increase the number of units sold. If this is done, how many units must be sold in order for a 15% return on investment to be earned?

8-37 Return on Investment; Transfer Pricing The Special Parts Division is an investment center of Conglomerate, Inc., a highly decentralized company. The division manufactures a single product, a part that it sells only to the Appliance Division. Normal volume is 100,000 units per year. The standard cost and transfer price for this part are as follows:

Variable Cost	$1.50
Fixed Cost	.50
Total Cost	$2.00
Profit	.25
Transfer Price	$2.25

The Special Parts Division has $150,000 invested in assets. The corporate headquarters charges all divisions 15% interest on invested assets.

The Appliance Division has found an outside supplier that will sell it the parts for $1.75 each. On this basis, the division expects to earn $325,000 on its $2,000,000 investment. The manager of the Appliance Division has indicated that unless the Special Parts Division lowers its price to $1.75, the division will buy the part from the outside supplier. The manager of the Special Parts Division refuses to sell below cost but is willing to negotiate a price that allows the division to at least meet the cost of capital. The Special Parts Division manager has appealed to top management, asking that the Appliance Division not be allowed to purchase from the outside because it would not be in the company's best interests.

Required:

a. Calculate return on investment for each division, assuming a transfer price of $2.25.

b. Calculate return on investment for each division, assuming a transfer price of $1.75.

c. Based on your answer to parts a and b, explain why each manager is unwilling to yield on the transfer price.

d. Is the Special Parts Division manager correct in stating that it is in the company's best interests for divisions to buy on the inside? Provide computations to support your answer.

e. You are the corporation's senior vice-president. You have been appointed by the president of the company to resolve this dispute. What is your decision? Why?

f. Assume that if the Appliance Division purchases the part on the outside, the Special Parts Division can manufacture another product for an outside customer. The division can sell 50,000 parts a year at $4.00 each, with a unit variable cost of $2.25. There will be no change in fixed costs or investment.

1. Calculate the return on investment for the Special Parts Division under this assumption.

2. Calculate the financial advantage or disadvantage to the company as a whole of this alternative versus the alternative of the Special Parts Division's continuing to sell the special part to the Appliance Division.

8-38 Transfer Pricing; Divisional Income A. R. Oma, Inc., manufactures a line of men's perfumes and after-shaving lotions. The manufacturing process is basically a series of mixing operations involving the addition of certain aromatic and coloring ingredients; the finished product is packaged in a company-produced glass bottle and packed in cases containing 6 bottles each.

A. R. Oma believes that the sale of its product is heavily influenced by the appearance and appeal of the bottle and has, therefore, devoted considerable managerial effort to the bottle production process. This has resulted in the development of certain unique bottle production processes in which management takes considerable pride.

The two areas (perfume production and bottle manufacture) have evolved almost independently over the years; in fact, a rivalry has developed between management personnel as to "which division is the more important" to A. R. Oma. This attitude is probably intensified because the bottle manufacturing plant was purchased intact 10 years ago, and no real interchange of management personnel or ideas (except at the top corporate level) has taken place.

Since the acquisition, all bottles produced have been transferred to the perfume manufacturing plant. Each area is considered a separate profit center and evaluated as such. As the new corporate controller, you are responsible for the definition of a proper transfer value to use in transferring bottles from the bottle production profit center to the packaging profit center.

At your request, the Bottle Division's general manager has asked certain other bottle manufacturers to quote a price for bottles of the quantity and sizes demanded by the perfume division. These competitive prices are:

Volume (in Cases)[a]	Total Price	Price per Case
2,000,000	$ 4,000,000	$2.00
4,000,000	7,000,000	1.75
6,000,000	10,000,000	1.67

A cost analysis of the internal bottle plant indicates that it can produce bottles at these costs:

Volume (in Cases)	Total Price	Cost per Case
2,000,000	$3,200,000	$1.60
4,000,000	5,200,000	1.30
6,000,000	7,200,000	1.20

Your cost analysts point out that these costs represent fixed costs of $1,200,000 and variable costs of $1 per case.

These figures have given rise to considerable corporate discussion as to the proper value to use in the transfer of bottles to the perfume division.

[a]A case contains 6 bottles.

This interest is heightened because a significant portion of a division manager's income is an incentive bonus based on profit center results.

The perfume division has the following costs in addition to the bottle costs:

Volume (in cases)	Total Cost	Cost per Case
2,000,000	$16,400,000	$8.20
4,000,000	32,400,000	8.10
6,000,000	48,400,000	8.07

After considerable analysis, the marketing research department has furnished you with the following price-demand relationships for the finished product:

Sales Volume (in Cases)	Total Sales Revenue	Sales Price per Case
2,000,000	$25,000,000	$12.50
4,000,000	45,600,000	11.40
6,000,000	63,900,000	10.65

Required:

a. The A. R. Oma Company has used market price to set transfer prices in the past. Using the current market prices and costs and assuming a volume of 6,000,000 cases, calculate the income for:
   1. The bottle division.
   2. The perfume division.
   3. The corporation.

b. Is this production and sales level the most profitable volume for:
   1. The bottle division?
   2. The perfume division?
   3. The corporation?

Explain your answer. (CMA adapted)

Part Three

Managerial Accounting Techniques for Decision Making

Chapter 9   Cost-Volume-Profit Analysis

Learning Objectives

The purpose of this chapter is to explain and illustrate the use of cost-volume-profit (CVP) analysis in internal decision making. The chapter describes and illustrates CVP applications for single-product firms and multiple-product firms. The use of graphical analysis is also shown. Studying this chapter will enable you to:

1. Describe the use of CVP analysis in internal decision making.
2. Apply CVP analysis to single products using the equation technique and the contribution margin technique.
3. Apply CVP analysis to multiple products using the equation technique and the contribution margin technique.
4. Apply CVP analysis while taking sales mix into account.
5. Describe and calculate operating leverage.
6. Describe the elements of a CVP graph.
7. Describe the elements of a profit-volume graph.
8. Describe the significance of and calculate the margin of safety.
9. Describe the assumptions in CVP analysis.

Chapter Topics

The major topics included in this chapter are:

> Description of Cost-Volume-Profit Analysis
> Single-Product Analysis
> Multiple-Product Analysis
> Operating Leverage
> Graphical Analysis
> Margin of Safety
> Applications of CVP Analysis
> Assumptions in CVP Analysis

This is the first of several chapters that describe techniques managers often use in making decisions. This chapter illustrates a way to analyze the effect of expected costs and volume on profit. The chapter relies strongly on the concepts of cost behavior, as discussed in Chapter 2. It illustrates analysis techniques for companies selling only one product, as well as for companies selling many products. A variety of applications of cost-volume-profit analysis are provided in order that you can see the many ways in which this technique can be used.

Description of Cost-Volume-Profit Analysis

Cost-volume-profit (CVP) analysis is a technique for evaluating the effect of changes in cost and volume on profit. **Costs** include variable and fixed costs that are expenses of the period. **Volume** represents the level of sales activity, either in units or in dollars. **Profit** for the firm may be net income or operating income. However, in some analysis, management is interested in the profit from the sale of one specific product, rather than all products.

A firm's total revenues must exceed total costs if it is to earn a profit. Once a firm is in business, certain costs are incurred regardless of volume. They are fixed costs. In addition, each sale usually includes variable costs. The amount of revenue resulting from each sale should be sufficient to cover the variable costs and provide a contribution margin that is applied toward the fixed costs. Total contribution margin must exceed fixed costs in order for the firm to earn a profit. If contribution margin is less than fixed costs, the firm incurs a net loss.

If the variable costs of a firm's product exceed its selling price, the firm will not stay in business long. Occasionally, a firm that sells a number of products may price one or more of them at less than variable cost in order to generate sales of the other products. Supermarkets often offer specials in which some items are priced at less than variable cost. By this technique, they encourage customers to shop at their stores and buy other products whose selling prices exceed variable costs. When products are sold intentionally below variable costs as a means of attracting customers, they are referred to as *loss leaders*.

The role of CVP analysis is to help managers answer questions that relate to certain decisions. For example, given the selling price, fixed costs, and variable costs of products, management can determine how many units must be sold to *break even*—to have a net income of zero. The **break-even point** is that level of volume (or sales) at which the firm earns zero profit. Analyzing costs and volume in order to determine the break-even point is referred to as **break-even analysis**. However, firms are not interested in merely breaking even; they are interested in making a profit. Therefore, CVP analysis is used in other applications as well.

Managers use CVP analysis to determine how many units must be sold to earn a specific net income or a minimum desired rate of return. CVP analysis can also be used to determine the necessary selling price of a product, given expected volume, costs, and desired profit. CVP analysis is also used to determine the effect of selling price on profit, given expected changes in variable or fixed costs. This chapter illustrates these applications of CVP analysis.

Some firms sell only one product. But most companies sell more than one. This discussion will start with the simple case of analyzing a single product and will go on to discuss analysis of multiple products in a subsequent section.

Single-Product Analysis

Single-product analysis can be applied to a firm that sells only one product or to a single product of a firm selling many products. Cost-volume-profit analysis uses one of two techniques—the equation technique or the contribution margin technique. The contribution margin technique is merely a short-cut version of the equation technique. As illustrated later, it provides a more direct approach than the equation technique.

Equation Technique

From previous study, you have seen that:

$$\text{Sales} - \text{Total Costs} = \text{Net Income}$$

This equation can be restated as follows:

$$\text{Sales} = \text{Total Costs} + \text{Net Income}$$

Total costs are composed of fixed costs and variable costs. Therefore, we can restate the equation again as follows:

$$\text{Sales} = \text{Fixed Costs} + \text{Variable Costs} + \text{Net Income}$$

This equation can be used to solve practically any type of cost-volume-profit problem. At this point, we will show how it is used to determine the break-even point and to determine sales required to achieve a desired profit.

Break-Even Point Mary Owens is considering an investment in Sports Press, a firm that will publish a new sports newspaper that will sell for $1.25 per copy. The company expects fixed costs of $60,000 per year and variable costs of $.75 per copy. Mary wants to know how many copies must be sold each year for the firm to break even. This can be determined by use of the equation technique. The equation to calculate the break-even point is as follows:

$$\text{Sales} = \text{Fixed Costs} + \text{Variable Costs} + \text{Desired Net Income}$$

This equation differs from the previous one only in its use of *desired* net income. This term represents the hoped for or expected net income, rather than an "after-the-fact" figure.

Sales includes two elements—selling price and number of copies needed to be sold. We know the selling price is $1.25. The number of copies to be sold is the unknown—that is what we are looking for. Therefore, we let x represent the number of copies that must be sold in order for the firm to break even. Fixed costs are $60,000; and variable costs are $.75 times x, the number needed to be sold. Since we are looking for the break-even point, desired net income is zero. Therefore, that part of the equation can be ignored in the calculation. The break-even point is determined as follows:

$$\$1.25x = \$60,000 + \$.75x$$
$$\$1.25x - \$.75x = \$60,000$$
$$\$.50x = \$60,000$$
$$x = \frac{\$60,000}{\$.50}$$
$$x = 120,000 \text{ Copies}$$

In order to break even, the firm must sell 120,000 copies of the newspaper per year. With this information, Mary can assess the potential market to see if a minimum of 120,000 copies is a reasonable expectation. Mary can determine total sales in dollars needed to break even by merely multiplying 120,000 copies by the selling price of $1.25 per copy, which results in a total of $150,000.

We can prove the break-even calculations merely by preparing an income statement that uses the assumptions and results of the calculation above. While it is not normally necessary to do this, it is done here to show the validity of the break-even calculation. The income statement is as follows:

Sales (120,000 × $1.25)	$150,000
Less: Variable Costs (120,000 × $.75)	90,000
Contribution Margin	$ 60,000
Less: Fixed Costs	60,000
Net Income	$ 0

The calculations above show that after selling 120,000 copies at $1.25 and subtracting the variable costs,,the company will be left with a contribution margin of $60,000. This amount is just enough to cover the fixed costs of $60,000 and results in a net income of zero, which is the break-even point.

Sales Required for Desired Net Income Mary Owens now knows that the paper must sell 120,000 copies per year to break even. However, she is interested in earning a net income of $18,000. She wants to know how many copies must be sold in order for this net income to be earned.

We use the same equation as before. However, in this case, desired net income is $18,000, rather than zero; and x becomes the number of copies that must be sold in order for $18,000 to be earned. The equation is as follows:

$$\$1.25x = \$60,000 + \$.75x + \$18,000$$
$$\$1.25x - \$.75x = \$60,000 + \$18,000$$
$$\$.50x = \$78,000$$
$$x = \frac{\$78,000}{\$.50}$$
$$x = 156,000 \text{ Copies}$$

Sports Press must sell 156,000 copies per year to earn a net income of $18,000. Dollar sales necessary to do this total $195,000 (156,000 copies × $1.25 per copy). You may wish to prove the validity of this calculation by determining net income when sales are $195,000.

At this point, Mary should examine the data to determine whether potential sales are likely to equal the number of copies calculated above. In other words, she needs to look at the market to determine the possibility of selling 156,000 copies. If it appears that the demand will be less than that, she will have to find ways to reduce costs or else accept a lower net income. In this respect, she might want to look at the long run. She may realize that the first year will be slow but that, as the paper gains acceptance and popularity, sales will increase. In any event, CVP analysis provides a starting point to help her make a decision.

Contribution Margin Technique

As previously described, contribution margin is the difference between sales and variable costs. It may be determined on both a total and a unit basis. In applying CVP analysis for a single product, you determine the unit contribution margin. For Sports Press, this margin is $.50 per copy ($1.25 − $.75). Every copy sold yields a contribution margin of $.50, which helps cover the fixed costs. When the fixed costs have been covered, the $.50 contribution margin of each additional copy sold results in profit. The $.50 per unit is not profit until the fixed costs have been covered.

The contribution margin technique is a short-cut method that can be used in CVP analysis. To illustrate, we will apply this technique to the situation described for the equation technique.

Break-Even Point In order for the firm to break even, it must cover its total fixed costs of $60,000. Each copy sold provides a $.50 contribution margin to apply toward the fixed costs. To determine the break-even point, we ask, in effect, "How many $.50s do we need in order to cover $60,000?". We calculate the break-even point by using the following formula:

$$\text{Break-Even Point} = \frac{\text{Fixed Costs}}{\text{Unit Contribution Margin}}$$

Using the data given for Sports Press, we calculate the break-even point as follows:

$$\text{Break-Even Point} = \frac{\$60,000}{\$.50}$$

$$= 120,000 \text{ Copies}$$

Notice that the calculation above is the same as the last two lines of the calculation using the equation technique (see page 256). The equation technique can normally be used to solve any CVP problem. However, when the data are given in a relatively simple form, the contribution margin technique may be quicker.

Sales Required for Desired Net Income When the contribution margin technique is used, the following formula is used to determine sales required to achieve a desired net income.

$$\text{Required Sales} = \frac{\text{Fixed Costs} + \text{Desired Net Income}}{\text{Unit Contribution Margin}}$$

Each copy sold provides a unit contribution margin that first applies towards fixed costs. After fixed costs have been covered, the contribution margin provides the net income. In this case, the fixed costs are $60,000; the desired net income is $18,000. Therefore, enough copies must be sold to provide total contribution margin of $78,000. To determine how many copies must be sold, the data are inserted in the equation as follows:

$$\text{Required Sales} = \frac{\$60,000 + \$18,000}{\$.50}$$

$$= 156,000 \text{ Copies}$$

As before, the calculation above is the same as the last two lines of the calculation using the equation technique. You may use either technique in working problems for single-product analysis. Use whichever is more convenient, based on the data provided.

Multiple-Product Analysis

As previously mentioned, a multiple-product firm may apply CVP analysis to a single product of its firm by using the techniques previously described. But for the company as a whole, the techniques are applied as described below.

Equation Technique

In this example, Franklin Company, a firm selling several products, incurs fixed costs of $450,000 per year. Its variable costs average 55 percent of sales. To apply the equation technique, we use the same basic equation as before:

$$\text{Sales} = \text{Fixed Costs} + \text{Variable Costs} + \text{Desired Net Income}$$

Break-Even Point As before, since the break-even point is a point at which net income is zero, the desired net income part of the equation is ignored. For a multiple-product company as a whole, we do not use unit data, because the selling prices and variable costs of the various types of units are likely to be different. Therefore, everything is looked at on a total basis. Sales represents total dollars of sales; and we let x equal the amount of total sales necessary for the firm to break even. Fixed costs are given as $450,000. For variable costs, we use the **variable cost ratio,** which is variable cost as a percentage of sales. This ratio is given as 55 percent. It is multiplied by sales, represented by x in the equation. With these data, we can determine the break-even point as follows:

$$x = \$450,000 + .55x$$
$$x - .55x = \$450,000$$
$$.45x = \$450,000$$
$$x = \frac{\$450,000}{.45}$$
$$x = \$1,000,000$$

The validity of this calculation is proven as follows:

Sales	$1,000,000
Less: Variable Costs (55% of $1,000,000)	550,000
Contribution Margin	$ 450,000
Less: Fixed Costs	450,000
Net Income	$ 0

Note that for multiple products, the break-even point is expressed in sales dollars. In contrast, the single-product analysis uses the contribution margin per unit and results in the break-even point's being given in units.

Sales Required for Desired Net Income   Franklin Company wants a net income of $900,000. Using the cost data above and letting x equal sales required to achieve a net income of $900,000, we calculate required sales as follows:

$$x = \$450,000 + .55x + \$900,000$$
$$x - .55x = \$450,000 + \$900,000$$
$$.45x = \$1,350,000$$
$$x = \frac{\$1,350,000}{.45}$$
$$x = \$3,000,000$$

In this case, desired net income is $900,000; so that amount is inserted in the equation. The company must have sufficient sales to cover its variable costs of 55 percent sales plus its fixed costs of $450,000 and its desired net income of $900,000. As shown above, this requires sales of $3,000,000. You may wish to prove the validity of this calculation by determining net income when sales are $3,000,000.

Contribution Margin Technique

The complement of the variable cost ratio is the **contribution margin ratio,** which represents total contribution margin as a percentage of sales. Together the variable cost ratio and the contribution margin ratio equal 100 percent. We use the contribution margin ratio to apply CVP analysis when we use the contribution margin technique for a multiple-product firm. The relationship among sales, variable costs, and contribution margin for the Franklin Company is as follows:

	Percent of Sales
Sales	100%
Variable Costs	55
Contribution Margin	45

The contribution margin ratio indicates how much contribution margin is received for every dollar of sales. In this case, the contribution margin ratio is 45 percent, which means that every dollar of sales provides a contribution margin of $.45. This relationship can be used to determine the break-even point and the sales required for desired net income.

Break-Even Point When the contribution margin technique is used, the formula for determining the break-even point for a multiple-product firm is:

$$\text{Break-Even Point} = \frac{\text{Fixed Costs}}{\text{Contribution Margin Ratio}}$$

The break-even point for the Franklin Company is calculated as follows:

$$\text{Break-Even Point} = \frac{\$450,000}{.45}$$

$$= \$1,000,000$$

Notice that again the calculation is the same as the last two lines of the calculation using the equation technique (see page 258). As with single-product analysis, the contribution margin technique is merely a short-cut approach to solving the problem.

Sales Required for Desired Net Income The amount of sales required to achieve a desired net income is determined by the following formula:

$$\text{Required Sales} = \frac{\text{Fixed Costs} + \text{Desired Net Income}}{\text{Contribution Margin Ratio}}$$

For Franklin Company, this becomes:

$$\text{Required Sales} = \frac{\$450,000 + \$900,000}{.45}$$

$$= \frac{\$1,350,000}{.45}$$

$$= \$3,000,000$$

As previously stated, either the equation technique or the contribution margin technique can be used. You should try to understand the concept behind each technique, however, rather than merely memorizing the formulas. If you understand the concept of contribution margin and contribution margin ratio, then you can solve any cost-volume-profit analysis problem with which you might be faced.

Sales Mix

The variable cost ratio and contribution margin ratio for a multiple-product company are based on an average for the company as a whole. Therefore, the percentages used in CVP analysis for a multiple-product firm depend on the sales mix the company uses.

Sales mix is the combination of a firm's products, each expressed as a percentage of total sales dollars. Franklin Company sells three products, A, B, and C. Product A provides 40 percent of total sales; Product B, 35 percent; and Product C, 25 percent. The selling price, variable cost, and contribution margin for each product are shown in Exhibit 9.1. The variable cost ratio ranges from a low of 40 percent for Product B to a high of 65 percent for Product A. Correspondingly, the contribution margin ratio varies from a high of 60 percent to a low of 35 percent.

To illustrate an application of sales mix, assume the company has sales of

Exhibit 9.1 Sales Mix

	A Dollars	A Percent	B Dollars	B Percent	C Dollars	C Percent
Sales Price	$10.00	100%	$8.00	100%	$15.00	100%
Variable Cost.	6.50	65	3.20	40	9.00	60
Contribution Margin	$ 3.50	35	$4.80	60	$ 6.00	40
Percent of Total Sales	40%		35%		25%	

$3,000,000, which we calculated earlier as the sales required to earn a net income of $900,000. If the sales mix is in the expected ratio of 40 percent, 35 percent, and 25 percent—for Products A, B, and C, respectively—results are as shown in Exhibit 9.2.

The variable costs shown for each product are based on the variable cost ratios given above—that is, 65 percent for Product A, 40 percent for Product B, and 60 percent for Product C. Total net income is $900,000, as expected. The variable cost ratio for the firm as a whole is 55 percent ($1,650,000 ÷ $3,000,000). Correspondingly, the firm's average contribution margin ratio is 45 percent.[1]

Exhibit 9.2 Sales Mix with $3 Million Total Sales

	A	B	C	Total	Percent
Sales Mix	40%	35%	25%	100%	
Sales	$1,200,000	$1,050,000	$750,000	$3,000,000	100%
Variable Costs	780,000	420,000	450,000	1,650,000	55
Contribution Margin	$ 420,000	$ 630,000	$300,000	$1,350,000	45
Fixed Costs				450,000	
Net Income				$ 900,000	

[1]The average contribution margin ratio can also be calculated by use of a weighted-average technique, as follows:

Product	Percent of Sales		CM Ratio		Average Contribution
A	40%	×	35%	=	14%
B	35	×	60	=	21
C	25	×	40	=	10
					45

Exhibit 9.3 Change in Sales Mix

	A	B	C	Total	Percent
Sales Mix	50%	30%	20%	100%	
Sales	$1,500,000	$900,000	$600,000	$3,000,000	100.0%
Variable Costs	975,000	360,000	360,000	1,695,000	56.5
Contribution Margin.	$ 525,000	$540,000	$240,000	$1,305,000	43.5
Fixed Costs.				450,000	
Net Income				$ 855,000	

Now assume that the company has $3,000,000 in sales but that its sales mix differs from the expected 40 percent, 35 percent, and 25 percent. Instead, it is 50 percent, 30 percent, and 20 percent for Products A, B, and C, respectively, as shown in Exhibit 9.3.

Although sales are $3,000,000, net income is only $855,000—$45,000 less than the desired $900,000. The overall contribution margin ratio has been reduced to 43.5 percent. The reason for this reduction is that more of Product A (the lower-profit product) was sold than expected and less of Products B and C (the higher-profit products) were sold than expected. In other words, there was a change in sales mix. This situation has two implications in CVP analysis. First, when CVP techniques are applied to a multiple-product firm, *an assumption is made that the sales mix will not change*. If this assumption is invalid, the results are also invalid. Second, management should analyze its sales mix and contribution margin percentages with an eye towards attempting to increase the proportion of the higher-profit products in the sales mix, even at the expense of the lower-profit products. Management should be aware of its sales mix and how changes in it may affect net income.

Operating Leverage

Managers often wonder what effect an increase or decrease in sales will have on profits. Naturally, they can prepare income statements at various sales levels to answer this question. However, they can answer it more directly by calculating operating leverage. **Operating leverage** represents a measurement of the effect on net income of changes in sales volume. For example, assume Franklin Company has sales of $1,500,000. Net income is $225,000, as shown below:

Sales	$1,500,000
Variable Costs (55%)	825,000
Contribution Margin	$ 675,000
Fixed Costs	450,000
Net Income	$ 225,000

Operating leverage is calculated as follows:

$$\text{Operating Leverage} = \frac{\text{Contribution Margin}}{\text{Net Income}}$$

Applying this formula to Franklin Company produces the following results:

$$\text{Operating Leverage} = \frac{\$675,000}{\$225,000} = 3$$

An operating leverage of 3 means that the percentage change in net income will be three times the percentage change in sales. For example, if Franklin Company anticipates a 20-percent increase in sales, net income will increase by 60 percent. In other words, if sales increase by $300,000 (20% × $1,500,000), net income will increase by $135,000 (60% × $225,000). This is proven as follows:

		Increase
Sales	$1,800,000	$300,000
Variable Costs (55%)	990,000	165,000
Contribution Margin	$ 810,000	$135,000
Fixed Costs	450,000	—
Net Income	$ 360,000	$135,000

As sales change, so does operating leverage. For example, if Franklin Company's sales are $1,800,000, its operating leverage is calculated as follows:

$$\text{Operating Leverage} = \frac{\$810,000}{\$360,000} = 2.25$$

The further away a firm is from the break-even point, the lower its operating leverage will be. This is because as a firm's net income increases, increases in contribution margin have a lower percentage effect on net income.

Operating leverage also applies to decreases in sales. For example, refer to the original illustration in which Franklin Company has sales of $1,500,000, net income of $225,000, and operating leverage of 3. If sales decrease by 20 percent, net income will decrease by 60 percent—a decrease of $135,000 (60% × $225,000). This is verified as follows:

		Decrease
Sales	$1,200,000	$(300,000)
Variable Costs	660,000	(165,000)
Contribution Margin	$ 540,000	$(135,000)
Fixed Costs	450,000	—
Net Income	$ 90,000	$(135,000)

In the operating leverage concept, management has a useful tool to quickly assess the effect on profits of changes in sales and thus to analyze different strategies the firm might be considering.

Graphical Analysis

The previously discussed techniques can be used to perform CVP analysis for any level of net income. However, graphs are frequently used to visually portray the CVP relationship. A graph provides a picture of the effect of changes in sales on net income. Graphs can be prepared for both single-product and multiple-product analysis.

Single-Product Analysis

Exhibit 9.4 illustrates a CVP graph for Sports Press, the firm previously discussed. An explanation of each item, as well as the way in which the various lines were determined, follows.

Total Sales Line To construct the total sales line, we start at the 0 point—the intersection of the horizontal axis and the vertical axis. We can select a sales activity of any amount; for this example, we will use 200,000 units, at which point total sales dollars equal $250,000 (200,000 × $1.25 per unit). A vertical and a horizontal dotted line are shown in Exhibit 9.4 for these items. Where these two dotted lines intersect, we put a point on the paper. We then draw a straight diagonal line from the 0 point through this point; the result is the total sales line.

Fixed Costs Line The fixed costs line is shown as a dashed line in the exhibit. By definition, fixed costs do not change over the relevant range. In this case, fixed costs are $60,000 for 0 units through 300,000 units. Therefore, a dashed line is drawn from the vertical axis at the $60,000 point from 0 units to 300,000 units.

Total Costs Line The total costs line represents the sum of fixed costs plus variable costs. To draw this line, we first determine variable costs at any level of activity. At 200,000 units of sales, variable costs are $150,000 (200,000 × $.75). At this level of sales, total costs are $210,000 ($150,000 variable costs plus $60,000 fixed costs). Therefore, we place a dot on the chart at the intersection of 200,000 units and $210,000. We then draw a straight diagonal line from the $60,000 point on the vertical axis through the dot. The line is drawn from the $60,000 mark because at 0 level of activity, total costs are $60,000—the fixed costs. At any point on this total costs line, we can determine the total costs for a particular volume of sales.

Break-Even Point The break-even point is the intersection of the total sales line and the total costs line. By definition, the break-even point is that point at which total sales equal total costs. For this example, this point is at 120,000 units, or $150,000.

Net Income Area The area to the right of the break-even point between the total sales line and the total costs line is the net income area. Any sales activity to the right of the break-even point results in net income. We can determine net income at any level of sales by reading the total sales dollars from the total sales line and subtracting the total costs read from the total costs line. For example, assume again that total sales are 200,000 copies.

Exhibit 9.4 CVP Graph–Single Product

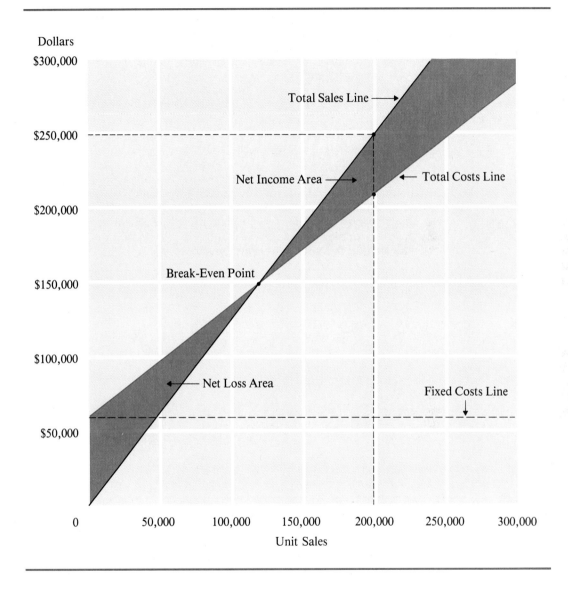

From the total sales line, we read on the vertical axis the figure $250,000. From the total costs line at 200,000 units, we read on the vertical axis a figure of $210,000. The difference between the total sales line and the total costs line is $40,000 ($250,000 − $210,000). Net income, then, is $40,000.

Net Loss Area The area to the left of the break-even point between the total sales line and the total costs line is the net loss area. Notice that the total costs line is above the total sales line to the left of the break-even point. The company is operating at a loss in this area, because total costs exceed total sales. We can determine amount of net loss for any level of activity below the break-even point by using the same procedures used for determining net income above the break-even point.

Multiple-Product Analysis

The CVP graph for a multiple-product analysis does not differ significantly from that for a single-product analysis. The primary difference is that the horizontal axis is labeled in terms of sales dollars rather than units, because the activity for the company as a whole, as well as the variable cost ratio, is measured in terms of total sales. A CVP graph for Franklin Company, a firm previously discussed, is shown in Exhibit 9.5.

This graph is constructed in the same way as that shown for single-product analysis. The explanation for the various items on the graph are also the same. In this case, the break-even point is at $1,000,000 of sales, as was previously determined mathematically. Any sales in excess of $1,000,000

Exhibit 9.5 CVP Graph–Multiple Products

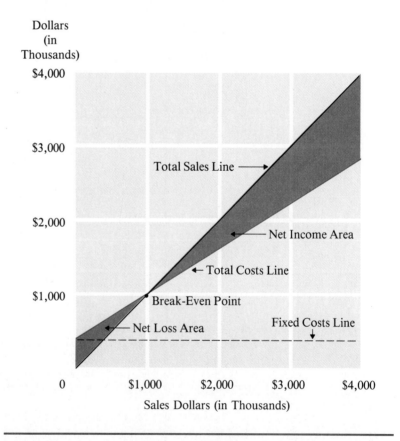

provide net income; any sales less than $1,000,000 result in a net loss. Remember however, that the amount of net income or loss, determined with the graph, is valid only if the sales mix remains the same throughout the entire length of the sales line.

Profit-Volume Graph   An alternative to the cost-volume-profit graph is the profit-volume graph, which shows the effect on net income of changes in volume. A profit-volume graph for Sports Press is shown in Exhibit 9.6.

Exhibit 9.6 Profit-Volume Graph

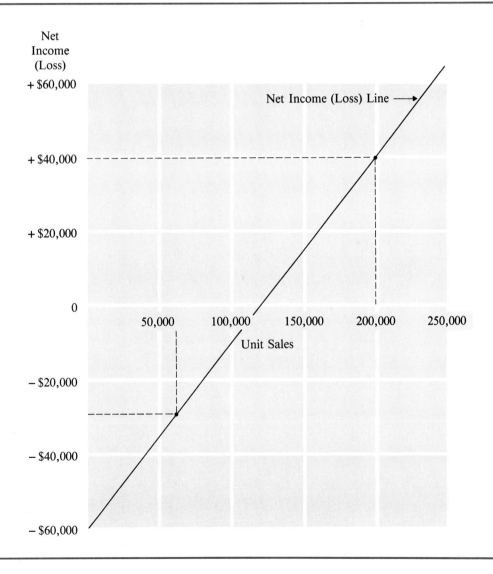

In this graph, the horizontal axis represents unit sales, as in the CVP graph. The vertical axis, however, represents net income or net loss. In Exhibit 9.6, the net income (loss) line crosses the horizontal axis at 120,000 units. By reading the vertical axis for that point, you can see that net income is $0.

The advantage of this graph is that it enables management to determine net income for any level of activity by merely reading the vertical axis for desired point of activity. For example, the vertical dotted line on the right side of the graph shows that at 200,000 units of sales, net income is $40,000. The vertical dotted line on the left side of the graph shows that at 60,000 units of sales, there is a net loss of $30,000. Many managers prefer this graph to the CVP graph because they can determine net income quickly for any level of activity. Notice that at 0 level of sales, there is a net loss of $60,000. This amount represents fixed costs.

We draw the profit-volume graph by plotting units on the horizontal axis and net income on the vertical axis. We determine the diagonal line by connecting the point representing the loss at 0 level of activity—that is, the fixed costs—to a point representing any known net income at a particular level of activity. We can mathematically determine net income from sales; for example, net income is $40,000 for sales of 200,000 units [$250,000 − $60,000 − ($.75 × 200,000 units) = $40,000]. The diagonal line increases based on contribution margin—in this case, $.50 per unit. In effect, the contribution margin is the slope of the line. For example, from the break-even point of 120,000 units to 150,000 units, net income increases by $.50 per unit, or $15,000 ($.50 × 30,000). At the 150,000-unit level, we can read the net income axis to find that net income is $15,000.

Margin of Safety

The **margin of safety** is the difference in sales between the present sales volume and the sales volume at the break-even point. It may be calculated either in sales dollars or units. For budgeting, margin of safety is the difference between expected sales and sales required to break even. It lets management know how far off its sales forecast can be before the firm will begin to suffer losses.

Assume that Sports Press expects to sell 150,000 copies the first year. At $1.25 per copy, this number of copies represents budgeted sales of $187,500. Break-even sales was previously calculated at 120,000 copies, or $150,000. The margin of safety for Sports Press, then, is calculated as follows:

$$\text{Margin of Safety (MS)} = \text{Budgeted Sales} - \text{Break-Even Sales}$$
$$\text{MS} = \$187,500 - \$150,000$$
$$= \$37,500$$

The margin of safety is often expressed as a percentage. This percentage is calculated for Sports Press as follows:

Percentage Margin of Safety (MS%)

$$= \frac{\text{Budgeted Sales} - \text{Break-Even Sales}}{\text{Budgeted Sales}}$$

$$MS\% = \frac{\$187,500 - \$150,000}{\$187,500}$$
$$= \frac{\$37,500}{\$187,500}$$
$$= 20\%$$

Note that margin of safety is expressed in dollar sales, not contribution margin. In the illustration above, if sales were 20 percent less than budgeted (20% × $187,500), the firm would still break even. However, a relatively low margin of safety, such as 3 or 4 percent, would indicate to management that there was not much room for error in its sales forecast. Since sales forecasting is difficult and inexact, a low margin of safety percentage indicates to management that it wouldn't take much error for a projected profit to become an actual loss. Thus, extra care should be taken in implementing plans to achieve a budgeted net income when the margin of safety is relatively low.

Applications of CVP Analysis

Previous illustrations showed how to use CVP analysis for determining the break-even point and for determining what sales level is required in order for the firm to achieve a desired net income. This section illustrates additional applications. Studying the examples provided here will enable you to better grasp the concepts of CVP analysis and thus to be able to apply the concepts in other situations.

Single-Product Analysis

You have already seen how the potential owner of Sports Press determined the break-even point and the sales required to achieve a desired net income of $18,000. This section uses the basic data already given and provides additional applications of CVP analysis for Sports Press. In the following examples, the equation technique is used. In many cases, however, the contribution margin technique would provide the answer more quickly.

Sales Required for Desired Rate of Return Assume Sports Press wants a 20 percent rate of return on sales. How many copies must it sell in order to achieve this desired rate of return?

In this situation, the desired net income is expressed as a percentage rather than as a total dollar amount. Since we are looking for the number of units that must be sold, x will represent these unknown units. In the equation, selling price is $1.25. Since the desired rate of return is 20 percent of sales, the desired net income in the equation becomes .20($1.25x). The problem is solved as follows:

$$\$1.25x = \$60,000 + \$.75x + .20(\$1.25x)$$
$$\$1.25x = \$60,000 + \$.75x + \$.25x$$
$$\$1.25x - \$.75x - \$.25x = \$60,000$$
$$\$.25x = \$60,000$$
$$x = \frac{\$60,000}{\$.25}$$
$$x = 240,000 \text{ Copies}$$

The example above showed rate of return on sales. Suppose, however, that Mary Owens invests $150,000 in this business. How many copies must be sold if she wants to earn a 15-percent rate of return on her investment?

In this case, desired net income is expressed in the equation as a percentage of $150,000. The level of sales required to achieve this net income is still expressed in the equation as the unknown, x. The problem is solved as follows:

$$\$1.25x = \$60,000 + \$.75x + .15(\$150,000)$$
$$\$1.25x = \$60,000 + \$.75x + \$22,500$$
$$\$1.25x - \$.75x = \$82,500$$
$$\$.50x = \$82,500$$
$$x = \frac{\$82,500}{\$.50}$$
$$x = 165,000 \text{ Copies}$$

In viewing the newspaper as a possible investment, Mary would consider whether she believed it was reasonable to expect to sell 165,000 copies. If this amount appeared reasonable, the investment would probably be made. However, if sales projections were less than 165,000 copies, Mary would either have to find a way to reduce costs, accept a lower rate of return, or not make the investment. Of course, this assumes the selling price remains at $1.25. A higher price might increase the rate of return; but it might lower sales, in which case it might actually decrease the rate of return.

Required Selling Price Now assume that costs are the same as before but that Mary has not decided on the selling price. She has estimated a sales level of approximately 140,000 copies a year. She wants to know what selling price would allow her to break even.

In this case, volume is known, but selling price is not. Thus, we let x represent the unknown selling price. Total sales are 140,000. The required selling price is calculated as follows:

$$140,000x = \$60,000 + \$.75(140,000)$$
$$140,000x = \$60,000 + \$105,000$$
$$140,000x = \$165,000$$
$$x = \frac{\$165,000}{140,000}$$
$$x = \$1.179 \text{ per Copy}$$

The result shows that the firm must sell each paper for approximately $1.18 in order to break even. It is unlikely that the firm will choose to sell each copy for $1.18. For one thing, an odd figure is not normally used as the selling price of a newspaper. But more importantly, $1.18 is the amount required to break even. Since the owner is interested in making a profit, the selling price will be something more than $1.18. If potential customers are unwilling to pay even $1.18, then the investment would not be a wise one.

Notice that in this problem, the variable cost of $.75 per copy is multiplied by the total number of copies to be sold, not by x, as it was in the previous examples. This is because x represents a selling price, not copies sold. Copies expected to be sold are 140,000.

Since the owner is interested in making a profit, she may want to expand this procedure to find the price she must charge for each copy in order to earn a rate of return of 15 percent on an investment of $150,000. She can do this as follows:

$$140,000x = \$60,000 + \$.75(140,000) + .15(\$150,000)$$
$$140,000x = \$60,000 + \$105,000 + \$22,500$$
$$140,000x = \$187,500$$
$$x = \frac{\$187,500}{140,000}$$
$$x = \$1.339$$

The owner must sell each copy for $1.34 in order to earn the desired rate of return. Again, it is unlikely she would charge this odd amount. Most likely, she would charge $1.35 per copy. If she believed she could charge $1.50 and not lose significant sales, she would probably use this amount. Suppose, however, she figured the market would not accept a price as high as $1.35 and that $1.25 would be a more reasonable price. A previous illustration showed that at $1.25 she would have to sell 165,000 copies in order to achieve a 15-percent return on investment. In this case, Mary would have to make a decision. If she believed $1.35 was too high a price, she would be forced to accept a lower rate of return or not go into business.

Change in Price For this example, assume Sports Press has been operating for a while, selling 150,000 copies a year at a price of $1.25 each. The owner plans to increase the price to $1.50 per copy. What effect will this increase have on the break-even point, which is 120,000 copies at a selling price of $1.25? Assume that fixed costs and variable costs do not change. The new break-even point is calculated as follows:

$$\$1.50x = \$60,000 + \$.75x$$
$$\$1.50x - \$.75x = \$60,000$$
$$\$.75x = \$60,000$$
$$x = \frac{\$60,000}{\$.75}$$
$$x = 80,000 \text{ Copies}$$

Notice that a $.25 increase per copy reduces the break-even point by one-third, from 120,000 copies to 80,000 copies. Suppose, however, that Mary expected the price increase to reduce sales from 150,000 to 125,000 copies. What would be the effect on current net income if this happened? In other words, would the company be better off to sell fewer copies at a higher price? This is determined as follows:

Current Net Income:

Contribution Margin (150,000 Copies × $.50 per Copy CM)	$75,000
Less: Fixed Costs	60,000
Net Income	$15,000

Net Income under Proposed Selling Price:

Contribution Margin (125,000 Copies × $.75 per Copy CM)	$93,750
Less: Fixed Costs	60,000
Net Income	$33,750

The company would be $18,750 ($33,750 − $15,000) better off with the new selling price. Even though sales would be reduced by 25,000 copies, the increased contribution margin (from $.50 to $.75) on the copies sold would more than offset the lost contribution margin on the 25,000 copies no longer sold.

Change in Fixed Costs Assume that the selling price is still $1.25 and the variable cost $.75 per copy, but that fixed costs have increased to $80,000 per year. How does this increase affect the firm's break-even point? The effect is calculated as follows:

$$\$1.25x = \$80,000 + \$.75x$$
$$\$1.25x - \$.75x = \$80,000$$
$$\$.50x = \$80,000$$
$$x = \frac{\$80,000}{\$.50}$$
$$x = 160,000 \text{ Copies}$$

Notice that an increase of $20,000 in fixed costs increases the firm's break-even point from 120,000 copies to 160,000 copies. We could also have determined this amount merely by calculating how many additional copies would have to be sold to cover the additional fixed costs. This calculation is shown as follows:

$$\frac{\$20,000}{\$.50} = 40,000 \text{ Additional Copies}$$

The additional fixed costs of $20,000 require an additional 40,000 copies to be sold. Since the break-even point was 120,000 copies, an additional 40,000 copies raises the break-even point to 160,000.

Change in Variable Costs Now assume selling price is $1.25 per copy and fixed costs are $60,000. Variable costs, however, have increased to $.90 per copy. How does this increase affect the break-even point? The new break-even point is calculated as follows:

$$\$1.25x = \$60,000 + \$.90x$$
$$\$1.25x - \$.90x = \$60,000$$
$$\$.35x = \$60,000$$
$$x = \frac{\$60,000}{\$.35}$$
$$x = 171,429 \text{ Copies}$$

An increase of $.15 per copy in variable costs increases the break-even point significantly—from 120,000 copies to 171,429 copies. Since management is frequently faced with increasing costs, it must be aware of how these costs affect its break-even point and net income. These considerations must figure in decisions regarding changes in selling price.

Combination of Changes Now let us look at the process Sports Press might go through when faced with several cost changes. In this case, assume fixed costs have increased to $75,000 and variable costs have increased to $.90 per unit. Mary wants a rate of return on sales of 20 percent. She estimates sales at 150,000 copies. Selling price is $1.25 per copy; but Mary wants to know what new selling price is required in order to cover the increased costs and provide the desired rate of return. The new selling price is represented by x. It is calculated as follows:

$$150,000x = \$75,000 + \$.90(150.000) + .20(150,000x)$$
$$150,000x = \$75,000 + \$135,000 + 30,000x$$
$$150,000x - 30,000x = \$210,000$$
$$120,000x = \$210,000$$

$$x = \frac{\$210,000}{120,000}$$

$$x = \$1.75 \text{ per Copy}$$

In this case, desired net income is 20 percent of total sales. Since the selling price is unknown, desired net income is expressed as 20 percent of the total unknown sales ($150,000x$). The result shows that the firm must now charge $1.75 per copy in order to cover costs and provide the desired rate of return. Mary must seriously question whether she can raise the price from $1.25 to $1.75 and still maintain sales of 150,000 copies. If she cannot, she may have to accept a lower rate of return or go out of business. Firms often find themselves in this type of situation. Their costs rise to such an extent that they price themselves out of the market. Whether this happens to a particular firm depends to a large extent on the type of product it sells. The demand for some products is such that higher prices will not reduce sales significantly. Management must explore this area thoroughly when making decisions of this type.

Multiple-Product Analysis

This section uses the Franklin Company to illustrate applications of CVP analysis for a multiple-product firm.

Sales Required for Desired Rate of Return Use the fixed costs of $450,000 and the variable cost ratio of 55 percent of sales determined earlier. Assume the company wants a 15-percent rate of return on sales. What level of sales is necessary in order to achieve this rate of return?

To solve this problem, let x equal the necessary sales. Desired net income is 15 percent of x. The required sales level is calculated as follows:

$$x = \$450,000 + .55x + .15x$$
$$x - .55x - .15x = \$450,000$$
$$.30x = \$450,000$$

$$x = \frac{\$450,000}{.30}$$

$$x = \$1,500,000$$

Using the same cost data as above, assume the firm wants a 20-percent rate of return on its investment of $3,000,000. Calculate the level of sales required to achieve this return on investment.

In this case, x is still required sales. Desired net income is 20 percent of $3,000,000, or $600,000. Required sales are calculated as follows:

$$x = \$450,000 + .55x + .20(\$3,000,000)$$
$$x = \$450,000 + .55x + \$600,000$$
$$x - .55x = \$1,050,000$$
$$.45x = \$1,050,000$$
$$x = \frac{\$1,050,000}{.45}$$
$$x = \$2,333,333$$

Change in Fixed Costs Previously, we calculated the break-even point for Franklin Company to be $1,000,000 when fixed costs were $450,000 and variable costs were 55 percent of sales. Management is considering spending an additional $90,000 for advertising in order to increase sales. If this amount is spent, how much must sales increase in order for the firm to break even?

The proposed $90,000 advertising expense is a fixed cost. To solve this problem, we merely use the equation as we did previously, except that fixed costs are now $90,000 more than they were before. The level of sales required to break even under these conditions is calculated as follows:

$$x = \$450,000 + \$90,000 + .55x$$
$$x - .55x = \$540,000$$
$$.45x = \$540,000$$
$$x = \frac{\$540,000}{.45}$$
$$x = \$1,200,000$$

You can see that the additional $90,000 of fixed costs increases the break-even point from $1,000,000 to $1,200,000. This means that for the advertising to pay for itself, it must generate at least $200,000 of sales. Otherwise, the firm will lose money on the additional advertising expense.

In this problem, we could have calculated the additional sales necessary to break even merely by determining the amount of sales necessary to cover $90,000 of fixed cost. You already know that with $450,000 of fixed costs, the firm needs $1,000,000 of sales to break even. The level of sales necessary to cover an additional $90,000 of fixed costs is calculated as follows:

$$\frac{\$90,000}{.45} = \$200,000$$

The calculation above shows that an additional $200,000 of sales is necessary to insure that the variable costs associated with those sales and the additional fixed costs of $90,000 are covered. When this $200,000 is added to the original break-even amount of $1,000,000, the new break-even amount becomes $1,200,000. In other words, $200,000 is the amount of sales necessary to break even on fixed costs of $90,000.

Change in Variable Costs As noted above, the original break-even point for Franklin Company was calculated at $1,000,000, assuming fixed costs of $450,000 and a variable cost ratio of 55 percent. Management is looking for ways to increase sales. In the past, its salespersons have all been paid a flat salary. Management is considering offering them a 10-percent commission on all sales in order to provide an incentive for them to sell more. If this is done, what amount of sales will be necessary for the firm to break even, assuming the same fixed costs of $450,000?

In this case, the additional 10-percent commission represents an increase in the variable costs. The variable cost ratio was 55 percent of sales; now, it is 65 percent. Sales are an unknown, represented by x. The level of sales required to break even is calculated as follows:

$$x = \$450,000 + .65x$$
$$x - .65x = \$450,000$$
$$.35x = \$450,000$$
$$x = \frac{\$450,000}{.35}$$
$$x = \$1,285,714$$

The purpose of the sales commission is to provide incentive for the salespersons to sell more. From the calculation above, you can see that in order for this incentive to pay off for the company, the salespersons must sell about $286,000 more than they needed to before for the firm to break even. If sales do not increase by $286,000, then the company is losing money by installing the commission program.

Combination of Changes As with Sports Press, any number of changes for Franklin Company might be proposed for use in CVP analysis. This illustration shows how to work with several such changes.

Management is interested in increasing sales. Consequently, it has proposed increasing advertising by $90,000 and providing salespersons with a 10-percent sales commission. Under these conditions, and with the original fixed costs of $450,000 and variable cost ratio of 55 percent, what amount of sales is necessary for the company to earn a rate of return of 15 percent on sales?

In this case, both fixed costs and variable costs are increased, and the firm has indicated its desired rate of return. The rate of return is expressed as 15 percent of x. With these data, the required sales level is calculated as follows:

$$x = \$450,000 + \$90,000 + .65x + .15x$$
$$x - .65x - .15x = \$540,000$$
$$.20x = \$540,000$$
$$x = \frac{\$540,000}{.20}$$
$$x = \$2,700,000$$

You may recall that, using fixed costs of $450,000 and the variable cost ratio of 55 percent, we previously calculated sales required to earn a 15-percent rate of return on sales to be $1,500,000. The calculation above shows that in order for the advertising and the commissions to be effective, they must increase sales by $1,200,000. Management must decide whether it believes this increase is reasonable. CVP analysis cannot make the decision. It merely shows what is necessary, given certain assumptions. If management believes the advertising and the commissions can indeed increase sales by $1,200,000, then the proposal will most likely be adopted. On the other hand, if it appears unlikely that this amount of increase in sales will occur, the proposal will probably not be adopted.

Assumptions in CVP Analysis

CVP analysis is a technique that helps management in decision making. Again, it is important to remember that the technique does not make the decisions. It merely provides information that management can analyze and on which management can base its final decision.

Certain assumptions underlie CVP analysis. The data resulting from the analysis are only as valid as these assumptions. This fact does not negate the usefulness of CVP analysis. As long as management understands the assumptions, it can adjust its final data to meet the actual situation under study. Some of these assumptions have been mentioned; some you may have inferred. However, to insure that you know the important assumptions in CVP analysis, they are presented here.

One assumption is that *costs have been accurately distinguished as variable or fixed.* As pointed out in Chapter 2, it is not always easy to separate costs between variable and fixed. Furthermore, some costs may be mixed and some may be step-variable. Thus, classification is not always accurate.

A second assumption is that *fixed costs remain constant within the relevant range of analysis.* This concept was discussed thoroughly in Chapter 2. Obviously, if fixed costs are expected to change, the changes must be considered in CVP analysis. However, the basic assumption is that they will not change.

CVP analysis also assumes that *total variable costs are affected only by changes in volume.* In other words, variable costs are always linear. This means that total variable costs increase or decrease only because of increases or decreases in the number of units sold. In reality, this is not always so. Changes in efficiency may result in a higher or lower total variable cost. As volume increases, material can sometimes be purchased for a lower price per unit. Thus, other factors normally affect total variable cost. But for CVP analysis, we ignore these factors. As always, management can adjust its data according to its own firm's circumstances.

Another assumption is that *revenues are linear*—that is, that selling price does not change over the range of activity. This, too, is not necessarily so. Sometimes economic factors require that the selling price be changed. Competition, for example, may require that management lower the selling price; or management may decide to change the selling price in order to increase volume. These factors can be considered as they apply to the individual firm.

CVP analysis assumes there is *no change in inventory levels.* In other words, whatever is produced in the current period is sold in the current period. Another way to describe this characteristic is to say that CVP analysis is really only applicable to variable costing. Under absorption costing, changes in inventory levels can affect net income. In using CVP analysis, we assume that inventory levels do not change, so that all fixed costs are subtracted from contribution margin in arriving at net income. This, in effect, is variable costing.

A final assumption is that *sales mix is constant* for multiple-product firms. As illustrated in the chapter, a change in sales mix affects CVP analysis. Thus, unless otherwise indicated, it is assumed that the percentage of total sales that each product provides will remain the same throughout the volume of activity under analysis.

Summary

Firms use cost-volume-profit analysis to determine the effect on profits of changes in volume and costs. Management must understand cost behavior patterns, as discussed in Chapter 2, in order to apply CVP analysis techniques. CVP analysis may be used by both single-product and multiple-product firms. In applying the techniques, firms can use the equation technique or the contribution margin technique. The equation technique is based on the equation:

$$\text{Sales} = \text{Fixed Costs} + \text{Variable Costs} + \text{Net Income}$$

The contribution margin technique is a short cut approach to applying CVP analysis. When performing the analysis for a multiple-product firm, management must be aware of its sales mix. Changes in the sales mix will change the results of the analysis.

The use of graphs provides helpful visualizations of the cost-volume-profit relationship. Either cost-volume-profit graphs or profit-volume graphs may be used.

The margin of safety represents the difference between the expected sales and sales at the break-even point. On a percentage basis, it allows management to know the margin of error in its sales forecast before expected profit turns into loss.

CVP analysis can be applied to a number of different types of situations. Several were illustrated in this chapter. An understanding of CVP concepts provides a background that can be applied to any situation for which appropriate data are at hand.

CVP analysis is only as valid as the assumptions that underlie it. Management must consider these basic assumptions. To the extent that any assumption is not valid in a specific situation, management must adjust its data to meet the realities of this situation.

In summary, CVP analysis is a useful technique for management. It must be remembered, though, that the technique does not make the decision; management does. With appropriate information, management can have more confidence in a decision based on the data resulting from CVP analysis.

Review Problem

Problem

Rusty's Radio Shop sells radios for $40 each. Variable costs are $25 per unit, and fixed costs are $22,500 a year. Rusty wants a net income that equals 20% of sales.

Required:

a. Determine how many radios must be sold each year in order for Rusty to break even.

b. Determine the amount of annual sales in units that Rusty needs in order to earn the desired net income.

c. If Rusty decides to spend $10,000 a year on advertising, how many units must he sell to earn the desired net income?

d. Last year Rusty sold 2,500 radios. He thinks he can sell 3,500 radios this year if he lowers the price. At what selling price can he sell 3,500 radios and earn a net income of $20,000 (rather than a net income of 20% of sales)?

Solution

For all requirements, let x equal the unknown item.

a.
$$\$40x = \$22,500 + \$25x$$
$$\$40x - \$25x = \$22,500$$
$$\$15x = \$22,500$$
$$x = \frac{\$22,500}{\$15}$$
$$x = 1,500 \text{ Units}$$

b.
$$\$40x = \$22,500 + \$25x + .20(\$40x)$$
$$\$40x = \$22,500 + \$25x + \$8x$$
$$\$40x - \$25x - \$8x = \$22,500$$
$$\$7x = \$22,500$$
$$x = \frac{\$22,500}{\$7}$$
$$x = 3,214 \text{ Units}$$

c.
$$\$40x = \$22,500 + \$10,000 + \$25x + .20(\$40x)$$
$$\$40x = \$22,500 + \$10,000 + \$25x + \$8x$$
$$\$40x - \$25x - \$8x = \$32,500$$
$$\$7x = \$32,500$$
$$x = \frac{\$32,500}{\$7}$$
$$x = 4,643 \text{ Units}$$

d.
$$3,500x = \$22,500 + \$25(3,500) + \$20,000$$
$$3,500x = \$22,500 + \$87,500 + \$20,000$$
$$3,500x = \$130,000$$
$$x = \frac{\$130,000}{3,500}$$
$$x = \$37.14 \text{ per Unit}$$

Note that this selling price does not guarantee sales of 3,500 units. A selling price of $37.14 on 3,500 units would cover all costs and result in a net income of $20,000. Rusty needs to question whether the price reduction from $40.00 to $37.14 would be enough to increase sales by 1,000 units a year.

Questions

9-1 What is meant by *cost-volume-profit analysis*?

9-2 If prices are determined by the marketplace, how can CVP analysis help management to determine prices?

9-3 Explain how CVP analysis might be used by a firm in determining how many units to produce.

9-4 Why is CVP analysis applied differently for multiple products than for single products?

9-5 What will be the effect on a firm's break-even point if selling price per unit increases by the same amount as variable cost per unit increases?

9-6 A firm's unit contribution margin is $.25. Fixed costs increase by $1,000 per year. What is the effect on the break-even point in terms of units?

9-7 A retailer, whose only variable cost is cost of goods sold, buys an item for $6 and sells it for $10. He remarks, "I make a $4 profit on every unit sold." Is he correct? Explain.

9-8 How is a firm with a high volume of sales often able to sell at a lower price than a firm with a low volume of sales, while earning the same total profit?

9-9 What is meant by *sales mix*? How does sales mix affect a firm's break-even point?

9-10 DEF Corporation sells Product A, with a 45% contribution margin, and Product B, with a 30% contribution margin. Current total sales are composed of 60% Product A and 40% Product B. What will happen to the firm's break-even point if the sales mix changes to 50%/50%? Explain.

9-11 Can the total costs line of a CVP graph ever be above the total sales line at any point to the right of the break-even point? Explain.

9-12 Refer to the profit-volume graph in Exhibit 9.6. Determine the firm's net income or loss for the following sales levels:
   a. 50,000 units.
   b. 100,000 units.
   c. 150,000 units.

9-13 In reviewing divisional budgets for next year, a firm's president noted that both of the firm's divisions project a satisfactory return on investment. However, the margin of safety is 10% for Division A and 2% for Division B. What is the significance of these facts?

9-14 "The fact that a number of assumptions must be valid for CVP analysis to be valid reduces the usefulness of the analysis." Do you agree with that statement? Why or why not?

Exercises

9-15 Single Product; Break-Even Point; Desired Profit Timothy Company sells its product for $5 per unit. Variable costs are $3.50 per unit; and fixed costs total $30,000 per year. Determine how many units must be sold each year to:

a. Break even.

b. Earn a profit of $15,000.

9-16 Single Product: Break-Even Point: Desired Profit Bixley Company sells its product for $8 per unit. Variable costs are $5 per unit; and fixed costs total $6,000 per year.

a. Determine the break-even point in:

1. Units.

2. Dollars.

b. Determine the number of units that must be sold for the firm to earn a net income of $40,000.

9-17 Single Product; Break-Even Point; Desired Profit Lucy's Clothing Store sells dresses at an average cost of $25 each, with a variable cost of $15 each. Fixed costs are $40,000 per year. Determine how many dresses must be sold each year in order for the firm to:

a. Break even.

b. Earn a profit of $25,000.

c. Earn a 20% return on sales.

9-18 Single Product; Required Selling Price John Baker is planning to sell a product with a variable cost of $4.25 per unit. Fixed costs are expected to be $50,000 per year. John estimates that he can sell 100,000 units per year. Determine the required selling price, assuming John wants:

a. A net income of $20,000.

b. A 15% return on sales.

c. A 10% return on his $150,000 investment.

9-19 Single Product; Required Selling Price Mary Evans opened a candy shop in which the variable cost per box is $3. She anticipates fixed costs of $10,000 per year and expects to sell 15,000 boxes per year. Determine the average selling price required to:

a. Break even.

b. Earn a net income of $12,000.

c. Earn a 10% return on sales.

9-20 Single Product; Increased Selling Price Region Company sells a product for $35 per unit, and the variable production and sales costs are $21 per unit. If Region adopts a 40% increase in the selling price of its product, by what percentage can unit sales decline before total profits decline? (CMA adapted)

9-21 Multiple Products; Break-Even Point; Desired Profit Hardy Company incurs fixed costs of $800,000 per year. Its variable cost ratio is 60%. Calculate:

a. Break-even sales.

b. Sales required to earn a profit of $200,000.

9-22 Multiple Products; Break-Even Point; Desired Profit Ace Corporation incurs fixed costs of $60,000 per year. Its variable costs average 65% of sales. Calculate:

a. Break-even sales.

b. Sales required to earn a profit of $20,000.

c. Sales required to earn a 20% return on sales.

9-23 Multiple Products; Break-Even Point Hanson Company's income statement for last year is as follows:

Sales		$300,000
Variable Costs	$165,000	
Fixed Costs	100,000	265,000
Net Income		$ 35,000

What was the company's break-even level of sales?

9-24 Determining Sales from Break-Even Point Tice Company is a medium-sized manufacturer of lamps. During the year, a new line called "Horalin" was made available to Tice's customers. The break-even point for sales of Horalin is $200,000, with a contribution margin of 40%. Assuming that the profit for the Horalin line for the year amounted to $100,000, determine total sales for the year. (AICPA adapted)

9-25 Operating Leverage Bakely Company had sales last year of $500,000. Variable costs totaled $300,000; and fixed costs were $160,000. Management projects a 20% increase in sales for the current year.

a. Determine the firm's operating leverage based on last year's results.

b. Use the operating leverage determined in part **a** to determine projected net income for the current year.

9-26 Explaining Profit Change Kary Company sells two products—Kary Sauce and Kary Juice. The contribution margin ratio is 30% for sauce and 20% for juice. In 19X1, sales of sauce were $60,000 and sales of juice were $40,000. Sales in 19X2 were $50,000 for each product.

a. Calculate the contribution margin ratio for the firm for 19X1.

b. How much was the increase or decrease in profit in 19X2, compared with 19X1?

c. Explain the reason for the change in profit.

9-27 Single Product; Break-Even Point; Margin of Safety; Operating Leverage Battle Company sells its product, Battlem, for $12 each. Variable costs are $9 per unit, and fixed costs are $75,000 per year. Next year it projects sales of $360,000. Calculate the following:

a. Break-even point in units and dollars.

b. Margin of safety.

c. Percentage of margin of safety.

d. Operating leverage.

9-28 Projecting Sales from Margin of Safety The Black Company manufactures and sells a specialty perfume. The company budgets a margin of safety of 20% for next year. Fixed costs are budgeted at $270,000 annually.

Variable costs are $6.60 per ounce. If the sales price per ounce is $12, what is the budgeted level of sales revenue for next year? (CMA adapted)

Problems

9-29 Single Product; Break-Even Point; Desired Profit Julie's China Shop sells china at $125 per set. Each set has a variable cost of $85. Julie's fixed costs are $15,000 per year. Last year the shop sold 600 sets of china.
Required:
   a. Determine the annual break-even point in units.
   b. How many sets of china must Julie sell in order to earn $20,000 a year?
   c. Julie is considering advertising next year. Assuming she spends $2,000 on advertising, how many additional sets must she sell in order to break even?
   d. In an effort to boost sales significantly, Julie is considering spending $5,000 on advertising next year and reducing the price to $100 per set. Calculate how many sets she must sell in order to:
      1. Break even.
      2. Earn $20,000.

9-30 Single Product; Break-Even Point; Desired Profit; Required Selling Price The B & Z Bookstore will open soon and will specialize in the buying and selling of used paperback books. Each book will cost the store $.50; and the owner is now considering several pricing strategies. Fixed costs are estimated at $8,000 a year.
Required:
   a. Assuming sales of 15,000 books a year, determine the selling price necessary for the owner to:
      1. Break even.
      2. Earn a profit of $10,000 a year.
   b. The owner thinks the price calculated in part a is too high. He wants to price each book at $.95 and increase volume. How many books would he need to sell to earn a profit of $10,000 a year?
   c. As another alternative, the owner is considering spending $2,500 a year on advertising and pricing each book at $1.25. Calculate the level of sales required for the owner to:
      1. Break even.
      2. Earn a profit of $10,000.

9-31 Single Product; Break-Even Point; Desired Profit; Change in Costs Carey Company sold 100,000 units of its product at $20 per unit. Variable costs are $14 per unit (comprising manufacturing costs of $11 and selling costs of $3). Fixed costs are incurred uniformly throughout the year and amount to $792,000 (comprising manufacturing costs of $500,000 and selling costs of $292,000). There are no beginning or ending inventories.
Required:
   a. Determine the break-even point in units and dollars.
   b. Determine the number of units that must be sold for the company to earn a net income of $60,000.

c. Labor costs are 50% of variable costs and 20% of fixed costs. Assume that wages and salaries increase by 10%. Determine the break-even point in units. (AICPA adapted)

9-32 Single Product; Break-Even Point; Desired Profit; Change in Costs
Laraby Company produces a single product. It sold 25,000 units last year with the following results:

Sales		$625,000
Variable Costs	$375,000	
Fixed Costs	150,000	525,000
Net Income		$100,000

In an attempt to improve its product, Laraby is considering replacing one of its component parts with a new and better one in the coming year. The part presently used has a cost of $2.50 per unit; the new part would cost $4.50 per unit. A new machine would also be needed to increase plant capacity. The machine would cost $18,000 with a useful life of 6 years and no salvage value. The company uses straight-line depreciation on all plant assets.

Required:
   a. What was Laraby Company's break-even point in number of units last year?
   b. How many units of product would Laraby Company have had to sell in the last year to earn $77,000 in net income?
   c. If Laraby Company holds the sales price constant and makes the suggested changes, how many units of product must it sell in the coming year to break even?
   d. If Laraby Company holds the sales price constant and makes the suggested changes, how many units of product will the company have to sell to make the same net income as last year?
   e. If Laraby Company wishes to maintain the same contribution margin ratio, what selling price per unit of product must it charge next year to cover the increased material costs? (CMA adapted)

9-33 Single Product; Break-Even Point; Desired Profit; Change in Costs
R. A. Ro and Company, maker of quality handmade pipes, has experienced a steady growth in sales for the past 5 years. However, increased competition has led Mr. Ro, the president, to believe that an aggressive advertising campaign will be necessary next year to maintain the company's present growth.

To prepare for next year's advertising campaign, the company's accountant has prepared and presented Mr. Ro with the following data for the current year:

Cost Schedule

Variable Costs (per Pipe):	
Direct Labor	$ 8.00
Direct Materials	3.25
Variable Overhead	2.50
Total Variable Costs	$13.75

Fixed Costs:	
Manufacturing	$ 25,000
Selling	40,000
Administrative	70,000
Total Fixed Costs	$135,000
Selling Price, per Pipe:	$25
Expected Sales, Current Year (20,000 units):	$500,000

Mr. Ro has set the sales target for next year at a level of $550,000 (or 22,000 pipes).

Required:

a. What is the projected net income for the current year?

b. What is the break-even point in units for the current year?

c. Mr. Ro believes an additional selling expense of $11,250 for advertising next year, with all other fixed costs remaining constant, will be necessary to attain the sales target. What will be net income next year if the additional $11,250 is spent?

d. What will be the break-even point in dollar sales next year if the additional $11,250 is spent for advertising?

e. If the additional $11,250 is spent for advertising next year, what level of dollar sales will be required for next year's net income to equal the current year's net income?

f. At a sales level of 22,000 units, what is the maximum amount that can be spent on advertising if a net income of $60,000 is to be earned? (CMA adapted)

9-34 Single Product; Break-Even Point; Desired Profit; Required Selling Price; Change in Costs All-Day Candy Company is a wholesale distributor of candy. The company services grocery, convenience, and drug stores in a large metropolitan area.

Small but steady growth in sales has been achieved by the company over the past few years, while candy prices have been increasing. The company is formulating its plans for the coming fiscal year. Presented below are the data used to project the current year's net income of $184,000.

Average Selling Price per Box		$4.00
Average Variable Costs (per Box):		
Cost of Candy		$2.00
Selling Expenses		.40
Total		$2.40
Annual Fixed Costs:		
Selling		$160,000
Administrative		280,000
Total		$440,000
Expected Annual Sales Volume (390,000 Boxes)		$1,560,000

Manufacturers of candy have announced that they will increase prices of their products by an average of 15% in the coming year because of increases in raw material (sugar, cocoa, peanuts, and the like) and labor costs. All-Day Company expects that all other costs will remain at the same rates or levels as those for the current year.

Required:

  a. What is All-Day Candy Company's break-even point in boxes of candy for the current year?

  b. What selling price per box must All-Day Candy Company charge to cover the 15% increase in the cost of candy and still maintain the current contribution margin ratio?

  c. What volume of sales in dollars must the All-Day Candy Company achieve in the coming year to maintain the same net income as projected for the current year if the selling price of candy remains at $4 per box and the cost of candy increases 15%? (CMA adapted)

9–35 Single Product; Break-Even Point; Desired Profit; Change in Costs Randy's Record Shop sells albums for $10 each. Each album costs Randy $7. Other variable costs average 5% of sales. One sales clerk is employed; she is paid $8,000 a year. Rent is $400 per month; insurance is $100 per month; and utilities average $3,500 a year. There are no other costs. Current sales are 12,000 albums a year.

Required:

  a. Calculate the annual break-even point in units.

  b. How many albums must be sold in order for Randy to earn $12,000 a year?

  c. In an effort to increase sales, Randy is considering paying the sales clerk a 10% commission on sales in addition to the salary. He hopes this will provide the clerk with an incentive to try to sell more. The clerk currently sells 60% of the albums sold, and Randy sells the other 40%. Randy does not expect to sell any more albums himself than he now does. If the commission is paid, how many albums must be sold in order for net income to be no less than it now is?

  d. Do you recommend that the sales commission plan be adopted? Why or why not?

9–36 Single Product; Break-Even Point; Desired Profit; Change in Costs; Required Price Kelly Williams is considering opening Kelly's Kerry Blue Kennels. She plans to raise and sell Kerry Blues, a distinguished breed of dogs. She believes she can do this in her spare time and still keep her regular job. She will sell Kerry Blues for $200 each. The variable cost of raising the dogs from birth until they are ready to sell is $60 per dog. Fixed costs are $500 a year.

Required:

  a. How many dogs must Kelly sell each year to break even?

  b. How many dogs must she sell each year in order to earn a net income of $3,500 a year?

  c. Kelly thinks that if she hired a part-time helper, she might be able to raise and sell more dogs. A part-time helper would cost $4 an hour and work 10 hours a week for 50 weeks a year. Expanding her facilities would increase Kelly's fixed costs by $500 a year. If these conditions were implemented, what would the following be?

    1. Break-even point in number of dogs.

    2. Number of dogs that must be sold for Kelly to earn a net income of $3,500 a year.

d. In addition to raising Kerry Blues, Kelly is also considering boarding dogs for people who are out of town. She estimates that she could keep 5 dogs each night for an average of 300 nights a year. The variable cost for each dog kept is $.50 per night. This alternative would require additional facilities and more hours of work from the part-time helper. Therefore, fixed costs would increase by $600 a year. What price must Kelly charge per dog per night to break even on boarding dogs?

e. As a practical matter, Kelly believes she is limited to selling a total of 35 Kerry Blues a year. Assume the same cost data as given in the problem and in parts c and d. What price must she charge for boarding dogs per dog per night to earn a total net income of $3,500 from selling Kerry Blues and boarding 5 dogs a night for 300 nights a year?

9-37 Single Product; Break-Even Point; Desired Profit; Required Selling Price; Change in Costs Bilt-Better Battery Company manufactures and sells automobile batteries. Financial data concerning the company are as follows:

Selling Price	$65 per Unit
Costs:	
Variable Manufacturing	$25 per Unit
Variable Selling and Administrative	$15 per Unit
Fixed Manufacturing	$200,000 per Year
Fixed Selling and Administrative	$150,000 per Year

Last year's sales were 20,000 units.

Required:

a. How many batteries must be sold each year for the firm to break even?

b. How many batteries must be sold each year for the firm to earn a 20% return on sales?

c. For next year, management is considering a 10% price increase. In order to offset customer resistance to the price increase, the firm will spend an additional $50,000 to advertise the exceptional quality of the battery. How many batteries must the company sell in order to earn net income equal to what it earned last year?

d. The company plans to improve the quality of the battery next year, but this improvement will increase variable cost by $5 a unit. Management believes that the improvement to the battery, along with increased advertising costing $100,000, will boost sales to 25,000 units. What selling price is needed for the firm to earn a net income of $200,000.

e. Do you recommend the company take the steps outlined in part d? Why or why not?

f. In order to improve sales next year, the company is considering offering a $5 rebate on every battery sold in March and April. It will spend an additional $100,000 to advertise the rebate offer. Regardless of the success (or lack of success) of the rebate, the company expects to sell at least 20,000 batteries.

1. How many batteries must be sold under the rebate offer in order for it to pay for itself?
2. Assuming that without the rebate offer, sales will not exceed 20,000 units, how many units must be sold under the rebate plan in order for the firm to earn $200,000 for the year?

9-38 Single Product: Break-Even Point: Amount of Discount; Coupon Redemption Big Brian's Pizza Parlor has done well in its several years of existence. An income statement for last year is shown below:

Big Brian's Pizza Parlor
Income Statement
for the Year Ended December 31, 19X2

Sales		$200,000
Cost of Food Sold	$60,000	
Wages	70,000	
Rent	6,000	
Depreciation	15,000	
Supplies	2,000	
Utilities	5,000	
Total Expenses		158,000
Net Income		$ 42,000

All expenses, except cost of food sold, are fixed. The average pizza sells for $5.

Required:

a. How many pizzas must be sold each year in order for Big Brian to break even?

b. How many pizzas must be sold in order for Big Brian to double net income from what it was in 19X2?

c. About 50 times a year, Big Brian is asked to use part of his facilities for special parties. Normally, each party results in sales of about $200; but $150 of regular sales are lost because of lack of space. The parties also ask for a discount. How much of a discount per pizza can Big Brian afford to give them?

d. Advertising for Big Brian's has always been by word of mouth. However, Big Brian is considering spending $10,000 for newspaper advertising next year. The advertisements will include coupons allowing $.50 off the regular price of a pizza. Big Brian estimates that 25% of the coupons will be redeemed by customers who would have bought a pizza at the regular price and 75% will be redeemed by customers who would not have bought a pizza at Big Brian's had it not been for the coupon. How many coupons must be redeemed by customers who otherwise would not have bought a pizza at Big Brian's in order for the coupon promotion to be worthwhile?

9-39 Multiple Products; Break-Even Point; Required Sales; Operating Leverage Conglom, Inc., sells a number of products, whose average contribution margin ratio is 40%. Fixed costs average $300,000 a year.

Required:

a. Calculate the annual break-even point.

b. Calculate sales required for the firm to earn $500,000.

c. Assume the firm has sales in 19X1 of $1,000,000. What is its operating leverage?

d. Because of an economic recession, management expects 19X2 sales to decline by 10% from the 19X1 level. Use the operating leverage calculated in part c to determine 19X2's expected net income.

9-40 Multiple Products; Break-Even Point; Desired Profit; Alternatives for Increasing Sales Last year's income statement for Super Office Supply Manufacturers is shown below.

Sales		$800,000
Variable Costs	$480,000	
Fixed Costs	400,000	880,000
Net Loss		$(80,000)

The loss is particularly disappointing in view of the fact that management had set a 10% return on sales as its profit goal. Management is now considering alternatives for next year, in hopes of achieving the profit objective.

Required:

a. Calculate the following:

1. Break-even sales.

2. Sales required to earn a 10% return on sales.

b. For each plan below, determine the level of sales required for the company to earn a 10% return on sales.

Plan A: In the past, salespersons were paid a salary with no commission. Plan A reduces these salaries by $50,000 a year and pays a 5% commission on sales.

Plan B: The firm's advertising budget has been relatively low. Plan B calls for a $200,000 advertising campaign to boost sales.

Plan C: Plan C combines Plans A and B—that is, it reduces salaries by $50,000 a year, pays a 5% commission on sales, and increases advertising by $200,000.

c. Which, if any, of the plans do you recommend? Why?

9-41 Multiple Products; Break-Even Point; Desired Profit; Change in Sales Mix; Change in Costs Rainbow Paint Company manufactures 2 lines of paint—Brite-White, which can be made into various colors when pigments are added, and Koat-Glos. Brite-White (BW) accounts for 70% of total sales and provides a 30% contribution margin. Koat-Glos (KG) accounts for remaining sales and provides a 40% contribution margin. Last year, sales totaled $1,000,000 and fixed costs totaled $200,000.

Required:

a. Calculate the overall contribution margin ratio for the firm.

b. What is the firm's break-even point in total sales?

c. Management wants a net income of $300,000.

1. What amount of total sales is necessary for the firm to achieve a net income of $300,000?

2. By how much must sales of each product increase over last year's sales for the firm to achieve a net income of $300,000?

d. Assuming total sales are $1,000,000, management would like to increase KG's share of sales to 40%. What is the maximum amount the firm could spend on advertising to achieve this sales mix while still earning a net income equal to last year's?

e. Fixed costs are expected to increase by $50,000 next year. Assuming that sales mix does not change, by how much must total sales increase in order for the firm to earn the same net income as last year?

9-42 Multiple Products; Break-Even Point; Desired Profit; Change in Sales Mix; Change in Costs The Alphabet Company sells three products, with prices, cost data, and sales mix as shown below:

	X		Y		Z	
Sales Price	$5.00	100%	$3.00	100%	$10.00	100%
Variable Cost	3.00	60%	2.40	80%	5.00	50%
Contribution Margin	$2.00	40%	$ .60	20%	$ 5.00	50%
Percent of Total Sales	30%		50%		20%	

Last year the company had sales of $400,000, fixed costs of $50,000, and a net income of $78,000.

Required:

a. Calculate the overall contribution margin ratio for the firm.

b. What is the firm's break-even point in:
   1. Total dollar sales
   2. Total unit sales

c. Assuming that sales mix does not change, how many units of each product must the firm sell in order to earn a net income of $100,000.

d. Calculate net income assuming that the price of Y is increased by 20%, resulting in a 10% decrease in units sold of Y and a 5% increase in units sold of X. There is no effect on sales of Z.

e. In an effort to increase the sales of Z, management is considering spending $20,000 to advertise it. This advertising is expected to increase unit sales of Z by 20% and decrease unit sales of X by 10%. There is no effect on sales of Y.
   1. Calculate net income under this assumption.
   2. Determine the break-even point in dollar sales under the new sales mix.
   3. Does this idea appear to be a good one? Explain.

f. Another alternative to increase sales of Z is under consideration. This plan calls for a 10% commission to be paid on sales of Z. How many units of Z must be sold for the firm to earn net income equal to last year's—that is, $78,000? There is no change in costs or sales of X and Y.

Chapter 10   Relevant Cost

Learning Objectives

The purpose of this chapter is to describe and illustrate the factors that must be considered when cost data is used as a basis for decision making. The chapter describes the concept of relevant cost and illustrates the application of this concept in several business situations. Studying this chapter will enable you to:

1. Distinguish the difference in cost considerations between long-run and short-run decisions.
2. Distinguish between quantitative and qualitative factors.
3. Describe the concept of relevant cost.
4. Apply relevant cost analysis in a variety of situations.
5. Describe joint product costs.
6. Apply the relative sales value method to cost allocation.
7. Describe opportunity cost.
8. Distinguish among various types of pricing policies.

Chapter Topics

The major topics included in this chapter are:

Cost Considerations in Decision Making
Description of Relevant Cost
Equipment Replacement
Segment Operations
~~Joint Product Costs~~
Make or Buy Decisions
Pricing
Limiting Factors

Many business and personal decisions are based on costs. In general, costs accumulated by the accounting system of a business may be used for external reporting, internal decision making, and controlling operations. As you have learned, the cost information needed for internal decision making frequently differs from that needed for external financial reporting. Management must be aware of what costs may appropriately be used for specific internal decisions.

This chapter discusses the concept of relevant cost. It illustrates the uses of cost data in several decision-making situations often encountered in business operations. A good understanding of relevant cost is the basis for good decisions.

Cost Considerations in Decision Making

A major consideration in looking at costs for making decisions is whether the decision is a long-run or a short-run decision. The specific costs to be considered, as well as the manner in which they are applied, may differ depending on the type of decision.

Long-Run Decisions

The primary objective of a business firm is to earn a profit. If a firm is to survive in the long run, its revenues must exceed its expenses. In addition, the profit it earns must represent a reasonable rate of return for the investment in the business. Otherwise, it is to the owner's benefit to withdraw the investment and place the funds elsewhere.

In arriving at the best long-run decisions, however, one must often look closely at the short run. An incorrect short-run decision may affect long-run profitability. Distinguishing between the necessary elements to use for short-run decisions and long-run decisions is described in this chapter.

Short-Run Decisions

Absorption costing requirements and long-run considerations often blur understanding of what cost data are necessary for making short-run decisions. Many short-run decisions can be made that will contribute to long-run profitability. Unfortunately, incorrect use of cost concepts often results in an incorrect decision that reduces total profit of the firm. This chapter illustrates how costs should be analyzed to determine whether the costs are appropriate to be used for making short-run decisions.

A major element of short-run decision making is the consideration of contribution margin concepts, including that of segment margin. You may recall that **segment margin** is the amount of contribution to total fixed costs and profit provided by a segment after the segment's variable and separable fixed costs are deducted from its revenues. In many instances, a short-run decision should be based on whether a segment margin will result from the decision. This chapter illustrates when contribution margin and segment margin should be the primary considerations and when long-run factors should be considered most important.

Quantitative and
Qualitative Factors

A **quantitative factor** can be measured numerically, such as with dollars, units, percentages, or ratios. For example, common quantitative measurements are net income and return on investment. There is no question that quantitative factors—the dollar-and-cent considerations—are important in any business decision. It is equally important, however, to consider qualitative factors.

A **qualitative factor** affects a decision but cannot be measured numerically. Many times, though, qualitative factors outweigh quantitative factors. Techniques presented later in this chapter relate to determining the appropriate quantitative factors to be used in decision making.

Quality itself is a qualitative factor. Suppose a firm must decide between two alternatives; one costs more than the other, but the more costly alternative provides greater quality. For example, in deciding which of two machines to buy, the firm may find that Machine A costs less than Machine B to buy and operate. However, Machine B results in a better-quality product that will translate into more sustained sales of product over a period of time. In this case, the qualitative factor (quality) may offset the quantitative factor (cost).

In making personal decisions, you may also consider quality more important than cost. Have you ever bought a high-priced product instead of a similar product that cost less? If so, why did you do it? Probably, you felt the more expensive product provided greater quality. In that instance, the qualitative factor outweighed the quantitative factor. Other qualitative factors such as **style, prestige,** and **image** often enter into decisions, especially at the personal level. For example, individuals have often bought expensive automobiles because of such factors when, most likely, less expensive but less prestigious automobiles would have provided the transportation they needed.

Service is another qualitative factor. You may pay a higher price for an item at a store at which you know you can obtain service if you have any problem with the product. Perhaps you could buy the same product at a lower price elsewhere; but if you do not believe that the lower-priced store would give you service you might need, you may decide that the lower price is not worth the accompanying risk. In that case, the qualitative factor of service would outweigh the quantitative factor of cost.

Human relations is another qualitative factor. Often a firm does not lay off employees even though quantitatively it would be the best thing to do. Laying off personnel provides a negative public relations image. Furthermore, it may result in problems with the employees' union. It may also create difficulties for the economy in the local community. Therefore, a firm sometimes will maintain people on its payroll even though it might be in the firm's economic interest to let them go. In these cases, the qualitative factors are more important than the quantitative factor (cost reduction) that might be achieved by the layoff.

The examples above are not all-inclusive. However, they illustrate how qualitative factors can influence a firm's decision. Qualitative factors are often forgotten in the analysis techniques for quantitative considerations. But when the final decision must be made, management should analyze all appropriate quantitative and qualitative factors.

Description of Relevant Cost

In decision making, a **relevant cost** is one that is pertinent to the decision being made. In other words, it relates to or has a bearing on the decision. The purpose of this section is to describe how costs are distinguished as relevant and to show how this concept is applied in practice. It should be pointed out that while the emphasis in this chapter is on relevant cost, relevant revenues are also important. When analyzing a decision that relates to revenues, management should consider only those revenues that have a bearing on the decision.

A *relevant cost* must be a *future expected cost* and must *differ between alternative decisions.* The process of analyzing relevant costs for the purpose of making decisions is referred to as **relevant cost analysis.**

Future Expected Cost

A decision to do something involves a future action. Therefore, a decision to incur costs should consider only costs that will be incurred in the future as a result of the decision. Frequently, incorrect decisions are based on the consideration of past costs. Past, or previously incurred, costs are referred to as **sunk costs.** These costs are usually the cost of assets already purchased. A sunk cost is irrelevant in a decision about the future. A cost previously incurred is not incurred again. The inclusion of sunk costs in decision making about the future leads to difficulties in relevant cost analysis.

irrelevant.

Any decision about the future should include the costs expected to be incurred in the future as a result of the decision. The problems arising from the incorrect inclusion of sunk costs in relevant cost analysis are illustrated later in this chapter.

Differ between Alternatives

To be relevant, a cost must differ between alternatives. For example, if you are moving from one city to another, you may find that the moving companies you are considering charge the same rates. Therefore, cost is irrelevant to your decision of which mover to choose. As a result, you will most likely select a mover based on qualitative factors such as on-time delivery, service, and past history of complaints.

On the other hand, if you are trying to decide whether to use a commercial mover or rent a truck and do it yourself, you will find there is a difference in cost. Most likely, cost will be substantially less if you do it yourself. Therefore, cost is relevant, because it differs between the alternatives. Whether you use a mover or do it yourself will probably depend on whether you think the money you will save by doing it yourself is worth the time, effort, and trouble (qualitative factors).

Illustration

To better understand the concept of relevant cost, consider the illustration presented in this section.

Jeff Perry has decided to visit relatives in another city. He is trying to decide whether to take a bus or a plane. In either case, he will be gone a total of fourteen days. The bus trip will require two days of travel each way. The round trip cost is $150; last year it was $120. If he goes by air, he can get there in less than a day and make his return trip in the same amount of time. It will cost $250 for a round-trip ticket, although it cost only $210 last year. Riding the bus will require that Jeff buy meals, which will cost a total of $60 for the round trip. There is no meal cost on the plane. Regardless of whether he goes by bus or air, his relatives will meet him and he will have no taxi fares. Before making the trip, Jeff plans to buy some new clothes that will cost $250 and a new suitcase that will cost $80. Furthermore, he will leave his pet hamster with a friend and pay him $1 a day for the fourteen days he is gone. The rent on his apartment is $400 a month. Since he will be gone for two weeks, he figures he is losing two weeks' rent.

In analyzing this situation, we must consider several matters. What is the quantitative difference in cost between taking a bus and a plane for this trip? What qualitative factors should be considered? The relevant costs for each alternative are as follows:

	Bus	**Air**
Fare	$150	$250
Meals	60	0
Total	$210	$250

There is a $40 difference in favor of taking the bus. Note that $210 and $250 are not the total costs of the trip. They are the relevant costs in deciding between the two alternatives. The cost of having his friend take care of his pet hamster, $14, will increase the total cost of the trip. But it is irrelevant between the two alternatives. The $330 he plans to spend for the clothes and suitcase is also irrelevant; it too is the same between alternatives. Whether the cost of these items is considered a cost of the trip depends on whether he would have bought them anyway. Last year's bus and air fares are irrelevant, because they are past costs, not expected future costs. The two weeks' lost rent on his apartment is irrelevant, because it will be incurred anyway.

If you had added the irrelevant costs that are future costs but that are the same between alternatives—that is, $14 + $250 + $80—total costs would be $554 by bus and $594 by air. The difference between the two alternatives would still be $40. Therefore, including those irrelevant items does not make the analysis wrong. However, it is usually better to include only the relevant factors in order that the analysis not be complicated with too much information. Frequently, inclusion of irrelevant data, while not necessarily incorrect, tends to confuse the problem and make it more difficult to understand the results.

Although it is $40 cheaper to go by bus, there are qualitative factors to consider. A primary qualitative factor is time. Going by bus will require at least two more full days than going by air. Jeff wants to visit his relatives, and going by air will provide him with additional time to be with them. Furthermore, since traveling is usually tiring, the additional cost of going by air may be outweighed by the qualitative factor of speed. On the other side, if Jeff has not made this trip before, the bus will offer him the chance to see scenery he cannot see by air. He may feel that in addition to saving money, he is getting a little extra with the scenery. If this last factor is important, Jeff may decide to go one way by bus and one way by air. This, of course, would provide different cost figures.

This illustration is one example of the application of relevant cost. The remainder of the chapter provides more detailed illustrations of relevant cost analysis to show how managers can use it in making decisions between alternatives.

Equipment Replacement

Equipment replacement involves a long-range decision that is discussed more fully in Chapter 11. However, it often provides difficulties in relevant cost analysis, because management tends to consider sunk costs when it should be analyzing future expected costs. This section provides an example of relevant cost analysis for equipment replacement.

The Nodden Company bought a machine for $15,000 six years ago. At the time it was bought, it had an expected useful life of ten years with no salvage value. Depreciation has been $1,500 per year, and accumulated depreciation totals $9,000 (6 years × $1,500). The current book value is $6,000 ($15,000 − $9,000). Operating costs for the machine are $2,500 per year. Because technological advances have made it out-of-date, it could be sold today for only $2,000.

A new, superior machine could be bought today for $6,000. It has only a four-year life; but its operating costs are only $1,000 per year. It would have no salvage value at the end of four years.

Management is trying to decide whether to replace the old machine with the new machine. It is concerned that disposing of the old machine now will result in a loss of $4,000 ($6,000 book value − $2,000 disposal value). Regardless of the decision, sales are expected to continue at $200,000 per year and cost of goods sold at $140,000 per year. Other operating costs (in addition to those of the machine) are expected to average $30,000 per year.

To analyze the quantitative factors, management should consider the relevant costs of each alternative. This relevant cost analysis is shown in Exhibit 10.1.

The company will be $2,000 better off over the next four years if it buys the new machine. The only relevant costs applicable to the old machine for the next four years are the operating costs of $2,500 per year—$10,000 for the four years. Parentheses are used in the exhibit to indicate costs. The new

Exhibit 10.1 Equipment Replacement Relevant Costs

	Old	New
Purchase of New Machine	—	$(6,000)
Disposal of Old Machine Now	—	2,000
Machine Operating Costs:		
Old—$2,500 × 4 years	$(10,000)	
New—$1,000 × 4 years		(4,000)
Total Relevant Costs	$(10,000)	$(8,000)

machine has a relevant cost of $8,000 for the four years. Notice that the initial price of $6,000 for the new machine is offset by the $2,000 disposal value for the old machine. The $2,000 is relevant because the firm receives $2,000 only if the new machine is purchased.

Notice the absence of the $4,000 loss on disposal for the old machine. The loss is an accounting loss that is reflected on the income statement. However, it is based on the book value of the old equipment, which is a past cost. As such, it is irrelevant in making decisions about the future. One point that is often overlooked when the loss on disposal is considered is that if the old machine is kept, the entire book value will be charged as an expense—depreciation expense—over the remaining life anyway. Therefore, the question really is whether to take part of the book value as a loss this year and recover part of it in the disposal or whether to charge the entire amount as an expense over the remaining life. Often the irrelevancy of book value in the analysis of data for equipment replacement decisions can best be seen by preparing income statements for each of the four years under each alternative, as is done in Exhibit 10.2.

Notice that the total four-year net income if the old machine is kept is $104,000. Total four-year net income for the new machine, however, is $106,000. The company is $2,000 better off if it buys the new machine. This result is the same as that shown in Exhibit 10.1. Note that although net

Exhibit 10.2 Four-Year Income Statements

	Old				
	Year 1	Year 2	Year 3	Year 4	Total
Sales	$ 200,000	$ 200,000	$ 200,000	$ 200,000	$ 800,000
Cost of Goods Sold	(140,000)	(140,000)	(140,000)	(140,000)	(560,000)
Other Operating Costs.	(30,000)	(30,000)	(30,000)	(30,000)	(120,000)
Machine Operating Costs.	(2,500)	(2,500)	(2,500)	(2,500)	(10,000)
Machine Depreciation	(1,500)	(1,500)	(1,500)	(1,500)	(6,000)
Net Income.	$ 26,000	$ 26,000	$ 26,000	$ 26,000	$ 104,000

	New				
	Year 1	Year 2	Year 3	Year 4	Total
Sales	$ 200,000	$ 200,000	$ 200,000	$ 200,000	$ 800,000
Cost of Goods Sold	(140,000)	(140,000)	(140,000)	(140,000)	(560,000)
Other Operating Costs.	(30,000)	(30,000)	(30,000)	(30,000)	(120,000)
Machine Operating Costs.	(1,000)	(1,000)	(1,000)	(1,000)	(4,000)
Machine Depreciation	(1,500)	(1,500)	(1,500)	(1,500)	(6,000)
Loss on Disposal of Old	(4,000)	—	—	—	(4,000)
Net Income.	$ 23,500	$ 27,500	$ 27,500	$ 27,500	$ 106,000

income in Year 1 is less with the new machine than with the old machine, this reduced income is offset by the higher incomes in subsequent years.

Although quantitatively the company is better off buying the new machine, there are qualitative factors to consider. One such factor is that often a new machine still has "bugs" in it. Operating costs for the new machine are estimated, while the actual operating costs for the old machine are known. If the operating costs for the new machine have been underestimated, the new machine will cost more than shown above. Management may feel more comfortable with a machine whose actual operating features it already knows.

Another qualitative factor is the psychological effect of recognizing the loss on the old machine. Although it is clearly to the advantage of the company to buy the machine (based on the validity of the assumptions), a psychological block against recognizing a loss in Year 1 often exists. Management must understand that it must make decisions that best further the overall profit objectives of the firm. There will always be technological advances in equipment. If the decision made several years ago was based on the best knowledge available at that time, management need feel no shame in recognizing that something better has come along six years later. Thus, management should overcome its concern about recognizing losses when disposing of equipment before the original estimated life has been completed. As mentioned above, the firm can recognize the loss now or depreciate the remaining book value over the equipment's remaining useful life. But in the latter case, it loses the advantage of having a superior machine with its related cost savings.

Relevant cost analysis provides management with appropriate data for making decisions on equipment replacement. The final decision is still management's. Using the quantitative data provided by relevant cost analysis, along with appropriate qualitative factors, management can make its decision based on what appears to be in the best interests of the firm.

Segment Operations

Chapter 8 illustrated the difficulties in analyzing cost data for the purpose of evaluating management performance. In this chapter, we want to look at the use of cost data to analyze the profitability of segment operations. A relationship often exists between segment profitability and management performance. However, at this point, we are concerned only with looking at profitability of a product line of a business, without considering its relationship to management performance.

Many firms prepare product-line income statements—that is, income statements showing sales and costs for each of its segments. Management may decide to drop a segment it considers unprofitable. The problem, however, comes in the determining whether a segment is unprofitable. This determination requires the proper application of relevant cost analysis. Unfortunately, this fact is not always understood, and occasionally incorrect decisions are made. This section illustrates relevant cost analysis for analyzing segment operations.

Dropping a Segment   In recent years, Harry's Hardware Store, which began a number of years ago selling only the general merchandise normally carried by hardware stores, has expanded into televisions and appliances, as well as toys. The toy department does particularly well at Christmas but is somewhat slow during the rest of the year. Harry is concerned about whether the toy department should be continued. His concern was generated by a recent product-line income statement that showed the toy department had lost $5,000 last year. This statement is shown in Exhibit 10.3.

Exhibit 10.3 Product-Line Income Statement with Allocated Common Fixed Costs

	General Merchandise	TV and Appliances	Toys	Total
Sales	$ 500,000	$ 300,000	$ 200,000	$1,000,000
Variable Costs	(300,000)	(195,000)	(150,000)	(645,000)
Contribution Margin	$ 200,000	$ 105,000	$ 50,000	$ 355,000
Fixed Costs:				
Separable	(50,000)	(35,000)	(25,000)	(110,000)
Common	(75,000)	(45,000)	(30,000)	(150,000)
Net Income	$ 75,000	$ 25,000	$ (5,000)	$ 95,000

The common fixed costs include such items as store rent, advertising, Harry's salary, and other administrative costs incurred for the store operation as a whole. Harry has always insisted on allocating these costs to each segment because "each department must carry its share of the load." The common fixed costs are allocated on the basis of sales.

It seems to Harry that the toy department should be dropped because it is losing money. Nevertheless, before making the decision, he has prepared a product-line income statement without the toy department, assuming that sales and costs of general merchandise and TV and appliances do not change. This statement is shown in Exhibit 10.4. It shows that if the toy department is dropped, net income for the store as a whole will fall from $95,000 to $70,000. Harry is puzzled by this result. He doesn't understand why dropping a money-losing operation would cause the store to reduce its net income.

The problem here is not unusual. In Exhibit 10.3, the common fixed costs of $30,000 that had been allocated to the toy department are irrelevant in determining its profitability. The $30,000 will be incurred regardless of whether the toy department is dropped or not. Total common costs are $150,000; this is what it costs to run the store for all departments. Notice in Exhibit 10.4 that total common costs are still $150,000. But in Exhibit 10.4, the costs are allocated to general merchandise and to TV and appliances. Dropping the toy department does not allow Harry to drop its $30,000 share of common fixed costs. However, its contribution margin of $50,000 and

Exhibit 10.4 Product-Line Income Statement after Dropping Toys

	General Merchandise	TV and Appliances	Total
Sales	$ 500,000	$ 300,000	$ 800,000
Variable Costs	(300,000)	(195,000)	(495,000)
Contribution Margin	$ 200,000	$ 105,000	$ 305,000
Fixed Costs:			
Separable	(50,000)	(35,000)	(85,000)
Common	(94,000)	(56,000)	(150,000)
Net Income	$ 56,000	$ 14,000	$ 70,000

separable fixed costs of $25,000 are dropped. The separable fixed costs are those incurred only for the operation of the department. They may include such things as the toy department manager's salary, depreciation on toy department fixtures, and similar items.

A short-cut method of analyzing the effect of dropping a product line is to look only at segment margin. If a department provides a segment margin, then that department is helping to cover common fixed costs. In such a case, the department should not be dropped if there are no alternative uses for its facilities. In this example, a proper analysis of whether to drop the toy department must begin with a determination of whether segment margin is being provided. This determination is made as follows:

Contribution Margin	$50,000
Separable Fixed Costs	25,000
Segment Margin	$25,000

The toy department provides a segment margin of $25,000. If the department is dropped, the company will lose the $25,000 segment margin but will not lose the $30,000 of common fixed costs. To analyze the effect of dropping the toy department, we must determine what the lost segment margin will do to total net income as follows:

Current Net Income	$95,000
Lost Segment Margin	25,000
New Net Income	$70,000

When the current net income of $95,000 is reduced by the lost segment margin of $25,000, the new net income is $70,000—the amount shown in Exhibit 10.4. It is not necessary, therefore, to prepare a complete product-line income statement to determine the effect of dropping one product line. By merely calculating the lost segment margin, we can arrive at the same solution.

The problems of cost allocation relative to managerial performance evaluation were described in Chapter 8. Some of the same pitfalls are present in product-line analysis. Naturally, total revenue must exceed total costs if the firm is to survive. Therefore, total segment margin must exceed total common fixed costs. A firm can, if it wishes, allocate common costs with the idea that each manager should be aware of the costs that must be covered by the firm. But decisions about the profitability of the segment should not be based on segment net income derived by allocating common fixed costs.

A better approach to showing product-line profitability is to prepare a product-line income statement that shows segment margin for each segment without an allocation of common fixed costs. Such a statement for Harry's Hardware Store is shown in Exhibit 10.5.

Exhibit 10.5 Product-Line Income Statement without Allocated Common Fixed Costs.

	General Merchandise	TV and Appliances	Toys	Total
Sales	$ 500,000	$ 300,000	$ 200,000	$1,000,000
Variable Costs . .	(300,000)	(195,000)	(150,000)	(645,000)
Contribution Margin	$ 200,000	$ 105,000	$ 50,000	$ 355,000
Separable Fixed Costs	(50,000)	(35,000)	(25,000)	(110,000)
Segment Margin	$ 150,000	$ 70,000	$ 25,000	$ 245,000
Common Fixed Costs				150,000
Net Income				$ 95,000

This statement clearly shows that each segment, including the toy department, provides a segment margin. Therefore, each segment is profitable. By looking at this exhibit, you can see that if any product line is dropped, net income will decrease by the amount of the segment margin.

Replacing a Segment   The toy department for Harry's Hardware Store is profitable. If the only alternatives are to drop the department or keep it, it should be kept. However, there may be other alternatives. The segment margin, then, should be analyzed on a return on investment basis. Harry may feel that although the toy department is earning a profit, his investment in it could be better used in some other way. Perhaps he could sell another product or expand one of the other departments. For this illustration, assume Harry is considering eliminating the toy department and expanding the TV and appliances department. He believes that by eliminating the toy department, he could increase sales of TV and appliances by $200,000 while maintaining the same variable cost ratio and the same separable fixed costs. An income statement prepared under these assumptions would appear as shown in Exhibit 10.6.

Exhibit 10.6 Expansion of TV and Appliances

	General Merchandise	TV and Appliances	Total
Sales	$ 500,000	$ 500,000	$1,000,000
Variable Costs	(300,000)	(325,000)	(625,000)
Contribution Margin	$ 200,000	$ 175,000	$ 375,000
Separable Fixed Costs	(50,000)	(35,000)	(85,000)
Segment Margin	$ 150,000	$ 140,000	$ 290,000
Common Fixed Costs			150,000
Net Income			$ 140,000

↑CM, ↑NI

The exhibit shows that expanding TV and appliances causes expected net income to be $140,000—an increase of $55,000 from the current net income of $95,000. The primary reason for this increase is that the contribution margin ratio for TV and appliances is 35 percent ($175,000 ÷ $500,000), whereas for the toy department it was 25 percent ($50,000 ÷ $200,000). The separable fixed costs for TV and appliances are $10,000 more than they were for toys; but this amount is more than offset by the increased contribution margin. Thus, based on the assumptions here, it would be in Harry's interest to drop the toy department and expand the TV and appliances department.

In summary, relevant cost analysis in segment operations regarding the dropping or adding of a product line requires analysis of the future expected revenues and costs that differ between alternatives. The primary difficulty managers face with relevant cost analysis of segment operations is the failure to consider that common fixed costs are irrelevant to the decision. They will be incurred whether or not a segment is dropped. An understanding of this concept is essential in determining segment profitability.

Joint Product Costs

Often raw materials can be processed into a number of products. For example, a barrel of crude oil can be processed into gasoline, diesel fuel, jet fuel, motor oil, and other products. A beef steer can be processed into various cuts of meat, such as sirloin steaks, T-bone steaks, roasts, and hamburger. In determining the cost of the final product, the firm may have a problem in deciding how much of the original raw material cost and the processing costs of the raw material should be considered part of the final product cost. For example, a steer may cost $750 at the stockyard and may require incurrence of $150 of processing costs before being split into separate products. How much of that $900 is to be a cost for each of the products made from the steer? The product cost associated with a number of final products is called a **joint product cost.** Determining how much of this cost should be charged to each resulting product presents an accounting problem. An illustration of these concepts is shown in Exhibit 10.7.

Exhibit 10.7 Joint Product Cost Illustration

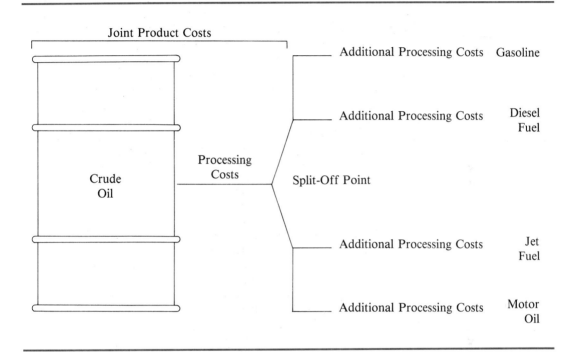

Relative Sales Value

The problem under discussion is one of cost allocation. As stated earlier, there are difficulties in making certain internal decisions on the basis of allocated costs. However, for inventory and product-costing purposes, as in manufacturing, joint product costs must be allocated to each of the final products. This allocation may be done in a number of ways. For example, the costs may be allocated on the basis of weight, units produced, or relative sales value. The use of relative sales value may be based on the sales value at the **split-off point,** that point at which the original raw material is separated into two or more products. The final sales value may also be used as the basis for cost allocation. Our example will use the sales value of the final product.

The Product Processing Company sells three products—A, B, and C—for $20, $25, and $50 per unit, respectively. Annual sales average 20,000 units, 10,000 units, and 7,000 units, respectively. Joint product costs total $150,000. The firm allocates the joint product costs to each product using the relative sales value method as shown in Exhibit 10.8.

Exhibit 10.8 Joint Product Cost Allocation

	Relative Sales Value		
Product	Number of Units	Selling Price	Sales Value
A	20,000 ×	$20 =	$ 400,000
B	10,000 ×	$25 =	250,000
C	7,000 ×	$50 =	350,000
Total Sales Value			$1,000,000

	Joint Product Cost Allocation		
A	$\dfrac{\$400,000}{\$1,000,000}$ ×	$150,000 =	$ 60,000
B	$\dfrac{\$250,000}{\$1,000,000}$ ×	$150,000 =	37,500
C	$\dfrac{\$350,000}{\$1,000,000}$ ×	$150,000 =	52,500
Total Joint Product Cost			$150,000

The exhibit shows that total cost is allocated to each product according to the proportion of its sales value to the total sales value of all products. In this case, we could simply have shown that products A, B, and C comprise 40 percent, 25 percent, and 35 percent of total sales value. These percentages, when multiplied by the joint product cost of $150,000, also result in the allocation shown above.

As previously mentioned, this type of allocation is often necessary for product costing and inventory purposes. However, as with any cost allocation, a danger is involved in using it for making internal decisions. For example, assume that additional processing costs (separable costs) for A, B, and C are $350,000, $190,000, and $260,000, respectively. If management were using the allocated costs above to determine the profitability of each product, it might prepare the product-line income statement shown in Exhibit 10.9.

The exhibit shows that Product A is losing $10,000. Management might be inclined to drop Product A. This problem is similar to that of Harry's Hardware, described earlier in the chapter. Specifically, segment profitability (and in this case the segments are products) should be measured on the basis of relevant cost. What costs are incurred that differ between the alternatives of selling the product and not selling the product? To answer this question, management should prepare a product-line income statement

Exhibit 10.9 Joint Product Net Income

	A	B	C	Total
Sales	$ 400,000	$ 250,000	$ 350,000	$1,000,000
Separable Costs	(350,000)	(190,000)	(260,000)	(800,000)
Joint Costs	(60,000)	(37,500)	(52,500)	(150,000)
Net Income	$ (10,000)	$ 22,500	$ 37,500	$ 50,000

showing the segment margins. For the Product Processing Company, this statement is shown in Exhibit 10.10.

The exhibit shows that rather than losing money, Product A provides a $50,000 segment margin that contributes to covering joint costs. The point is that in an analysis of the profitability of each product, the joint costs are irrelevant. The $150,000 cost is incurred in order that the products can be processed to a point at which Products A, B, and C can be processed further—that is, to the *split-off point*. The $150,000 cost is incurred regardless of whether A is produced or not. It does not differ between alternatives and is therefore irrelevant.

**Sales at
Split-Off Point**

Sometimes a firm can either process a product beyond the split-off point or sell it at the split-off point. The question of which alternative is more profitable then arises. The choice between these alternatives can be based on relevant cost analysis. Specifically, the firm can analyze each alternative to determine the expected future revenues and costs that differ between them.

Assume that Product Processing Company can sell Product B at the split-off point for $45,000. As previously mentioned, if it processes Product B further, it incurs additional costs of $190,000 and can sell the product for a total of $250,000. Using relevant cost analysis, Exhibit 10.11 shows the results of each alternative.

The exhibit shows that by processing further, the firm will earn a segment margin of $60,000, compared with the $45,000 segment margin it will earn if

Exhibit 10.10 Joint Product Net Income with Segment Margin

	A	B	C	Total
Sales	$ 400,000	$ 250,000	$ 350,000	$1,000,000
Separable Costs	(350,000)	(190,000)	(260,000)	(800,000)
Segment Margin	$ 50,000	$ 60,000	$ 90,000	$ 200,000
Joint Costs				150,000
Net Income				$ 50,000

Exhibit 10.11 Sale of Product B At Split-Off Point

	Process Further	Split-Off Point
Sales	$250,000	$45,000
Additional Costs	190,000	—
Segment Margin	$ 60,000	$45,000

it sells at the split-off point. Thus, the firm is $15,000 better off to process Product B further. Note that joint product costs did not enter into the analysis. They are irrelevant, because they will be incurred regardless of whether the firm processes Product B further or sells it at the split-off point.

Make or Buy Decisions

Manufacturing firms frequently require many items of direct material to produce a single product. A question sometimes arises as to whether certain items of direct material should be manufactured or bought from an outside supplier. The question of whether to manufacture a component part or subassembly or to buy it from another supplier is referred to as a **make or buy decision.** The answer to this question can best be obtained by use of relevant cost analysis.

Illustration

Balson Manufacturing Company currently manufactures 100,000 units of a certain part for use in one of its products. The cost of manufacturing these parts is shown in Exhibit 10.12.

A supplier has offered to sell 100,000 units per year of this part to Balson for $1.25 each. Balson is now faced with the question of whether to continue to make the part or to buy it from the outside supplier.

Exhibit 10.12 Cost to Make 100,000 Units

	Unit	Total
Direct Material	$ .35	$ 35,000
Direct Labor	.50	50,000
Variable Factory Overhead	.25	25,000
Fixed Factory Overhead:		
Separable	.10	10,000
Common	.30	30,000
Total	$1.50	$150,000

At first glance, it would appear that buying the part would benefit Balson. The unit cost of making it is shown in Exhibit 10.12 to be $1.50, compared with the cost to buy of $1.25. However, we must analyze the costs in Exhibit 10.12 to determine whether each cost is relevant to this decision. Which costs shown in Exhibit 10.12 are future expected costs that differ between the alternatives? Analysis reveals that the common fixed factory overhead costs are not relevant. By definition, common costs are incurred for the firm as a whole and are not direct costs of any one segment. If Balson decides to buy the part, it will continue to incur the $30,000 of common fixed factory overhead. In effect, these costs will be allocated to other products if production of the parts is discontinued.

The separable fixed factory overhead costs are relevant; they are incurred solely because this part is manufactured. Eliminating the manufacture of the part, then, will eliminate the $10,000 of separable fixed factory overhead cost. The variable costs of making the part are also relevant, since they are direct costs of the product. If the firm does not make the part, it does not incur the variable costs.

The appropriate way to analyze the make or buy decision in this case is to compare the relevant costs of making the part with the cost of buying it, as shown in Exhibit 10.13. The exhibit shows that the relevant costs of making total only $120,000, compared with the $125,000 cost of buying. The company will be $5,000 better off if it continues to make the part.

Exhibit 10.13 Make or Buy Analysis for 100,000 Units

	Make	Buy
Cost to Buy.	—	$125,000
Relevant Cost to Make	$120,000	—
Totals	$120,000	$125,000

This illustration has considered only quantitative data. Qualitative factors must be considered as well. One qualitative factor is whether the company wants to bother to continue making the part. It may feel that the convenience of letting someone else do it is worth the $5,000 difference. In addition, the company may find that the workers involved in manufacturing the part could be better employed elsewhere in the plant. On the other hand, discontinuing the manufacture of the part may result in the need to lay off workers. In that case, the company may continue making the part simply to maintain the stability of the work force. An important consideration in deciding whether to buy outside is whether the quality of the product the firm buys will be as good as the quality of the product it makes. Further, the company must be concerned about the stability of its supplier. If it buys on the outside, can it depend on its supplier to provide the part consistently on a timely basis?

Opportunity Cost

Another consideration in make or buy decisions is whether the firm has alternative uses for its facilities if it should decide to buy the product from an outside supplier. If it can use the facilities to earn additional revenue, it may be better to buy on the outside rather than lose this revenue. Lost revenue represents an **opportunity cost**—the segment margin foregone when one alternative is chosen over another. This cost does not represent a cash outlay. Rather, it represents the loss of potential segment margin that would have been received had the other alternative been chosen. For example, in the make or buy situation discussed above, assume that Balson Manufacturing Company has an alternative use for the facilities it now uses in making the part. If it buys the part on the outside, it can use its facilities to manufacture another product that will provide a segment margin of $25,000. If it continues to make the part, it will lose the opportunity to earn this additional segment margin. The potential segment margin of $25,000 represents an opportunity cost. Balson must consider this cost in its make or buy analysis. Such an analysis is illustrated in Exhibit 10.14.

Exhibit 10.14 Make or Buy Analysis for 100,000 Units with Opportunity Cost

	Make	**Buy**
Cost to Buy.	—	$125,000
Relevant Cost to Make	$120,000	—
Opportunity Cost of Making:		
Lost Segment Margin of Alternate Product	25,000	—
Totals.	$145,000	$125,000

You can see that when opportunity cost is considered, the cost of making is $145,000 and the cost of buying is $125,000. The company will be $20,000 better off if it buys the product on the outside. As always, qualitative factors must also be considered in making the final decision.

Some managers like to consider the opportunity cost a reduction in the cost of the buy alternative rather than an addition to the cost of the make alternative. It doesn't really matter how you do it; the results are the same. If you consider the opportunity cost a reduction in the cost of the buy alternative, you are saying that buying on the outside reduces total cost by $25,000 because of the segment margin received from the alternative use of the facilities. This approach is shown in Exhibit 10.15.

In this case, the total relevant cost of making is $120,000, compared with the cost of buying at $100,000. The difference is still $20,000 in favor of buying. It doesn't matter whether you use the approach shown in Exhibit 10.14 or the approach shown in Exhibit 10.15. The point to understand is that opportunity cost represents an additional cost of the make alternative. Whether you add it to "make" or subtract it from "buy," the relative difference in the two alternatives is the same.

Exhibit 10.15 Make or Buy Analysis for 100,000 Units with Opportunity Cost (Alternate Approach)

	Make	Buy
Cost to Buy.	—	$125,000
Relevant Cost to Make	$120,000	—
Opportunity Cost of Making:		
Segment Margin of Alternate Product	—	(25,000)
Totals.	$120,000	$100,000

Pricing

The price to charge for a product can be the easiest or the most complex decision management must make. In some cases, prices are set by a government agency. In other instances, severe competition limits the maximum price a firm can reasonably charge. But generally, management must make its own decisions about pricing. In doing so, it must consider a vast set of complex factors that include costs, competition, advertising, market demand, and the economy.

It is beyond the scope of this text to discuss the details and complexities of pricing. However, you should be aware of some of the overall concepts, particularly as they pertain to certain types of decisions. The following discussion concentrates on the cost factor in pricing decisions.

Normal Pricing

As previously discussed, a firm's total revenue must exceed its costs and provide a reasonable profit if it is going to survive. That means its prices must be high enough to meet these objectives. Chapter 9 illustrated one means of determining product price when given certain assumptions about costs and volume. That approach used contribution margin techniques to determine the necessary price.

There are a number of ways to determine prices. One popular method is to use what is called *cost-plus pricing*. Under cost-plus pricing, management prices its product at a certain markup, or percentage, above its cost. The cost used may be variable cost, manufacturing cost, or total cost. The percentage used is determined by management decision and may be somewhat arbitrary. For example, assume a firm prices its products at 25 percent above its total cost, to include manufacturing, selling, and administrative costs. If it sells a number of products, as most firms do, it must determine the cost of each product through the allocation process. Normal pricing that considers all costs is often called **full cost pricing.** Assume one product has a total cost of $100,000 for 50,000 units—a cost of $2 per unit ($100,000 ÷ 50,000 units). The price would be determined as follows:

$2.00 × .25 = $.50 Markup
$2.00 + $.50 = $2.50 Price

In this case, the selling price is $2.50 each. While this process may seem simple, remember that the firm must decide whether $2.50 is a reasonable price in view of the competition, the marketplace, and the economy. If competitors sell a similar product for $2.20 each, the firm may have difficulty with its $2.50 price, unless it can show consumers it has a better product. (This end may be achieved through advertising.) If a firm is selling hundreds or thousands of different products, pricing each one can become complex.

Special Pricing

Situations arise in which a firm is asked to provide a special price to a customer, either for a one-time purchase or a series of continuing purchases. Some manufacturers sell products under their own brand name and sell products to other firms with a different brand name at a lower price. Other special pricing situations involve bids whereby a potential buyer asks the firm to indicate the lowest price at which it is willing to sell a certain number of units.

In these situations, management must understand relevant cost concepts in order to make intelligent decisions about pricing. Some situations require that management sell below its normal price in order to improve the profitability of the firm as a whole. Qualitative factors should also be considered. But if management is going to achieve the long-run profit goals of the firm, it must understand how its decision to sell or not sell at a special price affects net income.

Special Situation   Walker Company has the capacity to manufacture 200,000 units of its product. Next year it anticipates sales of 150,000 units. It has determined, based on the cost data shown in Exhibit 10.16, that a selling price of $15 per unit is appropriate.

Variable selling and administrative costs include a sales commission of $1 per unit. Fixed factory overhead of $2 per unit is based on $300,000 of fixed

Exhibit 10.16 Target Selling Price

	Per Unit
Direct Material	$ 2.50
Direct Labor	3.00
Variable Factory Overhead	1.50
Fixed Factory Overhead	2.00
Total Manufacturing Costs	$ 9.00
Variable Selling and Administrative Costs	2.00
Fixed Selling and Administrative Costs	1.50
Total Costs	$12.50
20% Markup	2.50
Selling Price	$15.00

costs ($300,000 ÷ 150,000 units). Fixed selling and administrative costs of $1.50 per unit are based on $225,000 of fixed costs ($225,000 ÷ 150,000 units). A potential customer who does not normally buy from Walker Company has offered to buy 20,000 units at $11 per unit. Walker Company would not have to pay any sales commission on this sale. However, a special modification to the product is requested that would require incurrence of a fixed cost of $25,000. To the president of Walker Company, who is reluctant to agree to such a sale, it appears that the firm would not only lose $1.50 on each unit sold but would also have to make an additional outlay of $25,000 to meet the specifications of the buyer.

For this type of decision, relevant cost analysis is more appropriate than the normal costing procedure. The president should determine what costs will be incurred if Walker accepts the offer. In this case, there will be no sales commission; so variable costs will be $1 less than normal. The fixed factory overhead of $2 is based on total fixed factory overhead of $300,000; and fixed selling and administrative costs of $1.50 per unit are based on the total $225,000, as previously mentioned. These costs will be incurred regardless of whether the president accepts the offer. Thus, the $2 and $1.50 are irrelevant in this decision. The special modification costing $25,000 is a cost that would be incurred solely because of this order. An analysis of the relevant costs to be considered is shown in Exhibit 10.17.

Notice that this special sale will provide a contribution margin of $60,000. This amount is reduced by the $25,000 for the modification. The net effect is that accepting the offer will increase segment margin by $35,000. Thus, the president's original analysis is incorrect. This sale will cover the relevant costs and provide a profit.

The fact that the acceptance of the offer will increase segment margin by $35,000 does not mean it should be accepted. Other factors must be considered. If the firm establishes a policy of selling below its normal price, customers who normally pay $15 may request a special price. Often, a consideration of variable cost in special price analysis results in a philosophy of selling at variable cost or slightly above. This policy can be dangerous. All fixed costs must be covered in order for the firm to make a profit.

The point is that Walker Company's president may decide against accepting a special price offer for several reasons. But relevant cost analysis pro-

Exhibit 10.17 Special Price Analysis

Sales (20,000 × $11)	$220,000
Relevant Variable Costs (20,000 × $8)[a]	160,000
Contribution Margin	$ 60,000
Relevant Fixed Costs	25,000
Increase in Segment Margin	$ 35,000

[a]Direct Material	$2.50
Direct Labor	3.00
Variable Factory Overhead	1.50
Variable Selling and Administrative	1.00
Total	$8.00

vides the quantitative data that enter into the profitability aspect of the decision. A decision not to accept the offer should be made for the right reason. It should not be based on an incorrect analysis of data. In other words, if Walker Company decides to refuse the offer, it should not do so because it thinks it will lose money.

The kind of special pricing described above is often referred to as **incremental cost pricing**—a pricing strategy under which management considers only the incremental or additional costs that will be incurred in a given situation.

Bid Situation A bid situation is similar to the special situation described above. In this situation, a potential buyer asks several sellers to quote a price on a certain number of units. Generally, the company quoting the lowest price gets the sale. A selling company analyzes its costs to determine the lowest possible price it can offer. Normally, a firm will bid an amount greater than cost in order to earn a profit on the sale. The problem for the selling firm is that in order to have its offer accepted, its price must be lower than that of its competitors; and it does not know what price the competitors will bid.

In determining the lowest possible bid price, management must use relevant cost analysis. Otherwise, it may bid a price higher than it should because it is including costs that will not be incurred if the bid is accepted.

To illustrate, we will use the cost data for Walker Company illustrated above. Assume that the government has asked for a bid on 40,000 units of the product. No sales commission is attached to this sale, and no additional fixed costs will be incurred as a result of the sale. The relevant costs for management to consider in making the bid are shown in Exhibit 10.18.

In this case, the relevant costs are the variable costs to be incurred if the order is accepted—direct material; direct labor; variable factory overhead; and variable selling and administrative costs of $1 per unit, the sales commission having been excluded.

Most likely the bid price will be more than $8. The $8 figure tells management that it can bid as low as $8 and not lose any money. Naturally, the firm would like to earn a profit. Therefore, the $8 provides only the minimum price. Management wants the actual bid to be as high as possible, but not so high that it loses the bid to a competitor. As previously mentioned, the firm does not know exactly what its price should be. It will be something of a guess. Walker's bid will depend to some extent on how much it wants the

Exhibit 10.18 Relevant Costs for Bid

Direct Material	$2.50
Direct Labor	3.00
Variable Factory Overhead	1.50
Variable Selling and Administrative	1.00
Total	$8.00

sale. If the firm does not really need the work, it may bid a relatively high price; if it doesn't get the job at the price it bid, it doesn't care. On the other hand, if it is attempting to keep workers on the payroll because production is down in other areas, it may bid a price just barely above variable cost in order to increase the chances of having the bid accepted.

Relevant cost analysis will not tell management what price to bid. It will, however, provide management with the cost data it needs to make an intelligent decision. As with the special situation, the firm must know the minimum price it can bid and not lose money. However, as pointed out above, a danger is involved in considering a bid on the basis of variable cost. Both the special situation and the bid situation are based on short-run pricing decisions. As previously emphasized, long-run pricing decisions must consider total cost. But in certain instances, a short-run decision based only on the relevant costs for that decision can increase the total profitability of the firm.

Robinson-Patman Act

The Robinson-Patman Act is a federal law designed to prevent unfair price discrimination. Its purpose is to prevent sellers from offering the same product to different buyers at different prices. The act allows different selling prices to be charged when the differences are caused by differences in manufacturing costs, sale costs, or delivery costs. These differences may arise because the buyer has bought a different quantity or is having the goods delivered in a different manner from other customers. For example, high volume may reduce costs; this reduction may allow for a price difference. A buyer may pick up items at the seller's place of business rather than have the seller deliver them. This may also result in a price differential.

The act does not allow different prices to be charged because of incremental cost pricing. In other words, the prices must be based on full cost pricing. This text will not go into detail regarding provisions of the act. However, a firm must insure that in special pricing situations, it is meeting requirements of the law. The illustrations above are provided to show relevant cost data for special situations. Management must insure that any special price complies with the Robinson-Patman Act. In the exercises and problems at the end of the chapter, the Robinson-Patman Act is not considered, because their purpose is to emphasize an understanding of the cost concepts.

Limiting Factors

The profitability of a firm may be limited by several constraints. A store has a limited amount of selling space. It must, therefore, allocate this space to those products it believes will help it meet its profit goals. A manufacturing concern is limited by manufacturing space and by the number of machines or other equipment necessary to do the job. There are only twenty-four hours in a day; so the amount of manufacturing done per year is constrained by the amount of equipment the firm uses. Manufacturing requires certain skilled laborers. Inability to obtain people with the proper skills may result in production's being lower than desired. A firm needs a good sales force. If it is unable to hire qualified salespersons, it may not make as many sales as it would like.

Some limiting factors can be removed by expansion. For example, a store with limited selling space may rent or buy a larger store. A factory may expand and buy more equipment. These are long-run solutions. At this point, we want to look at the problems of limiting factors in short-run situations.[1] In other words, given certain constraints, what is the most profitable alternative for the firm? A manufacturing example will illustrate limiting factors in profitability analysis.

Dual Company can produce two products, A and B. Recently, demand for each product has exceeded the ability of production to meet that demand. In other words, the company believes that next year it can sell all of A that it can produce and all of B that it can produce. Its production facilities are limited; so management is trying to decide whether it should produce only A or only B. Unit product data are shown in Exhibit 10.19.

Exhibit 10.19 Unit Product Data

	A	B
Selling Price	$15	$10
Variable Costs	10	8
Contribution Margin	$ 5	$ 2
Contribution Margin Ratio	$33\frac{1}{3}$%	20%

Looking at the exhibit might lead you to believe that A is more profitable and thus is the product that should be produced. However, production of A requires one hour of machine time, while production of B requires twenty minutes. In other words, three units of B can be produced per hour; whereas only one unit of A can be produced per hour. Thus, the contribution margin is $5 per hour for A and $6 per hour for B (3 units × $2 per unit). If the company wants to maximize profitability for the year, it should produce only B. Total contribution margin from each product, assuming production capability of 4,800 hours per year, is shown in Exhibit 10.20.

For the year, Product B's contribution margin is $4,800 more than Product A's. Based strictly on the quantitative data, the company should produce only B and no A. The decision was based on a comparison of contribution margin *per hour,* although such comparisons are normally based on contribution margin per unit. Contribution margin per hour was used for comparison because in this case the scarce resource (limiting factor) is the restricted machine capacity needed to meet the demand for product.

Whether the firm will implement this decision depends on other factors. If great customer loyalty to Product A exists, refusal to produce any Product

---

[1]Chapter 12 discusses this problem in more detail under the topic "Linear Programming."

Exhibit 10.20 Profit Analysis with Limiting Factor

	A	B
Total Hours.	4,800	4,800
Units per Hour	× 1	× 3
Total Units.	4,800	14,400
Contribution Margin per Unit	× $5	× $2
Total Contribution Margin	$24,000	$28,800

A may result in bad public relations for the firm. Of course, if the firm is unable to satisfy the demand anyway, bad public relations may result from either alternative. Naturally, if demand for both products is as great as it appears, the company may want to consider long-run expansion. But in the short run, the analysis above shows that producing Product B would be more profitable.

Summary

In making decisions that involve cost data, management should use relevant costs, which are expected future costs that differ between alternatives. The use of irrelevant data in internal decision making may lead to inappropriate decisions.

All internal decision making involving cost data should include consideration of both quantitative and qualitative factors. Quantitative factors are the numerical factors on which dollar-and-cent amounts can be placed. Qualitative factors affect the decision but cannot be measured in terms of numbers; often they outweigh quantitative factors.

Relevant cost analysis can be applied to any decision a firm must make that includes cost data. This chapter provided illustrations of several applications. In equipment replacement, a major consideration is that the book value of old equipment is irrelevant. It is not an expected future cost; it is a sunk cost that has already been incurred and will not be incurred in the future. Thus, relevant cost analysis excludes consideration of book value in equipment replacement decisions.

Relevant cost analysis for segment operations requires analysis of those costs that will be incurred if the segment continues to operate and those that will be dropped if the segment no longer operates. A common fallacy in segment operation analysis is to assume that certain fixed costs will no longer be incurred when a segment has been dropped. It is therefore necessary to distinguish between separable fixed costs and common fixed costs. Allocation of the costs to the segments may mislead a manager into thinking that the cost is incurred because of the segment. Relevant cost analysis requires that common costs be recognized as irrelevant when dropping a segment is considered.

In make or buy analysis, the firm should consider only those costs that would be incurred under each alternative. Again, it is important to distinguish between separable and common fixed costs. An opportunity cost represents segment margin foregone because one alternative was chosen over another. It is often a consideration in make or buy analysis.

Pricing is a complex activity for any firm. A firm must establish a normal price that covers all costs and provides a reasonable profit and return on investment. Yet management must consider relevant costs in certain special pricing and bidding situations. In these special situations, a firm must also consider the Robinson-Patman Act, which prohibits price discrimination and requires adherence to certain specific price-costing concepts.

Firms sometimes do not have sufficient resources to provide all products demanded by customers. In these cases, a firm must consider the limiting factors. Management must analyze its products to determine which are the most profitable and will provide the greatest profit per limiting factor.

It must be remembered that relevant cost analysis merely provides data on which to base decisions; management still makes the final decision. This decision may be based on data other than costs, but cost is almost always a factor in it. Therefore, it is vitally important that appropriate costs be presented to management for its consideration.

Review Problem

Problem

JKL Corporation manufactures a product that normally sells for $50 each. The product's unit costs are shown below:

Direct Material	$12.00
Direct Labor	15.00
Variable Factory Overhead	2.00
Fixed Factory Overhead	2.50
Total Manufacturing Costs	$31.50
Variable Selling and Administrative Costs	2.00
Fixed Selling and Administrative Costs	1.50
Total Costs	$35.00

The firm currently produces 100,000 units annually, and fixed costs are charged to each product on the basis of this amount of production. The government has asked JKL and several of its competitors to bid on a contract for 20,000 units. That is, the government wants to buy 20,000 units from the firm offering to sell at the lowest price.

To produce an additional 20,000 units would require the firm to increase its fixed manufacturing costs by $5,000 for this year only. Fixed selling and administrative expenses would not change. Variable selling and administrative expenses would be only $.50 per unit for the special order. There would be no other changes in costs. The special order would not affect the firm's normal sales of 100,000 units a year.

Required:
  Determine the lowest unit price the firm could quote and not lose money
on the sale.

Solution
To arrive at a solution to this problem, we must determine the relevant
costs of producing and selling an additional 20,000 units, as shown below:

Direct Material	$12.00
Direct Labor	15.00
Variable Factory Overhead	2.00
Variable Selling and Administrative Costs	.50
Total Variable Costs per Unit	$29.50
	× 20,000 Units
Total Variable Costs	$590,000
Additional Fixed Manufacturing Costs	5,000
Total Cost of Order	$595,000

$$\text{Unit Cost of Order} = \frac{\$595,000}{20,000 \text{ Units}} = \$29.75$$

JKL could quote a price of $29.75 per unit and not lose money on the
order. This price would cover the total costs of $595,000 incurred in pro-
ducing and selling the additional 20,000 units. Note that the fixed factory
overhead and the fixed selling and administrative expenses incurred in producing and selling the current volume of 100,000 units are irrelevant to this
special order. These costs will be incurred regardless of whether the special
order is obtained.
  The firm will most likely bid a price higher than $29.75. The $29.75 only
recovers costs; it does not provide any profit. The amount of profit to include is a management decision. The objective in a bid situation is to quote
a price as high as possible, without losing the bid to another firm because
the bid is too high. This normally requires some guesswork; but relevant
cost analysis provides the basis for determining the lowest possible price to
recover costs.

Questions

10-1 Why is there a difference in cost considerations between long-run and
short-run decisions?

10-2 What is the difference between quantitative factors and qualitative
factors? Which is more important?

10-3 List three qualitative factors that may be important in decision making.

10-4 Since product quality ultimately affects sales, isn't quality really a
quantitative factor?

10-5 Define *relevant cost*.

10-6 What is a sunk cost? Why is it considered irrelevant to decisions
about the future?

10-7 How does the inclusion of data that are the same between alternatives affect relevant cost analysis?

10-8 A manager was heard to say, "I don't understand these accountants. They tell us how important it is to make a profit; and then they say that disposing of an asset at a loss is irrelevant." How would you respond to this comment?

10-9 Appleton Appliances is planning a big refrigerator sale. The first hundred customers who buy refrigerators will receive kitchen step-stools free. The store has 200 stools in stock. One hundred stools were purchased several months ago for $20 each. The other hundred were just recently received and cost the store $25 each. The stools are identical. Mr. Appleton has decided to give away the stools that cost $20 because, he says, "As long as I'm giving them away, I might as well give away the ones with a lower cost." Do you agree with his rationale? Explain.

10-10 "A product should never be dropped as long as it is providing a segment margin." Do you agree with this statement? Explain.

10-11 What is meant by *joint product cost*? Give an example. What is the accounting problem associated with joint product cost?

10-12 What is the primary criterion used to determine whether a product should be sold at the split-off point or processed further?

10-13 What is meant by *opportunity cost*? Why it is not accounted for in the formal accounting system?

10-14 Jerry Winter plans to buy a new car for $8,000. If she pays cash, she must use her savings, which have been earning 10% interest per year. If she borrows money to buy the car, she will pay 15% interest. What is Jerry's opportunity cost if she pays cash?

10-15 What is the difference between incremental cost pricing and full cost pricing? Which is better? Explain.

Exercises

10-16 Equipment Replacement Rodney Company purchased a machine 5 years ago for $20,000. It had an estimated useful life of 10 years with no salvage value. Operating costs are $12,000 per year. The machine could be disposed of today for $4,000. A new machine with a 5-year life and no salvage value at the end of 5 years could be bought today for $25,000. Its operating costs are estimated at $7,500 per year. Determine the relevant cost difference between keeping the old machine and buying the new one.

10-17 Equipment Replacement Maxwell Company has an opportunity to acquire a new machine to replace one of its present machines. The new machine would cost $90,000, have a 5-year life, and have no estimated salvage value. Variable operating costs would be $100,000 per year.

The present machine has a book value of $50,000 and a remaining life of 5 years. Its disposal value now is $5,000, but it will have no disposal value after 5 years. Variable operating costs are $125,000 per year.

Considering the 5 years in total, what will be the difference in the company's profit before income taxes if it acquires the new machine as opposed to retaining the present one? (AICPA adapted)

10-18 Segment Operations Colson Manufacturing Company produces a variety of products, of which "zlone" is one. Sales of zlone total $200,000 a year. Variable costs total $150,000 a year; separable fixed costs, $25,000 a year. Common fixed costs allocated to zlone total $40,000. Company management is considering dropping zlone, although it has no alternative use for the facilities.

a. Why do you think management is considering dropping zlone?

b. Do you recommend that it be dropped? Explain.

10-19 Segment Operations Operating results for the Westmeyer Writing Company were disappointing last year, as shown below:

	Pens	Pencils	Erasers	Total
Sales	$80,000	$60,000	$25,000	$165,000
Variable Costs	(60,000)	(45,000)	(20,000)	(125,000)
Contribution Margin	$20,000	$15,000	$5,000	$40,000
Fixed Costs:				
Separable	(10,000)	(8,000)	(3,000)	(21,000)
Common[a]	(5,000)	(5,000)	(5,000)	(15,000)
Net Income	$5,000	$2,000	$(3,000)	$4,000

[a]Allocated equally to all divisions.

In order to improve next year's profits, the president is considering dropping the Eraser Division. Assuming this action has no effect on the sales and costs of the other divisions and that total common fixed costs do not change, what will be next year's net income?

10-20 Relative Sales Value Paulson Products Company manufactures 3 products, A, B, and C. Final sales are $100,000 for A, $60,000 for B, and $40,000 for C. Joint product costs total $50,000. Separable costs are $60,000 for A, $35,000 for B, and $25,000 for C.

a. Allocate joint product costs to each product, based on the sales value of the final product.

b. Product C can be sold at the split-off point for $8,000. Determine whether the company is better off selling Product C at the split-off point or processing it further.

10-21 Relative Sales Value Helen Corporation manufactures products W, X, Y, and Z through a joint process. Additional information is as follows:

			If Processed Further	
Product	Units Produced	Sales Value at Split-off	Additional Costs	Sales Value
W	6,000	$ 80,000	$ 7,500	$ 90,000
X	5,000	60,000	6,000	70,000
Y	4,000	40,000	4,000	50,000
Z	3,000	20,000	2,500	30,000
	18,000	$200,000	$20,000	$240,000

Assuming that the company allocated total joint costs of $160,000 using the relative sales value at split-off approach, what were the joint costs allocated to each product? (AICPA adapted)

10-22 Make or Buy Decision Reggie's Restaurant serves delicious pies made by Reggie's own cooks. The cost of each pie has been calculated as follows:

Ingredients	$1.00
Electricity	.50
Labor	2.50
Total	$4.00

Cooks are paid $7.50 per hour, and each pie requires about 20 minutes of a cook's time. The cooks are paid for 8 hours work each day. Normally, they bake pies during the lull of business in the early afternoon.

A local bakery has offered to sell Reggie pies for $3 each. Reggie is considering accepting the offer because he will save $1 a pie.

a. Is Reggie's analysis correct? Explain.

b. What other factors should Reggie consider?

10-23 Make or Buy Decision; Opportunity Cost Golden, Inc., has been manufacturing 5,000 units per year of Part 10541, which is used in the manufacture of one of its products. At this level of production, the cost per unit of manufacturing Part 10541 is as follows:

Direct Materials	$ 2
Direct Labor	8
Variable Overhead	4
Fixed Overhead	6
Total	$20

Brown Company has offered to sell Golden 5,000 units of Part 10541 for $19 a unit. Golden has determined that it could use the facilities presently used to manufacture Part 10541 to manufacture Product RAC and generate an operating profit of $4,000. Golden has also determined that 2/3 of the fixed overhead will continue to be incurred even if Part 10541 is purchased from Brown. Determine the difference between the relevant costs to make and to buy. (AICPA adapted)

10-24 Special Pricing Willington Wastebasket Company manufactures wastebaskets with the following unit costs:

Cost of Goods Sold	$3.00
Selling and Administrative Expenses	1.50
Total	$4.50

Selling price is $5. Cost of goods sold includes $1 per unit of fixed overhead costs. Selling and administrative expenses include a 10% sales commission on the normal selling price, $.25 per unit of other variable costs, and $.75 per unit of fixed costs.

A large company has requested a bid price on 10,000 wastebaskets. If its bid is accepted, Willington will incur no additional fixed costs. However, the prospective customer has requested that its company seal be placed on each wastebasket, which would cost an additional $.25 each. There would be no sales commission on this order. The sale of these 10,000 units would not affect the normal annual volume of 100,000 units. Determine the minimum price Willington could bid and not lose money.

10-25 Special Pricing Boyer Company manufactures basketballs. The forecasted income statement for the year before any special orders is as follows:

	Amount	Per Unit
Sales	$4,000,000	$10.00
Manufacturing Cost of Goods Sold	3,200,000	8.00
Gross Profit	$ 800,000	$ 2.00
Selling Expenses	300,000	.75
Operating Income	$ 500,000	$ 1.25

Fixed costs included in the above forecasted income statement are $1,200,000 in manufacturing cost of goods sold and $100,000 in selling expenses.

A special offer to buy 50,000 basketballs for $7.50 each was made to Boyer. There will be no additional selling expenses if the special order is accepted. Assuming Boyer has sufficient capacity to manufacture 50,000 more basketballs, by what amount would operating income be increased or decreased as a result of accepting the special order? (AICPA adapted)

10-26 Limiting Factors Twin Company has been producing 2 popular products, Twink and Twank, for which it has been unable to keep up with demand. Twink sells for $2.50 each, has a variable cost of $1.50 per unit, and requires 1 1/2 hours of production time per unit. Each unit of Twank sells for $4.00, has a variable cost of $2.50, and requires 2 1/2 hours of production time. Prepare calculations to show which product is more profitable.

10-27 Limiting Factors E-Z Chair Manufacturing Company produces 2 types of chairs, both of which are much in demand. The firm uses a special type of direct material that results in a very comfortable chair. Variable unit costs are as follows:

	E-Z Sit	E-Z Rest
Direct Material	$ 80	$120
Direct Labor	110	110
Variable Factory Overhead	30	30
Variable Selling and Administrative Expenses	20	20
Total	$240	$280

Total fixed costs are the same regardless of which chair is produced. The E-Z Sit sells for $400; the E-Z Rest, for $480. Recently, there has been a shortage of direct material, and the company is unable to satisfy customer demand for either type of chair.

a. Assuming the firm decides to produce only one type of chair, which would be more profitable? Show computations.

b. Suppose purchases of direct material are limited to $18,000 a month. Calculate the difference in total profit between producing the more profitable chair and producing the less profitable one.

10-28 Obsolete Inventory The Lantern Corporation has 1,000 obsolete lanterns in inventory that had a manufacturing cost of $20,000. If the lanterns are remachined at a cost of $5,000, they can be sold for $9,000. If they are scrapped, they can be sold for $1,000. Which alternative is more desirable and what are the total relevant costs for that alternative? (AICPA adapted)

Problems

10-29 Equipment Replacement Robinson Company purchased a machine 2 years ago for $60,000. It had an estimated 6-year life and no salvage value. Operating costs are $20,000 a year. The company uses the straight-line method of depreciation.

The company now has a chance to buy a new machine for $40,000 that will reduce operating costs to $8,000 a year. The new machine has a 4-year life, with an estimated salvage value of $2,000 at the end of 4 years. The old machine could be sold for $10,000 today.

The president is not convinced the new machine should be bought, because it will result in a loss to be reflected on the income statement. Company sales total $150,000 a year. Cost of goods sold total $80,000 annually, and operating costs (other than for the machine) are $30,000.
Required:

a. Determine the loss on disposal of the old machine if the new machine is purchased.

b. Use relevant cost analysis to determine whether the old machine should be replaced.

c. Prepare 4-year income statements assuming nonreplacement and replacement to verify your answer to part **b**.

d. After looking at the results in part **c**, the president is upset. "This shows we incur a net loss for Year 1. The stockholders won't like that. I think we'd better keep the old machine." How would you respond to the president?

10-30 Equipment Replacement A division manager of a multidivision company with a strong system of responsibility accounting purchased a machine a year ago for $25,000. At the time, the machine had a 5-year life with no salvage value. The machine uses a process that requires all the working time of 4 workers, who are paid $12,000 a year each. Annual repair and maintenance costs total $1,500; and other machine operating costs are $500 a year.

A technologically superior machine that costs $40,000 is now available. The sales representative indicates that the machine requires the time of only 2 workers (each paid $12,000 a year). Repair and maintenance costs are estimated at only $600 a year, and other operating costs at $400 a year. Because the old machine is considered obsolete, it can be scrapped for only

$3,000. The new machine has an estimated 4-year life with no salvage value.

The division manager is not convinced. "I'll lose $17,000 on disposal of the old machine! How will that look on my performance report? I need to keep the old machine until I get my money out of it."

Required:

a. Prepare relevant cost analysis to indicate the difference between keeping and replacing the old machine.

b. Based on the results in part **a**, how would you respond to the division manager's objection?

10-31 Segment Operations All-State Sales Company began operations in the eastern part of the state and has expanded so that it now has 3 regional managers, each reporting to the president. The company does no manufacturing. Results in the western region have been disappointing in recent years; last year, a loss was reported. Serious consideration is being given to dropping operations in the western region. The company's most recent product-line income statement is shown below:

	(in Thousands of Dollars)			
	Western	Middle	Eastern	Total
Sales	$ 400	$1,000	$ 2,600	$ 4,000
Cost of Goods Sold	(240)	(600)	(1,560)	(2,400)
Gross Margin	$ 160	$ 400	1,040	$ 1,600
Selling and Administrative (S & A) Expenses.	(168)	(345)	(812)	(1,325)
Net Income (Loss)	$ (8)	$ 55	$ 228	$ 275

Cost of goods sold averages 60% of selling price. Selling and administrative expenses include the following items: (1) variable S & A of 12% of sales; (2) separable fixed costs of $40,000 for the western region, $100,000 for the middle region, and $260,000 for the eastern region; and (3) common fixed costs of $80,000 for the western region, $125,000 for the middle region, and $240,000 for the eastern region, allocated on the basis of sales.

Required:

a. Prepare a product-line income statement without allocating joint fixed costs.

b. Assume that dropping operations in the western region will not affect sales in either of the other two regions. Determine total net income under this alternative. Explain the reason for the difference between the new net income and current net income.

c. Assume that if the western region is dropped, sales can be increased to $1,200,000 in the middle region and to $3,000,000 in the eastern region. This alternative would require an increase in separable fixed costs of $10,000 for the middle region and $15,000 for the eastern region and an increase in common fixed costs of $25,000. Determine total net income under this alternative.

10-32 Segment Operations The officers of Bradshaw Company are reviewing the profitability of the company's 4 products and the potential effects of several proposals for varying the product mix. An excerpt from the income statement and other data follow:

	Totals	Product P	Product Q	Product R	Product S
Sales	$62,600	$10,000	$18,000	$12,600	$22,000
Cost of Goods Sold	44,274	4,750	7,056	13,968	18,500
Gross Profit	$18,326	$ 5,250	$10,944	$ (1,368)	$ 3,500
Operating Expenses	12,012	1,990	2,976	2,826	4,220
Income before Income Taxes	$ 6,314	$ 3,260	$ 7,968	$ (4,194)	$ (720)
Units Sold		1,000	1,200	1,800	2,000
Sales Price per Unit		$10.00	$15.00	$7.00	$11.00
Variable Cost of Goods Sold per Unit		$2.50	$3.00	$6.50	$6.00
Variable Operating Expenses per Unit		$1.17	$1.25	$1.00	$1.20

Each of the following proposals is to be considered independently of the others. Consider only the product changes stated in each proposal; assume the activity of other products remains stable. Ignore income taxes.
Required:
Determine the total effect on income of each of the following proposals:
a. Discontinue Product R.
b. Discontinue Product R with a consequent decrease of 200 units in sales of Product Q.
c. Increase sales price of R to $8, with a decrease in the number of units sold to 1,500.
d. Discontinue Product R. Use the plant in which R is produced to produce a new product, T. The total variable costs and expenses per unit of T will be $8.05, and 1,600 units can be sold at $9.50 each.
e. Part of the plant in which P is produced can easily be adapted to the production of S, but changes in quantities may make changes in sales prices advisable. Reduce production of P to 500 units (to be sold at $12 each), and increase production of S to 2,500 units (to be sold at $10.50 each).
f. Double the production of P by adding a second shift. Higher wages must be paid, increasing variable cost of goods sold to $3.50 for each of the additional units; 1,000 additional units of P can be sold at $10 each.
(AICPA adapted)

10-33 Make or Buy Decision Pelly Company manufactures a part, which it uses in other products, with the following costs:

Direct Material	$2.00
Direct Labor	3.50
Variable Factory Overhead	.50
Fixed Factory Overhead	1.50
Total	$7.50

Current usage is 50,000 units a year. An outside supplier has offered to sell Pelly these parts for $7 each.

Fixed factory overhead includes $20,000 for the salary of a supervisor, who will not be needed if the part is bought on the outside, and $5,000 for other separable fixed costs of the part. There is no other use for the facilities if the part is bought on the outside.

Required:

a. Prepare relevant cost analysis to show whether Pelly should make or buy the part.

b. Assume that Pelly can use the facilities in which it now makes the part to manufacture another product, which is expected to have the following costs:

Direct Material	$ 3.50
Direct Labor	4.00
Variable Factory Overhead	1.00
Fixed Factory Overhead	3.00
Total	$11.50

Fixed factory overhead includes $40,000 of separable fixed costs. The selling price of the new product would be $15, and projected sales total 30,000 units. Prepare relevant cost analysis to show whether Pelly should accept this alternative.

10-34 Special Pricing Allen Appliance Company manufactures washing machines with the following unit costs:

Direct Material	$ 50
Direct Labor	75
Variable Factory Overhead	25
Fixed Factory Overhead	20
Total Manufacturing Costs	$170
Variable Selling and Administrative Expenses	20
Fixed Selling and Administrative Expenses	15
Total Costs	$205

At the present time, this washing machine is Allen's only product. Current sales are 35,000 units a year, while manufacturing capacity is 50,000 units a year. Selling price is $250 each.

A large department store chain has offered Allen $200 per unit to manufacture 10,000 machines a year under the chain's name. Shipping costs would be $10 per machine higher because of the location of the chain's central distribution warehouse. No other costs would be affected.

Allen initially turned down the offer because it would lose $15 on each machine sold, for a total of $150,000; but it is now reconsidering because it thinks that maybe it has not looked at the numbers correctly.

Required:

a. You have been asked to analyze the data and determine the effect on Allen's net income of accepting the offer.

b. Assume Allen rejected the above offer because it had decided to manufacture a new model washer and needed the facilities. The new washer is a more expensive model. Unit costs are: direct material, $75; direct labor, $100; and variable factory overhead, $40. Fixed factory overhead would increase by $100,000 a year, and fixed selling and administrative expenses by $50,000 a year. In addition, the firm plans to spend $300,000 in advertising the new model the first year. Sales of the new model are not expected to affect sales of the old model. The sales goal is 10,000 units the first year, and the firm wants to provide a low introductory price. Calculate the minimum selling price for the new machine if the company wants a *total* net income of $1,500,000.

10-35 Relative Sales Value Superscent Perfume Company includes in its products 3 types of cologne, which incur a joint cost of $100,000. Each could be either sold at the split-off point or processed further. Appropriate data are as follows:

	Seabreeze	Rosemist	Moonglow
Number of Bottles:	10,000	5,000	30,000
Sales Value per Bottle at			
Split-off Point:	$2.00	$6.00	$5.00
Additional Processing Costs:	$20,000	$25,000	$40,000
Final Sales Value per Bottle:	$2.50	$10.00	$8.00

Required:

a. Determine the allocation of joint product cost to each product, assuming the cost is allocated on the basis of relative sales value at the split-off point.

b. If a product-line income statement was prepared based on the allocation in part a, and if all products were sold after additional processing, net income would be shown as follows: Seabreeze, ($5,000); Rosemist, $10,000; Moonglow $125,000. The manager of the Rosemist product line has complained about the allocation process. She claims net income would be higher if the allocation was based on units sold. Is that correct? Prepare calculations showing Rosemist's net income under the "units sold" allocation basis.

c. The company president is unhappy with the results of Seabreeze and Rosemist. He thinks the company should drop both of them and produce only Moonglow. If these 2 products are dropped and sales of Moonglow do not change, what will be the effect on the company's total net income? (*Note:* Do not consider sales at the split-off point.)

d. Should any product be sold at the split-off point? Prepare calculations to support your answer.

10-36 Segment Operations; Obsolete Inventory Elroy's Electronics sells a variety of products, including televisions, radios, stereos, and CBs. Lately, Elroy has been concerned because CB sales have declined, with a corresponding decline in profits. The latest product-line income statement is shown below. For simplicity, all products other than CBs have been combined on the statement; but Elroy does keep detailed data on all of them.

	Other Products	CBs	Total
Sales	$ 600,000	$100,000	$ 700,000
Variable Costs	(350,000)	(60,000)	(410,000)
Contribution Margin	$ 250,000	$ 40,000	$ 290,000
Fixed Costs:			
Separable	(60,000)	(20,000)	(80,000)
Common	(150,000)	(30,000)	(180,000)
Net Income	$ 40,000	$ (10,000)	$ 30,000

Common costs are allocated on the basis of sales. Elroy has commented that the only thing that's helped the CB line is that as sales have declined, common costs allocated to CBs have been lower.

Required:

a. Is Elroy's comment about lower allocated costs' helping the CB line valid? Explain.

b. If the CBs are dropped and sales of other products do not change, what will total net income be?

c. As an alternative, Elroy is considering dropping CBs and adding video recorders. He estimates sales of $200,000 with a variable cost ratio of 65%. Separable fixed costs would total $20,000. Calculate what total net income would result from adoption of this alternative.

d. If Elroy keeps the CB line, he has another problem. One type of CB becomes obsolete (from a sales viewpoint) on December 31, although owners of these models can still use them after that date. He has 100 of them on hand. He paid $60 each for them and would normally sell them for $90 each. After December 31, however, he can only sell them for parts for $15 each. He has begun lowering his price and plans a gigantic sale for the last week in December. What is the absolutely lowest price he can afford to sell them for?

10-37 Segment Operations Ocean Company manufactures and sells 3 products—Ex, Why, and Zee. Projected income statements by product line for next year are presented below:

	Ex	Why	Zee	Total
Unit Sales	10,000	500,000	125,000	635,000
Revenues	$925,000	$1,000,000	$575,000	$2,500,000
Variable Cost of Units Sold	285,000	350,000	150,000	785,000
Fixed Cost of Units Sold	304,200	289,000	166,800	760,000
Gross Margin	$335,800	$ 361,000	$258,200	$ 955,000
Variable and General Administrative (G & A) Expenses	270,000	200,000	80,000	550,000
Fixed G & A Expenses	125,800	136,000	78,200	340,000
Income (Loss) before Taxes	$ (60,000)	$ 25,000	$100,000	$ 65,000

Production costs are similar for all 3 products. The fixed G & A expenses are allocated to products in proportion to revenues. The fixed cost of units sold is allocated to products by various allocation bases, such as square feet for factory rent, machine hours for repairs, and so on.

Ocean management is concerned about the loss for product Ex and is considering the following alternative courses of corrective action:

Alternative A   Ocean would purchase some new machinery for the production of product Ex. This purchase would involve an immediate cash outlay of $650,000. Management expects that the new machinery would reduce variable production costs so that total variable costs (cost of units sold and G & A expenses for product Ex) would be 52% of product Ex's revenues. The new machinery would increase total fixed costs allocated to product Ex to $480,000 per year. No additional fixed costs would be allocated to products Why or Zee.

Alternative B   Ocean would discontinue the manufacture of product Ex. Selling prices of products Why and Zee would remain constant. Management expects that product Zee's production and revenues would increase by 50%. Some of the machinery presently devoted to product Ex could be sold at scrap value, which would equal its removal costs. The removal of this machinery would reduce fixed costs allocated to product Ex by $30,000 per year. The remaining fixed costs allocated to product Ex include $155,000 of rent expense per year. The space previously used for product Ex could be rented to an outside organization for $157,500 per year.

Required:

Prepare calculations showing the effects on projected total company income before tax of adopting Alternative A and of adopting Alternative B. (AICPA adapted)

10-38 Special Pricing   E. Berg and Sons build custom-made pleasure boats which range in price from $10,000 to $250,000. For the past 30 years, Mr. Berg, Sr., has determined the selling price of each boat by estimating the costs of material, labor, and a prorated portion of overhead and adding 20% to these estimated costs.

For example, a recent price quotation was determined as follows:

Direct Materials	$ 5,000
Direct Labor	8,000
Overhead	2,000
Total Costs	$15,000
Plus 20%	3,000
Selling Price	$18,000

The overhead figure was determined by estimating total overhead costs for the year and allocating them at 25% of direct labor.

If a customer rejected the price and business was slack, Mr. Berg, Sr., would often be willing to reduce his markup to as little as 5% over estimated costs. Thus, average markup for the year is estimated at 15%.

Mr. Berg, Jr., has just completed a course on pricing and believes the firm could use some of the techniques discussed in the course. The course emphasized the contribution margin approach to pricing; and Mr. Berg, Jr., believes such an approach would be helpful in determining the selling prices of their custom-made boats.

Total overhead, which includes selling and administrative expenses for the year, has been estimated at $150,000. Of this, $90,000 is fixed and the remainder is variable in direct proportion to direct labor.

Required:

a. Assume the customer rejected the $18,000 quotation in the example above and also rejected a $15,750 quotation (5% markup) made during a slack period. The customer countered with a $15,000 offer.

  1. What is the difference in net income for the year between accepting or rejecting the customer's offer?
  2. What is the minimum selling price Mr. Berg, Jr., could have quoted without reducing or increasing net income?

b. What advantages does the contribution margin approach to pricing have over the approach used by Mr. Berg, Sr.?

c. What pitfalls are there, if any, in using contribution margin pricing? (CMA adapted)

10-39 Special Pricing Anchor Company manufactures several styles of jewelry cases. Management estimates that during the third quarter of the current year, the company will be operating at 80% of normal capacity. Because the company wants higher utilization of plant capacity, it will consider accepting a special order.

Anchor has received special order inquiries from 2 companies. The first is from JCP, Inc., which would like to market a jewelry case similar to one of Anchor's cases. The jewelry case would be marketed under JCP's own label. JCP, Inc., has offered Anchor $5.75 per jewelry case for 20,000 cases to be shipped by October 1 of the current year. The cost data for the Anchor jewelry case, which are similar to the specifications for the JCP special order, are as follows:

Regular Selling Price per Unit	$9.00
Costs per Unit:	
Raw Materials	$2.50
Direct Labor (.5 Hours at $6 per Hour)	3.00
Overhead (.25 Machine Hours at $4 per Hour)	1.00
Total Costs	$6.50

According to the specifications provided by JCP, Inc., the special order case requires less expensive raw materials. Consequently, the raw materials will cost only $2.25 per case. Management has estimated that the remaining costs, labor time and machine time, will be the same as for the Anchor jewelry case.

The second special order was submitted by the Krage Company for 7,500 jewelry cases at $7.50 per case. These jewelry cases, like the JCP cases, would be marketed under the buyer's label and would have to be shipped by October 1 of the current year. However, the Krage jewelry case is different from any jewelry case in the Anchor line. The estimated per unit costs of this case are as follows:

Raw Materials	$3.25
Direct Labor (.5 Hours at $6 per Hour)	3.00
Overhead (.5 Machine Hours at $4 per Hour)	2.00
Total Costs	$8.25

In addition, Anchor will incur $1,500 in additional set-up costs and will have to purchase a $2,500 special device to manufacture the cases; this device will be discarded once the special order has been completed.

Anchor's manufacturing capabilities are limited to the total machine hours available. The plant capacity under normal operations is 90,000 machine hours per year, or 7,500 machine hours per month. The budgeted fixed overhead for the current year amounts to $216,000. All manufacturing overhead costs are applied to production on the basis of machine hours at $4 per hour.

Anchor will have the entire third quarter to work on the special orders. Management does not expect any repeat sales to be generated from either special order. Company practice precludes Anchor from subcontracting any portion of an order when special orders are not expected to generate repeat sales.

Required:

Should Anchor Company accept either special order? Justify your answer and show your calculations. (CMA adapted)

10–40 Special Pricing Nubo Manufacturing, Inc., is presently operating at 50% of practical capacity, producing about 50,000 units annually of a patented electronic component. Nubo recently received an offer from a company in Yokohama, Japan, that wants to purchase 30,000 components at $6 per unit, FOB Nubo's plant. Nubo has not previously sold components in Japan. Budgeted production costs for 50,000 and 80,000 units of output follow:

Units	50,000	80,000
Costs:		
Direct Material	$ 75,000	$120,000
Direct Labor	75,000	120,000
Factory Overhead	200,000	260,000
Total Costs	$350,000	$500,000
Cost per Unit	$7.00	$6.25

The sales manager thinks the order should be accepted, even if it results in a loss of $1 per unit, because he believes the sale may build up future markets. The production manager does not wish to have the order accepted, primarily because the order would show a loss of $.25 per unit when computed on the new average unit cost. The treasurer has made a quick computation indicating that accepting the order will actually increase gross margin.

Required:

a. Explain what apparently caused the drop in cost from $7.00 per unit to $6.25 per unit when budgeted production increased from 50,000 units to 80,000 units. Show supporting computations.

      b. 1. Explain whether the production manager, the treasurer, or both are correct in their reasoning.
         2. Explain why the conclusions of the production manager and the treasurer differ.

   c. Explain why each of the following may affect the decision to accept or reject the special order:
         1. The likelihood of repeat special sales or the likelihood of all sales to be made at $6 per unit.
         2. Whether the sales are made to customers operating in two separate, isolated markets or to customers competing in the same market.
         (AICPA adapted)

Chapter 11   Capital Budgeting

Learning Objectives

The purpose of this chapter is to describe and illustrate concepts and techniques for evaluating long-run alternatives. The chapter describes capital budgeting and illustrates various capital budgeting techniques, with emphasis on the discounted cash flow methods. The appendix describes the time value of money concept. Studying this chapter will enable you to:

1. Describe the purpose and significance of capital budgeting.
2. Describe the concepts behind the various capital budgeting techniques.
3. Apply the payback method.
4. Apply the unadjusted rate of return method.
5. Describe the significance and apply the techniques of the time value of money. (Appendix)
6. Apply the net present value method.
7. Apply the time-adjusted rate of return method.
8. Describe the effect of income taxes on capital budgeting.
9 Apply income tax considerations to capital budgeting.

Chapter Topics

The major topics included in this chapter are:

Description of Capital Budgeting
Payback Method
Unadjusted Rate of Return
Net Present Value
Time-Adjusted Rate of Return
Income Tax Considerations
Appendix: The Time Value of Money

Chapter 8 showed how to calculate return on investment by using "after-the-fact" techniques. It showed how to determine how profitable a particular investment has been. This chapter shows how to determine the expected profitability of the investment before it is made.

A firm usually has more investment opportunities than it has investment funds. Management must select investment alternatives that will best utilize the available investment funds to meet the long-run profit objectives of the firm. This chapter describes techniques available to management for these types of long-run decisions. The relevant cost concepts, described in Chapter 10, must be considered when investment alternatives are evaluated.

Description of Capital Budgeting

A **capital project** is a proposal for an expenditure that is expected to benefit the firm for a period longer than one year, such as an expenditure for property, plant, and equipment or new product development. **Capital budgeting** is defined as long-range planning for the *selection* and *financing* of capital projects.

As mentioned above, a firm usually has more alternatives than it has funds to invest in the alternatives. Thus, capital budgeting is used to help management decide which capital projects should be invested in. This chapter is concerned with how management can go about *selecting* capital projects. *Financing* of capital projects is a subject normally found in a course in business finance and is not discussed here.

This chapter illustrates several techniques for selecting capital projects. The projects may be similar; for example, management may be trying to decide which machine to purchase from a range of different models. Often, capital budgeting requires selection of one type of project from several dissimilar types of projects. For example, management may be trying to decide whether to buy a new machine for its processing division, build a new warehouse for its finished goods, or expand one of its sales facilities. Perhaps there is not enough money for all three projects. Capital budgeting would help determine which project to select.

The capital budgeting techniques presented in this chapter help management to evaluate quantitative factors. However, the discussion of qualitative factors in Chapter 10 is applicable here. Often, qualitative factors may outweigh quantitative factors.

The emphasis in capital budgeting is generally on cash flows. The techniques fall into two types—those that consider the time value of money and those that do not. The *payback method* and the *unadjusted rate of return method* do not consider the time value of money. The *net present value method* and the *time-adjusted rate of return method* are based on the time value of money concept.[1]

Payback Method

The **payback method** is a capital budgeting technique that determines how quickly a firm will recover its investment. The **payback period** is the length of time it takes for a firm to recover its investment. The payback method is

---

[1]If you are unfamiliar with the time value of money concept, you should read the appendix to this chapter before reading the sections on net present value and time-adjusted rate of return.

concerned with cash flows. It compares the *incremental* investment of a project with the annual *incremental* net cash inflows expected to result from the project. The incremental cash inflow is the *additional* cash expected to come into the firm as a result of the investment. A cash inflow may be revenue. On the other hand, it may be the reduction of a cash outflow. For example, if an investment in labor-saving machinery reduces labor costs by $3,000 a year, the $3,000 reduction in cash outflow is considered a cash inflow.

A particular investment may result in additional cash inflows and out-flows. Therefore, the terms *net cash inflows* and *net cash outflows* are used to represent the result of "netting" cash inflows and outflows. For example if an investment results in additional cash revenues of $10,000 and additional cash expenses of $6,000, the net cash inflow is $4,000. In practice, the terms *incremental cash inflows, net cash inflows,* and *annual cash inflows* are often used interchangeably to mean *annual incremental net cash inflows.*

The technique for applying the payback method depends on whether the annual cash inflows are even or uneven.

Even Cash Flows

The payback period for even cash inflows is determined by use of the following formula:

$$P = \frac{I}{CI}$$

In the formula, **P** is the payback period; **I** is the incremental investment; and **CI** represents the annual incremental net cash inflows from the invest-ment. Any estimated salvage value is ignored in determining the payback period.

To illustrate, Logan Company is considering the purchase of a new ma-chine for $40,000 (incremental investment) with an estimated useful life of ten years. The new machine would reduce cash operating costs by $10,000 per year (annual cash inflows). The payback period is calculated as follows:

$$P = \frac{\$40,000}{\$10,000} = 4 \text{ Years}$$

The calculation shows that the $40,000 investment will be recovered in four years. When the payback method is used to analyze alternative capital projects, the project with the shortest payback period is considered the most desirable. There is a disadvantage in using the payback method by itself, because it tells nothing about profitability. However, it does provide man-agement with an indication of how risky a proposed investment is. The greater the payback period, the longer it takes to recover the investment, and therefore, the greater the risk that the investment may not be recov-ered. Conversely, the shorter the payback period, the less the risk. (Advan-tages and disadvantages of the payback method will be further discussed later in the chapter.)

Notice that the payback method does not consider depreciation. Depreci-ation is an allocation of cost over the estimated useful life. The payback period determines how quickly the original cost will be recovered. There is not necessarily a relationship between the payback period and deprecia-tion.[2]

Uneven Cash Flows

The example above assumed that the reduced operating costs would be incurred evenly throughout the life of the machine. Assume now, however, that the incremental investment of $40,000 remains the same but that oper-ating costs will be reduced by $10,000 each year for the first two years and by $8,000 each year for the remaining life of the machine. A different procedure is needed to determine the payback period under these condi-tions.

To determine the payback period, determine each year's net cash inflow and the cumulative net cash inflows for all years until the investment is recovered. This procedure is shown in Exhibit 11.1.

Exhibit 11.1 Payback Method–Uneven Cash Flows

Year	Net Cash Inflows	Cumulative
1	$10,000	$10,000
2	10,000	20,000
3	8,000	28,000
4	8,000	36,000
5	8,000	44,000

Notice that by the end of the fourth year, $36,000 will have been recov-ered—$4,000 less than the incremental investment. By the end of the fifth year, however, $44,000 will have been recovered—$4,000 more than the incremental investment of $40,000. It is assumed that if $8,000 is recovered during the fifth year, $4,000 of it is recovered during the first half of the year. Therefore, $40,000 will be recovered in four and one-half years, which is the payback period.

Advantages and Disadvantages

A primary advantage of the payback method is its *simplicity*. For this rea-son, it is a popular project evaluation technique. Also, as mentioned earlier, it provides management with an *indication of the degree of risk* in the pro-posed investment. The disadvantages of the payback method are that it provides *no indication of profitability* and *ignores the time value of money*. A firm that is primarily interested in how quickly it can get its investment back, can get it back most quickly by not making it to begin with. If the payback period is less than the estimated useful life, then the firm is earning some return. But knowing that something is earned is not enough. Manage-

---

[2]As explained in a later section of this chapter, however, when the tax effect of cash flows is considered, the effect of depreciation in aftertax cash flows must be calculated.

ment needs some measure of profitability. Of course, if the payback period is longer than the estimated useful life of the project, the investment should not be made, because there is no chance of recovering the investment, let alone earning a return.

The payback method *can serve as a screening device.* Management may decide to require some minimum payback period regardless of other considerations. For example, a particular project may yield a 25-percent rate of return, but the payback period may be fifteen years. The longer the payback period, the greater the chance that the rate of return may not be achieved, or even that the initial investment may not be recovered. There is considerable uncertainty in business, and capital budgeting techniques rely on estimates. Thus, using some minimum payback period for any project helps to offset some of the uncertainty.

In summary, the payback period is an easy-to-use technique that provides an indication of risk. It may be helpful when used with other capital budgeting techniques. However, the payback period should not be the sole criterion by which management makes decisions among alternative capital projects.

Unadjusted Rate of Return

The **unadjusted rate of return method** is a technique for estimating the profitability of a capital project. It is sometimes called the *accounting method,* the *book value method,* the *financial statement method,* or the *simple rate of return method.* Like the payback method, it is easy to apply. Unlike the payback method, it does provide some measure of profitability. It is called *unadjusted* because it does not adjust the cash flows for the time value of money. As will be discussed later, this is its greatest disadvantage. The formula for determining the unadjusted rate of return is:

$$R = \frac{CI - D}{I}$$

R is the annual rate of return; **CI** represents the annual incremental cash inflows from the investment; **D** is the incremental depreciation on the investment; and **I** is the incremental investment. CI − D represents the amount of return resulting from the investment. It is similar to net income in that depreciation is subtracted.

Illustration

Using the data from the Logan Company example, you can determine the unadjusted rate of return as follows:

$$R = \frac{\$10,000 - \$4,000}{\$40,000} = \frac{\$6,000}{\$40,000} = 15\%$$

The straight-line method was used to calculate the depreciation of $4,000 ($40,000 ÷ 10 years). In order to make valid comparisons between years when using the unadjusted rate of return method, we must use the straight-line method of depreciation. The rate of return represents an annual average rate of return based on the initial investment of $40,000.

Instead of the initial investment, we can use the average investment. In this case, the average investment for ten years is $20,000. We determine the average by adding the initial investment ($40,000) to the book value at the end of ten years ($0) and dividing the sum by 2. The rate of return on the average investment is:

$$R = \frac{\$10,000 - \$4,000}{\$20,000} = \frac{\$6,000}{\$20,000} = 30\%$$

The rate of return is 30 percent—twice what it is when the original investment is used. For internal purposes, it does not matter which approach is used. In evaluating alternative projects, it is important to be consistent and use the same approach for all alternatives. Otherwise, the comparison of rates of return among alternatives would be meaningless.

In the example above, the new machine had no salvage value at the end of its estimated useful life. If a new machine is expected to have a salvage value, the estimated salvage value is subtracted from the investment cost in arriving at annual depreciation.

Advantages and Disadvantages

As with the payback method, the primary advantage of the unadjusted rate of return method is its *simplicity*. It also provides *some measure of profitability*. The primary disadvantage of the unadjusted rate of return method is that it *does not consider the time value of money*. It assumes that cash flows are the same regardless of the year in which they are spent or received. As described in the appendix to this chapter, the time value of money is an extremely important consideration in evaluating capital projects. Nevertheless, if a firm does not intend to use one of the methods that consider the time value of money, the unadjusted rate of return method offers an advantage over using only the payback method.

Although the payback method and the unadjusted rate of return method are not considered the best ones for evaluating capital projects, they are commonly used. Therefore, you should be aware of them; it is likely you may come across them at some point in the future.

Net Present Value

Before you proceed with this section, it is important that you understand the concept of the **time value of money.** Therefore, if you have not already done so, you should read the appendix to this chapter. The net present value method is one of the **discounted cash flow techniques.** These techniques discount future cash flows to their present value, based on an appropriate interest rate.

The **net present value method** determines the present value of the cash inflows and compares it to the present value of the cash outflows, using a specified rate of interest. The interest rate used may be the cost of capital or the desired minimum rate of return. The difference between the present value of the cash inflows and the present value of the cash outflows is called the **net present value.** If the net present value is positive, the investment alternative is expected to earn a return higher than the rate used in computing the present value of the cash flows. If the net present value is negative, the project provides a rate of return that is less than desired.

Positive Net
Present Value

Using the example of the Logan Company, we can compute the net present value of the proposed alternative. In that case, the cash inflows were the operating cost savings of $10,000 per year. The cash outflows consisted only of the original investment of $40,000. Assume the project has a ten-year life and management wants a 16-percent rate of return. The net present value is shown in Exhibit 11.2.

Exhibit 11.2 Positive Net Present Value

	Year(s)	Amount	PV Factor at 16%	Present Value
Operating Cost Savings	1–10	$ 10,000	4.833	$ 48,330
Investment	0	(40,000)	1.000	(40,000)
Net Present Value				$ 8,330

∴ rate of return >16%

The annual cost savings of $10,000 per year represent an annuity. Therefore, we use Table 2 in the appendix to determine the present value. The factor is 4.833. Multiplying this factor by the annuity of $10,000 results in a present value of cash inflows of $48,330. The investment is a cash outflow at one point in time. Theoretically, the investment is made today; so we designate today as Year 0. The factor is 1.000, because there is no discounting. The present value of any amount today is that amount. Therefore, the present value is $40,000. Parentheses are used to designate a cash outflow. When the present value of the cash outflow, $40,000, is subtracted from the present value of the cash inflows, $48,330, the net present value is $8,330.

It is important to understand the concept presented in the illustration. The cost savings will actually total $100,000 over ten years ($10,000 per year × 10 years). But the present value of these savings at 16 percent is only $48,330. Nevertheless, the present value of what the firm will receive, $48,330, is $8,330 greater than the present value of what it must give up, $40,000. This means that the rate of return is greater than 16 percent. If the net present value were exactly zero, the actual rate of return would be exactly 16 percent. When the net present value is negative, the actual rate of return is less than the required rate.

If investing in a project results in a cash inflow from disposal of an old asset, the amount of this inflow is considered in arriving at the net present value. For example, assume that if it invests in the machine described above, Logan Company can dispose of an old machine for $2,000. Net present value is calculated as shown in Exhibit 11.3.

Exhibit 11.3 Net Present Value with Disposal

	Year(s)	Amount	PV Factor at 16%	Present Value
Annual Net Cash Inflows	1–10	$ 10,000	4.833	$ 48,330
Disposal of Old – *cash inflow*	0	2,000	1.000	2,000
Investment	0	(40,000)	1.000	(40,000)
Net Present Value				$ 10,330

Negative Net Present Value

Assume that a company has the opportunity to invest $20,000 in a capital project that will yield net cash inflows of $5,000 per year each year for the next five years. The firm wants a minimum rate of return of 20 percent. The net present value of this proposal is shown in Exhibit 11.4.

Exhibit 11.4 Negative Net Present Value

	Year(s)	Amount	PV Factor at 20%	Present Value
Annual Net Cash Inflows	1–5	$ 5,000	2.991	$ 14,955
Investment	0	(20,000)	1.000	(20,000)
Net Present Value				$ (5,045)

return < 20%

In this case, the present value of the cash inflows is $14,955. Notice, however, that this amount is less than the present value of the investment, $20,000. This difference results in a negative net present value of $5,045. Realize that the firm is still earning a return on the investment. The firm receives a total of $25,000 for five years, which is $5,000 more than the investment. But considering the time value of money, this $5,000 return does not equal a 20-percent rate of return.

If the firm definitely will not accept projects that yield a rate of return less than 20 percent, the project will be rejected. Again, a negative net present value results when the present value of the cash outflows compared with the present value of the investment produces a rate of return lower than the one used in the calculations. As mentioned above, if net present value were exactly zero, the rate of return would equal the rate used as the discount factor.

Profitability Index

The **profitability index**—sometimes called the *present value index*—is the ratio between the present value of the cash inflows of an investment and the investment. It is expressed as follows:

$$\text{Profitability Index (PI)} = \frac{\text{Present Value of Cash Inflows (PVCI)}}{\text{Investment (I)}}$$

Using data from Exhibit 11.2, we can calculate the profitability index for the Logan Company's proposed project as follows:

$$PI = \frac{\$48,330}{\$40,000} = 1.21$$

If the profitability index is at least 1.00, the project is considered favorable. If it is less than 1.00, it is not considered favorable. However, in evaluating a single project using the net present value method, the firm need not determine the profitability index. It can make its decision based on the net present value.

The profitability index is most useful in evaluating several alternative projects. In this situation, the project with the largest net present value is not necessarily the most profitable, because it may require a substantially higher investment than other projects being considered. Therefore, the firm must determine the profitability index of each project in order to determine which is more profitable. Consider, for example, Exhibit 11.5.

The exhibit shows that Project A provides a net present value of $25,000, while Project B provides a net present value of only $20,000. With no further analysis, you might assume that Project A is more desirable than Project B. However, note that in order to obtain the net present value of $25,000, the firm must invest $60,000. Project B requires only a $30,000 investment. To equate the two projects in terms of profitability, the firm calculates the profitability index, as shown in Exhibit 11.5. Project B should be favored over Project A, because its profitability index is 1.67, compared with 1.42 for Project A. *The higher the profitability index, the more favorable the project.*

Exhibit 11.5 Profitability Index

	Project A	Project B
Present Value of Cash Inflows (PVCI)	$ 85,000	$ 50,000
Investment (I)	(60,000)	(30,000)
Net Present Value	$ 25,000	$ 20,000
Profitability Index:		
$\dfrac{\text{PVCI}}{\text{I}}$	$\dfrac{\$85,000}{\$60,000}$	$\dfrac{\$50,000}{\$30,000}$
	= 1.42	= 1.67

In calculating the profitability index, the *incremental* investment is used. If investing in a project results in a cash inflow from disposal of an old asset, the amount is subtracted from the investment in order to determine the incremental investment. Assume that in the above example, Project A includes disposal of an old asset for $3,000. The incremental investment is therefore $57,000 ($60,000 − $3,000). The profitability index is calculated as follows:

$$\frac{\$85,000}{\$57,000} = 1.49$$

Note again that for this calculation, $57,000 is used as the investment, not $60,000. The $3,000 disposal value of the old machine is subtracted from the $60,000 cost of the new machine.

Uneven Cash Flows

The previous illustrations provided examples in which the cash inflows were the same every year throughout the life of the project. If cash flows are uneven, the net present value method can still be easily applied. To illustrate, assume a company has an opportunity to invest $25,000 in a piece of equipment that will reduce operating costs by $5,000 per year each year for the next ten years. The equipment will need an overhaul costing $1,000 at the end of five years. The equipment can be disposed of at the end of ten years for $2,000. The company's cost of capital is 14 percent. Net present value is calculated as shown in Exhibit 11.6.

The present values of the annual net cash inflows and the investment are determined much as were similar values in previous illustrations. The overhaul in five years represents a cash outflow that occurs at one point in time. Therefore, Table 1 in the appendix, the present value of $1 table, is used to determine the appropriate factor at 14 percent. This factor is .519. We multiply the factor by the cost of the overhaul, $1,000, to obtain the present value of the overhaul in five years—$519. Note that this is a negative figure; it represents a cash outflow. The disposal value of $2,000 in ten years represents a cash inflow. To find the present value of this $2,000, we refer again to Table 1 to determine the present value factor of 14 percent in ten years. This factor is .270. Multiplying .270 by $2,000 results in the present value of the disposal value—$540. When the present value figures are added and subtracted, as appropriate, the net present value is determined to be $1,101.

Exhibit 11.6 Net Present Value with Uneven Cash Flows

	Year(s)	Amount	PV Factor at 14%	Present Value
Annual Net Cash Inflows	1–10	$ 5,000	5.216	$ 26,080
Overhaul	5	(1,000)	.519	(519)
Disposal of New	10	2,000	.270	540
Investment	0	(25,000)	1.000	(25,000)
Net Present Value				$ 1,101

The profitability index is calculated as before. The total present value of net cash inflows over ten years is $26,101 ($26,080 − $519 + $540). This amount is divided by the present value of the investment, $25,000. The profitability index is calculated as follows:

$$\text{Profitability Index} = \frac{\$26,101}{\$25,000} = 1.04$$

Advantages and Disadvantages

The net present value method *considers the time value of money*. Thus, using this method results in calculations that are more meaningful than those of techniques that do not consider the time value of money. The method *provides a means of insuring that the firm only accepts those projects that meet or exceed the predetermined cost of capital or minimum desired rate of return. Evaluating alternate projects is made easier by use of the profitability index. Application* of the method *is not difficult,* provided one understands the use of present value tables.

Another advantage of the net present value method is that determining the net present value presents *no problems when cash flows are uneven.* As described below, uneven cash flows make calculation of the time-adjusted rate of return more complicated.

There is no significant disadvantage to the net present value method. It does require that one understand how to apply the present value tables. But once this is learned, it is not a difficult task. *The only disadvantage* of this method *is that it does not give the exact rate of return.* The time-adjusted rate of return method must be used in order for the exact rate to be found. However, this presents no serious problems in either determining the acceptability of a project or in ranking projects.

Time-Adjusted Rate of Return

The **time-adjusted rate of return method** is a capital budgeting technique that determines the actual rate of return on a proposed investment, considering the time value of money. It is sometimes referred to as the *internal rate of return method.* Conceptually, it is similar to the net present value method. It differs in that, rather than determining whether a project meets a specified rate of return, such as the cost of capital, this method calculates the actual rate of return. The actual rate of return can then be compared with the cost of capital to determine whether the project is acceptable. For the project to be acceptable, the actual rate of return must at least equal, and preferably exceed, the cost of capital. The procedure for determining the time-adjusted rate of return depends on whether the project results in even cash flows or uneven cash flows.

Even Cash Flows

A firm is considering investing $14,420 in a project that will result in annual cash flows of $4,000 a year for the next five years. There is no expected salvage value, and no other cash flows are involved. Management wants to know the time-adjusted rate of return that is expected to be earned on this investment.

From previous discussion, we know that by multiplying the appropriate interest rate factor by the annuity, we arrive at the present value of the investment. The formula for determining the present value is:

$$\text{Present Value (PV)} = \text{Factor (F)} \times \text{Annuity}$$

In the present case, we know that an investment of $14,420 will result in cash inflows of $4,000 per year. Thus, $14,420 is the present value of $4,000 per year at an unknown interest rate. In terms of the formula, the present value is $14,420; the annuity is $4,000. The interest rate is represented by the unknown factor. To determine the interest rate, we solve first for the factor as follows:

$$\$14,420 = F \times \$4,000$$

$$F = \frac{\$14,420}{\$4,000}$$

$$F = 3.605$$

The factor of 3.605 represents the interest rate. By referring to Table 2 in the appendix, the present value of an annuity table, you can determine the interest rate. Go down the period column until you get to 5. This represents five years. Now go across horizontally in the five-year line until you get to 3.605. Read up to the interest line and you find 12 percent. The factor 3.605, then, represents an interest rate of 12 percent. In other words, an annuity of $4,000 a year for five years from an investment of $14,420 is a time-adjusted rate of return of 12 percent.

Understanding the time-adjusted rate of return is easier if you understand exactly what the concept involves. The firm has made an investment of $14,420. With annual cash flows of $4,000 per year, the payback period is 3.6 years ($14,420 ÷ $4,000). Since the project has a life of five years, you know a return is being earned on the investment. Each $4,000 cash flow represents a recovery of the initial investment and a return on the investment. The interest rate is applied to the amount of investment that has not yet been recovered, as illustrated in Exhibit 11.7.

Exhibit 11.7 Investment Recovery

Year	(1) Unrecovered Investment Beginning of Year	(2) Annual Net Cash Inflows	(3) Interest on Unrecovered Investment at 12%	(4) Investment Recovered This Year (2) − (3)	(5) Unrecovered Investment End of Year (1) − (4)
1	$14,420	$ 4,000	$1,730	$ 2,270	$12,150
2	12,150	4,000	1,458	2,542	9,608
3	9,608	4,000	1,153	2,847	6,761
4	6,761	4,000	811	3,189	3,572
5	3,572	4,000	428	3,572	0
		$20,000	$5,580	$14,420	

Study the exhibit closely. Notice. that in Year 1 the firm has invested $14,420. The net annual cash inflow is $4,000 (column 2). Interest of 12 percent is earned on that portion of the investment that has not yet been recovered. In Year 1, interest is $1,730 (12% × $14,420). The remaining $2,270 cash inflow represents the investment recovered in Year 1, as shown in column 4 ($4,000 − $1,730). Since $2,270 of the initial investment has been recovered in Year 1, at the end of the year $12,150 is still unrecovered, as shown in column 5 ($14,420 − $2,270). In Year 2, interest is earned on the unrecovered investment of $12,150. We see this in column 3 as $1,458 (12% × $12,150). Follow through the calculations for each year. At the end of Year 5, the entire investment has been recovered. The totals show that cash inflows of $20,000 for five years represent an investment recovery of $14,420 and interest of $5,580.

The illustration for determining the time-adjusted rate of return was made easier because the exact factor of 3.605 was found in the present value table. Most of the time, it will not be this way; you may have to interpolate to determine the actual rate of return.

To illustrate, assume that a $35,000 investment increases net cash inflows by $10,000 per year each year for the next five years. Management wants to know the time-adjusted rate of return on the proposed investment. Using the formula, you can determine the interest rate factor as follows:

$$PV = F \times \text{Annuity}$$
$$\$35,000 = F \times \$10,000$$
$$F = \frac{\$35,000}{\$10,000}$$
$$F = 3.500$$

Turn again to Table 2 and look for the 3.500 factor on the Period 5 line. You will note that it is not there. You will see the factors 3.605 at 12 percent and 3.433 at 14 percent. Since 3.500 lies between these two factors, the actual rate of return is between 12 percent and 14 percent. In many cases, this is enough information for management's needs. However, you can determine the actual rate of return more precisely by interpolation. Interpolation involves relating the difference in the factor at the actual rate, 3.500, to the difference in the factors at 12 percent and 14 percent. This process is illustrated as follows:

Factor at:	Present Value Factors	
12% Rate	3.605	3.605
Actual Rate	3.500	
14% Rate		3.433
Difference	.105	.172

$$\text{Actual Rate} = 12\% + \frac{.105}{.172}(2\%)$$
$$= 12\% + 1.2\%$$
$$= 13.2\%$$

The 2-percent difference between the 12-percent rate and the 14-percent rate is represented by a factor difference of .172. The difference between the 12-percent rate and the actual rate is represented by a factor difference of .105. This relationship is multiplied by the 2-percent difference to determine how much above 12 percent the actual rate is—1.2 percent. Therefore, the actual rate is 13.2%. Since capital budgeting includes many estimates, it is doubtful that the preciseness shown here is necessary in most instances. It is logical to round the results to the nearest percent.

Uneven Cash Flows

Determining the time-adjusted rate of return with uneven cash flows is more complicated than with even cash flows. You must use Table 1 in the appendix, the present value of $1 table, because the cash flows are not the same every year. This involves trial and error. First, select an interest rate you think may be close to the actual time-adjusted interest rate. Using this interest rate, calculate the present value of the cash flows. If the present value of the cash flows exceeds the present value of the investment, the interest rate you selected is too low. Seldom will the interest rate you select result in a present value of cash flows that exactly equals the present value of the investment. The idea is to find the two interest rates between which the actual interest rate lies and determine the actual interest rate through interpolation.

This process is illustrated with an example. A company has the opportunity to invest $60,000 in a project that will yield cash flows as follows:

Year	Cash Flows
1	$30,000
2	20,000
3	20,000
4	10,000
Total	$80,000

Total cash flows over four years are $80,000. Since this amount exceeds the $60,000 investment, the company is earning a return on its investment. Management wants to know the time-adjusted rate of return. It is difficult to determine the interest rate with which to begin the trial-and-error process. There is one way to approximate where to start: The $80,000 over four years represents an average cash flow of $20,000 per year. If the cash flow were $20,000 per year, the interest rate factor would be 3.000 ($60,000 investment ÷ $20,000 annual cash flow). Looking at the Period 4 line of Table 2, we can see that 3.000 is close to the factor 3.037, which represents an interest rate of 12 percent. However, we do not have even cash flows of $20,000 a year. Since the cash flow of $30,000 in Year 1 exceeds the average of $20,000 per year, the actual interest rate exceeds 12 percent. If the cash flows in the first year were less than the $20,000 average, it is likely that the actual interest rate would be less than 12 percent. Thus, we begin our trial and error calculations at an interest rate above 12 percent—say, 14 percent. The first step is to determine the total present value of cash flows at 14 percent, as follows:

	Net Cash	PV	Present
Year	Inflows	Factor	Value
1	$30,000	.877	$26,310
2	20,000	.769	15,380
3	20,000	.675	13,500
4	10,000	.592	5,920
Total Present Value			$61,110

*(columns headed under **14%**)*

Since the cash flows are not the same every year, we must calculate the present value on a year-by-year basis. The total present value for the four years is $61,110. Since this amount exceeds the present value of the investment of $60,000, the rate of return is greater than 14 percent.

Next, we determine the present value of the cash inflows at 16 percent, as follows:

	Net Cash	PV	Present
Year	Inflows	Factor	Value
1	$30,000	.862	$25,860
2	20,000	.743	14,860
3	20,000	.641	12,820
4	10,000	.552	5,520
Total Present Value			$59,060

*(columns headed under **16%**)*

The present value of the cash inflows at 16 percent totals $59,060. Since this amount is less than the present value of the investment of $60,000, the rate of return is less than 16 percent. The actual interest rate, then, lies between 14 percent and 16 percent. At this point, we must interpolate to determine the actual interest rate, as follows:

Interest Rate	Total Present Value	
14% Rate	$61,110	$61,110
Actual Rate	60,000	
16% Rate		59,060
Difference	$ 1,110	$ 2,050

$$\text{Actual Rate} = 14\% + \frac{\$1,110}{\$2,050} \, (2\%)$$

$$= 14\% + 1.1\%$$

$$= 15.1\%$$

The process of interpolation used here is similar to that used for determining the actual interest rate with even cash flows. The difference here, however, is stated in present values and not in factors. The actual interest rate lies between 14 percent and 16 percent. The difference between the actual rate and the 14-percent rate is $1,110 in present value. This amount is related to the difference in present values between 14 percent and 16 percent, $2,050. This difference represents a rate of return 1.1 percent over 14 percent. Thus, the actual rate of return is 15.1 percent.

Advantages and Disadvantages

The primary advantage of the time-adjusted rate of return method is that it *considers the time value of money* in determining the rate of return. For this reason, it is superior to techniques that do not consider the time value of money. Compared with the net present value method, it has the advantage that *management can determine the actual rate of return* on a proposed investment. Another advantage is that the time-adjusted rate of return method *makes it possible to compare projects requiring different amounts of investment on the same basis.* That is, management can compare the actual rates of return on several projects to see which ones yield the highest rate of return.

A major disadvantage of the time-adjusted rate of return method is that *it requires an assumption that all cash receipts from the project will be reinvested at the rate of return arrived at with the original investment.* This assumption is often unrealistic. The net present value method, on the other hand, assumes only that the cash inflows will be reinvested at the interest rate used in discounting the cash flows in the original calculation, such as the cost of capital. This assumption is more realistic.

The time-adjusted rate of return also has the disadvantage of being *somewhat complicated to calculate when cash flows are uneven,* which they will be most of the time. However, computers, as well as many types of hand calculators, have made this problem much less significant than it once was.

Income Tax Considerations

In order to most easily illustrate capital budgeting techniques, the previous sections excluded the effect of income taxes. However, income taxes have a major effect on cash flows. Any consideration of capital budgeting must consider the role of taxes. Although the examples in this section relate to discounted cash flow techniques, the tax effects are applicable to all capital budgeting techniques described in this chapter.

Aftertax Cash Flows

Increases in revenue result in increased income taxes. Therefore, the net cash flows after taxes are less than they were before taxes. A reduction in expenses also increases the amount of income subject to taxes; so a cost saving is actually reduced by the amount of taxes on the increased income.

The actual income tax rate depends on the type of organization, the amount of income, and current law. A corporation is the only type of organization that is taxed as a firm. However, the owners of proprietorships and partnerships pay taxes as individuals on the net income of their organization; so they too must be concerned about income taxes. The illustrations and problems here usually assume a 40-percent tax rate.

Assume that a firm can invest in a capital project that will result in cash inflows before taxes of $5,000 per year for the next five years. At a tax rate of 40 percent, income taxes total $2,000 (40% × $5,000). The aftertax cash inflows are $3,000 ($5,000 − $2,000 income taxes); $3,000, then, is the appropriate figure by which to multiply the present value factor.

Rather than calculating the income tax and subtracting it from the cash inflows, it is easier to *multiply the net cash inflows by the complement of the income tax rate*. This number will always be 100 percent minus the income tax rate. In the previous example, the complement of a 40-percent income tax rate is an aftertax cash effect of 60 percent (100% − 40%). Knowing this, we can calculate the aftertax cash flows with one computation. For example, in our current illustration, assume the company wants a minimum rate of return of 14 percent. The present value of the aftertax cash flows for five years at 14 percent are calculated as follows:

$$\$5,000 \times .6 \times 3.433 = \$10,299$$

The relationship of cash expenses to taxes must also be considered. An expense that is deductible for tax purposes reduces income taxes by the amount of the expense multiplied by the tax rate. Therefore, a cash expense results in a net cash outflow that is lower than it first appears. For example, if a machine requires an overhaul costing $1,000 at the end of four years, and if this cost is deductible in full for tax purposes, income taxes are reduced by $400 (40% × $1,000). *We can also calculate this amount more quickly by using the complement of the tax rate, 60 percent.* This results in the aftertax cash expense. Using the present value factor of 14 percent, we calculate the present value of the aftertax cash expense at the end of four years as follows:

$$\$1,000 \times .6 \times .592 = \$355.20$$

A cash expense that occurs every year in the same amount is multiplied by the present value of an annuity factor (Table 2).

Effect of Depreciation

To this point, we have ignored depreciation in considering discounted cash flow techniques. This is because depreciation, as such, does not represent a cash flow. It is merely an allocation of cost over the estimated useful life of the asset. When income taxes are considered, however, depreciation becomes important. Although depreciation itself neither provides nor uses cash, it is a deductible expense for income tax purposes. Therefore, it actually results in an increased cash inflow, because—and *only* because—it reduces income taxes. Thus, one must consider the effect of depreciation on income taxes, and therefore on cash flows, in applying capital budgeting techniques. The effect of depreciation on income taxes depends on whether the firm uses the straight-line method or one of the accelerated methods.[3]

---

[3]The Economic Recovery Tax Act of 1981 provided significant changes in requirements for depreciating newly acquired assets for tax purposes. It specifies the number of years over which assets can be depreciated and eliminates the traditional methods of accelerated depreciation, such as the sum-of-the-years'-digits and double-declining-balance methods. Instead, the act provides specific tables for accelerated depreciation. Nevertheless, the concept of the tax effect is unchanged; and this chapter illustrates the traditional methods, which can still be used for previously acquired assets.

Straight-Line Method *To determine the effect of straight-line depreciation on income taxes, we multiply the annual depreciation expense by the tax rate.* Note that this process differs from that used in the previous illustrations, where net cash inflows or cash expenses were multiplied by the complement of the tax rate. Since the straight-line method results in the same depreciation expense every year, we use the present value of an annuity table to determine the present value of the tax savings.

To illustrate the calculation of the present value of tax savings based on depreciation expense, let us assume that a firm purchases a machine costing $10,000 with an estimated four-year life and no expected salvage value. The present value of the tax savings is calculated as shown in Exhibit 11.8.

Note that the annual tax savings are $1,000. This means that the depreciation expense of $2,500 reduces taxable income by that amount and therefore reduces income taxes by $1,000. In other words, since taxable income is $2,500 less than it would have been without depreciation, income taxes are $1,000 per year less. The present value of the $1,000 per year at 14 percent is determined by use of the appropriate factor on the present value of an annuity table. The present value of tax savings over the four years is found to be $2,914.

Accelerated Methods Accelerated methods are generally more popular than the straight-line method because of their income tax effect. Accelerated methods reduce income taxes in the early years and therefore provide an increase in aftertax cash inflow in these years. This increased amount of cash can be invested.

Since the accelerated methods result in cash flows that are not the same each year, it is necessary to use the present value of $1 table to determine their effect on taxes. To illustrate, assume the same situation as above. The firm wishes to invest $10,000 in a machine with a four-year life and no salvage value. The sum-of-the-year's-digits depreciation method is used. The present value of the tax savings resulting from depreciation is shown in Exhibit 11.9.

Notice that each year's tax saving is calculated and multiplied by the appropriate factor. The total present value of the tax savings over the four years is $3,103—higher than for the straight-line method. That is because the sum-of-the-year's-digits method provides greater tax savings in the first two years. Therefore, the present value of these tax savings is higher.

Salvage Value

Chapter 10 indicated that the book value of equipment, and therefore the gain or loss on disposal of equipment, was irrelevant in internal decision making because it did not affect cash flows. Like depreciation, this concept

---

Exhibit 11.8 Straight-Line Depreciation Tax Effect

Annual Depreciation: $10,000 ÷ 4 Years = $2,500.
Annual Tax Savings: $2,500 × .4 = $1,000.
Present Value of Tax Savings at 14% = $1,000 × 2.914 = $2,914.

Exhibit 11.9 Sum-of-the-Years'-Digits Depreciation Tax Effect

Year	Depreciation	Tax Rate	Tax Savings	PV Factor at 14%	Present Value
1	$10,000 \times \dfrac{4}{10} = \$4,000$	40%	$1,600	.877	$1,403
2	$10,000 \times \dfrac{3}{10} = \$3,000$	40	1,200	.769	923
3	$10,000 \times \dfrac{2}{10} = \$2,000$	40	800	.675	540
4	$10,000 \times \dfrac{1}{10} = \$1,000$	40	400	.592	237

Total Present Value of Tax Savings $3,103

must be modified when the tax effect is considered. The gain on disposal of equipment does not provide cash; and the loss on disposal of equipment does not use cash. However, if the gain is taxable, the tax on the gain represents a cash outflow. If the loss is deductible, the loss reduces income that would otherwise be taxed. Therefore, the tax effect of the loss, like that of depreciation, increases cash inflows. The tax laws indicate when gains are taxable and losses deductible.[4] For our purposes, we assume all gains are taxable and all losses are deductible. If there is no gain or loss on the disposal of equipment, there is no tax effect.

To illustrate, assume that equipment is disposed of for $1,000 and that there is a $500 gain on the disposal. The net cash inflows resulting from the disposal are as follows:

Disposal of Equipment	$1,000
Tax on Gain on Disposal (40% × $500)	(200)
Net Cash Inflows	$ 800

Note that the disposal itself provides $1,000 cash inflow. By itself, the gain of $500 has no effect on cash flows. However, since the gain is taxable at the rate of 40 percent, it results in a $200 cash outflow in taxes. Thus, net cash inflow from disposal of equipment is $800.

Now assume that other equipment is disposed of for $3,000, resulting in a loss on disposal of $2,500. The result of this transaction is shown as follows:

Disposal of Equipment	$3,000
Tax Effect of Loss on Disposal (40% × $2,500)	1,000
Net Cash Inflows	$4,000

---

[4]Ther are special tax provisions for what are known as captial gains. For simplicity, we are considering all gains as taxable at the same rate.

The disposal provides a cash inflow of $3,000. The loss on disposal itself has no effect on cash flows. However, the loss is deductible and reduces taxable income by $2,500. Thus, $2,500 will not be taxed at 40 percent. This represents a positive cash inflow (reduced taxes) of $1,000. The net cash inflow from this transaction is $4,000.

Salvage value is often a factor in determining annual depreciation expense. Generally, expected salvage value is subtracted from cost to arrive at depreciable cost. In capital budgeting, the expected salvage value on equipment should be considered as a positive cash flow in the year in which it will be realized. If it is subtracted in arriving at annual depreciation expense, then the book value of the equipment is the same as the expected disposal value in the year of disposal. Thus, there is no tax effect. For example, assume that a firm expects a piece of equipment costing $12,000 with an expected salvage value of $2,000 will be used for five years. Annual depreciation is calculated as follows:

$$\frac{\$12,000 - \$2,000}{5 \text{ Years}} = \frac{\$10,000}{5 \text{ Years}} = \$2,000 \text{ per Year}$$

In capital budgeting, the salvage value of $2,000 would be shown as a positive cash flow with no tax effect. The book value at the end of five years will be $2,000. The expected salvage value is also $2,000. Therefore, there will be no gain or loss. If the firm used a 14-percent interest factor in determining net present value, the present value of the salvage value would be $1,038 ($2,000 × .519).

If salvage value is expected to be 10 percent or less of the original cost, it is often ignored in calculating annual depreciation expense. In this case, there is a tax effect on the disposal, because the book value is zero; and therefore, salvage value represents a gain. For example, assume a piece of equipment with a $20,000 cost has a $1,000 salvage value. In calculating annual depreciation expense, the firm may ignore the salvage value. In this case, depreciation expense is $4,000 per year ($20,000 ÷ 5 years). At the end of five years, the book value will be zero. If the equipment can be disposed of for $1,000 there will be a $1,000 gain on disposal. This gain is taxed, and the present value of the tax on the gain is calculated as follows:

$$\$1,000 \times .4 \times .519 = \$207.60$$

The tax on the gain is $400. Since the present value factor is 14 percent, this represents aftertax cash outflow of $207.60.

Illustration

In order to tie together the various tax considerations in capital budgeting, this section presents an illustration that includes these various considerations. Malto Company is considering investing in new equipment costing $45,000. It can dispose of its old equipment now for $2,000. Disposal of old equipment will result in a $500 loss. The new equipment can be disposed of in eight years for $5,000. The new equipment is expected to result in cost savings of $15,000 per year. It will, however, require an overhaul at the end of four years that will cost $1,500, which is fully deductible for tax purposes. The firm has a cost of capital of 16 percent. The net present value of this proposed investment is shown in Exhibit 11.10.

Exhibit 11.10 Net Present Value Method with Tax Effect

	Year(s)	Amount	Tax Factor	Aftertax Cash Flow	PV Factor at 16%	Present Value
Cost Savings	1–8	$ 15,000	.6	$ 9,000	4.344	$ 39,096
Depreciation Expense[a]	1–8	5,000	.4	2,000	4.344	8,688
Overhaul	4	(1,500)	.6	(900)	.552	(497)
Disposal of New	8	5,000	—	5,000	.305	1,525
Disposal of Old	0	2,000	—	2,000	1.000	2,000
Loss on Disposal of Old	0	500	.4	200	1.000	200
Investment	0	(45,000)	—	(45,000)	1.000	(45,000)
Net Present Value						$ 6,012

[a] $\dfrac{\$45,000 - \$5,000}{8 \text{ Years}} = \$5,000$ per Year

The illustration provides a good example of the effect of income taxes. Note that the cost savings of $15,000 a year amount to only $9,000 a year after taxes. The present value of these savings is only slightly over $39,000 for eight years. Without the tax effect of depreciation, the $45,000 investment would not be worthwhile. But this tax effect provides a cash flow of $2,000 per year. When discounted at 16 percent, this amount has a positive present value of almost $8,700. As shown in the exhibit, the combination of all elements in this situation results in a net present value of $6,012. Thus, the investment will provide a rate of return in excess of 16 percent.

Summary

Capital budgeting is the process of selecting and financing capital projects. Firms select capital projects by applying capital budgeting techniques.

The payback method is a relatively easy-to-apply technique that determines how quickly a firm will recover its investment in a capital project. It provides some measure of the risk of the investment. However, it provides no indication of profitability and does not consider the time value of money.

The unadjusted rate of return method calculates an average rate of return on investment based on the expected income from the project, after considering depreciation. It provides some clue as to profitability but does not consider the time value of money.

The discounted cash flow techniques are considered the best capital budgeting techniques, because they consider cash flows in relation to the time value of money. There are two discounted cash flow techniques: the net present value method and the time-adjusted rate of return method.

The net present value method discounts cash flows at a selected interest rate, such as the cost of capital. Under this method, the present value of cash inflows is compared with the present value of cash outflows to determine the net present value. If this difference is positive, the desired rate of return has been exceeded; if it is negative, the desired rate of return has not been met. If the net present value is zero, the expected rate of return on the project is exactly the desired rate of return. This method assumes that cash receipts will be reinvested at the rate used in discounting the cash flows.

The profitability index compares the present value of the cash inflows with the present value of the investment—the higher the index, the more attractive the alternative.

The time-adjusted rate of return method calculates the actual rate of return on investment, based on the time value of money. Rates of return that exceed the cost of capital or the minimum desired rate of return are attractive for investment. The highest rates of return are the most attractive. This method assumes that cash receipts will be reinvested at the rate of return calculated for the original investment.

Capital budgeting techniques should consider the effect of taxes on cash flows. Revenue, cost savings, and cash expenses are multiplied by the complement of the tax rate to determine the aftertax cash flow amount. Since depreciation expense is deductible for tax purposes, it provides a positive cash flow. Multiplying the depreciation expense by the tax rate gives the amount of this cash flow.

Salvage value of equipment provides a positive cash flow to the extent of the amount received on disposal. Gains and losses on disposal are multiplied by the tax rate to determine the reduction in cash flows resulting from the gain or the increase in cash flows resulting from the loss.

Accelerated methods of depreciation are generally preferable for tax purposes to the straight-line method, because they reduce income taxes in the early years. Reduced taxes result in more cash available for reinvestment.

In summary, capital budgeting techniques provide management with an indication of whether a project is worthwhile, based on quantitative factors. As always, the data provide management with an insight into expected results; but management must make the final decision based on all data available.

Appendix: The Time Value of Money

If you put money in a savings account, it will earn interest and the amount will grow. For example, if you deposit $100 at 6-percent interest, you will earn $6 interest during the year and have $106 at the end of the year, assuming interest is compounded (calculated) once a year. Interest may be calculated more frequently—perhaps quarterly or semiannually. Mathematical formulas exist that enable us to determine the amount to which any investment will grow, given an assumed interest rate. The amount can also be determined from tables.

The point is that money has value in relation to time. There is an interest factor attached to any investment. Money tied up in an investment could be earning interest in some alternative investment. Therefore, when considering alternative investments, management must consider the **time value of money**—a concept that recognizes that the value of cash flows depends on when they are received.

An investment is expected to result in cash inflows to the business. As cash is received, it can be reinvested in other projects. The more quickly cash is received, the sooner it can be reinvested. Thus, cash flows received earlier in a project's life are worth more than those received later, because of the interest factor.

Present Value Concepts   Suppose your rich uncle offers to give you $10,000. He offers to give it to you today or one year from today, whichever you wish. Which would be better? Intuitively, you probably know it is better to receive it today, because you can invest it today and earn interest on it. If the current interest rate is 10 percent, you can earn $1,000 interest between now and next year. If you receive the $10,000 today, you will have $11,000 one year from today. Obviously, if you wait for one year to receive the money, you will have only $10,000 one year from today.

In this situation, we calculated the future value of the $10,000. Another way to analyze the situation is to determine what each of the alternatives is worth today—that is, their **present value.** If you receive $10,000 today, its present value is $10,000. If you will receive $10,000 one year from today, the question is what amount must you invest today at 10-percent interest to have $10,000 one year from today. This can be calculated as follows:

$$x = \text{Amount to Be Invested}$$
$$x + .10x = \$10,000$$
$$1.10x = \$10,000$$
$$x = \frac{\$10,000}{1.10}$$
$$x = \$9,090.91$$

Investing $9,090.91 at 10 percent compounded annually will result in interest earnings of $909.09 for the year. This interest plus the investment total $10,000. The $9,090.91 represents the present value of $10,000 to be received one year from today at 10 percent. Comparing the two alternatives given to you by your rich uncle, you can see that the present value of $10,000 to be received today is $10,000. Assuming an interest rate of 10 percent, the present value of $10,000 to be received one year from today is $9,090.91. The first alternative is better, because its present value is higher.

Computing the present value is just another way of looking at alternatives and considering the interest rate factor. Instead of projecting the investment into the future to see what it grows to, we find the amount that, invested today, will grow to the amount to be received in the future. In business situations, using present value is very handy, because often a number of cash flows will occur at various times in the future. The present value concept provides a common denominator by which the firm can compare cash flows of various alternatives to see which is better.

It is not necessary to use a formula to compute present values; we can use tables instead. These tables are based on mathematical formulas. In this text, we are concerned with two of the tables—one that gives the present value of $1 and one that gives the present value of an annuity of $1.

Present Value of $1

The present value of $1 table is shown here as Table 1. To illustrate its application, let us assume the following situation. A firm has an alternative of investing in Project A, which will provide $2,000 at the end of two years, or Project B, which will provide $2,500 at the end of five years. The amount to be invested is the same for both projects. The firm is trying to determine which is the better alternative. Assuming the interest rate is 10

Table 1 Present Value of $1 *$ to be received at the end of X yrs.*

Period	5%	6%	8%	10%	12%	14%	16%	18%	20%	22%	24%	25%
1	.952	.943	.926	.909	.893	.877	.862	.847	.833	.820	.806	.800
2	.907	.890	.857	.826	.797	.769	.743	.718	.694	.672	.650	.640
3	.864	.840	.794	.751	.712	.675	.641	.609	.579	.551	.524	.512
4	.823	.792	.735	.683	.636	.592	.552	.516	.482	.451	.423	.410
5	.784	.747	.681	.621	.567	.519	.476	.437	.402	.370	.341	.328
6	.746	.705	.630	.564	.507	.456	.410	.370	.335	.303	.275	.262
7	.711	.665	.583	.513	.452	.400	.354	.314	.279	.249	.222	.210
8	.677	.627	.540	.467	.404	.351	.305	.266	.233	.204	.179	.168
9	.645	.592	.500	.424	.361	.308	.263	.225	.194	.167	.144	.134
10	.614	.558	.463	.386	.322	.270	.227	.191	.162	.137	.116	.107
11	.585	.527	.429	.350	.287	.237	.195	.162	.135	.112	.094	.086
12	.557	.497	.397	.319	.257	.208	.168	.137	.112	.092	.076	.069
13	.530	.469	.368	.290	.229	.182	.145	.116	.093	.075	.061	.055
14	.505	.442	.340	.263	.205	.160	.125	.099	.078	.062	.049	.044
15	.481	.417	.315	.239	.183	.140	.108	.084	.065	.051	.040	.035
16	.458	.394	.292	.218	.163	.123	.093	.071	.054	.042	.032	.028
17	.436	.371	.270	.198	.146	.108	.080	.060	.045	.034	.026	.023
18	.416	.350	.250	.180	.130	.095	.069	.051	.038	.028	.021	.018
19	.396	.331	.232	.164	.116	.083	.060	.043	.031	.023	.017	.014
20	.377	.312	.215	.149	.104	.073	.051	.037	.026	.019	.014	.012
21	.359	.294	.199	.135	.093	.064	.044	.031	.022	.015	.011	.009
22	.342	.278	.184	.123	.083	.056	.038	.026	.018	.013	.009	.007
23	.326	.262	.170	.112	.074	.049	.033	.022	.015	.010	.007	.006
24	.310	.247	.158	.102	.066	.043	.028	.019	.013	.008	.006	.005
25	.295	.233	.146	.092	.059	.038	.024	.016	.010	.007	.005	.004
30	.231	.174	.099	.057	.033	.020	.012	.007	.004	.003	.002	.001

percent, the present value of the return on each investment is calculated as follows:

Project A: $2,000 × .826 = $1,652.00 ← better investment
Project B: $2,500 × .621 =   1,552.50

Difference: $ 99.50

Look at Table 1. If you go along the Period 2 line to the 10-percent column, you will find a present value factor of .826. This factor is multiplied by $2,000 to arrive at a present value of $1,652. Going along the Period 5 line until you come to the 10-percent column, you will find a present value factor of .621. Multiplying this factor by the amount to be received, $2,500, gives a present value amount of $1,552.50. The present value of Project A is $99.50 higher than the present value of Project B, which means that Project A would be a better investment. Notice that although Project B provides a greater total return ($2,500 versus $2,000), Project A provides the return earlier. The return can be reinvested and can continue to earn interest. This example shows how important it is to consider the time value of money when considering cash flows to be received in the future.

This example used 10 percent as the interest factor. It is up to the firm's management to determine the appropriate interest rate. Typically, it will be the cost of capital or a specified desired minimum rate of return.

Present Value of an Annuity of $1

Many times, cash flows are received in equal amounts over a period of years. For example, assume a firm is considering two projects, C and D. Project C provides $4,000 a year each year for the next three years. Project D provides $3,000 a year each year for the next four years. It would appear that both investments are the same, since they both provide a return totaling $12,000. However, since Project D provides for the return in three years rather than four, it is probably better. But how much better is it?

To determine the answer to this question, we calculate the present value of the cash receipts. We could use the present value factor for each year at the appropriate interest rate (Table 1). However, the present value of an annuity of $1 table, Table 2, provides factors that can be used when the payments are received in equal amounts each year. An **annuity** is a series of equal cash flows. In effect, the factors in this table are the sums of the factors in the present value of $1 table. For example, using the 10-percent interest rate, we calculate the present value of each of the two alternatives in the example as follows:

Project C: $4,000 per Year for 3 Years = $4,000 × 2.487 = $9,948
Project D: $3,000 per Year for 4 Years = $3,000 × 3.170 =   9,510

Difference: $ 438

We determine the present value of Project C by finding the factor for three periods at 10 percent. Looking at Table 2 on the Period 3 line in the 10-percent column, you will find a factor of 2.487. Note that this factor is multiplied by the amount to be received each year, $4,000, resulting in a present value of $9,948. The present value of Project D uses the factor for four years at 10 percent from Table 2. This factor is 3.170. Multiplying it by the annual receipts of $3,000 results in a present value of $9,510. There is a present value difference of $438 in favor of Project C.

Let us look more closely at the relationship between the present value of $1 table and the present value of an annuity of $1 table. The present value of Project C could have been calculated from Table 1 as follows:

Year

1	$4,000 × .909 =	$3,636
2	$4,000 × .826 =	3,304
3	$4,000 × .751 =	3,004
	Total Present Value	$9,944

Table 2 Present Value of an Annuity of $1

Period	5%	6%	8%	10%	12%	14%	16%	18%	20%	22%	24%	25%
1	.952	.943	.926	.909	.893	.877	.862	.847	.833	.820	.806	.800
2	1.859	1.833	1.783	1.736	1.690	1.647	1.605	1.566	1.528	1.492	1.457	1.440
3	2.723	2.673	2.577	2.487	2.402	2.322	2.246	2.174	2.106	2.042	1.981	1.952
4	3.546	3.465	3.312	3.170	3.037	2.914	2.798	2.690	2.589	2.494	2.404	2.362
5	4.330	4.212	3.993	3.791	3.605	3.433	3.274	3.127	2.991	2.864	2.745	2.689
6	5.076	4.917	4.623	4.355	4.111	3.889	3.685	3.498	3.326	3.167	3.020	2.951
7	5.786	5.582	5.206	4.868	4.564	4.288	4.039	3.812	3.605	3.416	3.242	3.161
8	6.463	6.210	5.747	5.335	4.968	4.639	4.344	4.078	3.837	3.619	3.421	3.329
9	7.108	6.802	6.247	5.759	5.328	4.946	4.607	4.303	4.031	3.786	3.566	3.463
10	7.722	7.360	6.710	6.145	5.650	5.216	4.833	4.494	4.192	3.923	3.682	3.571
11	8.306	7.887	7.139	6.495	5.988	5.453	5.029	4.656	4.327	4.035	3.776	3.656
12	8.863	8.384	7.536	6.814	6.194	5.660	5.197	4.793	4.439	4.127	3.851	3.725
13	9.394	8.853	7.904	7.103	6.424	5.842	5.342	4.910	4.533	4.203	3.912	3.780
14	9.899	9.295	8.244	7.367	6.628	6.002	5.468	5.008	4.611	4.265	3.962	3.824
15	10.380	9.712	8.559	7.606	6.811	6.142	5.575	5.092	4.675	4.315	4.001	3.859
16	10.838	10.106	8.851	7.824	6.974	6.265	5.669	5.162	4.730	4.357	4.033	3.887
17	11.274	10.477	9.122	8.022	7.120	6.373	5.749	5.222	4.775	4.391	4.059	3.910
18	11.690	10.828	9.372	8.201	7.250	6.467	5.818	5.273	4.812	4.419	4.080	3.928
19	12.085	11.158	9.604	8.365	7.366	6.550	5.877	5.316	4.844	4.442	4.097	3.942
20	12.462	11.470	9.818	8.514	7.469	6.623	5.929	5.353	4.870	4.460	4.110	3.954
21	12.821	11.764	10.017	8.649	7.562	6.687	5.973	5.384	4.891	4.476	4.121	3.963
22	13.163	12.042	10.201	8.772	7.645	6.743	6.011	5.410	4.909	4.488	4.130	3.970
23	13.489	12.303	10.371	8.883	7.718	6.792	6.044	5.432	4.925	4.499	4.137	3.976
24	13.799	12.550	10.529	8.985	7.784	6.835	6.073	5.451	4.937	4.507	4.143	3.981
25	14.094	12.783	10.675	9.077	7.843	6.873	6.097	5.467	4.948	4.514	4.147	3.985
30	15.373	13.765	11.258	9.427	8.055	7.003	6.177	5.517	4.979	4.534	4.160	3.995

You will note a $4 difference between the amount calculated here and the amount calculated originally—$9,948. These amounts are different because the amounts shown in the tables have been rounded. As mentioned earlier, the present value factors are actually derived mathematically and can be carried out to many decimal places. For our purposes, they have been rounded to three places. Thus, occasionally differences occur because of rounding. The point is, however, that using Table 2 shortened the calculation. Consider how much longer it would take to use Table 1 to evaluate an alternative with a life of ten years or more.

It should be pointed out that the tables used here assume the cash flows occur at the end of each year. As a practical matter, cash flows occur at varying times during the year or evenly throughout the year. Tables are available to refine the process and make it more accurate than we have shown. For our purposes in this text, such refinement is not necessary.

The illustrations above showed only cash inflows (receipts). The present value of cash outflows is calculated in exactly the same manner. The chapter provides applications that use the present value tables to illustrate internal decision making through capital budgeting.

Summary

The time value of money is an important factor in the evaluation of investment alternatives. The two tables shown here are used in the chapter and in the problems at the end of the chapter for determining the present value of cash flows in certain situations. The present value of $1 table is used when a single amount is to be received or paid at one point in time in the future. The present value of an annuity of $1 table is used when a series of equal amounts is to be received or paid over a period of years in the future.

Review Problem

Problem

Dynamics, Inc., is considering the installation of new computer equipment at a cost of $100,000. The equipment to be replaced was purchased 3 years ago and has a book value of $18,000. It could be disposed of now for $12,000.

The new equipment is expected to reduce cash operating expenses by $35,000 a year. It has a 4-year life with no expected salvage value. The firm uses the straight-line method for depreciation. The tax rate is 40%. The firm's cost of capital is 14%.

Required:

For this proposed investment, calculate the following:

a. Net present value.

b. Profitability index.

c. Time-adjusted rate of return. (Interpolate to the nearest tenth of a percent.)

Solution

a.

	Year(s)	Amount	Tax Factor	Aftertax Cash Flow	PV Factor at 14%	Present Value
Cost Savings	1–4	$ 35,000	.6	$ 21,000	2.914	$ 61,194
Depreciation Expense[a]	1–4	25,000	.4	10,000	2.914	29,140
Disposal of Old Equipment	0	12,000	—	12,000	1.000	12,000
Loss on Disposal of Old Equipment[b]	0	6,000	.4	2,400	1.000	2,400
Investment	0	(100,000)	—	(100,000)	1.000	(100,000)
Net Present Value						$ 4,734

[a]$\dfrac{\$100,000}{4 \text{ Years}} = \$25,000$ per Year

[b]
Book Value of Old Equipment	$18,000
Disposal Value	(12,000)
Loss on Disposal	$ 6,000

b. The disposal value of the old equipment and the tax effect of the loss on the disposal result in a positive cash flow that is subtracted from the $100,000 investment. This results in an incremental investment of $85,600 to be used in calculating the profitability index as follows:

$$\text{Profitability Index} = \frac{\$61,194 + \$29,140}{\$100,000 - \$12,000 - \$2,400} = \frac{\$90,334}{\$85,600} = 1.06$$

c. The incremental investment of $85,600 determined above is used as the present value amount for calculating the time-adjusted rate of return, as shown below:

$$PV = F \times \text{Annuity}$$
$$\$85,600 = F \times (\$21,000 + \$10,000)$$
$$\$85,600 = F \times \$31,000$$
$$F = \frac{\$85,600}{\$31,000}$$
$$F = 2.761$$

The factor 2.761 falls between the factors 2.798 (16%) and 2.690 (18%) on the Period 4 line of Table 2 in the appendix. We interpolate as follows:

Factor at:		
16% Rate	2.798	2.798
Actual Rate	2.761	
18% Rate		2.690
Difference	.037	.108

$$\text{Actual Rate} = 16\% + \frac{.037}{.108}\,(2\%)$$
$$= 16\% + .7\%$$
$$= 16.7\%$$

Questions

11-1 Define *capital project* and *capital budgeting.*

11-2 How does capital budgeting help management to select capital projects for approval?

11-3 What is the effect of qualitative factors on capital budgeting?

11-4 Describe the advantages and disadvantages of the payback method.

11-5 Since the unadjusted rate of return method measures profitability, why is it not considered one of the better capital budgeting techniques?

11-6 Drole Company has used the unadjusted rate of return method in evaluating capital projects for several years. In the past, the firm used the initial investment to determine the rate of return. Recently, the president has stated that in the future all divisions will use the average investment because "we can double the rate of return this way." Comment on the validity of this statement.

11-7 What is meant by the statement, "Money has value in relation to time"? How does it affect capital budgeting?

11-8 (*Appendix*) Would you rather receive $2,000 a year for 3 years or $3,000 a year for 2 years? Does it make any difference? Explain. (*Note:* Do *not* use present value tables in answering the question.)

11-9 When the net present value method is used, a project with a negative net present value should be rejected. Do you agree? Explain.

11-10 Three projects under evaluation have net present values of $1,200, $5,000, and $25,000. Which project is best? Explain.

11-11 How does the time-adjusted rate of return method differ from the unadjusted rate of return method and from the net present value method? Which technique is best? Why?

11-12 A salesperson, when questioned about the apparently high maintenance cost of a machine he was selling, replied, "Don't worry about it. It's deductible." What did he mean by that? Do you agree that one should not worry about high costs if they are deductible? Explain.

11-13 If reducing expenses increases taxes, how can it be an advantage?

11-14 Since depreciation does not involve a cash flow, why is it considered in capital budgeting?

11-15 Since an asset cannot be depreciated below its estimated salvage value, regardless of the method used, why are accelerated depreciation methods generally considered more favorable for tax purposes than the straight-line method?

Exercises

Note: Ignore income tax implications in exercises and problems unless tax data are given.

11-16 Use of Tables (*Appendix*) Determine the present value of each of the following:

   a. $10,000 to be received at the end of 4 years at 8%.

b. $6,000 to be received each year for 6 years at 12%.
c. $4,200 to be received at the end of 12 years at 18%.
d. $2,800 a year to be received each year for 9 years at 14%.
e. $9,682 to be received at the end of 10 years at 6%.
f. $3,416 to be received each year for 15 years at 20%.

11-17 Use of Tables (*Appendix*) Determine the present value of each of the following:

a.	Amount	Received at End of Year:	Interest Rate
1.	$ 2,000	5	5%
2.	6,300	13	22%
3.	200,000	8	10%
4.	85,000	3	18%
5.	205	4	8%

b.	Amount	Received Each Year for:	Interest Rate
1.	$ 25,000	11 Years	12%
2.	2,100	4 Years	8%
3.	565	6 Years	14%
4.	165,000	10 Years	25%
5.	60,000	18 Years	6%

11-18 Sweepstakes-Winner (*Appendix*) You have just won a sweepstakes contest in which you have a choice of receiving $100,000 today or $15,000 a year for the next 10 years. The interest rate is 12%. Prepare calculations to show which would be a better choice from a financial viewpoint.

11-19 Investment Opportunities (*Appendix*) Linda Adams has 2 investment opportunities, each requiring the same amount of investment. Alternative A provides a return of $5,000 a year for 5 years. Alternative B provides a return of $6,000 a year for the first 2 years, $5,000 a year in Year 3, and $4,000 a year in Years 4 and 5. The interest rate is 8%. Prepare calculations to show which is the better alternative.

11-20 Investment Opportunities Able Andrews has 2 investment opportunities, each requiring the same initial investment. Alternative A provides $3,000 a year for 7 years and requires an additional outlay of $1,000 at the end of Year 4. Alternative B provides $2,500 a year for 10 years. The interest rate is 14%. Prepare calculations to show which is the better alternative.

11-21 Payback Method Determine the payback period in each of the following situations:

	Incremental Investment	Net Cash Inflows
a.	$ 3,000	$ 1,200
b.	10,000	2,000
c.	8,000	1,500
d.	35,000	6,000
e.	140,000	22,000

11-22 Payback Method; Uneven Cash Flows Determine the payback period in the situations shown below. Incremental investment was: (a) $35,000; (b) $60,000; (c) $180,000. Annual net cash inflows were as follows:

Year	a	b	c
1	$10,000	$20,000	$60,000
2	8,000	20,000	50,000
3	6,000	15,000	50,000 160 000
4	6,000	15,000	40,000
5	6,000	15,000	30,000
6	5,000		30,000
7	5,000		
8	5,000		

11-23 Payback Method; Unadjusted Rate of Return Barney Company is considering the purchase of a new machine at a cost of $20,000. Its expected life is 5 years, with no salvage value. Operating costs will be reduced by $8,000 a year.

a. Determine the payback period.

b. Determine the unadjusted rate of return based on the initial investment.

11-24 Payback Method; Unadjusted Rate of Return; Tax Effect Plastics, Inc., is considering the purchase of a $40,000 machine which will be depreciated on a straight-line basis over an 8-year period with no salvage value. The machine is expected to generate net cash income of $12,000 a year before income taxes. Assume that the income tax rate is 50%.

a. What is the payback period?

b. What is the unadjusted rate of return on the initial investment?
(AICPA adapted)

11-25 Net Present Value; Profitability Index Determine the net present value and the profitability index in each of the following situations:

	a	b	c
Investment:	$30,000	$85,000	$150,000
Annual Net Cash Inflows:	$6,000	$15,000	$40,000
Salvage Value (at End of Asset Life):	0	$2,000	$5,000 — 16
Asset Life (in Years):	8	10	6
Cost of Capital:	10%	12%	18%

11-26 Net Present Value; Profitability Index; Tax Effect Determine the net present value and the profitability index in each situation below. Assume straight-line depreciation and a 40% income tax rate. Salvage value is considered when determining annual depreciation.

	a	b	c
Investment:	$5,000	$20,000	$100,000
Annual Net Cash Inflows:	$1,500	$5,000	$2,500
Salvage Value (at End of Asset Life):	0	$2,000	$10,000
Asset Life (in Years):	5	8	10
Cost of Capital:	8%	10%	12%

11-27 Present Value of Aftertax Cash Flows; Independent Situations Determine the present value of the aftertax cash flows in each of the situations below. The tax rate is 40% in all cases. Use parentheses to indicate when your answer is a cash outflow.

a. $5,000 loss on disposal of an asset sold today at 12%.

b. $4,000 gain expected on an asset to be sold at the end of 3 years at 8%.

c. Depreciation (straight-line) on asset costing $12,000 with a 10-year life and no salvage value at 16%.

d. Second year depreciation (sum-of-the-years'-digits) on an asset costing $60,000 with a 5-year life and no salvage value at 22%.

e. Tax deductible cash outflows of $4,000 a year for 7 years at 12%.

f. Tax deductible cash outflows of $10,000 at the end of 6 years at 10%.

g. Cost savings of $8,000 a year for 12 years at 14%.

11-28 Net Present Value; Time-Adjusted Rate of Return; Independent Situations Determine the net present value and time-adjusted rate of return in each situation below. (Estimate the rate of return to the nearest percent without using interpolation.)

	Net Cash Inflows	Investment	Project Life (Years)	Cost of Capital
a.	$ 5,000	$18,000	5	10%
b.	8,000	50,000	10	12%
c.	15,000	70,000	8	16%
d.	2,000	6,600	4	6%
e.	3,500	15,000	7	12%

11-29 Net Present Value; Time-Adjusted Rate of Return; Tax Effect Hartley Company is reviewing a proposal to buy a new electric generator for its plant. The cost is $5,000; and the old generator can be salvaged for $500, its book value. The new generator will reduce power costs by $1,200 a year for the next 8 years, with no salvage value at that time. The company uses the straight-line method of depreciation. The tax rate is 40%. The firm's cost of capital is 12%. Determine the following:

a. Net present value.

b. Time-adjusted rate of return. (Estimate to the nearest percent without using interpolation.)

11-30 Net Present Value; Time-Adjusted Rate of Return; Tax Effect J. R. Jenson Sales Company would like to hire a new salesperson in order to help expand sales. Estimates show that a new person could result in increased sales of $50,000 a year, on which the firm averages a 40% contribution margin. The salesperson would be paid $15,000 a year plus an 8% commission (which is included in variable costs). Hiring a new salesperson means the firm would need to buy a new car for $10,500; it would have a 3-year life and no salvage value.

The firm uses the straight-line method of depreciation. The tax rate is 40%. J. R. has always required that any investment result in a rate of return of at least 16%. Use the (a) net present value method and (b) time-adjusted rate of return method to determine if a new salesperson should be hired. In using the latter method, estimate to the nearest percent without interpolation.

11-31 Determining Investment from Cash Flows Virginia Company invested in a 4-year project. Virginia's expected rate of return is 10%. Net cash inflows from the project are expected as follows:

Year	Net Cash Inflows
1	$4,000
2	4,400
3	4,800
4	5,200

The project resulted in a net present value of $1,000. Determine the amount of the original investment. (AICPA adapted)

Problems

11-32 Purchase of Typewriters BCB Company plans to buy 10 new typewriters at a cost of $1,000 each. The old typewriters can be disposed of for a total of $400 for all of them. The new typewriters are expected to last 5 years, with no salvage value at the end of that time. Because the new typewriters will increase efficiency and reduce costs, the incremental net cash inflows resulting from this investment are projected at a total of $3,000 a year. The firm's cost of capital is 14%.

Required:
Determine the following:
a. Payback period.
b. Unadjusted rate of return on the initial investment.
c. Net present value.
d. Profitability index.
e. Time-adjusted rate of return. (Estimate to the nearest percent without using interpolation.)

11-33 Purchase of Machine Yahoo Corporation is considering the purchase of a new machine. Two alternatives are available. Machine A costs $20,000 and would reduce operating costs by $6,000 a year. Its salvage value is $3,000. Machine B costs $30,000, would reduce operating costs by $9,000 a year, and has a disposal value of $1,000. Both machines have an estimated life of 5 years. The firm's cost of capital is 10%.

Required:
For each machine, calculate the following:
a. Payback period.
b. Net present value.
c. Profitability index.

11-34 Alternative Projects Bell Company is considering 2 alternative projects. Project A requires a $40,000 investment and would provide annual net cash inflows of $12,000 a year. Project B requires a $70,000 investment and would provide annual net cash inflows of $18,000 a year. Each project has an expected life of 5 years with no salvage value. The firm's cost of capital is 12%.

Required:

For each project, determine the following:

a. Net present value.

b. Profitability index.

c. Time-adjusted rate of return. (Interpolate to the nearest tenth of a percent.)

11-35 Single Project; Tax Effect Bellow Company is considering investing in a project at a cost of $90,000. The project is expected to provide annual incremental cash inflows of $35,000 a year for the next 8 years, with no salvage value at the end of that time. The firm uses the straight-line method of depreciation, and the tax rate is 40%. Management wants a minimum rate of return of 18%.

Required:

Calculate the following:

a. Net present value.

b. Profitability index.

c. Time-adjusted rate of return. (Interpolate to the nearest tenth of a percent.)

11-36 Truck Replacement; Loss on Disposal; Tax Effect Brown Company is considering the purchase of a new truck for $25,000. The old truck was bought 4 years ago and has a book value of $3,000. The firm uses the straight-line method of depreciation. At the time the old truck was bought, it was estimated to have a 5-year life with no salvage value. It can be disposed of now for $1,000.

The new truck is more efficient, can carry a greater load, and is less expensive to operate. It should increase net cash inflows by $8,000 a year. It has a 5-year life with no salvage value. The tax rate is 40%. The firm's cost of capital is 12%.

Required:

Calculate the following:

a. Net present value.

b. Profitability index.

c. Time-adjusted rate of return. (Interpolate to the nearest tenth of a percent.)

11-37 Purchase of Machine; Tax Effect Mother Bates' Home-Made Pies have become quite popular in a local community. Mother Bates has had difficulty in keeping up with the demand for pecan pies, one of the favorites. Because of the time it takes to shell the pecans, she is unable to bake as many pecan pies as people want to buy.

Recently, a pecan-shelling machine has come on the market that would allow Mother Bates to double her sales of pecan pies from 1,000 to 2,000 a year. However, sales of other pies would probably decline by 200 pies a year, because often customers buy something else when she is out of pecan pies. On the average, the pies sell for $5 and have a variable cost of $2 each.

Purchase of the machine would reduce labor costs by $4,000 a year. Repair and maintenance costs are estimated at $1,500 a year—somewhat high, but often shells get caught in the machine and jam it.

The cost of the machine is $10,000. It has an estimated life of 4 years with no salvage value. Mother Bates uses the straight-line method of depreciation, and her tax rate is 40%. She wants a minimum rate of return of 14% on all investments.

Required:

Calculate the following:

a. Net present value.

b. Profitability index.

c. Time-adjusted rate of return. (Interpolate to the nearest tenth of a percent.)

11-38 Basketball Player Contract; Tax Effect The Plakamine Pelicans are negotiating for the services of David Williams, a star basketball player in the Bayou Basketball League. David is demanding a $500,000 bonus upon signing and a salary of $200,000 a year for the next 5 years. The team owners think that David's presence on the team would increase yearly attendance from its present level as follows:

Year	Increase
1	50,000
2	50,000
3	30,000
4	20,000
5	10,000

Each ticket sells for $10, and there are virtually no variable costs. However, increased attendance would increase security and other fixed costs by $30,000 a year the first 3 years and $20,000 a year the last 2 years.

Contribution margin from concession sales are estimated to increase with the increased attendance as follows:

Year	Increase
1	$20,000
2	20,000
3	15,000
4	10,000
5	5,000

All payments to David are tax deductible. The tax rate is 40%. Because of the risk involved, the owners will not accept David's contract terms if they cannot earn at least a 20% rate of return on their investment.

Required:

Use the net present value method to determine whether David Williams' contract terms should be accepted.

11-39 New Product; Tax Effect Super Products Company is considering introducing a new product, which is expected to be on the market for 5 years. Sales for the first 2 years are forecast at $400,000 per year. Sales for the last 3 years are expected to be $250,000 per year. The variable cost ratio is 60%.

In order to produce the product, the company needs to add a building addition at a cost of $200,000. It must also buy new machinery for $150,000. The building would yield no cash flow at the end of the product's life, but the machinery could be sold for $30,000. The company uses the straight-line method of depreciation. The income tax rate is 40%.

An advertising campaign costing $100,000 will begin immediately. In addition, another $100,000 will be spent on advertising at the end of 3 years. Advertising is tax deductible.

The company requires a 10% rate of return on all capital projects.

Required:

Determine the net present value of the proposed capital project.

11-40 Machine Replacement; Tax Effect Hazman Company plans to re-place an old piece of equipment, which is obsolete and is expected to be unreliable under the stress of daily operations. The equipment is fully de-preciated, and no salvage value can be realized upon its disposal.

One piece of equipment being considered would provide annual cash savings of $7,000 before income taxes. The equipment would cost $18,000 and have an estimated useful life of 5 years. No salvage value would be used for depreciation purposes, because the equipment is expected to have no value at the end of 5 years.

Hazman uses the straight-line depreciation method on all equipment for both book and tax purposes. The company is subject to a 40% tax rate. Hazman has a cost of capital of 14%.

Required:

Calculate the following for Hazman Company's proposed investment in new equipment:

  a. Payback period.
  b. Unadjusted rate of return on the initial investment.
  c. Net present value.
  d. Profitability index.
  e. Time-adjusted rate of return; interpolate to the nearest tenth of a per-cent. (CMA adapted)

11-41 Machine Replacement; Tax Effect Rockyford Company must replace some machinery. This machinery has no book value, but its current market value is $1,800. One alternative is to invest in new machinery with a cost of $40,000. This new machinery would produce estimated annual pretax oper-ating cash savings of $12,500. The estimated useful life of the new machin-ery is 4 years. Rockyford uses straight-line depreciation for book purposes and the double-declining balance method for tax purposes.

The new machinery would have an estimated salvage value of $2,000 at the end of 4 years; however, the salvage value can be ignored for the pur-pose of depreciation, because it does not represent at least 10% of the cost of the asset. The investment in this new machinery would require an addi-tional investment in working capital of $3,000.

If Rockyford accepts this investment proposal, the disposal of the old machinery will take place on December 31 of the current year. The cash flows from the investment will occur during the next 4 calendar years (Years 1 through 4).

Rockyford is subject to a 40% income tax rate and has a 10% cost of capital. All operating and tax cash flows are assumed to occur at year end. (CMA adapted)

Required:

  a. Determine the present value of the following:
  1. Aftertax cash flow arising from the disposal of the old machinery on December 31 of the current year.
  2. Aftertax cash flows for all 4 years attributable to the operating cash savings.
  3. Effect of depreciation at the end of Year 1.
  4. Aftertax cash flows arising from the disposal of the new machinery at its salvage value at the end of Year 4.
  5. Income taxes related to the project for Year 2.
  b. Select the correct answer. Rockyford's additional investment in working capital of $3,000 required on December 31 of the current year is:
  1. A sunk cost that is not recovered.
  2. Considered part of the initial investment when determining the net present value.
  3. Spread over the 4-year life of the asset as a cash outflow.
  4. Depreciated as if it were part of the cost of the new machinery.
  5. Ignored.

11–42 New Product; Tax Effect The Baxter Company manufactures toys and other short-lived, fad-type items. The research and development department recently came up with an item that would make a good promotional gift for office equipment dealers. Aggressive and effective effort by Baxter's sales personnel has resulted in almost-firm commitments for this product for the next 3 years. It is expected that the product's value will be exhausted by that time.

In order to produce the quantity demanded, Baxter will need to buy additional machinery and rent some additional space. It appears that about 25,000 square feet will be needed; 12,500 square feet of presently unused, but leased, space is available now. (Baxter's present lease, with 10 years to run, costs $3 a square foot.) There is another 12,500 square feet adjoining the Baxter facility which Baxter will rent for 3 years at $4 per square foot per year if it decides to make this product.

The equipment will be purchased for about $900,000. It will require further expenditures of $30,000 for modifications, $60,000 for installation, and $90,000 for testing. All of these activities will be done by a firm of engineers hired by Baxter. All expenditures will be paid for on January 1 of the first year.

The equipment should have a salvage value of about $180,000 at the end of the third year. No additional general overhead costs are expected to be incurred.

The following estimates of revenues and expenses for this product for the 3 years have been developed:

	Year 1	Year 2	Year 3
Sales	$1,000,000	$1,600,000	$800,000
Material, Labor, and Incurred Overhead	400,000	750,000	350,000
Assigned General Overhead	40,000	75,000	35,000
Rent	87,500	87,500	87,500
Depreciation	450,000	300,000	150,000
Total Costs	$ 977,500	$1,212,500	$622,500
Income before Tax	$ 22,500	$ 387,500	$177,500
Income Tax (40%)	9,000	155,000	71,000
Net Income from Product	$ 13,500	$ 232,500	$106,500

Required:

a. Prepare a schedule that shows the incremental aftertax cash flows for this project for each year.

b. If the company requires a 2-year payback period for its investment, will it undertake this project? Prepare calculations to support your answer.

c. Calculate the aftertax accounting rate of return for this project.

d. A newly hired business school graduate recommends that the company consider the use of net present value analysis to study this project. If the company sets a required rate of return of 20% after taxes, will it accept this project? Show your supporting calculations clearly. (CMA adapted)

11-43 Additional Plant Capacity; Tax Effect Wisconsin Products Company manufactures several products. One of the firm's principal products sells for $20 per unit. The sales manager of Wisconsin Products has stated repeatedly that he could sell more units of this product if they were available. In an attempt to substantiate his claim, the sales manager conducted a market research study last year at a cost of $44,000 to determine potential demand for the product. The study indicated that Wisconsin Products could sell 18,000 units of the product annually for the next 5 years.

The equipment currently in use has the capacity to produce 11,000 units annually. The variable production costs are $9 per unit. The equipment has a book value of $60,000 and a remaining useful life of 5 years. The salvage value of the equipment is negligible now and will be zero in 5 years.

The company could purchase new machinery that would produce a maximum of 20,000 units per year. The new equipment costs $300,000 and has an estimated useful life of 5 years with no salvage value at the end of that time. Wisconsin Product's production manager has estimated that the new equipment would provide increased production efficiencies that would reduce the variable production costs to $7 per unit.

Wisconsin Products Company uses straight-line depreciation on all of its equipment for tax purposes. The firm is subject to a 40% tax rate, and its cost of capital is 15%.

The sales manager feels so strongly about the need for additional capacity that he has attempted to prepare an economic justification for the equipment, although that is not one of his responsibilities. His analysis, presented below, disappointed him, because it did not justify acquiring the equipment.

Required Investment

Purchase Price of New Equipment		$300,000
Disposal of Existing Equipment:		
Loss on Disposal	$60,000	
Less Tax Benefit (40%)	24,000	36,000
Cost of Market Research Study		44,000
Total Investment		$380,000

Annual Returns

Contribution Margin from Product:	
Using New Equipment	
[18,000 × (20 − $7)]	$234,000
Using Existing Equipment	
[11,000 × ($20 − $9)]	121,000
Increase in Contribution Margin	$113,000
Less Depreciation	60,000
Increase in before-Tax Income	$ 53,000
Income Tax (40%)	21,200
Increase in Income	$ 31,800
Less 15% Cost of Capital on Additional	
Investment Required (.15 × $380,000)	57,000
Net Annual Return of Proposed Investment	
in New Equipment	$(25,200)

Required:

  a. The controller of Wisconsin Products Company plans to prepare a discounted cash inflow analysis for this investment proposal. The controller has asked you to prepare corrected calculations of:

    1. The required investment in the new equipment.

    2. The recurring annual cash flows.

Explain the treatment of each item of your corrected calculations that is treated differently from the same item in the original analysis prepared by the sales manager.

  b. Calculate the net present value of the proposed investment in the new equipment. Discount factors for 15% (rounded) are shown below. (CMA adapted)

Period	Present Value of $1	Present Value of Annuity of $1
1	.87	.87
2	.76	1.63
3	.66	2.29
4	.57	2.86
5	.50	3.36

11–44 New Product; Uneven Cash Flows; Tax Effect Innovative Machine Company is considering producing electric pickle spears for removing pickles from jars. Primary customers would be fast food outlets whose ability to prepare hamburgers and other sandwiches would be speeded up with this machine.

A study of production costs indicates the spears could be produced at a variable cost of $13 each. The company would have to purchase special machinery for $60,000; it would have a 6-year life and a salvage value of $4,000. The firm uses the straight-line method of depreciation; and the salvage value would not be considered in calculating annual depreciation on this machine. Other separable fixed production costs are estimated at $100,000 a year. Facilities are available for production; but using them for this product would mean the firm would have to drop a product that has been providing a segment margin of $110,000 a year.

Market surveys suggest the selling price should be $25 per unit. A 6-year product life is estimated, with sales forecast as follows:

Year	Units
1	40,000
2	40,000
3	30,000
4	20,000
5	10,000
6	10,000

To achieve these sales levels would require advertising costs of $200,000 immediately, $100,000 at the end of Years 2 and 3, and $50,000 at the end of Years 4 and 5. The tax rate is 40%.

Required:

Calculate the time-adjusted rate of return. (*Note:* The cash flows are uneven; therefore, you must use the trial and error method.)

Chapter 12   Quantitative Techniques

Learning Objectives

The purpose of this chapter is to introduce you to several quantitative techniques that can be used by management in making decisions. The chapter describes and illustrates the use of probability theory and linear programming and the determination of economic order quantity and re-order point. Studying this chapter will enable you to:

1. Describe the use of probability theory in decision making and understand applicable terminology.

2. Calculate expected value.

3. Calculate the value of perfect information.

4. Prepare a payoff table.

5. Apply probability theory to capital budgeting.

6. Describe the use of linear programming in problem solving.

7. Solve problems using linear programming.

8. Describe the elements that are considered in determining economic order quantity and reorder point.

9. Determine economic order quantity.

10. Determine the reorder point.

Chapter Topics

The major topics in this chapter are:

Probability Theory
Linear Programming
Economic Order Quantity
Reorder Point

This chapter describes several techniques that can be used in addition to those discussed in previous chapters to help management in internal decision making. These techniques are called **quantitative techniques**—sophisticated mathematical approaches to problem solving. The chapter illustrates some of the more popular techniques: probability theory, linear programming, economic order quantity, and reorder point.

Strictly speaking, these are not accounting techniques; they are mathematical and statistical techniques. Nevertheless, the accountant should be aware of them, because the accountant is often the one who provides the relevant data for their application. Furthermore, the role of the management accountant is to help management make decisions that affect a firm's profitability. Quantitative techniques are tools that can be used in this role.

As with other decision-making techniques, the techniques in this chapter require that assumptions be made. As always, management must make the final decision. The techniques merely help management to make the decision; and the results determined by the techniques are only as valid as the assumptions.

Probability Theory

Probability theory is a concept that relates the projected outcome of a decision to the likelihood that the outcome will occur. In effect, this technique specifically takes uncertainty into consideration.

The probability of the occurrence of an outcome can be estimated with reasonable accuracy in some instances. For example, if you toss a coin, there is precisely one chance in two of its landing heads up and one chance in two of its landing tails up (provided, of course, that it is not loaded on one side). In other words, there is a 50-percent probability of heads and a 50-percent probability of tails. Dice have six sides each, and each side has a certain number of spots on it. When a die is tossed, there is one chance in six that a particular side will show on the face after the toss. For example, there is a 16 2/3-percent probability that the side with two spots will show up. In fact, there is a 16 2/3-percent probability of any one of the sides' showing up.

Unfortunately, most business situations do not lend themselves to such a precise assessment of probabilities. Nevertheless, for internal decision making, it is often necessary for management to assess the likelihood of the occurrence of certain events and of the outcome of certain actions. These probabilities are usually subjective, based on management's past experience and "feel" for the future.

Conditional Value

Conditional value is the amount that will result if a specific event occurs. For example, assume that a company expects to earn $75,000 per year if it produces a particular new product. The $75,000 represents the conditional value of the alternative—the amount that will result if the alternative is selected and results are as assumed. Note that probability does not enter into determining the conditional value.

To illustrate further, assume that Baker Company is considering offering a new product, Product A. Based on its analysis, management expects a contribution margin of either $100,000, $200,000, or $300,000. (As a practical matter, the contribution margin could range anywhere within these figures. However, for simplicity in illustrating the concept, we assume that the result will be only one of these three specific figures.) Fixed costs are estimated at $150,000. Each possibility that may occur is referred to as an

event. In this case, there are three events. One results in a contribution margin of $100,000; the second results in a contribution margin of $200,000; and the third results in a contribution margin of $300,000. The conditional value of each event is determined as follows:

Outcome

Event	Contribution Margin		Fixed Costs		Conditional Value
1	$100,000	−	$150,000	=	$(50,000)
2	200,000	−	150,000	=	50,000
3	300,000	−	150,000	=	150,000

Event 1 will result in a loss of $50,000. The $50,000 loss represents the conditional value of the event. Event 2 will result in a $50,000 profit; Event 3, in a $150,000 profit.

Understand that management usually does not know and cannot control which event will occur. Obviously, management would prefer to have the event occur that will result in $150,000 profit; and, of course, it would like to avoid the event that will result in a $50,000 loss. What management must do is assess the probability of each event's occurring. As mentioned earlier, this assessment is somewhat subjective but is based on past experience and management's knowledge of the market and other appropriate factors that may affect the outcome.

In this case, management has estimated the probabilities of each event as follows:

Event	Conditional Value	Probability
1	$(50,000)	.20
2	50,000	.30
3	150,000	.50

The data above show that, based on management's best judgment, if the firm makes Product A, there is a 20-percent chance that it will lose $50,000 per year, a 30-percent chance that it will earn $50,000 a year, and a 50-percent chance that it will earn $150,000 per year.

How are these data used in decision making and how does the firm compare them with other alternatives? These procedures are described in the following sections.

Expected Value

The next step in probability analysis is to determine each event's **expected value**—the weighted average of each conditional value of the event. Total expected value is the sum of expected values for each event. In other words, while conditional value shows the amount of profit or loss that will result if a specific event occurs, expected value shows the average profit or loss that would result on the basis of probabilities. Mathematically, we determine it by multiplying the probability of each event by the conditional value. For the Baker Company example, the result is shown as follows:

Event	Conditional Value	Probability	Expected Value
1	$(50,000)	.20	$(10,000)
2	50,000	.30	15,000
3	150,000	.50	75,000
Totals		1.00	$ 80,000

The calculations above indicate that if Baker Company decides to make this new product, it can expect an average profit of $80,000 per year. Realize that the actual results in any one year will be either a $50,000 profit, a $150,000 profit, or a $50,000 loss. But if the same conditions exist from year to year, the firm will earn a profit of $80,000 on the average.

It is sometimes easier to understand the concept of expected value by looking at it from another angle. The conditional values are the amounts that will result if contribution margin is $100,000, $200,000, or $300,000. If we look at a ten-year period, the probability is that in 20 percent of the years— that is, in two years out of ten, the firm will lose $50,000 per year. In three years out of ten, the firm will earn $50,000. Finally, in five years out of ten, the firm will earn a profit of $150,000 per year. Given this information, we can determine the ten-year income based on the probabilities as follows:

$$\$(50,000) \times 2 \text{ Years} = \$(100,000)$$
$$\$50,000 \ \times 3 \text{ Years} = \ \ \ 150,000$$
$$\$150,000 \ \times 5 \text{ Years} = \ \ \ 750,000$$
$$\text{10-Year Profit} \qquad \$ \ 800,000$$

If the firm decides to sell Product A, it will earn a total profit of $800,000 on it for the next ten years—an average of $80,000 per year, calculated as follows:

$$\frac{\$800,000}{10 \text{ Years}} = \$80,000 \text{ Average Profit per Year}$$

Notice that the average profit of $80,000 per year is the same as the total expected value previously calculated. This is because, by definition, the expected value is the *average* expected profit. It is important to realize that, based on the assumptions given, the firm will never earn $80,000 in any one year. Each year, it will have either a loss of $50,000, a profit of $50,000, or a profit of $150,000.

The calculations thus far indicate only that this alternative is a profitable one for the firm to pursue. For internal decision making, this alternative typically is compared with other alternatives. For example, assume that in addition to the alternative discussed, the firm has the alternative of selling another new product, Product B, that would result in contribution margin and probabilities as follows:

Event	Contribution Margin	Probability
1	$ 50,000	.20
2	250,000	.50
3	350,000	.30

Assuming the same fixed costs of $150,000, the conditional value of each event will equal the contribution margin less $150,000. The conditional value, when multiplied by the probability, results in the expected value of each event. In analyzing this alternative, management determines the total expected value, as follows:

Event	Conditional Value	Probability	Expected Value
1	$(100,000)	.20	$(20,000)
2	100,000	.50	50,000
3	200,000	.30	60,000
Totals		1.00	$ 90,000

This alternative results in a total expected value of $90,000, compared with a total expected value of $80,000 for Product A. On the average, then, Product B will provide $10,000 more profit per year to the company. On this basis alone, Product B would be selected.

Management may wish to look more closely at the probabilities to assess how it feels about the possibility that certain events will in fact occur. For example, although the probability of a $100,000 loss with Product B is only 20 percent, management may feel strongly that it does not wish to take a chance on losing $100,000 in any year. With Product A, the maximum loss in any year is $50,000. Based on this factor alone, management may prefer Product A simply because it wishes to minimize the risk of loss.

On the other hand, Product B is definitely more profitable on the average. There is an 80-percent chance it will earn at least $100,000 and a 30-percent chance it will earn as much as $200,000. There is only a 50-percent chance that Product A will earn $150,000, the maximum earnings possible. As you can see, the calculations do not provide a definite solution for management. They merely assess the probabilities of certain events' occurring, based on the best information available. As frequently mentioned, management must now consider what the various results would mean to the firm and make its decision based on the information available and the qualitative factors it considers appropriate.

Value of Perfect Information

Suppose that the products described above for Baker Company were of a type that incurred losses only in years of specific economic downturns. If the company knew beyond any doubt the years in which the downturns would occur, it could avoid losses by not selling those products in those particular years, assuming it could also avoid incurring the fixed costs of the products.

For example, if the firm had perfect information as to when Product A would result in a loss, it would only sell Product A when it knew it would make a profit. Therefore, the conditional value in 20 percent of the years would be zero, because the firm would not sell the product in those years. It is assumed that the fixed cost of $150,000 is incurred only if the product is sold. Total expected value in this situation is as follows:

Event	Conditional Value	Probability	Expected Value
1	$ 0	.20	$ 0
2	50,000	.30	15,000
3	150,000	.50	75,000
Totals		1.00	$90,000

By selling only in the profitable years, the company will average $90,000 per year, the expected value. The difference between the $90,000 the company can expect when it has perfect information and the $80,000 it can expect when it does not is $10,000. This $10,000 represents the **value of perfect information.** Theoretically, the company could spend up to $10,000 a year doing research to determine when it would be unprofitable to sell the product.

For Product B, the expected value with perfect information is calculated as follows:

Event	Conditional Value	Probability	Expected Value
1	$ 0	.20	$ 0
2	100,000	.50	50,000
3	200,000	.30	60,000
Totals		1.00	$110,000

Expected value with perfect information is $110,000. The value of perfect information in this case is $20,000 ($110,000 − $90,000).

It should be pointed out again that the techniques described above are used to help management arrive at a decision. As a practical matter, the firm cannot necessarily expect that a particular product could be sold for the next ten years. Neither can it expect that there will be no changes in costs and selling prices. Nevertheless, the analysis provides some objective method of distinguishing between the profitability of the two alternatives. But again, recognize that there are limitations in the technique.

Payoff Table

In the previous illustration, all possibilities of losses were caused by the inability of contribution margin to cover fixed costs. However, other causes for loss exist. Many firms sell products that are subject to deterioration. For example, certain bakery items, flowers, fruits and vegetables, meat, and other perishable goods, if unsold, will spoil and become worthless. Firms that sell such products must be concerned with losses on inventory caused by overstockage. Thus, in analyzing the number to stock, these firms must consider the profits on the expected sales, along with the losses on unsold items.

The example of Bill's Bakery will illustrate this concept. Among the numerous bakery items Bill sells is a special pastry he calls "Delectable Delights." These items have a variable cost of $.20 each and sell for $.50 each. They become stale very quickly, however, and any unsold at the end of the day must be thrown away. Thus, Bill loses $.20 on any that he makes but does not sell. Bill is trying to determine how many he should stock each day. Past experience has indicated that he can always expect to sell at least twenty per day. Past history also shows that he has never sold more than eighty per day. Based on his records, Bill assesses the probability of sales as follows:

Demand	Probability
20	.10
50	.60
80	.30

As a practical matter, of course, he could expect to sell between twenty and fifty or between fifty and eighty. But for simplicity in presenting the problem, we assume sales levels of either twenty, fifty, or eighty items.

In order to decide how many to stock each day, Bill needs to prepare a payoff table that shows the expected value for stockages of twenty, fifty, or eighty. A **payoff table** is a table that shows the conditional value for each alternative assuming each level of demand.[1] For Bill's Bakery, the payoff table is shown in Exhibit 12.1.

Exhibit 12.1 Payoff Table

	Course of Action: Stockage		
Demand	20	50	80
20	$6	$ 0	$(6)
50	6	15	9
80	6	15	24

To understand the significance of the payoff table, let's examine each column. Suppose Bill decides to stock twenty items per day. If there is a demand for twenty, he will sell them all. At a contribution margin of $.30 per item, this represents a profit of $6 ($.30 × 20). If there is a demand for fifty items, he will still sell only twenty, because that is all he has. Therefore, he will again make a profit of $6 per day. If there is a demand for eighty, he will still make $6 per day, because he can sell only twenty.

Suppose he decides to stock fifty per day. If there is a demand for twenty, he ends up with no profit or loss. This situation is demonstrated as follows:

Contribution Margin on 20 Items ($.30 CM × 20):	$ 6
Loss on 30 Items ($.20 VC × 30):	(6)
Profit:	$ 0

---

[1]Each level of demand is an event. It is not necessary to number each event as 1, 2, 3, and so on, as done previously. However, numbering the events often facilitates discussing them.

He makes $.30 on each of the twenty he sells, but he loses the $.20 variable cost on each of the thirty items that are unsold at the end of the day.

What if he stocks fifty items and the demand is for fifty items? He will make a profit of $15 ($.30 × 50). If he stocks fifty and the demand is for eighty, he will still make a profit of $15 on the fifty sold.

Now look at the third column. If he stocks eighty and the demand is for only twenty, he will lose $6, calculated as follows:

Contribution Margin on 20 Items ($.30 CM × 20): $ 6
Loss on 60 Items ($.20 VC × 60):   (12)
Loss: $ (6)

In this case, Bill makes a profit of $6 on the twenty sold but loses $12 on the sixty unsold, resulting in a loss for the day of $6.

If Bill stocks eighty and demand exists for only fifty, the profit for the day will be $9, calculated as follows:

Contribution Margin on 50 Items ($.30 CM × 50): $15
Loss on 30 Items ($.20 VC × 30):   (6)
Profit: $ 9

Here, the contribution margin on the fifty items sold is $15. But thirty items are unsold, resulting in a $6 loss. The profit for the day is $9.

If Bill stocks eighty and the demand is for eighty, he will make a profit of $24 ($.30 × 80).

Now that Bill has this information, what should he do? As you can see from Exhibit 12.1, the best alternative depends on the demand. To help him make a decision, he can now use probabilities of demand to determine the expected value for each conditional value under each course of action. This procedure is shown in Exhibit 12.2.

The conditional values (CV) in each column come from Exhibit 12.1. The expected values (EV) in each column come from multiplying the probability by the conditional value for each stockage level. The exhibit shows that the best alternative for Bill is to stock fifty items every day. By doing this, he will earn an average profit of $13.50 per day, which is higher than the averages for the other alternatives.

Exhibit 12.2 Expected Value of Each Course of Action

		Course of Action: Stockage					
Demand	**Probability**	**20**		**50**		**80**	
		CV	**EV**	**CV**	**EV**	**CV**	**EV**
20	.10	$6.00	$ .60	$ 0	$ 0	$(6.00)	$ (.60)
50	.60	6.00	3.60	15.00	9.00	9.00	5.40
80	.30	6.00	1.80	15.00	4.50	24.00	7.20
Totals	1.00		$6.00		$13.50		$12.00

To better understand the meaning of this expected value, assume Bill does stock fifty items every day for one hundred days. Based on the probabilities, ten days out of a hundred he will sell only twenty, and ninety days out of a hundred he will sell the fifty he stocks. His profit can be calculated as follows:

$$
\begin{array}{lll}
10 \text{ Days} \times \$0 & = \$ & 0 \\
90 \text{ Days} \times \$15 & = & \underline{1,350} \\
\text{Total Profit} & & \underline{\$1,350}
\end{array}
$$

$$\text{Average Profit per Day: } \frac{\$1,350}{100 \text{ Days}} = \$13.50$$

Over the hundred days, he will earn a total profit of $1,350—an average of $13.50 per day, the expected value shown in Exhibit 12.2. You may wish to perform a similar calculation for the stocking of eighty items. If you do, you will find that the average profit per day is $12.

The data in Exhibit 12.2 show that if Bill stocks twenty items every day, his profit will average $6.00 per day; if he stocks fifty items per day, his profit will average $13.50 per day; and if he stocks eighty items per day, his profit will average $12.00 per day. If Bill were able, he would really like to stock only twenty items on those days when there would be a demand for only twenty, to stock fifty items only on those days when there would be a demand for fifty, and to stock eighty only on those days when there would be a demand for eighty. Thus, if Bill had perfect information, he would stock only the amount demanded each day, thereby never losing any money because of unsold inventory. We can determine the expected value with perfect information as follows:

Demand	Probability	Conditional Value	Expected Value
20	.10	$ 6.00	$ .60
50	.60	15.00	9.00
80	.30	24.00	7.20
	1.00		$16.80

We determine the conditional value for each demand by multiplying the demand by the contribution margin of $.30 per unit.

If Bill knew exactly what days demand would be twenty, fifty, and eighty, he could earn an average profit of $16.80 per day. This can be proven as follows:

$$
\begin{array}{lll}
10 \text{ Days} \times \$6 & = \$ & 60 \\
60 \text{ Days} \times \$15 & = & 900 \\
30 \text{ Days} \times \$24 & = & \underline{720} \\
\text{Total Profit} & & \underline{\$1,680}
\end{array}
$$

$$\text{Average Profit per Day: } \frac{\$1,680}{100 \text{ Days}} = \$16.80$$

The expected value with perfect information is $16.80 per day. Therefore, the value of perfect information is $3.30 per day ($16.80 − $13.50). As before, this amount represents the difference between the expected value with perfect information and the expected value under the best alternative. Theoretically, Bill could afford to pay $3.30 per day in an effort to obtain perfect information about demand.

Capital Budgeting

Capital budgeting techniques can be expanded to include probability theory. For example, the illustrations of capital budgeting in Chapter 11 showed that cash inflows are an important element expected to result from investment in a specific project. As pointed out in that chapter, the expected cash flows are normally estimates. Management may believe that a range of cash flows, rather than just one cash flow amount, may result from the investment. In this case, it may assess the probabilities of these cash flows' occurring and then use the expected value of the cash flows in arriving at their present value.

Assume that a company has the alternative of investing $10,000 in a capital project. Cash flows are expected to be either $2,000, $3,000, or $4,000 per year for the next five years. The probability of these cash flows' occurring is 30 percent, 50 percent, and 20 percent, respectively. On this basis, the expected value of cash flows is calculated as follows:

Conditional Value	Probability	Expected Value
$2,000	.30	$ 600
3,000	.50	1,500
4,000	.20	800
Totals	1.00	$2,900

Now, rather than using either $2,000, $3,000, or $4,000 in determining the net present value, the firm uses the expected value, $2,900. The net present value for this project is calculated as shown in Exhibit 12.3:

Exhibit 12.3 Net Present Value

	Amount	PV Factor at 12%	Present Value
Cash Inflows	$ 2,900	3.605	$ 10,455
Investment	(10,000)	1.000	(10,000)
Net Present Value			$ 455

In this case, the net present value is $455. Since it is a positive figure, the desired rate of return of 12 percent has been exceeded. Thus, the project can be considered worthwhile.

Probability theory can be used in any capital budgeting application. The idea is to refine the projections so that probability is considered in determining the present value of cash inflows and outflows.

Linear Programming

Chapter 10 pointed out that sometimes management decisions must be based on the consideration of limiting factors. It illustrated a situation in which a firm could sell all that it could produce of two products. However, machine hours were limited, and the decision as to what to produce was based on contribution margin per hour. Frequently, more than one constraint exists, and another approach to problem solving must be taken.

Description of Linear Programming

Linear programming is a mathematical technique management can use in making decisions between alternatives that involve two or more constraints. Typically, these alternatives are designed to either maximize income or minimize costs. In any operation, management faces several limitations on the total amount of resources available. These include—but are not limited to—machine hours, raw materials, physical labor, and floor space. The objective of linear programming is to determine the most profitable combination of products, based on the specified conditions.

Linear programming problems can be quite complex. However, the availability of canned programs for most computers makes the use of linear programming techniques a common occurrence. This chapter illustrates the usefulness of linear programming by solving a relatively uncomplicated problem with the graphic approach.

Assume that Harrison Company produces two products, X and Y. Product X provides a contribution margin of $10 per unit and Product Y provides a contribution margin of $15 per unit. Because of machine constraints, production is limited to a total of 800 hours per month. Product X requires one-fifth of an hour of machine time per unit, and Product Y requires one-fourth of an hour per unit. The company likes to maintain one month's production in inventory at all times. Storage space for finished inventory is limited to 15,000 cubic feet. Each unit of Product X requires three cubic feet, and each unit of Product Y requires five cubic feet. The company wants to maximize its contribution margin per month by producing the optimal amounts of X and Y. Management wants to know, based on these constraints, how much X and how much Y it should produce each month.

Steps in Solving the Problem

There are four basic steps in solving linear programming problems:
1. Determine the objective function.
2. Determine the constraints.
3. Plot the constraints on a graph.
4. Calculate the optimal solution.

Determine the Objective Function (Step 1) In this step, we express the objective of the problem algebraically. For Harrison Company, the objective is to maximize contribution margin in the production of its two products, X and Y. This objective is expressed as follows:

Maximize:

Contribution Margin = $10X + $15Y

The equation above means that the firm wants the highest contribution margin possible from the combination of producing X and Y, with contribution margins of $10 and $15, respectively. Total contribution margin will be $10 multiplied by the number of units of X produced plus $15 multiplied by the number of units of Y produced. How many units of X and Y should be produced?

Determine the Constraints (Step 2) In this step, we set forth algebraically the constraints given in the problem. There are two constraints given in our problem; one is that total machine hours are limited to 800 hours per month, and the second is that total storage space is limited to 15,000 cubic feet. These constraints are expressed algebraically as follows:

$$\frac{1}{5}X + \frac{1}{4}Y \leq 800$$
$$3X + 5Y \leq 15,000$$

The symbol $\leq$ in the equation means "is equal to or less than." The first constraint says that one-fifth of an hour times the number of units of X produced plus one-fourth of an hour times the number of units of Y produced is equal to or less than 800 hours. Because capacity is limited to 800 hours, total production cannot exceed 800 hours. It is possible, however, that production could be less than 800 hours. The second constraint says that three cubic feet multiplied by the number of units of X plus five cubic feet multiplied by the number of units of Y is equal to or less than 15,000 cubic feet.

In addition to the constraints previously given, there are two other constraints, expressed as follows:

$$X \geq 0$$
$$Y \geq 0$$

These constraints say that the total production of X will be equal to or greater than zero and the total production of Y will be equal to or greater than zero. These constraints acknowledge that negative production is not possible. Thus, the firm may decide not to produce any X or Y; but it can never produce less than zero.

Plot the Constraints on a Graph (Step 3) To plot the first constraint, we first assume that the firm will produce only X and no Y. If this is so, then the firm can produce 4,000 units of X, calculated as follows:

$$\frac{1}{5}X + \frac{1}{4}Y = 800$$

If Y = 0, Then:

$$\frac{1}{5}X = 800$$

$$X = 5(800)$$
$$X = 4,000$$

Notice that in the equation above we assume that if no Y is produced, disregarding any other constraints, 800 hours will be used in producing X. If this is done, 4,000 units of X can be produced.

We plot this point on the graph by putting a dot on the X line at 4,000. Since Y is zero, the dot for it is placed on the very bottom line of the graph.

Next, assume that no X is produced. In this case, the maximum amount of Y that can be produced is 3,200, calculated as follows:

$$\frac{1}{5}X + \frac{1}{4}Y = 800$$

If X = 0, Then:

$$\frac{1}{4}Y = 800$$

$$Y = 4(800)$$
$$Y = 3,200$$

We plot this result by placing a dot on the Y axis at 3,200 when X is zero. Next a line is drawn from the 3,200 on the Y axis to the 4,000 on the X axis. The plotted constraint appears as follows:

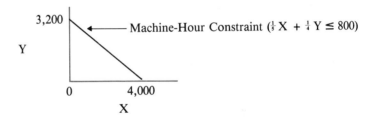

At this point, we can say that any production must fall to the left of this line. Any production to the right of the line would require more than 800 machine hours. Any production to the left of the line is within the 800-hour constraint and is possible, based on this constraint alone. However, we have another constraint to contend with—the cubic-feet constraint.

This constraint is plotted in the same manner as the machine-hour constraint. First, we determine how much Product X can be stored if no Product Y is stored. This is calculated as follows:

$$3X + 5Y = 15,000$$
$$\text{If } Y = 0, \text{ Then:}$$
$$3X = 15,000$$
$$X = \frac{15,000}{3}$$
$$X = 5,000$$

The warehouse can store 5,000 units of Product X if it does not have to store any units of Product Y. Now determine how much Y can be stored if no X is produced. This is calculated as follows:

$$3X + 5Y = 15,000$$
$$\text{If } X = 0, \text{ Then:}$$
$$5Y = 15,000$$
$$Y = \frac{15,000}{5}$$
$$Y = 3,000$$

If no X is produced, the warehouse can store 3,000 units of Y. We next plot these data on the graph.

On the X axis, we put a dot at 5,000 when Y is zero. On the Y axis, we put a dot at 3,000 when X is zero. Then we connect the two dots. This line is shown (without the machine-hour constraint line) as follows:

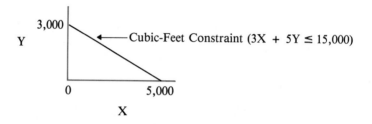

Based on this constraint alone, the firm can produce no combination to the right of the line and any combination to the left of the line.

To be meaningful, both constraints must be plotted on the same graph, as shown in Exhibit 12.4. The constraints produced by both lines are such that the only possible combinations of production are those included in the shaded area. Any combination of production within the shaded area is possible. The next step is to find the most profitable combination.

Determine the Optimal Solution (Step 4)   The objective is to determine the production at which the firm can obtain the maximum contribution margin. To make this determination, we calculate the contribution margin at each corner of the graph. A corner is a point at which two lines on the graph intersect. In Exhibit 12.4, there are four corners, as follows:

Corner	X	Y
1	0	0
2	0	3,000
3	1,000	2,400
4	4,000	0

The corners are: where X equals zero and Y equals zero; where X equals zero and Y equals 3,000, where X equals 1,000 and Y equals 2,400, and where X equals 4,000 and Y equals zero.

Next, we calculate the total contribution margin at each corner. The contribution margin for X is $10 per unit produced and for Y is $15 per unit

Exhibit 12.4 Linear Programming Graph

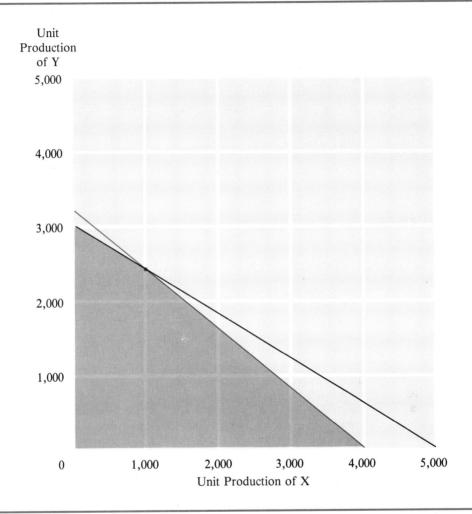

Unit Production of Y

Unit Production of X

produced. Contribution margin for each of the corners is shown in Exhibit 12.5. The maximum contribution margin is $46,000. It is obtained when 1,000 units of X and 2,400 units of Y are produced. Thus, this is the optimal production, because it will yield the maximum contribution margin.

The optimal solution will always occur at a corner, because the more produced, the greater the contribution margin. The corner represents a maximum point of production for a particular constraint. Thus, the corner showing the highest contribution margin will also have the maximum contribution margin that can be produced under the constraints given. It is possible that some combination other than a corner will yield the same

Exhibit 12.5 Calculation of Optimal Solution

Corner	Production		Contribution Margin		
	X	Y	X　+	Y　=	Total
1	0	0	$　0	$　0	$　0
2	0	3,000	0	45,000	45,000
3	1,000	2,400	10,000	36,000	46,000
4	4,000	0	40,000	0	40,000

maximum contribution margin as the corner. But no other combination will yield a contribution margin greater than that found at the optimal corner. Hence, we always compute contribution margin at each corner, knowing that the largest figure derived will be the optimal solution.

Economic Order Quantity

One of the complexities in selling is knowing how much inventory to keep on hand and when to order or manufacture more. We will consider the example of stocking inventory for a retail firm, but the principles are the same for inventory management of a manufacturer.

Let's look at the two extremes in inventory management. A manager might say, "I will not stock anything. I will merely order merchandise as customers require it and avoid inventory storage problems." What's wrong with this attitude? Well, as you might expect, most customers want what they want when they want it. They do not want to wait for merchandise to come in. Thus, a firm that has the philosophy of merely ordering merchandise as customers request it will most likely serve only a very limited number of customers.

The other extreme is to stock so many items of inventory that the firm never runs out. This practice provides customer satisfaction, because the firm always has what the customer wants when the customer wants it. The problem is that stocking inventory incurs costs—the more inventory stocked, the greater the costs.

Somehow management has to strike a happy balance between stocking enough to meet customer demands and not stocking so much that costs are too high. This section describes how to determine the amount of inventory the firm should order to minimize order costs and carrying costs by calculating the **economic order quantity (EOQ).** A subsequent section describes how to minimize the possibility of running out by maintaining a safety stock and calculating the reorder point.

Order Costs

Order costs are costs associated with ordering inventory. Basically, these costs include the cost of salaries paid to individuals whose job it is to place orders. Order costs also include the cost of forms used in ordering and may include telephone charges, if the telephone is used in the ordering process. In determining economic order quantity, we are concerned with incremental order costs—that is, those additional costs incurred simply because an order is placed. Calculating these costs is easier said than done; if a firm computes order cost for hundreds of different items, there is some problem in determining what incremental costs are attached to what order. To the extent that order costs are variable, the more frequently orders are placed, the greater the order cost. Conversely, making fewer orders reduces costs.

Carrying Costs	**Inventory carrying costs** include a number of items. The storage space itself is a cost—the more inventory on hand, the more space required. This cost may be measured in terms of depreciation for the storage area or rent. The salaries paid to individuals who work in the warehouse or storage area are another major cost of carrying inventory. Additional (incremental) storage space costs and salaries incurred for increased inventory are included in determining economic order quantity. Normally, there will be taxes and insurance on inventory. Most likely, the amount of taxes and insurance will depend on the dollar amount of inventory—the greater the inventory, the greater the cost.

Depending on the type of product, there is a risk of obsolescence and deterioration. Certain food items and drug items are dated. If too much inventory is bought and some items are not sold before their expiration date, a loss is incurred. There are clerical costs associated with maintaining inventory. Either individuals maintain inventory records, or computer time is used. Both represent a cost of carrying inventory. In other words, it costs to keep track of inventory on hand.

Another major cost of carrying inventory is the interest on the amount invested in it. As described in previous chapters, assets represent an investment. Money invested in inventory could have been invested elsewhere. For example, if the investment in inventory averages $200,000 a year, and the firm's cost of capital is 10 percent, there is a $20,000 annual interest cost on investment in inventory.

Firms can minimize the first category of inventory costs, order cost, by ordering large quantities at infrequent intervals; and they can minimize carrying costs by maintaining a very low inventory balance. The problem is to come up with the inventory amount that minimizes both costs at the same time.

Determining the Economic Order Quantity	There are three ways to determine the economic order quantity: by use of a table, a formula, or a graph. As previously discussed, order cost and carrying cost move in opposite directions. That is, the greater the quantity ordered, the smaller the annual ordering cost, because fewer orders are needed; but the greater the quantity ordered, the greater the annual carrying cost, because the average inventory is more. Thus, the objective of determining the economic order quantity is to find the order quantity at which the incremental annual order cost and the incremental annual carrying cost are the same. At this point, the total annual costs of ordering and stocking inventory are minimized.

Use of Table The construction of a table to determine the EOQ is a practical technique to use when the number of orders each year is not expected to be too high or when the number of items of inventory for which the EOQ is determined is not too many.

For example, assume a firm's inventory has the following characteristics:

Total Units Used per Year: 5,000
Cost per Order: $50
Annual Carrying Cost per Unit: $.30

It is unlikely that the firm would order more than the total annual usage at one time. Thus, in constructing the table, we assume the maximum number to be ordered at one time is 5,000, which represents one order per year. From there, we move sequentially through the number of orders per year, dividing the annual usage of 5,000 by the number of orders to determine the number that would be ordered each time. The economic order quantity is determined in Exhibit 12.6.

Exhibit 12.6 Table Determination of EOQ

(1) Orders per Year	(2) Units per Order [5,000 ÷ (1)]	(3) Average Inventory [(2) ÷ 2][a]	(4) Annual Order Cost [$50 × (1)]	(5) Annual Carrying Cost [$.30 × (3)]	(6) Total Annual Costs [(4) + (5)]
1	5,000	2,500	$ 50	$750	$800
2	2,500	1,250	100	375	475
3	1,667	833	150	250	400
4	1,250	625	200	188	388
5	1,000	500	250	150	400
6	833	417	300	125	425

[a]Calculation of average inventory assumes each order is used up before another order is received. Thus, the calculation is based on the beginning balance (the amount ordered) plus the ending balance (zero), with the total divided by two. For all practical purposes, this is the order quantity divided by two.

The exhibit shows the total annual cost for orders ranging from one per year to six per year. If the firm orders once per year, it must order 5,000 units. This represents an average inventory of 2,500 units per year. The annual order cost is $50, since only one order is placed. The annual carrying cost is $.30 per unit multiplied by the average inventory of 2,500 units ($750). These two costs, $50 and $750, are added together to arrive at the total annual cost of $800.

If two orders per year are placed, only 2,500 units are ordered each time, which reduces the average inventory to 1,250. Annual order cost is $100, because two orders are placed at $50 per order. The carrying cost is reduced because the average inventory is less; the exhibit shows it as $375. Total costs are $475.

Note that if four orders per year are placed, total annual cost is $388—the lowest total annual cost on the table. If three orders are placed, the cost is

$400; if five orders are placed, the cost again begins to rise. Notice that the annual order cost at four orders per year is $200 and the annual carrying cost is $188. Since these costs are not exactly equal, the economic order quantity is not exactly 1,250; but it is probably close enough. The formula method will determine the exact economic order quantity.

Use of Formula A mathematical formula has been derived to provide the precise economic order quantity. Exhibit 12.7 shows how this formula is used with the data from the previous illustration to determine the EOQ for our example.

Note that the economic order quantity determined by use of the formula is 1,291, compared with the EOQ of 1,250 determined by use of the table. Realize, however, that orders must frequently be made in round-lot sizes.

Exhibit 12.7 Formula Determination of EOQ

$$EOQ = \sqrt{\frac{2\ OU}{C}}$$

Where: O = Order Cost per Order.
$\quad\quad\quad U$ = Number of Units Used Annually.
$\quad\quad\quad C$ = Carrying Cost per Unit.

$$EOQ = \sqrt{\frac{2(\$50 \times 5,000)}{\$0.30}}$$

$$= \sqrt{\frac{2(\$250,000)}{\$0.30}}$$

$$= \sqrt{\frac{\$500,000}{\$0.30}}$$

$$= \sqrt{1,666,667}$$

$$= 1,291\ \text{Units}$$

Therefore, it may not be necessary to determine the EOQ exactly. For example, if the firm were required to order in lots of 100 units each, then it would probably order 1,300 units each time.

Use of Graph A graph can be used to determine the economic order quantity. As a practical matter, a firm would probably use the table or the formula to arrive at the amount. Nevertheless, the graph provides a visual display of the components that determine the economic order quantity and is helpful in illustrating these points. The economic order quantity determined by using the graph is shown in Exhibit 12.8.

Exhibit 12.8 Graphical Determination of EOQ

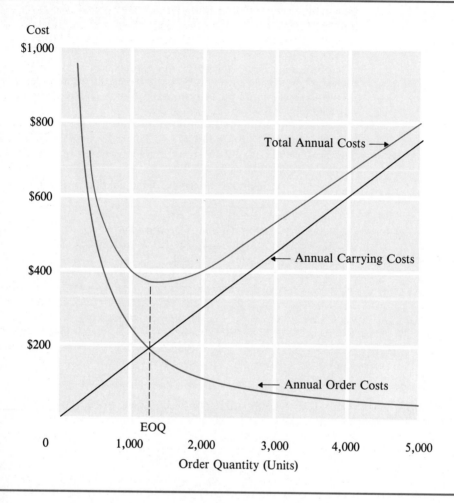

The three cost items are most easily plotted on the graph if a table is first constructed. The annual carrying cost is $.30 per unit of average inventory. Assuming that the order quantity is the same as in Exhibit 12.6, this cost ranges from $125 for six orders (of 833 units per order) to $750 for one order (of 5,000 units). (Of course, if there are no orders, there is no inventory, so this amount is zero.) Annual order costs range from $50 for one order to $300 for six orders. Note, however, that these costs are not plotted against the number of orders, but rather against the quantity ordered. Therefore, as the quantity ordered increases, the order cost decreases, as you can see on the graph. Total annual costs for quantity ordered are also shown on the graph. As you know, the economic order quantity is that point at which the annual order cost equals the annual carrying cost. On the graph, this point is at the intersection of these two lines. A dashed line is drawn vertically through this intersection. The economic order quantity is also the lowest point on the total annual cost curve.

As a practical matter, the exact economic order quantity is not necessarily the amount the firm will order. Most likely, it will order a practical amount somewhere along the bottom of the annual cost curve. From the graph, this appears to be from 1,000 to 2,000 units.

Reorder Point

As previously mentioned, the firm's other major inventory problem is running out of inventory—the **stockout.**

The immediate effect of not having a product in stock when it is requested is that the contribution margin on the product is lost if the customer goes elsewhere to buy the product. In addition, a firm that is always out of inventory loses customer goodwill. As a result, frequent stockouts may bring about a long-term loss of sales, as customers stop coming. Furthermore, dissatisfied customers will probably spread the word, and the firm will lose even further sales. The costs that result from this situation are opportunity costs. That is, the firm's not being able to sell a product because it doesn't have it on hand represents lost contribution margin that it would otherwise have earned. To avoid stockouts, a firm must maintain a safety stock and determine its optimal reorder point.

Safety Stock

Regardless of how many units represent the economic order quantity, the firm must have sufficient units on hand to meet demand between the time an order is placed and the time it is received. This difference in time is referred to as **lead time.** At some point before the inventory level reaches zero, the firm must place an order so that it will have sufficient time to receive the order before a stockout occurs. Because neither lead time nor daily usage can ever be exact, the firm normally maintains a safety stock.

Safety stock represents the amount the firm attempts to keep on hand so that if its normal stock runs out before an order is received, some stock will be on hand to meet customer demand. Naturally, there is a cost involved in maintaining the safety stock. But this cost is constant throughout the year, as long as the amount of safety stock does not change. A firm attempts to balance the cost of carrying safety stock against the cost of stockouts. The firm must determine the amount of safety stock based on the expected variance in lead time or in daily usage. In normal lead time is short, say two or three days, a smaller safety stock can usually be maintained. If lead time is longer, say twenty to thirty days, there is a greater risk of not having a sufficient amount on hand; in this case, a larger safety stock is required. Also, a larger safety stock is usually maintained for items with higher contribution margins, because the cost of running out is higher.

Calculating Reorder Point

The **reorder point** is that inventory level at which the firm places an order. It is based on the lead time and the safety stock. When the firm places an order, it should have just enough inventory on hand so that when the order is received the inventory is at the safety stock level. If there is a variance of several days, then some of the safety stock must be used.

The reorder point is determined as follows:

Reorder Point (RP) = Safety Stock + (Lead Time × Daily Use)

To illustrate the technique of determining the reorder point, let us assume that a company has an item of inventory with the following characteristics:

EOQ: 300 Units
Daily Usage: 10 Units
Lead Time: 5 Days
Safety Stock: 100 Units

The firm has previously determined its economic order quantity as 300 units. A lead time of five days means that it will use fifty units while it is waiting for an order to be received. Therefore, the order is placed when the inventory level is fifty units above the safety stock. The safety stock of 100 units allows for lead time to take longer than five days or for daily usage to go above ten units. The reorder point is calculated as follows:

RP = 100 + (5 × 10)
   = 150 Units

A reorder point of 150 units means that when the inventory level is down to 150, the firm places an order. Theoretically, it will use another fifty units before the order is received. At that time, it will have 100 units in stock—the safety stock level. If the order is not received on time, then some of the safety stock will be used. If the order is received on the day the inventory reaches the safety stock level, the inventory level will go up to 400 units upon receipt of the order. This process of ordering and usage is illustrated in Exhibit 12.9.

The initial order is for 400 units, the economic order quantity plus the 100-unit safety stock. Notice the diagonal line beginning at 400 and coming downward to the right. This line represents usage. When it reaches the 150 mark, 300 units are ordered. During the next five days, from day twenty-five to day thirty, an additional fifty units are used. This period is the lead time during which the order is being processed. Note that at the 100-unit inventory level, the inventory jumps from 100 to 400.

If everything goes as planned, it is at this 100-unit level that the order is received, five days after it has been ordered. The firm continues using ten units per day. You can see that at day fifty-five another order is placed. At day sixty, it is received and inventory again goes up to 400 units. Assuming there are no exceptions to the daily pattern of usage and lead time, the inventory cycle will continue in the manner shown in Exhibit 12.9. If, however, after the order has been placed at the reorder point of 150, the lead time is longer than five days or the daily usage is more than ten units, the company will use some of its safety stock to satisfy demand. A continual review of safety stock usage should be made to insure that safety stock is adequate. If safety stock appears to be too high, it can be reduced to save

Exhibit 12.9 Inventory Usage

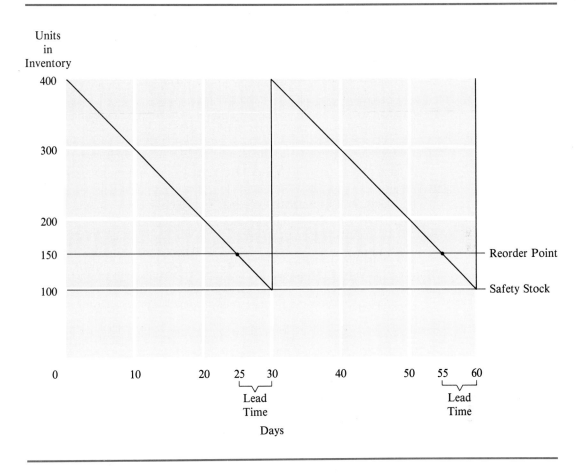

money. On the other hand, if safety stock frequently becomes low, the company should reevaluate its reorder point to determine whether lead time or daily usage exceeds the level originally planned for.

Summary

Quantitative techniques are mathematical approaches to solving certain management problems. In all cases, these techniques provide management with data on which to base a variety of internal decisions. As always, the techniques do not make decisions; management must do that.

This chapter illustrated four popular quantitative techniques. Probability theory provides management with a better insight into the likelihood that certain events will happen. With probability theory, management can determine expected outcomes of various alternatives. By comparing the expected values of these outcomes while considering the likelihood of the events' happening, the firm can decide which alternatives appear to be more profitable.

Management can also use probability theory to determine the expected outcome in the "best case" situation. In this situation, a determination of the value of perfect information can be made. This value represents an amount that management could spend in efforts to obtain better information regarding the likelihood of certain events' happening. Probability theory can be applied to capital budgeting as well. By discounting the probable cash flows, management gains a more realistic expectation of whether the firm will achieve the desired rate of return.

Linear programming is a mathematical technique used to determine maximum profitability when constraints exist. It is normally used to determine the maximum profit or the minimum cost. When the graphical technique is used, the constraints of the situation are drawn; and the more profitable combinations of inputs or outputs are determined to arrive at the optimal solution.

Inventory management is a major problem for firms that sell or manufacture. One concern is to minimize the costs of ordering and carrying inventory, while also minimizing the chance of running out. Since the ordering cost and carrying cost run in opposite directions, techniques have been developed to arrive at the order quantity that will equalize these two costs. These techniques include use of a table, use of a formula, and use of a graph.

The economic order quantity is the number of units that should be ordered each time to minimize both order cost and carrying cost. The reorder point is the inventory level at which the firm places an order. Determining this point requires knowledge of the economic order quantity, the lead time, and the desired safety stock.

Review Problem

Problem

Prakter Corporation is considering the introduction of a new product. Two products are being considered; however, because of limited funds, only one will be selected. Each requires an investment of $200,000 and has an expected life of 4 years. The firm's cost of capital is 12%. Expected annual net cash inflows after taxes, and their probabilities, are shown below for each product:

Prilltal		Brimax	
Net Cash Inflows	**Probability**	**Net Cash Inflows**	**Probability**
$ 40,000	.15	$ 30,000	.10
60,000	.25	60,000	.20
80,000	.50	90,000	.50
100,000	.10	120,000	.20

Required:
For each product, calculate the following:
a. Net present value.
b. Profitability index.

Solution
Before determining the net present value, we must determine the expected value of the net cash inflows, as shown below:

	Prilltal			Brimax	
Conditional Value	**Probability**	**Expected Value**	**Conditional Value**	**Probability**	**Expected Value**
$ 40,000	.15	$ 6,000	$ 30,000	.10	$ 3,000
60,000	.25	15,000	60,000	.20	12,000
80,000	.50	40,000	90,000	.50	45,000
100,000	.10	10,000	120,000	.20	24,000
Totals	1.00	$71,000		1.00	$84,000

a. The expected value of the cash flows is used as the amount to be multiplied by the present value factor in determining the net present value.

	Amount	PV Factor at 12%	Present Value Prilltal	Brimax
Cash Inflows:				
Prilltal	$ 71,000	3.037	$215,627	
Brimax	84,000	3.037		$255,108
Investment	(200,000)	1.000	(200,000)	(200,000)
Net Present Value			$ 15,627	$ 55,108

b. The profitability index is calculated as follows:

Prilltal: $\dfrac{\$215,627}{\$200,000} = 1.08$

Brimax: $\dfrac{\$255,108}{\$200,000} = 1.28$

Questions

12-1 How is probability theory helpful in management decision making?

12-2 Define *conditinal value* and *expected value*. Describe the difference between the two terms.

12-3 A firm has an investment opportunity with conditional values of annual profit for 3 possible events of $30,000, $50,000, and $80,000. By applying the expected probabilities to each event, it has arrived at total expected value of $65,000 if it decides on this investment. Since the actual outcome will be either $30,000, $50,000, or $80,000, of what use is the knowledge that expected value is $65,000?

12-4 What is meant by "the value of perfect information"? How is it help-ful in management decision making?

12-5 How can probability theory be applied to capital budgeting?

12-6 In what type of situations is linear programming normally used?

12-7 Since linear programming is a mathematical technique, why should an accountant be familiar with its use?

12-8 Why must the optimal solution to a linear programming problem al-ways be at a corner?

12-9 What elements must be considered in determining economic order quantity.

12-10 What are stockout costs?

12-11 The EOQ calculation includes elements that, as a practical matter, are difficult to determine with the precision implied in the calculation. Car-rying cost per unit is an example. Therefore, how is the EOQ calculation helpful to management?

12-12 What is the relationship between order costs and carrying costs—that is, how do they affect each other and how does their relationship affect eco-nomic order quantity?

12-13 What is the reorder point? How does it relate to economic order quantity?

12-14 What is meant by *safety stock*? How does it affect the economic order quantity?

Exercises

12-15 Expected Value of Project Wistful Company is considering a project that will result in possible annual net cash inflows as follows:

Net Cash Inflows	Probability
$10,000	.10
30,000	.20
50,000	.50
80,000	.20

Determine the expected value of this project.

12-16 Expected Value of New Product Benny Company anticipates intro-ducing a new product. The profit it might earn each year, along with the probabilities, are as follows:

Profit	Probability
$(20,000)	.10
10,000	.15
30,000	.25
50,000	.20
80,000	.15
90,000	.10
100,000	.05

a. Calculate the expected value of this product.

b. Assume top management is willing to introduce the product if there's a 50/50 chance it will earn at least $50,000. Will the product be introduced? Explain.

12-17 Expected Value of New Product Rogers Corporation has plans for a new product with the following possible profits and their probabilities:

Profit	Probability
$(20,000)	.15
20,000	.30
50,000	.40
80,000	.15

The reason for the possible loss is that product sales depend on the national economy, and in bad times sales will be lower.

a. Determine the expected value.

b. Determine the value of perfect information.

c. A consulting firm has offered to perform detailed research and analysis for Rogers Corporation to determine more accurately when slower economic activity might be expected. The firm would charge Rogers $5,000 for this work. Should Rogers hire the firm? Explain.

12-18 Expected Value of Machine Repair and Maintenance Costs Treadly Company has narrowed its decision in the purchase of a new machine to two choices, which are identical in terms of performance and expected costs, except for annual repair and maintenance costs. These costs, along with their probabilities, are shown below:

Repair and Maintenance Costs	Machine A	Machine B
$ 500	.10	.20
1,000	.15	.00
2,000	.40	.40
3,000	.30	.00
4,000	.05	.30
6,000	.00	.10

Management is pleased with the 20% probability that Machine B will incur only $500 of costs, but doesn't like the idea that its costs may be as high as $6,000. Determine which machine the firm should select based on expected repair and maintenance costs.

12-19 Expected Value of New TV Programs The Nationwide American Network (NAN) has its fall schedule lined up except for one half-hour slot. Two choices are being considered. The basic criterion for decision is the chance that the show will rate high. *Crazy Kids* has a better chance of being a hit but also a larger chance of being a flop. *Super Family* may not be a top-10 program, but it has a better chance of being in the next 20. The ratings affect advertising revenues. The probabilities of various ratings and associated revenues for each show are shown below:

| | | Probabilities | |
| | | Crazy Kids | Super Family |
Rating	Revenue	Crazy Kids	Super Family
1–10	$3,000,000	.30	.05
11–30	1,500,000	.20	.70
Lower Than 30	(500,000)	.50	.25

Which program should the network select? Support your answer with calculations.

12-20 Expected Value of Auto Repair Bob Tyler is having major problems with his car. He has taken it to Al's garage, where he has done business for years. He knows Al to be an honest mechanic. Al has made Bob the following offer: "I'll fix whatever's wrong with your car for $200 plus parts; or you can pay me $30 an hour for labor, plus parts. But you have to decide now." Al provides Bob with the following probabilities of time needed, based on his assessment of how the car runs and sounds:

Labor Time	Probability
4 Hours	.40
6 Hours	.20
8 Hours	.30
10 Hours	.10

a. Based on the probabilities, prepare calculations to show the least expensive alternative.

b. Why might Bob decide against the alternative you calculated in part a?

12-21 Expected Value of Parts Usage Thoran Electronics Company began producing pacemakers last year. At that time, the company forecast the need for 10,000 integrated circuits a year. During the first year, the company placed orders when the inventory dropped to 600 units so that it would have enough to produce pacemakers continuously during a 3-week lead time. Unfortunately, the company has run out of this component on several occasions, causing costly production delays. Careful study of last year's experience has resulted in the following expectations' being set for the coming year:

Weekly Usage	Related Probability of Usage	Lead Time	Related Probability of Lead Time
280 Units	.2	3 Weeks	.1
180 Units	.8	2 Weeks	.9
	1.0		1.0

a. Determine the expected average usage during a regular production week.

b. Determine the expected usage during lead time. (CMA adapted)

12-22 Linear Programming; Raw-Material Constraint A to Z Manufacturing Company manufactures 2 products—Bee and Cee. Each unit of Bee requires 2 units of raw material Jay and 4 Units of raw material Kay. Each unit of Cee requires 3 units of raw material Jay and 2 units of raw material Kay. There is a shortage of raw material, and the firm is unable to make monthly purchases exceeding 6,000 units of Jay and 8,000 units of Kay. Unit contribution margin is $3 for Bee and $5 for Cee.

   a. Assuming the firm wants to maximize contribution margin, determine the objective function.

   b. Determine the constraints.

   c. Regardless of whether it is the optimal amount, calculate the maximum amount of Bee that can be produced.

12-23 Linear Programming; Machine-Hour Constraint Combo Company produces two products—Algon and Grine—which provide contribution margins of $8 and $12 per unit, respectively. Each product goes through 2 processing departments. Each unit of Algon requires 1/2 machine hour in Department 1 and 2 machine hours in Department 2. Grine requires 1 hour in Department 1 and 3 hours in Department 2. A maximum of 1,000 hours in Department 1 and 1,500 hours in Department 2 are available each month.

   a. Assuming the firm wants to maximize contribution margin, determine the objective function.

   b. Determine the constraints.

   c. Regardless of whether it is the optimal amount, calculate the maximum amount of Algon that can be produced.

12-24 Linear Programming; Minimizing Material Cost The Beauty Company produces a cosmetic product in 60-gallon batches. The basic ingredients used are Material X, costing $7 per gallon, and Material Y, costing $17 per gallon. No more than 18 gallons of X can be used, and at least 15 gallons of Y must be used. How would the objective function (minimization of product cost) be expressed? (AICPA adapted)

12-25 Linear Programming; Machine-Hour Constraint Milligan Company manufactures 2 models, small and large. The models are processed as follows:

	Machining Department	Polishing Department
Small (X)	2 Hours	1 Hour
Large (Y)	4 Hours	3 Hours

The time available for processing the 2 models is 100 hours a week in the Machining Department and 90 hours a week in the Polishing Department. The contribution margin expected is $5 for the small model and $7 for the large model.

   a. How would the objective function (maximization of total contribution margin) be expressed?

   b. How would the restriction (constraint) for the Machining Department and for the Polishing Department be expressed? (AICPA adapted)

12-26 EOQ; Formula Rainey Company uses 10,000 units of X-lon a year at a purchase price of $30 each. The order cost is $15 per order, and inventory carrying cost is $3 per unit.

   a. Calculate the economic order quantity using the formula.

   b. How many times a year must an order be placed?

12-27 EOQ; Formula; Safety Stock; Reorder Point Brandon Company uses 24,000 units of Part 67K annually. In the past, it has ordered 2,000 units a month. Now, however, the inventory manager wonders whether this is the most economical thing to do. Order costs are $60 per order, and carrying costs are $8 per unit. It normally takes 3 days for an order to be received. Sometimes it takes longer; but it has never taken longer than 10 days.

   a. Use the formula to calculate the economic order quantity.

   b. Assuming the firm uses Part 67K on the basis of a 300-day year, determine the necessary safety stock.

   c. Calculate the reorder point.

12-28 Safety Stock; Reorder Point The following information relates to Eagle Company's Material A:

Annual Usage (in Units):	7,200
Working Days (per Year):	240
Normal Lead Time (in Working Days):	20
Maximum Lead Time (in Working Days):	45

Assuming that the units of Material A will be required evenly throughout the year, determine the safety stock and reorder point. (AICPA adapted)

12-29 Estimating Annual Usage Garmar, Inc., has determined the following data for a given year:

Economic Order Quantity (Standard Order Size):	5,000 Units
Total Cost to Place Purchase Orders for the Year:	$10,000
Cost to Place 1 Purchase Order:	$50
Cost to Carry 1 Unit for 1 Year:	$4

What is Garmar's estimated annual usage in units? (AICPA adapted)

Problems

12-30 Expected Value; Maintenance Contract Sure-All Insurance Company is negotiating a service contract for the repair and maintenance of all its office equipment. Three plans are being considered.

Plan A: A fixed rate of $1,000 a month.
Plan B: A fixed rate of $300 a month plus an additional $25 per hour.
Plan C: A rate of $40 per hour.

Under all plans, Sure-All would pay for parts. Based on past experience, the firm has developed the following probabilities of repair hours required per month:

Number of Hours	Probability
10	.20
20	.40
30	.30
40	.10

Required:
  a. Based on probabilities, which plan is the most favorable?
  b. What considerations might influence management to accept a plan other than the one you indicated in part a as the most favorable?

12-31 Expected Value; Alternative Machines Browbent Manufacturing Company is deciding which of 2 machines to buy for use in its plant. It is anticipated that the machine selected will increase efficiency and profitability by reducing costs and increasing the number of units produced. The probabilities for expected increases in profits from the Allego model are as follows:

Increase in Profits	Probability
$10,000	.20
30,000	.30
50,000	.40
80,000	.10

The Clexco model is subject to more uncertainty than the Allego model. In some instances, machine malfunctions have resulted in decreased profits. However, if it operates perfectly, profits might increase by as much as $100,000 a year. Probabilities for increased profits are as follows:

Increase in Profits	Probability
$(10,000)	.05
20,000	.25
50,000	.40
80,000	.20
100,000	.10

Required:
  a. Based on probabilities, which model should the company select?
  b. What other considerations might influence management's decision?
  c. Suppose that for $1,000, the firm could have the Clexco model modified to change the 5% probability of decreased profits to a 5% probability of no increase in profits. Should the $1,000 be spent for this purpose? Explain.

12-32 Expected Value; Value of Perfect Information Harry Clark operates a roadside fruit stand specializing in peaches. Harry pays $5 a bushel and sells for $8 a bushel. Because he has established a reputation for selling the "freshest peaches in the county," he gives any peaches unsold at the end of the day to nursing homes in the area.

Demand for the peaches has never been less than 20 bushels a day and has never exceeded 50 bushels a day. Harry has estimated demand probabilities as follows:

Demand	Probability
20	.20
30	.40
40	.30
50	.10

Required:

a. Construct a payoff table to determine the number of bushels of peaches Harry should stock.

b. How much could Harry pay to obtain better information regarding demand on specific days?

12-33 Expected Value; Value of Perfect Information Vendo, Inc., has been operating the concession stands at a university football stadium. The university has had successful football teams for many years; as a result, the stadium is always full. This university is located in an area that suffers no rain during the football season. From time to time, Vendo has found itself very short of hot dogs; and at other times, it has had many left. A review of the records of sales of the past 5 seasons revealed the following frequency of hot dogs sold:

Number of Hot Dogs Sold	Number of Games
10,000	5
20,000	10
30,000	20
40,000	15
	50

Hot dogs sell for $.50 each and cost Vendo $.30 each. Unsold hot dogs are given to a local orphanage without charge.

Required:

a. Assuming that only the 4 quantities listed were sold, prepare a payoff table to represent the 4 possible alternatives of ordering 10,000, 20,000, 30,000, or 40,000 hot dogs.

b. Use the expected value decision rule to determine the best alternative.

c. What is the dollar value of perfect information in this problem? (CMA adapted)

12-34 Expected Value; Alternative Machines; Net Present Value; Profitability Index Topman Corporation is considering the purchase of a new machine to help increase efficiency and cut costs. Two models are under consideration. Because these models have just recently been introduced on the market, actual operating experience is somewhat limited. However, the manufacturer has test data that provide probabilities as to potential annual cost savings of these machines. These data are shown below.

Z-100		Z-142	
Annual Cost Savings	Probability	Annual Cost Savings	Probability
$ 5,000	.20	$ 2,000	.30
8,000	.30	5,000	.25
10,000	.40	10,000	.15
15,000	.10	20,000	.30

The Z-100 costs $20,000, and the Z-142 costs $25,000. Neither machine is expected to have a salvage value at the end of its estimated useful life, which is 5 years. The company uses the straight-line method of depreciation, and the tax rate is 40%. The firm's cost of capital is 12%.

Required:

For each model, determine the following:

a. Net present value.

b. Profitability index.

(*Note:* Use the present value tables in the appendix of the preceding chapter in solving this problem.)

12-35 Expected Value; Net Present Value Mother Bates' Home-Made Pies have become quite popular in the local community. Last year, Mother Bates had difficulty in keeping up with the demand for pecan pies, a customer favorite. Therefore, she bought a pecan-shelling machine for $10,000. At the time of purchase, the machine had a 4-year life and no salvage value, and she has depreciated it for a year.

Although the pecan-shelling machine enabled her to double the sales of pecan pies from 1,000 to 2,000 a year, she still is unable to keep up with demand. A new machine has just come out that will put the pecans in the pies after it shells them. It is expected that this new machine will have the following probabilities of increasing the number of pecan pies sold each year:

Increase in Pies Sold	Probability
1,000	.30
2,000	.40
3,000	.20
4,000	.10

There will be no effect on the sales of other pies if the number of pecan pies sold increases. The pies sell for $5 each and have a variable cost of $2 each.

The new machine costs $15,000 and has an estimated life of 3 years with no salvage value. Repair and maintenance costs are $2,000 a year—$500 a year higher than for the old machine. There is an 80% probability that the old machine could be sold now for $2,500 and a 20% probability that it could be sold now for $3,500.

Mother Bates uses the straight-line method of depreciation. The tax rate is 40%, and she requires a 14% rate of return on all investments.

Required:

Use the net present value method to determine whether Mother Bates should buy the new machine. (*Note:* Use the present value tables in the appendix of the preceding chapter in solving this problem.)

12-36 Linear Programming Graph; Raw-Material Constraint Lakeville Corporation produces 2 products—Belnum and Ladnum. Data relative to each product are as follows:

	Belnum	Ladnum
Unit Contribution Margin:	$8	$12
Raw Material Units per Finished Unit:	3	5
Machine Hours per Finished Unit:	1 1/2	1 1/4

The company is limited to 2,400 units of raw material per month. Machine hours are limited to a total of 750 per month.

Required:

Construct a linear programming graph to determine how many units of each product should be produced to maximize total contribution margin.

12-37 Linear Programming Graph; Raw-Material Constraint Refer to Exercise 12–22.

Required:

Based on the data given in Exercise 12–22, construct a linear programming graph to determine how many units of each product should be produced to maximize total contribution margin.

12-38 Linear Programming Graph; Three Constraints The Frey Company manufactures and sells 2 products—a toddler bike and a toy high chair. Linear programming is employed to determine the best production and sales mix of bikes and chairs. This approach also allows Frey to speculate on economic changes. For example, management is often interested in knowing how variations in selling prices, resource costs, resource availabilities, and marketing strategies would affect the company's performance.

The demand for bikes and chairs is relatively constant throughout the year. The following economic data pertain to the products:

	Bike (B)	Chair (C)
Selling Price per Unit	$12	$10
Variable Cost per Unit	8	7
Contribution Margin per Unit	$ 4	$ 3
Raw Materials Required:		
Wood (in Board Feet)	1	2
Plastic (in Pounds)	2	1
Direct Labor Required (in Hours)	2	2

Estimates of the resource quantities available per month are:

Wood (in Board Feet)	10,000
Plastic (in Pounds)	10,000
Direct Labor (in Hours)	12,000

Required:
   a. Determine the objective function to maximize total contribution margin.
   b. Determine the constraints.
   c. Construct a graph with the constraints you developed in part b.
   d. Determine how many bikes and toy high chairs should be produced to maximize contribution margin. (CMA adapted)

12-39 EOQ; Table and Formula Mattson Company has been having problems lately with the management of its inventory. It has tried to order the right amount but always seems either to have too much or to have a stockout. You have been asked to assist them.
   Annual usage is 2,000 units. Order cost is $20 per order, and carrying cost is $.50 per unit.
Required:
   a. Construct a table to determine the number of units the firm should order.
   b. Use the formula to verify your results in part a.

12-40 EOQ; Graph Refer to Problem 12–39.
Required: Use a graph to determine the economic order quantity.

12-41 EOQ; Table and Formula Welton Company has been ordering inventory once a month in an effort to reduce carrying costs. Now, however, its order costs appear to be excessive. You have been asked to assist the firm in determining the economic order quantity. The following data are provided:

Annual Usage (in Units):	10,000
Cost per Order:	$100
Annual Carrying Cost per Unit:	$.10

Required:
   a. Construct a table to determine the number of units the firm should order.
   b. Use the formula to verify your results in part a.
   c. Based on your results in part a, how much will the firm save annually if it follows your recommendation?

12-42 EOQ; Formula; Reorder Point The Robney Company is a restaurant supplier that sells a number of products to various restaurants in the area. One of the products is a special meat cutter with a disposable blade.
   The blades are sold in packages of 12 blades for $20 per package. Over a number of years, it has been determined that the demand for the replacement blades is at a constant rate of 2,000 packages per month. The packages cost the Robney Company $10 each from the manufacturer and require a 3-day lead time from the date of order to date of delivery. The ordering cost is $1.20 per order, and the carrying cost is 10% per annum.
   Robney is going to use the economic order quantity formula.
Required:
   a. Calculate:
      1. The economic order quantity.
      2. The number of orders needed per year.
      3. The total cost of ordering and carrying the blades for the year.

b. Assuming there is no reserve (that is, no safety stock) and that the present inventory level is 200 packages, when should the next order be placed? (Use 360 days to equal a year.)

c. Discuss the problems most firms would have in attempting to apply this formula to their inventory problems. (CMA adapted)

Part Four

Cost Accounting Concepts

Chapter 13   Cost Accounting Systems

Learning Objectives

The purpose of this chapter is to provide you with an understanding of how manufacturing costs are accounted for by use of a job order cost system and a process cost system. The chapter also describes and illustrates the documentation used in cost accounting systems. Studying this chapter will enable you to:

1. Describe the documentation needed for a cost accounting system.
2. Describe a job order cost system and a process cost system.
3. Journalize and post transactions for a job order cost system.
4. Prepare a job cost sheet for a job order cost system.
5. Describe and calculate equivalent units of production and the equivalent cost per unit.
6. Journalize and post transactions for a process cost system.
7. Prepare a cost summary for a process cost system using FIFO. (Appendix)

Chapter Topics

The major topics included in this chapter are:

Documentation for a Cost Accounting System
Description of Job Order Costing
Illustration of Job Order Costing
Description of Process Costing
Illustration of Process Costing
Appendix: Process Costing Using FIFO

An introduction to accounting for manufacturing costs was presented in Chapter 3. This chapter expands the concepts presented there. The objective of a cost accounting system is to accumulate data for inventory valuation and product costing purposes, as well as to provide for proper control of manufacturing costs. Thus, transactions must be supported by appropriate documentation. The documentation needed in a cost accounting system is also described in this chapter.

Depending on the type of product manufactured, a firm normally uses one of two types of cost accounting systems: a job order cost system or a process cost system. This chapter describes and illustrates both.

Documentation for a Cost Accounting System

Any accounting system must have proper documentation in order for a firm to control its purchases and its assets. The concepts involved in documentation for a cost accounting system are no different from those for any other part of the accounting system. But because there are more complexities in cost accounting, there will be more documents.

A description of some of the types of documents used in cost accounting is provided in this section. The illustrations are merely examples; the exact format depends on the needs of the individual firm.

Raw Materials Inventory

The purchase of raw materials creates the need to account for purchases and inventory. Three basic documents used in this process are: the receiving report, the material requisition, and the material stores card. In addition, the purchase of raw materials must be controlled through a purchasing system that includes purchase orders. The requirement to control purchases does not differ from that for nonmanufacturing firms.

Receiving Report A **receiving report** is a document on which the firm records items and quantities of materials as they are received. The format does not differ from that which you may have studied in financial accounting for a merchandising firm. The material itself is placed in a raw materials warehouse, often referred to as the **stores warehouse** or **material stores.** The individual responsible for maintaining the stores warehouse, called the **stores supervisor** or the **storekeeper,** uses the receiving report as the basis for recording increases to the individual raw materials records, called **material stores cards** (described below). The accounting department receives a copy of the receiving report, which serves as one basis of support for making payment. The purchasing department also receives a copy, which is compared with the purchase order to insure that nothing has been received that was not ordered.

Material Requisition The **material requisition** is used by a manufacturing department to request raw material from the stores warehouse. An example is shown as Exhibit 13.1.

Requisitions should be prenumbered in order to increase control. A requisition must be signed by someone with authority to requisition material, usually a department supervisor or foreman. It will be in at least two copies. One copy is used by the stores supervisor as the basis for reducing the amount on hand in the records. It provides evidence of what happened to the material. The department issuing the requisition should maintain a

Exhibit 13.1 Material Requisition

	MATERIAL REQUISITION	NO. 36544

Date: 8/15/X2

Dept. Painting

Job. No. 5416

Description		Quantity	Unit Cost	Total Cost
Stock No.	Item			
25764	White paint	100 gal.	5.00	500.00

Requested by: *Jim Dealy*

Received by: *J. Evans*   Date: 8/16/x2

---

copy as a record of what material it has requested and received. A third copy may go to the accounting department.

Material Stores Card   The **materials stores card** is the subsidiary account for each item of raw material. It is a record on which receipts and issuances of raw material are recorded. An example is shown as Exhibit 13.2.

Note that it refers to the receiving reports and to the requisitions. The system is tied together through the material stores card. The monetary balance of all cards added together is the total of raw materials inventory that is shown in the general ledger control account.

The card also provides information that helps the stores supervisor to control inventory. The card shows the **reorder point.** When the amount on hand reaches this balance, additional items should be ordered. It also shows the amount that should be ordered. In this case, when the balance is down to 200 gallons, the company should order 500 gallons.

The illustrations shown here assume a manual accounting system. As a practical matter, such records are computerized in most firms. But this does not change the concepts. The same type of information is maintained by the computer, which allows more rapid and more accurate processing of the information.

Exhibit 13.2 Material Stores Card

MATERIAL STORES CARD

Description: Paint, white
Stock No.: 25764
Reorder Point: 200 gal.
Amount to Reorder: 500 gal.

Date	Received				Issued				Balance	
	Receiving Report No.	Quantity	Unit Cost	Total Cost	Req. No.	Quantity	Unit Cost	Total Cost	Quantity	Total Cost
8/1	Bal. fwd.								150	750.00
8/4	2564	500	5.00	2,500.00					650	3,250.00
8/11					36486	200	5.00	1000.00	450	2,250.00
8/15					36544	100	5.00	500.00	350	1,750.00

Direct Labor

Direct labor is accounted for through the use of a **time ticket.** An example is shown as Exhibit 13.3. The ticket is preprinted, and the appropriate information is written in for each situation. This example indicates that $20 is being charged to Job No. 5416 as direct labor for painting. The time ticket is approved by the department foreman, who is responsible for any costs incurred by the department. Possibly, the time ticket will be a computer-punched card with the appropriate information already prepunched. The foreman will write in the additional information, which will then be either punched or scanned and processed by the computer.

Time tickets are used for charging work-in-process inventory for direct labor costs. They are not the basis on which employees are paid. Employee hours worked will be recorded on typical time cards, which are found in nonmanufacturing firms as well. However, with the computer, another control feature is available. If an employee is paid for forty hours' work, it is

Exhibit 13.3 Time Ticket

Name Oscar A. Brown			Ticket No. 57432	
Employee No. 987-66-6255			Date 8/15/x2	
Department Painting				
Job. No. 5416				

Start Time	Stop Time	Total Time	Rate	Total Charge
8:00	10:30	2.5	8.00	20.00

Approved J. S. Kelly

possible to determine precisely where those forty hours were spent. Every hour paid can be accounted for.

The time ticket in this example shows that Mr. Brown spent two and one-half hours on Job No. 5416. Time tickets would also be completed for time spent by Mr. Brown on other jobs on this day. If Mr. Brown were to spend the entire week on the same job, then forty hours would be recorded on one time ticket.

Factory Overhead

The documentation to support the items included as factory overhead is no different from the documentation of similar types of items in a nonmanufacturing firm. It is important for the accounting department to be able to distinguish between manufacturing costs and selling and administrative expenses. The firm must also have a logical system for applying factory overhead to work-in-process inventory. The job order costing and process costing examples that follow illustrate how this is done.

Work-in-Process Inventory

As direct material, direct labor, and factory overhead are charged to work-in-process inventory, the cost accounting system requires documentation that accounts for these charges as a part of work-in-process inventory. This documentation is achieved with a *job cost sheet* for a job order cost system and a *cost summary* for a process cost system. Illustrations are provided in the examples of these two types of cost systems.

Finished Goods Inventory

Since finished goods inventory is similar to merchandise inventory for a merchandising firm, accounting for it poses no particular problems. As finished goods are completed, they are physically transferred to the finished goods warehouse. A document showing the quantity of finished goods and their cost is prepared and used as the basis for recording the entry to debit finished goods inventory and credit work-in-process inventory. The finished goods warehouse manager uses this document as the basis for adding to the subsidiary records maintained for each item of finished goods.

When finished goods are sold, the sales document serves as the authority to reduce finished goods in both the control and the subsidiary accounts.

Description of Job Order Costing

As mentioned previously, the two major types of costing systems are job order and process. A **job order cost system** accumulates costs for separate, identifiable jobs or batches. Costs are summarized at the completion of a job or batch. Printing, construction, and furniture manufacturing are examples of industries that normally use a job order cost system. A **process cost system,** on the other hand, accumulates costs for each production process over a period of time. In process costing, the completion of a time period, rather than the completion of production, usually determines when costs will be summarized. Companies that use a process cost system usually produce products that are homogeneous and indistinguishable from one another. Petroleum, chemicals, and paint are examples of industries that use process cost systems. This section discusses and illustrates the job order cost system. The following section covers the process cost system.

The primary accounting record used in a job order cost system to accumulate production costs for each job is a **job cost sheet.** As direct material and direct labor costs are incurred, they are recorded on the job cost sheet.[1] The application of factory overhead is also recorded there. The job cost sheet serves as the subsidiary account for work-in-process inventory. When the total costs for all job cost sheets are added together, the resulting total is the balance in the work-in-process inventory ledger account. An example of a job cost sheet for the Crystal China Company is shown as Exhibit 13.4.

When work-in-process inventory is debited for direct material used and direct labor cost incurred, the appropriate amounts are entered on the job cost sheet. Factory overhead is applied either on a period-of-time basis, such as weekly or monthly, or at the completion of the job. Factory overhead shown on Exhibit 13.4 was applied at the end of the job, because the job was completed before the end of the month.

The summary at the bottom of the cost sheet provides management with

---

[1]Under standard costing, as described in Chapters 6 and 7, the standard costs of direct material and direct labor are entered on the job cost sheet.

Exhibit 13.4 Job Cost Sheet

CRYSTAL CHINA COMPANY
Job Cost Sheet

NO. 27666

Job No.: 399
Product: Plates
Quantity: 1,000

Date Started: 2/2/X2
Date Completed: 2/13/X2

Direct Material

Date	Req. No.	Amount
2/1	2505	200.00
2/5	2540	300.00
2/10	2601	50.00
		550.00

Direct Labor

Date	Ticket No.	Hours	Amount
2/2–2/5	4560	20	140.00
2/2–2/6	4571	10	80.00
2/9–2/13	4577	40	300.00
			520.00

Factory Overhead

	Variable			Fixed	
Date	Application	Amount	Date	Application	Amount
2/13	50% x 520.00	260.00	2/13	25% x 520.00	130.00
		260.00			130.00

SUMMARY

Total Cost

Variable:
Direct Material	$ 550.00
Direct Labor	520.00
Factory Overhead	260.00
	$1,330.00

Fixed:
Factory Overhead	130.00
Total	$1,460.00

Unit Cost

Variable:
$ .55 ($550 ÷ 1,000)
.52 ($520 ÷ 1,000)
.26 ($260 ÷ 1,000)
$1.33

Fixed:
.13 ($130 ÷ 1,000)
Total $1.46

information on both a total basis and a unit basis. This information is important to management for making production and pricing decisions.

When a job is completed, the job cost sheet serves as the basis for the entry to transfer costs from work-in-process inventory to finished goods inventory. Based on Exhibit 13.4, the entry is:

Finished Goods Inventory	1,460	
Work-in-Process Inventory		1,460

Illustration of Job Order Costing

In order to help you understand a job order cost system, this section provides an illustration of journal entries and postings for a two-week period at the Crystal China Company. The subsidiary records—material stores cards and job cost sheets—are also shown. They are not as detailed as those illustrated previously; but they allow you to see how the system works. To simplify the example, we assume the company uses only two types of direct material and one type of indirect material.

On March 1, 19X2, the inventory balances are as follows:

Raw Materials Inventory:	
Clay	$1,500
Crystal	2,000
Indirect Material	500
Total	$4,000
Work-in-Process Inventory:	
Job No. 421	$1,000
Finished Goods Inventory:	
Completed Jobs:	
No. 419	$3,000
No. 420	4,000
	$7,000

Transactions and Entries

Transactions and journal entries for this illustration are provided in this section. Only transactions and ledger accounts relevant to the cost accounting process are shown.

March 2 Purchased raw material on account as follows:

Clay	$2,500
Crystal	3,000
Indirect Material	1,200
Total	$6,700

Raw Materials Inventory	6,700	
Accounts Payable		6,700

March 2 Began Job No. 422 with clay costing $1,200 and Job. No. 423
with crystal costing $1,800.

Work-in-Process Inventory	3,000	
Raw Materials Inventory		3,000

6 Direct labor for the week of March 2–6 was charged as follows:

Job No. 421	$ 500
Job No. 422	800
Job No. 423	1,000
	$2,300

Work-in-Process Inventory	2,300	
Accrued Payroll		2,300

6 Factory overhead was applied to jobs on the basis of direct labor
cost for the week:

Variable: 50 percent of direct labor cost.
Fixed: 25 percent of direct labor cost.

	Variable	**Fixed**
Job No. 421	$ 250	$125
Job No. 422	400	200
Job No. 423	500	250
	$1,150	$575

Work-in-Process Inventory	1,725	
Variable Factory Overhead		1,150
Fixed Factory Overhead		575

6 Job No. 421 was completed and transferred to finished goods inventory.

Finished Goods Inventory	1,875	
Work-in-Process Inventory		1,875

9 Finished goods from Job No. 419 were sold on account for $4,000.

Cost of Goods Sold	3,000	
Finished Goods Inventory		3,000
Accounts Receivable	4,000	
Sales		4,000

13 Direct labor for the week of March 9–13 was charged as follows:

Job No. 422	$1,100
Job No. 423	600
	$1,700

Work-in-Process Inventory	1,700	
Accrued Payroll		1,700

March 13 Factory overhead was applied as follows:

	Variable	Fixed
Job No. 422	$550	$275
Job No. 423	300	150
	$850	$425

Work-in-Process Inventory	1,275	
Variable Factory Overhead		850
Fixed Factory Overhead		425

13 Actual factory overhead costs for the period March 1–13 were as follows:

Variable: $2,100 ($400 indirect material; $1,500 indirect labor; $200 utilities).
Fixed: $1,150 ($500 rent; $650 managers' salaries).

Variable Factory Overhead	2,100	
Fixed Factory Overhead	1,150	
Raw Materials Inventory		400
Utilities Payable		200
Rent Payable		500
Accrued Payroll		2,150

13 Finished goods from Job No. 420 were sold for $5,300; finished goods from Job No. 421 were sold for $2,500.

Cost of Goods Sold	5,875	
Finished Goods Inventory		5,875
Accounts Receivable	7,800	
Sales		7,800

13 Job No. 422 was completed and transferred to finished goods inventory.

Finished Goods Inventory	4,525	
Work-in-Process Inventory		4,525

Ledger Accounts and Subsidiary Accounts

Raw Materials Inventory Note that the balance in the ledger account, $7,300, equals the sum of the balances of the material stores cards ($2,800 + $3,200 + $1,300).

Raw Materials Inventory

3/1 Balance	4,000	3/2	3,000
3/2	6,700	3/13	400
	10,700		3,400
Balance	7,300		

Material Stores Card			
Description: Clay			
Date	Received	Issued	Balance
3/1			1,500
3/2	2,500		4,000
3/2		1,200	2,800

Material Stores Card			
Description: Crystal			
Date	Received	Issued	Balance
3/1			2,000
3/2	3,000		5,000
3/2		1,800	3,200

Material Stores Card			
Description: Indirect Material			
Date	Received	Issued	Balance
3/1			500
3/2	1,200		1,700
3/13		400	1,300

Work-in-Process Inventory The job cost sheets serve as the subsidiary accounts for work-in-process inventory. Only the job cost sheet for the uncompleted job, Job No. 423, is shown here. Note that the balance in the ledger account, $4,600, equals the total of all costs on the job cost sheet ($1,800 + $1,600 + $800 + $400).

Work-in-Process Inventory

3/1	Balance	1,000	3/6	1,875
3/2		3,000	3/13	4,525
3/6		2,300		6,400
3/6		1,725		
3/13		1,700		
3/13		1,275		
		11,000		
	Balance	4,600		

Job Cost Sheet Job No. 423				
			Factory Overhead	
Date	**Direct Material**	**Direct Labor**	**Variable**	**Fixed**
3/2	1,800			
3/6		1,000	500	250
3/13		600	300	150
Totals	1,800	1,600	800	400

Finished Goods Inventory The amount in finished goods inventory, $4,525, is from Job No. 422 ($1,200 + $1,900 + $950 + $475). The job cost sheet on completed jobs is retained by the factory rather than by the finished goods warehouse. It is shown here, however, to show you how the total costs accumulated on the job equal the finished goods inventory balance as of March 13. The job cost sheets for finished goods that have been sold are not shown.

Finished Goods Inventory			
3/1 Balance	7,000	3/9	3,000
3/6	1,875	3/13	5,875
3/13	4,525		8,875
	13,400		
Balance	4,525		

Job Cost Sheet Job No. 422				
			Factory Overhead	
Date	**Direct Material**	**Direct Labor**	**Variable**	**Fixed**
3/2	1,200			
3/6		800	400	200
3/13		1,100	550	275
Totals	1,200	1,900	950	475

Factory Overhead

The factory overhead accounts are shown below. Any difference between overhead applied and overhead incurred is adjusted at the end of the year by use of the procedures shown in Chapter 3.

Variable Factory Overhead				Fixed Factory Overhead		
3/1	Balance	200	3/6 1,150	3/1 Balance 200	3/6	575
3/13		2,100	3/13 850	3/13 1,150	3/13	425

Description of Process Costing

A **process cost system** focuses on production departments for cost accumulation, rather than on specific jobs. As mentioned earlier, a typical feature of firms using process cost systems is that products flowing through a given production department during a given period of time are homogenous and indistinguishable from one another. Since all products are identical, there is no need to trace the cost for the production of each separate job, as is done with job order costing. Some examples of industries typically using process costing are the petroleum, chemical, paint, and cement industries.

In a process cost system, manufacturing costs are assigned to production centers (departments). At the end of a period, the total cost accumulated in a production center is assigned to all the units processed in that center during that period. Usually, not all units that were started during the period are completed at the end of the period; and not all units completed during the period were started in that period. One of the accounting problems connected with process costing is that at the end of the accounting period, the firm must determine both the cost of production that has been completed and transferred out of the production center and the cost of partially completed production that remains. This determination is made by use of equivalent units of production for the period.

Equivalent units of production, or **equivalent units,** represent a means of expressing partially completed units in terms of completed units. The concept of equivalent units can be illustrated with a simple example. Assume that a production department with no beginning inventory starts 1,000 units of product into production on May 1. At May 31, it has completed and transferred out 700 units. It has 300 units remaining in work in process that are only 60-percent complete. Manufacturing costs incurred during May totaled $2,640.

The 300 partially completed units in ending inventory represent 180 equivalent units (300 × 60%). Theoretically, it costs the same amount to produce 300 units to 60-percent completion as it does to produce 180 units to 100-percent completion. Therefore, total equivalent production for the period is calculated as follows:

Transferred Out (100% Complete)	700
Work-in-Process Inventory (300 × 60%)	180
Total Equivalent Units (e.u.)	880

The cost per equivalent unit is the total production cost for the period divided by the total equivalent units. In this case, cost per equivalent unit is $3 ($2,640 ÷ $880 e.u.). The cost of units transferred out and the cost of ending work-in-process inventory can now be calculated as follows:

Transferred Out:	700 e.u. × $3 =	$2,100
Work-in-Process Inventory:	180 e.u. × $3 =	540
Total Costs:		$2,640

The illustration above did not compute equivalent units separately for each cost element. Percentage of completion may differ for different cost elements. For example, all the required direct material for the product may be added at the beginning of the production process. In this case, equivalent units for direct material in work-in-process inventory will be the same as for completed units (100%). When the cost flows for various cost elements differ, equivalent units must be computed separately for each element. Thus, it may be necessary to compute equivalent units for direct material, direct labor, and factory overhead. In many cases, the cost flows for direct labor and factory overhead are the same, because factory overhead is applied on the basis of direct labor hours. In these cases, the two can be combined as conversion costs; equivalent units are then computed for direct material and for conversion costs.

The previous example did not include beginning work-in-process inventory. The procedure used for calculating equivalent units when there is beginning inventory (as there normally will be) depends on whether the firm uses the weighted-average or the first-in, first-out (FIFO) costing method. The weighted-average method is easier to apply and is used in the illustration below. The FIFO method is illustrated in the appendix to this chapter.

As in job order costing, the purpose of process costing is to match costs incurred with units produced. Two major steps are involved:
1. Determination of equivalent units of production.
2. Determination of unit cost and assignment of cost to all units.
The concepts of process costing and the application of the two steps above are best learned through the illustration presented in the next section.

Illustration of Process Costing

Palmer Paint Company puts direct material into production in the mixing department. After the mixing department has finished with it, the product is transferred to the finishing department. Here, additional material is added and the production is completed. It is assumed that the direct material added in the finishing department does not increase the total number of units produced.

Equivalent Units of Production

This example uses Palmer's production for April 19X1 to show the application of process costing. The production status for April for each department is described below.

Mixing Department On April 1, the mixing department had 1,000 gallons of product in beginning inventory. This inventory required no additional direct material; thus, it was 100-percent complete as to direct material. However, it was only 20-percent complete as to direct labor and factory overhead (conversion costs). During April, 5,000 additional gallons were started in production; and 3,000 gallons were completed and transferred to the finishing department. The ending inventory of 3,000 gallons on April 30 was 100-percent complete as to direct material and 80-percent complete as to conversion costs.

Finishing Department On April 1, the finishing department had 2,000 gallons in beginning inventory that were 100-percent complete as to direct material and 40-percent complete as to conversion costs. During the month, 3,000 gallons were transferred in from the mixing department; and 4,000 gallons were completed and transferred to finished goods inventory. Ending inventory on April 30 consisted of 1,000 gallons, which were 100-percent complete as to direct material and 30-percent complete as to conversion costs.

Since the beginning and ending inventories of each department are only partially complete, we must determine the number of equivalent units of production, as shown in Exhibit 13.5, before we can assign costs to production. Note that when the weighted-average method is used, beginning inventory is ignored when total equivalent units are computed. A different procedure is followed when the FIFO method is used (as described in the appendix).

Note also the transferred-in column for the finishing department. This information is shown because, in addition to the direct material and conversion costs the finishing department incurs in April, it also has transferred-in costs from the mixing department. The 5,000 equivalent units represent the number of transferred-in units that were in the department during April. The transferred-in costs will be assigned to these units.

Exhibit 13.5 Equivalent Units of Production–Weighted-Average Method

	Mixing		Finishing		
Palmer Paint Company **Equivalent Units of Production** **for the Month Ended April 30, 19X1**	**Direct Material**	**Conversion Costs**	**Transferred In**	**Direct Material**	**Conversion Costs**
Units Transferred Out (100% complete).	3,000	3,000	4,000	4,000	4,000
Add: Units in Ending Inventory:					
3,000 × 100%.	3,000				
3,000 × 80%.		2,400			
1,000 × 100%.			1,000	1,000	
1,000 × 30%.					300
Total Equivalent Units . .	6,000	5,400	5,000	5,000	4,300

Accounting for Costs   As previously mentioned, costs can be accounted for by use of either the weighted-average method or the FIFO method. When the weighted-average method is used, the total costs in the department for the period, including beginning inventory, are divided by the total equivalent units for the period to arrive at the cost per equivalent unit. This procedure is shown below for each department.

Mixing Department During April, costs for the mixing department were as follows:

	Total	Direct Material	Conversion Costs
Beginning Inventory	$ 2,600	$ 2,000	$ 600
Charged This Period	29,650	10,000	19,650
Totals	$32,250	$12,000	$20,250

The cost per equivalent unit is calculated as follows:

Direct Material: $12,000 ÷ 6,000 e.u. = $2.00 per e.u.
Conversion Costs: $20,250 ÷ 5,400 e.u. = 3.75 per e.u.
Total: $5.75 per e.u.

The number of equivalent units used above was determined in Exhibit 13.5. Cost per equivalent unit is $5.75; that is, completed production costs $5.75 per gallon. Thus, the cost of the 3,000 gallons transferred to the finishing department is $17,250 (3,000 × $5.75).

The journal entries to charge work-in-process inventory for direct material and conversion costs are similar to those used in job order costing. The entry to transfer the cost of units completed in the mixing department to the finishing department is as follows:

Work-in-Process Inventory—Finishing Department   17,250
    Work-in-Process Inventory—Mixing Department   17,250

Notice that the mixing department had total costs of $32,250 in April. They are accounted for as follows:

Transferred Out:	3,000 e.u. × $5.75	=		$17,250
Work-in-Process Inventory:				
Direct material:	3,000 e.u. × $2.00	=	$6,000	
Conversion Costs:	2,400 e.u. × $3.75	=	9,000	
Total Work-in-Process Inventory:				15,000
Total Costs				$32,250

Finishing Department The finishing department must include as part of its beginning inventory and costs for the period those costs that were transferred in from the mixing department. During April, costs for the finishing department were as follows:

	Total	Transferred In	Direct Material	Conversion Costs
Beginning Inventory	$14,075	$11,200	$2,050	$ 825
Charged This Period	29,550	17,250	3,450	8,850
Totals	$43,625	$28,450	$5,500	$9,675

The cost per equivalent unit is calculated as follows:

Transferred In: $28,450 ÷ 5,000 e.u. = $5.69 per e.u.
Direct Material: $5,500 ÷ 5,000 e.u. =   1.10 per e.u.
Conversion Costs: $9,675 ÷ 4,300 e.u. =   2.25 per e.u.

Total $9.04 per e.u.

The total cost of the 4,000 gallons that were transferred to finished goods inventory is $36,160 (4,000 × $9.04). The entry to record the transfer of this finished product is as follows:

| Finished Goods Inventory | 36,160 | |
| Work-in-Process Inventory—Finishing Department | | 36,160 |

The finishing department had total costs of $43,625 in April. They are accounted for as follows:

Transferred Out:	4,000 e.u. × $9.04 =		$36,160
Work-in-Process Inventory:			
Transferred In:	1,000 e.u. × $5.69 =	$5,690	
Direct Material:	1,000 e.u. × $1.10 =	1,100	
Conversion Costs:	300 e.u. × $2.25 =	675	
Total Work-in-Process Inventory			7,465
Total Costs			$43,625

Cost Summary

The cost information presented in the preceding pages is usually summarized by a firm on a document known as a **cost summary.** The format for the cost summary differs among companies. Cost summaries for the two departments of Palmer Paint Company are shown as Exhibits 13.6 and 13.7. The equivalent unit data shown on these two exhibits come from Exhibit 13.5.

Summary

A cost accounting system requires documentation that includes receiving reports, material requisitions, material stores cards, and time tickets. The material stores cards serve as subsidiary records for the raw materials inventory ledger account.

 There are two types of costing systems; job order and process. A job

Exhibit 13.6 Cost Summary–Mixing Department

Palmer Paint Company
Cost Summary
Mixing Department
for the Month Ended April 30, 19X1

	Total Cost	Equivalent Units	Cost per Equivalent Unit
Costs to Be Accounted For:			
Direct Material:			
Beginning Inventory	$ 2,000		
Charged This Period	10,000		
Total	$12,000	6,000	$2.00
Conversion Costs:			
Beginning Inventory	$ 600		
Charged This Period	19,650		
Total	$20,250	5,400	3.75
Total Costs to Be Accounted For	$32,250		$5.75
Costs Accounted For as Follows:			
Transferred Out	$17,250	3,000	$5.75
Work-in-Process Inventory:			
Direct Material	$ 6,000	3,000	$2.00
Conversion Costs	9,000	2,400	$3.75
Total	$15,000		
Total Costs Accounted For	$32,250		

order cost system accumulates costs for separate, identifiable jobs or batches. The primary document for a job order system is the job cost sheet, on which costs are accumulated for a job. Job costs sheets for completed jobs serve as the subsidiary records for the work-in-process inventory account.

A process cost system focuses on production departments, rather than on specific jobs, for cost accumulation. Products are usually homogeneous, such as petroleum, or chemicals. Process costing requires the calculation of equivalent units of production, which provide a means of expressing partially completed units in terms of completed units. The firm uses the cost per equivalent unit to determine the cost of product transferred out from a production center. The cost summary is the primary document used in accounting for costs of a production center.

Exhibit 13.7 Cost Summary-Finishing Department

Palmer Paint Company
Cost Summary
Finishing Department
for the Month Ended April 30, 19X1

	Total Cost	Equivalent Units	Cost per Equivalent Unit
Costs to Be Accounted For:			
Transferred In:			
Beginning Inventory	$11,200		
This Period	17,250		
Total	$28,450	5,000	$5.69
Direct Material:			
Beginning Inventory	$ 2,050		
Charged This Period	3,450		
Total	$ 5,500	5,000	1.10
Conversion Costs:			
Beginning Inventory	$ 825		
Charged This Period	8,850		
Total	$ 9,675	4,300	2.25
Total Costs to Be Accounted For	$43,625		$9.04
Costs Accounted For as Follows:			
Transferred Out	$36,160	4,000	$9.04
Work-in-Process Inventory:			
Transferred In	$ 5,690	1,000	$5.69
Direct Material	1,100	1,000	$1.10
Conversion Costs	675	300	$2.25
Total	$ 7,465		
Total Costs Accounted For	$43,625		

The procedure used for calculating equivalent units depends on whether the firm uses the weighted-average or FIFO costing method. The weighted-average method was used in the chapter; the appendix illustrates the FIFO method.

As part of your summary, you should review the detailed illustrations of the job order cost system and the process cost system included in the chapter.

Appendix: Process Costing Using FIFO

The FIFO method requires that beginning inventory costs and equivalent units be accounted for separately from current costs and equivalent units. Consequently, the total number of equivalent units represents current production. To arrive at this number, it is necessary to subtract equivalent units in beginning inventory. For Palmer Paint Company, equivalent units for April according to the FIFO method are calculated in Exhibit 13.8. The cost summary for the mixing department according to the FIFO method is shown as Exhibit 13.9.

Under the FIFO method, the beginning inventory of $2,600 must be accounted for; therefore, it is shown in that section of the cost summary. However, it is not averaged in as it was in Exhibit 13.6, which used the weighted-average method. Costs charged in April—$10,000 for direct material and $19,650 for conversion costs—are matched with the equivalent units for April (from Exhibit 13.8) of 5,000 for direct material and 5,200 for conversion costs. Thus, the cost per equivalent unit is calculated as $2 for direct material and $3.779 for conversion costs.

Exhibit 13.8 Equivalent Units of Production–FIFO Method

	Mixing		Finishing		
	Direct Material	Conversion Costs	Transferred In	Direct Material	Conversion Costs
Units Transferred Out (100% complete).......	3,000	3,000	4,000	4,000	4,000
Add: Units in Ending Inventory:					
3,000 × 100%.....	3,000				
3,000 × 80%.....		2,400			
1,000 × 100%.....			1,000	1,000	
1,000 × 30%.....					300
	6,000	5,400	5,000	5,000	4,300
Deduct: Units in Beginning Inventory:					
1,000 × 100%...	1,000				
1,000 × 20%...		200			
2,000 × 100%...			2,000	2,000	
2,000 × 40%...					800
Total Equivalent Units	5,000	5,200	3,000	3,000	3,500

Palmer Paint Company
Equivalent Units of Production
for the Month Ended April 30, 19X1

Exhibit 13.9 Cost Summary Using FIFO Method

Palmer Paint Company
Cost Summary
Mixing Department
for the Month Ended April 30, 19X1

	Total Cost	Equivalent Units	Cost per Equivalent Unit
Costs to Be Accounted For:			
Beginning Inventory	$ 2,600		
Charged This Period:			
Direct Material	$10,000	5,000	$2.000
Conversion Costs	19,650	5,200	3.779
Total	$29,650		$5.779
Total Costs to Be Accounted For	$32,250		
Costs Accounted For as Follows:			
Transferred Out:			
Beginning Inventory	$ 2,600		
Costs to Complete:			
Conversion Costs	3,023	800	$3.779
Total	$ 5,623		
Started and Completed	11,558	2,000	$5.779
Total Transferred Out	$17,181		
Work-in-Process Inventory:			
Direct Material	$ 6,000	3,000	$2.000
Conversion Costs	9,070	2,400	3.779
Total	$15,070		
Total Costs Accounted For	$32,251[a]		

[a]The $1 difference between total costs to be accounted for and total costs accounted for is caused by rounding.

In accounting for the costs, we consider first the cost to complete the beginning inventory. The 1,000 units in beginning inventory were only 20-percent complete as to conversion costs (200 equivalent units). Therefore, 800 equivalent units were required to complete beginning inventory. The 800 equivalent units are multiplied by the conversion cost per equivalent unit of $3.779 to arrive at the cost to complete of $3,023. By adding $3,023 to the $2,600 cost of beginning inventory, we find that the 1,000 units in beginning inventory have a completed cost of $5,623. Since we are using the FIFO method, these 1,000 units are included in the 3,000 units that were completed this period and transferred to the finishing department.

We know that 3,000 units were transferred out. Since 1,000 of them were in beginning inventory, then 2,000 units were started and completed in April. When 2,000 units are multiplied by the cost per equivalent unit of $5,779, the cost of units started and completed is determined to be $11,558. The total transferred-out cost, then, is $17,181 ($5,623 + $11,558).

Finally, work-in-process inventory consists of 3,000 units that are 100-percent complete as to direct material and 80-percent complete as to conversion costs. Direct material cost in work-in-process inventory totals $6,000 (3,000 e.u. × $2). The 2,400 equivalent units of conversion costs have a cost of $9,070 (2,400 e.u. × $3.779). Adding these two cost elements, we find the cost of work-in-process inventory to be $15,070. We arrive at total costs accounted—$32,251—for by finding the sum of costs transferred out—$17,181—and work-in-process inventory—$15,070.

The cost summary under FIFO for the finishing department would be prepared in a manner similar to that used in Exhibit 13.9. Of course, transferred-in costs would have to be considered, as they were when the weighted-average method was used. The preparation of this summary is the requirement set out in Problem 13–45.

Review Problem

Problem

Bramford Corporation uses a process cost system. The following information is available regarding production in Department A in October.

	Units	Cost
Work in Process, October 1	2,000	$10,800
Transferred Out in October	15,000	
Direct Material Used in October		81,500
Conversion Costs in October		51,700
Work in Process, October 31	5,000	

Work in process is always 100% complete as to direct material. Work in process on October 1 includes $8,500 for direct material and is 40% complete as to conversion costs. Work in process on October 31 is 60% complete as to conversion costs. The firm uses the weighted-average method in its process cost system.

Required:

a. Determine the cost per equivalent unit for October.

b. Determine the cost of work-in-process inventory as of October 31.

c. Prepare the journal entry as of October 31 to transfer completed units from Department A to Department B.

d. Prepare calculations to account for total costs in Department A.

Solution

Before determining the cost per equivalent unit, it is necessary first to determine total equivalent units, as shown below. Since the weighted-average method is used, beginning work in process is ignored in calculating total equivalent units.

	Direct Material	Conversion Costs
Units Transferred Out	15,000	15,000
Add: Units in Ending Inventory:		
5,000 × 100%	5,000	
5,000 × 60%		3,000
Total Equivalent Units	20,000	18,000

a.

	Direct Material	Conversion Costs
Cost of Work-in-Process Inventory, October 1	$ 8,500	$ 2,300[a]
Costs Charged This Period	81,500	51,700
Totals	$90,000	$54,000
Cost per Equivalent Unit	$\dfrac{\$90,000}{20,000} = \$4.50$	$\dfrac{\$54,000}{18,000} = \$3.00$

Total Cost per Equivalent Unit = $4.50 + $3.00 = $7.50

[a]$10,800 − $8,500 = $2,300

b. Work-in-process inventory on October 31 consists of 5,000 units, which are 100% complete as to direct material and 60% complete as to conversion costs. The cost of work-in-process inventory as of October 31 is calculated as follows:

Direct Material: 5,000 e.u.   × $4.50 = $22,500
Conversions Costs: 3,000 e.u.[a] × $3.00 =   9,000
Work-in-Process Inventory, October 31: $31,500

[a]5,000 × 60% = 3,000 e.u.

c. We determine the cost of units transferred to Department B by multiplying the number of units transferred by the total cost per equivalent unit. In this case, the cost is $112,500 (15,000 units × $7.50). The journal entry is:

Work-in-Process Inventory—Department B	112,500	
Work-in-Process Inventory—Department A		112,500

d. Costs in Department A in October totaled $144,000 ($10,800 + $81,500 + $51,700). They are accounted for as follows:

Work-in-Process Inventory, October 31	$ 31,500
Cost of Units Transferred Out	112,500
Total Costs Accounted For	$144,000

Note that the data calculated in this problem are similar to the data found on a formal cost summary. However, no formal cost summary was required.

Questions

13-1 What document is used to record raw material as it comes into the firm?

13-2 What is the difference between a material requisition and a material stores card?

13-3 The accounting department of JAY Company received an invoice from a supplier requesting payment of $500 for raw material purchased. An accounting clerk checked the files and found that JAY Company had issued a purchase order for the raw material. Should payment be made? Explain.

13-4 An accountant for Brannon Company recently added the balances of all material stores cards and compared the total with the balance of the raw materials inventory ledger account. The sum of the material stores cards was $300 less than the balance of the raw materials inventory account. Assuming no mathematical errors, provide one explanation for the discrepancy.

13-5 Would a time ticket be used to record indirect labor costs? Explain.

13-6 What is the purpose of a job cost sheet?

13-7 Warren Company has incurred $3,500 of direct material costs and $6,000 of direct labor costs in producing 250 units on Job #785. Factory overhead is applied at 75% of direct labor cost. What is the total cost per unit?

13-8 Describe how job cost sheets serve as subsidiary accounts for work-in-process inventory.

13-9 Describe the basic difference between a job order cost system and a process cost system.

13-10 What is meant by the term *equivalent units of production*?

13-11 Department 1 of Johnson Company began June with 1,500 units that were 60% complete in beginning work-in-process inventory. During June, the department completed and transferred 5,000 units to Department 2. Ending work-in-process inventory consisted of 1,000 units that were 25% complete. The company uses the weighted-average method. What were total equivalent units for June?

13-12 (*Appendix*) Refer to Question 13–11. Assume Johnson Company uses the FIFO method. What were total equivalent units for June?

13-13 Department A of ZXY Corporation transferred 3,000 units to Department B during October. Ending work-in-process inventory included 500 units that were 100% complete as to direct material and 80% complete as to conversion costs. The cost per equivalent unit was $1.25 for direct material and $2.75 for conversion costs. What was the cost of units transferred and the cost of ending inventory?

13-14 What is the purpose of a cost summary?

13-15 (*Appendix*) Briefly describe the primary difference between using the weighted-average method in process costing and using the FIFO method.

Exercises

13-16 Journal Entries for Underapplied or Overapplied Factory Overhead
Refer to the factory overhead accounts for the Crystal China Company on page 423. Prepare journal entries as of March 13 to adjust the cost of goods sold for the amount of underapplied or overapplied factory overhead.

13-17 Job Order Journal Entries The Evermore Company started Job No. 221 on April 1. During the first week, the following costs were incurred:

Direct Material	$3,500
Indirect Material	500
Direct Labor	4,000
Indirect Labor	600
Supervisory Salaries (Fixed)	1,000

The company applied variable factory overhead totaling $1,000 and fixed factory overhead totaling $800. Prepare journal entries to record the costs incurred and the application of factory overhead. Use April 7 as the date for your entries.

13-18 Job Order Journal Entries Using Account Numbers The following accounts are used by Ramsey Record Company in its job order cost system:
1. Raw Materials Inventory
2. Work-in-Process Inventory
3. Finished Goods Inventory
4. Cost of Goods Sold
5. Variable Factory Overhead
6. Fixed Factory Overhead
7. Accounts Payable
8. Accrued Payroll
9. Sales
10. Accounts Receivable

For each transaction below, use the account numbers above to show the accounts to be debited and credited.
 a. Raw materials were purchased on account.
 b. Direct material was issued for Job No. 46.
 c. Indirect material was used in the factory.
 d. Factory managers' salaries were incurred.
 e. Direct labor was incurred on Job No. 46.
 f. Variable and fixed overhead were applied to Job No. 46.
 g. Job No. 46 was completed.
 h. Finished goods were sold on account.

13-19 Job Order Journal Entries Below are abbreviated job cost sheets for jobs worked last month at Robert's Manufacturing Company. Factory overhead is applied at a combined rate.

Job No. 33			Job No. 34		
Direct Material	**Direct Labor**	**Factory Overhead**	**Direct Material**	**Direct Labor**	**Factory Overhead**
$1,000	$2,000	$1,500	$3,500	$5,000	$3,750

Both jobs were started during the month, and Job No. 33 was completed.

Using the data above, prepare journal entries to record the following transactions. (Prepare separate entries for each job.)

a. Direct material charged to production.
b. Direct labor charged to production.
c. Factory overhead charged to production.
d. Transfer of completed production to finished goods.

13-20 Calculating Job Costs and Inventory Balance Dressler Company began two jobs in July. There was no beginning work-in-process inventory. Costs were incurred as follows:

	Job No. 222	Job No. 223
Direct Material	$1,300	$2,100
Direct Labor	2,000	3,500

Factory overhead is applied at a combined rate of 50% of direct labor cost. Job No. 222 was completed in July, but Job No. 223 was still in process as of July 31.

a. Calculate the cost of finished goods completed for Job No. 222.
b. Determine the balance of work-in-process inventory as of July 31.

13-21 Calculating Unit Cost and Inventory Balance Tyson Company had 500 units in process on Job No. 645 as of May 31, with direct material costs of $300, direct labor costs of $600, and factory overhead costs of $450. During June, it completed Job 645 with additional direct material costs of $200 and additional direct labor costs of $400. Factory overhead is applied at a combined rate of 75% of direct labor cost.

The firm began Job No. 646 in June. As of June 30, direct material costs of $800 and direct labor costs of $1,200 had been charged to the job, which was still in process.

a. Calculate the unit cost of finished goods completed for Job No. 645.
b. Determine the balance of work-in-process inventory as of June 30.

13-22 Equivalent Units; Weighted-Average Method Hobbs Company began October with 2,000 units that were 40% complete. During October, 4,000 units were completed. At month end, there were 1,000 units 75% complete. Determine total equivalent units for the month, using the weighted-average method.

13-23 Equivalent Units; FIFO Method (*Appendix*) Refer to Exercise 13-22. Determine total equivalent units for the month using the FIFO method.

13-24 Equivalent Units; Weighted-Average Method Based on the data below, calculate total equivalent units. Use the weighted-average method.

	Units	Percent Complete Direct Material	Percent Complete Conversion Costs
Beginning Inventory	5,000	100%	60%
Transferred Out	20,000		
Ending Inventory	4,000	100%	20%

13-25 Equivalent Units; FIFO Method (*Appendix*) Refer to Exercise 13-24. Assume the firm uses the FIFO method. Calculate total equivalent units.

13-26 Equivalent Units; Weighted-Average Method Based on the data below, calculate total equivalent units. Use the weighted-average method.

	Units	Percent Complete	
		Direct Material	**Conversion Costs**
Beginning Inventory	2,000	80%	40%
Transferred Out	20,000		
Ending Inventory	6,000	70%	60%

13-27 Equivalent Units; FIFO Method (*Appendix*) Refer to Exercise 13–26. Assume the firm uses the FIFO method. Calculate total equivalent units.

13-28 Equivalent Units; Weighted-Average Method The Wiring Department is the second stage of Flem Company's production cycle. On May 1, beginning work in process contained 25,000 units, which were 60% complete as to conversion costs. During May, 100,000 units were transferred in from the first stage of Flem's production cycle. On May 31, ending work in process contained 20,000 units, which were 80% complete as to conversion costs. Material costs are added at the *end* of the process. Using the weighted-average method, determine total equivalent units for May and select the correct answer below. (AICPA adapted)

	Transferred-In Costs	**Materials**	**Conversion Costs**
a.	100,000	125,000	100,000
b.	125,000	105,000	105,000
c.	125,000	105,000	121,000
d.	125,000	125,000	121,000

13-29 Process Costing Journal Entry; Weighted-Average Method The cost summary of Department 1 of the Proso Manufacturing Company showed 6,000 equivalent units for May at a cost of $15,000. The company transferred 4,000 units to Department 2 on May 31. The firm uses the weighted-average method in its process cost system.

a. Determine the cost per equivalent unit.

b. Prepare the journal entry to transfer the completed units to Department 2.

13-30 Process Costing Journal Entries; Weighted-Average Method Abra Manufacturers, Inc., transferred 3,000 units of product from the mixing department to the finishing department in October. The cost per equivalent unit for the department was $2.50. The finishing department began October with 1,000 units with a transferred-in cost of $2.30 per unit. It completed and transferred out 4,000 units to finished goods. The department's cost per equivalent unit (not including transferred-in cost) was $4 per unit. Prepare journal entries as of October 31 to record the above transfers of product.

13-31 Process Costing Journal Entries The following data are available from the production records of the Taylor Tyler Tool Company for the month ended March 31.

	Cost per Equivalent Unit	
	Department 1	**Department 2**
Direct Material	$1.25	$2.50
Direct Labor	2.00	5.00
Factory Overhead	1.00	3.00

Department 1 transferred 2,000 units to Department 2 during the month. Department 2, which had no beginning work-in-process inventory, transferred 1,500 units to finished goods. Prepare journal entries as of March 31 to record the above transfers of product.

Problems

13-32 Job Order Journal Entries Bellamy Company uses a job order cost system. Data for jobs started in November are shown below. There was no work-in-process inventory as of November 1.

	Job No. 777	**Job No. 778**	**Job No. 779**
Direct Material Cost	$1,000	$3,000	$2,400
Direct Labor Cost	$480	$600	$360
Direct Labor Hours	80	100	60
Units	600	1,200	800

Variable factory overhead is applied at the rate of $3 per direct labor hour. Fixed factory overhead is applied at the rate of $1.50 per direct labor hour. During November, the firm completed Jobs 777 and 779.
Required:
    a. Prepare the journal entry to apply factory overhead to work in process for November. Use only one entry; but as an explanation, indicate the amount charged to each job.
    b. Prepare the journal entry to transfer the costs of Job No. 777 and Job No. 779 to finished goods inventory.
    c. Calculate the balance of work-in-process inventory as of November 30.

13-33 Job Order Journal Entries Costs on the three jobs in process as of March 1 for Delane Company are shown below.

	Job No. 166	**Job No. 167**	**Job No. 168**
Direct Material	$1,600	$750	$1,230
Direct Labor	1,000	350	900
Factory Overhead	400	140	360

Factory overhead is applied at a combined rate of $2 per direct labor hour. The following transactions occurred during March:
    1) Direct labor was charged as follows:

Job No.	Hours	Amount
166	40	$200
167	100	500
168	60	300

2) Additional direct material costing $300 was added to Job No. 167.

3) Factory overhead was applied to each job.

4) Jobs 166 and 167 were completed.

Required:

a. Prepare journal entries for the above transactions. A single entry may be made for each numbered transaction, but data should be shown for individual jobs as an explanation for the entry.

b. Calculate the balance of work-in-process inventory as of March 31.

13-34 Job Order Journal Entries; Job Cost Sheet Below is a job cost sheet (abbreviated) for the Milo Manufacturing Company for the period July 1–14.

Job No. 250				
			Factory Overhead	
Date	**Direct Material**	**Direct Labor**	**Variable**	**Fixed**
7/1	$40			
7/1–7/7		$100		
7/10	60			
7/8–7/14		125		

During the remainder of July, the following transactions related to Job No. 250 occurred:

July 15 Direct material of $30 was put into production.

   21 Direct labor for the period July 15–21 totaled $80.

   24 Direct material of $50 was put into production.

   28 Direct labor for the period July 22–28 totaled $95.

   28 Variable factory overhead was applied at the rate of 30% of direct labor cost.

   28 Fixed factory overhead was applied at the rate of 50% of direct labor cost.

   28 The job was completed and 50 finished units were transferred to the finished goods warehouse.

   30 Thirty finished units were sold on account for $25 each.

Required:

a. Prepare a job cost sheet similar to the one shown above. Insert the data included on the job cost sheet above.

b. Prepare journal entries to record the transactions for the period July 15–30. As you prepare each entry, insert the appropriate data on the job cost sheet.

c. Prepare a summary on the job cost sheet (similar to that shown in Exhibit 13.4).

13-35 Job Order Journal Entries Handmire's, Incorporated, uses a job order cost system. The balance sheet as of December 31, 19X3, includes the following items:

Raw Materials Inventory $3,000
Work-in-Process Inventory   650
Finished Goods Inventory   500

A look at the company's records reveals that work in process consists of one job, Job No. 44. The job cost sheet is shown below:

Job No. 44					
		Direct Labor		**Factory Overhead**	
Date	**Direct Material**	**Hours**	**Amount**	**Variable**	**Fixed**
1/1 Balance	$100	50	$250	$100	$200

Unsold finished goods from Job No. 43 represent finished goods inventory. Transactions for January 19X4 are as follows:

January 3 Issued direct material for Job No. 44, $1,000.

5 Issued direct material for Job No. 45, $600.

10 Finished goods from Job No. 43 were sold on account for $700.

15 Direct labor for the period January 1–15 was as follows:

Job No. 44   60 Hours $300
Job No. 45   40 Hours   200

16 Issued direct material as follows:

Job No. 44 $200
Job No. 45   300
Job No. 46   800

18 Raw materials costing $750 were purchased on account.

20 Direct labor for the period January 16–20 for Job No. 44 was 15 hours at a cost of $75.

20 Factory overhead was applied to Job No. 44. The variable overhead rate is $2 per direct labor hour; the fixed overhead rate is $4 per direct labor hour. The job was completed.

25 Direct material costing $150 was issued to Job No. 46.

27 All completed goods from Job No. 44 were sold on account for $3,800.

31 Direct labor for the period January 16–31 was as follows:

Job No. 45   100 Hours $500
Job No. 46   50 Hours   250

31 Factory overhead was applied to Jobs 45 and 46; but neither job is complete.

31 Indirect material used in January totaled $300. The only other variable overhead cost in January was indirect labor, which totaled $350.

31 Fixed factory overhead incurred in January was as follows:

Manager's Salary	$800
Depreciation on Plant and Equipment	400

31 Cost of goods sold was adjusted for the amount of under-applied or overapplied factory overhead for the month.

Required:

a. Using the format shown above for Job No. 44, prepare job cost sheets for Jobs 44, 45, and 46.

b. Prepare journal entries to record the transactions for January. Where appropriate, enter data on job cost sheets.

c. Post the journal entries to appropriate ledger accounts. Be sure to enter the beginning balances of the inventory accounts.

d. Prepare calculations showing that the balance of all job cost sheets on uncompleted jobs equals the balance of the work-in-process inventory ledger account.

13-36 Job Order; Questions on Selected Data The multiple-choice questions below are based on the following data:

Department 203–Work in Process–Beginning of Period

Job No.	Material	Labor	Overhead	Total
1376	$17,500	$22,000	$33,000	$72,500

Department 203–Costs for 19X7

	Material	Labor	Other	Total
Incurred by Jobs:				
1376	$ 1,000	$ 7,000	—	$ 8,000
1377	26,000	53,000	—	79,000
1378	12,000	9,000	—	21,000
1379	4,000	1,000	—	5,000
Not Incurred by Jobs:				
Indirect Materials and Supplies	15,000	—	—	15,000
Indirect Labor	—	53,000	—	53,000
Employee Benefits	—	—	$23,000	23,000
Depreciation	—	—	12,000	12,000
Supervision	—	20,000	—	20,000
Total	$58,000	$143,000	$35,000	$236,000

Department 203–Overhead Rate for 19X7

Budgeted Overhead:	
Variable:	
Indirect Materials	$ 16,000
Indirect Labor	56,000
Employee Benefits	24,000
Fixed:	
Supervision	20,000
Depreciation	12,000
Total	$128,000
Budgeted Direct Labor Dollars	$80,000
Rate per Direct Labor Dollar ($128,000 ÷ $80,000)	160%

Required:

Select the correct answer for each item below. Provide calculations to support your selection.

a. The actual overhead for Department 203 for 19X7 was:
   1. $156,000.
   2. $123,000.
   3. $70,000.
   4. $112,000.
   5. None of the above.

b. Department 203's overhead for 19X7 was:
   1. $11,000 underapplied.
   2. $11,000 overapplied.
   3. $44,000 underapplied.
   4. $44,000 overapplied.
   5. None of the above.

c. Job 1376 was the only job completed and sold in 19X7. What amount was included in cost of goods sold as the total cost of this job?
   1. $72,500.
   2. $91,700.
   3. $80,500.
   4. $19,200.
   5. None of the above.

d. The value of work-in-process inventory at the end of 19X7 was:
   1. $105,000.
   2. $180,600.
   3. $228,000.
   4. $205,800.
   5. None of the above.

e. Assume that overhead was underapplied in the amount of $14,000 for Department 203. If underapplied overhead was distributed between cost of goods sold and inventory, how much of the underapplied overhead was allocated to the year-end work-in-process inventory?
   1. $9,685.
   2. $4,315.
   3. $12,600.

4. $1,400.

5. None of the above. (CMA adapted)

13-37 Job Order; Cost of Goods Manufactured Statement The Rebeccca Corporation is a manufacturer that produces special machines made to customer specifications. All production costs are accumulated by means of a job order costing system. The following information was available at the beginning of October 19X4:

Direct Materials Inventory, October 1	$16,200
Work in Process, October 1	3,600

A review of the job order cost sheets revealed that the composition of the work-in-process inventory on October 1 was as follows:

Direct Materials	$1,320
Direct Labor (300 Hours)	1,500
Factory Overhead Applied	780
	$3,600

Activity during the month of October was as follows:

Direct materials costing $20,000 were purchased.
Direct labor for job orders totaled 3,300 hours at $5 per hour.
Factory overhead was applied to production at the rate of $2.60 per direct labor hour.

On October 31, inventories consisted of the following components:

Direct Materials Inventory	$17,000
Work-in-Process Inventory:	
Direct Materials	$4,320
Direct Labor (500 Hours)	2,500
Factory Overhead Applied	1,300
	$8,120

Required:
Prepare in good form a detailed statement of the cost of goods manufactured for the month of October. (AICPA adapted)

13-38 Process Costing; Equivalent Units and Cost Data; Weighted-Average Method The Bolo Company incurred costs of $18,200 in Department A during June. Department A began June with 3,000 equivalent units at a cost of $5,200. During June, 10,000 units were started; and 8,000 units were transferred to Department B. The company uses the weighted-average method in its process cost system. Direct material and conversion costs are incurred evenly throughout the process; so there is no division between them in equivalent unit calculations. Ending work-in-process inventory is 50% complete.

Required:
  a. Determine the total equivalent units in June.
  b. Determine the cost per equivalent unit for June.

  c. Determine the cost of work-in-process inventory as of June 30.

  d. Prepare the journal entry to transfer completed units to Department B.

  e. Prepare calculations to account for total costs in Department A.

(*Note:* Do not prepare a formal cost summary.)

13–39 Process Costing; Equivalent Units and Cost Data; Weighted-Average Method The Alcorn Company uses a process cost system. The following information is available regarding production in Department 1 for December.

	Units	Cost
Work in Process, December 1	500	$1,500
Transferred Out in December	3,000	
Direct Material Used in December		3,850
Conversion Costs in December		6,640
Work in Process, December 31	1,000	

Work in process is always 100% complete as to direct material. Cost of beginning work in process includes $550 for direct material. Beginning work-in-process inventory is 50% complete as to conversion costs, and ending work-in-process inventory is 30% complete as to conversion costs. The company uses the weighted-average method in its process cost system.

Required:

  a. Determine the cost per equivalent unit for December.

  b. Determine the cost of work-in-process inventory as of December 31.

  c. Prepare the journal entry as of December 31 to transfer completed units from Department 1 to Department 2.

  d. Prepare calculations to account for total costs in Department 1.

(*Note:* Do not prepare a formal cost summary.)

13–40 Process Costing; Equivalent Units and Cost Data; Weighted-Average Method Belfair Industries uses a process cost system. The following information is available regarding production in Department 2 for March.

	Units	Cost
Work in Process, March 1	2,000	$10,000
Transferred In from Department 1 during March	13,500	8,000
Transferred Out in March	12,000	
Direct Material Used in March		19,200
Conversion Costs in March		36,200
Work in Process, March 31	3,500	

Work in process is always 100% complete as to direct material. Cost of beginning work in process includes $2,500 for direct material and $1,300 of transferred-in costs. Beginning work-in-process inventory is 25% complete as to conversion costs, and ending work-in-process inventory is 60% complete as to conversion costs. The company uses the weighted-average method in its process cost system.

Required:

  a. Determine the cost per equivalent unit for March.

b. Determine the cost of work-in-process inventory as of March 31.

c. Prepare the journal entry as of March 15 to transfer completed units from Department 1 to Department 2.

d. Prepare the journal entry as of March 31 to transfer completed units from Department 2 to finished goods inventory.

e. Prepare calculations to account for total costs in Department 2.

(*Note:* Do not prepare a formal cost summary.)

13–41 Process Costing; Cost Summary; Weighted-Average Method The assembly department of Hoe Humm Manufacturers is the first processing department into which direct material is introduced. On May 1, 19X6, the assembly department had a work-in-process inventory of 6,000 units that was 100% complete as to direct material and 40% complete as to conversion costs. Cost of beginning inventory was $17,500, of which $5,500 was for direct material. During May, 20,000 additional units were started in production, and 22,000 units were completed and transferred to the painting department. The ending inventory of 4,000 units was 100% complete as to direct material and 70% complete as to conversion costs.

During May, direct material costs of $25,000 and conversion costs of $90,000 were incurred in the department. Factory overhead is applied at the rate of 50% of direct labor cost. The company uses the weighted-average method in its process cost system.

Required:

a. Prepare a formal cost summary for the assembly department for the month ended May 31, 19X6. (*Note:* Round equivalent unit cost calculations to the third decimal place.)

b. Prepare journal entries to record transactions charging the department for costs in May and transferring units to the painting department. (Ignore the dates of the entries.)

c. Prepare the work-in-process inventory ledger account for the assembly department, including the beginning balance. Post May transactions to the account.

13–42 Process Costing; Cost Summary; Weighted-Average Method Refer to Problem 13–41. On May 1, 19X6, the painting department of Hoe Humm Manufacturers had a work-in-process inventory of 3,000 units that was 50% complete as to direct material and 40% complete as to conversion costs. Beginning inventory included transferred-in costs of $15,000, direct material costs of $900, and conversion costs of $3,600. During May, 22,000 units were transferred in from the assembly department. On May 31, there was an ending inventory of 10,000 units, which was 60% complete as to direct material and 50% complete as to conversion costs. Completed units were transferred to finished goods inventory.

The cost of direct material used during May totaled $12,000. Direct labor costs incurred during May totaled $40,000, and factory overhead was applied at the rate of 50% of direct labor cost.

Required:

a. Prepare a formal cost summary for the painting department for the month ended May 31, 19X6. (*Note:* Round equivalent unit cost calculations to the third decimal place.)

b. Prepare journal entries to record transactions charging the department for costs in May and transferring units to finished goods inventory. (Ignore the dates of the entries.)

c. Prepare the work-in-process inventory ledger account for the painting department, including the beginning balance. Post May transactions to the account.

13-43 Process Costing; Equivalent Units and Cost Data; FIFO Method (*Appendix*) Refer to Problem 13-39. Assume that the company uses the FIFO method in its process cost system.

Required:

a. Determine the cost per equivalent unit for December. (*Note:* Round equivalent unit cost calculations to the third decimal place.)

b. Determine the cost of work-in-process inventory as of December 31.

c. Prepare the journal entry as of December 31 to transfer completed units from Department 1 to Department 2.

d. Prepare calculations to account for total costs in Department 1.

(*Note:* Do not prepare a formal cost summary.)

13-44 Process Costing; Equivalent Units and Cost Data; FIFO Method (*Appendix*) Refer to Problem 13-40. Assume that the company uses the FIFO method in its process cost system.

Required:

a. Determine the cost per equivalent unit for March. (*Note:* Round equivalent unit cost calculations to the third decimal place.)

b. Determine the cost of work-in-process inventory as of March 31.

c. Prepare the journal entry as of March 15 to transfer completed units from Department 1 to Department 2.

d. Prepare the journal entry as of March 31 to transfer completed units from Department 2 to finished goods inventory.

e. Prepare calculations to account for total costs in Department 1.

(*Note:* Do not prepare a formal cost summary.)

13-45 Process Costing; Cost Summary; FIFO Method (*Appendix*) Refer to the Palmer Paint Company example in the chapter and to the illustration of use of the FIFO method for the mixing department of the Palmer Paint Company in the appendix to the chapter.

Required:

Prepare a formal cost summary for the finishing department of the Palmer Paint Company using the FIFO method. (*Note:* Round equivalent unit cost calculations to the third decimal place. Also, assume that the beginning balance of work-in-process inventory on April 1 has the same cost as it did under the weighted-average method, $14,075.)

Chapter 14   Cost Allocation

Learning
Objectives

The purpose of this chapter is to provide you with an understanding of how factory overhead costs are allocated to product costs. The chapter describes why cost allocation is necessary and illustrates the process. Studying this chapter will enable you to:

1. Describe the need for cost allocation.
2. Describe the effect of the standards of the Cost Accounting Standards Board.
3. Define *cost objective*.
4. Contrast direct costs with indirect costs.
5. Describe the process of cost allocation.
6. Contrast three methods of cost allocation.
7. Apply cost allocation concepts in specific situations.
8. Describe the role of cost allocation in nonmanufacturing entities.

Chapter Topics

The major topics included in this chapter are:

The Need for Cost Allocation
Cost Allocation Concepts
The Process of Cost Allocation
Allocation of Administrative Expenses
Cost Allocation in Nonmanufacturing Entities

Chapters 3 and 13 discussed cost accounting systems and emphasized that manufacturing costs must be accounted for separately from selling and administrative costs. Included in manufacturing costs are factory overhead costs, which are normally charged to production at a predetermined overhead rate.

In determining a factory overhead rate in Chapter 3, we merely estimated the total amount of factory overhead expected to be incurred during the period and estimated the total activity to be used as a basis for charging the overhead costs. In practice, the process is more complicated than that.

There are many classifications of overhead, and all must be considered in determining the overhead rate. To arrive at a final overhead rate, factory overhead costs throughout the company must be assigned ultimately to each product. This process is called **cost allocation.**

The Need for Cost Allocation

The process of cost allocation can sometimes be complicated. You may wonder why it is necessary.

Required by Generally Accepted Accounting Principles

Generally accepted accounting principles (GAAP) require that manufacturing firms use absorption costing. Under absorption costing, all factory costs are charged to the cost of production. If a firm produced only one product, this process would not be difficult to carry out. However, large companies produce hundreds and even thousands of different products. These companies must have cost allocation systems that appropriately assign factory costs to the products. The difficulty comes in the allocation of factory overhead costs.

Required by Standards of the Cost Accounting Standards Board

The Cost Accounting Standards Board (CASB) was created by Congress in 1970. Its primary role was to issue cost accounting standards applicable to defense contracts with the federal government, including contracts with the Department of Defense, the Department of Energy, and the National Aeronautics and Space Administration. In some instances, other government agencies, through their own administrative authority, have extended the CASB's standards to nondefense contracts as well.

As an agency, the CASB went out of existence in 1980. However, the standards it issued are still in force for firms with government contracts that meet the criteria spelled out in the law. In theory, CASB standards are applicable only to certain government contracts and therefore are not binding on all firms or on nongovernment contracts. As a practical matter, however, companies using CASB standards for government contracts may logically use them for their nondefense work as well. As a result, the influence of the CASB may extend beyond its statutory authority.

Since one of the disputed areas in government contracts in prior years was the allocation of costs, the CASB gave considerable attention to this area. Many companies are now required to comply with CASB standards regarding cost allocation. As mentioned above, they may use these same standards in their nondefense production as well.

Relationship to Management Decision Making

The allocation of all factory costs to the cost of products is a fact of life. It is a part of absorption costing. As previously discussed, there is justification for absorption costing. Nevertheless, certain management decisions should be based on information reported on a basis other than that of absorption costing. Some pitfalls in using absorption costing were illustrated at the end of Chapter 4 and expanded on in Chapters 8 and 10.

A student of managerial accounting should be familiar with absorption costing and with the required accounting and reporting requirements under generally accepted accounting principles. However, information for internal decision making generally does not rely on absorption costing.

Cost Allocation Concepts

The problems of cost allocation pertain primarily to absorption costing, because it requires that all manufacturing costs, fixed and variable, be included in product cost. The ultimate objective is to determine the cost of goods manufactured, which is necessary in order to prepare an income statement that shows the cost of goods sold. It is also needed in order to know whether the current pricing policy is adequate to cover the cost of manufacturing. (However, pricing considerations are sometimes affected by other factors, as was discussed in Chapter 10.) The first step in the cost allocation process is to identify cost objectives. *Cost objective*, *direct cost*, and *indirect cost* were defined in Chapter 8. However, their importance in the cost allocation process warrants further discussion of these terms.

Cost Objective

The Cost Accounting Standards Board defined a cost objective as "a function, organizational subdivision, contract, or other work unit for which cost data are desired and for which provision is made to accumulate and measure the cost of processes, products, jobs, capitalized projects, etc."[1] Simply stated, a **cost objective** is anything for which a firm wishes to accumulate costs. For a manufacturing firm, the ultimate or **final cost objective** for manufacturing costs is the product cost; the firm accumulates costs in order to determine the cost of the product. Determining the final cost of products, however, requires that the costs associated with intermediate cost objectives be determined. The **intermediate cost objectives** are the various manufacturing segments, which are also incurring costs. The Board defined **allocate** to mean "to assign an item of cost, or a group of items of cost, to one or more cost objectives."[2]

In Chapters 1 and 8, we discussed the concept of responsibility accounting. Under responsibility accounting, costs are accumulated for each segment. In a manufacturing firm, the segments we are concerned with are those that incur manufacturing costs. These segments are referred to as *cost centers* and are intermediate cost objectives. For example, the manufacture of any product normally requires that costs be incurred for depreciation or rent of factory space, depreciation of equipment, indirect labor in the stores warehouse, indirect labor for plant guards, and utility costs, to name but a few. These various types of costs are accumulated in cost centers and must somehow be allocated to the various products.

[1] *4 Code of Federal Regulations.* Section 400. 1 (1981 ed.)
[2] *Ibid.*

**Direct and
Indirect Costs**

The assignment of costs to cost objectives is easier for direct costs, more difficult for indirect costs. A **direct cost** is one that benefits a specific cost objective or is caused by the activities of a specific cost objective. The criterion for determining a direct cost is the **traceability** of that cost to a given cost objective. In other words, can the benefit of the cost or the incurrence of the cost be traced directly to a specific cost objective?

An **indirect cost** is one that benefits or is caused by the activities of more than one cost objective but cannot be traced to a specific cost objective. The problem of cost allocation for a manufacturing firm is to assign factory overhead costs to the appropriate cost objectives in the appropriate amounts in order to determine an overhead rate by which to apply these costs to the cost of the product.

We have seen examples of direct costs in earlier chapters. For example, direct material and direct labor are direct costs of the final cost objective, the product for which they are incurred. However, if a company is producing several products, the electricity used benefits all products and cannot be traced to a specific one. Therefore, the electricity cost must be allocated among all of the products—it is an indirect cost to the products.

Costs not directly identified with final cost objectives should be grouped into logical and homogeneous expense pools and allocated accordingly.[3] These expense pools are often called indirect cost pools. Many of them are referred to as service centers. For example, plant security is a service center. Plant security costs, such as salaries, uniforms, weapons, operation of vehicles, and depreciation on the security office and vehicles, are accumulated in an indirect cost pool and allocated to the appropriate cost objectives.

To classify a cost as direct or indirect, the firm must analyze the cost objective to which it is applicable. For example, a plant guard's salary is a direct cost of plant security. However, it is an indirect cost of the products; it benefits more than one product, but the benefit cannot be traced specifically to individual products.

Note that the terms *direct* and *indirect* are not related to cost behavior. Both direct and indirect costs can be either variable or fixed. The direct/indirect terminology has to do with the traceability of a cost to a specific cost objective.

The Process of Cost Allocation

Cost allocation requires a systematic process for the accumulation of costs by intermediate cost objectives and the distribution of those costs to other intermediate and final cost objectives. Management must decide on logical centers for accumulating costs. Since the initial cost centers are frequently responsibility centers, individuals are normally held accountable for costs incurred by the cost centers for which they are responsible. The allocation system is also crucial. The problems of cost allocation in regard to responsibility accounting and managerial performance measurement were discussed in Chapter 8.

---

[3]Cost Accounting Standards Board, *Restatement of Objectives, Policies, and Concepts*, May 1977, p. 6.

A manufacturer's objective in cost allocation is to determine the factory overhead rate to be used in applying overhead to the producing departments. There are five steps in the overhead allocation process:

1. Determine budgeted indirect factory overhead costs.
2. Select the basis for allocation.
3. Select the method of allocation.
4. Allocate general factory costs and service center costs.
5. Determine the overhead rate.

To show the process of cost allocation, this section will apply in an illustration of the Munson Appliance Company, a manufacturer of small appliances.

Costs to be Allocated (Step 1)

A cost accounting system should accumulate indirect factory costs into indirect cost pools.[4] As mentioned earlier, indirect cost pools are cost centers that incur costs that benefit or are caused by more than one final cost objective.

There are three classifications of indirect costs: (1) general factory costs, (2) service center costs, and (3) production center costs.

ins. on fac. bldg
deprec " " "
prop. taxes " " "
salaries of VP of mfg.
production supt.
office staff salaries

General Factory Costs Indirect costs that cannot be traced directly to a specific sevice center or production center are called **general factory costs.** These costs, often called *factory occupany costs*, are necessary in order for the firm to have a place in which manufacturing can occur. They include depreciation, insurance, and taxes on the factory building and on any equipment that is used by all departments. In addition, they include salaries of the vice-president of manufacturing and the plant superintendent, as well as any costs associated with running their offices, such as salaries for their secretaries.

provide services to
the production dept.
maint, security, custodians,

Service Center Costs Costs incurred in providing services to the producing departments and to other service centers are **service center costs.** These services include maintenance, power plant, plant security, materials warehouse, and custodial.

direct cost of the dept.
but indirect of product

Production Center Costs Each production center also incurs costs that are direct costs of the department but indirect costs of the product. For example, machinery in the cutting department of a furniture manufacturer is used to cut wood to various shapes for specific pieces of furniture. Depreciation on this machinery is a direct cost of the cutting department. However, it is an indirect cost to the specific products, because it benefits all products. Thus, although the production center costs are not allocated to other departments, these costs are included in determining the overhead rate to be applied to the product.

The final cost objectives for the Munson Appliance Company are the specific products it manufactures. Thus, the company wants to determine

[4]The term *indirect* is used here because factory overhead costs that are *indirect* to the product are being allocated. When the final cost objective is not specified, it is generally understood that the final cost objective is the product.

the cost of producing toasters, mixers, can openers, and the other appliances it makes.

The company incurs general factory costs and also has three service centers—(1) a utilities department, (2) a custodial department, and (3) a maintenance department. There are three producing departments: (1) molding, (2) painting, (3) and assembly. The objective of cost allocation for the company is to allocate general factory costs to the service centers and to the producing departments. Next, service center costs are allocated to other service centers (where appropriate) and to the producing departments. Once all of these costs have been allocated to the producing departments, they are combined with the direct overhead costs of the producing departments (which are also indirect product costs). Then, an overhead rate is established for applying the costs to each product.

Since the overhead rate is an estimate, its development must be based on the estimated costs to be incurred during the next period. The first step is to estimate costs by natural classifications, such as salaries, supplies, and insurance. These estimated costs are, in effect, budgeted costs. A budget of indirect costs for the Munson Appliance Company for 19X5 is shown in Exhibit 14.1.

Exhibit 14.1 Budgeted Indirect Costs

	Variable	Fixed	Total
General Factory Costs	$ 50,000	$ 250,000	$ 300,000
Service Center Costs:			
Utilities	$200,000	$ 50,000	$ 250,000
Custodial	50,000	100,000	150,000
Maintenance	100,000	300,000	400,000
Total Service Center Costs	$350,000	$ 450,000	$ 800,000
Production Center Costs:			
Molding	$ 75,000	$ 200,000	$ 275,000
Painting	25,000	150,000	175,000
Assembly	50,000	100,000	150,000
Total Production Center Costs	$150,000	$ 450,000	$ 600,000
Total Indirect Costs	$550,000	$1,150,000	$1,700,000

The costs are budgeted according to cost behavior, variable and fixed. In this illustration, an overhead application rate will be developed for each of the two cost behavior patterns. Some firms, however, may use a combined rate.

Basis for Allocation (Step 2)

The basis used for allocating indirect costs directly affects the costs allocated to the final cost objectives. The Cost Accounting Standards Board indicated its preference for allocation bases, which are summarized in order of preference as follows:[5]

1. *A measure of activity of the cost center.* For example, the primary activity of the custodial department is measured in labor hours of custodial personnel. Thus, an appropriate basis for allocating costs of the custodial department is the number of hours spent by custodial personnel in the other departments.

electricity

2. *A measure of output of the cost center.* For example, utility costs are usually allocated on the basis of usage. Electricity costs are allocated based on the number of kilowatt hours used by the receiving departments.

3. *An activity of the cost center receiving the service.* For example, machine hours may be the basis for allocating maintenance costs to the production centers.

The CASB also indicated that some indirect costs—for example, the general factory costs—may not be allocable on the basis of a specific beneficial or causal relationship. The CASB stated that "these costs should be grouped in relation to the activities managed and the base selected to measure the allocation of these indirect costs to cost objectives should be a base representative of the entire activity being managed."[6] The Board believed that total cost of plant activities might be a reasonable base for such allocation. Frequently, the base used is the number of square feet in the factory.

It should be recognized that for costs such as general factory costs, the base selected is quite arbitrary. By definition, there is no cause or benefit relationship between the cost and the activities. Nevertheless, allocation is required for external reporting purposes under generally accepted accounting principles (absorption costing) and for firms with government contracts that must comply with the standards issued by the CASB.

General Factory Costs   The Munson Appliance Company uses the total square feet in its factory for allocating general factory costs to cost centers. The number of square feet in each cost center is shown below:

	Number of Square Feet
Service Centers:	
Utilities	25,000
Custodial	10,000
Maintenance	20,000
Production Centers:	
Molding	70,000
Painting	50,000
Assembly	75,000
Total	250,000

[5]Cost Accounting Standards Board, *Restatement of Objectives*, pp. 7–8
[6]*Ibid.*, p. 8.

Service Center Costs Utilities costs are allocated on the basis of kilowatt hours.[7] Since internal decision making requires a knowledge of cost behavior, both a variable rate and a fixed rate are determined. In this way, management knows that if a using department reduces its electricity usage, costs to the company as a whole are reduced, based on the variable rate. Reduction of electricity usage by a using department will also reduce the amount of fixed costs allocated to it, based on the fixed rate. However, it most likely will not reduce total fixed costs of the utilities department (and, therefore, of the company as a whole). Thus, in making decisions that affect the company as a whole, it is helpful if management knows which allocated costs are variable and which are fixed.

Custodial services are allocated on the basis of the number of hours spent by the custodial department personnel in the using departments. These are referred to as custodial service-hours (CSH). As with general factory costs, the custodial department should separate variable and fixed costs. However, the amount of custodial services to the other departments does not vary in relation to any activity of the other departments. It is doubtful that any action by a using department would affect total costs of the custodial department (and the company as a whole). Thus, total costs of the custodial department are combined, and only a fixed allocation rate is calculated.

Maintenance costs are allocated on the basis of machine hours. The theory is that the more hours machines are run, the greater the maintenance cost. As with the utilities department, both a variable and a fixed allocation rate are calculated for the maintenance department. Variable costs will vary in relation to an activity (machine usage) of the using departments, and this information should be available to management.

The total activity of each department to which general factory costs and service center costs will be allocated is shown in Exhibit 14.2. These are the budgeted activities; they reflect the amount of activity expected during the next year. In addition, the exhibit shows budgeted direct labor hours for each production center, because direct labor hours are the basis on which the overhead rate is determined.

Note that none of a department's cost is allocated to the department itself. In addition, since this example uses sequential allocation, as described below, no costs are allocated back to a center once that center's costs have been allocated. For example, some of the utilities department's cost will be allocated to the custodial department. But none of the custodial department's costs are allocated to the utilities department.

Method of Allocation (Step 3)

Since general factory costs apply to all elements of the factory, they are allocated to each service center and production center on the basis of square feet, as described above. However, a problem arises in the allocation of service center costs. Some service centers serve only production centers; but

---

[7]Utilities costs include those for electricity, heating, and water. However, in order to simplify the example, the illustration shows only the allocation of electricity costs.

Exhibit 14.2 Basis for Allocation and Overhead Rate Determination

	Square Feet	Kilowatt Hours	Custodial Service Hours	Machine Hours	Direct Labor Hours
₱ 300,000					
Service Centers:					
Utilities	25,000	–	–	–	–
Custodial	10,000	10,000	–	–	–
Maintenance	20,000	20,000	2,000	–	–
Production Centers:					
Molding	70,000	80,000	6,000	20,000	70,000
Painting	50,000	50,000	5,000	15,000	60,000
Assembly	75,000	90,000	7,000	25,000	100,000
Totals	250,000	250,000	20,000	60,000	230,000

some service centers serve other service centers as well as production centers. In many cases, there is cross-servicing among service centers.

Munson Appliance Company's maintenance department provides maintenance services only to production centers. Maintenance of the utility plant is provided by individuals within the utilities department. The utilities department provides utilities to all other service centers as well as to production centers. The custodial department also provides services to each service center and to production centers. How, then, do we allocate the costs of the service centers? There are three ways: direct allocation, simultaneous allocation, and sequential allocation.

Direct Allocation When **direct allocation** is used, service center costs are allocated directly to production centers, and other service centers that may be served by the one whose costs are being allocated are ignored. For example, the costs of Munson's custodial department would be allocated directly to production centers, even though other service centers receive custodial services. The direct method is the easiest to apply, but it is the least theoretically appropriate.

Simultaneous Allocation When **simultaneous allocation** is used, reciprocal relationships of the service centers are recognized. This method uses simultaneous equations to compute the amount of service center costs to be allocated among service centers. Under this method, each service center that receives service from another receives part of the cost of the other service center. This method is the most theoretically sound. However, it is somewhat complex, and an illustration of it is beyond the scope of this text.

In some cases, it is questionable whether the increased accuracy gained by the more complex method is worth the additional time and cost needed to obtain it. However, with the use of calculators and computers, simultaneous allocation is not as time consuming as it once was.

this is the one we use: ⌐STEP -DOWN METHOD⌐ or STEP METHOD.

Sequential Allocation When **sequential allocation** is used, the cost of one service center is first allocated to all other service centers and to the production centers. When the costs for the first service center have been allocated, the costs for the next service center are allocated. The term *sequential* describes the process of each service center's costs being allocated in a predetermined sequence. Sequential allocation is also called the *step method* and the *step-down method*.

A disadvantage of this method is that it does not recognize all reciprocal relationships. For example, assume that the utilities department's costs are allocated to the custodial department, and then the custodial department's costs are allocated to the maintenance department. Under this arrangement, the costs of the custodial department that were incurred in the utilities department are never charged to the utilities department.

The sequence of allocation should be based on service. The costs of the service department that provides the most service to other departments will be allocated first. The costs of the service department that provides the second most service will be allocated next. For example, if it is assumed that the amount of utilities service to the custodial department exceeds the amount of custodial services to the utilities department, then utilities should be allocated to custodial. As you might expect, measuring the amount of service between departments may not be easy; and the judgment of who provides most service may be arbitrary. This is another disadvantage of sequential allocation.

Munson Appliance Company uses sequential allocation. First, utilities costs are allocated to the custodial department, the maintenance department, and the production departments. Custodial costs are then allocated to maintenance and production. Finally, maintenance costs are allocated to production.

Allocation of Costs (Step 4)

General Factory Costs To determine the allocation rate per square foot, divide total factory costs of $300,000 (from Exhibit 14.1) by 250,000 square feet (from Exhibit 14.2). This calculation results in the following allocation rate:

$$\frac{\$300,000}{250,000 \text{ Square Feet}} = \$1.20 \text{ per Square Foot}$$

The amount of general factory costs allocated to each cost center is determined by multiplying $1.20 per square foot by the number of square feet in each cost center. The results of this process are shown in Exhibit 14.3.

Note that although there are variable general factory costs, these costs were combined with the fixed costs to determine the allocation rate. It is necessary to distinguish between variable and fixed costs in each cost center, because certain internal decisions may be based on the cost behavior

Exhibit 14.3 Allocation of General Factory Costs

	Number of Square Feet	Rate	Allocated General Factory Cost
Service Centers:			
Utilities	25,000	$1.20	$ 30,000
Custodial	10,000	1.20	12,000
Maintenance	20,000	1.20	24,000
Production Centers:			
Molding	70,000	1.20	84,000
Painting	50,000	1.20	60,000
Assembly	75,000	1.20	90,000
Totals	250,000		$300,000

within the center. However, there is not necessarily any need to have separate allocation rates. Whether an allocated cost is variable to another department depends on whether an activity in the other department causes changes in the cost. In this case, it does not. A cost allocated on the basis of square feet is a fixed cost to the other departments.

Utilities Costs The next step is to determine the allocation rate for the utilities department. As previously discussed, two rates are established. The budgeted variable cost of $200,000 (from Exhibit 14.1) is divided by the expected usage of 250,000 kilowatt hours (from Exhibit 14.2). The budgeted fixed utilities cost of $50,000 (from Exhibit 14.1) must first be added to the $30,000 of general factory cost allocated to the utilities department (from Exhibit 14.3). This results in a total fixed utilities cost of $80,000 to be allocated to the other departments. The allocation rates are calculated as follows:

$$\text{Variable: } \frac{\$200,000}{250,000 \text{ KWH}} = \$.80 \text{ per KWH}$$

$$\text{Fixed: } \frac{\$80,000}{250,000 \text{ KWH}} = \$.32 \text{ per KWH}$$

To allocate utilities costs to the other departments, multiply the rate per kilowatt hour by the expected kilowatt usage in each department (Exhibit 14.2). Thus, utilities costs are allocated as follows:

Custodial
Variable: 10,000 KWH × $.80 per KWH = $8,000
Fixed: 10,000 KWH × $.32 per KWH = $3,200

Maintenance
Variable: 20,000 KWH × $.80 per KWH = $16,000
Fixed: 20,000 KWH × $.32 per KWH = $6,400

Molding
Variable: 80,000 KWH × $.80 per KWH = $64,000
Fixed: 80,000 KWH × $.32 per KWH = $25,600

Painting
Variable: 50,000 KWH × $.80 per KWH = $40,000
Fixed: 50,000 KWH × $.32 per KWH = $16,000

Assembly
Variable: 90,000 KWH × $.80 per KWH = $72,000
Fixed: 90,000 KWH × $.32 per KWH = $28,800

The allocation of utilities costs is summarized in Exhibit 14.4.

Exhibit 14.4 Allocation of Utilities Costs

	Variable	Fixed	Total
Custodial	$ 8,000	$ 3,200	$ 11,200
Maintenance	16,000	6,400	22,400
Molding	64,000	25,600	89,600
Painting	40,000	16,000	56,000
Assembly	72,000	28,800	100,800
Totals	$200,000	$80,000	$280,000

Custodial Costs Next, custodial costs are allocated. As mentioned previously, since custodial costs are not really incurred at a variable rate by the using departments, only a fixed rate is calculated. To the budgeted custodial costs of $150,000 (Exhibit 14.1) must be added the $12,000 allocation of general factory costs (Exhibit 14.3) and the $11,200 allocation of utilities cost (Exhibit 14.4). Thus, the total custodial costs to be allocated are $173,200 ($150,000 + $12,000 + $11,200).

Custodial costs are allocated on the basis of budgeted custodial service-hours to be spent in the using department. From Exhibit 14.2, we know this is 20,000 service-hours. The allocation rate is calculated as follows:

$$\frac{\$173,200}{20,000 \text{ CSH}} = \$8.66 \text{ per CSH}$$

The allocation rate of $8.66 per service-hour is multiplied by the expected number of service-hours to be spent in the using departments, resulting in an allocation of custodial costs as shown in Exhibit 14.5.

Exhibit 14.5 Allocation of Custodial Costs

	Custodial Service Hours	Rate	Allocated Cost
Maintenance	2,000	$8.66	$ 17,320
Molding	6,000	8.66	51,960
Painting	5,000	8.66	43,300
Assembly	7,000	8.66	60,620
Totals	20,000		$173,200

Maintenance Costs The final allocation of service center costs is for the maintenance department. Its costs are allocated at both a variable rate and a fixed rate on the basis of 60,000 machine hours being used (Exhibit 14.2). As with the other departments, we must first determine the total costs to be allocated, as follows:

	Variable	Fixed
Budgeted Maintenance Overhead Costs	$100,000	$300,000 (Exhibit 14.1)
Allocation of:		
General Factory Costs		24,000 (Exhibit 14.3)
Utilities Costs	16,000	6,400 (Exhibit 14.4)
Custodial Costs		17,320 (Exhibit 14.5)
Totals	$116,000	$347,720

With this information, we can calculate the variable and fixed allocation rates as follows:

$$\text{Variable: } \frac{\$116,000}{60,000 \text{ Machine Hours}} = \$1.93333 \text{ per Hour}$$

$$\text{Fixed: } \frac{\$347,720}{60,000 \text{ Machine Hours}} = \$5.79533 \text{ per Hour}$$

At this point, a question arises: To how many decimal places should the allocation rates be carried? Generally, we carry decimal places out far enough so that when the rates are multiplied by the activity, errors caused by rounding are minimized. In this example, we carried the rates out to enough decimal places that there were no errors due to rounding. In practice, since this whole process is one of estimation anyway, the firm may not need to carry a decimal past two, three, or four places. It depends on how the final results might be affected by rounding.

We can now allocate the maintenance costs to each of the production centers by multiplying the allocation rates determined above by the expected activity—machine hours (from Exhibit 14.2)—in each department. Thus, maintenance costs are allocated as follows:

Molding

Variable: 20,000 Machine Hours × $1.93333 per Hour = $38,667

Fixed: 20,000 Machine Hours × $5.79533 per Hour = $115,907

Painting

Variable: 15,000 Machine Hours × $1.93333 per Hour = $29,000

Fixed: 15,000 Machine Hours × $5.79533 per Hour = $86,930

Assembly

Variable: 25,000 Machine Hours × $1.93333 per Hour = $48,333

Fixed: 25,000 Machine Hours × $5.79533 per Hour = $144,883

The results of this process are shown in Exhibit 14.6.

Exhibit 14.6 Allocation of Maintenance Costs

	Variable	Fixed	Total
Molding	$ 38,667	$115,907	$154,574
Painting	29,000	86,930	115,930
Assembly	48,333	144,883	193,216
Totals	$116,000	$347,720	$463,720

Determination of the Overhead Application Rate (Step 5)

Since all factory overhead costs have now been charged to production centers, the overhead application rate to be used by each department in product costing can be determined. The total factory overhead costs that have been charged to the production centers are shown in Exhibit 14.7.

The general factory costs and the service department costs shown in Exhibit 14.7 are those that have been allocated by the process shown above. The direct costs shown in Exhibit 14.7 are the direct factory overhead costs charged to each department; they were shown originally in Exhibit 14.1. Note that although they are direct costs of each production center, they are indirect costs for each of the final products. In fact, all costs shown in Exhibit 14.7 are indirect product costs. This, of course, is the purpose of the entire allocation process—to allocate indirect product costs to the final product costs. If the totals of all department costs (the bottom line of Exhibit 14.7) are added, they will total $1,700,000, the amount of indirect costs shown in Exhibit 14.1. Thus, we know that all indirect costs have been allocated to the production centers.

We charge these indirect costs to the final cost objective—the product—by applying factory overhead on the basis of a predetermined rate, which we determine by dividing factory overhead cost by the budgeted activity on which the overhead will be applied—in this case, direct labor hours. The determination of factory overhead rates for each production center is shown in Exhibit 14.8.

Exhibit 14.7 Total Factory Overhead Costs Charged to Production Centers

	Molding		Painting		Assembly	
	Variable	**Fixed**	**Variable**	**Fixed**	**Variable**	**Fixed**
General Factory		$ 84,000		$ 60,000		$ 90,000
Utilities	$ 64,000	25,600	$ 40,000	16,000	$ 72,000	28,800
Custodial		51,960		43,300		60,620
Maintenance	38,667	115,907	29,000	86,930	48,333	144,883
Direct	75,000	200,000	25,000	150,000	50,000	100,000
Totals	$177,667	$477,467	$ 94,000	$356,230	$170,333	$424,303

Again, the question of rounding arises. It is doubtful whether a firm needs to carry out the overhead rate to five decimal places as shown below. That was done here to point out that the factory overhead rates do not generally come out to nice round figures. In the problems and examples in this text, we normally use overhead rates of only two or three decimal places in order to simplify the calculations.

The calculation of the overhead application rate is the last step in the allocation process. The overhead rate is used to apply factory overhead to work-in-process inventory as products are manufactured. This process was illustrated in Chapters 3 and 13. The rates used in the illustrations in those chapters would have been derived through the process you have seen here.

A summary of the allocation process for Munson Appliance Company is shown in Exhibit 14.9. The information presented in the exhibit is the same as that shown in the previous exhibits. However, it allows you to see at a glance how the total factory overhead cost of $1,700,000 (from Exhibit 14.1) has been allocated to arrive at the final overhead application rates for each production department.

Exhibit 14.8 Determination of Factory Overhead Rates

	Variable	Fixed
Molding:	$\dfrac{\$177,667}{70,000 \text{ DLH}} = \$2.5381$ per DLH.	$\dfrac{\$477,467}{70,000 \text{ DLH}} = \$6.82096$ per DLH.
Painting:	$\dfrac{\$94,000}{60,000 \text{ DLH}} = \$1.56667$ per DLH.	$\dfrac{\$356,230}{60,000 \text{ DLH}} = \$5.93717$ per DLH.
Assembly:	$\dfrac{\$170,333}{100,000 \text{ DLH}} = \$1.70333$ per DLH.	$\dfrac{\$424,303}{100,000 \text{ DLH}} = \$4.24303$ per DLH.

Exhibit 14.9 Summary of Cost Allocation

	General Factory	Utilities		Custodial	Maintenance		Molding		Painting		Assembly	
		Variable	Fixed		Variable	Fixed	Variable	Fixed	Variable	Fixed	Variable	Fixed
Budgeted Departmental Overhead Costs	$ 300,000	$ 200,000	$ 50,000	$ 150,000	$ 100,000	$ 300,000	$ 75,000	$200,000	$25,000	$150,000	$ 50,000	$100,000
Allocation of:												
General Factory Costs	$(300,000)		30,000	12,000		24,000		84,000		60,000		90,000
Utilities Costs		$(200,000)	$(80,000)	11,200	16,000	6,400	64,000	25,600	40,000	16,000	72,000	28,800
Custodial Costs				$(173,200)		17,320		51,960		43,300		60,620
Maintenance Costs					$(116,000)	$(347,720)	38,667	115,907	29,000	86,930	48,333	144,883
Total Production Center Overhead Costs							$177,667	$477,467	$94,000	$356,230	$170,333	$424,303
Budgeted Direct Labor Hours							70,000		60,000		100,000	
Factory Overhead Rate (per DLH)							$2.5381	$6.82096	$1.56667	$5.93717	$1.70333	$4.24303
Allocation Basis	Square Feet	Kilowatt Hours		Custodial Service Hours	Machine Hours							

Allocation of Administrative Expenses

Most manufacturing firms show administrative expenses as a period cost on the income statement. They do not allocate this cost to manufacturing. In one of its early statements, the Cost Accounting Standards Board recognized that "the allocation of all period costs to the products and services of the period is not a common practice either for public reporting or for internal management purposes; yet this has long been the established cost principle for costing defense procurement."[8] Thus, administrative expenses (referred to as general and administrative expenses by CASB) incurred under contracts that require adherence to CASB standards must be allocated to the final cost objectives. This allocation process is referred to as the **full costing concept.**

Since the allocation of manufacturing cost is, to a large degree, arbitrary, you can imagine the problems in allocating administrative costs. Because the allocation of administrative costs is not a standard practice in accounting, such procedures are not included in this text. But you should be aware that some firms are required by law to allocate administrative costs in certain contractual situations.

In addition to administrative expenses, CASB standards also require an allocation of home office expenses to operating segments. As described in Chapter 8, this practice can create problems in evaluating management performance. It is important that the objective of one accounting procedure (cost allocation) not interfere with the objective of another management function (performance evaluation).

Cost Allocation in Nonmanufacturing Entities

Since generally accepted accounting principles, as well as CASB standards, require allocation of manufacturing costs to products, discussion in this chapter has focused on that process. However, cost allocation concepts are applicable to nonmanufacturing organizations as well.

Hospitals are very concerned about cost allocation. They receive reimbursement from the federal government for Medicare patients, and the amount reimbursed is often based on costs determined through the allocation process. Utility firms are also concerned with cost allocation. Their rates are based on costs; so cost allocation plays a role in determining the rate calculation.

There is no accounting nor legal requirement for a retailing firm to allocate its costs to selling departments. Nevertheless, it is sometimes done. The practice of allocating costs within a retail store is based on the idea that all selling departments generate revenue. In order to determine the profitability of each department, management may allocate to each department its share of all costs. There is merit in the concept of insuring that all costs are being covered and that each department is bearing its "fair share of the

---

[8]Cost Accounting Standards Board, *Statement of Operating Policies, Procedures and Objectives,* March 1973, p. 16.

load." However, as always, the process of cost allocation can result in faulty internal decision making, as described in Chapters 8 and 10.

To illustrate cost allocation for a merchandising firm, we can think of a retail department store as being divided into service departments and selling departments. The service departments may consist of the credit department, accounting department, personnel department, and an employees' cafeteria. The selling departments, of course, are the departments that sell merchandise, such as the furniture department, appliance department, sporting goods department, women's clothing department, and men's clothing department. In addition, some general store costs (similar to general factory costs) are incurred; they include the salaries of the store manager and the assistant store manager, rent or depreciation on the store building, and depreciation of store fixtures not related to the service or selling departments.

The allocation procedure is similar to that for a manufacturing firm. General store costs are allocated to the service departments and the selling departments. Service department costs are allocated to other service departments and to selling departments. As with a manufacturing firm, the basis for allocation should, where possible, be related to an activity of either the service department or the selling department. However, again, as with a manufacturer, the allocation base may be somewhat arbitrary.

In summary, the process of cost allocation in nonmanufacturing entities is based on the same concept as cost allocation for manufacturing firms. The idea is to try to charge the costs of the firm against those activities that benefit from the cost in proportion to the benefit received. This is quite often easier said than done.

Summary

Generally accepted accounting principles require that manufacturing firms allocate factory overhead costs to the final cost objectives, the products. In addition, standards of the Cost Accounting Standards Board spell out specific requirements for cost allocation on certain government contracts. Although the CASB no longer exists, its standards are still applicable.

Costs may be classified as direct or indirect. A cost is direct when a cost objective benefits from or causes the cost. An indirect cost, on the other hand, benefits or is caused by more than one cost objective. The determination of whether a cost is direct or indirect depends on the specific cost objective and is based on the traceability of the cost.

For allocation purposes, the costs are accumulated in indirect cost pools, which can generally be classified as: (1) general factory costs; (2) service center costs; and (3) production center costs. General factory costs are allocated to the service centers and production centers. Service center costs are allocated to other service centers and to production centers. Finally, production center costs (including those allocated to the production centers) are used to determine the factory overhead rate to apply to the product.

The bases for allocating indirect costs are: (1) measure of activity of the cost center allocating the costs; (2) measure of output of the cost center allocating the cost; and (3) measure of activity of the cost center receiving the cost. Costs that cannot be allocated on any of the above three bases, such as general factory costs, should be allocated on the basis of the entire activity to be managed.

Service center costs may be allocated directly, sequentially, or simultaneously. Direct allocation ignores allocation of service center costs to other service centers. In sequential allocation, the sequence of allocation is based on the benefit or service to other service centers. Simultaneous allocation uses simultaneous equations to insure that all service center costs are appropriately allocated to all other service centers benefiting from these costs.

As part of your summary, you should review the allocation process illustrated in this chapter for the Munson Appliance Company. Be sure you understand the concepts and procedures involved.

Nonmanufacturing entities may also allocate costs. The process is similar to that for manufacturing firms. For example, merchandising firms allocate general store costs to service departments. Service department costs are allocated to other service departments and to selling departments.

Cost allocation may provide useful information to both manufacturing firms and merchandising firms. However, allocated costs do not necessarily represent the actual costs that the cost center has incurred. Thus, cost allocation can often be misleading when the results are used as a basis for certain types of internal decisions.

Review Problem

Problem

Berrymade Manufacturing Company has prepared factory overhead budgets for 19X4, as shown below. It allocates general factory costs and service department costs sequentially in the order shown below, using a combined rate and using the bases indicated. Overhead rates for production departments are based on direct labor hours.

	Costs	Square Feet	CSH	KWH	DLH
General Factory Costs	$ 15,000	—	—	—	—
Custodial Department	30,000	4,000	—	—	—
Utilities Department	40,000	15,000	400	—	—
Assembly Department	20,000	30,000	1,600	40,000	15,000
Painting Department	16,000	26,000	2,000	60,000	12,000
Totals	$121,000	75,000	4,000	100,000	27,000

Required:

a. Allocate general factory costs and service department costs in the sequence shown above. That is, allocate general factory costs to each department; then allocate custodial department costs to the other departments, and so on. (Round the allocation rates to 3 decimal places and round allocated costs to the nearest dollar.)

b. Determine the factory overhead rate for each production department. (Round to 3 decimal places.)

c. Prepare calculations to prove that the overhead rates determined in part b will cover all factory overhead costs, assuming actual production equals expected production.

Solution

a. General factory costs are allocated as follows:

$$\text{Allocation Rate: } \frac{\$15,000}{75,000 \text{ Square Feet}} = \$.20 \text{ per Square Foot}$$

Custodial: 4,000 Square Feet × $.20 = $ 800
Utilities: 15,000 Square Feet × $.20 =   3,000
Assembly: 30,000 Square Feet × $.20 =   6,000
Painting: 26,000 Square Feet × $.20 =   5,200

Total Allocated Cost $15,000

In determining the custodial department rate, it is necessary to add the $800 of allocated general factory costs to the $30,000 of expected departmental costs. **Custodial department** costs are allocated as follows:

$$\text{Allocation Rate: } \frac{\$30,000 + \$800}{4,000 \text{ CSH}} = \frac{\$30,800}{4,000 \text{ CSH}} = \$7.70 \text{ per CSH}$$

Utilities: 400 CSH × $7.70 = $ 3,080
Assembly: 1,600 CSH × $7.70 =   12,320
Painting: 2,000 CSH × $7.70 =   15,400

Total Allocated Cost $30,800

Note that in this example, custodial department costs are allocated to the utilities department; whereas in the chapter illustration, utilities costs were allocated to the custodial department. This represents a management decision based on the amount of service provided by departments to each other.

As with the custodial department, the costs allocated to the utilities department must be included in calculating the overhead rate for the utilities department. **Utilities department** costs are allocated as follows:

$$\text{Allocation Rate: } \frac{\$40,000 + \$3,000 + \$3,080}{100,000 \text{ KWH}} = \frac{\$46,080}{100,000 \text{ KWH}} =$$
$$\$.461 \text{ per KWH}$$

Assembly: 40,000 KWH × $.461 = $18,440
Painting: 60,000 KWH × $.461 =   27,660

Total Allocated Cost $46,100[a]

[a]The $20 difference from the $46,080 above is caused by rounding.

b. We determine the overhead rate for each production department by adding previously allocated service department costs to the expected production department costs and dividing by the appropriate base—in this case, direct labor hours.

Assembly Department Overhead Rate: $\dfrac{\$20,000 + \$6,000 + \$12,320 + \$18,440}{15,000 \text{ DLH}}$

$$= \frac{\$56,760}{15,000 \text{ DLH}} = \$3.784 \text{ per DLH}$$

Painting Department Overhead Rate: $\dfrac{\$16,000 + \$5,200 + \$15,400 + \$27,660}{12,000 \text{ DLH}}$

$$= \frac{\$64,260}{12,000 \text{ DLH}} = \$5.355 \text{ per DLH}$$

c. Expected production is indicated by the expected direct labor hours for each production department. Expected factory overhead costs total $121,000. We determine total expected overhead to be applied by multiplying the overhead rate of each department by the expected direct labor hours. If the overhead rates are correct, total overhead expected to be applied should equal $121,000, the total budgeted overhead for the period. The calculation is as follows:

$$\text{Assembly: } 15,000 \text{ DLH} \times \$3.784 = \$\ 56,760$$
$$\text{Painting: } 12,000 \text{ DLH} \times \$5.355 = \underline{\quad 64,260}$$
$$\text{Total Overhead to Be Applied} \quad \underline{\underline{\$121,020^a}}$$

ᵃThe $20 difference from the budgeted $121,000 is caused by rounding.

The solution above, as well as the example of the Munson Appliance Company in the chapter, illustrated and described the allocation process in some detail in order to help you understand the process.

As a practical matter, the mechanics of cost allocation can be simplified by use of a worksheet. Although the procedures do not differ, all allocations are shown on one piece of paper; and the use of columns makes it easier to determine the total amount to be allocated by each segment.

The solution to parts a and b of this review problem are shown on a worksheet on the next page so that you can see how one is used. You may find a worksheet useful in solving problems at the end of the chapter.

Questions

14-1 Why is cost allocation needed?

14-2 Of what significance are CASB standards today?

14-3 Why do you suppose that the Cost Accounting Standards Board was created?

14-4 Define *cost objective.*

14-5 Distinguish between a final cost objective and an intermediate cost objective.

14-6 What is meant by *full costing?*

14-7 What is the difference between a direct cost and an indirect cost? Give an example of each.

14-8 What is meant by the *traceability* of a cost?

Berrymade Manufacturing Company
Cost Allocation Worksheet
for the Year Ended December 31, 19X4

	General Factory	Custodial	Utilities	Assembly	Painting	Total
Total Budgeted Overhead Costs	$15,000	$30,000	$40,000	$20,000	$16,000	$121,000

General Factory Costs
Allocation Rate:

$$\frac{\$15,000}{75,000 \text{ Square Feet}} = \$.20 \text{ per Square Ft.}$$

	General Factory	Custodial	Utilities	Assembly	Painting	Total
Allocated as Follows:	(15,000)					
Custodial: 4,000 Square Feet × $.20		800				
Utilities: 15,000 Square Feet × $.20			3,000			
Assembly: 30,000 Square Feet × $.20				6,000		
Painting: 26,000 Square Feet × $.20					5,200	

Custodial Department
Allocation Rate: $30,800

$$\frac{\$30,800}{4,000 \text{ CSH}} = \$7.70 \text{ per CSH}$$

	General Factory	Custodial	Utilities	Assembly	Painting	Total
Allocated as Follows:	(30,800)					
Utilities: 400 CSH × $7.70			3,080			
Assembly: 1,600 CSH × $7.70				12,320		
Painting: 2,000 CSH × $7.70					15,400	

Utilities Department
Allocation Rate: $46,080

$$\frac{\$46,080}{100,000 \text{ KWH}} = \$.461 \text{ per KWH}$$

	General Factory	Custodial	Utilities	Assembly	Painting	Total
Allocated as Follows:	(46,080)					
Assembly: 40,000 KWH × $.461				18,440		
Painting: 60,000 KWH × $.461					27,660	
Total Overhead Costs				$56,760	$64,260	$121,020[a]

Overhead Rate Calculated as Follows:

Assembly: $\dfrac{\$56,760}{15,000 \text{ DLH}} =$ $3.784 per DLH

Painting: $\dfrac{\$64,260}{12,000 \text{ DLH}} =$ $5.355 per DLH

[a]The $20 difference from the budgeted $121,000 is caused by rounding.

14-9 What is an indirect cost pool? Give an example.

14-10 How can the same cost be a direct cost of one cost objective but an indirect cost of another cost objective? Give an example.

14-11 "Direct costs are variable and indirect costs are fixed." Discuss the validity of this statement.

14-12 Name the basic classifications of indirect costs.

14-13 List, in order of preference, the bases that may be used for cost allocation.

14-14 How do direct allocation, simultaneous allocation, and sequential allocation differ?

14-15 Is cost allocation required for merchandising firms? Explain.

Exercises

14-16 Classifying Cost Objectives Indicate whether each item in the list below would be an intermediate cost objective or a final cost objective.
   a. Maintenance department of a factory.
   b. Cost of one model produced by an automobile manufacturer.
   c. Cost of 500 airplanes produced by a defense contractor.
   d. Custodial costs in a factory.
   e. Total cost of a sporting goods department for a department store.
   f. Costs of credit department of a department store.

14-17 Classifying Costs and Cost Objectives Indicate whether each item in the list below is a direct cost or an indirect cost to the intermediate cost objective and to the final cost objective. In some cases, the cost may not be applicable to either the intermediate or the final cost objective. Item a is shown as an example.

	Intermediate Cost Objective	Final Cost Objective
a. Plant guard's salary, to the security department.	Direct	Indirect
b. Glass used in manufacturing bottles.		
c. Salary of the vice-president of manufacturing, to the maintenance department.		
d. Sweeping compound, to the custodial department.		
e. Wages of sander in a furniture factory.		
f. Depreciation of fence around factory, to the utilities department.		

14-18 Classifying Costs Indicate which of the items below are considered direct costs and which are considered indirect costs of producing television sets. The company also produces other appliances.

a. Paint for the cabinets.

b. Glass over the picture tubes.

c. Depreciation of raw materials warehouse.

d. Glass for factory windows.

e. Tubes for TV sets.

f. Wages of individuals inserting tubes.

g. Free coffee for early morning shift of assembly line workers making TV sets.

h. Employer's share of FICA (social security taxes) paid on wages of custodial personnel.

14-19 Selecting Cost Allocation Bases The chapter listed the following as appropriate bases for allocating costs:

A. A measure of activity of the cost center.

B. A measure of output of the cost center.

C. An activity of the cost center receiving the service.

D. A basis of the entire activity being managed.

For each cost center listed below, select the activity listed on the right that should serve as the basis of allocation. Also, indicate which of the bases listed above is applicable to the activity selected. Some items may be used more than once; some may not be used at all. As an example, the correct answer to item a is:

a. Maintenance Department   7   C

Cost Center	**Activity**
a. Maintenance Department	**1.** Number of service-hours worked by the cost center providing the service.
b. Employees' Cafeteria	**2.** Number of employees in cost centers receiving the service.
c. Plant Security	**3.** Number of square feet in cost center receiving the service.
d. Custodial Department	**4.** Total cost of center receiving the service.
e. Stores Warehouse	**5.** Number of employees served from the center receiving the service.
f. First Aid Station	**6.** Kilowatt hours used by center receiving the service.
g. General Factory Costs	**7.** Machine hours used by center receiving the service.
h. Utilities Department	**8.** Number of service-hours worked in center receiving the service.
	9. Total number of direct labor hours worked in factory.
	10. Cost of raw materials used by centers receiving raw materials.

14-20 Calculating Allocation Rates For each of the service center costs shown below, determine the allocation rate. Consider each item independently.

	Costs	Allocation Basis
a. Utilities Department	$10,000	200,000 Kilowatt Hours
b. Factory Day Care Center	2,500	50 Children
c. Maintenance Department	25,000	7,500 Machine Hours
d. Custodial Department	40,000	250,000 Square Feet
e. Factory Superintendent's Office	30,000	$300,000 Total Factory Cost

14-21 Allocating Costs; Manufacturing Firm A company has 2 service departments and 2 producing departments. The budgeted costs to be allocated and the basis of allocation for the service departments are as follows:

	Costs	Allocation Basis
Service Department No. 1	$10,000	Square Feet
Service Department No. 2	40,000	Direct Labor Hours

Costs of Service Department No. 1 are allocated to Service Department No. 2 and to the producing departments. Costs of Service Department No. 2 are allocated to the producing departments. Information regarding square feet and direct labor hours is as follows:

	Square Feet	DLH
Service Department No. 2	10,000	—
Producing Department A	40,000	7,500
Producing Department B	50,000	13,000
Totals	100,000	20,500

Determine the amount of cost to be allocated to each department.

14-22 Allocating Costs; Department Store Diamond Department Store allocates its general store costs to the credit department, to "hard-line merchandise" (furniture, appliances, and the like), and to "soft-line merchandise" (clothing, kitchenwares, and the like) on the basis of square feet. Credit department costs are allocated to hard-line and soft-line merchandise on the basis of credit sales. Data for the store are as follows:

	Costs	Square Feet	Credit Sales
General Store Costs	$200,000	—	—
Credit Department	150,000	5,000	—
Hard-Line Merchandise	—	60,000	$350,000
Soft-Line Merchandise	—	35,000	150,000
Totals	$350,000	100,000	$500,000

Determine the amount of cost to be allocated to each department.

14-23 Allocating Costs; Manufacturing Firm Information regarding factory overhead costs and the basis for allocation for the Alaloc Company is shown below. The costs shown do not include allocated costs.

	Costs	KWH	CSH
Utilities	$ 5,000	—	—
Custodial	3,120	2,000	—
Melting	8,100	5,000	500
Molding	12,540	10,000	800
Finishing	10,930	8,000	900
Totals	$39,690	25,000	2,200

a. Allocate utilities costs to the other 4 departments.

b. Allocate custodial costs to the other 3 departments.

c. Determine the total costs of each production department after allocation of service department costs.

14-24 Allocating Costs; Manufacturing Firm In the situation below, general factory costs and service department costs (except custodial) of the Maknothing Company have already been allocated to the custodial department and the 2 producing departments. The company uses a combined allocation rate. Information regarding the allocated costs and the overhead costs expected to be incurred is as follows:

	Costs Already Allocated	Costs Expected to Be Incurred
Custodial	$18,500	$41,300
Shaping	27,000	46,000
Assembly	41,000	58,000

Custodial costs are allocated on the basis of square feet. The shaping department contains 38,000 square feet; the assembly department, 54,000 square feet. Budgeted direct labor hours are 24,000 hours for shaping and 35,000 hours for assembly.

a. Determine the allocation rate for the custodial department.

b. Determine the amount of custodial costs to be allocated to each producing department.

c. Determine the factory overhead rate for each producing department, using direct labor hours as the base. (Round to 3 decimal places.)

14-25 Allocating Costs; Manufacturing Firm; Variable and Fixed Allocation Rates In the situation below, general factory costs and service department costs (except maintenance) of the Makall Company have already been allocated to the maintenance department and the 2 producing departments. Information regarding the allocated costs and the overhead costs expected to be incurred is as follows:

	Costs Already Allocated		Budgeted Costs to Be Incurred	
	Variable	Fixed	Variable	Fixed
Maintenance	$15,000	$40,000	$35,000	$60,000
Molding	14,000	7,000	6,000	8,000
Finishing	20,000	12,000	15,000	13,000

Maintenance costs are allocated on the basis of machine hour usage. Budgeted machine hours for the molding department are 13,000 hours and for the finishing department, 27,000 hours. Budgeted direct labor hours are 10,000 hours for molding and 15,000 hours for finishing.

a. Determine the variable and fixed allocation rates for the maintenance department.

b. Determine the amount of maintenance costs to be allocated to each producing department.

c. Determine the variable and fixed factory overhead rates for each producing department, using direct labor hours as the base. (Round to 3 decimal places.)

Problems

14-26 Allocating Costs; Manufacturing Firm The Allo Kate Company has prepared factory overhead budgets for 19X1 as shown below. The firm allocates general factory costs and service department costs sequentially in the order shown below, using a combined rate and the bases indicated. The production departments' overhead rates are based on direct labor hours.

	Costs	Square Feet	CSH	Machine Hours	DLH
General Factory Costs	$ 12,000	—	—	—	—
Custodial Department	20,000	3,000	—	—	—
Maintenance Department	35,000	8,000	500	—	—
Production Department 1	18,000	15,000	2,100	3,000	12,500
Production Department 2	22,000	22,000	3,500	3,600	16,800
Totals	$107,000	48,000	6,100	6,600	29,300

(combined, DLH — handwritten notes)

Required:

a. Allocate general factory costs and service department costs in the sequence shown above. (Round the allocation rates to 3 decimal places and round allocated costs to the nearest dollar.)

b. Determine the factory overhead rate for each production department. (Round to 3 decimal places.)

14-27 Allocating Costs; Manufacturing Firm; Variable and Fixed Allocation Rates The Koolkat Corporation has prepared factory overhead budgets for 19X1 as follows:

	Variable	Fixed
General Factory Costs	—	$10,000
Plant Security	—	15,000
Utilities Department	$19,000	25,000
Production Department 1	5,000	10,000
Production Department 2	6,000	8,000
Totals	$30,000	$68,000

The firm allocates overhead costs sequentially, using a variable and a fixed rate, as appropriate, in the order shown above. The bases used for the service departments' allocation and for determining the production departments' overhead rates are shown below. Note that general factory costs are allocated on the basis of total department costs.

	Total Department Costs	Square Feet	KWH	DLH
General Factory Costs	—	—	—	—
Plant Security	$15,000	—	—	—
Utilities Department	44,000	10,000	—	—
Production Department 1	80,000	22,000	60,000	25,000
Production Department 2	61,000	18,000	45,000	18,500
Totals	$200,000	50,000	105,000	43,500

Required:

a. Allocate general factory costs and service department costs in the sequence shown above. (Round allocation rates to 3 decimal places and round allocated costs to the nearest dollar.)

b. Determine the variable and fixed factory overhead rates for each production department. (Round to 3 decimal places.)

14-28 Allocating Costs; Applying Factory Overhead to Job Caufield Corporation has prepared factory overhead budgets for 19X5 as shown below. The bases for service department allocation and for production department overhead rate determination are also shown.

	Costs	Square Feet	CSH	Machine Hours	DLH
General Factory Costs	$20,000	—	—	—	—
Custodial Department	28,000	5,000	—	—	—
Maintenance Department	40,000	10,000	500	—	—
Assembly Department	65,000	20,000	2,500	6,000	30,000
Finishing Department	110,000	15,000	2,000	4,000	45,000
Totals	$263,000	50,000	5,000	10,000	75,000

The firm allocates overhead costs sequentially, using a combined rate, in the order shown above. It uses a job order cost system. During January, the company began Job No. 81-1 and incurred the following direct costs in the assembly department:

Direct Material	$800
Direct Labor (60 DLH)	400

Required:

a. Allocate general factory costs and service department costs in the sequence shown above.

b. Determine the factory overhead rate for each production department. (Round to 3 decimal places.)

c. Determine the amount of factory overhead to be applied to Job No. 81–1 in the assembly department for January.

14-29 Allocating Costs; Process Cost System; Variable and Fixed Allocation Rates Beautiflo Products Company uses a process cost system in the manufacture of its beauty lotions. For 19X9, factory overhead costs of all service departments have already been allocated, except for the maintenance department. The company uses both variable and fixed overhead allocation rates. Information regarding the allocated costs and overhead costs expected to be incurred is as follows: *used to determine rates*

	Costs Already Allocated		Costs Expected to Be Incurred	
	Variable	**Fixed**	**Variable**	**Fixed**
M/C Hrs Maintenance	$ 5,000	$ 9,000	$11,500	$12,000
Blending	27,000	22,300	4,700	3,500
Finishing	29,400	27,800	2,900	4,400

Maintenance costs are allocated on the basis of machine hours. Factory overhead rates of the production departments are based on the direct labor cost they incur. The budget for these items is as follows:

	Blending	**Finishing**	**Total**
Machine Hours:	2,000	8,000	10,000
Direct Labor Cost	$250,000	$175,000	$425,000

During January, the production departments incurred the following direct labor costs for the number of equivalent units shown below:

	Blending		**Finishing**	
	Cost	**E.U.**	**Cost**	**E.U.**
Direct Material	$40,000	2,500	$60,000	4,000
Direct Labor	25,000	1,500	32,000	1,200

Required:
   a. Allocate maintenance department costs to each production department.
   b. Determine the variable and fixed overhead rates for each production department. *DLC*
   c. Determine the amount of factory overhead applied to each department in January.
   d. In January, 1,000 units were transferred from the blending department to the finishing department. Assuming that the number of equivalent units is the same for factory overhead as it is for direct labor, determine the total cost of units transferred to the finishing department in January. (Round unit costs to 3 decimal places.)

14-30 Allocating Costs; Department Store Debbie's Department Store allocates its general store costs to all departments; it allocates the costs of its service departments, personnel and credit, to the 2 selling departments, clothing and furniture. The budgeted costs for next year, along with the allocation bases, are shown below:

	Costs	Square Feet	Number of Employees	Amount of Credit Sales
General Store Costs	$35,000	—	—	—
Personnel Department	20,000	800	—	—
Credit Department	33,500	1,200	20	—
Clothing Department	—	10,000	25	$240,000
Furniture Department	—	16,000	15	600,000
Totals	$88,500	28,000	60	$840,000

Required:

a. Allocate general store costs and service department costs in the sequence shown above.

b. Determine the total amount of cost allocated to each selling department.

14–31 Allocating Costs Based on Sales Triproducts Appliance Company manufactures toasters, electric mixers, and electric can openers. There is considerable competition among the managers of these divisions. In 19X3, divisional results were as follows:

	Division		
	Toaster	Mixer	Can Opener
Sales	$200,000	$300,000	$300,000
Variable Costs	120,000	180,000	180,000
Contribution Margin	$ 80,000	$120,000	$120,000
Fixed Costs	40,000	55,000	55,000
Net Income	$ 40,000	$ 65,000	$ 65,000

Each division incurred fixed costs of $10,000, which were direct costs of the division. All other fixed costs of the company were accumulated in an indirect cost pool and allocated to each division on the basis of sales. There were no beginning or ending inventories.

In 19X4, the manager of the toaster division launched an aggressive advertising campaign and doubled sales. Managers of the other divisions, satisfied with their 19X3 results, did nothing differently. Their sales fell by $100,000. The 19X4 results were as follows:

	Division		
	Toaster	Mixer	Can Opener
Sales	$400,000	$200,000	$200,000
Variable Costs	240,000	120,000	120,000
Contribution Margin	$160,000	$ 80,000	$ 80,000
Fixed Costs	135,000	40,000	40,000
Net Income	$ 25,000	$ 40,000	$ 40,000

The manager of the toaster division is furious over the results. He recognizes that the increased advertising cost of $65,000 increased the fixed costs;

but this increase was more than offset by the $80,000 increase in contribution margin. There were no other increases in direct fixed costs for any division or in indirect fixed costs for the company. There were no beginning or ending inventories.

You have been asked to explain what happened.

Required:

   a. Determine the amount of indirect fixed costs allocated to all divisions.

   b. Show how indirect fixed costs were allocated to each division in 19X3.

   c. Show how indirect fixed costs were allocated to each division in 19X4.

   d. Prepare calculations that show why the net income of the toaster division declined by $15,000.

   e. Does the manager of the toaster division have a good reason to be upset over the 19X4 results? Explain.

14-32 Allocating Costs; Manufacturing Firm; Variable and Fixed Allocation Rates Sasnakra Corporation has budgeted its factory indirect costs for 19X2 as follows:

	Variable	Fixed	Total
General Factory Costs	$ 25,000	$175,000	$200,000
Service Center Costs:			
Custodial	$ 20,000	$ 62,000	$ 82,000
Maintenance	80,000	180,000	260,000
Materials Handling	30,000	70,000	100,000
Total Service Center Costs	$130,000	$312,000	$442,000
Production Center Costs:			
Shaping	$ 20,000	$ 40,000	$ 60,000
Welding	35,000	90,000	125,000
Finishing	45,000	60,000	105,000
Total Production Center Costs	$100,000	$190,000	$290,000
Total Indirect Costs	$255,000	$677,000	$932,000

The basis for allocation and overhead rate determination is shown below:

	Square Feet	CSH	Machine Hours	Tons Handled	DLH
General Factory Costs	—	—	—	—	—
Service Centers:					
Custodial	5,000	—	—	—	—
Maintenance	12,000	800	—	—	—
Materials Handling	6,000	200	2,000	—	—
Production Centers:					
Shaping	34,000	1,400	13,000	10,500	22,000
Welding	42,000	2,000	15,000	14,000	28,000
Finishing	26,000	1,600	10,000	18,000	24,000
Totals	125,000	6,000	40,000	42,500	74,000

Costs are allocated in the sequence shown. The variable and fixed general factory costs and custodial costs are combined and allocated at a fixed rate only. Maintenance costs and materials-handling costs are allocated at both a variable rate and a fixed rate. Machine hours for materials handling represent the number of hours the various materials-handling machines (such as fork lifts) are run.

Required:

  a. Allocate general factory costs and service center costs in the sequence shown above. (Round allocation rates to 3 decimal places and round allocated costs to the nearest dollar.)

  b. Determine the variable and fixed factory overhead rates for each production center. (Round to 3 decimal places.)

14–33 Allocating Hospital Costs; Variable and Fixed Allocation Rates Mendenheel Hospital has 3 service centers—Security, Custodial, and Food Service. In addition, the hospital incurs other general costs, such as utilities, administrative salaries, and other administrative costs. These costs are accumulated in an indirect cost pool called General Hospital Costs.

  There are 5 basic revenue centers—Cafeteria, Pharmacy, X-ray, Laboratory, and Patient Care. Patient Care includes such items as surgery, emergency room, and hospital convalescence. (The hospital maintains records of revenue and costs for each category of Patient Care; but this problem is limited to the major classification.)

  Food Service provides meals to the cafeteria (where customers pay for them) and to Patient Care (which includes their cost as part of the room cost).

  The budget of costs for 19X6 and the bases for allocation are shown below. The budgeted amounts for the revenue centers are the direct costs of the centers.

	Costs		Basis		
	Variable	Fixed	Square Feet	CSH	Meals Served
General Hospital Costs	$150,000	$200,000	—	—	—
Security	—	61,000	3,000	—	—
Custodial	30,000	120,000	4,000	—	—
Food Service	231,000	150,000	10,000	3,000	—
Cafeteria	—	—	12,000	3,600	20,000
Pharmacy	—	—	2,000	600	—
X-Ray	—	—	4,000	1,200	—
Laboratory	—	—	5,000	1,600	—
Patient Care	—	—	100,000	30,000	190,000
Totals	$411,000	$531,000	140,000	40,000	210,000

General Hospital Costs are allocated to all service centers and revenue centers. Service center costs are allocated sequentially in the order shown above, except that Food Service costs are allocated only to Cafeteria and to Patient Care. Both General Hospital Costs and Security costs are allocated on the basis of square feet.

  Food Service costs are allocated at both a variable rate and a fixed rate. All other costs are combined and allocated at a fixed rate only.

Required:

   a. Allocate General Hospital Costs and service center costs in the sequence shown above. (Round to 3 decimal places.)

   b. Determine the total amount of cost allocated to each revenue center.

   c. Assume that the hospital budgets direct variable costs of $171,000 and direct fixed costs of $240,000 for x-ray services. The hospital expects that 18,000 x-rays will be taken. Assuming the hospital is not trying to make a profit, determine the amount that patients will probably be charged for each x-ray.

14-34 Calculating Promotion Department Costs The promotion department of the Doxolby Company is responsible for the design and development of all promotional materials for the corporation, including all promotional campaigns and related literature, pamphlets, and brochures. Top management is reviewing the effectiveness of the promotion department to determine if the department's activities could be managed better and more economically by an outside promotion agency. As a part of this review, top management has asked for a summary of the promotion department's costs for the most recent year. The following cost summary was supplied:

Promotion Department
Costs for the Year Ended November 30, 19X8

Direct Department Costs	$257,500
Charges from Other Departments	44,700
Allocated Share of General Administrative Overhead	22,250
Total Costs	$324,450

The direct department costs consist of costs that can be traced directly to the activities of the promotion department, such as supplies, staff and clerical salaries and related employee benefits, and so on. The charges from other departments represent the costs of services provided by other departments of Doxolby at the request of the promotion department. The company has developed a charging system for such interdepartmental uses of services. For instance, the in-house printing department charges the promotion department for the promotional literature printed. All such services provided to the promotion department by other departments of Doxolby are included in charges from other departments. General administrative overhead comprises such costs as top management salaries and benefits, depreciation, heat, insurance, property taxes, and the like. These costs are allocated to all departments in proportion to their number of employees.

Required:

   Discuss the usefulness of the cost figures as presented for the promotion department as a basis for comparison with a bid from an outside agency to provide the same type of activities. (CMA adapted)

14-35 Allocating Hospital Costs The administrator of Wright Hospital has presented you with a number of service projections for the year ending June 30, 19X2. Estimated room requirements for inpatients by type of service are:

Type of Patient	Total Patients Expected	Average Number of Days in Hospital		Percent of Regular Patients Selecting Types of Service		
		Regular	Medicare	Private	Semiprivate	Ward
Medical	2,100	7	17	10%	60%	30%
Surgical	2,400	10	15	15%	75%	10%

Of the patients served by the hospital, 10% are expected to be Medicare patients, all of whom are expected to select semiprivate rooms. Both the number and proportion of Medicare patients have increased over the past 5 years. Daily rentals per patient are: $40 for a private room, $35 for a semi-private room, and $25 for a ward.

Operating room charges are based on personnel-minutes (number of minutes the operating room is in use multiplied by number of personnel assisting in the operation). Charges are $.13 per personnel-minute for inpatients and $.22 for outpatients. Studies for the current year show that operations on inpatients are divided as follows:

Type of Operation	Number of Operations	Average Number of Minutes per Operation	Average Number of Personnel Required
A	800	30	4
B	700	45	5
C	300	90	6
D	200	120	8
	2,000		

The same proportion of inpatient operations is expected for the next fiscal year, and 180 outpatients are expected to use the operating room. Outpatient operations average 20 minutes in length and require the assistance of 3 persons.

The budget for the year ending June 20, 19X2, by departments, is:

General Services:		
Maintenance of Plant	$	50,000
Operation of Plant		27,500
Administration		97,500
All Others		192,000
Revenue-Producing Services:		
Operating Room		68,440
All Others		700,000
		$1,135,440

The following information is provided for cost allocation purposes:

	Square Feet	Salaries
General Services:		
Maintenance of Plant	12,000	$ 40,000
Operation of Plant	28,000	25,000
Administration	10,000	55,000
All Others	36,250	102,500
Revenue-Producing Services:		
Operating Room	17,500	15,000
All Others	86,250	302,500
	190,000	$540,000

Basis of Allocations:
   Maintenance of Plant—Salaries
   Operation of Plant—Square Feet
   Administration—Salaries
   All Others—8% to Operating Room;
      92% to All Other Revenue
      Producing Services

Required:
   Prepare schedules showing the computation of the following:
   a. The number of patient-days (number of patients multiplied by average stay in hospital) expected by type of patients and service.
   b. The total number of personnel-minutes expected for operating room services for inpatients and outpatients. For inpatients, show the breakdown of total operating room personnel-minutes by type of operation.
   c. Expected gross revenue from routine services.
   d. Expected gross revenue from operating room services.
   e. Cost per personnel-minute for operating room services, assuming that the total personnel-minutes computed in part b is 800,000 and that the step-down (sequential) method of cost allocation is used (that is, costs of the general services departments are allocated in sequence first to the general services departments that they serve and then to the revenue producing departments). (AICPA adapted)

Part Five

Special Topics

Chapter 15   Statement of Changes in Financial Position

Learning Objectives

The purpose of this chapter is to describe and illustrate the statement of changes in financial position. The chapter shows how the statement is used to explain the sources and uses of working capital. Studying this chapter will enable you to:

1. Describe the nature and purpose of the statement of changes in financial position.
2. Calculate and explain increases and decreases in working capital.
3. Prepare a schedule of changes in working capital.
4. Describe the sources and uses of working capital.
5. Describe significant changes that do not affect working capital.
6. Prepare a statement of changes in financial position using the working capital approach.
7. Prepare a statement of changes in financial position using the cash approach.

Chapter Topics

The major topics included in this chapter are:

Nature and Purpose of Statement of Changes in Financial Position
Increases and Decreases in Working Capital
Sources of Working Capital
Uses of Working Capital
Significant Changes Not Affecting Working Capital
Preparation of the Statement of Changes in Financial Position
Relationship of the Statement of Changes in Financial Position to the Balance Sheet
Cash Approach

The **statement of changes in financial position** is an external financial statement that describes changes in balance sheet items between two balance sheet dates in terms of working capital. Although the income statement and the balance sheet are the two most commonly known external financial statements, the statement of changes in financial position is also a primary external statement. Firms presenting their statements in conformity with generally accepted accounting principles must present a statement of changes in financial position. Generally, financial analysts consider this statement of equal importance with the income statement and the balance sheet, because it indicates where working capital came from during the year and how it was used.

Nature and Purpose of Statement of Changes in Financial Position

Description

As mentioned above, in order for firms to present their financial statements in conformity with generally accepted accounting principles, they must present a statement of changes in financial position. *APB Opinion No. 19* requires that the statement disclose all important aspects of financing and investing activities of the firm.[1] Several approaches may be used to report the financing and investing activities of a firm on the statement of changes in financial position. This chapter illustrates the working capital approach and the cash approach.

Although the preferred title is the statement of changes in financial position, the statement is still referred to by other terms, such as the *statement of source and application of working capital; statement of source and application of funds;* or, more simply, *funds statement.*

The statement of changes in financial position is important because it shows where working capital came from and where it went. In fact, it is sometimes referred to informally as the "where got and where gone" statement. **Working capital** is the difference between current assets and current liabilities. It represents the excess of current assets available to carry on the day-to-day operations of the business. Working capital is an important element of business operations, because without adequate working capital, a firm will soon go out of business. Because working capital is the life-blood of a business, the analyst is interested in this statement.

Illustration

To provide a frame of reference, Exhibit 15.1 shows an example of a statement of changes in financial position.

At this point, do not be concerned with the details of the statement; they will be explained later in the chapter. Rather, concentrate on the type of information the statement provides. Remembering the importance of working capital to a firm, notice that the statement shows that working capital for Gild Company has increased by $44,000 during 19X2. It also shows why it has increased. Specifically, operations provided $37,000 of working capital. The sale of equipment, a mortgage, and the issuance of common stock provided another $92,000. The firm used working capital totaling $85,000 to purchase land, retire bonds, and declare dividends. The difference between the sources of working capital, $129,000, and the uses of working capital, $85,000, is an increase in working capital, $44,000.

---

[1] *Reporting Changes in Financial Position: Opinions of the Accounting Principles Board, 19* (New York: American Institute of Certified Public Accountants, 1971), para. 8.

Exhibit 15.1 Statement of Changes in Financial Position

Gild Company
Statement of Changes in Financial Position
for the Year Ended December 31, 19X2

Sources of Working Capital:			
Operations:			
Net Income (as Reported)		$27,000	
Adjustments for Items Not Providing or Using Working Capital:			
Depreciation.	$12,000		
Gain on Sale of Equipment	(2,000)	10,000	
Working Capital Provided by Operations			$ 37,000
Other Sources:			
Sale of Equipment		$15,000	
Mortgage for Land Purchase		50,000	
Issuance of Common Stock		27,000	
Working Capital Provided by Other Sources. .			92,000
Total Working Capital Provided			$129,000
Uses of Working Capital:			
Purchase of Land		$50,000	
Retirement of Bonds		30,000	
Declaration of Dividends		5,000	
Total Working Capital Used			85,000
Increase in Working Capital			$ 44,000

Schedule of Changes in Working Capital

	19X2	19X1	Increase (Decrease) in Working Capital
Current Assets:			
Cash	$ 22,000	$ 14,000	$ 8,000
Accounts Receivable (Net)	126,000	155,000	(29,000)
Inventory	185,000	133,000	52,000
Prepaid Expenses	12,000	13,000	(1,000)
Totals	$345,000	$315,000	$ 30,000
Current Liabilities:			
Accounts Payable	$140,000	$160,000	$ 20,000
Accrued Liabilities	16,000	10,000	(6,000)
Totals	$156,000	$170,000	$ 14,000
Working Capital	$189,000	$145,000	$ 44,000

The **schedule of changes in working capital,** shown at the bottom of the exhibit, is an integral part of the statement of changes in financial position. It shows specific changes in the working capital items (current assets and current liabilities). Again, the details of this schedule will be described later.

Consider the difference in the types of information provided by the statement of changes in financial position, the income statement, and the balance sheet. The income statement summarizes revenue and expenses for the period and shows the resultant net income or net loss. The balance sheet shows the firm's financial position at a point in time in terms of assets, liabilities, and owners' equity. But neither the income statement nor the balance sheet provides details concerning working capital nor explains changes that have taken place in the balance sheet items. This information is provided by the statement of changes in financial position. The remainder of the chapter will explain the details of the statement of changes in financial position and provide a step-by-step illustration of its preparation.

Increases and Decreases in Working Capital

The schedule of changes in working capital in Exhibit 15.1 shows that Gild Company has six working capital items. Current assets include four items: cash, accounts receivable, inventory, and prepaid expenses. Current liabilities include two items: accounts payable and accrued liabilities. The schedule shows the increase or decrease in working capital resulting from the change in each item. It is important to understand how changes in current assets and current liabilities result in increases and decreases in working capital.

Working capital is the difference between current assets and current liabilities. The total increase in working capital for Gild Company between 19X1 and 19X2 is $44,000, calculated as follows:

	19X2	19X1	Increase in Working Capital
Current Assets	$345,000	$315,000	
Current Liabilities	156,000	170,000	
Working Capital	$189,000	$145,000	$44,000

The firm wants to know the specific increases and decreases in the working capital items that resulted in the $44,000 increase in working capital. At this point, it is important to understand the effect on working capital of an increase or decrease in a working capital item. These effects are as follows:

1. An increase in a current asset results in an increase in working capital.
2. A decrease in a current asset results in a decrease in working capital.
3. An increase in a current liability results in a decrease in working capital.
4. A decrease in a current liability results in an increase in working capital.

The first two items are probably easy to understand, since working capital is the difference between the current assets and current liabilities. Increases in current assets would naturally increase working capital, and decreases would decrease working capital. You may need to study items 3 and 4 a little more to be sure you understand why they are valid. Increases in current liabilities result in decreases in working capital because an increase in a current liability reduces the amount of current assets available for day-to-day operations. For example, assume that a firm's current assets total $100,000 and its current liabilities total $60,000. Working capital is $40,000, as shown below:

Current Assets	$100,000
Current Liabilities	60,000
Working Capital	$ 40,000

Now, assume that current assets remain the same but current liabilities increase to $75,000. Working capital is now $25,000, as shown below:

Current Assets	$100,000
Current Liabilities	75,000
Working Capital	$ 25,000

A decrease in current liabilities has the opposite effect—that is, it increases working capital because a smaller amount is being deducted from current assets.

Sources of Working Capital

Any financial activity that results in an increase in current assets or a decrease in current liabilities is a **source of working capital.** When the statement of changes in financial position shows sources of working capital, it is showing where working capital came from during the current period. We say that these activities *provide* working capital. The four most common sources of working capital are:
1. Operations.
2. Sale of noncurrent assets.
3. Long-term borrowing.
4. Issuance of stock.

Operations

A primary source of working capital for most businesses is operations. Selling merchandise or providing services increases working capital because it results in increases in cash and accounts receivable. Operations uses working capital in the form of expenses. Paying expenses with cash and creating current liabilities result in decreases in working capital. Therefore, the net income of a firm—the difference between revenue and expenses—summarizes many individual changes in working capital during the period and represents a major source of working capital. Note in Exhibit 15.1 that operations provided Gild Company $37,000 of working capital.

The net income figure alone, however, is usually not the amount of working capital resulting from operations. Normally, adjustments must be made for items included on the income statement that were deductions from revenue but that did not use working capital and for items included as revenue that did not provide working capital. Such items include depreciation, gain or loss on sale of assets, amortization of intangible assets, and amortization of bond discount or premium.

To illustrate, consider the following simplified income statement:

Sales	$ 50,000
Expenses (Other Than Depreciation)	(40,000)
Depreciation Expense	(4,000)
Net Income	$ 6,000

Net income is $6,000. However, depreciation expense uses neither cash nor any other form of working capital and therefore should not be deducted from sales in arriving at working capital provided by operations. Working capital provided by operations is really the difference between sales and cash expenses. In the example, this amount is $10,000 ($50,000 − $40,000). It would be possible to determine the working capital provided by operations by subtracting all the working-capital expenses on the income statement from all revenue that provided working capital; but this procedure would be cumbersome and time consuming. The common practice to determine working capital provided by operations is to add back to net income those items deducted in arriving at net income that did not use working capital. In this case, that would be the $4,000 depreciation expense. Thus, in this illustration, working capital provided by operations is $10,000—net income of $6,000 plus depreciation expense of $4,000.

It is important to realize that depreciation does *not* provide working capital. It is added back solely because, although it was subtracted in arriving at net income, it did not use working capital.

Some items of revenue do not provide working capital. Consider the following example:

Sales	$80,000
Gain on Sale of Truck	2,000
Total Revenue	$82,000
Expenses (Including $4,000 Depreciation)	65,000
Net Income	$17,000

In this case, depreciation requires an adjustment to net income, as before. In addition, the firm has reported a gain of $2,000 on the sale of the truck. Let's look at how that gain was determined.

Selling Price of Truck	$5,000
Book Value of Truck	3,000
Gain on Sale	$2,000

The $2,000 gain is the difference between the $5,000 selling price and the $3,000 book value. Note that the sale of the truck provided $5,000 of working capital. This will be shown in another section on the statement of changes in financial position. The gain itself, however, does not provide working capital. However, the $17,000 net income includes this $2,000 gain. Since our objective is to determine the amount of working capital provided by operations, we must subtract the $2,000 gain from net income as an adjustment. To determine working capital provided by operations in this example, we adjust net income for depreciation expense and for the gain on the sale of the truck as follows:

Net Income (as Reported)		$17,000
Adjustments for Items Not Providing or Using Working Capital:		
Depreciation	$ 4,000	
Gain on Sale of Truck	(2,000)	2,000
Working Capital Provided by Operations		$19,000

In this case, working capital provided by operations is $19,000. As before, it would be possible to reconstruct the income statement showing only revenue items that provided working capital and deducting only items that used working capital. But the process shown above is more practical.

Sale of Noncurrent Assets

The sale of noncurrent assets also provides working capital. For example, in the previous illustration, the sale of the truck for $5,000 cash provided $5,000 working capital. The sale of equipment by Gild Company (Exhibit 15.1) provided $15,000 of working capital.

It is important to note that working capital is provided from the sale of a noncurrent asset regardless of whether a gain or loss results from the sale. In the previous illustration, the truck's sale resulted in a gain of $2,000. The $2,000 gain was not what provided working capital, however; the sale for $5,000 provided working capital. The gain was included in revenue and was subtracted from net income in arriving at working capital provided by operations.

If an asset is sold at a loss, working capital is still provided by the sale. For example, assume the following situation:

Sale of Equipment	$ 2,500
Book Value	4,000
Loss on Sale	$(1,500)

In this illustration, the sale of equipment provided $2,500 working capital; therefore, it is a source of working capital. The loss on the sale did not provide or use working capital. However, the loss is subtracted from revenue in arriving at net income for the period. It represents an expense that did not use working capital. Therefore, the loss should be added back to net income as an adjustment in the operations section of the statement of changes in financial position, similar to depreciation.

Long-Term Borrowing

The issuance of long-term debt is a source of working capital. Sometimes firms borrow to improve their working capital positions. They find it advantageous to incur long-term obligations in order to increase the amount of working capital available for current needs.

Issuance of Stock

Another major source of working capital is the issuance of stock, either common or preferred. Note in Exhibit 15.1 that Gild Company issued common stock for $27,000. On the statement of changes in financial position, it does not matter whether the stock is issued for par or more than par. Recording the issuance of stock in the accounts requires a separation between par value and paid-in capital in excess of par. But on the statement of changes of financial position, the entire amount received from the sale of stock is shown as a source of working capital.

Uses of Working Capital

The statement of changes in financial position shows how working capital was used during the period. Any financial activity that results in a decrease in current assets or an increase in current liabilities is a **use of working capital.** Uses of working capital are sometimes called **applications** of working capital. The five primary uses of working capital are:
1. Loss from operations.
2. Purchase of noncurrent assets.
3. Payment of long-term debt.
4. Retirement of stock.
5. Declaration of cash dividends.

Loss from Operations

Normal business operations are conducted in the hope that a profit will be made. In most instances, revenue exceeds expenses. Net income, with adjustment for the non-working-capital items, is a major source of working capital. However, if a firm incurs a net loss, then working capital has been used in operations rather than provided by operations. A loss means that expenses, which use working capital, have exceeded revenue, which provides working capital. The net loss, therefore, represents a use of working capital. However, just as net income must be adjusted for non-working-capital items, so also must a net loss be. Consider the following illustration:

Sales	$ 60,000
Expenses (Including $8,000 Depreciation)	74,000
Net Loss	$(14,000)

In this case, the firm has lost $14,000. However, expenses include $8,000 of depreciation, which did not use working capital. Therefore, the net loss must be adjusted to determine the amount of working capital used for operations. This is done as follows:

Net Loss	$(14,000)
Adjustments for Items not Providing or Using Working Capital:	
Depreciation	8,000
Working Capital Used for Operations	$ (6,000)

After the depreciation adjustment, working capital used for operations is $6,000, rather than the net loss of $14,000.

Purchase of Noncurrent Assets

When noncurrent assets are purchased, working capital is used. This major use of working capital must be reflected on the statement of changes in financial position.

**Payment of
Long-Term Debt**

When a firm makes payments on its long-term debt or retires long-term debt, it is using working capital. Note that Gild Company used $30,000 to retire bonds (Exhibit 15.1).

Retirement of Stock

Another use of working capital is the retirement of stock. When a firm retires common or preferred stock, it pays cash to the stockholders whose stock is being retired. This reduces working capital. The purchase of treasury stock, while technically not a retirement, is nevertheless a use of working capital as well.

**Declaration of
Cash Dividends**

Declaration of cash dividends uses working capital because it increases current liabilities. Notice that working capital is reduced when a cash dividend is declared, not when it is paid. The payment of dividends is not a use of working capital, but rather a change in the working capital items—that is, a decrease in cash and a decrease in current liabilities. Gild Company declared dividends totaling $5,000 in 19X2; this is shown as a use of working capital in Exhibit 15.1.

Significant Changes Not Affecting Working Capital

The statement of changes in financial position should show all important aspects of financing and investing activities that have occurred during the period. We have described transactions that provide or use working capital. However, there are often transactions that do not, by themselves, increase or decrease working capital. Nevertheless, they represent significant financing or investing activities and, as such, should be shown on the statement of changes in financial position. Several types of such transactions are described below. The list is not all-inclusive.

One such transaction is the *purchase of an asset by incurrence of long-term debt*. For example, assume that a firm purchases equipment and signs a long-term note. Technically, there has been no change in working capital. However, for the purposes of the statement of changes in financial position, we assume the firm issued the note for cash and then used cash to purchase equipment. Thus, on the statement of changes in financial position, the firm will show the issuance of the note as a source of working capital and the purchase of equipment as a use of working capital. This is what Gild Company did; it purchased land by issuing a mortgage note (Exhibit 15.1).

Another such activity is the *sale of an asset for which a long-term note rather than cash is received*. In this case, the firm would show the sale of the asset of a source of working capital and the investment in the note as a use of working capital.

A third significant change not affecting working capital is the *issuance of debt for the retirement of debt*. For example, when bonds become due, a firm may issue additional bonds, using the proceeds to pay off the old bonds. It may also exchange new bonds for old bonds. In either case, the issuance of new debt is shown as a source of working capital and the retirement of old debt is shown as a use of working capital.

Another such transaction is the *purchase of an asset by issuance of stock*. For example, a firm might make an investment by buying a substantial amount of another firm's stock. If the firm makes this investment by issuing stock, the issuance of stock represents a source of working capital; and the investment in the other firm is a use of working capital.

Stock dividends also do not affect working capital. The declaration of such dividends is considered to be merely a change from one stockholders' equity account to another. Therefore, stock dividends are not shown on the statement of changes in financial position.

Preparation of the Statement of Changes in Financial Position

The previous sections illustrated the statement of changes in financial position for the Gild Company and described the type of information shown on the statement. This section will illustrate the procedures Gild Company used to prepare this statement. There are four steps, as follows:

1. Prepare comparative balance sheets.
2. Prepare the schedule of changes in working capital.
3. Analyze data in ledger accounts and journal entries.
4. Prepare the statement of changes in financial position.

Comparative Balance Sheets (Step 1)

The balance sheet is sometimes called the *statement of financial position*. It shows only the amounts for assets, liabilities, and owners' equity as of a specific date. The statement of changes in financial position relates directly to the balance sheet, because it describes how the balance sheet amounts have changed since the last balance sheet date. The purpose of the statement of changes in financial position is to illustrate what changes have taken place in the noncurrent balance sheet items and to describe these changes in terms of working capital.

The first step is to prepare comparative balance sheets and to show the dollar difference in each balance sheet item as an increase or decrease. Comparative balance sheets for Gild Company for the past two years, as well as the income statement for the most recent year, are presented in Exhibits 15.2 and 15.3.

Schedule of Changes in Working Capital (Step 2)

The schedule of changes in working capital is an integral part of the statement of changes in financial position. However, as a practical matter, the firm may prepare it before it prepares the formal statement used for external reporting purposes. The schedule shows the increase or decrease in working capital resulting from the change in each working capital item. Gild Company's schedule was shown in Exhibit 15.1 but for convenience of discussion is shown again in Exhibit 15.4.

The exhibit shows that working capital increased as a result of increases in cash and inventory and decreases in accounts payable. Working capital decreased because of decreases in accounts receivable and prepaid expenses and increases in accrued liabilities. The net effect of the increases and de-

Exhibit 15.2 Comparative Balance Sheets

Gild Company
Balance Sheets
December 31, 19X2 and 19X1

	19X2	19X1	Increase (Decrease)
Current Assets:			
Cash.	$ 22,000	$ 14,000	$ 8,000
Accounts Receivable (Net)	126,000	155,000	(29,000)
Inventory.	185,000	133,000	52,000
Prepaid Expenses	12,000	13,000	(1,000)
Total Current Assets	$345,000	$315,000	$ 30,000
Property, Plant, and Equipment:			
Land.	$200,000	$150,000	$ 50,000
Plant and Equipment (Net).	175,000	200,000	(25,000)
Total Property, Plant, and Equipment	$375,000	$350,000	$ 25,000
Total Assets.	$720,000	$665,000	$ 55,000
Current Liabilities:			
Accounts Payable	$140,000	$160,000	$(20,000)
Accrued Liabilities	16,000	10,000	6,000
Total Current Liabilities	$156,000	$170,000	$(14,000)
Long-Term Debt:			
12% Bonds Payable	$120,000	$150,000	$(30,000)
Mortgage Payable	50,000	—	50,000
Total Long-Term Debt	$170,000	$150,000	$ 20,000
Stockholders' Equity:			
Common Stock, $5 Par	$215,000	$200,000	$ 15,000
Additional Paid-In Capital	92,000	80,000	12,000
Retained Earnings.	87,000	65,000	22,000
Total Stockholders' Equity	$394,000	$345,000	$ 49,000
Total Liabilities and Stockholders' Equity	$720,000	$665,000	$ 55,000

creases in the individual working capital items resulted in an increase in working capital of $44,000 for the year.

The purpose of the statement of changes in financial position is to illustrate what changes in the noncurrent items resulted in increases in working capital and what changes resulted in decreases in working capital. The net effect of changes in the noncurrent items resulted in an increase in working capital of $44,000. The next step, therefore, is to analyze data to determine what transactions affected working capital.

Exhibit 15.3 Income Statement

Gild Company
Income Statement
for the Year Ended December 31, 19X2

Sales		$500,000
Cost of Goods Sold:		
Inventory, January 1, 19X2	$133,000	
Purchases.........................	352,000	
Cost of Goods Available for Sale	$485,000	
Less: Inventory, December 31, 19X2	185,000	
Cost of Goods Sold		300,000
Gross Margin		$200,000
Operating Expenses:		
Selling Expenses	$ 60,000	
Administrative Expenses.................	82,000	
Total Operating Expenses		142,000
Operating Income		$ 58,000
Other Income and Expenses:		
Gain on Sale of Equipment	$ 2,000	
Interest Expense	(18,000)	16,000
Income before Taxes....................		$ 42,000
Income Tax Expense....................		15,000
Net Income............................		$ 27,000

Exhibit 15.4 Schedule of Changes in Working Capital

Gild Company
Schedule of Changes in Working Capital
for the Years Ended December 31, 19X2 and 19X1

	19X2	19X1	Increase (Decrease) in Working Capital
Current Assets:			
Cash.......................	$ 22,000	$ 14,000	$ 8,000
Accounts Receivable (Net)	126,000	155,000	(29,000)
Inventory......................	185,000	133,000	52,000
Prepaid Expenses	12,000	13,000	(1,000)
Totals.....................	$345,000	$315,000	$ 30,000
Current Liabilities:			
Accounts Payable	$140,000	$160,000	$ 20,000
Accrued Liabilities	16,000	10,000	(6,000)
Totals.....................	$156,000	$170,000	$ 14,000
Working Capital....................	$189,000	$145,000	$ 44,000

**Analysis of Data
(Step 3)**

In practice, the data for preparing the statement of changes in financial position can be obtained by analysis of the appropriate ledger accounts and journal entries. Often, there is only one logical explanation for a change in a noncurrent item. For example, if land, as shown on the balance sheet, has increased, and no other information about this increase is available, one can assume that land was purchased. What is not known from the data available is whether land was sold and purchased, with the increase being the difference between the two transactions. For our purposes, you will either be given the necessary data regarding changes in accounts or, where appropriate, will be expected to make a reasonable assumption as to the reason for the change.

The following data are based on an examination of Gild Company's records:

1. Net income for the year is shown in Exhibit 15.3 as $27,000, including a gain of $2,000 on the sale of equipment. Assume that operating expenses include depreciation expense of $12,000.
2. The firm purchased land for $50,000 and signed a mortgage note in order to acquire the land.
3. The firm used cash to retire $30,000 of its bonds outstanding.
4. The firm issued 3,000 shares of common stock at $9 a share.
5. Equipment with a book value of $13,000 was sold for $15,000 cash.
6. Dividends of $5,000 were declared and paid.

**Statement of Changes
in Financial Position
(Step 4)**

The statement of changes in financial position is divided into two major parts—*sources of working capital* and *uses of working capital. Sources of working capital* is further divided into two sections—*operations* and *other sources. Uses of working capital* is not normally subdivided.

One approach to preparing the statement is to determine where each of the items that affect working capital will be shown on the statement. This is done for each of the six items listed in the previous section.

1. Net income with adjustments—source (operations).
2. Purchase of land—use.
   Issuance of mortgage note—source (other sources).
3. Retirement of bonds—use.
4. Issuance of stock—source (other sources).
5. Sale of equipment—source (other sources).
6. Declaration of dividends—use.

There is no prescribed order for listing items under *other sources* or for listing the uses of working capital. However, if there is a net loss, it is listed as the first use of working capital.

With the information above, the statement of changes in financial position can be prepared. It was shown in Exhibit 15.1 and is repeated here as Exhibit 15.5.

The statement of changes in financial position for Gild Company shows that during the past year $129,000 of working capital was provided. Of this, $37,000 came from operations. The additional $92,000 was provided from: sale of equipment, $15,000; a mortgage issued for the purchase of land, $50,000; and the sale of common stock, $27,000. The statement also shows how the working capital was used. Specifically, $50,000 was used to buy

Exhibit 15.5 Statement of Changes in Financial Position

Gild Company
Statement of Changes in Financial Position
for the Year Ended December 31, 19X2

Sources of Working Capital:			
Operations:			
Net Income (as Reported)		$27,000	
Adjustments for Items Not Providing or Using Working Capital:			
Depreciation.	$12,000		
Gain on Sale of Equipment	(2,000)	10,000	
Working Capital Provided by Operations			$ 37,000
Other Sources:			
Sale of Equipment		$15,000	
Mortgage for Land Purchase		50,000	
Issuance of Common Stock		27,000	
Working Capital Provided by Other Sources. .			92,000
Total Working Capital Provided			$129,000
Uses of Working Capital:			
Purchase of Land		$50,000	
Retirement of Bonds		30,000	
Declaration of Dividends		5,000	
Total Working Capital Used			85,000
Increase in Working Capital			$ 44,000

Schedule of Changes in Working Capital

	19X2	19X1	Increase (Decrease) in Working Capital
Current Assets:			
Cash	$ 22,000	$ 14,000	$ 8,000
Accounts Receivable (Net)	126,000	155,000	(29,000)
Inventory	185,000	133,000	52,000
Prepaid Expenses	12,000	13,000	(1,000)
Totals	$345,000	$315,000	$ 30,000
Current Liabilities:			
Accounts Payable	$140,000	$160,000	$ 20,000
Accrued Liabilities	16,000	10,000	(6,000)
Totals	$156,000	$170,000	$ 14,000
Working Capital	$189,000	$145,000	$ 44,000

land; $30,000, to pay off bonds; and $5,000, to declare dividends. The uses total $85,000. The difference between the amount of working capital provided and the amount of working capital used is $44,000. Note that this amount is the same as the increase in working capital shown in the schedule of changes in working capital.

Relationship of the Statement of Changes in Financial Position to the Balance Sheet

The statement of changes in financial position explains the changes that have occurred in the noncurrent items on the balance sheet. At this point, it is useful to analyze each change in the noncurrent items on the Gild Company balance sheet and show where that change is explained on the statement of changes in financial position. This procedure is illustrated in Exhibit 15.6.

The exhibit relates each of the balance sheet changes to the statement of changes in financial position. Thus, we not only know where working capital came from and where it went, but we also know why the noncurrent items on the balance sheet changed by the amounts they did. This information is valuable for management as it analyzes its working capital position and for financial analysts as they assess the overall financial position and operating results of the firm.

Cash Approach

As previously mentioned, there are several approaches to the preparation of the statement of changes in financial position. The working capital approach is one of the most popular and has thus been illustrated in detail. However, you should also be familiar with the cash approach. The cash approach to preparing the statement of changes in financial position illustrates where cash came from during the year and where it went. Because of the need to have adequate cash for conducting operations, some firms prefer to use the cash approach to prepare the statement of changes in financial position.

The balance sheet in Exhibit 15.2 shows that the cash balance for Gild Company increased by $8,000 between 19X1 and 19X2. This section will illustrate the preparation of the statement of changes in financial position that explains this increase.

The primary difference between the cash approach and the working capital approach is in the operations section of the statement. The other items are unchanged. The terminology used also changes slightly. For example, where the working capital approach shows that the sale of equipment provided working capital, the cash approach shows that the sale of equipment provided cash.

Two items on the income statement that were adjusted because they did not provide or use working capital have already been considered. These adjustments are the same for the cash approach as they were for the working capital approach. Specifically, depreciation expense did not use cash;

Exhibit 15.6 Balance Sheet Changes Related to Statement of Changes in Financial Position

	Balance Sheet			Statement of Changes in Financial Position	
	19X2	**19X1**	**Change**		
Land	$200,000	$150,000	+ $50,000	Purchase of Land	$50,000
Plant and Equipment (Net)	$175,000	$200,000	− $25,000	Sale of Equipment Depreciation	$13,000 12,000 $25,000
12% Bonds Payable	$120,000	$150,000	− $30,000	Retirement of Bonds	$30,000
Mortgage Payable	$ 50,000	—	+ $50,000	Mortgage for Land Purchase	$50,000
Common Stock	$215,000	$200,000	+ $15,000	Issuance of Common Stock	$27,000
Additional Paid-In Capital	$ 92,000	$ 80,000	+ $12,000		
Retained Earnings	$ 87,000	$ 65,000	+ $22,000	Net Income Declaration of Dividends	$27,000 (5,000) $22,000

therefore, it is added back to net income. The gain on the sale of equipment of $2,000 did not provide cash; so it is subtracted from net income.

It is necessary now to consider the other income statement items that did not provide or use cash and adjust them according to the changes in current assets and the current liabilities. The current assets and the current liabilities sections of the Gild Company balance sheets from Exhibit 15.2 are shown below as Exhibit 15.7. Note that the right-hand column in the exhibit represents the increases and decreases in the account balances, which are not necessarily the same as the increases and decreases in working capital described previously.

The adjustments to net income in the operations section require some explanation. The income statement is prepared on the accrual basis, which means that revenue is recognized when earned, regardless of when cash is received. In effect, it is necessary to convert the income statement prepared on an accrual basis to a cash basis. The income statement for Gild Company is shown in Exhibit 15.3. Sales and the cost of goods sold section from the income statement are shown as Exhibit 15.8.

Exhibit 15.7 Comparative Partial Balance Sheets

	19X2	19X1	Increase (Decrease)
Current Assets:			
Cash	$ 22,000	$ 14,000	$ 8,000
Accounts Receivable (Net)	126,000	155,000	(29,000)
Inventory	185,000	133,000	52,000
Prepaid Expenses	12,000	13,000	(1,000)
Total Current Assets	$345,000	$315,000	$ 30,000
Current Liabilities:			
Accounts Payable	$140,000	$160,000	$(20,000)
Accrued Liabilities	16,000	10,000	6,000
Total Current Liabilities	$156,000	$170,000	$(14,000)

Let us first convert sales, shown in Exhibit 15.8 to be $500,000. For most firms, this item consists of cash sales and credit sales. Since we know that the Gild Company has accounts receivable, we know that some sales are credit sales. In determining the cash received from sales, then, we must consider the change in accounts receivable. Theoretically, beginning accounts receivable of $126,000 were collected. The ending balance of $155,000 represents amounts sold but not yet collected. Sales on the income statement are converted to a cash basis as follows:

Accounts Receivable, January 1, 19X2	$155,000
Sales	500,000
Total Possible Cash Receipts	$655,000
Less: Accounts Receivable, December 31, 19X2	126,000
Cash Receipts from Sales and Collections of Accounts Receivable	$529,000

Exhibit 15.8 Partial Income Statement

Sales		$500,000
Cost of Goods Sold:		
Inventory, January 1, 19X2	$133,000	
Purchases	352,000	
Cost of Goods Available for Sale	$485,000	
Less: Inventory, December 31, 19X2	185,000	
Cost of Goods Sold		300,000
Gross Margin		$200,000

The amount of cash collected from sales and collections of accounts receivable totals $529,000, rather than the $500,000 shown as sales on the income statement. In other words, the beginning balance of $155,000 resulted in cash collections. Of the $500,000 sold in this period, $126,000 has not been collected. Thus, a total of $529,000 cash was received this year from sales and accounts receivable collections.

It is not necessary to recalculate cash receipts as done above. You can merely look at the change in accounts receivable and add that change to or subtract it from net income. In this case, accounts receivable decreased by $29,000. This means $29,000 more cash was collected this year than reflected in the sales figure on the income statement. Therefore, we must make an addition to net income when converting it to the cash basis. An increase in accounts receivable would be subtracted from net income, because the total cash collected from sales would have been less than the amount of sales.

The next item on the income statement, as shown in Exhibit 15.8, is cost of goods sold, $300,000. This amount is not the amount paid for merchandise. We want to adjust the cost of goods sold figure to arrive at the amount of cash payments. Notice in Exhibit 15.7 that inventory increased from $133,000 to $185,000. Theoretically, this increase represents an additional cash outlay of $52,000. However, we must also examine the change in accounts payable. If accounts payable increased, then the amount of increased purchases paid for is less than $52,000. If accounts payable decreased, then not only did the firm pay for $52,000 more inventory, it also paid more on account.

Examining accounts payable, you see that they decreased from $160,000 to $140,000. This decrease represents a $20,000 increase in cash outflow. Increase in inventory and decrease in accounts payable result in an adjustment to cost of goods sold totaling $72,000, as follows:

Cost of Goods Sold	$300,000
Increase in Inventory	52,000
Decrease in Accounts Payable	20,000
Cash Payments for Merchandise	$372,000

We say, then, that although cost of goods sold was $300,000, payments for merchandise totaled $372,000. In adjusting the income statement to the cash basis, we must decrease net income by $52,000 and $20,000 for the inventory and accounts payable items, because they represent additional cash outlays.

Another current asset item that changed during the year is prepaid expenses, which went down from $13,000 to $12,000. Thus, although total operating expenses on the income statement (Exhibit 15.3) are $142,000, the cash paid for operating expenses must be adjusted for the noncash items. One of these, depreciation expense of $12,000, was described earlier. The reduction of prepaid expenses from $13,000 to $12,000 means that the income statement includes $1,000 of expenses for which cash was not paid in this period. Therefore, net income is increased by $1,000 to arrive at cash payments for operating expenses.

Finally, accrued liabilities increased from $10,000 to $16,000. This increase means that there are $6,000 of expenses on the income statement for which cash was not paid during this period. From the information given, we do not know the exact nature of these expenses. They could represent wages, interest, or taxes that have been incurred but not paid. In any event, the $6,000 represents an amount to be added to net income in arriving at the amount of cash provided by operations.

Now that the adjustments to net income have been analyzed, the statement of changes in financial position based on the cash approach can be prepared, as shown in Exhibit 15.9. Notice that the increase in cash shown in Exhibit 15.9 corresponds with the $8,000 increase in cash shown in the partial balance sheets in Exhibit 15.7. This statement is also called the *statement of cash flow* or, more simply, the *cash flow statement*.

Exhibit 15.10 summarizes the adjustments that must be made to convert net income calculated on the accrual basis to cash provided by operations. It can be stated simply that to arrive at cash provided by operations, *decreases*

Exhibit 15.9 Statement of Changes in Financial Position–Cash Approach

Gild Company			
Statement of Changes in Financial Position–Cash Approach			
for the Year Ended December 31, 19X2			
Sources of Cash:			
Operations:			
Net Income (as Reported)		$27,000	
Adjustments for Items Not Providing or Using Cash:			
Depreciation.	$12,000		
Gain on Sale of Equipment	(2,000)		
Decrease in Accounts Receivable	29,000		
Increase in Inventory	(52,000)		
Decrease in Prepaid Expenses	1,000		
Decrease in Accounts Payable	(20,000)		
Increase in Accrued Liabilities	6,000	(26,000)	
Cash Provided by Operations			$ 1,000
Other Sources:			
Sale of Equipment		$15,000	
Mortgage for Land Purchase		50,000	
Issuance of Common Stock		27,000	
Cash Provided by Other Sources			92,000
Total Cash Provided			$93,000
Uses of Cash:			
Purchase of Land		$50,000	
Retirement of Bonds		30,000	
Payment of Dividends		5,000	
Total Cash Used			85,000
Increase in Cash			$ 8,000

Exhibit 15.10 Adjustment of Net Income to Cash Provided by Operations

Net Income (as Reported)

    Add: Depreciation Expense

    Add: Loss on Sale of Assets
    Subtract: Gain on Sale of Assets

    Add: Decrease in Accounts Receivable
    Subtract: Increase in Accounts Receivable

    Add: Decrease in Inventory
    Subtract: Increase in Inventory

    Add: Decrease in Prepaid Expenses
    Subtract: Increase in Prepaid Expenses

    Add: Increase in Accounts Payable
    Subtract: Decrease in Accounts Payable

    Add: Increase in Accrued Liabilities
    Subtract: Decrease in Accrued Liabilities

Cash Provided by Operations

---

in current assets and increases in current liabilities are added to net income and increases in current assets and decreases in current liabilities are subtracted from net income. Rather than memorize these adjustments, though, it is better to understand the rationale behind them, as described on the previous pages. As mentioned, the adjustments for depreciation expense and for the gain or loss on the sale of assets are the same for the cash approach as for the working capital approach.

Summary

The statement of changes in financial position is a primary external financial statement that shows where working capital came from and how it was used during the period. The statement explains changes in the noncurrent items of the balance sheet. It is used by management and financial analysts to better understand the firm's working capital position.

    Working capital is the difference between current assets and current liabilities. It represents the excess of current assets available to the firm for its day-to-day operations. The statement of changes in financial position includes a schedule of changes in working capital. This schedule shows the increases and decreases in each current asset and current liability item and how these increases and decreases affect the amount of working capital.

The statement of changes in financial position includes two major parts: sources of working capital and uses of working capital. The sources of working capital include the operating results, the sale of noncurrent assets, long-term borrowing, and the issuance of stock. Operating results are measured primarily by net income. However, net income must be adjusted for items that did not provide or use working capital during the year.

The primary applications of working capital include the loss from operations, the purchase of noncurrent assets, the payment of long-term debt, the retirement of stock, and the declaration of cash dividends.

Some transactions do not by themselves affect working capital directly; yet, they represent significant financing or investing activities that should be described on the statement of changes in financial position. These transactions include the purchase of an asset for debt or for stock, the sale of an asset for debt, and the issuance of new debt for the retirement of old debt.

Some firms prepare a statement of changes in financial position using the cash approach. The cash approach shows where cash came from and where it went. When the cash approach is used, the operations section of the statement of changes in financial position begins with net income. However, it must be adjusted for items that did not use or provide cash.

In summary, the statement of changes in financial position is an important financial statement. It is useful both internally to management and externally to stockholders and others interested in how well the company has done.

Review Problem

Comparative balance sheets for Paul's Pool & Patio Shop for the years ended December 31, 19X4 and 19X5, are shown below:

Paul's Pool & Patio Shop
Balance Sheets
December 31, 19X4 and 19X5

	19X5	19X4
Cash	$ 1,800	$ 800
Accounts Receivable (Net)	6,500	7,200
Inventory	13,600	9,800
Prepaid Expenses	300	500
Fixtures and Equipment (Net)	8,500	8,000
Delivery Truck (Net)	13,500	16,500
Total Assets	$44,200	$42,800
Accounts Payable	$ 3,200	$ 2,500
Salaries Payable	500	800
Taxes Payable	750	600
Notes Payable (Long Term)	9,000	10,000
Paul Pierson, Capital	30,750	28,900
Total Liabilities and Capital	$44,200	$42,800

During 19X5, the following financial activities occurred:

1. Net income was $19,850. Paul withdrew $18,000 for his personal use.

2. Depreciation totaled $1,000 on the fixtures and equipment and $3,000 on the delivery truck.

3. Paul purchased new fixtures at a cost of $2,000. Old fixtures with a book value of $500 were sold for $300.

4. Payments on the note totaled $1,000.

Required:

    a. Prepare a schedule of changes in working capital.

    b. Prepare a statement of changes in financial position using the working capital approach for the year ended December 31, 19X5.

Solution

    a.

Paul's Pool & Patio Shop
Schedule of Changes in Working Capital
for the Year Ended December 31, 19X5

	19X5	19X4	Increase (Decrease) in Working Capital
Current Assets:			
Cash	$ 1,800	$ 800	$1,000
Accounts Receivable (Net)	6,500	7,200	(700)
Inventory	13,600	9,800	3,800
Prepaid Expenses	300	500	(200)
Totals	$22,200	$18,300	$3,900
Current Liabilities:			
Accounts Payable	$ 3,200	$ 2,500	$ (700)
Salaries Payable	500	800	300
Taxes Payable	750	600	(150)
Totals	$ 4,450	$ 3,900	$ (550)
Working Capital	$17,750	$14,400	$3,350

b. The schedule of changes in working capital is a part of the statement of changes in financial position. However, since it was prepared in part a, it is not repeated here.

Paul's Pool & Patio Shop
Statement of Changes in Financial Position
for the Year Ended December 31, 19X5

Sources of Working Capital:
  Operations:
    Net Income (as Reported) $19,850
    Adjustments for Items Not Using
      Working Capital:
      Depreciation $4,000
      Loss on Sale of Fixtures   200   4,200

Working Capital Provided by Operations		$24,050
Other Sources:		
Sale of Fixtures		300
Total Working Capital Provided		$24,350
Uses of Working Capital:		
Purchase of Fixtures	$ 2,000	
Payments on Note	1,000	
Withdrawals by Owner	18,000	
Total Working Capital Used		21,000
Increase in Working Capital		$ 3,350

Note that the loss on sale of fixtures, $200, is treated similarly to depreciation. It represents an expense that was deducted in arriving at net income, but one that did not use working capital. Thus, it is added back to net income in arriving at working capital provided by operations. The $200 loss was determined by subtracting the $500 book value from the $300 received from the sale of the fixtures.

This problem uses statements of a proprietorship rather than a corporation. The preparation of the statement does not change. Only some items are different. For example, rather than declaration of dividends, the proprietorship statement shows withdrawals by owner. Naturally, the proprietorship balance sheet shows only one owner's equity account, for capital, rather than accounts for common stock and retained earnings.

Questions

15-1 What is the purpose of the statement of changes in financial position? How does it differ from the income statement and the balance sheet?

15-2 What is a funds statement?

15-3 Is it possible for a firm to show a net income on the income statement, yet show a decrease in working capital? Explain.

15-4 Why does a decrease in current liabilities increase working capital?

15-5 List the primary sources of working capital.

15-6 List the primary uses of working capital.

15-7 An individual was heard to remark, "Depreciation provides working capital. That's why it is added to net income in the sources section of the statement of changes in financial position." Do you agree? Explain.

15-8 Why is a gain on the sale of an asset subtracted from net income on the statement of changes in financial position?

15-9 Why is the declaration of a cash dividend considered a use of working capital before the dividend has been paid?

15-10 When a firm purchases a building by issuing a mortgage, why is the transaction shown on the statement of changes in financial position? After all, the firm did not receive or use working capital in the transaction.

15-11 Why are decreases in inventory and increases in accounts payable added to net income under the cash approach?

15-12 Roe Company prepared a statement of changes in financial position under the working capital approach. It showed an increase in working capital of $5,000. The firm also prepared a statement under the cash approach; but it showed a decrease in cash of $3,000. How do you explain what might be considered by some to be a discrepancy?

15-13 Would a declared but unpaid cash dividend be shown on the statement of changes in financial position using the cash approach? Explain.

Exercises

15-14 Increases and Decreases in Working Capital Items Below are balances of the working capital items for Blaine Company as of December 31, 19X2 and 19X3:

	19X3	19X2
Cash	$100,000	$ 80,000
Accounts Receivable (Net)	240,000	265,000
Inventory	175,000	120,000
Prepaid Expenses	15,000	11,000
Accounts Payable	260,000	215,000
Accrued Liabilities	45,000	60,000

For each item, indicate whether the change between 19X2 and 19X3 resulted in an increase or a decrease in working capital.

15-15 Schedule of Changes in Working Capital The balances of the working capital items for Crane Company as of December 31, 19X7 and 19X8 are shown below:

	19X8	19X7
Cash	$ 62,000	$ 94,000
Accounts Receivable (Net)	135,000	115,000
Inventory	169,000	185,000
Prepaid Expenses	22,000	16,000
Accounts Payable	180,000	156,000
Accrued Liabilities	33,000	40,000

Prepare a schedule of changes in working capital for the year ended December 31, 19X8.

15-16 Effects of Transactions on Working Capital Items Indicate whether each transaction below increases working capital, decreases working capital, or has no effect on working capital.
  a. Purchase of equipment for cash.
  b. Purchase of inventory on account.
  c. Payment of a long-term note.
  d. Recording of depreciation expense.
  e. Payment of accounts payable.

    f. Collection of accounts receivable.

    g. Sale of common stock for cash.

    h. Sale of bonds for cash.

    i. Payment of short-term note.

    j. Sale of equipment at a loss.

15–17 Sources and Uses of Working Capital Indicate whether each transaction below would appear on the statement of changes in financial position as a *source* of working capital, a *use* of working capital, or *both*. If the transaction affects only working capital items, indicate *working capital change*.

    a. Purchase of a truck for cash.

    b. Net income.

    c. Sale of stock for cash.

    d. Payment of cash dividend declared last year.

    e. Issuance of common stock for land.

    f. Payment of a 6-month note.

    g. Conversion of bonds for common stock.

    h. Retirement of bonds.

15–18 Calculating Working Capital Provided or Used For each item below, calculate the amount of working capital *provided by* or *used in* operations.

	Net Income (Loss)	Depreciation	Other
a.	$20,000	$3,000	
b.	$45,000	$10,000	$3,000 Gain on Sale of Asset
c.	$112,000	$15,000	$3,000 Amortization of Bond Discount
d.	$55,000	$6,000	$7,000 Loss on Sale of Investment
e.	$80,000	$8,000	$4,000 Amortization of Bond Premium
f.	$(12,000)	$10,000	$3,000 Loss on Sale of Assets
g.	$(20,000)	$3,000	$4,000 Gain on Sale of Assets
h.	$2,000	$3,000	$10,000 Gain on Sale of Assets

15–19 Working Capital Provided by Operations Diamond Company's net income for the year ended December 31, 19X9, was $2,500,000. Additional information is as follows:

Depreciation of Fixed Assets	$2,900,000
Dividends Paid on Preferred Stock	200,000
Long-Term Debt:	
Bond Discount Amortization	50,000
Interest Expense	800,000
Provision for Doubtful Accounts on	
Long-Term Receivables	250,000
Amortization of Goodwill	90,000

Calculate the amount of working capital provided by operations for the statement of changes in financial position for the year ended December 31, 19X9. (AICPA adapted)

15-20 Calculating an Increase in Working Capital The following information on selected cash transactions for 19X8 has been provided by the Smith Company:

Proceeds from Short-Term Borrowings	$1,200,000
Proceeds from Long-Term Borrowings	4,000,000
Purchases of Fixed Assets	3,200,000
Purchases of Inventories	8,000,000
Proceeds from Sale of Smith's Common Stock	2,000,000

What is the increase in working capital for the year ended December 31, 19X8, that resulted from the above transactions? (AICPA adapted)

15-21 Sources and Uses of Working Capital The following information was taken from the accounting records of Oregon Corporation for 19X9:

Proceeds from Issuance of Preferred Stock	$4,000,000
Dividends Declared on Preferred Stock	400,000
Bonds Payable Converted to Common Stock	2,000,000
Purchases of Treasury Stock, Common	500,000
Sale of Plant Building	1,200,000
2% Stock Dividend on Common Stock	300,000

For Oregon's statement of changes in financial position for the year ended December 31, 19X9, determine the sources and uses of working capital, based on the information above. (AICPA adapted)

15-22 Sale of Fixed Assets Consider the situation below. Select and explain the correct answer.

Token Company sold some of its fixed assets during 19X7. Their original cost was $750,000, and accumulated depreciation at the date of sale was $600,000. The proceeds from the sale of the assets were $210,000. The information concerning the sale of the fixed assets should be shown on Token's statement of changes in financial position for the year ended December 31, 19X7, as:

a. A subtraction from net income of $60,000 and a source of $150,000.
b. An addition to net income of $60,000 and a source of $150,000.
c. A subtraction from net income of $60,000 and a source of $210,000.
d. A source of $150,000. (AICPA adapted)

15-23 Determining Items for the Cash Approach Marie Williams is preparing a statement of changes in financial position for her business. She uses the cash approach. Below are data for the company's records for the year 19X1.

Cost of Goods Sold	$ 60,000
Accounts Payable, January 1	35,000
Accounts Payable, December 31	48,000
Inventory, January 1	23,000
Inventory, January 31	30,000
Sales	110,000
Accounts Receivable, January 1	18,000
Accounts Receivable, December 31	25,000

a. Determine the amount of cash received from sales and collected from receivables.

b. Determine the amount of cash paid for merchandise.

15-24 Cash Provided by Operations Below are listed the current assets and current liabilities for Ashford Company as of December 31, 19X2 and 19X3.

	19X3	19X2
Cash	$20,000	$16,000
Accounts Receivable (Net)	77,000	85,000
Inventory	65,000	45,000
Prepaid Expenses	9,000	6,000
Accounts Payable	31,000	35,000
Accrued Liabilities	12,000	7,000

Net income for the year ended December 31, 19X3, was $38,000. Depreciation for the year totaled $9,000. Calculate the amount of cash provided by operations.

15-25 Total Cash Provided Blandon Company uses the cash approach in preparing the statement of changes in financial position. Last year, net income was $120,000; and depreciation totaled $15,000. Current asset and current liability balances as of December 31, 19X4 and 19X5, are as follows:

	19X5	19X4
Cash	$15,000	$12,000
Accounts Receivable (Net)	68,000	60,000
Inventory	49,000	52,000
Prepaid Expenses	4,000	3,000
Accounts Payable	35,000	28,000
Accrued Liabilities	14,000	16,000

The following transactions also occurred:

Sale of Common Stock for Cash	$50,000
Purchase of Equipment with Long-Term Note	35,000
Dividends Declared and Paid	10,000
Cash Borrowed on Long-Term Note	20,000

Determine the amount to be shown as total cash provided on the statement of changes in financial position for the year ended December 31, 19X5.

Problems

15-26 Statement of Changes in Financial Position; Working Capital Approach Comparative condensed data from the balance sheets of Lybrand Corporation as of December 31, 19X2 and 19X3, are shown below:

	19X3	19X2
Current Assets	$250,000	$235,000
Property, Plant, and Equipment (Net)	680,000	560,000
Total Assets	$930,000	$795,000
Current Liabilities	$100,000	$ 95,000
Long-Term Debt	200,000	150,000
Stockholders' Equity	630,000	550,000
Total Liabilities and Stockholders' Equity	$930,000	$795,000

Net income for 19X3 was $100,000, and depreciation totaled $40,000. Dividends of $20,000 were declared and paid. The firm bought new equipment at a cost of $160,000 and borrowed $50,000 cash on a long-term note.

Required:

   a. Determine the increase or decrease in working capital for the year. (No formal schedule of changes in working capital is required.)

   b. Prepare a statement of changes in financial position using the working capital approach for the year ended December 31, 19X3.

15-27 Statement of Changes in Financial Position; Working Capital Approach Michelle Smith owns Smith's Sewing Center, which sells sewing machines and other sewing items. The balance sheets as of December 31, 19X2 and 19X3, are shown below:

Smith's Sewing Center
Balance Sheets
December 31, 19X2 and 19X3

	19X3	19X2
Cash	$ 900	$ 800
Accounts Receivable (Net)	5,000	2,100
Inventory	6,300	4,000
Prepaid Expenses	150	300
Store Building (Net)	75,000	80,000
Store Fixtures and Equipment (Net)	15,500	15,000
Total Assets	$102,850	$102,200
Accounts Payable	$ 2,000	$ 1,300
Salaries Payable	600	800
Taxes Payable	350	200
Notes Payable (Short-Term)	4,500	3,000
Mortgage Payable	45,000	50,000
Michelle Smith, Capital	50,400	46,900
Total Liabilities and Capital	$102,850	$102,200

During 19X3, the following financial activities occurred:

   1. Net income was $12,000. Michelle withdrew $8,500 for personal use.

2. Depreciation was $5,000 on the building and $2,000 on equipment.

3. Equipment costing $3,000 was purchased. Old equipment with a book value of $500 was sold for that amount.

4. Payments on the mortgage totaled $5,000.

5. Michelle borrowed an additional $1,500 from the bank on a short-term note.

Required:

a. Prepare a schedule of changes in working capital.

b. Prepare a statement of changes in financial position using the working capital approach for the year ended December 31, 19X3. (Do not repeat the schedule of changes in working capital.)

15-28 Statement of Changes in Financial Position; Working Capital Approach; Explaining Problems Data from Hazlecraft Corporation's balance sheets for the past 2 years are shown below:

	19X9	19X8
Cash	$ 2,000	$ 6,000
Accounts Receivable (Net)	157,000	165,000
Inventory	163,000	140,000
Prepaid Expenses	8,000	7,000
Land	115,000	115,000
Building and Equipment (Net)	285,000	250,000
Total Assets	$730,000	$683,000
Accounts Payable	$195,000	$165,000
Accrued Liabilities	30,000	28,000
Long-Term Note Payable	50,000	100,000
Common Stock, $10 Par	300,000	200,000
Additional Paid-in Capital	50,000	50,000
Retained Earnings	105,000	140,000
Total Liabilities and Stockholders' Equity	$730,000	$683,000

At the end of 19X8, management was dissatisfied with the working capital position. The company issued additional common stock in 19X9 in an attempt to improve this situation. The following information is available regarding financial activities for 19X9:

1. The firm suffered a net loss of $35,000. Depreciation totaled $40,000.

2. Equipment was sold for its book value of $10,000.

3. New equipment costing $85,000 was purchased. Management would have preferred to delay this purchase, but it was delayed last year and the need was critical.

4. Half the amount owed on the long-term note became due and was paid.

5. Fifteen thousand shares of common stock were offered for sale, but only 10,000 shares could be sold. They were sold at par.

Required:

a. Prepare a schedule of changes in working capital.

b. Prepare a statement of changes in financial position using the working capital approach for the year ended December 31, 19X9. (Do not repeat the schedule of changes in working capital.)

c. Despite efforts to improve the working capital position, the situation at the end of 19X9 was worse. Why?

15-29 Statement of Changes in Financial Position; Working Capital Approach Data from comparative balance sheets for Grandberry Company as of December 31, 19X4 and 19X5, are shown below:

	19X5	19X4
Cash	$ 18,000	$ 15,000
Marketable Securities	150,000	—
Accounts Receivable (Net)	98,000	90,000
Inventory	112,000	80,000
Prepaid Expenses	2,000	6,000
Investments	72,000	50,000
Land	250,000	300,000
Buildings and Equipment (Net)	660,000	500,000
Total Assets	$1,362,000	$1,041,000
Accounts Payable	$ 115,000	$ 80,000
Accrued Liabilities	10,000	14,000
Bonds Payable	100,000	300,000
Mortgage Payable	200,000	—
Common Stock	550,000	400,000
Retained Earnings	387,000	247,000
Total Liabilities and Stockholders' Equity	$1,362,000	$1,041,000

Net income for the year ended December 31, 19X5, was $185,000. Depreciation totaled $90,000. In addition, the following financial activities took place.

1. Investments with a cost of $20,000 were sold for $25,000. Additional investments costing $42,000 were made.

2. An office complex costing $250,000 was added to the buildings. This addition required a $200,000 mortgage.

3. Land costing $50,000 was sold for $40,000.

4. Bonds with a face value of $200,000 were retired.

5. Common stock was issued for $150,000.

6. Dividends of $45,000 were declared and paid.

Required:

a. Prepare a schedule of changes in working capital.

b. Prepare a statement of changes in financial position using the working capital approach for the year ended December 31, 19X5. (Do not repeat the schedule of changes in working capital.)

15-30 Statement of Changes in Financial Position; Working Capital Approach; Net Loss Blakeview Company's comparative balance sheets as of December 31, 19X1 and 19X2, are shown below.

Blakeview Company
Balance Sheets
December 31, 19X1 and 19X2

	19X2	19X1
Cash	$ 2,000	$ 5,000
Accounts Receivable (Net)	36,000	45,000
Inventory	40,000	62,000
Prepaid Expenses	2,000	12,000
Buildings (Net)	415,000	340,000
Equipment (Net)	235,000	210,000
Total Assets	$730,000	$674,000
Accounts Payable	$ 35,000	$ 39,000
Salaries Payable	20,000	12,000
Taxes Payable	1,000	4,000
Bonds Payable	200,000	100,000
Common Stock	350,000	350,000
Retained Earnings	124,000	169,000
Total Liabilities and Stockholders' Equity	$730,000	$674,000

The following financial activities occurred during 19X2:

1. The firm showed a net loss of $35,000. Depreciation totaled $20,000 on the buildings and $25,000 on the equipment.

2. The net loss included an uninsured fire loss that destroyed a building with a book value of $30,000 and equipment with a book value of $15,000.

3. Bonds with a face value of $100,000 were issued to buy a new building.

4. A new building was bought at a cost of $125,000.

5. New equipment was bought for $65,000.

6. Despite the net loss, dividends of $10,000 were declared and paid.

Required:

a. Prepare a schedule of changes in working capital.

b. Prepare a statement of changes in financial position using the working capital approach for the year ended December 31, 19X2. (Do not repeat the schedule of changes in working capital.)

15–31 Statement of Changes in Financial Position; Working Capital Approach Comparative balance sheets for Trendy Corporation as of December 31, 19X1 and 19X2, are shown below:

Trendy Corporation
Balance Sheets
December 31, 19X1 and 19X2
(in Thousands)

	19X2	19X1
Current Assets:		
Cash	$ 45	$ 50
Marketable Securities	425	200
Accounts Receivable (Net)	580	500
Inventory	420	350
Prepaid Expenses	7	10
Total Current Assets	$1,477	$1,110
Investments	$2,075	$2,000
Property, Plant, and Equipment:		
Land	$ 410	$ 550
Buildings	1,220	1,000
Accumulated Depreciation	(350)	(300)
Equipment	370	360
Accumulated Depreciation	(125)	(120)
Total Property, Plant, and Equipment	$1,525	$1,490
Intangible Assets:		
Patents	$ 70	$ 80
Total Assets	$5,147	$4,680
Current Liabilities:		
Accounts Payable	$ 400	$ 330
Notes Payable	50	80
Accrued Liabilities	40	50
Total Current Liabilities	$ 490	$ 460
Long-Term Debt:		
Bonds Payable (Net of Unamortized Premium)	$2,396	$2,400
Mortgage Payable	200	—
Total Long-Term Debt	$2,596	$2,400
Stockholders' Equity:		
Preferred Stock, $100 Par	$ 200	$ 300
Common Stock, $10 Par	1,030	1,000
Additional Paid-in Capital	376	250
Retained Earnings	455	270
Total Stockholders' Equity	$2,061	$1,820
Total Liabilities and Stockholders' Equity	$5,147	$4,680

The following financial activities occurred during 19X2:

1. Net income totaled $400,000. Depreciation was $50,000 on buildings and $30,000 on equipment.

2. Amortization of bond premium totaled $4,000. Patent amortization was $10,000.

3. Land that had been bought for $140,000 was sold for $200,000.

4. A new building costing $220,000 was purchased. The firm paid $20,000 cash and signed a mortgage for the balance.

5. Equipment with a cost of $30,000 was sold for $3,000. Accumulated depreciation at the time of sale was $25,000.

6. New equipment costing $40,000 was purchased.

7. One thousand shares of preferred stock were retired at par.

8. Three thousand shares of common stock were sold for $52 per share.

9. The firm made long-term investments totaling $125,000. Investments with a cost of $50,000 were sold for $35,000.

10. Dividends declared totaled $15,000 on preferred and $200,000 on common.

Required:

a. Prepare a schedule of changes in working capital.

b. Prepare a statement of changes in financial position using the working capital approach for the year ended December 31, 19X2. (Do not repeat the schedule of changes in working capital.)

15–32 Statement of Changes in Financial Position; Working Capital Approach; Purchase of Business The financial statements presented below were provided to the Sparton Corporation, which is considering purchasing ARCHCO, Inc. The statements presented did not include a statement of changes in financial position. Sparton's controller would like to have this statement, as well as other relevant financial information, before making a financial analysis of ARCHCO, Inc.

ARCHCO, Inc.
Statement of Financial Position
December 31, 19X6 and 19X7
(in Thousands)

	19X7	19X6
Assets		
Cash	$ 16,800	$120,000
Accounts Receivable	81,900	73,200
Inventories	119,700	97,500
U.S. Treasury Bills	33,450	79,500
Total Current Assets	$251,850	$370,200
Land	217,500	195,000
Plant and Equipment (Net)	391,500	387,000
Patents (Less Accumulated Amortization)	28,500	31,500
Total Assets	$889,350	$983,700

Liabilities and Owners' Equity

Accounts Payable	$136,500	$198,500
Taxes Payable	3,000	2,500
Interest Payable	6,000	4,500
Notes Payable	30,000	21,750
Total Current Liabilities	$175,500	$227,250
Deferred Income Taxes	11,400	9,750
Long-Term Bonds	150,000	300,000
Total Liabilities	$336,900	$537,000
Preferred Stock	111,000	45,000
Common Stock	360,000	337,500
Retained Earnings	81,450	64,200
Total Liabilities and Owners' Equity	$889,350	$983,700

Income Statement
for the Year Ended December 31, 19X7
(in Thousands)

Sales	$441,600	
Gain on Retirement of Bonds	9,900	$451,500
Expenses, Taxes, and Losses:		
Cost of Goods Sold	$252,000	
Wages and Salaries	51,000	
Depreciation	18,000	
Amortization	3,000	
Other	28,200	
Interest	19,500	
Loss on Sale of Equipment	3,600	
Income Taxes	16,950	392,250
Net Income		$ 59,250

The following information is available to explain the ARCHCO, Inc., financial results for 19X7.

1. The significant decline in cash and treasury bills occurred because funds from these sources were used to retire the bonds at a favorable time.

2. Equipment with a cost of $35,000 and a book value of $18,000 was sold for $14,400.

3. A portion of the preferred stock was issued to provide cash to purchase outstanding bonds in the market. The remaining amount was issued to JIS, Inc., for land and the related plant and equipment on the land.

4. Cash dividends of $4,500 and $15,000 were paid to the preferred and common shareholders, respectively. The common shareholders received a stock dividend with a market value of $22,500.

5. The income tax expense account and the deferred income tax account that appear in the statements properly account for all income tax situations of ARCHCO, Inc.

Required:

a. Prepare, in good form, a statement of changes in financial position for the year ended December 31, 19X7. Use the working capital approach.

b. Identify and explain the probable reasons why the Sparton controller would want a statement of changes in financial position of ARCHCO, Inc. (CMA adapted)

15–33 Working Capital Provided by Operations; Early Repayment of Bonds Data from comparative balance sheets are presented for Shelby, Inc., a calendar-year company.

	December 31	
	19X4	**19X3**
	Dr. (Cr.)	**Dr. (Cr.)**
Current Assets	$ 237,000	$ 160,000
Equipment	615,000	600,000
Accumulated Depreciation	(218,000)	(210,000)
Goodwill	240,000	250,000
	$ 874,000	$ 800,000
Current Liabilities	$(180,000)	$ (80,000)
Bonds Payable	(200,000)	(300,000)
Discount on Bonds	—	4,000
Common Stock	(550,000)	(550,000)
Retained Earnings	56,000	126,000
	$(874,000)	$(800,000)

You have discovered the following facts:

1. During 19X4, Shelby sold, at no gain or loss, equipment with a book value of $38,000; it purchased new equipment costing $75,000.

2. During 19X4, bonds with a face value of $100,000 were extinguished. They were not current liabilities prior to their extinguishment.

3. Retained earnings were affected only by the 19X4 net income or loss.

Required:

a. How much working capital was provided by operations during 19X4?

b. Assume that $100,000 face value of bonds became current at December 31, 19X4, to be repaid in early 19X5. What would be the change in working capital under this assumption? (AICPA adapted)

15–34 Statement of Changes in Financial Position; Cash Approach; Explaining Cash Decrease Comparative balance sheets for Dantzler Corporation as of December 31, 19X5 and 19X6, are shown below:

Dantzler Corporation
Balance Sheets
December 31, 19X5 and 19X6

	19X6	19X5
Cash	$ 400	$ 3,200
Accounts Receivable (Net)	10,300	8,800
Inventory	13,200	11,000
Prepaid Expenses	500	800
Equipment (Net)	12,700	12,000
Total Assets	$37,100	$35,800
Accounts Payable	$ 7,000	$ 6,500
Accrued Liabilities	1,400	2,100
Notes Payable (Long-Term)	4,000	5,000
Common Stock	20,000	20,000
Retained Earnings	4,700	2,200
Total Liabilities and Stockholders' Equity	$37,100	$35,800

The following financial activities took place during 19X6:

1. Net income totaled $4,500. Depreciation was $1,500.
2. Equipment costing $3,000 was purchased.
3. Equipment with a book value of $800 was sold for that amount.
4. Payments on notes payable totaled $1,000.
5. Dividends of $2,000 were declared and paid.

The president has expressed concern that the cash balance has fallen so low. He does not understand this, especially since net income was $4,500.

Required:

a. Determine the increase or decrease in each current asset and current liability item. (See Exhibit 15.7 for an example. This is *not* a schedule of changes in working capital.)

b. Prepare a statement of changes in financial position for the year ended December 31, 19X6, using the cash approach.

c. How would you explain the decrease in cash to the president?

15-35 Statement of Changes in Financial Position; Cash Approach Refer to Problem 15-27.

Required:

a. Determine the increase or decrease in each current asset and current liability item. (See Exhibit 15.7 for an example. This is *not* a schedule of changes in working capital.

b. Prepare a statement of changes in financial position for the year ended December 31,19X3, using the cash approach.

15-36 Statement of Changes in Financial Position; Cash Approach Refer to Problem 15-28.

Required:

a. Determine the increase or decrease in each current asset and current liability item. (See Exhibit 15.7 for an example. This is *not* a schedule of changes in working capital.)

b. Prepare a statement of changes in financial position for the year ended December 31, 19X9, using the cash approach.

15-37 Statement of Changes in Financial Position; Cash Approach Refer to Problem 15-29.

Required:

a. Determine the increase or decrease in each current asset and current liability item. (See Exhibit 15.7 for an example. This is *not* a schedule of changes in working capital.)

b. Prepare a statement of changes in financial position for the year ended December 31, 19X5, using the cash approach.

15-38 Statement of Changes in Financial Position; Cash Approach Refer to Problem 15-31.

Required:

a. Determine the increase or decrease in each current asset and current liability item. (See Exhibit 15.7 for an example. This is *not* a schedule of changes in working capital.)

b. Prepare a statement of changes in financial position for the year ended December 31, 19x2, using the cash approach.

Chapter 16   Financial Statement Analysis

Learning Objectives

The purpose of this chapter is to show how we can use financial statements to learn about a business firm's financial condition. The chapter illustrates applications of the most commonly used techniques for evaluating a firm's financial position and operating results. Studying this chapter will enable you to:

1. Perform and understand the results of horizontal and vertical analysis.
2. Analyze common-size statements and understand the results.
3. Calculate and understand the meaning of ratios that relate to a firm's short-run financial stability.
4. Calculate and understand the meaning of ratios that relate to a firm's long-run financial stability.
5. Calculate and understand ratios that relate to a firm's operating and financial performance.
6. Calculate earnings per share, to include extraordinary items.
7. Describe the advantages and limitations of comparing financial statements among firms.

Chapter Topics

The major topics included in this chapter are:

> Comparative Statements
> Short-Run Financial Stability
> Long-Run Financial Stability
> Operating Performance
> Comparison among Firms

Financial statements, such as the income statement, balance sheet, and statement of changes in financial position, communicate information about a firm. The format of the statements is fairly well standardized, and the terminology has specific technical meanings. Therefore, anyone with a background in accounting can look at a firm's financial statements and determine how well or how poorly the firm has performed in the most recent period, as well as determine how strong or how weak its current financial position is.

Financial statement analysis is the process of comparing relationships among financial statement items in order to evaluate a firm's financial position and operating performance. This process is most often performed by individuals outside the firm to assist them in making credit and investment decisions. However, management also uses financial statement analysis internally so that it can learn the financial strengths and weaknesses of the firm.

The process of analyzing financial statements includes the development of ratios. A **ratio** describes the relationship between one financial statement item and another. Ratios may be expressed in a number of ways, such as in percentages, in single whole numbers, or in an expression relating one number to another number (for example, 3 to 1).

The previous chapter illustrated the statement of changes in financial position and described its use in analyzing the flow of working capital and cash for the most recently ended year. This chapter emphasizes the concepts and procedures for analyzing the income statement and balance sheet. This analysis, along with that of the statement of changes in financial position, allows management and outsiders to assess both the short-run and long-run prospects of the firm.

Comparative Statements

A starting point in financial statement analysis is to prepare **comparative statements**—financial statements of two or more years presented side by side. Typically, statements of the current year and the previous year are compared. The purpose of preparing comparative statements is to determine whether there have been significant changes that may warrant additional investigation. Two methods are used in looking at comparative statements. One is to analyze dollar and percentage changes of each item. A second is to prepare common-size statements. Each of these methods is described below.

Dollar and Percentage Changes

An analysis of dollar and percentage changes is referred to as **horizontal analysis.** When horizontal analysis is used, the analyst goes across the financial statements for each item, comparing the dollar change in amounts and the percentage change between years. To illustrate, financial statements for the last two years for Star Company, a merchandising firm, are presented in Exhibits 16.1 and 16.2.

Comparative Balance Sheets To determine the dollar change, the analyst subtracts the amounts of the base year (in this case, 19X1) from the amounts in the most recent year (19X2). The dollar increases and decreases in Exhibit 16.1 were arrived at by subtracting the figures for 19X1 from the figures for 19X2. The percentage change is determined by dividing the dollar change by the amount in the base year (19X1). For example, the increase of 32 percent in current assets was arrived at by dividing $72,000,

Exhibit 16.1 Comparative Balance Sheets

<table>
<tr><td colspan="5" align="center">**Star Company**
Balance Sheets
December 31, 19X2 and 19X1</td></tr>
<tr><td></td><td></td><td></td><td colspan="2" align="center">**Increase
(Decrease)**</td></tr>
<tr><td></td><td>**19X2**</td><td>**19X1**</td><td>**Dollars**</td><td>**Percent**</td></tr>
<tr><td>Current Assets:</td><td></td><td></td><td></td><td></td></tr>
<tr><td>Cash . . . .</td><td>$ 40,000</td><td>$ 35,000</td><td>$ 5,000</td><td>14%</td></tr>
<tr><td>Accounts Receivable (Net) . . . .</td><td>150,000</td><td>110,000</td><td>40,000</td><td>36</td></tr>
<tr><td>Inventory . . . .</td><td>100,000</td><td>75,000</td><td>25,000</td><td>33</td></tr>
<tr><td>Prepaid Expenses . . . .</td><td>10,000</td><td>8,000</td><td>2,000</td><td>25</td></tr>
<tr><td>Total Current Assets . . . .</td><td>$300,000</td><td>$228,000</td><td>$72,000</td><td>32</td></tr>
<tr><td>Property, Plant, and Equipment:</td><td></td><td></td><td></td><td></td></tr>
<tr><td>Land . . . .</td><td>$100,000</td><td>$100,000</td><td>—</td><td>—</td></tr>
<tr><td>Plant and Equipment (Net) . . . .</td><td>350,000</td><td>380,000</td><td>$(30,000)</td><td>(8)</td></tr>
<tr><td>Total Property, Plant, and
Equipment . . . .</td><td>$450,000</td><td>$480,000</td><td>$(30,000)</td><td>(6)</td></tr>
<tr><td>Total Assets . . . .</td><td>$750,000</td><td>$708,000</td><td>$42,000</td><td>6</td></tr>
<tr><td>Current Liabilities:</td><td></td><td></td><td></td><td></td></tr>
<tr><td>Accounts Payable . . . .</td><td>$120,000</td><td>$ 88,000</td><td>$32,000</td><td>36</td></tr>
<tr><td>Accrued Liabilities . . . .</td><td>20,000</td><td>17,000</td><td>3,000</td><td>18</td></tr>
<tr><td>Total Current Liabilities . . . .</td><td>$140,000</td><td>$105,000</td><td>$35,000</td><td>33</td></tr>
<tr><td>Long-Term Debt:</td><td></td><td></td><td></td><td></td></tr>
<tr><td>10% Bonds Payable . . . .</td><td>$300,000</td><td>$300,000</td><td>—</td><td>—</td></tr>
<tr><td>Total Liabilities . . . .</td><td>$440,000</td><td>$405,000</td><td>$35,000</td><td>9</td></tr>
<tr><td>Stockholders' Equity:</td><td></td><td></td><td></td><td></td></tr>
<tr><td>8% Preferred Stock, $100 Par,
500 Shares . . . .</td><td>$ 50,000</td><td>$ 50,000</td><td>—</td><td>—</td></tr>
<tr><td>Common Stock, $10 Par, 10,000
Shares . . . .</td><td>100,000</td><td>100,000</td><td>—</td><td>—</td></tr>
<tr><td>Additional Paid-In Capital . . . .</td><td>40,000</td><td>40,000</td><td>—</td><td>—</td></tr>
<tr><td>Retained Earnings . . . .</td><td>120,000</td><td>113,000</td><td>$ 7,000</td><td>6</td></tr>
<tr><td>Total Stockholders' Equity . . . .</td><td>$310,000</td><td>$303,000</td><td>$ 7,000</td><td>2</td></tr>
<tr><td>Total Liabilities and Stockholders'
Equity . . . .</td><td>$750,000</td><td>$708,000</td><td>$42,000</td><td>6</td></tr>
</table>

the change between 19X1 and 19X2, by $228,000, the amount of the total current assets at the end of 19X1.

Not all changes are significant. Comparative balance sheets show only the amounts and percentages of change. Further analysis is needed to arrive at the reasons for and significance of changes. In the case of Star Company,

Exhibit 16.2 Comparative Income Statements

Star Company
Income Statements
for the Years Ended December 31, 19X2 and 19X1

	19X2	19X1	Increase (Decrease) Dollars	Percent
Sales	$800,000	$740,000	$ 60,000	8%
Cost of Goods Sold	450,000	420,000	30,000	7
Gross Margin	$350,000	$320,000	$ 30,000	9
Operating Expenses	260,000	220,000	40,000	18
Operating Income	$ 90,000	$100,000	$(10,000)	(10)
Interest Expense.	30,000	30,000	—	—
Income before Taxes.	$ 60,000	$ 70,000	$(10,000)	(14)
Income Taxes (40%)	24,000	28,000	(4,000)	(14)
Net Income.	$ 36,000	$ 42,000	$ (6,000)	(14)
Other Data:				
Preferred Dividends:				
Total	$4,000	$4,000		
Per Share	$8.00	$8.00		
Common Dividends:				
Total	$25,000	$25,000		
Per Share	$2.50	$2.50		

the total increase in assets is 6 percent, a relatively small amount. However, it is noteworthy that accounts receivable increased 36 percent; inventory, 33 percent; and total current assets, 32 percent. In looking at percentages, consider the dollar changes also. For example, prepaid expenses increased 25 percent. But this is really only an increase of $2,000, from $8,000 to $10,000, and is probably not significant.

Look at liabilities. Notice that accounts payable increased 36 percent and total current liabilities increased 33 percent. These increases appear to be significant.

At this point, we cannot speculate on the reasons for the changes; nor can we discern whether apparently significant changes really are significant. Additional analysis is necessary before meaningful conclusions can be formed.

Comparative Income Statements Comparative income statements normally provide more information than do comparative balance sheets. One reason for this is that a primary goal of most firms is to increase net income, which is reported on the income statement. We can look at comparative income statements and tell immediately whether this goal has been achieved.

Exhibit 16.2 shows the sales increased by 8 percent. However, net income decreased by 14 percent. Management will want to know why net income decreased, particularly when there was an increase in sales. It can obtain some information as to the reasons by analyzing the comparative income statements.

An increase in sales should result in a similar increase in gross margin. In this case, the 8-percent in sales resulted in a 9-percent increase in gross margin, because the cost of goods sold increased slightly less than sales—that is, 7 percent versus 8 percent. If there were a significant increase in cost of goods sold without a corresponding increase in sales, it would be an indication that selling prices were not keeping up with increases in the cost of merchandise purchased. As described later, it might also mean that inventory is being stolen. As described in Chapter 3, the net income of manufacturing firms using absorption costing is also affected by changes in inventory levels.

The firm's operating problem in 19X2 appears to be with operating expenses. Notice that they increased 18 percent, resulting in a 10-percent decrease in operating income. Operating expenses consist of the selling and administrative expenses necessary to run the firm on a day-to-day basis. Management needs to analyze each specific expense item to determine whether some are unreasonably high. Perhaps expenses can be reduced in some areas. On the other hand, there may be rising operating costs, such as those for utilities or wages, that management can do nothing about. In this event, prices may have to be raised to help cover increased operating costs, provided the quantity sold does not decline too much because of the price increase.

Exhibit 16.2 shows no other significant changes for our consideration. Income before taxes decreased because operating income decreased. Income taxes are less because income before taxes is less. Thus, we might conclude that the reason net income decreased by 14 percent is because of the increase in operating expenses for the year.

Common-Size Statements

Common-size statements are financial statements that show each item as a percentage rather than a dollar amount. Each asset item is shown as a percentage of total assets, which are shown as 100 percent. Each liability and owner's equity item is shown as a percentage of total liabilities and owner's equity. The income statement shows all items as a percentage of sales, which is shown as 100 percent. This type of analysis is referred to as **vertical analysis,** because we analyze the financial statements up and down, rather than across, as was done for horizontal analysis.

Common-Size Balance Sheet Comparative common-size balance sheets are shown for Star Company in Exhibit 16.3. Significant changes between years should be investigated. Looking at Exhibit 16.3, you see that accounts receivable is 20 percent of total assets in 19X2; whereas it was only 15 percent in 19X1. This increase may be significant. Further analysis may provide us with an indication of how significant it is. Look at property, plant, and

Exhibit 16.3 Comparative Common-Size Balance Sheets

Star Company
Common-Size Balance Sheets
December 31, 19X2 and 19X1

	Percentages	
	19X2	**19X1**
Current Assets:		
Cash	5%	5%
Accounts Receivable (Net)	20	15
Inventory	13	11
Prepaid Expenses	2	1
Total Current Assets	40	32
Property, Plant, and Equipment:		
Land	13	14
Plant and Equipment (Net)	47	54
Total Property, Plant, and Equipment	60	68
Total Assets	100%	100%
Current Liabilities:		
Accounts Payable	16%	13%
Accrued Liabilities	3	2
Total Current Liabilities	19	15
Long-Term Debt:		
10% Bonds Payable	40	42
Total Liabilities	59	57
Stockholders' Equity:		
8% Preferred Stock, $100 Par, 500 Shares	7	7
Common Stock, $10 Par, 10,000 Shares	13	14
Additional Paid-In Capital	5	6
Retained Earnings	16	16
Total Stockholders' Equity	41	43
Total Liabilities and Stockholders' Equity	100%	100%

equipment. Note that it went down from 54 percent to 47 percent. This decrease may not be significant, because it only represents the depreciation for the year. On the other hand, it may indicate that the growth in the business's facilities is not keeping pace with the deterioration of buildings and equipment. A continuous decrease over the years would warrant further investigation. The total liabilities percentage and the total stockholders' equity percentage, as they relate to the long-run stability of the firm, will be discussed later.

Common-Size Income Statement Comparative common-size income statements for Star Company are shown in Exhibit 16.4. These statements include several items that management, as well as outside financial analysts, frequently look at as a means of evaluating how well the firm has done.

Exhibit 16.4 Comparative Common-Size Income Statements

	Percentages	
	19X2	**19X1**
Sales	100%	100%
Cost of Goods Sold	56	57
Gross Margin	44	43
Operating Expenses	33	30
Operating Income	11	13
Interest Expense.	4	4
Income before Taxes.	7	9
Income Taxes (40%)	3	4
Net Income.	4%	5%

Star Company Common-Size Income Statements for the Years Ended December 31, 19X2 and 19X1

Cost of Goods Sold Percentage The **cost of goods sold percentage** indicates the total cost of goods sold as a percentage of sales. This percentage is usually fairly standard for firms within a specific type of industry. Normally, a firm does not have a significant control over cost of goods sold; therefore, the percentage should not vary greatly from year to year. The use of quantity discounts and good buying techniques may keep this percentage to a minimum. For Star Company, it declined slightly from 19X1 to 19X2. Shoplifting losses and other thefts will be reflected in the cost of goods sold percentage. If this percentage is abnormally high, it may indicate that inventory is being lost through theft. Increases in this percentage may also mean that selling prices are not keeping up with the cost of merchandise purchased.

Gross Margin Percentage The **gross margin percentage** (frequently called the *gross margin ratio*) is the relationship of gross margin to sales. It is the complement of the cost of goods sold percentage. It represents the percentage of sales available to cover operating expenses and provide the net income.

Operating Expense Ratio The **operating expense ratio** is the relationship of operating expenses to sales. It is an important ratio, because operating expenses is one area over which management normally has some control.

Operating expenses consist of selling and administrative expenses. By controlling them, management can increase the firm's profitability. Notice that the operating expense ratio for Star Company increased from 30 percent in 19X1 to 33 percent in 19X2. While this may not be significant, remember that net income decreased from $42,000 to $36,000. As previously mentioned, management should analyze each operating expense item to determine where the potential problem may lie. These individual operating expenses are not provided here.

Return on Sales The relationship of net income to sales is called the **return on sales.** This percentage varies from one industry to another. Notice that return on sales for Star Company declined from 5 percent in 19X1 to 4 percent in 19X2. This decline is a direct result of the increase in the operating expense ratio. The return on sales reflects the effects of cost of goods sold and operating expenses on the profitability of the firm. It is often referred to in business reports.

Short-Run Financial Stability

Short-run creditors—that is, those lending money to be paid back within a year or those selling merchandise on credit—are especially interested in the firm's short-run financial stability. In other words, they are interested in the ability of the firm to repay debts due in the near future. They are interested in the liquidity of the firm. **Liquidity** is defined as the firm's ability to convert assets into cash. Several ratios are useful in determining the firm's short-run debt-paying ability.

Working Capital

Working capital is the difference between current assets and current liabilities. It represents the excess of current assets available to carry on the day-to-day operations of a business. The amount of working capital for Star Company increased from 19X1 to 19X2, as shown below:

	19X2	19X1
Current Assets	$300,000	$228,000
Current Liabilities	140,000	105,000
Working Capital	$160,000	$123,000

Looking at the dollar amount of working capital by itself does not usually provide sufficient information for the analyst. It is necessary to consider other short-term ratios along with this one. It is also important to know where working capital came from and where it went during the year. This information is provided by the statement of changes in financial position, which is described in Chapter 15.

Current Ratio

The **current ratio,** the relationship of current assets to current liabilities, is calculated by dividing current assets by current liabilities. It is a widely used measure of a firm's short-term debt-paying ability. Current assets represent cash, those assets expected to be converted to cash during the next year, and prepaid expenses. Current liabilities represent those debts expected to be paid in the next year. Therefore, you can see how knowing the relationship between these two items is helpful. The current ratio for Star Company is calculated as follows:

	19X2	**19X1**
$\dfrac{\text{Current Assets}}{\text{Current Liabilities}}$	$\dfrac{\$300,000}{\$140,000} =$	$\dfrac{\$228,000}{\$105,000} =$
Current Ratio	2.14 to 1	2.17 to 1

There has been a slight decline in the ratio; but it is insignificant. One rule of thumb used for many years is that, generally, a firm's current ratio should not fall below 2 to 1. There are many exceptions, however; and the ratio depends to some extent on the type of firm. For example, public utilities seldom have a current ratio as high as 2 to 1; but this is not considered detrimental. Because of the nature of their business, a high current ratio is not generally necessary. In any event, the analyst should look at more than just the current ratio.

Acid-Test Ratio

The **acid-test ratio,** often called the *quick ratio,* is the ratio of quick assets to current liabilities. **Quick assets** are cash and those assets that can be converted to cash within a short period of time; they consist of cash, marketable securities, and accounts receivable. Marketable securities are included because the firm can sell them quickly, usually by merely making a phone call. Accounts receivable also can be sold within a short period of time to banks or finance companies. On the other hand, inventory is not a quick asset, because it normally takes longer to convert inventory to cash. Prepaid expenses are never really converted to cash; rather, they conserve cash by paying for items in advance.

The idea behind the acid-test ratio is to determine whether a firm could pay all its current liabilities, if necessary, within a very short period of time. Practically, it would never have to do this. But as a measure of short-term financial stability, a firm's ability to do it is important to the short-term creditor. The acid-test ratio for Star Company is calculated below:

	19X2	**19X1**
$\dfrac{\text{Quick Assets}}{\text{Current Liabilities}}$	$\dfrac{\$190,000}{\$140,000} =$	$\dfrac{\$145,000}{\$105,000} =$
Acid-Test Ratio	1.36 to 1	1.38 to 1

There has been virtually no change in the acid-test ratio from 19X2 to 19X1. Creditors normally like to see an acid-test ratio of at least 1 to 1. Such a ratio means that a firm has the ability to pay off all its current liabilities very quickly.

Inventory Turnover

Inventory represents a substantial investment for merchandising and manufacturing firms. There are several costs attached to holding inventory; they are described fully in Chapter 12. They generally include the interest cost associated with the investment; the cost of storage space, such as rent on a warehouse; and the cost of obsolescence and deterioration, which occur with many products. Thus, it is essential for management to properly manage inventory. Inventory turnover is a measure of inventory management. **Inventory turnover** represents the number of times inventory is replaced during the year. Generally, a higher inventory turnover is preferred to a lower inventory turnover. However, an abnormally high inventory turnover may indicate that, at times, the firm is running out of inventory during the year and thereby losing sales and creating customer ill-will.

To calculate inventory turnover, the firm must first determine average inventory. Management usually has monthly inventory figures and can use them to determine the average for the year. External analysts, however, do not usually have access to monthly figures; therefore, they use beginning inventory and ending inventory and merely divide the sum of these two figures by two to obtain an average. Assume that beginning inventory in 19X1 for Star Company was $105,000. The balance sheet in Exhibit 16.1 shows ending inventory for 19X1 as $75,000. This becomes beginning inventory for 19X2. Exhibit 16.1 shows ending inventory for 19X2 as $100,000. Average inventory is calculated as follows:

	19X2	**19X1**
	$\dfrac{\$75,000 + \$100,000}{2} =$	$\dfrac{\$105,000 + \$75,000}{2} =$
	$\dfrac{\$175,000}{2} =$	$\dfrac{\$180,000}{2} =$
Average Inventory	$87,500	$90,000

Inventory turnover indicates how many times this average inventory was replaced. It is calculated by dividing cost of goods sold by average inventory, as follows:

	19X2	**19X1**
$\dfrac{\text{Cost of Goods Sold}}{\text{Average Inventory}}$	$\dfrac{\$450,000}{\$87,500} =$	$\dfrac{\$420,000}{\$90,000} =$
Inventory Turnover	5.14	4.67

Inventory turnover for Star Company has increased slightly from 19X1 to 19X2. This is not a significant increase, but it suggests a favorable trend. It was probably caused by the increase in sales.

Another calculation, related to inventory turnover, is the **number of days to turnover.** This calculation indicates how long it took, on the average, to sell inventory. It is calculated for Star Company below:

	19X2	**19X1**
$\dfrac{\text{Days in a Year}}{\text{Inventory Turnover}}$	$\dfrac{365}{5.14} =$	$\dfrac{365}{4.67} =$
Number of Days to Turn Over	71	78

This calculation parallels inventory turnover. That is, if inventory turnover has increased, it will naturally take fewer days for inventory to turn over. As you see, this figure decreased from 78 days to 71 days.

Accounts Receivable Turnover

Accounts receivable is another major asset representing a considerable investment for most firms. Accordingly, it is important to properly manage this asset. A measure of credit management, and therefore accounts receivable management, is **accounts receivable turnover,** which measures how quickly accounts receivable are being collected. It is similar to inventory turnover in that a high receivable turnover is regarded as favorable and a low turnover is regarded as unfavorable.

Average accounts receivable must first be calculated. For Star Company, assume that the beginning balance of accounts receivable in 19X1 was $90,000. Exhibit 16.1 shows the ending balance as $110,000. This becomes the beginning balance for 19X2. The ending balance for 19X2 is shown on Exhibit 16.1 as $150,000. The amount of average accounts receivable is calculated as follows:

	19X2	**19X1**
	$\dfrac{\$110,000 + \$150,000}{2} =$	$\dfrac{\$90,000 + \$110,000}{2} =$
	$\dfrac{\$260,000}{2} =$	$\dfrac{\$200,000}{2} =$
Average Accounts Receivable	$130,000	$100,000

Accounts receivable turnover is calculated by dividing credit sales for the year by average accounts receivable. For Star Company, assume all sales are credit sales. In this case, the accounts receivable turnover is calculated as follows:

	19X2	**19X1**
$\dfrac{\text{Credit Sales}}{\text{Average Accounts Receivable}}$	$\dfrac{\$800,000}{\$130,000} =$	$\dfrac{\$740,000}{\$100,000} =$
Accounts Receivable Turnover	6.15	7.4

Turnover has decreased from 7.4 to 6.15. At this point, we cannot say that this is necessarily unfavorable, although a lower turnover is generally regarded as less favorable than a higher one. It appears that in order to increase sales, the company has eased its credit restrictions, which is not in itself bad. In fact, a very high turnover may indicate that credit restrictions are too tight and that sales are being lost unnecessarily. The point is that, as a measure of accounts receivable management, decreasing turnover is a factor that needs to be watched.

Another way of looking at this measurement is to calculate the **average collection period** of accounts receivable, which is determined by dividing the number of days in the year by the accounts receivable turnover. This calculation is shown below for Star Company:

	19X2	19X1
$\dfrac{\text{Days in a Year}}{\text{Accounts Receivable Turnover}}$	$\dfrac{365}{6.15} =$	$\dfrac{365}{7.4} =$
Average Collection Period	59.3 Days	49.3 Days

The average collection period has increased from 49.3 days to 59.3 days. This increase appears to be significant. Again, with the limited information available, we cannot say there is a problem. However, if the firm's normal collection period is sixty days, customers, on the average, are paying just within the required time. Since few customers will pay early, and some will always be slow, it is not uncommon for the average collection period to exceed the credit terms slightly. Nevertheless, Star Company should be careful in granting future credit to insure that it does not allow an unreasonably large number of questionable accounts to be added to accounts receivable.

Long-Run Financial Stability

Bondholders and long-term note holders are naturally interested in the firm's long-run ability to pay its debts. In addition, before granting long-term credit, a potential lender wants some assurance that the loan will be repaid. A creditor is also interested in the firm's ability to meet periodic interest payments. Long-term creditors can use several ratios to assess a firm's long-run financial stability.

Debt-Asset Ratio

The **debt-asset ratio,** sometimes called the *debt ratio*, is the relationship between total liabilities and and total assets. It is calculated by dividing total liabilities by total assets.

The debt-asset ratio provides the creditor with some indication as to the probability of collecting the amount owed to the event the firm must liquidate its assets (sell its assets if it goes out of business). In liquidation, assets are normally sold for less than the amount shown on the books. Creditors receive payment before stockholders. The greater the debt-asset ratio, the less likely a creditor will receive the full amount owed. Therefore, a creditor prefers a low debt-asset ratio to a high debt-asset ratio. There is no standard as to what constitutes a high or low ratio. It depends to some extent on the overall financial condition of the company, as well as the industry. Nevertheless, if the debt ratio exceeds 60 percent, creditors may want to look closely before granting additional credit. The debt-asset ratio for Star Company is calculated as follows:

	19X2	19X1
$\dfrac{\text{Total Liabilities}}{\text{Total Assets}}$	$\dfrac{\$440,000}{\$750,000} =$	$\dfrac{\$405,000}{\$708,000} =$
Debt-Asset Ratio	58.7%	57.2%

The debt-asset ratio for Star Company has increased from 57.2 percent to 58.7 percent. This means that creditors are providing 59 percent of the assets. Star Company's debt-asset ratio approaches the 60-percent mark mentioned above. The ratio is not necessarily significant unless a firm goes into liquidation. However, if the debt-asset ratio is too high, and if operating performance is poor, a company may be forced into liquidation because it is unable to pay its debts on time.

Subtracting the debt-asset ratio from 100 percent provides the **equity-asset ratio.** It is based on the same concept as the debt-asset ratio but is looked at from the stockholder's viewpoint. That is, it measures the percentage of assets provided by the stockholders. The equity-asset ratio is just another way of measuring the firm's long-run financial position.

If a firm is able to meet its debts and interest payments, a high debt-asset ratio may work to the benefit of stockholders because of the leverage factor. This situation is described in a later section.

Debt-Equity Ratio

The **debt-equity ratio** is the relationship between total liabilities and total stockholders' equity. It provides the same type of measurement as the debt-asset ratio in that it relates the assets provided by creditors to the assets provided by stockholders. The ratio is determined by dividing total liabilities by total stockholders' equity, as follows:

	19X2	19X1
$\dfrac{\text{Total Liabilities}}{\text{Total Stockholders' Equity}}$	$\dfrac{\$440,000}{\$310,000} =$	$\dfrac{\$405,000}{\$303,000} =$
Debt-Equity Ratio	1.42	1.34

Star Company's debt-equity ratio has increased from 1.34 to 1.42. This means that the creditors have provided 1.4 times as many assets as the stockholders. The significance of the debt-equity ratio is similar to that of the debt-asset ratio. Both measure the relative financing of the firm by creditors and stockholders. Therefore, a high debt-equity ratio is generally not considered favorable by creditors; but, again, it may benefit stockholders if the firm is able to properly use leverage, as described later. Naturally, it only benefits stockholders if the firm is able to meet its debts and interest payments on a timely basis.

Times Interest Earned

Times interest earned, a measurement for determining the relationship between operating income and the interest requirements, is calculated by dividing operating income by interest expense. It measures the relative safety of the interest payment for creditors. The creditors expect that the greater the interest coverage, the more likely they will receive their interest payments on time.

Notice that operating income, rather than net income, is used in the calculation. The reason for this is that the analyst wants to know how many times interest has been earned. Thus, the interest deduction should not be included. Furthermore, interest is deductible for tax purposes, and taxes are calculated after interest is deducted. Therefore, the operating income figure is more appropriate to use in the calculation than the net income figure. The times interest earned for the Star Company is calculated below:

	19X2	19X1
$\dfrac{\text{Operating Income}}{\text{Interest Expense}}$	$\dfrac{\$90,000}{\$30,000}=$	$\dfrac{\$100,000}{\$30,000}=$
Times Interest Earned	3 Times	3.33 Times

Here the times interest earned has gone down from 3.33 to 3. As with most ratios, there is no magic number that constitutes an appropriate times interest earned. However, in measuring the creditors' likelihood of receiving interest payments, the higher the times interest earned, the better. Times interest earned for Star Company is not very high. This does not necessarily indicate a problem; but, when coupled with the debt-asset ratio of 59 percent, it might cause a potential creditor to be somewhat cautious about extending a substantial amount of long-term credit at this time.

Operating Performance

Creditors are interested in the operating performance of a firm, because it is through profitable operations that the firm generates sufficient cash to repay debts and meet interest payments. Stockholders and potential investors are also interested in operating performance, since it is through profitable operations that they receive a return on their investment in the form of dividends or an increase in the price of the stock in the marketplace. There are a number of measurements that help evaluate operating performance.

Earnings per Share

Earnings per share represents the amount of net income that one share of common stock has earned for the period. Rightly or wrongly, it is probably the most frequently looked at measure of operating performance. The calculation of earnings per share depends on whether the firm has a simple capital structure or a complex capital structure.

Simple Capital Structure A firm with a **simple capital structure** does not have any securities that are convertible into common stock. If the firm has only common stock outstanding, then earnings per share is calculated by merely dividing net income for the year by the average number of shares outstanding for the year.[1] For example, if a firm has net income of $100,000 and an average of 20,000 shares outstanding for the year, earnings per share is $5 ($100,000 ÷ 20,000).

---

[1]The average number of shares outstanding is a weighted average, not a simple average. For example, if a firm has 10,000 shares outstanding for three months and 20,000 shares outstanding for nine months, the average number of shares for the year is 17,500, calculated as follows:

$$3 \text{ Months} \times 10,000 = 30,000$$
$$9 \text{ Months} \times 20,000 = \underline{180,000}$$
$$\underline{\underline{210,000}}$$

$$\frac{210,000}{12 \text{ Months}} = 17,500 \text{ Shares}$$

When preferred stock is outstanding, we must first subtract the preferred dividend requirement from net income to arrive at **income available to common shares** and then divide this amount by the average number of common shares outstanding to determine earnings per share. Since Star Company has preferred stock outstanding, its earnings per share is calculated as follows:

	19X2	19X1
Net Income	$36,000	$42,000
Preferred Dividends	−4,000	−4,000
Income Available to Common Shares	$32,000	$38,000

$$\frac{\text{Income Available to Common Shares}}{\text{Average Number of Common Shares Outstanding}} \quad \frac{\$32,000}{10,000} = \quad \frac{\$38,000}{10,000} =$$

Earnings per Share (EPS)	$3.20	$3.80

In this case, earnings per share has declined from $3.80 to $3.20. This decline would normally be regarded negatively by potential investors. Normally, earnings per share for the current year is compared with those of several prior years to determine the trend. For example, assume that the Star Company had the following earnings per share for 19X2 and the four prior years:

19X2	19X1	19X0	19W9	19W8
$3.20	$3.80	$3.50	$3.00	$2.60

The current year's decline in earnings is definitely a disappointment when compared with the rising trend of the last four years. The question arises as to whether this year's decline represents a new trend or whether it is an isolated phenomenon. In other words, can the company take steps to reverse this downward trend and again begin earning more than in previous years?

Complex Capital Structure A **complex capital structure** includes securities that are convertible to common stock. It is not unusual for firms to issue preferred stock or bonds with a convertible feature. This feature allows the holders of the securities to convert their security into common stock at some point in the future. These types of securities are sold in order to raise capital and provide an attractive alternative for the buyer. For example, a bondholder may not be interested in common stock at the current time but may become interested if it appears the company is going to be particularly profitable. Therefore, convertible bonds are attractive in that the bondholder has the safety of earning interest and principal as a creditor but still has the option of becoming a common stockholder if that alternative appears to become more favorable.

These types of securities present a problem in calculating earnings per share; if converted to common stock, they will dilute earnings per share from what it otherwise would be. Therefore, in order to fully inform the financial statement reader, firms are required to calculate both primary earnings per share and fully diluted earnings per share.

Primary earnings per share is the earnings per share calculation based on the assumption that none of the convertible securities will be converted. In effect, this calculation is the same as the one shown for the simple capital structure. For example, assume that Star Company's 500 shares of preferred stock are convertible into 2,000 shares of common stock. Primary earnings per share is calculated under the assumption that none of the preferred will be converted. Thus, the calculation is exactly the same as in the previous section—that is, $3.20 per share for 19X2 and $3.80 per share for 19X1.

Fully diluted earnings per share is calculated under the assumption that all convertible securities are converted to common stock. Under those conditions, no preferred stock and 12,000 shares of common stock (10,000 + 2,000) are outstanding. Therefore, there is no preferred dividend requirement. Fully diluted earnings per share is calculated for Star Company as follows:

	19X2	**19X1**
$\dfrac{\text{Net Income}}{\text{Average Number of Common Shares Outstanding}}$	$\dfrac{\$36,000}{12,000} =$	$\dfrac{\$42,000}{12,000} =$
Fully Diluted Earnings per Share	$3.00	$3.50

You now have the following earnings per share figures for the complex capital structure:

	19X2	**19X1**
Earnings per Share (EPS)	$3.20	$3.80
Fully Diluted EPS	$3.00	$3.50

You may ask, "Well, is earnings per share for 19X2 $3.20 or $3.00?" The answer depends on your assumption. The reason for the dual calculation is to alert the reader that the $3.20 figure will be inappropriate if the preferred stock is converted. If only some of the stock is converted, then earnings per share will lie between $3.00 and $3.20. Thus, depending on what the preferred shareholders do, earnings per share may be as high as $3.20 or as low as $3.00.

Extraordinary Items In the operation of a firm, extraordinary items may appear. **Extraordinary items** are defined as events that affect the financial statements but that are unusual and nonrecurring in nature. A primary example of an extraordinary item is a disaster loss, such as one caused by a fire, flood, or earthquake. Generally accepted accounting principles require that extraordinary items be shown separately on the income statement and that earnings per share be calculated separately for extraordinary items. This practice helps the financial analyst to assess the normal operating results of a firm versus extraordinary results that will not normally be expected to occur again.

To illustrate, let us assume that in 19X2 Star Company suffered a hurricane loss totaling $20,000. An extraordinary item is shown on the income statement net of its tax effect. In this case, the $20,000 loss is deductible for tax purposes. Therefore, the loss reduces otherwise taxable income by

$20,000. Since the tax rate is 40 percent, a $20,000 reduction is taxable income results in an $8,000 reduction in taxes (40% × $20,000). This means that without the loss the firm would pay an additional $8,000 in taxes. Thus, the aftertax loss is only $12,000 ($20,000 − $8,000). The section on the income statement that reports the extraordinary item is shown below:

Income before Extraordinary Item	$36,000
Extraordinary Item:	
Hurricane Loss (Net of Tax)	(12,000)
Net Income	$24,000

The $36,000 shown above was shown in Exhibit 16.2 as net income. However, in this case, it is income before extraordinary item. The extraordinary item is deducted, net of tax, resulting in a net income of $24,000.

Earnings per share is now calculated as follows:

Earnings per Share before Extraordinary Item	$3.20
Extraordinary Item:	
Hurricane Loss (Net of Tax)	(1.20)
Earnings per Share	$2.40

The $12,000 loss caused by the extraordinary item reduced earnings per share by $1.20 ($12,000 ÷ 10,000 shares) to $2.40 per share. This type of presentation helps the financial analyst, whose concern is for the long-run profitability of the firm. Since, by definition, extraordinary items are unusual and nonrecurring, the $1.20 per share loss will most likely be disregarded in assessing future earnings potential. Thus, in looking at the future, the financial analyst considers the $3.20, rather than the $2.40, as the important element.

Recognize that the firm did in fact lose $1.20 per share this year; it has $12,000 less income because of the hurricane. However, with regard to the future, this $12,000 loss may not be significant.

It is also important to separate an extraordinary gain on the income statement. If an unusual or nonrecurring gain were not shown as a separate item, the financial analyst might assume that the earnings per share shown was from normal operations. Again, in assessing the future earnings potential of the firm, it would be misleading to include as ordinary earnings a gain that is not expected to occur again.

Reporting extraordinary items is unrelated to whether a capital structure is simple or complex. Unusual and nonrecurring items must be reported as extraordinary under both types of capital structures.

Price-Earnings Ratio   The **price-earnings ratio** is the relationship of the market price per share of common stock to its earnings per share. This ratio is typically calculated on primary earnings per share. However, an analyst can calculate on primary, fully diluted, or both. The calculation involves dividing market price per share by earnings per share. Assume that at the end of 19X1 Star Company common stock was selling for $35 per share. At the end of 19X2, it was selling for $25 per share. The price-earnings ratio is calculated as follows:

	19X2	**19X1**
$\dfrac{\text{Market Price}}{\text{Earnings per Share}}$	$\dfrac{\$25.00}{\$3.20}=$	$\dfrac{\$35.00}{\$3.80}=$
Price-Earnings Ratio	7.8	9.2

The illustration shows that at the end of 19X2, one share of Star Company common stock is selling for 7.8 times its earnings. The price-earnings ratio by itself is generally not significant. It is important to compare it with past price-earnings ratios, as well as with what is "normal" for the industry. In this case, the price-earnings ratio has declined from what it was at the end of 19X1. The market price has also declined. These declines were probably caused by the decreased earnings this year. Thus, investors' perception of the future potential of this stock has declined somewhat because of the firm's lower earnings. Therefore, they are unwilling to pay as much as they were previously.

The price-earnings ratio varies among industries. Companies involved in new technology or new product development often have high price-earnings ratios. Investors bid up the price of the stock in the belief that the companies will have higher future earnings.

A stock whose price-earnings ratio is beneath its average price-earnings ratio may currently be priced too low. Consequently, it might represent a good buy. However, one needs to determine why the stock is priced low. If it is low because the future of the company is in doubt, then certainly the stock is not a good buy. At other times, temporary conditions may result in a stock's price being depressed, as reflected in the price-earnings ratio. The stock might be a good buy if its future performance is expected to improve. In any event, one should not make investment decisions on the basis of only one ratio. Other factors should be considered.

Dividends

Dividends are distributions of a company's earnings. One major reason for buying stock of a corporation is the expectation of receiving dividends. Dividends are normally quoted on the basis of dividends per share. For preferred stock, the dividend is usually stipulated in the description of the stock; "8-percent preferred," for example, means that the stock pays a dividend of 8 percent of par value when dividends are declared.

Common stock dividends per share are calculated by dividing the total amount of dividends declared by the number of common shares outstanding. As a practical matter, however, the board of directors normally declares dividends per share, based on earnings per share. Thus, total common dividends declared are normally based on the dividend per share multiplied by the number of common shares outstanding. Exhibit 16.2 showed that preferred dividends per share in both 19X1 and 19X2 were $8. Common dividends were $2.50 per share in both years.

Two ratios are significant in regard to common stock dividends—the dividend payout ratio and the dividend yield.

Dividend Payout Ratio   The **dividend payout ratio** is the ratio of dividends per share to earnings per share. It is calculated by dividing dividends per share by earnings per share.[2] The percentage of earnings paid out by a firm in the form of dividends depends, to a large extent, on the firm's philosophy. Many growth-oriented firms reinvest a major portion of their earnings into new product development and therefore pay very little in dividends. Supposedly, the increased future earnings resulting from this investment in the company will result in higher stock prices and dividends in future years. Other firms pay a fairly consistent percentage of earnings in dividends over the years. Many manufacturing firms pay about 40 percent to 60 percent of earnings in dividends; but this varies from firm to firm. The dividend payout ratio for Star Company is shown below:

	19X2	**19X1**
Dividends per Share / Earnings per Share	$\dfrac{\$2.50}{\$3.20} =$	$\dfrac{\$2.50}{\$3.80} =$
Dividend Payout Ratio	78.1%	65.8%

The dividend payout ratio went up from 19X1 to 19X2 because earnings went down. Often, a company will reduce its dividends if its earnings have decreased. However, if the decline in earnings is considered temporary, it is not unusual for a firm to continue with the same dollar amount of dividends per share in order not to upset stockholders. Naturally, if earnings decline every year, a reduction in dividends will ultimately be necessary.

Dividend Yield The **dividend yield** represents dividends as a percentage of the market price of the stock. It is determined by dividing dividends per share by market price per share. The dividend yield for Star Company is shown below:

	19X2	**19X1**
Dividends per Share / Market Price per Share	$\dfrac{\$2.50}{\$25.00} =$	$\dfrac{\$2.50}{\$35.00} =$
Dividend Yield	10%	7.1%

When market price is $25 per share, a stockholder receives a dividend return of 10 percent. We might compare this return with that on an investment in a savings account or certificates of deposit, which pay interest of between 5 and 12 percent. Star Company's 19X2 dividend yield is higher than that from a low-interest savings account. In addition, the earnings reinvested by the company may result in increased future earnings from dividends, which may cause the price of the stock to go up. An increase in the market price of the stock benefits stockholders when they sell their stock. However, a risk is involved in stock-market investment. In the Star Company example, stockholders who held shares of Star Company stock at the end of 19X1 have seen their investment fall from $35 per share to $25 per share.

Notice that the yield has increased from 7.1 percent to 10 percent. It has increased because the dividend per share has stayed the same but the mar-

---

[2]In a complex capital structure, the dividend payout ratio is usually based on primary earnings per share.

ket price has fallen. It is important to realize that the dividend yield is based on the current market price, not on the price the stockholder paid for the stock. This is because the current market price represents the amount for which stockholders could sell the stock now and reinvest the proceeds. In other words, it represents the stockholders' current investment. Thus, for yield to be an accurate portrayal of the stockholders' return, it must be based on the current market price.

Return on Assets

Return on assets is the relationship of operating income to total assets. It is calculated by dividing operating income by total average assets and is used to measure how well the assets employed in the business have been used. There are several other ways of calculating this return. Some analysts merely divide net income by average assets. Others add back interest expense to net income and divide this amount by average assets. However, by using operating income, we determine how well management has used the assets of the business to earn income from doing what it is in business to do. Financial management, which relates to interest expense, must be measured separately from operating management. Income taxes must be paid, of course, but the operating managers have no control over taxes. Thus, the use of operating income provides shareholders with some indication of managerial performance in using assets.

To calculate return on assets, it is necessary first to determine the average assets for the year. Assume that beginning assets for Star Company in 19X1 were $700,000. Ending assets for 19X1 are shown on the balance sheet in Exhibit 16.1 as $708,000. Beginning and ending assets for 19X2 are shown in Exhibit 16.1 as $708,000 and $750,000, respectively. The amount of average assets is calculated as follows:

	19X2	**19X1**
	$\dfrac{\$708{,}000 + \$750{,}000}{2} =$	$\dfrac{\$700{,}000 + \$708{,}000}{2} =$
	$\dfrac{\$1{,}458{,}000}{2} =$	$\dfrac{\$1{,}408{,}000}{2} =$
Average Assets	$729,000	$704,000

Operating income is shown on the income statements in Exhibit 16.2 as $100,000 for 19X1 and $90,000 for 19X2. With these data, return on assets can be calculated as follows:

	19X2	**19X1**
$\dfrac{\text{Operating Income}}{\text{Average Assets}}$	$\dfrac{\$90{,}000}{\$729{,}000} =$	$\dfrac{\$100{,}000}{\$704{,}000} =$
Return on Assets	12.3%	14.2%

Return on assets has declined from 19X1 to 19X2 primarily because of the decline in operating income. Notice, however, that the increase in average assets also contributes to the decline. There is a smaller amount of income on a larger amount of assets, which reduces return on assets.

Return on Equity

Return on equity, often called *return on common equity* or *return on common shareholders' equity*, is a measurement that indicates how well the company has used the common stockholders' investment. It is calculated by dividing income available to common shares by average common stockholders' equity. If preferred stock is outstanding, preferred dividends are deducted from net income to arrive at income available for common stockholders. If there is no preferred stock, then net income is the income available to common shares.

For Star Company, common stockholders' equity consists of common stock, additional paid-in capital, and retained earnings. Assume that these items totaled $240,000 at the beginning of 19X1. From the balance sheet on Exhibit 16.1, we can calculate this total for the end of 19X1 as $253,000 ($100,000 + $40,000 + $113,000). The beginning balance of common stockholders' equity in 19X2 is the ending balance from 19X1, $253,000. The ending balance in 19X2 can be calculated from Exhibit 16.1 to be $260,000 ($100,000 + $40,000 + $120,000). Average common equity is calculated as follows:

	19X2	**19X1**
	$\dfrac{\$253,000 + \$260,000}{2} =$	$\dfrac{\$240,000 + \$253,000}{2} =$
	$\dfrac{\$513,000}{2} =$	$\dfrac{\$493,000}{2} =$
Average Common Equity	$256,500	$246,500

Because preferred stock is outstanding, preferred dividends of $4,000 must be subtracted from net income to arrive at income available to common shares. As shown on page 537, this figure is $38,000 for 19X1 and $32,000 for 19X2. The return on equity is calculated below:

	19X2	**19X1**
$\dfrac{\text{Income Available to Common Shares}}{\text{Average Common Equity}}$	$\dfrac{\$32,000}{\$256,500} =$	$\dfrac{\$38,000}{\$246,500} =$
Return on Equity	12.5%	15.4%

Return on equity declined primarily because net income declined. Note, however, that return on equity after taxes for 19X2, 12.5 percent, exceeds return on assets before taxes, 12.3 percent. Thus, the firm may have used leverage to its advantage. **Leverage,** often called *trading on the equity,* is the process by which a firm uses funds obtained from creditors and preferred stockholders to earn a rate of return greater than the cost of such funds. To determine how successfully leverage was used, we must calculate the aftertax return on assets by multiplying the complement of the tax rate by the return on assets percentage. With a tax rate of 40 percent, the complement is 60 percent (1 − .40). Thus, the aftertax return on assets for 19X2 is 7.4 percent (60% × 12.3%). Let's see how successful Star Company was in using leverage.

There is no interest expense on current liabilities—that is, accounts payable and accrued liabilities. Thus, the firm is earning 7.4 percent on the assets provided by current liabilities without paying any interest. Bonds payable have a 10-percent interest rate; but the interest is deductible for tax purposes. Aftertax interest cost is really only 6 percent.[3] For the $300,000 in assets provided by bondholders, the firm is paying an effective interest rate of 6 percent and earning 7.4 percent. Preferred stock dividends are not deductible for tax purposes; thus the 8-percent dividend rate on preferred is more than the 7.4 percent earned on assets. This difference does not benefit the common stockholders.

A firm that uses debt wisely can benefit from it. There are risks involved, of course, because the interest must be paid and the debt must eventually be repaid. Therefore, a firm that incurs too much debt may run into trouble. However, it is a fallacy to say a firm is better off if it incurs no debt. If it can earn more on its assets than it is paying in interest cost on debt, stockholders benefit from this difference.

Book Value per Share

Book value per share represents the net assets attributable to one share of common stock. Theoretically, it represents the assets provided by one share of common stock. It is determined by dividing net assets (total assets minus total liabilities) by the number of common shares outstanding. Since net assets equal stockholders' equity, book value can be determined by dividing stockholders' equity by the number of shares outstanding. If preferred stock is also outstanding, preferred stockholders' equity must be subtracted from net assets to determine the amount of net assets applicable to common stockholders.

Total stockholders' equity in Star Company at the end of 19X1 is $303,000. Of this, $50,000 is for preferred stock. Thus, total common stockholders' equity is $253,000 ($303,000 − $50,000). Common stockholders' equity at the end of 19X2 is $260,000 ($310,000 − $50,000). Book value per share for Star Company is calculated as follows:

	19X2		19X1	
$\dfrac{\text{Total Common Equity}}{\text{Common Shares Outstanding}}$	$\dfrac{\$260,000}{10,000}$	=	$\dfrac{\$253,000}{10,000}$	=
Book Value per Share	$26.00		$25.30	

Book value per share is calculated as of a specific date. It is based on total common stockholders' equity as of that date, rather than on average common stockholders' equity for the year. The example shows that at the end of 19X2, each share of common stock represents ownership of $26 of assets. Theoretically, if all assets could be sold for the amount shown on the balance sheet, then after all liabilities and preferred stockholders were paid, common stockholders would receive $26 per share. Practically, it never happens this way, because assets are seldom sold for the amount shown on the balance sheet, especially if the firm is going out of business.

---

[3]Interest payments are deductible for tax purposes. Thus, if the $30,000 in interest were not paid, the firm would have $30,000 more income, on which it would pay $12,000 in taxes (40% × $30,000). Thus, the effective interest expense (after the $12,000 tax saving has been deducted) is $18,000. The effective interest rate is 6 percent ($18,000 ÷ $300,000 long-term debt).

Book value per share is an often-calculated figure; it is found in annual reports of most firms. As a practical matter, it has little significance in financial statement analysis. Normally, analysts are interested in assessing the future potential, especially the earning power, of a firm. Book value merely indicates the amount at which net assets appear on the books at a particular time. Other statement ratios provide more information for analysts to use in assessing the potential of a firm.

Comparison among Firms

In our analysis of Star Company, we have compared data for 19X2 with data for 19X1. Financial analysts, as well as management, frequently compare ratios of a firm with those of other firms or with industry-wide averages. Publications are available that provide industry averages for such items as operating expense ratio, return on equity, return on assets, return on sales, inventory turnover, accounts receivable turnover, and many other ratios.[4]

It is sometimes helpful to compare one firm's ratios with industry averages in order to see if there are significant deviations about which the firm should be concerned. For example, if the industry average for the operating expense ratio is 25 percent, then Star Company should look closely at why its operating expense ratio is 33 percent. While comparisons with other firms may be helpful, they must be tempered with judgment and common sense. Differences in accounting methods among firms will affect ratios. For example, depreciation methods and inventory methods vary among firms. This variation affects ratio calculations and, if ignored, distorts the significance of comparisons. Therefore, when comparing firms we should try to determine whether they use similar accounting procedures. Where they don't, adjustments must be made in the analysis. If information is not available, then we must consider the possibility that results may differ simply because differing accounting techniques are used.

Summary

Financial statement analysis is the process of analyzing relationships among items on financial statements of a firm in order to evaluate the firm's financial position and operating performance. This chapter has analyzed the financial statements of the hypothetical Star Company.

Typically, financial analysis begins with the preparation of comparative statements for the two most recently ended years. Dollar percentage changes are analyzed horizontally to detect any significant differences between years. Common-size statements, in which all items are stated as a

[4]For example, Robert Morris Associates annually provides such ratios in its publication *RMA Annual Statement Studies.* Dun & Bradstreet, Inc., publishes retailing, wholesaling, and manufacturing ratios periodically in *Dun's Review,* a monthly business magazine.

percentage of a base, are prepared in order to relate each item to other items on the statement.

Financial statement analysis also involves comparing ratios. A ratio is the relationship between one financial statement item and another. In financial statement analysis, a number of ratios are commonly used in assessing the financial position and operating performance of the firm.

Some ratios focus on short-run financial stability; others focus on long-run financial stability. A number of ratios are calculated to help assess operating performance. This chapter provided illustrations and applications of the most commonly used ratios. As part of your summary, you should review these ratios and be familiar with not only how they are calculated but also what they mean.

Frequently, analysts compare ratios of one firm with those of other firms or with industry-wide averages. This helps them to determine whether the firm being analyzed is "in the ballpark" insofar as certain specific items are concerned.

Financial statement analysis is a useful tool for both internal and external use. However, it is important to understand the limitations of financial statement analysis. The ratios provide indications. No single ratio should be used alone as the basis for making a decision. The idea of financial statement analysis is for analysts to look at enough items so that they can form a picture of the firm's overall financial health insofar as position and performance are concerned.

Review Problem

Problem

Garland Corporation's income statement and balance sheet for the current year are shown below.

Garland Corporation
Income Statement
for the Year Ended December 31, 19X1

Sales	$1,500,000
Cost of Goods Sold	880,000
Gross Margin	$ 620,000
Operating Expenses	400,000
Operating Income	$ 220,000
Interest Expense	60,000
Income before Taxes	$ 160,000
Income Tax Expense	40,000
Net Income	$ 120,000

Garland Corporation
Balance Sheet
December 31, 19X1

Assets

Cash	$ 80,000
Marketable Securities	200,000
Accounts Receivable (Net)	450,000
Inventory	600,000
Prepaid Expenses	40,000
Land	300,000
Buildings (Net)	450,000
Total Assets	$2,120,000

Liabilities and Stockholders' Equity

Accounts Payable	$ 480,000
Accrued Liabilities	60,000
12% Bonds Payable	500,000
8% Preferred Stock	300,000
Common Stock	500,000
Additional Paid-in Capital	100,000
Retained Earnings	180,000
Total Liabilities and Stockholders' Equity	$2,120,000

All sales are credit sales. Balances for the following items as of January 1, 19X1, were as follows:

Accounts Receivable (Net)	$ 350,000
Inventory	520,000
Total Assets	1,880,000
Total Common Equity	750,000

On January 1, 19X1, the firm had 3,000 shares of preferred stock and 50,000 shares of common stock outstanding. There were no changes in the number of shares outstanding of either class of stock during the year. Required dividends on preferred stock were declared; and dividends totaling $66,000 were declared on common stock.

Required:

Calculate the following ratios:

a. Current ratio.
b. Acid-test ratio.
c. Inventory turnover.
d. Accounts receivable turnover.
e. Average collection period.
f. Debt-asset ratio.
g. Times interest earned.
h. Return on assets.
i. Return on equity.
j. Operating expense ratio.
k. Return on sales.

l. Book value per share.
m. Earnings per share.
n. Dividend payout ratio.

Solution

a. Current Assets:

$80,000 + $200,000 + $450,000 + $600,000 + $40,000 = $1,370,000
Current Liabilities: $480,000 + $60,000 = $540,000

Current Ratio: $\dfrac{\$1,370,000}{\$540,000} = 2.54$

Note that the current ratio and the acid-test ratio are often expressed as a single figure, as shown above. It is understood that the ratio is 2.54 to 1.

b. Quick Assets: $80,000 + $200,000 + $450,000 = $730,000

Acid-Test Ratio: $\dfrac{\$730,000}{\$540,000} = 1.35$

c. Average Inventory: $\dfrac{\$520,000 + \$600,000}{2} = \dfrac{\$1,120,000}{2} = \$560,000$

Inventory Turnover: $\dfrac{\$880,000}{\$560,000} = 1.57$

d. Average Accounts Receivable:

$\dfrac{\$350,000 + \$450,000}{2} = \dfrac{\$800,000}{2} = \$400,000$

Accounts Receivable Turnover: $\dfrac{\$1,500,000}{\$400,000} = 3.75$

e. Average Collection Period: $\dfrac{365}{3.75} = 97.3$ Days

f. Total Liabilities: $480,000 + $60,000 + $500,000 = $1,040,000

Debt-Asset Ratio: $\dfrac{\$1,040,000}{\$2,120,000} = 49.1\%$

g. Times Interest Earned: $\dfrac{\$220,000}{\$60,000} = 3.67$

h. Average Assets:

$\dfrac{\$1,880,000 + \$2,120,000}{2} = \dfrac{\$4,000,000}{2} = \$2,000,000$

Return on Assets: $\dfrac{\$220,000}{\$2,000,000} = 11\%$

i. Common Equity, December 31, 19X1:
$500,000 + $100,000 + $180,000 = $780,000
Average Common Equity:

$\dfrac{\$750,000 + \$780,000}{2} = \dfrac{\$1,530,000}{2} = \$765,000$

Income Available to Common Shares:

Net Income	$120,000
Preferred Dividends (8% × $300,000)	24,000
Income Available to Common Shares	$ 96,000

Return on Equity: $\dfrac{\$96,000}{\$765,000} = 12.5\%$

j. Operating Expense Ratio: $\dfrac{\$400,000}{\$1,500,000} = 26.7\%$

k. Return on Sales: $\dfrac{\$120,000}{\$1,500,000} = 8\%$

l. Book Value per Share: $\dfrac{\$780,000}{50,000} = \$15.60$

m. Earnings per Share: $\dfrac{\$96,000}{50,000 \text{ Shares}} = \$1.92$

n. Dividends per Share: $\dfrac{\$66,000}{50,000 \text{ Shares}} = \$1.32$

Dividend Payout Ratio: $\dfrac{\$1.32}{\$1.92} = 68.8\%$

Questions

16-1 Since financial statement analysis is applied to data resulting from past performance, how does it help individuals make credit and investment decisions regarding the future?

16-2 Of what value to the financial analyst is knowledge of percentage changes?

16-3 If cost of goods sold has increased by a slightly higher percentage than sales, what is the most likely reason?

16-4 What is the operating expense ratio? Why is it an especially important ratio for management's consideration?

16-5 Suppose that a firm's current assets are less than its current liabilities. What is the significance of this situation?

16-6 Axton Corporation had an inventory turnover of 12 last year. The average turnover for firms in the same industry as Axton was 6. Is Axton's turnover favorable? Explain.

16-7 Bretton Company's credit policy requires that customers pay their accounts within 30 days. The firm grants no discount for early payment. Last year, the average collection period was 10 days. Would you regard this situation as favorable? Explain.

16-8 Moxley Corporation has a debt-asset ratio of 10%. As a potential stockholder, do you regard this as a favorable situation? Explain.

16-9 The common stock of some fairly strong companies provides very low dividend yields. Why are investors willing to invest in companies in which the dividend yield is less than they could earn on a savings account or certificate of deposit?

16-10 An extraordinary gain is, in fact, income to a firm. Therefore, why is it not really considered by financial analysts when they evaluate a firm's operating results?

16-11 What is the difference between primary earnings per share and fully diluted earnings per share? Why are both reported? Doesn't reporting both just confuse the investor? Explain.

16-12 In looking at the financial statements of Nanton Company, you note that book value per share is $10; yet the stock is selling for $5 per share. It appears the firm could sell all its assets and make a profit. Do you consider the stock a good buy?

16-13 Since annual bond interest must be paid only once, why does it matter what "times interest earned" is, as long as it is at least 1?

16-14 A firm recently issued bonds to increase working capital. This issuance brought the current ratio from 1.3 to 1 to 2.1 to 1 and the debt-asset ratio to 35%. Other ratios appear reasonable. Comment on the wisdom of issuing the bonds.

16-15 Why should ratios of a firm be compared with an industry average? What problems are involved in such comparisons?

Exercises

16-16 Current Ratio; Acid-Test Ratio Selected data from the balance sheet of Blankner Company as of December 31 of its most recently ended year are as follows:

Cash	$30,000
Marketable Securities	50,000
Accounts Receivable (Net)	180,000
Inventory	150,000
Prepaid Expenses	10,000
Accounts Payable	175,000
Accrued Liabilities	20,000

   a. Calculate the current ratio.
   b. Calculate the acid-test ratio.
   c. Comment as to whether the ratios you calculated appear favorable.

16-17 Operating Performance Ratios Consider the following income statement:

Flora Corporation
Income Statement
for the Year Ended December 31, 19X1

Sales	$500,000
Cost of Goods Sold	280,000
Gross Margin	$220,000
Operating Expenses	130,000
Operating Income	$ 90,000
Interest Expense	20,000
Income before Taxes	$ 70,000
Income Tax Expense	25,000
Net Income	$ 45,000

Average assets for the year totaled $1,000,000. Calculate the following ratios:

a. Cost of goods sold percentage.
b. Operating expense ratio.
c. Return on sales.
d. Return on assets.
e. Times interest earned.

16-18 Inventory Turnover The following data pertain to the Danville Company's last 3 years:

	19X3	19X2	19X1
Cost of Goods Sold	$980,000	$900,000	$800,000
Ending Inventory	250,000	180,000	140,000

Calculate inventory turnover and the number of days to turn over for 19X2 and 19X3. Comment on the change between the 2 years.

16-19 Accounts Receivable Turnover In 19X5, Matteran Company undertook to increase sales by increasing the number of credit customers. Data for the last 3 years are shown below:

	19X5	19X4	19X3
Credit Sales	$700,000	$620,000	$600,000
Accounts Receivable (Net)	85,000	45,000	40,000
Net Income	38,000	32,000	30,000

The normal credit period is 30 days.

a. Determine the percentage increase in sales and net income for 19X5.
b. Determine accounts receivable turnover and the average collection period for 19X4 and 19X5.
c. Comment on the apparent results of the action to increase sales.

16-20 Earnings per Share; Dividend Payout Ratio Felton Corporation had net income of $600,000 last year. The company had an average of 150,000 shares of common stock outstanding for the year. It also had outstanding 5,000 shares of $100 par, 10% preferred stock convertible to common on the basis of 5 shares of common for each share of preferred. Dividends of $1 per share were declared on common stock. Calculate the following:

  a. Primary earnings per share.
  b. Fully diluted earnings per share.
  c. Dividend payout ratio.

16-21 Earnings per Share During 19X4, Bittersweet, Inc., had outstanding 50,000 shares of common stock. Income before extraordinary item was $250,000. The firm incurred an extraordinary loss by fire of $40,000. The tax rate is 40%.

  a. Calculate net income.
  b. Calculate earnings per share.

16-22 Operating Performance Ratios Selected data from the financial statements of Rosen, Incorporated, for the year ended December 31, 19X2, are shown below:

Sales	$365,000
Operating Expenses	$200,000
Operating Income	$100,000
Net Income	$40,000
Average Assets	$550,000
Average Common Equity	$800,000
Average Common Shares Outstanding	25,000

Calculate the following ratios:

  a. Operating expense ratio.
  b. Return on sales.
  c. Return on assets.
  d. Return on equity.
  e. Earnings per share.

16-23 Long-Term and Operating Performance Ratios Selected data from the financial statements of Lorsten Company for the year ended December 31, 19X2, are shown below:

Average Assets	$1,600,000
Total Assets, December 31, 19X2	$2,000,000
Average Common Equity	$650,000
Total Common Equity	$700,000
Total Liabilities, December 31, 19X2	$900,000
Interest Expense	$85,000
Operating Income	$320,000
Net Income	$150,000
Preferred Stock, December 31, 19X2	$200,000
Preferred Dividends	$15,000
Common Shares Outstanding	50,000

Calculate the following ratios:

  a. Debt-asset ratio.
  b. Times interest earned.
  c. Return on assets.
  d. Return on equity.

    e. Earnings per share.

    f. Book value per share.

16–24 Earnings per Share; Dividend Ratios Caltel Corporation showed net income of $240,000 for its most recently ended year. The company had an average of 60,000 shares of common stock outstanding during the year. It began and ended the year with 5,000 shares of $100 par, 10% preferred outstanding. Dividends of $2 per share were declared on common stock, and the most recent market price was $40 per share.

Calculate the following:

    a. Earnings per share.

    b. Price-earnings ratio.

    c. Dividend payout ratio.

    d. Dividend yield.

16–25 Calculating Dividends from the Dividend Payout Ratio Growing, Inc., had net income for 19X7 of $10,600,000 and earnings per share on common stock of $5. Included in net income was $1,000,000 of bond interest expense related to the firm's long-term debt. The income tax rate for 19X7 was 50%. Dividends on preferred stock were $600,000. The dividend payout ratio on common stock was 40%. What were the dividends on common stock in 19X7? (AICPA adapted)

16–26 Current Ratio Relationships Each lettered item below describes an independent situation. For each situation, one factor is denoted X and the other factor is denoted Y. For each situation, compare the factors to determine whether X is greater than, equal to, or less than Y. Explain your answer.

    a. Delta Corporation wrote off a $100 uncollectible account receivable against the $1,200 balance in its allowance account. Compare the current ratio *before* the write off (X) with the current ratio *after* the write off (Y).

        1. X greater than Y.

        2. X equals Y.

        3. X less than Y.

        4. Cannot be determined.

    b. Epsilon Company has a current ratio of 2 to 1. A transaction reduces the current ratio. Compare the working capital *before* this transaction (X) with the working capital *after* this transaction (Y).

        1. X greater than Y.

        2. X equals Y.

        3. X less than Y.

        4. Cannot be determined.

(AICPA adapted)

Problems

16–27 Various Ratios Settler Corporation's income statement and balance sheet for the current year are shown below:

Settler Corporation
Income Statement
for the Year Ended December 31, 19X4

Sales	$980,000
Cost of Goods Sold	600,000
Gross Margin	$380,000
Operating Expenses	250,000
Operating Income	$130,000
Interest Expense	50,000
Income before Taxes	$ 80,000
Income Tax Expense	25,000
Net Income	$ 55,000

Settler Corporation
Balance Sheet
December 31, 19X4

Assets

Cash	$ 35,000
Marketable Securities	100,000
Accounts Receivable (Net)	360,000
Inventory	400,000
Prepaid Expenses	30,000
Land	200,000
Buildings (Net)	650,000
Total Assets	$1,775,000

Liabilities and Stockholders' Equity

Accounts Payable	$ 340,000
Accrued Liabilities	60,000
10% Bonds Payable	500,000
Common Stock	400,000
Additional Paid-in Capital	200,000
Retained Earnings	275,000
Total Liabilities and Stockholders' Equity	$1,775,000

All sales are credit sales. Balances for the following items as of January 1, 19X4, were as follows:

Accounts Receivable (Net)	$ 280,000
Inventory	350,000
Total Assets	1,425,000
Total Common Equity	720,000

Required:

Calculate the following ratios:

a. Current ratio.
b. Acid-test ratio.
c. Inventory turnover.
d. Accounts receivable turnover.
e. Average collection period.
f. Debt-asset ratio.
g. Times interest earned.
h. Return on assets.
i. Return on equity.
j. Operating expense ratio.
k. Return on sales.

16–28 Various Ratios Baldwin Company's income statement and balance sheet for the current year are shown below:

Baldwin Company
Income Statement
for the Year Ended December 31, 19X3

Sales	$220,000
Cost of Goods Sold	125,000
Gross Margin	$ 95,000
Operating Expenses	60,000
Operating Income	$ 35,000
Interest Expense	15,000
Income before Taxes	$ 20,000
Income Tax Expense	4,000
Net Income	$ 16,000

Baldwin Company
Balance Sheet
December 31, 19X3

Assets	
Cash	$ 8,000
Accounts Receivable (Net)	15,000
Inventory	12,000
Prepaid Expenses	3,000
Equipment (Net)	50,000
Total Assets	$88,000
Liabilities and Stockholders' Equity	
Accounts Payable	$ 9,000
Accrued Liabilities	2,000
Long-Term Notes Payable	35,000
Common Stock, $10 Par	30,000
Retained Earnings	12,000
Total Liabilities and Stockholders' Equity	$88,000

Credit sales average 80% of total sales. There has been no change in the number of shares outstanding during the year. In addition, balances for the following items as of January 1, 19X3, were as follows:

Accounts Receivable (Net)	$11,000
Inventory	9,500
Total Assets	85,000
Total Common Equity	30,000

Required:

Calculate the following ratios:

a. Current ratio.

b. Acid-test ratio.

c. Inventory turnover.

d. Accounts receivable turnover.

e. Average collection period.

f. Debt-asset ratio.

g. Return on assets.

h. Return on equity.

i. Return on sales.

j. Operating expense ratio.

k. Earnings per share.

16-29 Various Ratios Brief Company's balance sheet and income statement for the current year are shown below:

Brief Company
Balance Sheet
December 31, 19X1

Assets

Cash	$ 106,000
Accounts Receivable	566,000
Inventories	320,000
Plant and Equipment, Net of Depreciation	740,000
Patents	26,000
Other Intangible Assets	14,000
Total Assets	$1,772,000

Equities

Accounts Payable	$ 170,000
Federal Income Tax Payable	32,000
Miscellaneous Accrued Payables	38,000
Bonds Payable (4%, Due 19X9)	300,000
Preferred Stock ($100 Par, 7% Cumulative Nonparticipating and Callable at $110)	200,000
Common Stock (No par, 20,000 Shares Authorized, Issued, and Outstanding)	400,000
Retained Earnings	720,000
Treasury Stock (800 Shares of Preferred)	(88,000)
Total Equities	$1,772,000

Brief Company
Income Statement
for the Year Ended December 31, 19X1

Net Sales	$1,500,000
Cost of Goods Sold	900,000
Gross Margin on Sales	$ 600,000
Operating Expenses (Including Bond Interest Expense)	498,000
Income before Federal Income Taxes	$ 102,000
Income Tax Expense	37,000
Net Income	$ 65,000

Additional Information: There are no preferred dividends in arrears, and the balances in the accounts receivable and inventory accounts are unchanged from January 1, 19X1. There were no changes in the bonds payable, preferred stock, or common stock accounts during 19X1.

Required:

Calculate the following ratios:

a. Current ratio as of December 31, 19X1.

b. The number of times bond interest was earned during 19X1.

c. The number of times bond interest and preferred dividends were earned during 19X1.

d. The average number of days' sales in ending inventories as of December 31, 19X1.

e. The book value per share of common stock as of December 31, 19X1.

f. The rate of return for 19X1 based on the year-end common stockholders' equity.

g. The debt-equity ratio as of December 31, 19X1. (AICPA adapted)

16-30 Various Ratios; Comparative Statements The Printing Company is listed on the New York Stock Exchange. The market value of its common stock was quoted at $10 per share at December 31, 19X5 and 19X4. Printing's balance sheet at December 31, 19X5 and 19X4, and its statement of income and retained earnings for the years then ended are presented below:

Printing Company
Balance Sheet
(in Thousands)

	December 31	
	19X5	19X4
Assets		
Current Assets:		
Cash	$ 3,500	$ 3,600
Marketable Securities	13,000	11,000
Accounts Receivable (Net)	105,000	95,000
Inventories	126,000	154,000
Prepaid Expenses	2,500	2,400
Total Current Assets	$250,000	$266,000
Property, Plant, and Equipment (Net)	311,000	308,000
Investments	2,000	3,000
Long-Term Receivables	14,000	16,000
Goodwill and Patents (Net)	6,000	6,500
Other Assets	7,000	8,500
Total Assets	$590,000	$608,000
Liabilities and Stockholders' Equity		
Current Liabilities:		
Notes Payable	$ 5,000	$ 15,000
Accounts Payable	38,000	48,000
Accrued Expenses	24,500	27,000
Income Taxes Payable	1,000	1,000
Payments Due within 1 Year on Long-Term Debt	6,500	7,000
Total Current Liabilities	$ 75,000	$ 98,000
Long-Term Debt	169,000	180,000
Deferred Income Taxes	74,000	67,000
Other Liabilities	9,000	8,000
Total Liabilities	$327,000	$353,000
Stockholders' Equity:		
Common Stock, Par Value $1 per Share; Authorized 20,000,000 Shares; Issued and Outstanding 10,000,000 Shares	$ 10,000	$ 10,000
5% Cumulative Preferred Stock, par Value $100 per Share; $100 Liquidating Value; Authorized 50,000 Shares; Issued and Outstanding 40,000 Shares	4,000	4,000
Additional Paid-in Capital	107,000	107,000
Retained Earnings	142,000	134,000
Total Stockholders' Equity	$263,000	$255,000
Total Liabilities and Stockholders' Equity	$590,000	$608,000

Printing Company
Statement of Income and Retained Earnings
(in Thousands)

	Year Ended December 31	
	19X5	**19X4**
Net Sales	$600,000	$500,000
Costs and Expenses:		
Cost of Goods Sold	$490,000	$400,000
Selling, General, and Administrative Expenses	66,000	60,000
Other Expenses	7,000	6,000
Total Costs and Expenses	$563,000	$466,000
Income before Income Taxes	$ 37,000	$ 34,000
Income Taxes	(16,800)	(15,800)
Net Income	$ 20,200	$ 18,200
Retained Earnings at Beginning of Period	134,000	126,000
Dividends on Common Stock	(12,000)	(10,000)
Dividends on Preferred Stock	(200)	(200)
Retained Earnings at End of Period	$142,000	$134,000

Required:
Based on the above information, compute (for the year 19X5 only) the following:

a. Current ratio.
b. Acid-test ratio.
c. Average collection period, assuming all sales on account.
d. Inventory turnover.
e. Book value per share.
f. Earnings per share.
g. Price-earnings ratio per share.
h. Dividend payout ratio. (AICPA adapted)

16–31 Comparative Common-Size Income Statements; Explaining Changes
Comparative income statements for Hanson Company for the last 2 years are shown below:

Hanson Company
Income Statements
for the Years Ended December 31, 19X1 and 19X2

	19X2	**19X1**
Sales	$121,000	$100,000
Cost of Goods Sold	75,000	60,000
Gross Margin	$ 46,000	$ 40,000
Operating Expenses	42,000	32,000
Income before Taxes	$ 4,000	$ 8,000
Income Tax Expense (25%)	1,000	2,000
Net Income	$ 3,000	$ 6,000

The company president, who is quite upset with the results, has commented, "I don't understand it. We increased advertising expense by $5,000 in an effort to increase sales. Apparently, that was successful. Yet, our net income went down."

Required:

a. Determine the percentage change for each item on the income statements.

b. Prepare common-size income statements for each year.

c. Comment on those items that would help to explain the decrease in net income to the president.

d. Do you recommend that the increased advertising expense be continued? Explain.

16–32 Comparative Common-Size Income Statements; Various Ratios
Masonfield Corporation's income statements and balance sheets for the past 2 years are shown below:

Masonfield Corporation
Income Statements
for the Years Ended December 31, 19X3 and 19X4

	19X4	19X3
Sales	$300,000	$250,000
Cost of Goods Sold	175,000	150,000
Gross Margin	$125,000	$100,000
Operating Expenses	80,000	75,000
Operating Income	$ 45,000	$ 25,000
Interest Expense	5,000	—
Income before Taxes	$ 40,000	$ 25,000
Income Tax Expense (20%)	8,000	5,000
Net Income	$ 32,000	$ 20,000

Masonfield Corporation
Balance Sheet
December 31, 19X3 and 19X4

	19X4	19X3
Assets		
Cash	$ 8,000	$ 15,000
Accounts Receivable (Net)	65,000	53,000
Inventory	70,000	60,000
Prepaid Expenses	4,000	12,000
Property, Plant and Equipment (Net)	375,000	300,000
Total Assets	$522,000	$440,000

Liabilities and Stockholders' Equity

Accounts Payable	$ 60,000	$ 55,000
Dividends Payable	15,000	10,000
10% Bonds Payable	50,000	—
Common Stock	300,000	300,000
Retained Earnings	97,000	75,000
Total Liabilities and Stockholders' Equity	$522,000	$440,000

Required:

a. Determine the percentage change for each item on the income statements.

b. Prepare common-size income statements for each year.

c. Calculate the following ratios for each year:

1. Current ratio.
2. Acid-test ratio.
3. Debt ratio.

d. Calculate the following ratios for the year ended December 31, 19X4:

1. Return on assets.
2. Return on equity.

e. One stockholder has complained, "Our debt ratio is higher than last year, and now we've got interest to pay. Issuing bonds was not a good idea." As president, how would you respond? In your response, include comments regarding the overall performance and financial position of the firm.

16–33 Common-Size Income Statements; Different Companies; Times Interest Earned and Return on Assets Data from income statements of 2 firms in the same industry are shown below:

	Beta Company	Gamma Company
Sales	$500,000	$1,200,000
Cost of Goods Sold	260,000	700,000
Gross Margin	$240,000	$ 500,000
Operating Expenses	100,000	150,000
Operating Income	$140,000	$ 350,000
Interest Expense	50,000	75,000
Income before Taxes	$ 90,000	$ 275,000
Income Tax Expense (40%)	36,000	110,000
Net Income	$ 54,000	$ 165,000

Average assets totaled $2,000,000 for Beta Company and $3,700,000 for Gamma Company.

Required:

a. Prepare common-size statements for each company.

    b. For each company, calculate:
       1. Times interest earned.
       2. Return on assets.
    c. Comment on the performance of each company. To the extent possible, provide reasons for differences between the companies.

16–34 Comparative Common-Size Income Statements and Balance Sheets; Different Companies; Various Ratios Data from income statements and condensed balance sheets for the past 2 years for 2 similar companies in the same industry are shown below:

	(in Thousands)			
	Baker Company		**Kramer Company**	
	19X3	**19X2**	**19X3**	**19X2**
Sales	$9,000	$6,000	$8,500	$8,000
Cost of Goods Sold	5,700	4,200	5,200	5,000
Gross Margin	$3,300	$1,800	$3,300	$3,000
Operating Expenses	1,800	900	1,500	1,300
Operating Income	$1,500	$ 900	$1,800	$1,700
Interest Expense	450	150	90	100
Income before Taxes	$1,050	$ 750	$1,710	$1,600
Income Tax Expense (40%)	420	300	684	640
Net Income	$ 630	$ 450	$1,026	$ 960

	(in Thousands)			
	Baker Company		**Kramer Company**	
	19X3	**19X2**	**19X3**	**19X2**
Current Assets	$ 3,000	$2,000	$4,200	$4,000
Property, Plant, and Equipment (Net)	9,500	7,000	5,100	4,700
Total Assets	$12,500	$9,000	$9,300	$8,700
Current Liabilities	$ 1,800	$1,000	$1,600	$1,500
Long-Term Debt	3,700	1,250	750	1,200
Stockholders' Equity	7,000	6,750	6,950	6,000
Total Liabilities and Stockholders' Equity	$12,500	$9,000	$9,300	$8,700

The companies are staunch competitors. In 19X3, Baker Company made an all-out effort to outsell Kramer Company. It sold bonds to modernize and improve its plant and equipment. Kramer Company, on the other hand, has tried to reduce its long-term debt. Long-term debt of both companies carries a 12% interest rate. Neither company has preferred stock outstanding.

Required:

a. Prepare common-size income statements and balance sheets for both companies for both years.

b. Calculate the following ratios for each company for each year:

    1. Current ratio.

    2. Debt ratio.

    3. Times interest earned.

c. Calculate the following ratios for each company for the year ended 19X3:

    1. Return on assets.

    2. Return on equity.

d. Comment on the performance and financial position of each company. Does the issuance of additional debt appear to have been in the best interest of Baker Company? Explain.

e. As a potential investor, in which company would you prefer to invest? (Disregard market price and dividends, for which you have no data.) Explain.

16–35 Ratio Comparisons and Explanations; Different Companies Below are selected ratios for 2 companies in the same industry for the most recently ended year, along with industry averages.

	Seaton Company	Walter Company	Industry Average
Current Ratio	3.3 to 1	1.9 to 1	2.4 to 1
Acid-Test Ratio	1.5 to 1	.8 to 1	1.2 to 1
Debt-Asset Ratio	32%	51%	40%
Operating Expense Ratio	41%	45%	43%
Times Interest Earned	6	2	4
Inventory Turnover	10	16	11
Accounts Receivable Turnover	11	8	12
Return on Assets	13%	18%	14%
Return on Equity	10%	12%	11%
Dividend Payout Ratio	20%	80%	60%
Price-Earnings Ratio	12	6	10

Required:

Compare financial strength and operating results between Seaton Company and Walter Company and between each company and the industry average. In your discussion, provide a possible explanation for the fact that Walter Company has a low price-earnings ratio, although its return on assets and return on equity are relatively high.

16–36 Ratio Comparisons and Explanations; Same Company Below are selected ratios and financial data for Roundout Corporation for the past 3 years.

	19X7	19X6	19X5
Current Ratio	1.8 to 1	1.5 to 1	2.0 to 1
Acid-Test Ratio	.9 to 1	.7 to 1	1.1 to 1
Debt-Asset Ratio	55%	55%	40%
Operating Expense Ratio	37%	40%	35%
Depreciation Expense	$2,000,000	$2,000,000	$1,000,000
Times Interest Earned	4	2	6
Return on Assets	9%	7%	12%
Return on Equity	6%	4%	8%
Earnings per Share	$1.40	$.80	$2.50
Dividend Payout Ratio	10%	0%	60%
Price-Earnings Ratio	8	5	10

Required:

Provide possible explanations for the changes that took place between 19X5 and 19X6 and between 19X6 and 19X7.

16-37 Ratio Comparisons and Explanations; Same Company Thorpe Company is a wholesale distributor of professional equipment and supplies. The company's sales have averaged about $900,000 annually for the 3-year period 19X3–19X5. The firm's total assets at the end of 19X5 amounted to $950,000.

The president of Thorpe Company has asked the controller to prepare a report that summarizes the financial aspects of the company's operations for the past 3 years. This report will be presented to the board of directors at their next meeting.

In addition to comparative financial statements, the controller has decided to present a number of relevant financial ratios to assist in the identification and interpretation of trends. At the request of the controller, the accounting staff has calculated the following ratios for the 3-year period 19X3–19X5:

	19X3	19X4	19X5
Current Ratio	2.00	2.13	2.18
Acid-Test Ratio	1.20	1.10	.97
Accounts Receivable Turnover	9.72	8.57	7.13
Inventory Turnover	5.25	4.80	3.80
Percent of Total Debt to Total Assets	44%	41%	38%
Percent of Long-Term Debt to Total Assets	25%	22%	19%
Sales to Fixed Assets (Fixed Asset Turnover)	1.75	1.88	1.99
Sales as a Percent of 19X3 Sales	100%	103%	106%
Gross Margin Percentage	40.0%	38.6%	38.5%
Net Income to Sales	7.8%	7.8%	8.0%
Return on Total Assets	8.5%	8.6%	8.7%
Return on Stockholders' Equity	15.1%	14.6%	14.1%

In the preparation of the report, the controller has decided first to examine the financial ratios independently of any other data to determine if the ratios themselves reveal any significant trends over the 3-year period.

Required:

Answer the following questions. Indicate in each case which ratio (or ratios) you used in arriving at your conclusion.

a. The current ratio is increasing while the acid-test ratio is decreasing. Using the ratios provided, identify and explain any factors that might contribute to this apparent divergence.

b. In terms of the ratios provided, what conclusions can be drawn regarding the company's use of financial leverage during the 19X3–19X5 period?

c. Using the ratios provided, what conclusions can you draw regarding the company's net investment in plant and equipment? (CMA adapted)

16–38 Supplying Missing Data Below is a balance sheet with certain data missing.

Calvin Company
Balance Sheet
December 31, 19X8

Assets	
Cash	$ 50,000
Accounts Receivable (Net)	?
Inventory	240,000
Prepaid Expenses	10,000
Property, Plant, and Equipment (Net)	?
Total Assets	?
Liabilities and Stockholders' Equity	
Accounts Payable	$200,000
10% Bonds Payable	?
Retained Earnings	30,000
Common Stock	?
Total Liabilities and Stockholders' Equity	?

The following additional information is available for your consideration:

Current Ratio:	2.5 to 1
Acid-Test Ratio:	1.25 to 1
Debt-Asset Ratio:	60%
Operating Income:	$85,000
Interest Expense:	$30,000
Cost of Goods Sold:	$600,000

Interest expense includes $2,000 on a short-term note.

Required:

Calculate the missing items for the balance sheet. Determine these amounts in the following order:

a. Accounts receivable.

b. Bonds payable.

c. Total assets.

d. Property, plant, and equipment (net).

e. Common stock.

Chapter 17   Inflation Accounting

Learning Objectives

The purpose of this chapter is to illustrate the effects of inflation on financial statements and provide you with an understanding of how to prepare and interpret inflation-adjusted statements. Studying this chapter will enable you to:

1. Describe inflation accounting.
2. Describe how a price index is developed and construct an index.
3. Adjust financial statement items for price-level changes.
4. Prepare constant dollar financial statements.
5. Define monetary items.
6. Describe and calculate the purchasing power gain or loss.
7. Prepare current cost financial statements.
8. Describe and calculate holding gains and losses.
9. Contrast constant dollar statements with current cost statements.
10. Describe the requirements of the FASB for inflation accounting. (Appendix)

Chapter Topics

The major topics included in this chapter are:

The Need for Inflation Accounting
Use of a Price Index
Constant Dollar Statements
Current Cost Statements
Appendix: FASB Requirements for Inflation Accounting

Generally accepted accounting principles require that financial statements be based on historical cost. That is, assets are recorded at the amount of their original cost and are depreciated on that basis. The income statement reflects expenses on the basis of the original cost of the item expensed. Accountants have used historical cost because it is objective and is relatively easy to apply.

With an ever-increasing rate of inflation, however, the need for financial statements that consider the effects of inflation has increased. Consequently, in 1979, the Financial Accounting Standards Board (FASB) prescribed that certain firms provide supplemental inflation-adjusted data along with their historical cost statements.[1]

There are several ways to adjust financial statements for inflation. This chapter illustrates two methods. In addition, the appendix to this chapter describes the FASB requirements for companies that must prepare inflation-adjusted data.

The Need for Inflation Accounting

Inflation accounting is an accounting procedure that considers the effects of changing prices on items reported on financial statements. The reason for the current emphasis on inflation accounting is that, because of the high inflation rates experienced in recent years, historical cost statements do not adequately reflect the current financial position of a firm and its operating results, based on up-to-date costs. Internally, management needs to know the current position of the firm and whether revenues provided by the firm are sufficient to cover current costs of operations. Management decisions may be affected by inflation-adjusted data. For example, pricing and investment decisions based on inflation-adjusted data may differ from those based on historical cost data. Segment performance, too, may be viewed differently when the effects of inflation are shown.

Historical cost statements present problems for external users of financial statements. They are unable to appropriately compare financial statements of different firms because the dollar figures represent different levels of purchasing power. Furthermore, financial statements based on historical cost include the addition and subtraction of dollars whose value is unequal because of inflation. Thus, trying to evaluate a firm's trend or trying to compare companies in terms of dollars is less meaningful than it otherwise might be.

To illustrate, assume that a firm bought a piece of land in 1930 for $10,000. It also bought land in 1982 for $50,000. These two purchases represent the only land owned by the firm. Under historical cost accounting, land is shown on the firm's balance sheet at $60,000. However, the land purchased in 1930 would no doubt have cost significantly more if purchased in 1982. In order to show more properly the firm's financial position regarding the land it owns, it is more appropriate to restate the land at its current cost, or at what one might expect to pay for it in 1982. Assuming the land bought in 1930 would cost $45,000 in 1982, land is more appropriately shown on the balance sheet at $95,000 ($45,000 + $50,000).

The problem with historical cost is illustrated by this situation, in which 1930 dollars are added to 1982 dollars. We would not add 10,000 pesos to 50,000 francs and say the result is 60,000 dollars. Yet, we do something

---

[1]"Financial Reporting and Changing Prices," *Statement of Financial Accounting Standards No. 33* (Stamford, Conn.: Financial Accounting Standards Board, 1979).

similar to that when we add dollars of different years that have been affected greatly by inflation.

Inflation accounting seeks to equate dollars on the income statement and the balance sheet to amounts that can be appropriately added and subtracted and, therefore, appropriately used in decision making. There are several techniques for adjusting statements for inflation. The pages that follow illustrate two techniques; however, they are not the only approaches to inflation accounting.

Use of a Price Index

One approach to accounting for inflation is to adjust historical cost data with a price index. Constant dollar statements, described later, use this approach. At this point, what an index is, how it is developed, and how it is used will be explained.

A **price index,** also called a **price-level index,** is a measure of prices of a number of selected items. The index for one year becomes the base year against which increases and decreases in subsequent years are measured. **Purchasing power** represents the amount of goods and services that can be bought with a stated sum of money. A price index measures changes in purchasing power. The price index can best be understood through an illustration of its development and use.

Developing the Index   A price index does not attempt to measure the prices of all goods and services. Rather, it selects a representative number of items. The most commonly known index in the United States is the Consumer Price Index for All Urban Consumers, most commonly referred to simply as the Consumer Price Index (CPI). The CPI is prepared monthly by the U.S. Bureau of Labor Statistics and reported widely through the news media. It represents a general price-level index that shows changes in the prices of a "market basket" of goods and services normally bought by the U.S. consumer.

A price-level index can be prepared for a specific type of good or service, such as housing construction, machine tools, food, or doctors' fees. The concept for developing an index is the same whether it is for a general price-level index, such as the CPI, or for a specific price-level index.

To illustrate, assume we must develop a price index for a market basket of items labeled A, B, C, D, and E. The prices of each item for 19X1 and 19X2, the percentage change, and the price index for each year are shown in Exhibit 17.1.

The price for the market basket of goods in 19X1 was $16.70. This same market basket of goods cost $17.40 in 19X2. The percentage change for each individual item is shown in the exhibit. The price for 19X1 is considered the base year and represents a price index of 100. Although the percentage change on individual items ranged from a decrease of 11 percent to an increase of 20 percent, the percentage increase in all items averaged 4 percent. Therefore, the price index for 19X2 is 104. The calculation shown in the footnote to the exhibit is the typical way to compute the price index for

Exhibit 17.1 Price Index

Item	Unit Price		Percent Change
	19X2	**19X1**	
A	$ 3.20	$ 3.00	+ 7%
B	1.60	1.50	+ 7
C	2.40	2.50	− 4
D	6.00	5.00	+20
E	4.20	4.70	−11
	$17.40	$16.70	
Price Index	104ª	100	

ª$\frac{\$17.40}{\$16.70} \times 100 = 104$

a year other than the base year. However, it may be easier to understand the 19X2 price index if calculated as follows:

$$
\begin{array}{ll}
19X2 & \$17.40 \\
19X1 & \underline{16.70} \\
\text{Increase} & \$\ \ .70
\end{array}
$$

Percent Increase: $\dfrac{\$.70}{\$16.70} = .04 = 4\%$

19X2 Price Index: $100 + 4 = 104$

The market prices for all five items increased a total of $.70 from 19X1 to 19X2, an increase of 4 percent. Since 19X1 is the base year, with an index of 100, the 19X2 index is 100 plus the 4-percent current increase, or 104. In the example above, percentages have been rounded to the nearest percent. Traditionally, price indexes are calculated to the nearest tenth of one percent.

On the basis of the cost of the five items in the market basket of goods for the eleven-year period of 19W5 through 19X5, a price index, with 19X1 as the base year, is constructed as follows:

19W5	78
19W6	82
19W7	87
19W8	90
19W9	95
19X0	98
19X1	100
19X2	104
19X3	110
19X4	120
19X5	135

The indexes above indicate that prices were lower prior to 19X1 and higher since 19X1. Specifically, the cost of the five items in 19X5 are 35 percent higher than they were in 19X1. In other words, it takes $1.35 in 19X5 to buy what $1.00 would buy in 19X1. Or it can be said that a 19X1 dollar is worth only $.74 ($1 × 100/135) in 19X5; the purchasing power of the dollar declined $.26 from 19X1 to 19X5.

Using the Index

The general price-level index measures the average increase in prices of only those items included in the index. Thus, the current index number would not really apply to someone who did not buy the five items measured by the index. For example, the consumer price index measures a "typical" market basket of goods and services bought by the U.S. public. If the index for a certain year has increased by 12 percent, we say that the country has experienced a 12-percent inflation rate for that year. The actual inflation experienced by any individual depends on the extent to which that individual purchased the items included in the CPI market basket. Thus, individuals and businesses are affected by inflation depending on the items they buy, which are not necessarily the items included in the index.

Despite its shortcomings, the CPI measures a broad range of goods and services. Therefore, it is considered an indication of the inflation rate of the country as a whole. It is applied broadly to individuals and business firms, even if it does not measure their specific inflation rates.

To see how the price index might be used in adjusting financial statement data, assume that a firm bought land in 19W7 for $5,000. To determine the price-level-adjusted cost (or the constant dollar cost) of the land in 19X5, we use the index for 19X5 and 19W7 as follows:

$$\$5,000 \times \frac{135}{87} = \$7,759$$

Land purchased for $5,000 in 19W7 has a price-level-adjusted cost of $7,759 in 19X5. As mentioned above, one shortcoming of price-level adjustments is that they measure the average price changes in the market basket included in the index. Thus, applying the index to land bought in 19W7 does not necessarily indicate its cost in 19X5. Nevertheless, it does provide an overall measurement of cost increases caused by inflation and of declines in purchasing power.

Constant Dollar Statements

Constant dollar statements are financial statements that have been adjusted for general price level changes. They are sometimes called *general price-level-adjusted statements*. The consumer price index is used to adjust both the income statement and the balance sheet to reflect the increase or decrease in the general price level.

The term *constant dollar* is used to indicate that all dollars of varying time periods are converted to an equal basis. In the preceding section, the land illustration showed how 19W7 dollars were converted to 19X5 dollars. After all items on the balance sheet had been converted to 19X5 dollars, the items could legitimately be added to determine the firm's financial position.

Exhibit 17.2 Historical Cost Income Statement

Lockner Company
Income Statement
for the Year Ended December 31, 19X4

Sales		$100,000
Cost of Goods Sold:		
Inventory, January 1, 19X4	$10,000	
Purchases	60,000	
Cost of Goods Available for Sale	$70,000	
Less: Inventory, December 31, 19X4	15,000	
Cost of Goods Sold		55,000
Gross Margin		$ 45,000
Operating Expenses		20,000
Income before Taxes		$ 25,000
Income Tax Expense		5,000
Net Income		$ 20,000

Income Statement

An income statement prepared on a historical cost basis for Lockner Company is shown as Exhibit 17.2. Our objective is to adjust this income statement to reflect changes in the general price level. The price-level indexes needed to do this are as follows:

January 1, 19X3	118
December 1, 19X3	128
January 1, 19X4	130
December 1, 19X4	142
December 31, 19X4	145
Average for 19X4	140

In the sections that follow, each income statement item is analyzed to show the adjustment step by step.

Sales Sales occur throughout the year. Theoretically, each sales transaction should be adjusted based on the price level at the date of sale and the price level at the end of the year. Because of the volume of sales transactions, this procedure is usually not practical. Furthermore, price-level data are usually available only on a monthly basis. As a practical matter, if sales occur relatively evenly throughout the year, the use of the averge price-level index for the year is appropriate. The adjustment for Lockner Company's sales is based on the price-level index at December 31, 19X4, and the average index of 140 for 19X4. Sales are adjusted as follows:

$$\text{Sales: } \$100,000 \times \frac{145}{140} = \$103,571$$

The calculation shows that sales of $100,000, when adjusted for the rise in the price level during the year, result in an adjusted sales figure of $103,571. This is the sales amount to be used on the constant dollar income statement.

Cost of Goods Sold Cost of goods sold includes three separate items that require adjustment—beginning inventory, purchases, and ending inventory. Beginning inventory is shown in Exhibit 17.2 as $10,000. To determine the price-level-adjusted cost of beginning inventory at December 31, 19X4, the price-level index at that date—145—and the price-level index at December 1, 19X3, its date of purchase—128—are used as follows:

$$\text{Inventory, January 1, 19X4: } \$10,000 \times \frac{145}{128} = \$11,328$$

Theoretically, each purchase transaction should be adjusted. However, assuming Lockner Company's purchases occurred evenly throughout the year, the same price-level indexes that were used for sales—that is, 145 and 140—can be used for purchases. Purchases are adjusted as follows:

$$\text{Purchases: } \$60,000 \times \frac{145}{140} = \$62,143$$

Ending inventory should be adjusted based on its purchase date. Lockner Company uses the first-in, first-out (FIFO) inventory valuation method. Ending inventory shown on the balance sheet at December 31, 19X4, was purchased on December 1, 19X4. Therefore, to adjust ending inventory to constant dollars at December 31, 19X4, we use the year-end index of 145 and the December 1 index of 142, as follows:

$$\text{Inventory, December 31, 19X4: } \$15,000 \times \frac{145}{142} = \$15,317$$

Constant dollar figures for cost of goods sold can now be calculated as follows:

Inventory, January 1, 19X4	$11,328
Purchases	62,143
Cost of Goods Available for Sale	$73,471
Less: Inventory, December 31, 19X4	15,317
Cost of Goods Sold	$58,154

Note that cost of goods available for sale is the sum of the two adjusted amounts of beginning inventory and purchases. Cost of goods sold is the result of subtracting the adjusted ending inventory amount from cost of goods available for sale. Although cost of goods sold is $55,000 on a historical cost basis, it is $58,154 after adjustment for the increase in the price level.

Operating Expenses Depreciation expense is considered separately from other operating expenses, because operating expenses generally occur evenly throughout the year while depreciation expense is based on the acquisition of an asset at some specific time in the past. Depreciation expense should be adjusted based on the date of acquisition of the asset being depreciated.

Lockner Company had depreciation expense of $5,000. Operating expenses other than depreciation amounted to $15,000. Assuming these expenses occurred evenly throughout the year, they are adjusted by use of the year-end price-level index of 145 and the average price-level index for the year of 140, as follows:

$$\text{Operating Expenses (Less Depreciation): } \$15,000 \times \frac{145}{140} = \$15,536$$

Depreciation expense of $5,000 is based on assets that were bought on January 1, 19X3 with an expected 10-year life and no salvage valve. At that time, the price level was 118. Therefore, to adjust depreciation expense to constant dollars at December 31, 19X4, it is necessary to use the year-end index of 145 and the index at the time of purchase, 118. This is done as follows:

$$\text{Depreciation Expense: } \$5,000 \times \frac{145}{118} = \$6,144$$

Note that depreciation expense is now $6,144, rather than $5,000. When we adjust the items on the balance sheet, you will see that this is the appropriate expense based on the adjusted cost of the asset. Operating expenses, as adjusted, total $21,680 ($15,536 + $6,144).

Income Tax Expense The adjustment for income tax expense depends on when the tax is paid. If it is paid on the last day of the year, no adjustment is necessary. Typically, however, firms make payments throughout the year—at least quarterly, and perhaps monthly. In this example, assume that income tax expense has been paid throughout the year. Therefore, the adjustment uses the year-end index of 145 and the average index of 140. The adjustment is as follows:

$$\text{Income Tax Expense: } \$5,000 \times \frac{145}{140} = \$5,179$$

A comparison of the constant dollar income statement with the historical cost income statement is shown in Exhibit 17.3.

On a historical cost basis, net income is $20,000. However, net income on a constant dollar basis is only $18,558. Because of the rise in prices, the firm has not really done as well as it first appeared. One advantage of comparing constant dollar income statements of various years is that a firm can determine whether there is a real growth in sales and earnings or whether increases in these items are merely caused by inflation.

Balance Sheet

The balance sheet is converted to a constant dollar basis in much the same way as the income statement. However, before considering the individual assets, liabilities, and stockholders' equity items, we must look at a new concept, monetary items.

Monetary Items **Monetary items** are cash and claims to receive or obligations to pay a fixed sum of money. **Monetary assets,** then, are cash and those assets that will be received in a fixed dollar amount. Examples of

Exhibit 17.3 Constant-Dollar Income Statement

Lockner Company
Income Statement
for the Year Ended December 31, 19X4

	Historical Cost		Adjustment Factor	Constant Dollar
Sales		$100,000	145/140	$103,571
Cost of Goods Sold:				
Inventory, January 1, 19X4 . .	$10,000		145/128	$11,328
Purchases.	60,000		145/140	62,143
Cost of Goods Available for Sale	$70,000			$73,471
Less: Inventory, December 31, 19X4	15,000		145/142	15,317
Cost of Goods Sold		55,000		58,154
Gross Margin		$ 45,000		$ 45,417
Operating Expenses		20,000	a	21,680
Income before Taxes.		$ 25,000		$ 23,737
Income Tax Expense		5,000	145/140	5,179
Net Income		$ 20,000		$ 18,558

^aAs calculated on page 574:

Operating Expenses (Less Depreciation)	$15,536
Depreciation Expense	6,144
Total	$21,680

monetary assets, in addition to cash, are accounts receivable and notes receivable. The need to identify monetary assets arises from the fact that at the balance sheet date, no adjustment is needed for these items. The dollar amount on the balance sheet represents the current purchasing power of cash or the current amount expected to be received at some time in the future. As will be described later, holding monetary assets may result in a purchasing power gain or loss.

Monetary liabilities represent fixed claims. They are shown on the balance sheet without adjustment, because the amount of the liability represents the amount that will be paid, regardless of the level of inflation. As with monetary assets, holding monetary liabilities may result in a purchasing power gain or loss. Examples of monetary liabilities are accounts payable, notes payable, and bonds payable.

All other assets and liabilities are considered **nonmonetary items,** because they do not represent either claims to receive or obligations to pay fixed amounts in the future. Nonmonetary items are adjusted to a constant dollar basis, based on the price-level index.

Purchasing Power Gain or Loss Holding monetary items results in a purchasing power gain or loss caused strictly by inflation. For example, assume an individual holds $1,000 cash at a date when the price-level index is 100. If the $1,000 is held for one year, during which the index rises to 110, it will be affected by an inflation rate of 10 percent. It will now take $1,100 ($1,000 × 110/100) to buy what could have been bought for $1,000 a year ago. Therefore, the individual has suffered a purchasing power loss of $100 simply from holding $1,000 cash for the year.

Assume also that this same individual owes $5,000 on a note at a time when the price index is 100. One year later, when the price index is 110, the purchasing power represented by the note is $5,500 ($5,000 × 110/100). But the individual must pay only $5,000 to satisfy the creditor's claim. In this case, the individual has experienced a purchasing power gain of $500.

This leads to the generalization that holding monetary assets in a time of inflation results in purchasing power losses. Correspondingly, holding monetary liabilities during an inflationary period results in purchasing power gains. The net difference between purchasing power gains and purchasing power losses is the purchasing power gain or loss for the year. In constant dollar accounting, it is necessary to determine the purchasing power gain or loss.

Comparative balance sheets for Lockner Company as of December 31, 19X3 and 19X4, are shown in Exhibit 17.4. Lockner Company's balance sheet includes two monetary assets—cash and accounts receivable—and two monetary liabilities—accounts payable and note payable. Whether assets or liabilities are current or long-term is not important in determining the purchasing power gain or loss resulting from holding these items during an inflationary period.

Exhibit 17.4 Historical Cost Balance Sheets

Lockner Company
Comparative Balance Sheets
December 31, 19X3 and 19X4

	19X4	19X3
Cash	$ 6,000	$ 2,000
Accounts Receivable (Net)	32,000	23,000
Inventory	15,000	10,000
Land	100,000	60,000
Equipment	50,000	50,000
Less: Accumulated Depreciation	(10,000)	(5,000)
Total Assets	$193,000	$140,000
Accounts Payable	$ 15,000	$ 18,000
Five-Year Note Payable	40,000	—
Common Stock	100,000	100,000
Retained Earnings	38,000	22,000
Total Liabilities and Stockholders' Equity	$193,000	$140,000

Note that the items were not just held during the period, they also increased or decreased. To determine the purchasing power gain or loss, it is necessary to adjust the beginning balance by the price index at the date of the balance. Theoretically, changes in each item should be adjusted on the basis of the price index at the date of each increase or decrease. In this example, assume that cash, accounts receivable, and accounts payable increased or decreased evenly throughout 19X4. Therefore, we can use the average price index for the year—140—for adjusting these changes. Note payable had a zero balance as of December 31, 19X3. It is assumed that the note shown on the balance sheet at December 31, 19X4, was incurred on January 1, 19X4. Therefore, it is adjusted on the basis of the price level index at that date—130.

The purchasing power gain or loss for 19X4 is shown in Exhibit 17.5.[2] The exhibit shows that there were purchasing power losses for cash and accounts receivable. To understand the meaning of these losses, look at cash. The exhibit shows that on the historical cost balance sheet, cash is $6,000. Because of inflation, cash is increased to $6,374 on a constant dollar basis.

Exhibit 17.5 Purchasing Power Gain or Loss

	Historical Cost	Adjustment Factor	Constant Dollar	Gain or Loss
Cash:				
Balance, 1/1/X4	$ 2,000	145/130	$ 2,231	
Increase for 19X4	4,000	145/140	4,143	
Balance, 12/31/X4	$ 6,000		$ 6,374	$ (374)
Accounts Receivable:				
Balance 1/1/X4	$23,000	145/130	$25,654	
Increase for 19X4	9,000	145/140	9,321	
Balance, 12/31/X4	$32,000		$34,975	(2,975)
Accounts Payable:				
Balance, 1/1/X4	$18,000	145/130	$20,077	
Decrease for 19X4	(3,000)	145/140	(3,107)	
Balance, 12/31/X4	$15,000		$16,970	1,970
Notes Payable:				
Balance, 1/1/X4[a]	$40,000	145/130	$44,615	
Change for 19X4	—		—	
Balance, 12/31/X4	$40,000		$44,615	4,615
Purchasing Power Gain				$ 3,236

[a]Incurred on 1/1/X4.

[2]*FASB Statement No. 33* illustrates a short-cut method for calculating purchasing power gain or loss. However, separate calculations are shown above in order to illustrate the effect of each item.

However, the amount of cash on December 31, 19X4, is not $6,374; it is still $6,000. The firm would need $6,374 to buy what $6,000 would have bought a year ago. Therefore, there is a purchasing power loss of $374.

Accounts receivable is similar to cash. The amount shown on the balance sheet at December 31, 19X4, is $32,000. Although inflation has increased the purchasing power of this amount to $34,975, the firm's customers will repay only $32,000. Therefore, the firm has suffered a purchasing power loss of $2,975.

Lockner Company shows purchasing power gains on its monetary liabilities. When adjusted for inflation, accounts payable increase to $16,970. But the firm must repay only $15,000, resulting in a purchasing power gain of $1,970.

To keep pace with inflation, the firm should have to pay $44,615 on its note payable. But since it only pays back $40,000, it has a purchasing power gain of $4,615.

The result of all purchasing power gains and losses on monetary items results in a purchasing power gain of $3,236 for the year. Theoretically, a purchasing power gain or loss may be shown as an income statement item or added or subtracted directly to or from retained earnings. In this illustration, the latter approach is followed, as shown later.

Assets Monetary assets are shown on the constant dollar balance sheet at the same amount as on the historical cost balance sheet. Thus, at December 31, 19X4, cash is shown as $6,000 and accounts receivable as $32,000. The nonmonetary assets must be adjusted on the basis of the price-level indexes.

Inventory at December 31, 19X4, was purchased on December 1, 19X4. It is adjusted based on the price-level index at that date, 142, as follows:

$$\text{Inventory: } \$15,000 \times \frac{145}{142} = \$15,317$$

Land is shown on the balance sheet in Exhibit 17.4 at December 31, 19X4, as $100,000, an increase of $40,000 from the previous year. The land balance results from two transactions. Land was purchased on January 1, 19X3, for $60,000 and on January 1, 19X4, for $40,000. Each purchase of land must be adjusted on the basis of the price index at the date of purchase, as follows:

$$\text{Land, January 1, 19X3: } \$60,000 \times \frac{145}{118} = \$\ 73,729$$

$$\text{Land, January 1, 19X3}\quad 40,000 \times \frac{145}{130} = \quad 44,615$$

$$\text{Total:} \qquad\qquad\qquad\qquad\qquad \underline{\underline{\$118,344}}$$

Equipment has not changed during the year. The $50,000 on the balance sheet represents the equipment purchased on January 1, 19X3. Accumulated depreciation is based on this equipment. Therefore, both items are adjusted on the basis of the price index at January 1, 19X3—118—as follows:

$$\text{Equipment: } \$50,000 \times \frac{145}{118} = \$61,441$$

$$\text{Accumulated Depreciation: } \$10,000 \times \frac{145}{118} = \$12,288$$

Earlier, we calculated price-level-adjusted depreciation expense for 19X4 as $6,144. This figure is verified by the fact that one year's depreciation on $61,441 is $6,144 ($61,441 ÷ 10 years).

Liabilities Lockner Company has two liabilities—accounts payable and note payable. Both are monetary liabilities. Therefore, each will be shown on the constant dollar balance sheet at the same amount as on the historical cost balance sheet. A gain from holding these monetary items has already been calculated as part of the purchasing power gain for the year.

Owners' Equity Since Lockner Company is a corporation, owners' equity is stockholders' equity. It is divided into two parts—paid-in capital and retained earnings. Paid-in capital consists only of common stock, which is shown as $100,000 on the balance sheet at December 31, 19X3. There were no changes in 19X4. The common stock was issued at the date of incorporation, January 1, 19X3. There have been no changes since that date. Therefore, it is adjusted based on the price index at that date, as follows:

$$\text{Common Stock: } \$100,000 \times \frac{145}{118} = \$122,881$$

Retained earnings is adjusted based on the items that comprise it. The retained earnings balance shown on the historical cost balance sheet at December 31, 19X3, is $22,000. We do not have a constant dollar balance sheet as of December 31, 19X3. Therefore, we will assume that the $22,000 retained earnings balance at December 31, 19X3, would have been adjusted to a constant dollar amount of $22,667 as of that date.

To adjust the December 31, 19X3, balance of retained earnings to December 31, 19X4, we use the price indexes at those dates, which are 130 and 145, respectively. This adjustment results in a restated beginning retained earnings balance of $25,282 ($22,667 × 145/130) at December 31, 19X4.

Constant dollar net income for 19X4 is shown in Exhibit 17.3 as $18,558. A purchasing power gain of $3,236 for 19X4 is shown in Exhibit 17.5.

During the year, the firm paid dividends of $4,000. To determine the constant dollar amount, we adjust each dividend payment according to the index at the date of payment. Since we do not have the price index for each payment date, we use the average for the year, 140. This adjustment results in a constant dollar amount of $4,143 ($4,000 × 145/140).

The result of these adjustments provides a constant dollar retained earnings balance of $42,933 at December 31, 19X4, as shown below:

Retained Earnings, December 31, 19X3	
$22,667 (restated) × $\frac{145}{130}$	$25,282
Net Income, 19X4, Constant Dollar, per Exhibit 17.3	18,558
Purchasing Power Gain, 19X4, per Exhibit 17.5	3,236
Less: Dividends, 19X4 $\left(\$4,000 \times \frac{145}{140}\right)$	(4,143)
Retained Earnings, December 31, 19X4	$42,933

Exhibit 17.6 Constant Dollar Balance Sheet

Lockner Company
Balance Sheet
December 31, 19X4

	Historical Cost	Adjustment Factor	Constant Dollar
Cash	$ 6,000	—	$ 6,000
Accounts Receivable (Net)	32,000	—	32,000
Inventory	15,000	145/142	15,317
Land	100,000	a	118,344
Equipment	50,000	145/118	61,441
Less: Accumulated Depreciation	(10,000)	145/118	(12,288)
Total Assets	$193,000		$220,814
Accounts Payable	$ 15,000	—	$ 15,000
Five-Year Note Payable	40,000	—	40,000
Common Stock	100,000	145/118	122,881
Retained Earnings	38,000	b	42,933
Total Liabilities and Stockholders' Equity	$193,000		$220,814

[a]As calculated on page 578.
[b]As calculated on page 579.

The constant dollar balance sheet can now be prepared. It is shown in Exhibit 17.6. The exhibit shows the restated amounts for assets, liabilities, and stockholders' equity. The asset amounts do not necessarily represent the value of the assets at the balance sheet date. Since they were adjusted with a general price-level index, they show only the purchasing power represented by the assets, based on the index. The actual cost to replace specific assets may be more or less than the amount shown on the balance sheet.

Summary of Constant Dollar Statements

Adjusting historical cost statements with a general price-level index is one means of reflecting a more current basis, in terms of purchasing power, for the amounts shown on the statements. The results of adding and subtracting the items on the statements are more meaningful because they are all stated in the same type of dollars, constant dollars. Comparisons among periods are more meaningful because dollars of equal purchasing power are used.

The effect of inflation on a firm's monetary assets and liabilities is also reflected on constant dollar statements, providing the firm's management, owners, and interested creditors and investors with an insight as to the effects of inflation on the firm.

One major reason the accounting profession has clung to historical cost is that it provides an objective measurement. Historical cost is readily determinable and used consistently from one year to the next. Constant dollar accounting also provides objectivity, because it uses indexes based on government-generated data. The indexes are available to all firms. If the regulating authorities want to do so, they can provide specific procedures for firms to follow in applying the price indexes. Such procedures will help strengthen objectivity and consistency.

Constant dollar accounting has disadvantages. Changes in the general price level do not necessarily reflect changes in the firm's individual assets. Nor do the adjusted amounts necessarily represent the cost of the specific assets at the balance sheet date. Similarly, determining the purchasing power gain or loss on the basis of a general price-level index does not necessarily provide a representative gain or loss for the firm. A firm's purchasing power gain or loss really depends on the increase or decrease in the prices of the specific assets it owns.

Current Cost Statements

An alternative to constant dollar accounting is current cost accounting. It solves some of the problems associated with constant dollar accounting but causes other problems not associated with constant dollar accounting.

With **current cost accounting,** expenses are shown on the income statement at their cost at the time of expense, while assets are reported at the amount it would cost to buy them at the balance sheet date. The concept is based on measuring the amount the firm would have to pay to replace the service potential in the assets it owns. In effect, current cost accounting measures the specific price changes of assets, rather than general price changes. The items most affected under current cost accounting are inventories and property, plant, and equipment.

Current cost means the cost of replacing old assets with similar assets that have the same service potential. For example, under current cost accounting, the cost of a three-year-old machine is shown on the balance sheet at the amount a similar three-year-old machine would cost. If a firm is unable to determine the cost for a similar three-year-old machine, it can use the cost of a similar new machine with the same service potential. In this case, current cost would be the cost of the new machine, less three years' depreciation.

Income Statement

The two items affected on the income statement prepared under current cost accounting are cost of goods sold and depreciation expense. Cost of good sold is measured at the current cost of the items sold on the date they were sold. For example, assume an item of inventory with a historical cost of $150 is sold on July 1. Assume also that at the time of sale the firm would have to pay $165 for that same item. The amount to be shown as cost of goods sold on the income statement is $165, its current cost, not $150, its historical cost.

Depreciation expense is based on the current cost of the asset. For example, Lockner Company has equipment with a historical cost of $50,000. At December 31, 19X4, the firm determines the current cost of similar equipment to be $65,000. Therefore, depreciation expense is $6,500 ($65,000 ÷ 10 years), compared with $5,000 under historical cost.

Lockner Company has determined that its beginning inventory of $10,000 had a cost of $11,000 when it was sold. During the year, the company purchased merchandise with a historical cost of $60,000, of which $15,000 is on hand as of December 31, 19X4. The current cost of purchases is determined to be $68,000; that of ending inventory, $15,300. The latter amount is included in the purchases figure. The remaining amount of purchases, $52,700 ($68,000 − $15,300), represents the current cost of purchases at the time the inventory purchased was sold.

Operating expenses other than depreciation are considered to be at their current cost at the time they are expensed. For Lockner Company, this amount is $15,000. Adding depreciation expense of $6,500 (as calculated above) results in current cost operating expenses of $21,500.

On the basis of the data provided, the current cost income statement can be prepared, as shown in Exhibit 17.7. Notice that net income is considerably less on a current cost basis than on a historical cost basis. This difference is caused by the increases in cost of goods sold and depreciation expense. The gross margin percentage on the historical cost income statement is 45 percent ($45,000 ÷ $100,000), but it is only 36.3 percent on the current cost income statement ($36,300 ÷ $100,000). Return on sales is 20 percent ($20,000 ÷ $100,000) for the historical cost statement, versus 9.8 percent ($9,800 ÷ $100,000) for the current cost statement. This raises a question as to whether revenues are sufficient to adequately meet the rising costs of resources used in the operations of the firm.

Exhibit 17.7 Current Cost Income Statement

Lockner Company
Income Statement
for the Year Ended December 31, 19X4

	Historical Cost		Current Cost	
Sales		$100,000		$100,000
Cost of Goods Sold:				
Inventory, January 1, 19X4	$10,000		$11,000	
Purchases	60,000		68,000	
Cost of Goods Available for Sale	$70,000		$79,000	
Less: Inventory, December 31, 19X4	15,000		15,300	
Cost of Goods Sold		55,000		63,700
Gross Margin		$ 45,000		$ 36,300
Operating Expenses		20,000		21,500
Income before Taxes		$ 25,000		$ 14,800
Income Tax Expense		5,000		5,000
Net Income		$ 20,000		$ 9,800

Holding Gains and Losses

Under current cost accounting, holding certain assets may result in a gain or loss. For Lockner Company, the current cost of goods sold, $63,700, is $8,700 higher than the historical cost of goods sold. The reason for this increase is that inventory had a higher cost at the time of sale than at the time of purchase. However, since the firm purchased the inventory at a lower cost, it realized a gain of $8,700 from holding the inventory.

A **realized holding gain or loss** results from the disposal of an asset with a current cost higher or lower than its historical cost. An **unrealized holding gain or loss** results from holding, but not disposing of, assets whose current cost is more or less than their historical cost.

The inventory as of December 31, 19X4, has a historical cost of $15,000 and a current cost of $15,300. Therefore, there is an unrealized holding gain of $300 on that inventory.

Assume that Lockner Company's equipment, with a historical cost of $50,000, had a current cost of $50,000 at December 31, 19X3. Thus, there was no holding gain on equipment for 19X3. The current cost at December 31, 19X4, is $65,000, an increase of $15,000. Historical cost and current cost data for the equipment after two years are as follows:

	Historical Cost	Current Cost	Increase
Cost	$50,000	$65,000	$15,000
Accumulated Depreciation	10,000	13,000	3,000
Book Value	$40,000	$52,000	$12,000

Current cost depreciation for 19X4 is $6,500; historical cost depreciation is $5,000. This difference is recognized as depreciation expense $1,500 in 19X4. Since accumulated depreciation is $3,000 higher under current cost than under historical cost, there is a $1,500 unrecognized holding gain on first-year depreciation. It is unrecognized because it was never charged on the income statement, since historical cost and current cost were the same at the end of the first year. In effect, we must "catch up" depreciation for the prior year on the increase in the current cost of the asset. **Catch-up depreciation** (also referred to as *backlog depreciation*) is not shown on the income statement. Thus, it is unrecognized. The increase in book value of $12,000 also represents an unrecognized holding gain. The holding gain on equipment is summarized as follows:

Increase in Cost		$15,000
Recognized as Depreciation in 19X4		$ 1,500
Unrecognized Catch-up Depreciation	$ 1,500	
Unrecognized Increase in Book Value	12,000	
Total Unrecognized Holding Gain		13,500
Total Holding Gain for 19X4		$15,000

Lockner Company owns land that it acquired in two transactions—one on January 1, 19X3, with a historical cost of $60,000 and one on January 1, 19X4, with a historical cost of $40,000. The land acquired in 19X3 had a current cost of $68,000 at December 31, 19X3. Current costs at December 31, 19X4, and the holding gains for 19X4 are as follows:

	Historical Cost	Current Cost 12/31/X3	Current Cost 12/31/X4	Holding Gain for 19X4
First Purchase	$ 60,000	$68,000	$ 80,000	$12,000
Second Purchase	40,000	—	50,000	10,000
Totals	$100,000	$68,000	$130,000	$22,000

For 19X3, the firm had an unrealized holding gain on land of $8,000 ($68,000 − $60,000). In 19X4, the unrealized holding gain on land was $22,000, comprising $12,000 on the first purchase and $10,000 on the second purchase.

The holding gains for Lockner for 19X4 are summarized as follows:

Realized Holding Gains:		
Inventory Sold	$ 8,700	
Depreciation in 19X4	1,500	$10,200
Unrealized Holding Gains:		
Inventory	$ 300	
Equipment	13,500	
Land	22,000	35,800
Total Holding Gains		$46,000

Note that adding the realized holding gains of $10,200 to the current cost net income of $9,800 (from Exhibit 17.7) results in the historical cost net income of $20,000. If the current cost of an asset is less than its historical cost, the firm shows a holding loss. Lockner Company had no holding losses in 19X4.

There is controversy over what constitutes the proper reporting for holding gains and losses. Some accountants believe that such gains and losses should be included on the income statement. Others believe that including them is misleading and that current operations are not affected by the holding of assets. The latter view holds that such gains and losses should be reported separately and then added to or subtracted from retained earnings. The theory is that holding gains or losses represent increases or decreases in assets and equity caused by something other than operations. In fact, *FASB Statement No. 33* (described in the appendix) refers to such changes as "increases and decreases in current costs" and does not use the terms holding gains or holding losses.

Balance Sheet

The balance sheet reflects assets at their current costs. As previously mentioned, inventory and property, plant, and equipment are primarily affected. Retained earnings, however, must be calculated on the basis of current cost net income, and is also affected by holding gains and losses for the year.

Exhibit 17.8 Current Cost Balance Sheet

Lockner Company
Balance Sheet
December 31, 19X4

	Historical Cost	Current Cost
Cash	$ 6,000	$ 6,000
Accounts Receivable (Net)	32,000	32,000
Inventory	15,000	15,300
Land	100,000	130,000
Equipment	50,000	65,000
Less: Accumulated Depreciation	(10,000)	(13,000)
Total Assets	$193,000	$235,300
Accounts Payable	$ 15,000	$ 15,000
5-Year Note Payable	40,000	40,000
Common Stock	100,000	100,000
Retained Earnings	38,000	80,300
Total Liabilities and Stockholders' Equity	$193,000	$235,300

The historical cost retained earnings balance at December 31, 19X3, was $22,000 (from Exhibit 17.4). We will assume that this balance would be $28,500 on a current cost basis. Therefore, the beginning balance of retained earnings on a current cost basis at January 1, 19X4, is $28,500. The current cost retained earnings balance at December 31, 19X4, is determined to be $80,300, as follows:

Retained Earnings, January 1, 19X4 (Current Cost)	$28,500
Net Income, 19X4, per Exhibit 17.7	9,800
Realized Holding Gains	10,200
Unrealized Holding Gains	35,800
Less: Dividends, 19X4	(4,000)
Retained Earnings, December 31, 19X4	$80,300

The current costs of inventory, land, and equipment at December 31, 19X4, were previously given as $15,300, $130,000, and $65,000, respectively. The current cost balance sheet for Lockner Company as of December 31, 19X4, is shown in Exhibit 17.8.

The current cost balance sheet provides readers current cost data on the specific assets used by the firm. In this respect, it is considered superior to both historical cost and constant dollar balance sheets.

Summary of Current Cost Statements

As previously described, current cost statements provide more up-to-date data on a firm's costs than do either historical cost or constant dollar statements. The current cost statements have the advantage of providing managers with data that allow them to analyze the firm's pricing structure for goods and services to insure that it is consistent with the current cost of providing these goods and services. Furthermore, readers of financial statements are able to determine the effects of inflation on specific assets of the firm.

The major difficulty with current cost statements is that they are less objective than either historical cost or constant dollar statements. Determining the current cost of assets is not an easy job, especially for specialized types of equipment in manufacturing firms. In the Lockner Company illustration, current costs were given. In practice, determining current costs may take considerable time and may sometimes require the use of estimates of questionable validity.

Current cost statements, while giving recognition to increases and decreases in costs of specific assets, do not recognize the overall changes caused by inflation. Thus, unlike constant dollar statements, they do not contain adjustments in monetary items for inflation.

Summary

Generally accepted accounting principles require that financial statements for external reporting be prepared on the basis of historical cost. Historical cost provides an objective measurement that is easy to understand and apply. However, historical cost statements are distorted in periods of inflation. Therefore, alternatives to historical cost statements have been developed to measure the effects of inflation on the financial statements.

One way to account for inflation is to use constant dollar statements, which adjust financial statement items on the basis of a general price-level index. As a result, the statements reflect net income and assets, liabilities, and owners' equity in terms of current purchasing power. Financial statements adjusted for the general price level also consider purchasing power gains or losses that result from holding monetary items. However, the use of a general price-level index does not necessarily reflect the actual price change of a specific item.

Current cost statements are based on the changes in cost of specific items on the financial statements. Items are adjusted according to the current cost at the time of the expense or at the balance sheet date. Current cost statements primarily affect inventory and property, plant, and equipment. The use of current costs results in holding gains and losses, which result from the firm's holding nonmonetary assets. These gains or losses represent the difference between the current cost of an asset and its current cost at a prior balance sheet date.

The primary disadvantage of current cost statements is that determining the current cost of some assets is difficult. Often, estimates must be made that are not as objective as desired.

FASB Statement No. 33 requires that certain inflation-adjusted financial data be reported as supplementary information to the historical cost financial statements. Some data are adjusted on the basis of constant dollars, some on the basis of current costs. The requirements of *Statement No. 33* are described in the appendix to this chapter.

Historical cost statements will still be used for some time to come. However, continuing inflation results in a need for adjustments to historical cost to reflect the effects of inflation. By using both historical cost data and inflation-adjusted data, the financial statement reader is provided with more useful and meaningful information.

Appendix: FASB Requirements for Inflation Accounting

The illustrations in this chapter show two approaches to adjusting historical cost statements for inflation. Other approaches or adaptations of the procedures presented here may serve the purpose equally well. At present, generally accepted accounting principles do not require comprehensive financial statements reflecting the effects of inflation. However, as previously mentioned, the Financial Accounting Standards Board issued *Statement of Financial Accounting Standards No. 33* in 1979. It requires certain adjustments to financial statements for inflation, but it does not require a complete restatement of historical cost statements.

Statement No. 33 applies only to companies with inventories and property, plant, and equipment (before deduction of accumulated depreciation) of $125 million or companies with total assets (after deduction of accumulated depreciation) of more than $1 billion. These firms' financial statements will still be presented on a historical cost basis, in accordance with generally accepted accounting principles, as has been done in the past. However, in addition to the historical cost statements, the firms are required by the FASB to supply certain supplementary information. Specifically, *Statement No. 33* requires the following disclosures of firms that meet the above criteria.[3]

1. *Income from continuing operations on a constant dollar basis.* Income from continuing operations excludes extraordinary items, the cumulative effect of accounting changes, and discontinued operations. It is similar to net income calculated on a constant dollar basis, as shown in Exhibit 17.3. However, for purposes of meeting the requirements, it is assumed that sales and operating expenses (other than depreciation) are generally stated at the current dollar amount on the historical cost income statement. Therefore, adjustments are required only for cost of goods sold and depreciation expense. *Statement No. 33* allows adjustment to be made in either average-for-the-year constant dollars or in end-of-the-year constant dollars. This means that the firm does not have to use two or more different indexes in making the adjustments, as was done in Exhibit 17.3.

[3]"Financial Reporting and Changing Prices," *Statement of Financial Accounting Standards No. 33* (Stamford, Conn.: Financial Accounting Standards Board, 1979), para. 29–35.

2. *Purchasing power gain or loss on monetary items.* A purchasing power gain or loss on a monetary item is similar to the amount calculated in Exhibit 17.5. *Statement No. 33* specifies that the purchasing power gain or loss shall *not* be included in income from continuing operations. It will be shown as a separate amount and not included as a part of the income statement.

3. *Income from continuing operations on a current cost basis.* Income from continuing operations shown on a current cost basis is similar to current cost net income, shown in Exhibit 17.7. The restatement is required only for cost of goods sold and depreciation expense.

4. *Current costs of inventory and property, plant, and equipment at the balance sheet date.* The current costs of inventory and property, plant, and equipment at the balance sheet date are similar to the amounts shown for inventory, land, and equipment in Exhibit 17.8.

5. *Increases or decreases in the current costs of inventory and property, plant, and equipment, net of inflation.* Increases or decreases in the current costs of inventory and property, plant, and equipment, net of inflation, relate to the holding gains and losses described on pages 583–584. However, *Statement No. 33* refers to "increases or decreases in current cost" and does not use the terms *holding gain* and *holding loss.* Also, under *Statement No. 33*, these increases or decreases must be shown net of inflation.

For example, land is shown on the balance sheet in Exhibit 17.8 at a current cost of $130,000 on December 31, 19X4. The holding gain on land from January 1, 19X4, was calculated as $22,000. To meet the requirements of *Statement No. 33*, it is necessary to adjust the January 1 balance by the inflation for the year to determine the current cost on December 31, net of inflation. This adjustment is made as follows:

Current Cost, December 31, 19X4 $130,000
Current Cost, January 1, 19X4, Adjusted for 19X4 inflation:

$$\$108,000 \times \frac{145}{130} = \qquad 120,462$$

Increase in Current Cost (Holding Gain), Net of Inflation $ 9,538

The illustration shows that the cost of land would have to rise to $120,462 just for purchasing power to be maintained. In Lockner Company's case, the land's cost increased to $130,000. Therefore, there was a holding gain, net of inflation, of $9,538. *Statement No. 33* states that holding gains and losses are *not* to be included in income from continuing operations. Like purchasing power gains or losses, holding gains or losses are shown separately.

6. *A five-year-summary of selected data.* The selected data should include:[4]
  a. Net sales and other operating revenues.
  b. Constant dollar information on:
    1) Income from continuing operations.
    2) Income per common share from continuing operations.
    3) Net assets at year end.
  c. Current cost information on:
    1) Income from continuing operations.

[4]Ibid., para. 35.

2) Income per common share from continuing operations.

3) Net assets at year end.

4) Increases or decreases (holding gains or losses) in current cost amounts of inventory and property, plant, and equipment, net of inflation.

d. Other information, to include:

1) Purchasing power gain or loss on net monetary items.

2) Cash dividends declared per common share.

3) Market price per common share at year end.

4) Consumer price index for each year.

An example of required reporting of income statement data, taken from *Statement No. 33*, is shown in Exhibit 17.9. The data presented in Exhibit 17.9 conform with requirements 1 through 5 described on the previous pages. An example of the required five-year data, also taken from *Statement No. 33*, is shown in Exhibit 17.10. Because *Statement No. 33* requires

Exhibit 17.9 Adjusted Income Statement Data from *FASB Statement No. 33*

**Statement of Income from Continuing Operations Adjusted for Changing Prices
for the Year Ended December 31, 1980
(In 000s of Dollars)**

	As Reported in the Primary Statements	Adjusted for General Inflation	Adjusted for Changes in Specific Prices (Current Costs)
Net Sales and Other Operating Revenues	$253,000	$253,000	$253,000
Cost of Goods Sold	197,000	204,384	205,408
Depreciation and Amortization Expense	10,000	14,130	19,500
Other Operating Expense	20,835	20,835	20,835
Interest Expense	7,165	7,165	7,165
Provision for Income Taxes	9,000	9,000	9,000
	244,000	255,514	261,908
Income (Loss) from Continuing Operations	$ 9,000	$ (2,514)	$ (8,908)
Gain from Decline in Purchasing Power of Net Amounts Owed		$ 7,729	$ 7,729
Increase in Specific Prices (Current Cost) of Inventories and Property, Plant, and Equipment Held during the Year[a]			$ 24,608
Effect of Increase in General Price Level			18,959
Excess of Increase in Specific Prices over Increase in the General Price Level			$ 5,649

[a]At December 31, 1980, current cost of inventory was $65,700, and current cost of property, plant, and equipment, net of accumulated depreciation was $85,100.

Source: "Financial Reporting and Changing Prices," *Statement of Financial Accounting Standards No. 33* (Stamford, Conn.: Financial Accounting Standards Board, 1979), p. 33.

Exhibit 17.10 Five-Year Data from *FASB Statement No. 33*

**Five-Year Comparison of Selected
Supplementary Financial Data Adjusted for Effects of Changing Prices
(In 000s of Average 1980 Dollars)**

	Years Ended December 31,				
	1976	**1977**	**1978**	**1979**	**1980**
Net Sales and Other Operating Revenues	$265,000	$235,000	$240,000	$237,063	$253,000
Historical Cost Information Adjusted for General Inflation:					
Income (Loss) from Continuing Operations				(2,761)	(2,514)
Income (Loss) from Continuing Operations per Common Share				$ (1.91)	$ (1.68)
Net Assets at Year-End				55,518	57,733
Current Cost Information:					
Income (Loss) from Continuing Operations				(4,125)	(8,908)
Income (Loss) from Continuing Operations per Common Share				$ (2.75)	$ (5.94)
Excess of Increase in Specific Prices over Increase in the General Price Level				2,292	5,649
Net Assets at Year-End				79,996	81,466
Gain from Decline in Purchasing Power of Net Amounts Owed				7,027	7,729
Cash Dividends Declared per Common Share	$ 2.59	$ 2.43	$ 2.26	$ 2.16	$ 2.00
Market Price per Common Share at Year-End	$ 32	$ 31	$ 43	$ 39	$ 35
Average Consumer Price Index	170.5	181.5	195.4	205.0	220.9

Source: "Financial Reporting and Changing Prices," *Statement of Financial Accounting Standards No. 33* (Stamford, Conn.: Financial Accounting Standards Board, 1979), p. 34.

that five-year data be reported beginning with 1979, Exhibit 17.10 does not include adjusted data for the years 1976, 1977, and 1978.

There is no agreement among accountants as to whether the constant dollar basis or the current cost basis is a better means of accounting for inflation. The FASB has indicated its reason for requiriing data on both bases as follows:

The requirement to present information on both a constant dollar basis and a current cost basis provides a basis for studying the usefulness of the two types of information. The Board intends to study the extent to which the information is used, the types of people to whom it is useful, and the purpose for which it is used. The requirements of this Statement will be reviewed on an ongoing basis and the Board will amend or withdraw requirements whenever that course is justified by the evidence. This Statement will be reviewed comprehensively after a period of not more than five years.[5]

Because of the subjectivity involved in the preparation of statements adjusted for inflation, and the uncertainty as to their usefulness, not everyone agrees that the requirements outlined in *FASB Statement No. 33* are necessary or helpful. Nevertheless, the FASB believes that this statement is a first step in providing more meaningful financial information to users. In the Statement, the FASB summarized its position as follows:

> The Board believes that this Statement meets an urgent need for information about the effects of changing prices. If that information is not provided: Resources may be allocated inefficiently; investors' and creditors' understanding of the past performance of an enterprise and their ability to assess future cash flows may be severely limited; and people and government who participate in decisions on economic policy may lack important information about the implication of their decisions. The requirements of the Statement are expected to promote a better understanding by the general public of the problems caused by inflation: Statements by business managers about those problems are unlikely to have sufficient credibility until financial reports provide quantitative information about the effects of inflation.[6]

Review Problem

Problem

The historical cost income statement for Robinson Company for the year ended December 31, 19X4, is shown below:

Robinson Company
Income Statement
for the Year Ended December 31, 19X4

Sales		$100,000
Cost of Goods Sold:		
Inventory, January 1, 19X4	$ 6,000	
Purchases	80,000	
Cost of Goods Available for Sale	$86,000	
Less: Inventory, December 31, 19X4	20,000	
Cost of Goods Sold		66,000
Gross Margin		$ 34,000
Operating Expenses		20,000
Income before Taxes		$ 14,000
Income Tax Expense		3,000
Net Income		$ 11,000

[5]Ibid., para. 15.
[6]Ibid., p. ii.

Beginning inventory was purchased on December 1, 19X3, when the price index was 110. Inventory was purchased evenly throughout the year. Ending inventory was purchased on December 1, 19X4, when the price index was 125. Operating expenses include depreciation expense of $5,000 on equipment purchased when the price index was 85. Income taxes were paid on December 31, 19X4.

Monetary assets increased during the year from $10,000 to $14,000. Monetary liabilities also increased during the year, from $6,000 to $9,000. The price index was 112 on January 1, 19X4, and 130 on December 31, 19X4. The average for 19X4 was 120.

Required:

a. Prepare a constant dollar income statement for the year ended December 31, 19X4.

b. Determine the purchasing power gain or loss for 19X4.

Solution

A formal approach to preparing a constant dollar income statement, along with the corresponding historical cost statement, is shown in Exhibit 17.3. For the purpose of working problems, however, when only the constant dollar statement is prepared, the adjustments may be shown in parentheses next to each item or as a footnote to each item. In the solution below, parentheses are used. It is assumed that sales in this problem occur evenly throughout the year. (Unless otherwise stated, that will be the assumption in the questions, exercises, and problems that follow this review problem.)

a.   **Robinson Company**
                Constant Dollar Income Statement
                for the Year Ended December 31, 19X4

Sales ($100,000 × 130/120)		$108,333
Cost of Goods Sold:		
Inventory, January 1, 19X4 ($6,000 × 130/110)	$ 7,091	
Purchases ($80,000 × 130/120)	86,667	
Cost of Goods Available for Sale	$93,758	
Less: Inventory, December 31, 19X4 ($20,000 × 130/125)	20,800	
Cost of Goods Sold		72,958
Gross Margin		$ 35,375
Operating Expenses:		
Depreciation ($5,000 × 130/85)	$7,647	
Other ($15,000 × 130/120)	16,250	23,897
Income before Taxes		$ 11,478
Income Tax Expense		3,000
Net Income		$ 8,478

b. The method for calculating purchasing power gain or loss is shown in Exhibit 17.5. This calculation can be done in a less formal way, as shown below. Note that the illustration below uses total monetary assets and liabilities, rather than calculating the gain or loss for each individual item.

Monetary Assets:

Adjusted Balance, January 1, 19X4: $10,000 × 130/112	=	$11,607
Adjusted Increase, 19X4: $4,000 × 130/120	=	4,333
		$15,940
Balance, December 31, 19X4		14,000 $(1,940)

Monetary Liabilities:

Adjusted Balance, January 1, 19X4: $6,000 × 130/112	=	$ 6,964
Adjusted Increase, 19X4: $3,000 × 130/120	=	3,250
		$10,214
Balance, December 31, 19X4		9,000 1,214
Purchasing Power Loss		$ (726)

Questions

17-1 Define *inflation accounting*. How does it differ from accounting using historical costs?

17-2 Why has more emphasis been placed on using inflation accounting in recent years?

17-3 How does a price index measure inflation?

17-4 Assume the consumer price index rises by 9% in a given year. Since this index measures the prices of a selected market basket of goods and services, how can it be said that any one individual suffered a 9% inflation rate?

17-5 What are monetary items? Distinguish between monetary assets and monetary liabilities.

17-6 What is the difference between a current asset and a monetary asset? Why isn't inventory considered a monetary asset?

17-7 Why does holding cash during an inflationary period result in a purchasing power loss?

17-8 Daniel Fisher bought a home, taking out a mortgage that required monthly payments of $500 for the next 25 years. The interest rate on his mortgage will not change during this period. Based only on this financing arrangement, would Daniel benefit from inflation during the next 25 years. Explain.

17-9 What is the difference between a purchasing power gain and a holding gain?

17-10 What is the difference between a realized holding gain and an unrealized holding gain?

17-11 Briefly describe the difference in concept between constant dollar statements and current cost statements.

17-12 Briefly compare the advantages and disadvantages of constant dollar statements with those of current cost statements.

17-13 (*Appendix*) Why do you suppose the FASB requires only that supplementary inflation-adjusted data accompany historical cost statements, rather than that completely inflation-adjusted statements be prepared in lieu of historical cost statements.

17-14 (*Appendix*) What is the purpose of adjusting the holding gain for inflation, as required by *FASB Statement No. 33*? (See requirement 5 in the appendix.)

17-15 (*Appendix*) Hilden Company's 5-year data on income per share from continuing operations on both a historical cost and a constant dollar basis are shown below. 19X1 is the base year.

	19X5	19X4	19X3	19X2	19X1
Historical Cost	$2.75	$2.00	$1.50	$1.20	$1.00
Constant Dollar	$1.50	$1.25	$1.15	$1.10	$1.00

Briefly describe the significance of the data shown above.

Exercises

17-16 Price Index Prices for items A through E for the last 3 years are shown below. Using 19X1 as the base year, develop a price index for each year.

	Unit Price		
Item	19X3	19X2	19X1
A	$1.60	$1.25	$1.00
B	.75	.60	.55
C	8.00	6.80	5.50
D	2.20	2.60	2.90
E	9.50	9.00	8.60

17-17 Price Index A market basket of goods had the following total prices for each year listed below:

19W7	$15
19W8	$18
19W9	$20
19X0	$25
19X1	$30
19X2	$32
19X3	$38
19X4	$45

Using 19X0 as the base year, construct the price index for each year.

17-18 Price-Level Adjustments; Balance Sheet Items Blanton Company purchased land for $15,000 on January 1, 19X1, when the price level was 123. It purchased equipment on January 1, 19X2, for $20,000 when the price level was 135. The equipment had a 5-year life with no salvage value and is depreciated using the straight-line method. The price level on December 31, 19X2, was 150. Determine the amount to be shown on the firm's 19X2 constant dollar financial statements for the following:

a. Land.

b. Depreciation expense.

c. Equipment.

17–19 Price-Level Adjustments; Income Statement Items Radner Company had sales of $240,000 in 19X2. Operating expenses other than depreciation totaled $110,000. Depreciable equipment bought on January 1, 19W7, cost $150,000 and had an estimated 10-year life and no salvage value. Depreciable equipment bought on January 1, 19X0, cost $30,000 and had an estimated 6-year life and no salvage value. Price indexes were as follows:

January 1, 19W7	85
January 1, 19X0	110
January 1, 19X2	130
December 31, 19X2	148
Average for 19X2	137

Determine the amount to be shown on the 19X2 constant dollar income statement for the following:

a. Sales.

b. Operating expenses (other than depreciation).

c. Depreciation expense.

17–20 Price-Level Adjustments; Sales In 19X0, Warren Corporation had sales of $250,000. At that time, the president set a long-range goal of increasing sales by 50% by 19X5. Actual sales in 19X5 were $400,000. The average price level in 19X0 was 118; in 19X5, it was 200. Should the president be pleased with the results? Prepare calculations to support your answer.

17–21 Price-Level Adjustments; Balance Sheet Items Index Company was formed on January 1, 19X7. Selected balances from the historical cost balance sheet at December 31, 19X7, were as follows:

Cash	$60,000
Marketable Securities, Stocks (Purchased January 1, 19X7)	70,000
Marketable Securities, Bonds (Purchased January 1, 19X7, and Held for Price Speculation)	80,000
Long-Term Receivables	90,000

Assume the general price-level index was 100 at December 31, 19X6, and 110 at December 31, 19X7. Determine the amount at which each of the above accounts should be shown on a constant dollar balance sheet at December 31, 19X7. (AICPA adapted)

17–22 Purchasing Power Gain or Loss On January 1, 19X3, when the price index was 165, Coe Company had monetary item balances as follows:

Cash	$ 3,500
Accounts Receivable (Net)	16,000
Accounts Payable	22,800

On December 31, 19X3, when the price index was 172, the balances were the same. Calculate the purchasing power gain or loss for the year.

17-23 Purchasing Power Gain or Loss Carlton Company showed balances of monetary items on its 2 most recent balance sheets as follows:

	December 31	
	19X2	**19X1**
Cash	$16,000	$10,000
Accounts Receivable (Net)	22,000	25,000
Accounts Payable	23,000	15,000

Applicable price indexes were as follows:

December 31, 19X1	120
December 31, 19X2	130
Average for 19X2	126

Calculate the purchasing power gain or loss for the year.

17-24 Purchasing Power Gain or Loss with Changes in Balances Selected items from the 2 most recent balance sheets for Stromler Corporation are shown below:

	December 31	
	19X8	**19X7**
Cash	$ 7,000	$ 5,000
Accounts Receivable (Net)	8,000	13,000
Land	60,000	60,000
Accounts Payable	14,000	20,000
Note Payable	30,000	30,000
Common Stock	150,000	100,000

Applicable price indexes were as follows:

December 31, 19X7	160
December 31, 19X8	180
Average for 19X8	172

Calculate the purchasing power gain or loss for the year.

17-25 Holding Gains and Losses Kolt Company began operations on January 1, 19X2. On that date, it purchased land for $80,000 and equipment for $20,000. The equipment had an estimated 10-year life with no salvage value. The firm uses the straight-line method of depreciation. During the year, the firm bought and sold inventory with a historical cost of $155,000 and a current cost of $163,000. At December 31, 19X2, current costs were as follows:

Inventory (Historical Cost, $7,000)	$ 8,000
Equipment (Gross)	22,000
Land	75,000

Calculate the realized and unrealized holding gains and losses for the year.

17-26 Holding Gains On January 1, 19X4, Whitman Company bought land for $50,000 and a building for $80,000. The building had a 20-year life with no expected salvage value. The firm uses the straight-line method of depreciation. It sold inventory during the year that had a historical cost of $220,000 and a current cost of $245,000. Ending inventory had a historical cost of $30,000 and a current cost of $32,000. There was no beginning inventory.

At December 31, 19X4, current cost of land was $60,000; of building, $85,000. Calculate realized and unrealized holding gains for the year.

17-27 Holding Gains Tamber Company began business on January 1, 19X2, selling heavy equipment. On that date, it purchased land at a cost of $150,000 and a building at a cost of $200,000. The building had an estimated 20-year life with no salvage value. The firm uses the straight-line method of depreciation.

Inventory purchased and the current cost on the date sold in 19X3 was as follows:

Historical Cost	Current Cost
$20,000	$21,500
17,000	19,000
21,800	23,000
22,000	*Not Sold as of* 12/31/X2

At December 31, 19X2, current cost of land was $175,000; of buildings, $215,000; and of inventory, $23,000. Calculate realized and unrealized holding gains for the year.

17-28 Holding Gains Fair Value, Inc., paid $1,200,000 in December 19X6 for certain of its inventory. In December 19X7, half of the inventory was sold for $1,000,000 when the current cost of the original inventory was $1,400,000. Using current cost accounting, calculate the following for 19X7:

a. Gross margin on inventory sold.
b. Realized holding gain on inventory.
c. Unrealized holding gain on inventory. (AICPA adapted)

Problems

17-29 Constant Dollar; Depreciation; Gain or Loss on Sale of Assets
Rambert Company purchased equipment at a cost of $300,000 on January 1, 19X1, when the price index was 70. The equipment had an estimated 5-year life with no salvage value. The firm uses the straight-line method of depreciation.

The equipment was sold on December 31, 19X4, for $75,000. Price indexes as of December 31 for each year the equipment was held were as follows:

19X1	80
19X2	100
19X3	125
19X4	140

Required:

a. Calculate depreciation expense for each year on a constant dollar basis.

b. Calculate the gain or loss from the sale of the equipment on both a historical cost and a constant dollar basis.

17-30 Constant Dollar; Depreciation; Gain or Loss on Sale of Assets Banter Company bought 2 identical parcels of land for a total of $220,000 and equipment for $100,000 on January 1, 19X1, when the price index was 100. The equipment had a 5-year life with no salvage value. The firm uses the straight-line method of depreciation.

One parcel of land was sold on December 31, 19X3, for $150,000. The equipment was sold on December 31, 19X4, for $8,000. Price indexes at December 31 during this period were as follows:

19X1	115
19X2	135
19X3	150
19X4	160

Required:

Calculate the following:

a. Depreciation expense on a constant dollar basis for each year.

b. Gain or loss on the sale of the equipment on both a historical cost and a constant dollar basis.

c. Gain or loss on the sale of land on both a historical cost and a constant dollar basis. (Describe the significance of your results.)

d. Price-level-adjusted cost of land as of December 31, 19X4.

17-31 Constant Dollar; Gain or Loss on Sale of Assets The 3 situations described below are independent, but for all of them use the following information on price-level indexes at the end of the 5 indicated years:

19X1	100
19X2	110
19X3	115
19X4	120
19X5	140

Situation 1: In December 19X4, the Meetu Corporation purchased land for $300,000. The land was held until December 19X5, when it was sold for $400,000.

Situation 2: On January 1, 19X2, the Silver Company purchased equipment for $300,000. The equipment was being depreciated over an estimated life of 10 years by the straight-line method, with no estimated salvage value. On December 31, 19X5, the equipment was sold for $200,000.

Situation 3: An analysis of the Gallant Corporation's machinery and equipment account as of December 31, 19X5, follows:

Machinery and Equipment:	
Acquired in December 19X2	$400,000
Acquired in December 19X4	100,000
Balance	$500,000

Accumulated Depreciation:

On Equipment Acquired in December 19X2	$160,000
On Equipment Acquired in December 19X4	20,000
Balance	$180,000

Required:

a. For Situation 1, determine the gain or loss on the sale of land to be shown on the constant dollar income statement for the year ended December 31, 19X5.

b. For Situation 2, determine the gain or loss on the sale of equipment to be shown on the constant dollar income statement for the year ended December 31, 19X5.

c. For Situation 3, determine the amount to be shown as machinery and equipment, net of accumulated depreciation, on the constant dollar balance sheet as of December 31, 19X5. (AICPA adapted)

17-32 Constant Dollar Income Statement A historical cost income statement for Calter Company is shown below:

Calter Company
Income Statement
for the Year Ended December 31, 19X8

Sales	$50,000
Cost of Goods Sold	30,000
Gross Margin	$20,000
Operating Expenses	15,000
Income before Taxes	$ 5,000
Income Tax Expense	1,000
Net Income	$ 4,000

There was no beginning or ending inventory. Inventory was purchased evenly throughout the year. Operating expenses include depreciation expense of $3,000 on equipment purchased on January 1, 19X3, when the price index was 110. Income taxes were paid evenly throughout the year.

Monetary assets increased from $20,000 at December 31, 19X7, to $25,000 at December 31, 19X8. Monetary liabilities increased from $15,000 to $18,000 during that same year. The price index was 160 on January 1, 19X8, and 172 on December 31, 19X8. The average index for 19X8 was 165.

Required:

a. Prepare a constant dollar income statment for the year ended December 31, 19X8.

b. Determine the purchasing power gain or loss for 19X8.

17-33 Constant Dollar Income Statement Hart Company's historical cost income statement is shown below:

Hart Company
Income Statement
for the Year Ended December 31, 19X2

Sales		$80,000
Cost of Goods Sold:		
Inventory, January 1, 19X2	$10,000	
Purchases	50,000	
Cost of Goods Available for Sale	$60,000	
Less: Inventory, December 31, 19X2	8,000	
Cost of Goods Sold		52,000
Gross Margin		$28,000
Operating Expenses		18,000
Income before Taxes		$10,000
Income Tax Expense		2,000
Net Income		$ 8,000

Beginning inventory was purchased on December 31, 19X1, when the price index was 105. Purchases of inventory were made evenly throughout the year. Ending inventory was purchased on November 1, 19X2, when the price index was 120. Operating expenses include depreciation expense of $4,000 on equipment purchased when the price index was 90. Income taxes were paid on December 31, 19X2.

Monetary assets decreased from $8,000 at December 31, 19X1, to $5,000 a year later. Monetary liabilities decreased from $12,000 to $10,000 during that same time period. The price index was 107 on January 1, 19X2, and 121 on December 31, 19X2. The average for 19X2 was 115.

Required:

a. Prepare a constant dollar income statement for the year ended December 31, 19X2.

b. Determine the purchasing power gain or loss for 19X2.

17-34 Constant Dollar Balance Sheet Comparative balance sheets for PLI, Inc., are shown below:

PLI, Inc.
Comparative Balance Sheets
December 31, 19X2 and 19X3

	19X3	19X2
Cash	$ 2,500	$ 1,800
Accounts Receivable (Net)	8,600	5,200
Inventory	4,600	4,000
Land	15,000	15,000
Equipment	5,000	5,000
Less: Accumulated Depreciation	(1,000)	(500)
Total Assets	$34,700	$30,500

Accounts Payable	$ 3,500	$ 2,700
Note Payable	10,000	10,000
Common Stock	15,000	15,000
Retained Earnings	6,200	2,800
Total Liabilities and Stockholders' Equity	$34,700	$30,500

The price index at the date the ending inventory was purchased was 130. The price index when land and equipment were purchased and common stock was issued was 95. The price index at December 31, 19X2, was 120; at December 31, 19X3, it was 135. The average price index for 19X3 was 125.

Restated retained earnings at December 31, 19X2, were $3,200. Constant dollar net income for 19X3 was $4,012. No dividends were declared or paid in 19X3.

Required:

a. Determine the purchasing power gain or loss for the year. (*Note:* To save time, you may use total monetary assets and total monetary liabilities, rather than calculating each item separately.)

b. Determine the constant dollar retained earnings balance at December 31, 19X3.

c. Prepare a constant dollar balance sheet as of December 1, 19X3.

17-35 Constant Dollar Balance Sheet Comparative balance sheets for Clay Company are shown below:

Clay Company
Comparative Balance Sheets
December 31, 19X5 and 19X6

	19X6	19X5
Cash	$ 6,000	$ 4,000
Accounts Receivable (Net)	35,000	28,000
Inventory	36,000	40,000
Buildings	180,000	150,000
Equipment	60,000	60,000
Accumulated Depreciation	(46,000)	(30,000)
Total Assets	$271,000	$252,000
Accounts Payable	$ 16,000	$ 25,000
Note Payable	60,000	80,000
Common Stock	150,000	120,000
Retained Earnings	45,000	27,000
Total Liabilities and Stockholders' Equity	$271,000	$252,000

The firm began business on January 1, 19X4, issuing 12,000 shares of $10 par common stock. Equipment and buildings were also bought on that date. An additional building was bought on June 1, 19X6, at which time 3,000 shares of common stock were also issued. Accumulated depreciation on the new building at December 31, 19X6, was $1,000. Ending inventory was purchased on November 15, 19X6. A $20,000 payment on the note was made on September 1, 19X6.

Retained earnings at December 31, 19X5, restated on a constant dollar basis was $30,000. Constant dollar net income for 19X6 was $27,179. Dividend payments of $2,000 were made every 3 months beginning with March 1, 19X6. Each payment was declared in 19X6.

Applicable price indexes were as follows:

January 1, 19X4	140
December 31, 19X5	160
March 1, 19X6	162
June 1, 19X6	165
September 1, 19X6	170
November 15, 19X6	173
December 1, 19X6	175
December 31, 19X6	177
Average for 19X6	168

Required:

a. Determine the purchasing power gain or loss for the year. (*Note*: To save time, you may use total monetary assets and total monetary liabilities, rather than calculating each item separately.)

b. Determine the constant dollar retained earnings balance at December 31, 19X6.

c. Prepare a constant dollar balance sheet as of December 31, 19X6.

17–36 Constant Dollar Balance Sheet Wheat Company is a new business enterprise which started operations on January 1, 19X3. While the operating returns are below industry average, company management is pleased with the first 2 years' results. The income statement for 19X4 and comparative balance sheets for 19X3 and 19X4 appear below.

Wheat Company
Income Statement
for the Year Ended December 31, 19X4

Revenue from Sales		$84,000
Cost of Goods Sold:		
Inventory, January 1, 19X4	$21,000	
Purchases	48,000	
Cost of Goods Available	$69,000	
Inventory, December 31, 19X4	25,000	44,000
Gross Margin		$40,000
Operating Expenses:		
Wages and Salaries	$24,000	
Depreciation	7,000	31,000
Income before Taxes		$ 9,000
Income Taxes		1,800
Net Income		$7,200

Wheat Company
Balance Sheet
December 31, 19X3 and 19X4

	19X4	19X3
Assets		
Cash	$13,800	$10,000
Accounts Receivable (Net)	17,000	20,000
Inventory	25,000	21,000
Fixed Assets (Net)	38,000	45,000
Total Assets	$93,800	$96,000
Equities		
Accounts Payable	$ 9,600	$19,000
Long-Term Debt	33,000	33,000
Contributed Capital	40,000	40,000
Retained Earnings	11,200	4,000
Total Equities	$93,800	$96,000

The economy experienced a high rate of inflation in each of the past 2 years. The management believes that reports of the operating results and financial position distort the true picture, because the effect of inflation is not fully recognized in the statements. They would like to communicate the magnitude of this distortion to the stockholders. Consequently, the company is considering issuing supplementary financial statements restated for price-level changes.

The company accountant has assembled the following information:
1. Wheat Company's sales, purchases, and expenses occur evenly throughout the year.
2. The inventory is valued at cost using the first-in, first-out (FIFO) method. The inventory on December 31, 19X3, was acquired at June 30, 19X3, prices; and the inventory on December 31, 19X4, was acquired at September 30, 19X4, prices.
3. All of the fixed assets were acquired on January 1, 19X3.
4. The indexes which measure the change in the price level for selected dates are as follows:

January 1, 19X3	100
January 1, 19X4	110
December 31, 19X4	130

The price level has risen evenly throughout each year.
Required:
 a. Prepare the balance sheet for December 31, 19X4, restated to reflect changes in the price level.
 b. Calculate the purchasing power gain or loss for the year ended December 31, 19X4. (CMA adapted)

17–37 Current Cost Income Statement The historical cost income statement for Anderson, Inc., is shown below:

Anderson, Inc.
Income Statement
for the Year Ended December 31, 19X9

Sales		$940,000
Cost of Goods Sold:		
Inventory, January 1, 19X9	$ 60,000	
Purchases	650,000	
Cost of Goods Available for Sale	$710,000	
Less: Inventory, December 31, 19X9	85,000	
Cost of Goods Sold		625,000
Gross Margin		$315,000
Operating Expenses		215,000
Income before Taxes		$100,000
Income Tax Expense		40,000
Net Income		$ 60,000

The current cost of beginning inventory when it was sold was $62,000. Purchases had a current cost on the date of sale or on December 31, 19X9, as follows:

Purchases	Current Cost
$100,000	$105,000
125,000	133,000
210,000	225,000
130,000	137,000
85,000	90,000
$650,000	$690,000

Depreciation expense was $30,000 on a historical cost basis and $35,000 on a current cost basis.

Required:

   a. Prepare a current cost income statement for the year ended December 31, 19X9.

   b. Determine the effective tax rate (that is, income tax expense as a percentage of income before taxes) for the historical cost and the constant dollar income statement. Comment on the significance of these calculations.

17-38 Current Cost Balance Sheet A historical cost balance sheet for Topper Company at the end of its first year of operations is shown below:

Topper Company
Balance Sheet
December 31, 19X4

Cash	$ 12,000
Accounts Receivable (Net)	60,000
Inventory	45,000
Land	115,000
Building	240,000
Equipment	120,000
Accumulated Depreciation	(20,000)
Total Assets	$572,000
Accounts Payable	$ 30,000
Mortgage Payable	250,000
Common Stock	280,000
Retained Earnings	12,000
Total Liabilities and Stockholders' Equity	$572,000

Historical cost of goods sold was $130,000. At the time of sale, the merchandise would have cost $138,000. Other current costs at December 31, 19X4, were:

Inventory	$ 47,000
Land	118,000
Building	252,000
Equipment	124,000

On January 1, 19X4, the date of purchase, the building had an estimated useful life of 30 years; equipment, of 10 years. Neither had an expected salvage value at the end of the estimated useful life. The firm uses the straight-line method of depreciation.

Current cost net income for 19X4 was $3,200. No dividends were declared.

Required:

a. Calculate the recognized and unrecognized holding gains for 19X4.

b. Determine the amount of current cost retained earnings at December 31, 19X4.

c. Prepare a current cost balance sheet as of December 31, 19X4.

17-39 Current Cost Income Statement and Balance Sheet Johnson Company began operations on January 1, 19X2. Its historical cost income statement and balance sheet are shown below:

Johnson Company
Income Statement
for the Year Ended December 31, 19X2

Sales	$315,000
Cost of Goods Sold	180,000
Gross Margin	$135,000
Operating Expenses	75,000
Income before Taxes	$ 60,000
Income Tax Expense	15,000
Net Income	$ 45,000

Johnson Company
Balance Sheet
December 31, 19X2

Cash	$ 13,000
Accounts Receivable (Net)	95,000
Inventory	76,000
Land	180,000
Equipment	40,000
Less: Accumulated Depreciation	(4,000)
Total Assets	$400,000
Accounts Payable	$ 60,000
Notes Payable	100,000
Common Stock	200,000
Retained Earnings	40,000
Total Liabilities and Stockholders' Equity	$400,000

At the time merchandise was sold, it had a current cost of $190,000. At December 31, 19X2, the current cost of inventory was $80,000; of land, $195,000; and of equipment, $42,000. Dividends of $5,000 were declared and paid during the year.

Required:

a. Prepare a current cost income statement for the year ended December 31, 19X2.

b. Calculate the holding gain or loss for 19X2.

c. Calculate the current cost retained earnings balance as of December 31, 19X2.

d. Prepare a current cost balance sheet as of December 31, 19X2.

17–40 Current Cost Income Statement Refer to Problem 17–33. The current cost of beginning inventory was $11,500; of ending inventory, $8,500. The current cost of purchases was $56,200. The current cost of equipment at December 31, 19X2, was $50,000. The equipment had historical cost depreciation of $4,000. It is 2 years old and had an estimated life of 10 years at the date of purchase with no salvage value. Current cost at December 31, 19X1, was $40,000.

Hart Company also owns land that it bought for $70,000 and that had a current cost of $75,000 at December 31, 19X1, and of $73,500 at December 31, 19X2.

Required:

   a. Prepare a current cost income statement for the year ended December 31, 19X2.

   b. Calculate the holding gain or loss for 19X2.

   c. After reviewing the current cost income statement, the company president was quite upset. He does not understand why the firm must pay more in income taxes than it has earned in income. Explain this situation to him.

17–41 Analysis of Inflation Accounting Description Published financial statements of United States companies are currently prepared on a stable-dollar assumption, even though the general purchasing power of the dollar has declined considerably because of inflation in recent years. To account for this changing value of the dollar, many accountants suggest that financial statements should be adjusted for general price-level changes.

Three independent, unrelated statements regarding general price-level-adjusted financial statements follow. Each statement contains some fallacious reasoning.

Statement I

The accounting profession has not seriously considered price-level-adjusted financial statements before because the rate of inflation usually has been so small from year to year that the adjustments would have been immaterial in amount. Price-level-adjusted financial statements represent a departure from the historical cost basis of accounting. Financial statements should be prepared from facts, not estimates.

Statement II

If financial statements were adjusted for general price-level changes, depreciation charges in the earnings statement would permit the recovery of dollars of current purchasing power and, thereby, would equal the cost of new assets to replace the old ones. General price-level-adjusted data would yield amounts on the statement of financial position that closely approximated current values. Furthermore, management could make better decisions if general price-level-adjusted financial statements were published.

Statement III

When financial data are adjusted for general price-level changes, a distinction must be made between monetary and nonmonetary assets and liabilities. Under the historical cost basis of accounting, these items have been identified as "current" and "noncurrent." When the historical cost basis of accounting is used, no purchasing power gain or loss is recognized in the accounting process; but when financial statements are adjusted for general price-level changes, a purchasing power gain or loss will be recognized on monetary and nonmonetary items.

Required:

   Evaluate each of the independent statements, identify the areas of fallacious reasoning in each, and explain why the reasoning is incorrect. Complete your discussion of each statement before proceeding to the next statement. (AICPA adapted)

Glossary

This glossary provides a quick reference for terms used in the text. Since accounting terms have technical meanings, you can often best understand them by referring to the context within which they are used. Therefore, the chapter in which each term is defined, explained, or illustrated, as well as the page number on which it can be found, is shown in parentheses following the definition.

Absorption costing A cost accounting procedure under which fixed factory overhead is considered a product cost and "absorbed" into the cost of the product. (Chapter 3, p. 52)

Accounts receivable turnover A measure of accounts receivable management. Measures how quickly accounts receivable are being collected. (Chapter 16, p. 533)

Acid-test ratio The ratio of quick assets to current liabilities; a measure of a firm's ability to pay its current liabilities within a short period of time. (Chapter 16, p. 531)

Actual cost system A cost accounting procedure under which actual factory overhead is charged to work-in-process inventory as it is incurred. (Chapter 3, p. 54)

Actual/normal cost system A cost system in which direct material and direct labor are charged to work-in-process inventory at actual costs, and factory overhead is charged at a predetermined rate based on normal activity. (Chapter 3, p. 57; Chapter 7, p. 193)

Allocate Assign an item of cost to one or more cost objectives. (Chapter 14, p. 449)

Application of factory overhead The charging of factory overhead to work in process on an estimated basis. (Chapter 3, p. 58)

Asset turnover See *investment turnover*.

Authority The power or right to make decisions. (Chapter 1, p. 11)

Average collection period The number of days it takes, on the average, to collect accounts receivable. (Chapter 16, p. 533)

Book value per share The amount of net assets attributable to one share of common stock. (Chapter 16, p. 544)

Break-even analysis The process of analyzing costs and volume in order to determine the break-even point. (Chapter 9, p. 254)

Break-even point That level of volume (or sales) at which the firm earns zero profit. (Chapter 9, p. 254)

Budget A formal expression of planned operations, expressed in financial terms. (Chapter 5, p. 115)

Capital budgeting Long-range planning for the selection and financing of capital projects. (Chapter 11, p. 334)

Capital project A proposed expenditure that is expected to benefit the firm for a period longer than one year, such as for property, plant, and equipment or new product development. (Chapter 11, p. 334)

Capital turnover See *investment turnover*.

Catch-up depreciation In current cost accounting, depreciation resulting from current increases in an asset's cost that were not previously recognized on the income statement. (Chapter 17, p. 583)

Centralized firm A firm in which most decisions are made by top management, with little delegation of authority. (Chapter 8, p. 214)

Committed costs Fixed costs that must be incurred for a firm to accomplish its long-range organizational goals. (Chapter 2, p. 22)

Common fixed cost A fixed cost that benefits more than one segment and is not a direct cost of any one specific segment. (Chapter 8, p. 221)

Common-size statements Financial statements that show each item as a percentage rather than a dollar amount. (Chapter 16, p. 527)

Comparative statements Financial statements of two or more years that are presented side by side. (Chapter 16, p. 524)

Complex capital structure A capital structure that includes securities that are convertible to common stock. (Chapter 16, p. 537)

Conditional value In probability theory, an amount that will result if a specific event occurs. (Chapter 12, p. 374)

Constant dollar statements Financial statements that have been adjusted for general price-level changes. (Chapter 17, p. 571)

Contribution approach income statement An income statement that classifies expenses according to cost behavior. (Chapter 4, p. 84)

Contribution margin The differ-ence between sales and variable costs; represents an amount available to cover fixed costs for the period and provide a profit. (Chapter 4, p. 84)

Contribution margin ratio Contribution margin as a percentage of sales. (Chapter 4, p. 90; Chapter 9, p. 259)

Controllable cost A cost that an individual manager has the ability to influence within a specified time period. (Chapter 8, p. 222)

Controller The individual in charge of the accounting function in a large firm. (Chapter 1, p. 15)

Controlling The process of comparing actual results with planned expectations and taking corrective action, where necessary, when results differ significantly from the plan. (Chapter 1, p. 13; Chapter 5, p. 118)

Conversion cost The combination of direct labor and factory overhead; called conversion cost because these costs are incurred in the conversion of direct material into finished product. (Chapter 3, p. 51)

Cost The amount of resources given up in order to receive some good or service. (Chapter 2, p. 20)

Cost accounting cycle The process of accounting for the flow of manufacturing costs from initial incurrence to ultimate disposition as cost of goods sold. (Chapter 3, p. 53)

Cost allocation The process of assigning factory overhead costs to production. (Chapter 14, p. 448)

Cost behavior The reaction of cost to changes in activity. (Chapter 2, p. 20)

Cost center A responsibility center in which a manager is responsible for costs incurred by the segment. (Chapter 8, p. 215)

Cost objective Anything for which a firm wishes to accumulate costs. (Chapter 8, p. 221; Chapter 14, p. 449)

Cost of capital The interest rate that a firm must pay for its funds. (Chapter 8, p. 224)

Cost of goods manufactured The manufacturing cost assigned to goods that were completed during a particular accounting period. (Chapter 3, p. 64)

Cost of goods sold percentage Cost of goods sold as a percentage of sales. (Chapter 16, p. 529)

Cost summary A document for accounting for direct material, direct labor, and factory overhead charged to work-in-process inventory in a process cost system. (Chapter 13, p. 427)

Cost-volume-profit (CVP) analysis A technique for evaluating the effect on profit caused by changes in costs and volume. (Chapter 9, p. 254)

Current cost The cost of replacing old assets with similar assets that have the same service potential. (Chapter 17, p. 581)

Current cost accounting An accounting procedure by which expenses are shown on the income statement at their cost at the time of expense, while assets are reported at the amount it would cost to buy them at the balance sheet date. (Chapter 17, p. 581)

Currently attainable standards Standards that allow for the fact that some inefficiency is inescapable. (Chapter 6, p. 155)

Current ratio The relationship of current assets to current liabilities; a measurement of a firm's short-run financial condition. (Chapter 16, p. 530)

Debt-asset ratio Total liabilities as a percentage of total assets. A measurement of long-run debt-paying ability. (Chapter 16, p. 534)

Debt-equity ratio The relationship between total liabilities and total stockholders' equity. (Chapter 16, p. 535)

Decentralized firm A firm in which managers at the lower levels have more authority to make decisions regarding their particular operation. (Chapter 8, p. 214)

Direct cost A cost that benefits or is caused by the activities of a specific cost objective. (Chapter 8, p. 221; Chapter 14, p. 450)

Direct costing See *variable costing.*

Directing The issuing of instructions to specific employees to carry out certain actions. (Chapter 1, p. 13)

Direct labor The cost of wages for the individuals who work in the manufacture of a specific product. (Chapter 3, p. 50)

Direct labor budget A budget of direct labor costs needed to meet the production budget. (Chapter 5, p. 125)

Direct material Raw material that becomes an integral part of the final product. (Chapter 3, p. 50)

Direct materials budget A budget of direct materials that must be purchased in order to meet the requirements of the production budget. (Chapter 5, p. 124)

Discounted cash flow technique A capital budgeting technique that discounts future cash flows to their present value, based on an appropriate interest rate. (Chapter 11, p. 338)

Discretionary fixed costs Fixed costs that management has the option of modifying from one year to the next without changing the firm's ability to accomplish its long-range goals. (Chapter 2, p. 24)

Dividend payout ratio The ratio of dividends per share to earnings per share. (Chapter 16, p. 540)

Dividend yield Dividends as a percentage of the market price of the stock; an indication of the investors' return on the stock. (Chapter 16, p. 541)

Earnings per share The amount of net income that one share of common stock has earned for the period. (Chapter 16, p. 536)

Economic order quantity (EOQ) The amount of inventory that should be ordered in order to minimize order costs and carrying costs. (Chapter 12, p. 388)

Entity Any organization for which financial information is needed. (Chapter 1, p. 7)

Equity-asset ratio Stockholders' equity as a percentage of total assets. (Chapter 16, p. 535)

Equivalent units of production A means of expressing partially completed units in terms of complete units. (Chapter 13, p. 423)

Event In probability theory, each possibility that may result from a specific decision. (Chapter 12, pp. 374–375)

Expected value In probability theory, the weighted average of the conditional value of each event. (Chapter 12, p. 375)

Expired costs Costs that have been incurred and "used up." Expenses are expired costs. (Chapter 2, p. 20)

Extraordinary items Events that affect financial statements but are unusual and nonrecurring in nature. (Chapter 16, p. 538)

Factory burden See *factory overhead.*

Factory overhead Any manufacturing cost that is not direct material or direct labor. (Chapter 3, p. 50)

Feedback The process of gathering information, comparing the results against the budget, and communicating these results to management. (Chapter 5, p. 119)

Financial statement analysis The process of comparing relationships among financial statement items in order to evaluate a firm's financial position and operating performance. (Chapter 16, p. 524)

Finished goods Completed manufactured items. (Chapter 3, p. 49)

Finished goods inventory An account that represents the cost of completed but unsold products. (Chapter 3, p. 49)

Fixed cost A cost that does not change in total in relation to changes in a specific activity within a relevant range of time or activity. (Chapter 2, p. 22)

Fixed factory overhead Factory overhead costs that do not change in relation to production activity within a given time period or relevant range of activity. (Chapter 3, pp. 50–51)

Fixed factory overhead account The account for recording incurred (debit) and applied (credit) fixed factory overhead. (Chapter 3, p. 59)

Fixed factory overhead applied The estimated amount of fixed factory overhead charged to work-in-process inventory at a predetermined rate on a timely basis, under actual/normal and standard cost systems. (Chapter 3, p. 60)

Fixed factory overhead incurred The amount of fixed factory overhead cost actually incurred. (Chapter 3, p. 59)

Fixed overhead budget variance The difference between actual fixed overhead cost incurred and the budgeted fixed overhead cost. (Chapter 7, p. 189)

Fixed overhead total variance The difference between actual fixed overhead cost incurred and the amount of fixed overhead cost applied. (Chapter 7, p. 192)

Flexible budget A budget or series of budgets for different levels of activity. (Chapter 6, p. 150)

Full costing concept The process of allocating all costs, including administrative expenses, to final cost objectives. (Chapter 14, p. 463)

Full cost pricing A pricing strategy that considers all costs. (Chapter 10, p. 309)

Fully diluted earnings per share The earnings per share assuming that all convertible securities will be converted to common stock. (Chapter 16, p. 538)

Goal congruence A concept under which the segment managers' goals conform with the goals of the company as a whole. (Chapter 8, p. 235)

Gross margin percentage Gross margin as a percentage of sales. (Chapter 16, p. 529)

Horizontal analysis The analysis of financial statement items across the page, rather than up and down. (Chapter 16, p. 524)

Ideal standards Standards that can be achieved only with absolute peak performance and efficiency under perfect conditions. (Chapter 6, p. 155)

Income available to common shares Net income remaining for common shares after the preferred dividend requirement has been subtracted. (Chapter 16, p. 537)

Incremental cost pricing A pricing strategy under which management considers only the incremental or additional costs that will be incurred in a given situation. (Chapter 10, p. 312)

Indirect cost A cost that benefits or is caused by the activities of more than one cost objective but that cannot be traced to a specific cost objective. (Chapter 8, p. 221; Chapter 14, p. 450)

Indirect cost pools Groups of costs not directly identified with final cost objectives. (Chapter 14, p. 450)

Indirect labor The cost of wages paid to individuals who work in the manufacturing process but who do not work directly on a specific product. (Chapter 3, p. 51)

Indirect manufacturing cost See *factory overhead.*

Indirect material Raw material used in the manufacturing process that does not become a part of the final product. (Chapter 3, p. 49)

Inflation accounting An accounting procedure that considers the effects of changing prices on items reported on financial statements. (Chapter 17, p. 568)

Inventory turnover The number of times that inventory is replaced during the year; a measurement of inventory management. (Chapter 16, p. 532)

Investment center A responsibility center in which a manager is responsible for earning a rate of return on the segment's investment in assets. (Chapter 8, p. 215)

Investment turnover The relationship of sales to investment, calculated by dividing sales by investment; a measurement of the amount of sales generated by investment. (Chapter 8, p. 224)

Job cost sheet The primary accounting record used in a job order cost system for accumulating production costs on each job. (Chapter 13, p. 416)

Job order cost system A cost accounting system that accumulates costs for separate, identifiable jobs or batches. (Chapter 13, p. 416)

Joint product cost A product cost associated with a number of final products. (Chapter 10, pp. 302–303)

Labor efficiency standard The number of hours of direct labor needed to complete one unit of finished product. (Chapter 6, p. 156)

Labor efficiency variance The difference between the actual number of hours worked and the standard number of hours allowed for in the flexible budget, multiplied by the standard rate. (Chapter 6, p. 164)

Labor rate standard The expected direct labor cost per hour. (Chapter 6, p. 156)

Labor rate variance The difference between the actual labor rate and the budgeted labor rate, multiplied by the number of actual hours worked. (Chapter 6, p. 163)

Lead time The difference in time between the time an order is placed and the time it is received. (Chapter 12, p. 393)

Leverage The process by which a firm uses funds obtained from creditors and preferred stockholders to earn a rate of return greater than the cost of such funds. (Chapter 16, p. 543)

Linear programming A mathematical technique that helps management in making decisions between alternatives when there are two or more constraints. (Chapter 12, p. 383)

Liquidity The firm's ability to convert assets into cash. (Chapter 16, p. 530)

Management A collective group of individuals who direct the operations of an entity. (Chapter 1, p. 11)

Management by exception A concept used in responsibility accounting under which management concentrates its time and efforts in exceptional (or problem) situations. (Chapter 5, p. 119; Chapter 8, p. 215)

Manufacturing burden See *factory overhead.*

Manufacturing overhead See *factory overhead.*

Margin of safety The difference in sales between present sales volume and sales volume at the break-even point. (Chapter 9, p. 268)

Master budget A series of budgets for all financial activities of a firm for the budget period. (Chapter 5, p. 120)

Material price standard The amount the firm expects to pay for one unit of direct material. (Chapter 6, p. 156)

Material price variance The difference between the actual quantity purchased at the actual price and the actual quantity purchased at the standard price. (Chapter 6, p. 159)

Material requisition A document used by a manufacturing department to request raw material from the stores warehouse. (Chapter 13, p. 412)

Material stores card A subsidiary record used to account for an individual item of raw material. (Chapter 13, p. 413)

Material usage standard The quantity of material needed for each unit of finished product. (Chapter 6, p. 156)

Material usage variance The difference between the amount of direct material used and the amount that should have been used for the quantity of finished units produced, based on the standard price. (Chapter 6, p. 160)

Method of least squares A statistical technique that provides a straight-line formula for a mixed cost; used in determining the fixed and variable elements of a mixed cost. (Chapter 2, pp. 34 and 35)

Mixed cost A cost that contains both fixed and variable elements. (Chapter 2, p. 26)

Monetary assets Cash and those assets that will be received in a fixed dollar amount. (Chapter 17, p. 574)

Monetary items Cash and claims to receive (monetary assets) or obligations to pay (monetary liabilities) a fixed sum of money. (Chapter 17, p. 574)

Monetary liabilities Obligations to pay a fixed amount. (Chapter 17, p. 574)

Net income variance The difference between budgeted net income and actual net income. (Chapter 6, p. 151)

Net present value The difference between the present value of cash inflows of a capital project and the present value of cash outflows. (Chapter 11, p. 338)

Net present value method A capital budgeting technique that determines the present value of the cash inflows and compares it to the present value of the cash outflows, using a specified rate of interest. (Chapter 11, p. 338)

Noncontrollable cost A cost that an individual manager does not have the ability to influence within a specified time period. (Chapter 8, p. 222)

Nonmonetary items Assets and liabilities that are not considered monetary items. (Chapter 17, p. 575)

Number of days to turn over A figure that indicates, on the average, how long it took to sell inventory. (Chapter 16, p. 532)

Operating expense budget A budget of selling and adminis-trative expenses. (Chapter 5, p. 127)

Operating expense ratio The relationship of operating expenses to sales; an indication of management's ability to control operating expenses. (Chapter 16, p. 529)

Operating leverage A measurement of the effect on net income of changes in sales volume. (Chapter 9, p. 262)

Opportunity cost Segment margin foregone when one alternative is chosen over another. (Chapter 10, p. 308)

Organizing The functions of (1) establishing an organizational structure and (2) communicating plans to people responsible for its implementation. (Chapter 1, p. 13)

Overapplied overhead The difference between the amount of factory overhead incurred and the factory overhead applied, when the amount applied is greater than the amount incurred. (Chapter 3, p. 61)

Overhead See *factory overhead.*

Overhead efficiency variance The difference between the cost of variable factory overhead for the actual hours worked and the cost of variable factory overhead for the number of hours that should have been worked, based on the standard rate. (Chapter 6, p. 167)

Overhead spending variance The difference between the actual variable factory overhead cost incurred and the cost that should have been incurred, based on the actual hours worked at the standard rate. (Chapter 6, p. 166)

Payback method A capital budgeting technique that determines how quickly a firm will recover its investment. (Chapter 11, p. 334)

Payback period The length of time it takes for a firm to recover its investment. (Chapter 11, p. 334)

Payoff table In probability theory, a table that shows the conditional value for each alternative, assuming each level of demand. (Chapter 12, p. 379)

Performance report A document that shows budgeted expectations, actual results, and deviations from the budget for some segment of the firm. (Chapter 5, p. 119)

Period costs Costs incurred during a specific accounting period that are considered to benefit the firm for that period and are charged against revenue for that period. Always includes selling and administrative costs. Under variable costing, includes fixed factory overhead. (Chapter 3, p. 52)

Planning As a function of management, determining, in advance, what steps are needed in order to satisfy goals. (Chapter 1, p. 13) In budgeting, a primary purpose of budgeting. (Chapter 5, p. 117)

Present value The value of an amount of cash today, as opposed to its value in the future, based on a specified rate of interest. (Chapter 11, p. 355)

Price-earnings ratio The relationship of the market price per share of common stock to its earnings per share. (Chapter 16, p. 539)

Price index A measure of prices of a number of selected items. (Chapter 17, p. 569)

Primary earnings per share The earnings per share assuming that none of the convertible securities will be converted to common stock. (Chapter 16, p. 538)

Prime cost The combination of direct material and direct labor. (Chapter 3, p. 50)

Probability theory A concept that relates the projected outcome of a decision to the likelihood that the outcome will occur. (Chapter 12, p. 374)

Process cost system A cost accounting system that accumulates costs for each production process over a period of time. (Chapter 13, pp. 416 and 423)

Product costs Manufacturing costs that are considered to attach to the product. (Chapter 3, p. 52)

Production budget A budget showing required production in units for the budget period. (Chapter 5, p. 122)

Profitability index The ratio between the present value of the cash inflows of an investment and the amount of the investment. (Chapter 11, p. 341)

Profit center A responsibility center in which a manager is responsible for the amount of profit earned. (Chapter 8, p. 215)

Programmed costs See *discretionary fixed costs.*

Purchasing agent The individual responsible for buying raw materials for the company. (Chapter 6, p. 156)

Purchasing power The amount of goods and services that can be bought with a stated sum of money. (Chapter 17, p. 569)

Qualitative factor A decision-making factor that cannot be measured numerically. (Chapter 10, p. 293)

Quantitative factor A decision-making factor that can be measured numerically, such as with dollars, units, percentages, or ratios. (Chapter 10, p. 293)

Quantitative techniques Sophisticated mathematical approaches to problem solving. (Chapter 12, p. 373)

Quick assets Cash and those assets that can be coverted to

cash within a short period of time. (Chapter 16, p. 531)

Quick ratio See *acid-test ratio.*

Rate of return on sales See *return on sales.*

Ratio The relationship between one financial statement item and another. (Chapter 16, p. 524)

Raw materials The items that a manufacturer has purchased to use in producing a product. (Chapter 3, p. 48)

Raw materials inventory The control account for raw materials, the balance of which represents the total cost of raw materials on hand. (Chapter 3, p. 49)

Realized holding gain or loss A gain or loss that arises from the disposal of an asset with a current cost higher or lower than its historical cost. (Chapter 17, p. 583)

Receiving report A document on which the firm records items and quantities of materials as they are received. (Chapter 13, p. 412)

Relevant cost A cost that is pertinent to the decision being made. To be relevant, a cost must be a future expected cost that differs between alternatives. (Chapter 10, p. 294)

Relevant cost analysis The process of analyzing relevant costs for the purpose of making decisions. (Chapter 10, p. 294)

Relevant range A period of time or range of activity within which a fixed cost does not change. (Chapter 2, p. 22)

Reorder point The inventory level at which additional items should be ordered. (Chapter 12, p. 394; Chapter 13, p. 413)

Replacement cost The cost of replacing assets now in use with similar assets. (Chapter 8, p. 230)

Residual income The difference between actual income (segment margin) earned on an investment and the desired income on the investment, based on the minimum desired rate of return. (Chapter 8, p. 226)

Responsibility The requirement to be answerable or accountable for the results of decisions. (Chapter 1, p. 11)

Responsibility accounting A system of accounting under which managers are given decision-making authority and responsibility for activities occurring within specific areas of a company. (Chapter 1, p. 11; Chapter 8, p. 215)

Responsibility center That segment for which a specific manager is responsible. (Chapter 8, p. 215)

Return on assets Operating income as a percentage of total assets. A measurement of how well the assets have been used by a firm. (Chapter 16, p. 542)

Return on common equity See *return on equity*.

Return on equity Income available to common shares divided by average common equity; a measurement that indicates how well the company has used the common stockholders' investment. (Chapter 16, p. 543)

Return on investment (ROI) Income (segment margin) as a percentage of investment; a measurement of management performance. (Chapter 8, p. 224)

Return on sales Internally, segment margin as a percentage of sales. (Chapter 8, p. 224) Externally, net income as a percentage of sales. (Chapter 16, p. 530)

ROI See *return on investment*.

Safety stock The amount of inventory that a firm always attempts to keep on hand so that if its normal stock runs out before an order is received, some stock will be on hand to meet cus-

tomer demand. (Chapter 12, p. 393)

Sales margin See *return on sales*.

Sales mix The combination of a firm's products, each expressed as a percentage of total sales dollars. (Chapter 9, p. 260)

Sales variance The difference between budgeted units and actual units, multiplied by the contribution margin per unit. (Chapter 6, p. 152)

Scatter chart A method by which the fixed and variable elements of a mixed cost can be estimated by a visual process. Also used to determine whether a straight-line relationship exists between the variable element of a mixed cost and the activity against which it is assumed the variable elements varies. (Chapter 2, p. 28)

Scatter graph See *scatter chart*.

Schedule of changes in working capital A part of the statement of changes in financial position; it shows specific changes in working capital items. (Chapter 15, p. 488)

Segment An area of activity of a firm about which accounting information is desired. (Chapter 1, p. 9)

Segment margin The difference between the revenue of a segment and the direct cost of the segment. Represents the amount of income that has been earned by the particular segment. (Chapter 8, p. 219)

Semivariable cost See *mixed cost*.

Separable fixed cost A direct fixed cost of a segment. (Chapter 8, p. 221)

Simple capital structure A capital structure in which the firm does not have any securities that are convertible into common stock. (Chapter 16, p. 536)

Source of working capital Any financial activity that results in an increase in current assets or a decrease in current liabilities. (Chapter 15, p. 489)

Split-off point The point at which the product resulting from the original raw material is separated into two or more products. (Chapter 10, p. 303)

Standard cost The expected cost of producing one unit. (Chapter 6, p. 155)

Standard cost system An accounting system under which all manufacturing costs are charged to production at standard cost. (Chapter 6, p. 155; Chapter 7, p. 194)

Statement of changes in financial position An external financial statement that describes changes in balance sheet items between two balance sheet dates in terms of working capital. (Chapter 15, p. 485)

Static budget A budget prepared for only one level of activity. (Chapter 6, p. 150)

Step-variable cost A cost that changes as a particular activity changes but not in direct proportion to changes in the activity. (Chapter 2, p. 24)

Storekeeper See *stores supervisor*.

Stores supervisor The individual with the responsibility of maintaining the warehouse in which raw materials are stored. (Chapter 13, p. 412)

Strategic planning Long-range planning that considers a firm's strategy for achieving its organizational goals. (Chapter 1, p. 13)

Sunk cost A past, or previously incurred, cost. Normally used when referring to previously purchased assets. (Chapter 10, p. 294)

Time-adjusted rate of return method A capital budgeting

technique that determines the actual rate of return on a proposed investment, considering the time value of money. (Chapter 11, p. 343)

Times interest earned A measurement for determining the relationship between operating income and the interest requirements; calculated by dividing operating income by interest expense. (Chapter 16, p. 535)

Time ticket The document on which direct labor hours are recorded. (Chapter 13, p. 414)

Time value of money A concept that recognizes that the value of cash flows depends on when they are received. (Chapter 11, p. 355)

Transfer price The amount used to record the transfer of product between segments of a firm based on cost, market price, variable cost, or a price negotiated between the segment managers. (Chapter 8, p. 230)

Unadjusted rate of return method A capital budgeting technique that estimates the profitability of a capital project, without considering the time value of money. (Chapter 11, p. 337)

Underapplied overhead The difference between the amount of factory overhead incurred and the amount of factory overhead applied, when the amount incurred is greater than the amount applied. (Chapter 3, p. 61)

Unexpired costs Costs that have been incurred but not "used up." Assets are unexpired costs. (Chapter 2, p. 20)

Unrealized holding gain or loss A gain or loss that arises from holding, but not disposing of, assets whose current cost is more or less than their historical cost. (Chapter 17, p. 583)

Value of perfect information The difference between expected value with perfect information and expected value without perfect information. (Chapter 12, p. 378)

Variable cost A cost that changes in total in direct proportion to changes in a specific activity. (Chapter 2, p. 21)

Variable costing A cost accounting method under which fixed factory overhead is considered a period cost rather than a product cost. Only variable factory costs are considered product costs. (Chapter 3, p. 52; Chapter 4, p. 80)

Variable cost of production budget A budget of variable production costs required to meet the production budget. (Chapter 5, p. 126)

Variable cost ratio Variable cost as a percentage of sales. (Chapter 4, p. 90; Chapter 9, p. 258)

Variable factory overhead account The account for recording incurred (debit) and applied (credit) variable factory overhead. (Chapter 3, p. 57)

Variable factory overhead applied The estimated amount of variable factory overhead that is charged to work-in-process inventory at a predetermined rate on a timely basis under an actual/normal and standard cost system. (Chapter 3, p. 58)

Variable factory overhead incurred The amount of variable factory overhead costs actually incurred. (Chapter 3, p. 57)

Variance A deviation from the budget. (Chapter 5, p. 119)

Vertical analysis The analysis of financial statement items up and down the page, rather than across. (Chapter 16, p. 527)

Visual fit See *scatter chart*.

Volume A level of sales or production activity. (Chapter 2, p. 20; Chapter 9, p. 254)

Volume variance The difference between the budgeted fixed overhead cost and the amount of fixed overhead cost applied. (Chapter 7, p. 190)

Working capital The difference between current assets and current liabilities. It represents the excess of current assets available to carry on the day-to-day operations of a business. (Chapter 15, p. 486; Chapter 16, p. 530)

Work in process Started but unfinished production. (Chapter 3, p. 49)

Work-in-process inventory The cost of unfinished production. (Chapter 3, p. 49)

Index

In addition to the terms listed below, see also the glossary for descriptions of key terms and phrases.

10-29 b. $20,000 in favor of new
10-30 a. $63,000 in favor of new
10-31 b. $203,000 new net income c. $321,000 new net income
10-32 a. Increase by $900; c. Increase by $1,650; e. Decrease by $1,515
10-33 b. $130,000 in favor of buy
10-34 b. $252.50 per machine
10-35 b. Rosemist net income, $13,889; c. $30,000 decrease
10-36 b. $10,000; c. $60,000
10-37 Alternative A, increase income by $24,000; Alternative B, decrease income by $10,000
10-38 a. 1. $1,200 in favor of accepting
10-39 Krage Co. order, $625 loss
11-16 a. $7,350; c. $575.40; e. $5,402.56
11-17 a. 2. $472.50; 4. $51,765; b. 2. $6,955.20; 4. $589,215
11-19 Alternative B, PV, $20,332
11-20 Alternative B, PV, $13,040
11-21 b. 5 yr.; d. 5.8 yr.
11-22 b. 3 1/3 yr; c. 3 1/2 yr.
11-23 b. 20%
11-24 a. 4.7 yr.; b. 8.75%
11-25 a. NPV, $2,010; PI, 1.07 c. NPV, $(8,230); PI, .95
11-26 a. NPV, $191; PI, 1.04; c. NPV, $(67,965); PI, .32
11-27 b. $(1,270.40); d. $4,300.80; f. $(3,384)
11-28 a. $955, 12%; c. $(4,840), 14%; e. $974, 14%
11-29 a. $319; b. 14%
11-30 a. $(618); b. 12%
11-31 $13,427
11-32 b. 10.4%; c. $699; e. 17%
11-33 b. A, $4,609; B, $4,740 c. A, 1.23; B, 1.16
11-34 a. A, $3,260; B, ($5,110) c. A, 15.3%; B, 9%
11-35 a. $13,989; c. 22.9%
11-36 a. $1,314; c. 14.3%
11-37 a. $1,481; c. 21.1%
11-38 NPV, $(35,211), or $(35,523)
11-39 NPV, $(49,424)
11-40 a. 3.2 yr; c. $1,363; e. 17.1%
11-41 a. 1. $1,080; 3. $7,272; 5. $826
11-42 b. 1.95 yr.; d. $39,150
11-43 a. 2. $87,000; b. $16,320
11-44 19.0%
11-45-S a. $296; c. $(5,402)
11-46-S NPV, $500
11-47-S NPV, $(675)
11-48-S NPV, $17,708
11-49-S NPV $2,000

12-15 $48,000
12-16 a. $43,000
12-17 a. $35,000
12-18 Machine A, expected cost, $2,100
12-19 Crazy Kids, EV, $950,000
12-20 a. Expected value of hourly rate, $186
12-21 b. 420 units
12-22 c. 2,000 units
12-23 c. 750 units
12-26 b. 32 times
12-27 a. 600 units; b. 560 units
12-28 Safety stock, 750 units
12-29 Annual usage, 1,000,000 units
12-30 a. Plan B, average cost, $875
12-31 a. Clexco, EV, $50,500
12-32 a. EV, 30 bushels, $74
12-33 a. EV, 30,000 units, $4,000; c. $1,800
12-34 a. Z-100, NPV, $5,019
12-35 NPV, $22
12-36 Produce 200 units of B and 360 units of L
12-37 Produce 10,000 units of C and no units of B
12-38 d. Produce 4,000 bikes and 2,000 chairs
12-39 a. EOQ, 400 units
12-40 EOQ, 400 units
12-41 a. EOQ, 5,000 units; b. EOQ, 4,472 units; c. $792
12-42 a. 1. 240 units; 3. $240; b. Immediately
13-20 b. $7,350
13-21 a. $4.50 per unit
13-22 4,750 e.u.
13-23 3,950 e.u.
13-24 Conversion costs, 20,800 e.u.
13-25 Conversion costs, 17,800 e.u.
13-26 Direct material, 24,200 e.u.
13-27 Direct material, 22,600
13-29 a. $2.50 per e.u.
13-30 Debit Finished Goods Inventory, $25,800
13-31 Debit Finished Goods Inventory, $22,125
13-32 c. $4,050
13-33 b. $2,910
13-34 c. Total cost, $900
13-35 c. Balance, work-in-process inventory, $3,940; d. Balance, Job No. 45, $2,440
13-36 a. 2; e. 3
13-37 Cost of goods manufactured, $39,760
13-38 b. $2.229 per e.u.; c. $5,573
13-39 a. $3.40 per e.u.; b. $1,790
13-40 a. $5.007 per e.u.; b. $13,315
13-41 a. Cost of units transferred out, $116,292
13-42 a. Cost of units transferred out, $135,690
13-43 a. $3.277 per e.u.; c. Cost of units transferred out, $10,237